THE SOVIETS

by Albert Rhys Williams

Harcourt, Brace and Company, New York

2

DK
266
.W5
1937

113A

Designed by Robert Josephy

Contents

II. ECONOMIC LIFE

CONTENTS vii

42. What is the Condition of the Railways, Waterways, Airways and Roads? 188
43. What is the Rôle of Science in Developing the Economic Life of the Country? 201
44. What Are the Functions of the Labor Unions? 212
45. What is the Cause of the Low Productivity of the Russians—and Its Cure? 214
46. How Are the Labor Unions Organized and Run? 223
X 47. How Are the People Insured Against Illness, Accident, Old Age, Unemployment? 230
X 48. How Are the People Clothed and Fed? 234
49. How Are the People Housed? 249
50. What Incentives to Work Has the Soviet Citizen? 258
51. Where Does All the Money Come From—and Go To? 269
52. What is the Rôle of Money, Banks, and Credits? 275
53. Will the Machine and Industrialization Under the Soviets Standardize People, Create Conflict Between Classes, and Lower Aesthetic Values? 281

III. SOCIAL LIFE

54. What is the Status of Women Under the Soviets? 287
X 55. How Are Marriages Made in the Soviet Union? 294
56. How Are People Divorced? 297
57. What is the Attitude Toward Sex? 298
X 58. What About Birth Control and Abortion? 301
59. What Are the Soviets Doing to Combat Disease and Promote Health? 306
60. How do the Soviets Deal with the Liquor Problem? 316
61. Are the Church and Religion Persecuted in the Soviet Union? 319
62. What Are the Causes of the Antagonism of the Revolution to the Church? 322
63. How Was the Campaign Against Religion Carried On? 326

Foreword

The aim of this book is to give a picture of Soviet life and institutions, how they came into being, the plans and prospects for the future. It started out as a simple pamphlet of questions and answers, like one I wrote twenty years ago. But like the country it describes, the material was too large and complex to squeeze into any pamphlet. So it grew into this good-sized volume. The reader who wishes to confine himself to the 200 pages of large print can obtain a fairly good idea of the general situation and set-up. If he wishes more, he can delve into the 300 pages of small print for illustration, elaboration, and anecdote. There, too, the expert may find something new about Soviet peoples and folkways picked up during my five years' sojourn in the villages.

In the foreground are put the ideals and achievements of the Revolution, its positive rather than its negative features. In doing this there is always the danger of creating too fair and idyllic a picture. That is a disservice both to the Soviets and to the reader, especially one who is led to believe that everything is for the best in the best of all possible worlds, that all the age-old problems of humanity are there solved or on the way to solution.

With such romantic notions he goes to the Soviet Union, expecting to find a people filled with the "dear love of comrades," with starlit faces marching toward the millennium. Instead he sees them going about their affairs much as they do elsewhere, intent on food, clothes, amusements. He runs into churlish, fumbling officials, turning the simplest transaction into an ordeal. He discovers red tape, bureaucracy, censorship, gross inefficiency, three persons often not doing the work of one. He observes beggars in the streets, women doing the work of men, over-crowded street cars and houses. Returning to his hotel he may find the elevator out of order, bugs in his bed, a cockroach in the soup, no stopper in the bath-tub and two kinds of cold water running into it. "So this is Communism!" he exclaims and goes forth to tell the world his sorrow and disillusion. All these and other negative aspects of Soviet life are set down in this book. If they are in the background it is because there is nothing peculiarly new or original about them in Russia, or for that matter in the world. See Question 88, "What Books to Read about the Soviets?"

In contrast to the sad failures and defects of the Revolution stands a long list of its accomplishments in all spheres of human endeavor. To the positive-minded it is these things that are of real and lasting significance and interest. To state some of them briefly: The rapid transformation of a backward, agrarian, poverty-stricken country into a leading industrial nation. A system of planning working toward an ordered, wasteless development of the nation's resources and industries. Elimination of crises and depressions by striking a balance between production and consumption—putting money in the hands of the people to buy back the goods as fast as they make them. Abolition of unemployment with the right of every citizen to work, education and leisure written into the Constitution.

The merging of 25,000,000 tiny peasant holdings into 250,000 big scale farms, equipped with modern machinery and power. The advance of science, art, and the "Lenin light," into the 300,000 "dark" villages. Teaching a hundred million illiterates to read and write, publication of 45,000 new titles a year, the reduction of 58 languages to writing. The practical disappearance of racial and national antagonisms between Jews, Russians, Tatars, Armenians and 185 other peoples now living together in peace and amity. The mobilization of millions for the colossal tasks of culture and construction, calling forth those heroic and self-sacrificing qualities in the human spirit usually manifested only in times of war.

Most of these things are now a matter of record. They have been set forth in a vast array of books, some stressing the achievements, others the costs in privation and suffering by which they were attained. Frequently one subject has been singled out for special treatment with the result that the information the reader may be seeking is scattered through many volumes. "The Soviets" essays to gather into one volume all the salient facts in all fields of Soviet activity and to present them in concise and easily accessible form.

For constant help in gathering the material in Russia and preparing the manuscript I am indebted to Lucita Squier. Among many others to whom I am greatly indebted are Professor H. H. Fisher of the Hoover War Library and Stanford University; Professor Alexander Kaun of the Slavic Department of the University of California; Professor Bruce Hopper of Harvard University; General Victor A. Yakhontoff of the old Russian Army; Avrahm Yarmolinsky of the New York Public Library; Kathleen Barnes of the Institute of Pacific Relations; George Soule of *The New Republic;* and most of all to Dorothy Erskine of San Francisco. From them I received advice, criticisms, protests—sometimes heeded and sometimes not. So the responsibility for the spirit and tone of the book, as well as whatever errors may have crept into it, rests on myself.

I. Government, Party, and Nations

1. What is the U.S.S.R.?

The Union of Soviet Socialist Republics—*not* the United States of Soviet Russia! Because Russia is its largest part it is popularly known as Soviet Russia. Correctly abbreviated, it is called the Soviet Union.

Its territory is the same as the former Empire of the Tsars, except for the loss of Finland and the Baltic Provinces of Estonia, Latvia, and Lithuania, which have become independent states; five border provinces, now part of the new Poland; Bessarabia, now incorporated into Rumania; and 7,780 square miles ceded to Turkey.

These regions comprised but one-thirtieth of the former area of the country, a trifling loss. Even the alienation of the 28 million people they contained was not a serious blow. Very serious, however, was the blow to the economic life. In losing these provinces the Soviet Union lost a fifth of her railway trackage, a fourth of her manufactures, and important sections of the metal industry. To repair these great losses quickly and then to push on to higher levels was the reason for the swift pace of the Five-Year Plans, the emphasis on industrialization, and the Stakhanov movement for raising the output of labor.

2. How Large is the Country?

About one-sixth the land surface of the globe, 8,241,644 square miles. It is larger than the combined areas of Canada, the United States including Alaska, and Central America; it is the largest continuous domain in the world. In the Post-Gatty round-the-world flight, 45 of 106 hours' flying time were spent over Soviet territory. As land boundaries, it has Finland, Poland, Rumania, Turkey, Iran, China, and Japan, while less than five miles of water in the Bering Strait separates Little Diomede Island owned by the United States from Big Diomede Island owned by the

Soviets. So extensive is the Soviet Union that many of its citizens live farther away from their capital city, Moscow, than do the people of New York or Capetown. It has a chain of radio stations beyond the Polar Circle, and along its Southern borders flourish big tea plantations and groves of citrus fruit. As the astronomer Alexander von Humboldt pointed out, it is larger than the face of the moon at its full. If there are grounds for the building of Socialism in any one country then it is here. For in the words of an old peasant proverb, "Russia is not a country, it is a world."

One glance at the map shows this immensity. But it should be a new map. The old ones have been made obsolete by the Revolution—"the whirlwind that swept everything before it"—carrying away the old imperial names and replacing them with new. Most striking are the changes in the names of cities. No longer are they called after the Tsars but after the leaders of the Revolution. Petrograd, the city of Peter, has become Leningrad, the city of Lenin, and Tsaritsin, on the Volga, is now called Stalingrad, in token of Stalin's part in saving it from capture by the Whites. There is also a Stalinabad, Stalino, Stalinsk. Altogether a full score of cities, towns, mountain peaks, and canals have acquired the names of Stalin and Lenin.

If they are the chief gainers in the rechristening process, it is Catherine the Great who has been the greatest loser. To Karl Marx she lost Ekaterinstadt, now called Marxstadt, in the German Republic on the Volga. Ekaterinfeld is now Luxemburg in honor of the German "Red Rosa." Ekaterinodar, "gift of Catherine," becomes Krasnodar, "gift of the Reds." Ekaterinoslav, "the glory of Catherine," now glorifies a mammoth steel and rolling-mill under the name of Dneipropetrovsk. Ekaterinburg, where Tsar Nicholas was executed, is now Sverdlovsk, after the President of the Soviet Congress that sanctioned the execution.

The town of Nikolaevsk takes the name of Pugachevsk, after the Cossack who was drawn and quartered for leading the peasant revolt against the Great Catherine. Romanovsky Khutor goes to the anarchist prince and philosopher who fought the Romanovs all his life, Kropotkin. Nizhni-Novgorod, which sounds romantic but in Russian simply means Lower Newtown, as the birthplace of the "grandfather of proletarian literature," is now the city of Gorky. Vyatka, as the birthplace of the leader assassinated in 1935 by the "terrorist group," is now the city of Kirov. The park where the imperial family and their retainers lived was known as Tsarskoye Selo, Village of the Tsars. Their palaces and houses turned into schools and orphan-homes are now known as Detskoye Selo, Village of the Children.

In wholesale fashion, too, have been rebaptized the streets, public squares, provinces, and even peoples (See page 333). Out of the revolutionary font they emerge with names of great rebels, humanitarians, poets, and scientists. The rivers, however, are still allowed to flow under their ancient names, though not always in their ancient channels. Untouched, so far at any rate, are also the names of most of the Ukrainian cities and Moscow, the "white-walled" Mother City of the Russians. It was the capital of Russia until Peter the Great moved the seat of government to his newly built town on the Neva and called it Saint Petersburg—the name of which was changed in 1914 to Petrograd.

In March, 1918, to escape the menace of the German armies and to be nearer the center of the country, Lenin moved the capital back again to Moscow—to the Kremlin. This is a sort of acropolis with a high crenellated wall enclosing arsenal, palaces, and the cathedrals topped with golden crosses where the Tsars were crowned and many lie buried. Here, with a huge piece broken from its side, stands the biggest bell in Russia and an equally useless "king of cannons." Hence the saying, "Tsar Bell does not ring, Tsar Cannon does not shoot, and Tsar Nicholas does not reign." In the words of another old Russian saying, "Above Moscow lies the Kremlin, above it lie only the stars." This is doubly true now for, in place of the imperial two-headed eagles, the Kremlin's green-tiled towers now hold high the Soviet's five-pointed stars. Once more it is the heart of the pulsing activities of the nation. In its gold-and-marble former throne room assemble the delegates of the Supreme Council and other important congresses. From it go forth the laws, orders, and decrees that govern the eleven Soviet republics.

3. When and How Was the U.S.S.R. Established?

On November 7, 1917, when the Provisional Government of Kerensky was overthrown and the Soviet Congress declared itself the sole power in the country. According to the Julian calendar by which the Russians then reckoned time, this occurred on October 25 and is therefore called the October Revolution. It must be distinguished from the overthrow of the Tsar which occurred on March 12, 1917—known as the February Revolution.

At first the country was known as the R.S.F.S.R.—the Russian Socialist Federated Soviet Republic. With the ratification of a new constitution six years later it officially received its present name. To be technically correct then, one must say that the U.S.S.R. was established on July 6, 1923. But that is a legal nicety. Not by signatures affixed to a document did it come into being, but by guns in the hands of the insurgent masses—by a momentous act of revolution.

Three Points About the October Revolution

It was a spontaneous elemental uprising of the masses. Hungry, war-sick, disillusioned, and desperate, with volcanic fury, a hundred million men and women pressed forward to the goal of their long unfulfilled dreams "like a flow of molten lava that could not be dammed or turned aside." (Ross)

It was guided by the Communists or Bolsheviks—a party of some 200,000 members, literally a handful amongst the 175 millions of Russia, less than two per cent. Hence the charges against the Revolution as being "the arbitrary act of a coterie of iron-willed zealots," "the tyranny of an infinitesimal fraction." There is no gainsaying that the Bolsheviks were a handful, zealous and arbitrary enough. But that they gratuitously superimposed themselves upon a protesting people is erroneous. This very persistent idea comes from focusing all attention upon the numbers in the Party. But this was absolutely no index of Bolshevik sentiment in the country. For every Bolshevik officially enrolled in the Party there were fifty in the general population. "Non-Party Bolsheviks" Stalin now calls them.

The dangers, the hard duties, and discipline of the Party made the masses chary of joining it. But they voted heavily for it. In the summer of 1917 the big cities like Moscow and Petrograd gave a clear majority to the Bolsheviks not only in the Soviets but in the municipal elections where all citizens went to the polls. In June, 1918, the Allies overthrew the Vladivostok Soviet and after imprisoning the Bolshevik leaders and closing their papers, held a "free democratic election." Whereupon the Bolsheviks rolled up a greater vote than all the other sixteen parties combined.

More important than casting their votes for the Bolsheviks was the readiness of the masses to shoulder a gun for them. The armies and garrisons were Bolshevik—so were the workers in the basic industries. With the key positions, the bayonets, and the effective vital forces on their side, the Party felt that it had a clear mandate to carry on the Revolution in the Bolshevik way—which in so many ways coincided with the demands and desires of the masses.

It launched straightway a series of radical measures aimed at the immediate destruction of the old order and construction of the new on wholly new foundations. Two of these were of tremendous effect in maintaining the continued loyalty of the insurgent masses and insuring the stability of the new government. The first, issued on November 8, while the smoke had scarcely faded from the guns of the cruiser *Aurora* firing over the Winter Palace, was the *Decree on Land* declaring "the lands of the crown, the monasteries, and the landlords are henceforth the property of the nation forever." Even to the Westerner, the significance of thus satisfying the age-old longing of the hundred million peasants is apparent.

Quite as important was the second measure, appearing seven days later, November 15, signed by Lenin and Stalin. This was *The Declaration of Rights of the Peoples of Russia* proclaiming "the right to free development of national minorities, their free self-determination including separation." The significance of this is difficult to overestimate. By removing the grievances and satisfying the national aspirations of the 188 non-Russian peoples in the country, it rallied to the Soviets this host of powerful allies. The full import of this has never been grasped by the West which is even yet but dimly aware of the vast congeries of peoples that made up the former empire of the Tsars —and which is not familiar with the long history of oppressions suffered by these peoples.

4. What Peoples, Races, and Nations Inhabit the Country?

I. THE SLAVS. Out of a population of 175 millions, about three-fourths are Slavs, divided into three main branches, speaking distinct languages. The six million White Russians, holding the marches to the West, are fair-skinned, blue-eyed, and closest to the original stock. They are not to be confused with the emigrant "White Russians," who fled abroad during the Revolution. The 35 million Ukrainians, or Little Russians, as they were formerly called, occupying the fertile Black Earth zone in the South, are taller, short-headed, and dark-haired. The 80 million Great Russians, with Scandinavian, Tatar, and Finnish elements in their blood-stream, were pre-eminently conquerors, pioneers, and colonizers. Having established Tsarism and the Patriarchate in Moscow, they extended their dominion over all the others.

Steadily, from the days of Ivan the Terrible, they pushed the frontiers of the Empire out to the Pacific and down to the gates of India, bringing new lands and peoples under the Russian tricolor. In the vanguard of this advance moved the cavalry of the Cossacks from their eleven "camps" on the Don, the Terek, the Amur, and other military outposts. In these Cossacks was effected one of the strange transformations of history. Once freedom-lovers, fleeing to the frontiers from tyranny of the Tsar, they became his trusted janissaries in the conquest of new territories. Once rebels, they stood ready with their savage *nagaikas*—whips of leather thongs, tipped with steel—to suppress the first signs

of rebellion in others. Freebooters and champions of the Orthodox Faith, with one saber-stroke cleaving the infidel to the heart,
they slashed a way for the Russian priests with the cross, for the
vodka-traders, merchants, and governors.

Tirelessly, for more than three centuries, Imperial Russia
added to its domains at the rate of sixty square miles a day. And
still land-hungry it entered the Great War with the objective,
"to plant the Russian cross on the dome of the Great Mosque
in Constantinople." This Pan-Slavic dream was rudely shattered
by the Revolution. Even so, in the vast territory it inherited, live
189 peoples, speaking 150 languages, and adhering to 40 religions
—or, to be more correct, in process of disavowing them. Roughly
the non-Slavic peoples fall into the following main ethnic groups.

II. THE FINNO-UGRIANS, numbering about three million,
were the original masters of the forests and fenlands of Russia.
Some were driven out by the Slavs pressing up from the South.
Others commingling amicably with the invaders had a part in
forming the Great Russian type, leaving their imprint on the
features as they did their names on the rivers. This infusion of
Finnish blood is not large, but enough so it may be said "scratch
a Russian and you will find a Finn." On the other hand, a score
of these peoples, less assimilable, still retain their distinctive customs, rites and languages.

Around the lakes beyond Leningrad live the Karelians, carrying
a duck and drake as symbols of fertility in their wedding processions
and placating the spirit of the bear they have killed. From their runes
or rhapsodic ballads collected in the "Kalevala," Longfellow derived
the rhythm for "Hiawatha." Along the Arctic coast are the flat-faced
Lapps, and reindeer-rearing Nentsi, with great herds feeding on moss
dug out of the frozen tundras with their hoofs. In the wilds of Siberia
live the Ugrian Voguls and Ostiaks, primitive trapping and hunting
tribes, in winter living in "dug-outs" roofed with birch-bark.

At the other extreme are the urbanized Estonians, strongly influenced by German culture. Occupying the basins of the rivers whose

names begin with V—the Vetluga, Vyatka, Vychegda, and Upper Volga—are the Mordvins, the Mari, the Votiaks, Zyrians, and Permians. Driven into the hinterland as the Russians moved up the valleys, they were forced to pay annually a heavy fur-tribute or become serfs of the great proprietors like the Stroganovs. Joining the peasant rebellion under Pugachev, they swept towards Moscow, firing the manor houses, hanging officials and landlords to the lintels. With the suppression of this revolt the government sought forcibly to Christianize them.

Whole villages, herded into the rivers by the gendarmes, were baptized *en masse* by bishops on the banks. Hurriedly emerging, they shook off the water so the new religion would not "take." Mission schools were opened in which, contrary to usual policy, instruction was given in the native tongue. Nominally Orthodox, they were often duped by crafty Russians into buying seats in the Christian heaven, selling their last cow to obtain a choice reservation. At the same time not to offend their own pagan deities they continued to lay food offerings for them beneath the white birches of their ancient sacred groves. With these may be classed the Chuvash, whose Turkic origin is almost obscured by the amount of Finnic blood in their veins and words in their language.

III. THE TURCO-TATARS, numbering 18 million, are mostly descendants of the hordes which swept out of Asia led by the great warriors Tamerlane, "The Earth-Shaker," and Genghis Khan, "Emperor of All Men," who said "as there is one ruler in heaven, so there should be but one on earth"—and nearly became that one. After crashing the gates of Europe, they fell back to Central Asia to pasture their flocks and herds on the steppes, to mingle their blood with the native stocks, and for 300 years from their strongholds along the Volga, to levy tribute on the Russians.

Largely followers of Islam, with its fatalism inclining them to passivity and resignation, they have been quiescent for centuries. But in their veins runs the blood of conquerors, statesmen, and administrators. Now it is being roused and quickened by the Revolution. From Mecca their youths are turning to Moscow, embracing the doctrines of Marx as ardently as their fathers embraced the doctrines of Mohammed. With long dormant energies now galvanized into action the world may feel afresh the powerful impact of these peoples. It is worth while then to note the strange and alien names they bear.

Most numerous are the Uzbeks who built their fabled cities in the fertile oases among the arid deserts of Central Asia: Holy Bokhara, from whose highest minaret, the Tower of Death, law-breakers were hurled 200 feet to the pavement below; Kokand, in the mountain-walled Vale of Ferghana; "Jeweled" Samarkand, with its Registan, called by Lord Curzon "the most impressive public square in the world." On all sides rise the Moslem colleges, mosques, and memorial tombs—majestic monuments of rough simplicity, topped with slender minarets and turquoise domes, with arches and portals tiled in brilliant blue and white and friezes of marble slabs in a hundred intricate geometric patterns. At dawn and sunset the call of the muezzin mingles with the cries of the water-carriers plodding through the knee-deep dust. The bazaars flash with rainbow-tinted raw silk robes which in winter are cotton-wadded against the cold. Above the tinkling of camel-bells and the wailing of the old men around the tomb of Tamerlane ring the songs of the irrigation shock-brigades marching out to make the sandy wastes grow cotton, the "white gold" of Uzbekistan.

Over the adjacent steppes roam the supple, sport- and laughter-loving Kazakhs, or "Freemen," delighting in hawking and hunting. With one stroke of their short whips they break the back of a fleeing animal and at full gallop lift the carcass from ground to saddle. Today encamped on a river-bottom, and next day rolling up their circular felt huts, bound for the foothills of the Pamirs, "the roof of the world," five hundred miles away. In 1936 Kazakhstan became one of the eleven constituent republics and is fast on the way to industrialization with machine-tractor stations, wind-motors, coal-mines, and a huge copper plant for smelting 100,000 tons yearly. Around its Aral Sea live the Kara-Kalpaks, or "Black Bonnets," after the shaggy sheepskin caps they wear.

Along the Chinese frontier dwell the Kirghiz, drinking the milk of mares, ewes, and yaks, and cooking their meat over fires of camel-dung. About Lake Issik-Kul they grow barley and opium poppy and graze their fat-tailed sheep upon the plains till these wither up under the blazing sun. Then, along the same trails beaten by their ancestors more than a thousand years ago they drive their great flocks, led by big bucks and flanked by weary-eyed dogs, up to the cool springs and succulent grass of the mountain meadows. Elevated to the status of a constituent republic in 1936 Kirghizia is now organizing huge livestock farms; planting a half million acres with fiber crops, cotton, Italian hemp, kenaf, and kendyr; building silk factories and tanneries.

Northward to the Urals, the Bashkirs pasture their half-wild horses on the silvery feather-grass and ferment the milk of their mares into an invigorating drink known as *koumiss*. They are indolent, peace-loving, lavish in hospitality. To show their guest that the goat or sheep is perfect they cut its throat in his presence, and cooking it whole, tear it to pieces with their hands as they feast squat-legged on the earth. As token of highest esteem, choice morsels like the cold boiled eye are ceremoniously thrust in the guest's mouth with their fingers.

Occupying the enormous basin of the Lena, are the gifted Yakuts, preferring to clear the forests for tillage rather than to hunt in them. Unlike many of the tribes in Siberia which have decimated by the poisons of vodka and syphilis introduced by advancing civilization, they retain their pristine health and vigor. Increasing in numbers, they spread their language and customs, not only among the backward natives, but even among the Russian settlers.

Most cultured are the descendants of the Golden Horde, the Tatars of Kazan, who supplied the Moslem East with priests, the Volga wharves with sinewy stevedores, and the cafés of the big cities with waiters. Skilled in tanning and dyeing leather, they are celebrated for their saddles and gay morocco boots sewn out of a hundred varie-gated pieces. Like the rest of the Moslems, they jealously guarded their women, but they exploited them less, allowing them leisure for the graces of living and the arts of seduction. Even in remote villages one sees the girls with eyebrows penciled black, with henna- or vermilion-tinted finger nails, bringing water from the well. Still more apparent is this predilection for the pleasures and amenities of life among the Tatars of the Crimea. In the old capital, Bakhchisarai, stands the lat-ticed Palace of the Khan, with its golden cabinet, coffee-room, and the Fountain of Tears described in a poem of Pushkin about the Khan's beloved Polish captive, Marie. It is interesting to observe how the mosques in the South are built of sun-baked brick with melon-domes while in the forests of the North they are wooden with sharp slanting roofs to fend off the heavy snowfalls.

An altogether different breed are the Turcomans on the east shore of the Caspian Sea, half-savage, half-literate, and crowned with massive sheepskin shakos that make them look like giants. They are adroit in evading the laws against the purchase of brides and until recently mercilessly exploited their women, who were the weavers of the rugs of Merv and Tekke renowned for richness of design and coloring.

Across the Caspian, above deep reservoirs of oil—the "black gold" of the Caucasus—live the Azerbaijan Tiurks. In this "Land of Fire," as it was known to the ancients, still stands the Temple of the Fire-Worshipers, whose flames were fed by natural gas. Till recently here was celebrated the Festival of Ali, in which Moslem fanatics, working themselves into a frenzy, slashed their flesh with daggers and danced through the streets with blood-streaming bodies. Other Turkic tribes of the Caucasus are the Kumiks and Karachayevs.

IV. THE JAPHETIC PEOPLES OF THE CAUCASUS. To the ancients the mountains of the Caucasus were the cradle of humanity, "the stony girdle of the globe." Here, isolated from the world and each other by barriers of ice and granite, forty races numbering about six million cling to the traditions and customs of their ancestors—reaching back to legendary ages. For this is the flaming Colchis to which came the Argonauts in quest of the Golden Fleece, and where Prometheus was eternally torn by the vultures.

Across this land rolled the conquering armies of the world—the Roman legions, the hosts of Persia and Macedonia, the Mongols, and the Crusaders. A hundred times its cities have been sacked and pillaged—every pass and hill and highroad soaked in blood. This warring past is reflected in the ruins of fortresses that crown the heights; in the national costume, slashed with a row of cartridge-pockets across the breast and a gleaming dagger at the belt; in the salutation to the passerby, "Be victorious!" and in the gallant answer, "May the victory be yours!"; in the blood-feuds that raged amongst the hill-tribes always so quick with the knife or trigger to avenge an insult or defend their honor.

Ceaseless conflict with human forces and with nature—matching their wits and strength against the mountain wastes—has made these people sinewy, resourceful, adroit, and artful. At the same time they are singularly courteous and hospitable—lovers of music, of dancing, of feasting, and of wine, "red blood of the earth," that in the fertile valleys pours from the ground like water. Proud of their glamorous past, they glorify it in poetry and song, and with deft hands fashion copper and silver into objects of beauty and weapons incrusted with jewels.

Amongst the swarms of peoples in this human hive the story of the Armenians, their feuds and massacres by the Turks, is already well known to the West. More recently it has come to know that not only the inhabitants of the State of Georgia, but a powerful cultured race in the Caucasus are likewise called Georgians. In 345 they were Christianized by St. Nina with her grape-vine cross. They look back almost a thousand years to the Golden Age of arts and literature when Rustaveli wrote the national epic, "The Man in the Panther's Skin," and a noble architecture arose under David the Builder and the Great Queen Tamara. Cultured and valorous as this little country was, it could not withstand the pressure of the colossus reaching down from the North. With the penetration of trading and industrial capital, followed by an alliance between its nobles and the Russians, Georgia became a vassal of the Tsars. But the oppressed peasantry and the liberty-loving mountaineers kept up an incessant struggle against autocracy in all its forms. Schooled in revolutionary theory and practice, and with a flair for politics evolved through centuries of dealing with all kinds of states and rulers, these Georgians have developed a grasp of statecraft that amounts to genius.

On the rain- and sun-drenched Black Sea slopes live the Abkhasians, in a semi-tropic paradise which produces a luxuriant growth of camel and phoenix palms, tangerines, tea, pomegranates—and centenarians.

One of them, Nicholas Chapkovsky, was 142 years of age, when Henri Barbusse visited him in 1928. Scientists are now investigating other cases of extreme longevity in this district, among which is Ekun Shoua, reputed to be 157 years and still taking his daily two-mile walk in the mountains. The oldest man in the world in the cradle of the human race!

In the mountains of Daghestan live the metal-working Lezghians, and 28 other peoples formerly lumped together under this name, although each spoke a distinctly different dialect. United by their murids, a hierarchy of holy men to whom they were bound by vows of strict obedience, they held back the Russian conquest of the Caucasus for a quarter of a century. Even more furious was the resistance of the democratic Chechens, led by Shamil, "The Thunder-Bolt," whose cunning in outwitting the best Russian generals and annihilating their armies is the theme of a thousand songs and legends.

With them were allied the Adygei and Cherkess, better known abroad as Circassians. Their women, commanding the highest prices in the slave-markets of the East, were the big-eyed beauties of the Sultan's harems. Most of these clans emigrated to Turkey rather than bow to the Russian yoke. Others kept up a guerilla struggle against the conquerors, suddenly pouncing down on baggage-trains, slaying officers, robbing travelers—acting generally as the Robin Hoods of the mountains. Often this political banditry degenerated into sheer brigandage; neighbors as well as the Russians were looted. Most notorious were the Ingushi, whose country was called a "den of thieves and cut-throats."

In a granite bowl, ringed about by glaciers and eight peaks higher than Mount Blanc, lie the white-gleaming villages of the Svans. Alongside each house rises a lofty massive tower into which the family fled for refuge from the onslaughts of raiders riding over the high passes. In a still more shut-in stone-girt cauldron live the Khevsurs, wearing medieval helmets, chain armor, and white Frankish crosses on their costumes. Are these the heritage from a hard-pressed band of Crusaders, driven into the mountains and absorbed by the natives who gave them sanctuary? This theory once deemed plausible is now assailed by more careful students who, after long groping into the origins of all these mysterious peoples of the mountains, are now compelled in many cases to admit they are baffled. There is no gainsaying, however, that the Khevsurs are an accommodating people. To them, fleeing for their lives, have come political refugees of all stripes—from monarchists to Bolsheviks—always sure of finding a safe asylum. Not less eclectic were they in matters of religion. In addition to their pagan holidays they observed the Friday of the Moslems, the Saturday of the Jews, and the Sunday of the Christians—which made them easily the champion religionists of the world.

Around the highest peak, Elbruz, live the aristocrats of the mountains, the Kabardins, whose various weapons and dress were appropriated by the Russians—also their celebrated radio-active mineral springs, now converted into magnificent spas and health-resorts. On both sides of the Pass of the Cross, over which runs the Georgian Military Road, are the Iranian Ossetines, Christianized by Queen Tamara and then converted to Islam.

But it is a well-nigh hopeless task to name all these peoples or fragments of peoples, "ethnic islands in a sea of history." And it is not necessary. They are important chiefly to the ethnographer, the linguist, or the traveler seeking out the picturesque and exotic.

V. JEWS, GERMANS, TAJIKS, AND MONGOLS.

Long before anyone ever heard of Russians or Tsars, the Jews were in Russia. In the eighth century the rulers of the powerful Khazars were converted to Judaism, establishing a regime tolerant of all religions. Their tutors were possibly the ancestors of the present Crimean Jews who disclaimed responsibility for the crucifixion as they were settled in the land before Jesus was born. In the Caucasus live the so-called Mountain Jews, claiming descent from the lost ten tribes of Israel. There are also Karaite Jews, Georgian-speaking Jews, and the Persian-speaking, silk-weaving Jews of Bokhara.

All told they number less than a hundred thousand, as against some three million speaking Yiddish—a Germanic vernacular with Hebrew letters. These were largely confined to a Pale of Settlement in certain specified provinces, and within this pale another pale was created by expelling them from the village. They were not allowed to own or lease land, to be officers in the army, nor to enter branches of government service, like the railways, the postal and telegraph services, as these were state-owned. On a limited quota basis their children were admitted to the schools while Jewish girl students sometimes resorted to the "yellow passport" of the prostitute in order to reside in the university towns.

In spite of all handicaps, through loopholes in the law, bribery of officials, submitting to Christian baptism, and sheer ability, great numbers of Jews became doctors, lawyers, bankers, and owners of factories. Under the "liberal" Tsars, life, too, became more tolerable for the masses, thanks to the lifting of certain disabilities and laxity in enforcing the law. But again the offensive was resumed and many Jews seeking deliverance through revolution turned to the parties of the Left. This furnished a pretext for further repressions, pogroms, and massacres which raised indignant protests from such leaders as Tolstoy, James Bryce and Cardinal Manning. Little changed, however, was the Imperial attitude, fairly well reflected by Pobedonostzev, Procurator of the Holy Synod, in his advocacy of a policy that would "convert a third of the Jews to Christianity, destroy another third by starvation, and drive the last third into emigration."

The Germans (1,300,000) are largely descendants of the artisans and engineers imported by Peter the Great and of the farm colonists invited into Russia by Catherine the Great in order to infect her peasants with German industry and order, but whose example was never very contagious. They were largely Lutherans, like the Letts, whose hatred against the double tyranny of the Baltic barons and the Tsar imbued them with a strong revolutionary ardor. The mainstay of the Roman Catholics were the Poles (780,000) and the Lithuanians.

The pure Mongols, moon-faced, slant-eyed, and mostly Buddhists, are represented by three branches: The horse-breeding Kalmucks, who, held back by an early break-up of ice, could not cross the Volga in time to join the main horde in its memorable stampede back to China, so vividly described in De Quincey's "Revolt of the Tatars." In the Altai Mountains live the Oriots who appear in the travels of

Marco Polo. Around Lake Baikal are the Buriats whose lamas, learned in the Indian philosophies, engaged from sunset to sunrise in cycles of disputes on the problems of life. All told, there are only a half-million Mongols but, by reason of the influence they exercise upon their kinsmen just across the borders in the People's Republics of Tannu-Tuva and Outer Mongolia, which are closely bound to the Soviet Union by trade and, in the latter case, by pledges of mutual assistance in event of attack by Japan or any other power—they are politically important. So are the Moldavians (250,000), now separated by the Dneister River from their fellow countrymen in the former Russian province of Bessarabia.

In the Pamirs the million Tajiks play the same significant rôle in relation to their racial and religious brethren across the Afghan frontier and in India. Fanatical Moslems, their eyes are frequently as blue as any Nordic's, for they spring from the same Iranian stock as the English, Swedes, and Germans. Dignified and gracious in manner, great numbers still cling to the customs of pre-Biblical times, as tenaciously as their villages do to the steep slopes of the mountains. Their houses are built without nails or windows, with each flat roof forming a courtyard for the one above it. They still cross the swift rivers on the inflated skins of goats and asses, and they saw their first wheeled vehicles when the airplanes flew into their fastnesses.

Thus the Soviet Union is made up of all kinds of peoples representing all levels of culture at all stages of social evolution: From the Paleo-Asiatic tribes of Kamchatka on the island of Sakhalin, just emerging from the Stone Age, to the Imeretians of the Caucasus, who possessed a developed art and literature while Anglo-Saxons were yet barbarians. From the roving reindeer and whale-hunting Chuckchi of the Arctic littoral to settled peoples like the Greeks, building their stone cities in the Crimea on the ruins of those built by their fathers seven centuries before the Christian era. On the one hand the patriarchal Avars, forbidding their women to sit, eat, or speak in the presence of men and on the other hand a survival of the matriarchate of the Yasai, or "women race," where the mothers and daughters do the trading and food-getting and the males are relegated to tending the household. At one extreme are hunting tribes like the Siberian Tunguz now called Evenki, with millions of square miles of virgin forest to wrest a living from while at the other are the intensive soil-tilling Ajarians, with rows of corn amidst their orchards, red-flowered beans climbing up to the corn-stalks, and a net of melon and pumpkin vines stippling the ground with green and yellow.

Such a multiplicity of peoples that one can do barely more than enumerate them. Aiysors, Aleuts, Balkars, Bessermen, Chuvants, Crishens, Dargins, Dungans. . . . Thus runs the list of nationalities many of whose names even were quite unknown under the old regime. Nor was it concerned in knowing them. To the Great Russians they were simply Inorodtzy "aliens by origin," the lesser breeds without the law. And the whole aim of Tsarist policy was how most quickly to bring them in subjugation to the imperial law. Acquired by force, they were ruled by force.

5. What is the Policy of the Soviets Toward Jews, Tatars, Kazakhs, Armenians, and the Other 185 Peoples?

"The equality and sovereignty of all peoples." "Their right to complete self-determination." "The abolition of all national privileges and restrictions." "The full free cultural development of every people." In putting into effect these four principles proclaimed by the October Revolution, the Soviets are finding a solution of the vexing problem of national and race antagonisms. How completely this is revolutionizing the status and attitude of the 188 former subject peoples can be grasped only by understanding their position under the Empire.

Toward all these peoples *the policy of the Tsars was forcible Russification.* "One Tsar, one religion, one language," or, in the more abstract formula, Autocracy, Orthodoxy, and Nationalism, meaning by the last, the culture, customs, and institutions of the Great Russians. These they sought to superimpose upon their own

Slav kinsmen—the White Russians and the Little Russians—as well as upon the dark-skinned races. With this objective the autocracy drove ahead rough-shod and ruthless. But not always. It was compelled at times to act cautiously and with cunning.

Fearful of rousing the Moslems to revolt, it interfered little with their practice of polygamy, wife-purchase, and child marriage. Finding that the non-resistance and resignation of Buddhism was a potent aid in pacifying the rebellious, it ordered the proselytizing arm of the church to leave that religion alone. Making alliances with native ruling classes—the emirs, khans, beys, and chieftains—it did not curtail their privileges so long as they kept their subjects in order. And in order to combat German influence along the Baltic, and Turkish influence in the Caucasus, a measure of cultural freedom was granted to these provinces on the borders.

But these were gestures of liberality, deviations from the declared policy dictated by expediency. Pausing for a moment the Great Russian steam-roller again resumed its onward course trampling down and rooting out the culture, traditions, and languages of the subject races, striving to supplant them with its own. To insure docility and obedience it kept them/ like the peasants, in a state of abysmal ignorance and economic vassalage.

With the age-old device of "divide and rule," it fomented strife between Turks and Armenians, Poles and Ukrainians. It incited one against the other and all against the Jews, who were perhaps the worst treated of all the step-children of the Empire. It played upon that "dislike of the unlike" in human beings, emphasizing the alien creed and customs of the Jews. It charged them with "ritual murder," the use of Christian blood in their religious ceremonies. It represented them as exploiters and parasites, and not without reason, since being practically forbidden access to the soil they turned in great numbers to trading, shop-keeping, and vodka-distilling. On these grounds it was easy to make the masses believe that the Jews were the authors of their hardships and miseries. Thus the outcast and outlawed race served at times as a veritable godsend to the autocracy. Whenever hard-pressed it wanted to divert the rising discontent and wrath of the people away from itself, the Jews could be used. They were made the scapegoats in times of famine, pestilence, and military defeat, and the populace, inflamed against them by the Black Hundreds, was led into their quarters to slay, pillage, and burn.

In all this, it may be said, there was nothing peculiarly Slavic or original. The Tsars were simply doing their bit in carrying the "white man's burden," employing the usual methods of imperial powers in dealing with alien peoples from the days of the Roman Empire to modern Italy and Japan. Furthermore, they did hold together the motley concourse of tribes and nations within the bonds of the Empire. But in it was no organic unity. The peoples were crushed, but not assimilated. It was a "Roman Peace" maintained by the Cossack whip and sword. As late as 1916 a third of the revolting Kirghiz were exterminated and whole tribes fled across the frontier. National passions and hatred of the oppressor, long smoldering beneath the surface, awaited only the downfall of the Tsar to break out in conflagration. The vast mosaic of nationalities "held together by violence, fraud and injustice fell to pieces" (Dillon). Through the centrifugal forces of the Revolution, first the states along the Baltic, then everywhere, began detaching themselves from the center. The great Eurasian plain extending across two continents threatened to resolve itself into another Balkan or Central Europe, crazy-quilted with a hundred warring states.

This catastrophe was averted by the *policy of the Soviets assuring self-determination and autonomy to all peoples.* This perhaps is the most significant achievement of Communist statecraft for it at once put a stop to the process of disintegration. Instead of breaking up into separate nations, Russia was welded into a single political-economic system. This was accomplished by completely reversing the old imperial system. The supremacy of the Great Russians was disavowed. No one people, henceforth, was to dominate another. To each was guaranteed the right to its own language, culture, and institutions. Subject races no longer, but as equals they were invited into "a free union of free peoples," called the Russian Socialist Federated Soviet Republics, and later, the Union of Soviet Socialist Republics.

6. What is Meant by UNION in the Name "Union of Soviet Socialist Republics"?

As the United States is a union of 48 states and the British Empire is a commonwealth of six nations, in a similar way the U.S.S.R. is an alliance of eleven Soviet republics. It was created in July, 1923, by a treaty or covenant between the four chief republics then existing—Russia, White Russia, the Ukraine, and Transcaucasia. Two more were admitted in 1925, another in 1929, and in 1936 the number was extended to eleven. In entering this Union the members give jurisdiction over certain matters to the federal government.

In its own domain each of these eleven republics is master of its own affairs. Each has its own written constitution and a complete set-up of legislative and executive organs. Each has its own *Sovnarkom* or cabinet of fourteen Commissariats, four of which—Education, Social Welfare, Local Industry, and Communal Economy—have no counterpart in the federal cabinet and are administered by its own officials in conformity with its own conditions and customs. Each has its own budget, its own courts, and the power of pardon and amnesty. And though doubtless a republic would have a hard time in seceding, Article 17 of the Constitution flatly guarantees to each the right of free withdrawal from the Union. Following are the eleven constituent republics:

Republic	Capital	Area (Sq. kilometers)
R.S.F.S.R.	Moscow	16,499,400
Ukraine	Kharkov	443,100
White Russia	Minsk	126,800
Uzbekistan	Tashkent	370,000
Turkmenia	Ashkhabad	443,600
Tajikistan	Stalinabad	143,900
Georgia	Tbilisi (Tiflis)	69,600
Armenia	Erevan	30,000
Azerbaijan	Baku	86,000
Kazakhstan	Alma-Ata	2,744,000
Kirghizia	Frunze	196,700

Within the limits of the new federal Constitution, there is self-government for the eleven nationalities after whom the above constituent republics are named. But what is the status of the hosts of others? They are by no means forgotten. On a similar home-rule basis, with a similar but less complete state apparatus, they manage their own affairs. The more advanced peoples are organized into Autonomous Soviet Socialist Republics each with its Supreme Council cabinet of commissars and courts. The less advanced into Autonomous Regions, not having as yet attained the full republican status. The more backward or smaller units into National Districts.

Within the borders of the Russian Soviet Federated Socialist Republic there are the *Autonomous Republics* of the Karelians, Tatars, Volga-Germans, Yakuts—seventeen in all. There are also six *Autonomous Regions* such as the Cherkess, Oirots, Jews. Within these more limited self-governing areas and the twenty-four other territories and provinces comprising this enormous federated republic are enclaves of peoples of alien stock and language, often formed into *National Districts,* such as the Koriaks, Ostiak-Voguls. Thus the R.S.F.S.R. is a huge agglomeration of peoples, each provided with the machinery of government adapted to its present cultural level and political maturity.

On the same principle the other ten constituent republics are sometimes divided into lesser units. New national districts and regions are formed while older ones schooled by experience in managing their affairs are promoted to the status of autonomous republics. These in turn, further demonstrating their self-governing capacities, may in course of time take their places as full-fledged constituent republics alongside the other eleven. By this device some fifty peoples, comprising 98 per cent of the population, are already enjoying a large measure of national autonomy. No more orphan nations! Each now has its special fatherland with its own capital, conducting its affairs in its own mother tongue—in some cases even with its own flag, coat-of-arms and native troops—working out its own destiny, according to its own traditions, in its own way.

7. What Power do the Small Nations Exercise in the Central Government in Moscow and How Are They Represented?

While enjoying a large measure of power in their own domains, the small nations exercise a definitely limited and conditioned power in the Central Government. For, in the last analysis, the Soviet Union is a highly centralized state, and in belonging to it, the republics necessarily give up some of their sovereign powers. These are enumerated in Article 14 of the new Constitution. The federal government arrogates to itself the sole power of declaring war, directing foreign relations, regulating trade, transport, posts, and telegraphs. It also lays down the basic principles governing the chief aspects of social life. Having delegated these vital matters to the federal government, what part in turn do the republics have in deciding them?

Obviously in population these republics differ greatly. There are ten times as many Kazakhs as Yakuts, 30,000,000 Ukrainians against 72,000 Ajarians. How hopelessly outvoiced and outvoted the small ones would be in the federal government were they represented in it on the basis of numbers alone! But they are not. Regardless of size, they meet in Moscow on the same footing when they come together to consider their common affairs and to legislate. Just as each American state, big or little, sends two representatives to the Senate, so to the Council of Nationalities each of the eleven constituent republics sends 25 deputies, each of the twenty-two autonomous republics sends 11, each of the nine autonomous regions sends 5, each of the national districts sends 1. In this body each nationality, the smallest as well as the largest, has its own delegation to advance its claims, safeguard its interests, and express its viewpoint on the larger issues of state. Each here wields the same power.

"But not real power!" interject those critics to whom the whole Soviet structure is but an imposing façade and a camouflage, cleverly devised to make the people believe they are governing themselves, deceiving them with the forms of democracy but withholding from them its substance. Neither this Council of Nationalities nor any other Soviet body, they insist, exercises any real authority. It is lodged solely in the Communist Party, particularly in the Polit-Bureau of the Party which is the real citadel of power. It dominates and determines everything regardless of the will of the people. That is the calumny of enemies or of those who do not understand the principles and dynamics of Soviet democracy. But even if this charge were altogether true, the minor nationalities could have no ground for complaint. The All-Union Communist Party is composed of members of all races and peoples, and great pains are taken to see that even the small and backward nations have their due representation. In the Polit-Bureau there have always been representatives of the non-Russian peoples—Jews, Georgians, Letts, Ukranians. And of course practically all the presidents and commissars of the national republics, regions, and districts are of the same stock and blood as the inhabitants.

At this point, one may cite the dictum of the monarchists: "The Russian nation is the only sovereign and ruling nation. Power in the State belongs to it alone." This doctrine is repudiated by the phalanx of non-Russians in high posts in the Soviet state, and by most of the 575 deputies who sit in the Council of Nationalities. Clearly a tremendous change has been wrought by the Revolution in the political status of the former subject peoples—symbolized by the change in name of the country.

8. Why Was the Name of the Country Changed from Russia to U.S.S.R.?

It signalized the passing of the domination of the country by the Russians, and the entry of the other 188 peoples into full partnership invested with equal powers and privileges. It declared that no longer was any one nation the sole proprietor and guardian of the State, but that henceforth it was the joint enterprise of them all. A visible and outward sign of this change in status is the change in name.

It makes easier the way for other peoples to enter this League of Soviet Nations, as Litvinov described his country to the League in Geneva. For large as it already is, the Soviet Union regards itself as only a nucleus which may grow into a larger world-wide federation. But a nation might well be reluctant to join if in doing so it had to sacrifice its name and identity. It does not have to. A nation is not invited to join Russia, but the Union of Soviet Socialist Republics. Thus the door is open wide for the present independent People's Republics of Tannu-Tuva and Mongolia, or any other that may rise in the future. It can come into the Union assured not only of preserving its name but all its national interests, economic and cultural, and developing them.

9. What Are the Effects of Soviet Policy upon the Industries, Culture, and Languages of the 189 Peoples?

In these fields they have most completely come into their own. For it is here that full scope and free play are given to the principle of autonomy. Far more so than in the political, because as already noted, the federal government reserves to itself control over the vital issues of war, diplomacy, communications. But in these other spheres—industry, language, education, and the arts —not only are there to all intents no reservations or restraints, but by every means they are fostered and stimulated. With what far-reaching results may best be seen in each case by contrast with the old regime.

The resources and industries of the minor nationalities are being developed at a tremendous rate. Under the Tsars they were treated as agrarian colonies and sources of raw materials. Their industrialization was artificially retarded in order to provide the Russians with freer markets for their own wares and finished goods. By heavy taxation their wealth was systematically drained away to the center.

Now the current is reversed. Out of Moscow, capital is pouring into the far reaches of the Union. Once desolate regions are being dotted by grain-elevators, the derricks of oil-wells, the smoke-stacks of furnaces and smelters. The once wasted waters of great rivers, impounded into dams and turned into power and light in hydro-electric stations, are setting the steppes humming with wires. Or sluiced through irrigating canals they are turning the parched lands into orchards and plantations. In their own gins the cotton of the Uzbeks is cleaned, and it is woven into cloth by looms made in their own factories. In its own "Daghestan Fires" the quartz-sands of Daghestan are melted into liquid glass, window-panes, and bottles—10,000 tons a year. In its own shops the tobaccos of Sukhumi are blended and rolled into cigarettes.

In the Pamirs and Altais trails are being widened into auto-roads and highways blasted over the mountains through passes of perpetual snow. The open ranges and free pastures seized by the land-grabbing Cossacks are being restored to their former occupants. The mountaineers are being given access to the plains. The vagrant streams that "do not know their places" are being curbed and set in proper channels. The vagrant Gypsies are being lured from their roving ways into wood-working artels and collectives. The ox and the bullock are giving way to the tractor. Locomotives are driving the camel from the desert and even the nomad is being converted into an industrialist—still too often an inefficient and indolent one. But Asiatic languor and laziness, begotten in part by the malaria mosquito, as it is by the hook-worm in Georgia, is being exorcised by quinine and draining of marshes. And those ancient scourges sweeping out of the East —bubonic plague, cholera, and typhus—are being checked no longer by prayers and incantations but by chemicals, quarantine, and doctors.

Among the Jews is going on a most radical change in their ways of getting their living. Contrary to general impression, they suffered greatly at the hands of the Revolution. While it swept away all the old disabilities, and made anti-Semitism a criminal offense, on the other hand it came down most heavily on the class to which so many of the Jews belonged—the traders, shop-keepers, speculators, *luftmenschen*. Many found places in the bureaus and offices vacated by those striking against the Soviets. Others, retrained as mechanics and metallists, are being absorbed in the big industries. Most significant is the transformation of the former ghetto-dwellers into tillers of the soil. Instead of the handful in the few old colonies under the Tsar, hundreds of thousands are now engaged in husbandry all the way from the Crimea to the far reaches of Siberia, where a center of Jewish life is growing up in Birobijan, named after two rivers flowing through this territory which abounds in timber, furs, and fish with adjoining deposits of iron, coal, gold, graphite, and marble.

Into this virgin wilderness are coming thousands of Jewish settlers each year. Some, recoiling from the hardships of pioneer life—cold, mud, and mosquitoes—give up and go back to their old homes. Most of them, conquering their long-inbred aversion to physical labor, are rejoicing in their new-found freedom on the land. They are building tractor-stations, power-houses, brick kilns, and creameries. They are pushing back the forests with big farms of wheat, soybeans, and rice, and in wood-working artels are turning their cedar and oak into wagons, window-frames, furniture. . . . In a new world on new foundations they are creating a new homeland that in a few decades may support millions of Jews. Raised from a Jewish National District to an Autonomous Region with its own schools, courts, libraries, and art museum, it is scheduled in due time to be elevated to the status of a republic.

"Scheduled also" interjected its traducers "to serve as a buffer state against Japan and become an area of conflict in event of a war." In rejoinder, Lord Marley points out that any assault would be launched far to the East or the West. For those however to whom this looms as a valid objection to going to Birobijan, there are other colonies and Jewish National Districts open to them. Among them are Stalindorf, Kalinindorf, and Larindorf, named after the leading men active in this historic undertaking—the return of the Jews to the land.

More revolutionary still is the economic transformation taking place among the primitive tribes of the North. Through Arctic seas, ice-breakers are smashing a way for the fifty steamers now plying to the mouth of the Yenisei. There the city of Igarka, with 20,000 inhabitants, is rising on foundations hewn from the frozen earth by axes. On summer nights it is lit by the midnight sun, in winter by electricity from its new power-house. Further inland a Great North Dog-and-Reindeer-Sledge-Route, 8,500 miles in length, is linking the Bering Sea with the Baltic. From the hunters and trappers at points more inaccessible airplanes are bringing their pelts to the markets. By establishing big sanctuaries for birds and beast, the supplies of game and fur for the future is assured. By prohibiting the sale of vodka and by checking the spread of syphilis—as ravaging to the natives of Siberia as to the Pacific Islanders and the Indians of America—the general level of health and well-being has been lifted. The monotony of diet is relieved by the introduction of vegetables and cereals now grown around the Polar Circle, thanks to the labors of Michurin and Vavilov. The natives are moving out of their igloos and sod "dug-outs" into windowed houses. The fishermen are throwing away their fish-hooks made of the breastbone of birds to use drag-nets and seines. Artels are being formed for graphite-mining, gold-dredging, and polishing the ivory of mammoth tusks dug from the frozen tundras.

Thus skipping a whole period of evolution, the aborigines are passing from their crude tools to the most modern machines, from the reindeer to the airplane, from a primitive life to a socialized economy. Omitting entirely the intermediate stage of capitalism, at one bound out of tribal feudalism they are leaping into Socialism.

In the second place an intensive campaign of education is bringing literacy to even the most inert and backward peoples. Under the Tsars, like the peasants, they were kept in a woeful state of ignorance. "Knowledge is like salt," declared a leading Tsarist statesman. "It is good only in small doses, according to the position of each social group and the need for it. Efforts to educate the masses would bring more trouble than benefit." True, a scheme for general education was projected but it was never put into effect. Even among the Ukrainians and White Russians, only one in three were literate, while among the Kazakhs, Kirghiz, and Yakuts not one in a hundred. Of the half-million women of Turkmenistan less than a score could read or write.

Now with a compulsory schooling for all children and an elaborate system of adult education, the Soviets are on the threshold of universal literacy. The number of Moldavian schoolmasters has risen from eleven to six hundred, the universities in the trans-Caucasus from one to twenty-two. In the Ukraine, besides 16,500 elementary schools in its own language, there are hundreds conducted in German, Yiddish, and Polish—and scores of them in Greek, Tatar, even in Swedish and French. So it is in all the republics. Wherever in a community there are enough children of a given nationality, a school must be opened in its language. That is a cardinal principle in the Soviet scheme. To each child in school and to each litigant in court the right to his native tongue.

To each people then, however small, is assured its own language. Under the Tsars the slogan was "one nation, one language!" Not only was Russian the sole medium of official business in state and court, but every effort was made to introduce it in the few native theatres, public halls, and schools that existed. A Kalmuck boy caught speaking his own dialect in class or at play had to wear around his neck the sign, "It is forbidden to speak Kalmuck," and go dinnerless. Even cultivated tongues like the Georgian were frowned upon and a minister of Nicholas I solemnly declared: "There never was, there is not now, and there never can be, a separate Ukrainian language. It is Russian corrupted by Polish." At one time the Gospels in Ukrainian had to be smuggled across the frontier; and in concerts, even the folk-songs sung in French! (Yarmolinsky.)

Now 336 newspapers, twelve art and literary magazines, and over 7,000 books yearly are published in Ukrainian. In the annual list of new titles, this hitherto almost unknown country stands eighth among all the countries of the world. More books are printed in Yiddish for the three million Soviet Jews than for all the other fourteen million Jews combined. Besides their own schools, the Gypsies have their own theatre, traveling in summer on a circuit from Leningrad to Odessa, and their own newspaper, *The New Trek*. Altogether publication goes on in 108 languages. In order to make them more accessible to all, most of them have been modernized, unified, and Latinized. No longer do the Mongol and Iranian languages appear in their former intricate characters, but in the same simple alphabet as the English. The cursive Arabic script—delicate and graceful, but difficult to master —was necessarily the monopoly of a scholastic caste. To make it easier for the toiling masses—also for the typist and typesetter— twenty-two of the Turco-Tatar tongues have been Latinized. So have Western Chinese, Korean, Kurd, Mountain Hebrew, and many others.

Likewise Russian, for the benefit of non-Slavs who are learning it. In his celebrated poem "Unto Myself I Reared a Monument" Pushkin wrote:

> The rumor of my fame will sweep through vasty Russia,
> And all its peoples speak this name, whose light shall reign
> Alike for haughty Slav, and Finn, and savage Tungus,
>   And Kalmuck riders of the plain.
>
> I shall be loved, and long the people will remember
> The kindly thoughts I stirred—my music's brightest crown,
> How in this cruel age I celebrated freedom,
>   And begged for ruth toward those cast down.
>
> —tr. by Babette Deutsch

This prophecy is now come true. Not only do the Tungus and the Kalmuck riders know the name of Pushkin but they may read his tales and poems now translated into 52 of the native languages. And conversely, into Pushkin's native language are being translated their own stories, songs and verses.

Still more striking is the host of new peoples now making its debut in the field of letters. The Golds and the Gilyaks, the Izhorians, Digorians, Vespians, and Tabassarians, the Yakugirs, Yagnobians, and Yazgulyanians, the Kets, the Kumands, and the Karagas. These are queer, fantastic-sounding names, as if they were invented by romantic writers for dwellers on another planet. But they are real peoples, occupying in some cases areas bigger than Belgium and with oral traditions reaching into the misty past. One reason one never heard of them is that hitherto they had no written medium through which to make themselves known to the world. Their languages were only spoken and without alphabet or script existed only in the realm of sound. Now 58 of them have been reduced to writing and supplied with grammars, primers, and dictionaries. Unabated this work goes on among the tribes of the far-off steppes, the forests, and the mountains. Soviet scholars living with them and listening to their speech are transfixing it on paper. In the same manner the music and folksongs which had no written notation, or which, like that of the Uzbeks, perished centuries ago, is being given one. Thus to the most obscure peoples is assured a vehicle through which to tell the story of its past, to voice its hopes and dreams and show whatever genius it may possess.

"To each people its own language!" The extremes to which the Soviets have gone in their determination to realize this objective is revealed to the casual traveler from the windows of the railway-car. As the train passes through regions of mixed populations, he can glimpse the names of stations in half a dozen languages. It is difficult however to grasp the colossal expenditure all this involves. Besides the tremendous outlay of money for the printing of literature, textbooks, manuals, and newspapers in a hundred vernaculars, there is the output of time and energy on the part of Russian officials in learning the languages of the peoples amongst whom they are working. And not less so upon the part of these peoples in the learning of Russian, generally taught as a secondary language in the schools so that all citizens may have a common medium of communication.

The Soviet justifies these great costs by the ends it seeks to attain. In the words of Stalin, "Socialist culture cannot be nationless culture." Only through its own language can the *ethos* and *genius* of a people unfold and express themselves in the realms of art and literature.

As a result of all this there is a veritable renaissance of the national cultures. Under the Tsars the drama, songs, and art of the dominant race were magnified to the detriment of the rest. True, the Russians were wont to applaud Gypsy choirs and Lezghian dances and sometimes affected the dress costume of the Kabardins and the gay skull cap of the Tatars. In this there was much of the spirit of patronage and condescension towards the bizarre and exotic. In general, the native cultures were neglected, discouraged, and vigorously suppressed.

In complete reversal of this attitude each people is now encouraged to develop its own culture—"national in form and socialist in content." This does not mean the preservation and cultivation of all the elements in the old cultures. The Communists maintain that it is impossible for the Turco-Tatars steeped in the Koran and the Arabic language and clinging to the tenets and ways of Islam to take their proper place in the new society. By the same token neither can the Jews, continuing in the Talmudic traditions, make their rightful contribution to the new life. To all intents a ban is placed upon the study of Hebrew—for the present at any rate—and Zionism is regarded as a form of bourgeois chauvinism. The aim is to sever the ties binding the peoples to their theocratic, feudal, or capitalist past, to wean them from the caste ideas and ethics of their former privileged and priestly classes. At the same time in keeping with Lenin's dictum, "No one can hope to be Communist without mastering the heritage of the past," the aim is to preserve and foster all the popular and social values in the old culture.

To this end hundreds of national and regional museums and scores of national theatres are being established. Expeditions from the Academy of Science are ferreting into remote places, recovering the secrets of the ancient handicrafts, reviving the folklore and music that were dying out. To the Art Olympiads and the Theatre of Folk Art in Moscow with gay variegated costumes and weird musical instruments come the troupes from the far reaches of the land; Uzbek shepherds re-enacting the drama of their struggles to reclaim their stolen pasture lands; Georgian mountaineers in felted *bourkas* and silvered daggers, reciting their epic, "Man in the Panther's Skin," a classic centuries before Shakespeare was born; the mass choirs of the Abkhasians singing without words.

Alongside the old, so carefully cherished, are the first fruits of the new culture growing out of the nascent life and ferment of ideas now stirring the peoples. The half-heathen Mari chanting the wonders of the "Lenin light," as they call the electricity now illumining their dark forests beyond the Volga. Tatar poets reading verses dedicated to the tractor—the "iron horse of Socialism." Gypsies describing their new venture as tillers of the soil in "Sunrise Over the Marshes." Squat-legged story-tellers from the bazaars of the East, alternating their heroic tales of Tamerlane with new legends about the mighty deeds of Lenin.

From Ashkhabad, 3,000 miles away, a cavalcade of thirty-four horsemen in high long-haired caps and raw silk rainbow robes comes riding into Moscow bringing with them their desert songs and dances. How they traversed the parched and roadless deserts, going thirsty while they gave their horses the last drops from their flagons and swaddled them against the icy night winds in their own blankets while they slept shivering on the sands; how they pushed on, now without sighting a single person for days, now through multitudes flocking out to cheer them; how after three months their horses' hoofs clattered on the stone pavements of the capital, and to the "mighty men," Stalin, Molotov, and Voroshilov, they gave their salutations and their best *kolhoz* steeds, receiving from them in turn awards and golden watches—all this becomes the theme of new sagas and legends told in the oases and teashops of Turkmenia and sung by the cotton pickers in the new collectives.

Besides the regional Olympiads of Art in which the various peoples of Central Asia and the Caucasus vie with one another there are the Spartakiads of Sport in which they meet to demonstrate their prowess in the sphere of physical culture. A Buriat may win the pole-vault, a Kazakh the discus-throw, a Little Russian make a Big Russian take the count in the wrestling match, while a fleet-footed Tungus runner outstrips the field. Alongside of these regular track and field events there is a revival of those feats of skilled strength by which the ancestors of the present day athletes entertained themselves in olden times. Among these is Georgian wrestling which is conducted with something of the pomp and ceremony of a bull-fight, the contestants in special attire timing their movements to the roll of the *zurni,* an orchestra of drums.

This encouragement to self-expression along national lines leads Stalin to remark, "It may seem strange that we—advocates of the merging of all cultures into one common culture with one common language—are at the same time partisans of the flourishing of national cultures. But there is nothing strange in this. National cultures must be allowed to unfold and develop, to make apparent all their potential qualities." To the extent that each reaches its full fruition will the society of the future be enriched. And in the present the opportunity of each people to see and understand the culture and achievements of the others serves as a powerful factor in promoting a spirit of mutual respect and esteem.

10. What is the Significance of the Soviet Solution of the Problem of Race and Nationality?

It demonstrates that the national aspirations and interests of the most diverse peoples can be satisfied, and that, at the same time, these peoples can be held together in a single political-economic system, with each enjoying all the benefits accruing from this union. Thus to a world torn by national strife and dissensions and with the frontiers of all states bristling with bayonets, forts, and tariff-walls, the Soviet Union presents the spectacle of 189 peoples living and working together in peace and amity.

As the Soviet Constitution of 1924 rhetorically puts it: "There —in the camp of Capitalism—reign national enmity, inequality, colonial slavery, chauvinism, national oppression, pogroms, imperialist brutalities, and wars. Here—in the camp of Socialism— prevail mutual confidence and concord, national freedom and equality, a dwelling together of the peoples in peace and their brotherly collaboration." A rather exultant and sweeping assertion. Like all generalizations, it has its exceptions.

Some Disruptive Factors

The Revolution has not driven out all the devils of nationalism. The prejudices and barriers between races trained for centuries to look upon each other with rancor and envy are not melted down in a day or a decade. Armenians still carry bitter memories of bloody massacres perpetrated on them by the Kurds and Turks—and vice versa. The old blood-feuds and vendettas still linger on in the mountains. The old epithets of contempt—*Zheed* for the Jew, *Samoyed* meaning "cannibal" for the Nentsi, *Sart,* or "yellow dog," for the Uzbek—are still whispered, albeit furtively. In the factory dining-rooms the older

Moslems, abhorring pork like the Jews, refuse to sit at the same tables with the sausage-eaters, or go to the same baths.

With rankling memories of the past, minor nationalities still harbor suspicions of the good intentions of the Russians. And not without reasons. For the old superior domineering attitude still survives in some members of the former ruling nation, even among the Communists. On the other hand, these once suppressed and humiliated peoples are themselves sometimes infected by the same spirit they resent in the Russians. Pride in their new-found strength and achievements easily grows into national arrogance and chauvinism, and breaks out into undue self-glorification in their speeches, poems, and plays. Nationalities just liberated from thraldom are not averse to lording it over minority groups within their borders. Although comprising less than ten per cent of the population, the Finns in Karelia sought to make their language obligatory for all.

Against these aberrations or "deviations from the correct national line," as they are called, the Soviets proceed in many ways: by exposure in the press of all manifestations of national contempt and jingoism, and by holding them up to merciless scorn and ridicule; by haling offenders into the courts, inflicting on them drastic penalties, even capital punishment, for the "stirring up of racial or religious strife"; by directing the energies and emotions of each people to the total reconstruction of its life. Occupied in this colossal task little time remains to indulge in the old feuds, hates, and grievances and they die of inanition. Other factors, still more positive and powerful, are operating to fuse the heterogeneous units into one.

Forces Making for Unification and Consolidation

Obviously there are many material advantages for each nation in belonging to the huge federation which pools the strength and resources of them all: The large funds to draw upon for investment in capital projects and in case of some national calamity; the free flow of goods over one-sixth of the globe unimpeded by tariff-walls and customs-barriers; the economy of supporting a single corps of foreign ambassadors, consuls, and commercial agents instead of separate ones for each of the eleven constituent and twenty-two autonomous republics.

The economic interdependence of all is fostered by the policy of developing the particular resources of each region to the fullest. This assures to each the maximum growth but on the other hand prevents any one from being wholly self-sustaining and sufficient to itself. Cotton-raising Uzbekistan looks to timber-growing Karelia for lumber and to the iron-smelting Urals for metals. All three look to grain-growing Ukrainia for rye and wheat. With each dependent upon the others a thousand economic ties are binding them closer together.

Social intercourse, intermarriage, and intermingling of the blood-streams are now taking place on a tremendous scale between peoples who formerly regarded one another as "aliens," "infidels," and "pariahs." Constantly they increase with the breaking-down of the divisive influence of caste and religion and by the building-up of mutual respect through the spread of education in the spirit of Communism. From the Institute of Northern Peoples in Leningrad thousands of youths carry the new doctrine of fraternity back to their villages along the Arctic littoral and into the *taiga* of Siberia. From the Institute of Eastern Peoples in Moscow it is borne down to the mountains of Afghanistan and into the grazing lands of Mongolia. Jews who once quailed before the dreaded whips of the Don Cossacks are now joined in friendly competitions with their erstwhile enemies in plowing, reaping, and even in horsemanship. Radio and press are battering away at the old taboos and discriminations. Railways and airways are weaving stronger the strands of good-will and understanding. In a thousand ways the processes of mutual adaptation and assimilation are accelerated.

All these forces make for a growing solidarity of feeling and interests among the 189 peoples. They have much the same problems to grapple with and the same enemies to guard against. They are animated by a common purpose, conscious of the same historic mission, and give allegiance to a single leadership—the one All-Union Communist Party. Under its unified direction they are engaged in the same great enterprise—the building of Socialism.

11. What is Meant by SOCIALIST in the Name "Union of Soviet Socialist Republics"?

(A planned system of national economy in which the prime motive in the production of goods is not the making of profits but use. This is based on the social ownership of means of production. In Stalin's words to Roy Howard in 1936, "Our society is Socialist because private ownership of factories, plants, land, banks, and transportation has been abolished in our country and replaced by public property." There are two main forms: The giant mills, mines, railways, airways, oil-fields, tractor stations, forests, and state farms are all owned and operated by the government. The cooperative form in which the stores, the peasant collective farms with their barns, cattle, and "the use of the land forever," and the *artels* of artisans with their workshops and implements turning out leather, lace, lacquers, are all jointly owned and managed by their members.)

Thus, in contrast to capitalist countries, in the Soviet Union all but an infinitesimal fraction of the means of creating wealth are socially-owned. Privately owned are one's personal belongings, furniture, savings, most houses and living quarters. What the Soviet citizen earns by his own labor is his to use, to enjoy, and to dispose of as he sees fit. What he is prevented from doing is appropriating the fruits of other people's labors. He cannot own or buy shares in the wealth-producing properties such as land, forests, oil, coal, water-power, or big industries. But if this Socialist system takes away this ancient right of exploiting one's fellows, on the other hand it gives him a number of new unique rights. These are the rights to work, to leisure, to education, to material security from infancy to old age. All of these for the first time in history are written into the constitution of the nation. To ensure them for all citizens, all those services ministering to the general welfare such as schools, medicine, and science are organized on Socialist lines, making them practically free and accessible to all.

Outside this "socialized sector," as it is called, still exists the "private sector"—individual craftsmen, shopkeepers, private practitioners, and a small fraction of the peasants still tilling the soil "on their own," in the old primitive traditional fashion. Just as in other countries state and municipally-owned schools, post offices, and railways are islands of Socialism in the sea of capitalism, so in the Soviet Union still remain these tiny islands of capitalism. Not for long, however. In the Soviet program of complete socialization, they are slated to disappear at the earliest possible moment. With the country already predominantly Socialist it is entitled to the name it bears.

But why is the name Socialist used at all? Why isn't it the Union of Soviet *Communist* Republics? One reason is that for fifty years the revolutionary struggle of the workers has been chiefly waged under the Socialist banner. By keeping that name, the Soviet Union keeps its connection with the historic movement, declares that it is the natural logical outcome.

Another reason is that the Soviet Union is still far distant from the goals of Communism. Communism envisages an ideal society in which each person gives according to his ability and receives according to his needs. In the Soviet Union inequality of earnings still exists, people are paid as elsewhere according to the quality and quantity of their work. Communism is a stateless society in which the state has disappeared and "the government over persons is replaced by an administration of things." In the Soviet Union the state is still all-powerful, regulative, coercive. Communism is a classless society in which all privileges of birth, wealth, and unequal education are abolished. In the Soviet Union, while most of these inequalities are being swept away, there are still remnants of the old classes, and many vestiges of the old order still survive in the customs and consciousness of the people.

For these reasons the word *Communist* in the name of the country would be very much of a misnomer. Up until recently the word Socialist was also a misnomer. It was merely a declaration of the objective toward which the Soviet peoples have been struggling for these twenty years. Even yet, as Stalin points out, they have not completely arrived. But they are so near to it that the new Constitution opens with the simple statement that the U.S.S.R. "is a Socialist state of workers and peasants."

12. What is Meant by SOVIET in the Name "Union of Soviet Socialist Republics"?

(Soviet is the Russian word for council.) In old days there were Soviets of bee-keepers, medical workers, a Soviet of ministers of the Tsar. On the main Kremlin gate was a celestial figure—the Angel of the Soviet! In 1905 the word took on a distinctly revolutionary meaning when it was applied to the groups—virtually strike-committees—that directed that first general uprising against the Tsar. These first Soviets were crushed.

With the downfall of the Tsar, in 1917, immediately they sprang into life again all over the land: in little towns upon the Black Sea coast and along the rivers reaching into the depths of the Archangel forest; in regiments of soldiers at the front and on battleships of the fleet; among miners, railwaymen, iron-molders, peasants, teachers. It was a remarkable phenomenon, but there was nothing mysterious or inscrutable about it.

The Soviets were formed spontaneously, just as they might be in any other country in a similar emergency. Something had to be done and done quickly. Naturally the people came together right on the spot where they happened to be working—for instance in the big spinning room of a textile factory. Naturally they wanted to get and keep in contact with the ideas and sentiment in other factories, shops, offices, and barracks around them. Quite as naturally they selected one or more of their fellow-workers whom they trusted to do this. So they did in every other institution in the vicinity. All these delegates elected directly from their jobs constituted a local Soviet or council. It set to work at once enforcing order, securing supplies, rationing food—acting in place of the old apparatus that was falling to pieces.

As the Soviets rose everywhere out of the same condition, to deal with the same problems, everywhere they were alike. Almost exact replicas of the Soviets around Petrograd were those around Vladivostok, 6,000 miles away, at the other end of the Trans-Siberian line. These local Soviets, through delegates sent up to Petrograd, were united in a central body, the All-Russian Congress of Soviets. Rapidly they grew in power and prestige, increasingly rallied around them the support of the masses, more and more assumed the functions of government; and, on November 7, 1917, they became the government.

As Lenin perceived, these organs that rose so elementally at the outset of the Revolution were admirably adapted for carrying it on. Along the same lines, then, on which they were first organized, they continued to function for twenty years. The basis of representation was occupational—not territorial. A man voted according to where he worked, not where he resided; not passively as a "mere inhabitant," but functionally as a producer. The Soviets were elected not from wards or precincts, but by individuals who met at the polls once every two or four years. They were elected from factories, offices, regiments, universities, farms —by groups that met daily on the job. Thus each group, through close contact, could pick the man who best represented its specific interests, one whom it knew and who knew his business. The theory being that, as economic interests are more vital and fundamental than any other and as the state deals primarily with economic problems, direct economic representation is the most effective.

The fundamental principles and set-up are not essentially changed by the new Constitution of 1936. The country is still governed by Soviets from the bottom up to the Supreme Soviet or Supreme Council in Moscow. As members of labor unions in factories, as tillers of the soil on the collective farms, as professors in academic societies, as housewives in certain localities

. . . they assemble to nominate their candidates for the Soviets. The chief difference is that they now vote directly for the deputies to all Soviets up to the top; they vote secretly; and everybody has a vote. These changes in the electoral system are only a reflection of changes in the general economy of the country and in the status of its citizens. As all, or practically all, are now regarded as engaged in "socially useful labor" to all is now given the means for the "social control" of the state enunciated by Lenin in 1918.

Lenin Expounds the Soviet Idea to Raymond Robins

". . . We may be overthrown in Russia, by our backwardness or by foreign force, but eventually the idea in the Russian Revolution will break and wreck every political social control in the world. Our method of social control dominates the future."

"But," said Robins, "my government is democratic. Do you really say that the idea in the Russian Revolution will destroy the democratic idea in the government of the United States?"

"The American government," said Lenin, "is corrupt."

"That is simply not so," said Robins. "Our national and our local governments are elected by the people, and most of the elections are honest and fair, and the men elected are the true choices of the voters. You cannot call the American government a bought government."

"Oh, Colonel Robins," said Lenin, "you do not understand. It is my fault. I ought not to have said corrupt: I do not mean that your government is corrupt in money. I mean that it is decayed and corrupt in thought. It is living in the political thinking of a bygone political age. It is living in the age of Thomas Jefferson. It is not living in the present economic age. Therefore it is lacking in intellectual integrity. How shall I make it clear to you? Well, consider this:

"Consider your states of New York and Pennsylvania. New York is the center of your banking system. Pennsylvania is the center of your steel industry. These are two of your most important things, banking and steel. They are the base of your life. They make you what you are. Now if you really believe in your banking system, and respect it, why don't you send Mr. Morgan to your Senate? And if you really believe in your steel industry, in its present organization, why don't you send Mr. Schwab to the Senate? Why do you send men who know less about banking and less about steel, and who protect the bankers and the steel manufacturers and pretend to be independent of them? It is inefficient. It is insincere. It refuses to admit the fact that the real control is no longer political. That is why I say your system is lacking in integrity. That is why our system is superior. That is why it will destroy yours."

"Frankly," said Robins, "I don't believe it will."

"It will," said Lenin. "Do you know what ours is?"

"Not very well yet," said Robins. "You've just started."

"I'll tell you," said Lenin. "Our system will destroy yours because it will consist of a social control which recognizes the basic fact that the real power today is economic and that the social control of today must therefore be economic also. So what do we do? Who will be our representatives in our national Soviet, from the district of Baku, for instance?

"The district of Baku is oil. Oil makes Baku. Oil rules Baku. Our representatives from Baku will be elected by the workers in the oil industry. You ask, 'Who are these workers?' I say, the men who manage and the men who obey the orders of managers—the superintendents, engineers, artisans, manual laborers. All the persons actually engaged in the actual work of production, by brain or hand—they are workers. Persons not so engaged, but who try to live off it without labor, by speculation, by royalties, by investment unaccompanied by any work of management or by any work of daily toil—they are not workers. They may know something about oil, or they may not. Usually they do not. In any case, they are not engaged in the actual production of oil. Our republic is a producers' republic.

"You will say that your republic is a citizens' republic. Very well. I say that man as producer is more important than man as citizen. The most important citizens in your oil districts—who are they? Are they not oil men? We will represent Baku as oil. Similarly, we will represent the coal basins of the Don as coal. They will be representatives of the coal industry. Again, from the country districts, our representatives will be chosen by peasants who grow crops. What is the real interest of the country districts? It is not storekeeping. It is not money-lending. It is agriculture. From our country districts our Soviets of peasants will send representatives chosen by agriculture to speak for agriculture.

"This system is stronger than yours because it admits reality. It seeks out the sources of daily human work-value and, out of those sources directly, it creates the social control of the state. Our government will be an economic social control for an economic age. It will triumph because it speaks the spirit, releases and uses the spirit, of the age that now is.

"Therefore, Colonel Robins, we look with confidence at the future. You may destroy us in Russia. You may destroy the Russian Revolution. It will make no difference. A hundred years ago the monarchies of Britain, Prussia, Austria, and Russia overthrew the government of revolutionary France. They restored a monarch, who was called a legitimate monarch to power in Paris. But they could not stop, and they did not stop, the revolution of middle-class democracy, which had been started at Paris by the men of the French Revolution of 1789. They could not save feudalism.

"Every system of feudal aristocratic social control in Europe was destined to be destroyed by the political democratic social control worked out by the French Revolution. Every system of political democratic social control in the world today is destined now to be destroyed by the economic producers' social control worked out by the Russian Revolution.

"Colonel Robins, you do not believe it. I have to wait for events to convince you. You may see foreign bayonets parading across Russia. You may see the Soviets, and all the leaders of the Soviets, killed. You may see Russia dark again as it was before. But the lightning out of that darkness has destroyed political democracy everywhere. It has destroyed it not by physically striking it, but simply by one flash of revealment of the future." (*Raymond Robins' Own Story as told to William Hard*)

13. Who Votes for the Soviets, and How?

Universal, equal, direct, and secret suffrage. This was called the "four-tailed" franchise by the old revolutionary parties of Russia and was an objective of their struggle for decades. It is at last put into effect by the new Constitution.

Universal means the extension of the franchise to every Soviet citizen after reaching eighteen years of age. That gives a vote to over 100,000,000 persons, the largest electorate in the world. The only exceptions are imbeciles and those deprived by special order of the court.

Equal means that the vote of every person counts one whether he is a peasant or worker, priest or atheist, Communist or non-Communist, foreigner or citizen.

Direct means that all members of the Soviets, from the lowest to the highest, are chosen directly by the people. So are all the People's Judges, while moot questions are to be decided by popular referenda.

Secret means that with a list of candidates named by Labor Unions, Cooperatives, organizations of youth, cultural societies, and the Communist Party—which, as will appear later, is unlike a political party in our sense of the term—each citizen enters the polls to mark his ballot for the ones he prefers.

All this seems very much like the technique of elections in Western countries. But it is a radical change in the Soviet form, reflecting the fundamental transformation that has taken place in the social-economic system. It marks the passing of the special status and privileges of the working class and the entry of the peasants, professional classes, and civil servants into full partnership in the business of governing the state. Power is now the prerogative of the whole people, shared by all alike.

From the Old Constitution to the New

The first constitutions of 1918 and 1924, based on the Declaration of Rights of Toiling and Exploited Peoples written by Lenin, did not promise freedom, equality, and political rights to all. Frank and militant class documents, they were designed to secure the "dictatorship of the proletariat," the rule and government of the working class. By this is meant primarily the industrial workers. On them, according to Marxist theory, is laid the historic mission of ushering in the new social order. As the greatest sufferers from exploitation under capitalism, or the most aware of it, they have the greatest incentive for overthrowing it. Also as they are strategically placed at the engines, dynamos, switches, and pumps, they have the power to do so. They are therefore the natural "grave-diggers" of the old order. Furthermore, working together in factories and mines begets in them a receptivity to new ideas, a sense of solidarity, and a social outlook essential to the building of Socialism. They are therefore the natural "architects" of the new order. As Stalin explained this Marxist theory to H. G. Wells, "The transformation of the world is a great, complicated, and painful process. For this great task a great class is required."

This statement of Stalin was based on what actually occurred in Russia. It was the workers primarily who made the Revolution, and on them devolved the chief responsibility for defending it and carrying it through to its goal. Therefore all means were utilized to make them conscious of the historic rôle they were playing, and to secure the dominance of their interests and ideas in the organs of state. To this end those classes whose interests, occupations, cast of mind or temperament rendered them hostile to the building of Socialism were disfranchised outright. The following could not vote or be voted for: Persons guilty of the cardinal Communist sin of exploiting their fellow men—all who lived on unearned income, by "speculation," or in any way extracting gain from the labor of others—owners of factories and stores, kulaks, and middlemen. . . . Persons who were the bulwarks or retainers of the Tsar's regime—members of the royal family, the gendarmes, and agents of the old detective and punitive organs, and most officers who fought in the White Armies against the Soviets. . . . Persons who, from the building of the good society in this world, diverted the minds and energies of the people to a paradise in the next world—all monks, priests, rabbis, lamas, and leaders of the hundred Russian sects and cults.

With the loss of the ballot went the loss of food-cards, labor-union and other privileges. So serious were these disabilities for the "deprived ones," as they were styled, that it evoked a lively desire to obtain the franchise, and each year considerable numbers who proved their loyalty to the Soviets were given it. Altogether, the names appearing in the lists of the disfranchised ran from two to five per cent of the adult population. This was a drastic device but still it failed to realize the Communist aim of putting control in the hands of the workers. For three-fourths of the population were peasants and on an equal suffrage basis they could easily outvote and swamp the workers.

Therefore a *limited franchise* was given the peasants, whose instinctive conservatism rendered them at best lukewarm to the building of Socialism. This limitation did not apply to the local Soviets in charge of local affairs. For them every peasant—except the kulak—voted, and every vote counted one. The discrimination came in the method of electing representatives to the higher Soviets. They were chosen by a system that gave to 100 *voters* in the towns the same voting power as 500 *inhabitants* in the villages. This meant roughly that while the peasants' vote counted one, the workers' vote counted three. In this way the ascendancy of the working class—with the Communist Party as its vanguard—was ensured in the organs that legislated, laid down broad policies, and put them into effect.

All these restrictions and disabilities are now completely swept away. In the words of Article 135 of the new Constitution "every citizen has the right to elect and be elected, irrespective of his race or nationality, his religion, educational, or residential qualifications, his social origin, property status, and past activity." By this broadening of the franchise to include every citizen at last is realized the pledge of Lenin in 1919 "to work systematically for the abolition of this inequality in voting."

Abolished likewise is the old method of voting. Formerly it was by acclamation or show of hands which often deterred the cautious person from voting as he really wanted, for fear of offending a neighbor, a high official, or a Communist. Now, with secret balloting, without fear or favor, he can vote for the person or policy that he really wants. And finally, also, abolished is the old indirect system of elections whereby the local Soviet chose the delegates who composed the Soviet of the rayon or province and these in turn sent up the delegates composing the Soviet of the republics, and so on. This system was not without its advantages. By filtering out the less capable along the way it secured for the higher Soviets the more efficient and zealous administrators, and also their control by the better organized workers and the Communists. Only in the organs at the base of the Soviet pyramid were the deputies directly elected. At the apex they were several removes away from the people and their control. Now all the way from bottom to top they are directly elected by and responsible to the people.

Because of these changes the new Constitution is hailed as a great stride forward toward real democracy. And it is. But it must be remembered that under the "dictatorship of the proletariat," even in its heyday, there was a large amount of democracy. That is evident in the ways by which the people managed their affairs under the old Constitution, which are preserved in all essentials and more widely extended under the new. The basic self-governing unit is the "general meeting" of all members of a small community, collective farm, or factory. Here in line with the traditions of the old *mir,* or village-gathering, or of the old New England town-meeting, they meet to consider their mutual interests—schools, roads, taxes; building a new bridge, "laboratory hut," or radio station; reading of reports on the Five-Year Plan, foreign relations, the menace of war.

Out of these free-for-all discussions emerges a consensus of opinion as to what should be done. The business of doing it is the function of the local Soviets. To these organs candidates are nominated by various groups, their vices and virtues often hotly debated, and sometimes only after a series of meetings do the elections take place. In this way a half million "general meetings" serve as forums and training-schools in which "the masses are teaching themselves how to rule themselves." They afford the people an intimate first-hand contact with the problems that concern them and from the list of candidates they can select those they best know and trust to manage their common property and run their local affairs. To their constituencies these elected deputies, two or three times yearly, give an account of their stewardship. They also report on the activities of the higher Soviets, taking back with them thousands of "instructions" and proposals for new laws and changes in the old. Thus continuously and at all points is the pressure of public opinion brought to bear upon the apparatus of government.

In the multifarious activities of the 70,000 Soviets, besides the million or more regularly elected deputies, several million more citizens are enlisted as volunteers. About the same procedure is followed in the labor unions, cooperatives, the innumerable civic societies and leagues. Because of this wide participation of the masses, observers like the Webbs maintain that the term "dictatorship" was always a misnomer. Rather it was really a democracy, different in form and technique from the West, but nevertheless a democracy in the sense that it gave the people the opportunity to express their will and determine the conditions of work and life. Certainly in the administration of local affairs, insofar as their decisions did not run counter to higher laws and directives, control was in the hands of the people. As for those larger affairs of state, such as the insistent pursuit of a policy of peace, the long successful effort to avoid war at any cost, the concentration on the building of Socialism instead of on World-Revolution, there are few to deny that these policies represent the real wishes of the Soviet peoples.

This expression of the popular will is made more easy, direct, and effective by the new Constitution. How fully and quickly all its statutes will be put into effect depends upon a number of factors, chiefly war. In any case the Soviet Union is not and in no wise pretends to be a "complete" democracy. That, according to Communist theory, will come only with the coming of a completely classless society and an economy of abundance. As Lenin puts it, "Only in a Communist Society where there are no longer classes can one speak of freedom. Then people will become accustomed to the observance of those elementary rules of social life known for centuries, repeated for thousands of years in all sermons. They will observe them without force, without subjection, without constraint, without the special apparatus of compulsion called the State, which will wither away and disappear."

Having served its purpose, the State, in the words of Engels, will take its place in the museum of history alongside the bronze ax and the spinning-wheel. Then "the government over persons will be replaced by an administration of things." That, in all likelihood, is destined to occur only in some more or less distant future. But it is interesting to note that just as the present move toward a fuller democracy was preluded by long discussions in Soviet theoretical journals, now in these same journals are appearing articles about the next steps on the road leading to the ultimate abolition of the State and the Party.

14. How is the Soviet State Organized?

It is built like a pyramid with its base formed by some 70,000 local Soviets of Toilers' Deputies. Above them stand the Soviets of the *rayons,* or townships; above them the Soviets of the *oblasts,* regions, provinces, territories; above them the Soviets of the republics. Thus tier upon tier the structure rises up to the Supreme Council, *Verkhovny Soviet* of the U.S.S.R.

These Soviets vary in size from some 20 members in the villages up to 300 or more in the larger areas while the city of Moscow has 2,116 deputies. Their work is far more extensive than that of similar bodies in non-Socialist lands, as it embraces wide fields of enterprise elsewhere left in private hands. Yet their sessions are short as most of the deputies elected from their jobs return to their jobs. The worker goes back to his factory, farm, or fishing-fleet; the teacher turns again to his school; the judge to his law-court; the actor to his theatre; others to their posts in the Red Army, Party, and Cooperatives.

The aim of this is to avoid the sharp differentiation of the people into "the governing" and "the governed," to avoid the creation of a professional caste of law-makers and officials. But the activities of these Soviets are continuous and must have continuous direction. For this purpose each Soviet chooses from its members a strong, standing Executive Committee, the supreme authority in the intervals between sessions. From the bottom up every Soviet is responsible to the one above it. On the other hand, every member of a higher Soviet reports back to the constituency from which he came and is subject to recall by it.

The apex of the whole pyramid apparatus is the All-Union Supreme Council, the sovereign power in the country. From it all legislative and executive organs derive their authority. Unless specially convened it assembles twice a year in sixty-day sessions in the former Imperial Throne Room of the Moscow Kremlin. This parliament composed of about 1,200 members, elected for a term of four years, is divided into two chambers. The *Council of the Union* consists of some 600 deputies elected directly by the people every four years, one deputy for 300,000 inhabitants. The *Council of Nationalities* consists likewise of about 575 directly elected members on the basis of twenty-five deputies from each constituent republic, eleven from each autonomous republic, five from each autonomous region and one from each national district. Its function is to introduce and temper legislation to fit the special interests, culture, and customs of the 189 races or ethnic groups.

A bill becomes a law by a majority vote in both chambers. Any member may address a question to a commissar or other high official to which an oral or written reply must be given within three days. In case of a conflict between the two chambers it goes to a conciliation commission made up of an equal number of representatives from each house. If disagreement persists, as a final resort, new elections are called for. In each chamber work is directed by a chairman and two vice-chairmen. These chairmen preside in turn over the joint session of the two houses among whose duties is the election of the powerful *Presidium of the Supreme Council* consisting of 37 members. As the supreme authority of the country when the parliament is not sitting, in this small body is focused tremendous power. It convenes sessions, interprets laws, conducts referenda on its own initiative or on demand of the republics, awards decorations grants pardons, ratifies treaties, appoints and removes the high command of the armed forces, and can even declare war in case of an attack on the Soviet Union or on any country with which it has a treaty of mutual assistance.

Responsible to and appointed by the Supreme Council is the chief executive organ of the country, the *Council of People's Commissars, Sovnarkom,* corresponding to the cabinet in other countries. Besides the usual administrative duties, it issues "decrees" which, save in emergencies, must be ratified by the Supreme Council. There are eighteen commissariats, divided into two groups:

1. Eight *All-Union Commissariats* deal with matters over which the federal government has sole jurisdiction: Foreign Affairs; Defense; Foreign Trade, a state monopoly; Railways; Waterways; Communication, post and telegraph; Heavy Industry, oil, coal, iron, and steel; Defense Industry. These direct their work throughout the country by their own appointed representatives.

2. Ten *Unified or Joint Commissariats* existing both in the federal cabinet in Moscow and in the cabinets of the eleven constituent republics to whose Supreme Councils they are responsible. These are the Commissariats of Light Industry; Timber; Food; Agriculture; State Grain and Livestock Farms; Finance; Home Trade; Home Affairs; Justice; Health. This federal cabinet has a chairman, a vice-chairman, and includes also the heads of five important auxiliary organs: The State Planning Commission, Gosplan; The Soviet Control Commission, which checks up on the execution of all decrees, orders, and ordinances to verify how much has actually been accomplished, and acts to strengthen the general morale and discipline; The Committee for Purchasing Agricultural Products; The Committee on Arts; The Committee on Higher Education, which supervises the technical institutes and training centers of university standing maintained by the commissariats.

Appointed by the Supreme Council are the judges of the *Supreme Court,* for terms of five years, and a chief Prosecutor or State Attorney, for seven years. The court advises on the legality of proposed legislation, decides disputes between republics, and hears accusations against high officials. The Prosecutor is vigilant to see that no commissariat, nor any institutions under them, nor individuals holding office, fail to observe the federal law. He appoints a federal prosecutor, in each republic and autonomous region, who is responsible, not to local authorities, but to him alone, for five years.

This, in skeleton form, is the state apparatus of the Central Government. After this pattern is constructed that of each of the eleven republics with practically the same machinery. The one outstanding difference is the make-up of the Councils of People's Commissars in these republics. In addition to the above-mentioned ten Unified or Joint Commissariats, and the representatives of the All-Union Commissariats and two of its Committees, appear four that have no counterpart in the federal cabinet—the Commissariats of Education, Local Industry, Communal Economy, and Social Welfare.

There were also Commissariats of Labor up to 1934 when they were dissolved and their functions handed over to the labor unions. More striking than the absence of this department often found in foreign cabinets is the presence of several that have no counterpart in England or America. These are the industrial commissariats which have steadily increased in number, indicating a trend in the state to occupy itself less proportionately with political affairs and more with economic, a process of evolution from a "government over persons to an administration of things." Pertinent in this connection are the words of Lenin in 1918, "Not only politicians and administrators, but engineers and agronomists will in the future speak from the tribune of our congresses. This is the beginning of a most happy epoch when there will be less and less politics, when people will not speak about politics so often and so long. Engineers and agronomists will speak much more."

15. What is the Force That Holds the Huge Soviet Apparatus Together and Keeps It Going?

Manifestly something powerful is needed to run the huge apparatus, complicated in itself and all its parts. This applies not only to the state, but as will appear later, to Soviet organizations in the field of industry, transport, trade, education, science—to every Soviet institution except the courts and the Red Army. They are all intricate and involved. And, intricate as they seem on paper, they are not less so in reality.

With every opportunity for red tape, friction, legislative dead-locks, endless dispute and dissension, one wonders why the whole vast machine does not get hopelessly gummed up or break down altogether. That it does not is due to a body of men, described by Pilnyak as "pick of the flabby, uncouth Russian folk—men in leather jackets who function energetically." These are the Communists, the engineers directing the whole machinery, the repair-crew ready for every emergency, the constant source of dynamic energy, infusing life and motion into all the parts.

The Communists are Distinct from the Soviets. This difference should be clearly grasped at the outset. There are 175 million citizens of the Soviet Union, of which only some two million are members of or candidates for the Communist Party. By fact of birth or residence in the Soviet Union one is a citizen; through choice one belongs to the Party. The official Soviet newspaper in Moscow is *Izvestia* (*News*); the official Communist newspaper is *Pravda* (*Truth*). From the center down into the provinces and out into the remotest villages these two institutions run parallel—each with its own papers, magazines, headquarters, organs, officials. It is the Soviet Government, however, that is the sovereign power in the country. It alone can pass laws, send the army and navy into action, give orders to the police. Over these affairs the Communist Party has no legal jurisdiction whatever. Nor has it over Soviet citizens, or for that matter over its own members.

The Communists Control the Soviets. Though distinct from the government, they dominate it—infinitely more than the Democrats do the American Government or the Conservatives the British. There is no secret about this. "The Party openly admits," says Stalin, "that it guides and gives general direction to the government." This is putting it modestly. As a matter of course, almost automatically, the Party decisions of today become the Soviet laws of tomorrow. Almost exactly as the Five-Year Plans are outlined by the Party, they are adopted by the Government. This is achieved not by arbitrary imposition of its will but by using its tremendous authority and prestige. Prior to any meeting of a Soviet or other body in which there are non-party members the Communist "fraction" or group holds a caucus to decide the course it will follow. Then entering the general meeting to work and vote as a unit the Communists are usually able to put through the measure they sponsor and elect the candidates they nominate.

All the People's Commissars and nearly all the heads of trusts and universities, the general staff and high commanders of the Red Army, are members of the Party. They likewise hold most of the key positions in the Labor Unions, Cooperatives, Machine-Tractor Stations, and the press which, with the Soviets, are known as the "levers," "conveyors," "belts," transmitting ideas and directives to the masses. Upon its members in these organizations—"using their influence and all their arts of persuasion" (Stalin)—the Party depends for carrying out its policies. If they do not, it straightway discredits, demotes, or deposes them. So authoritative is the Party that at its bidding the Association of Proletarian Writers melted away. For a copy of the newspapers containing the call to curb the excesses of collectivization, peasants in remote places paid as much as ten rubles. And this was only a letter signed by the secretary, Stalin. More powerful than a *ukase* of the Tsar is a *directive* of the Party. Thus is put into effect the "dictatorship of the proletariat." The Communist Party is conceived of as its vanguard and through it dictatorship or control is exercised.

16. Why is the Communist Party So Powerful?

It is the only legal party and enjoys a complete monopoly in the political field. As is said half-humorously, "There can be several parties in the Soviet Union, but on the sole condition that one is in power and the others in jail." As Stalin explains it, political parties are the expression of the interests of opposing classes. In the Soviet Union the interest of all its citizens is in the building of Socialism and there is no necessity for more than one party.

It is a compact, iron-disciplined body, with all its parts moving into action as a single unit, presenting a solid front on every issue. At the same time it is highly flexible, able to adapt itself to swift changes in circumstances and public opinion.

It is close to the masses, a sensitive instrument for ascertaining and articulating their ideas and wishes. "Amongst them," said Lenin, "we are a drop in the sea and we can govern only if we adequately express what they feel." Standing, not above and apart from the people, but penetrating into the farthest reaches of the land with its 130,000 local units, it knows at first hand their wants and needs.

It knows exactly what it wants and out of its analysis of social laws and forces has charted a way for getting it. Its aim is Communism, the creation of a new society by a change in its property basis and with a complete change in the superstructure of ethics and institutions. Toward this goal it drives forward often changing its tactics but never its objective. With its sole criterion "the progress of the Revolution," it waives aside precedent, quashes legal obstacles, and rides rough-shod over age-old traditions. Anything that advances Communism is good. Anything that retards it is bad.

Like Whom Are the Communists?

That they are more than a political party is at once evident. The Webbs call upon their readers to think of its membership "as a united confraternity, a widely spread companionship, or as a highly disciplined order professing a distinct and dogmatic political creed, and charged with a particular vocation, rather than as a political party." In order to bring this home to the Western mind, writers have ransacked history to find an analogy. By focusing attention on some one trait or feature the Party has been likened to the Order of Jesuits, to Plato's Guardians, or to Cromwell's Ironsides with their Spartan rigor and Puritan outlook. In some aspects the Communist Party does resemble each of these organizations. In others it is quite the reverse.

Like the Jesuits, the Communists are bound together by allegiance and fealty to a common doctrine. But the doctrine of the Communists is based on materialism and science, completely abjuring the mystical and supernatural—any idea of God. Like the Guardians, those supermen in reason and intelligence devised by Plato to rule his ideal republic, so the Communists govern the affairs of this Soviet Republic. But, quite the opposite of the Guardians who came from a privileged caste, the Communists are mostly of lowly proletarian and peasant origin.

More often the Party is pictured as an army strictly regimented from top to bottom: Stalin is the Commander-in-Chief; the Polit-Bureau serves as the General Staff; the provincial, regional, and *rayon* secretaries as captains, lieutenants, and corporals; the two million members as soldiers of the rank-and-file carrying out with unquestioning obedience the orders of its commanders. But, totally unlike any army, these Communist commanders and officers are for the most part elected. And still more unlike an army, it is hard for one to get into the Party and easy to get out of it. At any moment in any crisis a member may leave it of his own free will.

None of these analogies hold good. At some point each of them breaks down completely. As Brailsford remarks, "Nothing like the Communist Party exists on the earth today or ever before our time made its appearance in history. It is unique in its aims, its methods, its morale, its organization."

17. How is the All-Union Communist Party Organized?

The basic unit formerly called the "cell" and now the "primary party organ" comprises all Communists in a given village, office, Soviet, Labor Union, regiment, ship, or hospital. In a large enterprise like a State Farm or factory there may be one in each of its workshops—brigades, teams, or shifts. It serves as the vitalizing force, the carrier of Party ideas to the larger social unit to which it belongs. Altogether there are about 135,000 of them. They elect the delegates comprising the Party Committees of the *rayons,* wards, or cities. These in turn elect the Party Committee of the province or territory. From these are sent the delegates who compose the Party Congress in each of the several republics. Thus each higher Party organ is elected by, and at the same time has jurisdiction over, the ones below it. It may alter or reject any of their decisions insofar as they conflict with Party rulings. This is known as "democratic centralism."

At the apex of this Party pyramid stands the *All-Union Congress,* convened every two to four years and composed of about 2,000 delegates and alternates. Since the founding of the Party in 1898, there have been 17 of these congresses and the whole history of the Revolution may be written around them. Prior to the Congress is the Party Conference of chairmen and secretaries and a wide discussion of current problems and ways of meeting them in the "cells" and press. This is carried into the Congress, often with a great deal of acrimony, until finally emerges a definite policy known as the "Party Line." With its adoption all debate abruptly ceases and the Party swings into action with every member obligated to support every decision by every means at his command. Before dissolving, the Congress elects the following three organs:

The Central Committee, meeting several times a year, is composed of 70 members and 68 "alternates" to fill the places of absentees. When the Congress is not sitting it is the supreme authority of the Party enjoying a prestige that almost always assures to it blanket approval of its activities and resolutions. Attached to it are nine departments with sub-sections such as Propaganda, "many ideas for the few," and agitation, "few ideas for the many," charged with general campaigns among the masses and intensive education of all its members. Other departments are the Agricultural, Industrial, Transport, Planning— on a small scale paralleling those in the cabinet of the Soviet Government.

The Auditing Commission of 22 members watches over the treasury and checks up on the finances of all organs.

The Commission of Party Control consisting of 61 members serves as the collective keeper of the "Party conscience," maintaining the morale and discipline of its members. It keeps a record of all Party members, explains the Communist code of ethics, oversees the "cleansings" and "purgings." It is empowered to send its representatives into any meeting of any committee or Party organ to see that its activities conform to the instructions and "line" laid down by the Party. It may summon any Communist at any time to give an account of his public activities and even his personal life, and is the court of final appeal in cases of expulsion. It secures for the Party supervision over all state institutions by concerted action with the Commission of Soviet Control, the one case in which Soviet and Party are officially connected.

The Central Committee of the Communist Party appoints the following:

The Polit-Bureau of 10 members and 5 "alternates," the supreme authority when the Central Committee is not sitting. As all major policies of State and Party are first debated and often decided by this body, it is—or was, at any rate up till the election of the Presidium of the Supreme Council of the U.S.S.R.—the most powerful single organ in the whole country.

The Secretariat of 4 members of which Stalin is the head.

The Organization Bureau of 10 members and 2 alternates forms with the Secretariat a close interlocking directorate, superintending the affairs of the vast network of Party cells and committees. It appoints the paid workers to their positions, receives reports, gives advice, and issues detailed instructions.

The Party Delegates to the Third Communist International.

The Editors of the chief Party papers.

To qualify for most of these offices a Communist must have a Party standing of ten years. This puts control of the commanding heights largely into the hands of men of long tested wisdom and loyalty. With them rests the decision of every important issue from high policies of State to terms of admission into the Party.

18. How Does One Become a Member of the Communist Party?

Feeling the urge to join, with the recommendation of three to five members, one appears before the local branch of the Party as an *applicant*. After a check-up on character, conduct, and loyalty to Communist aims and principles, he is entered on the rolls as a *candidate*. Thereupon he becomes a student in a "school of political grammar," while his manner of life is kept under close scrutiny. This period of instruction and probation lasts from one to five years, depending on whether one is a worker, farmer, engineer, Red Armyist, or civil servant. It ends with an examination: "In joining the Party is he motivated by ideas of his own self-advancement? Is he grounded in Leninist theory and tactics? Does he understand his civic duties? Is he addicted to drink or religion? What company does he keep? Has he any traces of bourgeois mentality?" If he is approved by a majority vote he receives the red card of a full-fledged *member*.

Who May Join the Party?

Not everybody may even apply for membership. To private traders, speculators, priests, kulaks, and the Tsar's gendarmes, the gates of entry are completely closed. To others the way into the Party is made hard or easy depending on whether or not they are regarded as good material for the building of Socialism. That is determined largely on the basis of occupation and parentage which are divided into four categories:

1. Most drastic are the tests for persons of bourgeois origin—those belonging to the official and professional classes, and civil servants in general. Fearing the influx and influence of elements alien to its aims and ideology, the Party requires that they be vouched for by 5 members of ten years' standing and wait outside the gates as candidates for five years.

2. Less stringent are the terms of admission for collective farmers, small craftsmen, and primary school teachers. However, as they are usually of peasant antecedents, and may still have deep attachment to private property and an innate conservatism begotten of their old individualistic ways of getting a living, the Party is cautious about letting them in too readily. They must furnish 5 sponsors who have been members for five years, together with the recommendation of a representative of the *rayon* committee or Machine-Tractor Station and stand as candidates for two years.

3. Somewhat easier are the tests for farm laborers, Red Armyists, engineer-technicians in the field, and those who have been industrial workers for less than five years. They enter on the same basis as those in the second category, except that they do not furnish any recommendations other than those of their five sponsors.

4. The gates of the Party swing open wide to the "aristocracy of labor"—those working in mines, mills, and factories for five years or more. They are preferred because their instinctive class-consciousness, and the spirit of solidarity and cooperation created by long working together, makes them naturally the bearers of the collective idea. With only 3 sponsors of one year's standing and after only one year as candidates, they are welcomed into the fold.

This assures a preponderance of manual workers who constitute on the basis of origin some 60 per cent of the membership as against 20 per cent peasants and 20 per cent intelligentsia and civic servants. However, as the promotion of workers and farmers to responsible posts in all branches of the national life is the fixed policy of the Party, about 50 per cent of the membership, on the basis of present occupation, are actually engaged directly in tilling the soil and in industry. Great efforts are made to raise the proportion of women to 20 per cent and also to secure a due representation from each of the 189 nationalities.

Why the Party is Small in Numbers. In the Soviet Union there are tens of millions who call themselves Communists, and to all intents they are. Of these only some two million are actually enrolled as members, candidates, and "sympathizers" of the Party, a new category created in 1934. Obviously by lowering its standards, it could quickly double or triple its size. But always the stress has been on quality rather than quantity. Only once were the bars let down to all comers. That was when the White Army of Denikin was marching on Moscow, and all Communists were in imminent danger of being shot or hanged. To join at such a moment was supreme evidence of one's sincerity and devotion to the cause. On other occasions the bars have been lowered a bit to facilitate the admission of "workers from the bench and the plow." Such was the "Lenin levy" after his death when 200,000 new candidates were recruited. Also the "mass enlistments" on the Tenth Anniversary of the Revolution, and at the end of the first year of the Five-Year Plan brought great numbers into the Party. How long they stay in the Party is another question. That depends upon how they live up to their duties and obligations.

19. What Are the Duties, Privileges, and Ethics of a Communist?

The Communist must carry out all orders and instructions of the Party. From the moment he becomes a member, his time, talents, and energies are no longer his own to do with as he sees fit. They are at the disposal of the Party. What it dictates to him he must do, regardless of danger, risk, or personal desire. His own aptitudes and inclinations will be considered, but the last word lies with the Party. Where it sends him he must go, and without murmuring. Comfortably living in Moscow today, tomorrow he may be drafted to one of the fighting fronts. At an hour's notice he must pack up his things and start for some lone trading-station in the Arctic, a blast-furnace in the Urals, an army post on the Manchukuo border. And wherever he goes, it is no ordinary service that is demanded of him.

The Communist must be an "activist." Always Lenin insisted there was no place in the Party for the mere believer or well-wisher—only for the man of deeds. Outside of earning a living at his regular job he must actively engage in some definite social work. It may be as organizer of a shock-brigade, as secretary of the Anti-Alcohol League, as speaker for the Air and Chemical Defense or collector of funds in aid of the Spanish workers. Hardly an able Communist without at least two or three extra assignments over and above his routine work in the "cell" or basic unit to which he belongs. It is a terrific drain upon one's strength and vitality—putting verve into mass meetings, whipping up interest in loans and drives, inducing fellow-workers to enter the Stakhanov courses, sitting through late-into-the-night conferences so essential to the Russian way of doing things. And what is it all for? To explain that to the satisfaction of others, the Communist must first understand it himself—theory, tactics, and current events. To zeal, all the time he must be adding knowledge.

The Communist must always keep studying. As he had to go to school before joining the Party, so he has to keep going. For this purpose, quite apart from the Soviets, an elaborate educational system is run and supported by the Party itself: Primary schools with gray-beards learning to spell out the words on the red banners under which they march. Graded schools of "political grammar," teaching the class struggle, the Communist Manifesto, the rôle of the tractor in the liberation of the villages, the influence of such writers as Tolstoy or Gorky. And so on up to the Communist Universities and the institutes of research. "A school for every Communist and every Communist in school." This includes the higher officials who have their own Marx-Lenin "circles," seminars, and reading courses. With theory goes an intensive study of the Party program, so that every member may know what to do and exactly why he is doing it. At the same time there is practical training in problems of leadership and management, whereby a man of diligence and ability may rise to high positions of trust and responsibility. But that does not necessarily imply a corresponding rise in his income. The knowledge acquired is to accrue primarily to the benefit of the Commonwealth and Party, not to the material weal of the Communist.

The Communist must lead a life of relative simplicity. It is difficult to do otherwise. Up till 1933 no matter how much a Communist earned he could retain no more than the "Party-Maximum"—fixed then at 900 rubles a month. This was the limit for the most brilliant head-surgeon in a hospital or the most capable director of a factory, if he were a Communist, although under him might be non-Party specialists receiving five times as much. Any surplus he earned, aside from a portion he might pick up from his writings, went into a pension-fund for old and disabled comrades. While this limitation no longer obtains, it is generally observed in spirit. Woe to the Communist who shows that his interest in a position is because it is lucrative.

As monthly dues to the Party, every member is assessed from 20 copeks up to three per cent of his income, a mere trifle alongside the contributions he is called upon to make to the numerous societies and causes. Then there are special collections—for building a dirigible, a Lenin memorial, a house for homeless children; for food and medicines for the Spanish Loyalists. In all these good works, by generous giving, the Communist is expected to set an example for others. With his income eaten into on all sides, the

Communist is often forced to lead a frugal, if not ascetic, life. In a comparatively poor country, to give up the idea of luxury or amassing a competence is not such a great sacrifice. But it is a sacrifice to give up one's personal convictions, and one that the Communist may be called upon to make.

The Communist must always hew to the "Party Line." That means the line of action by which the policies mapped out by the Party congress are made effective. Although this line often changes, pursuing today a trade or tax measure that yesterday it opposed, the Communist must change with it. He must be ready to fall in with the new tactics to meet new conditions. They may not accord with his previous convictions, he may have even furiously agitated against them, but once the majority of the Party has spoken the matter is settled. As fervently as he denounced a measure he must now support it—or get out. Although he deems it wrong he must act as if he believed it right. This insistence on Party fealty may put a strain on conscience and a premium on mere conformity. So be it. The Party holds that the fate of the Revolution rests upon unity of mind and action, that any "deviation" spells disruption and disaster. Not for a moment will it tolerate any individual, however brilliant he may be, who sets up his own will and judgment against the collective wisdom of the Party. It requires every member unreservedly to accept its decisions and unwaveringly to carry out its directives. This is particularly true in critical moments, as in 1930 when Collectivization was in danger, and in 1937, with the Fascist powers threatening an assault from the East and West. With the very existence of the Soviet State at stake, any contumacy—not to speak of defiance of or conspiracy against the "Party line"—is regarded as treachery of the deepest dye.

Privileges of the Communist. Heavy as are the burdens and obligations he takes upon himself, they are balanced by certain compensations. If he must bear the onus for the blunders and failures of the Party, he shares also the glory of its successes.

A certain prestige comes to him as a "Leninist." He is usually chosen by his fellows as their spokesman. His red card is a passport opening many doors closed to the ordinary citizen. If he must work hard he is always assured of a job, and a good one. His chances for promotion are greater, for high positions of trust are preferentially given to Communists. Attached to them are certain perquisites in the form of better quarters, automobiles, secretaries—serving to magnify one's feelings of self-importance and power. If there is any priority in admission to rest homes, hospitals, or schools, it will probably favor the Party man. If at all times the member has to put first the interests of the Party, it is likewise to the interest of the Party to look out for its members.

These advantages are alluring enough to tempt an ambitious, power-loving man to weasel his way into the Party, even if his heart is not in the cause. With his eye on the main chance he may try by outward conformity and lip-service to make for himself a career and enjoy its rewards. But it is a hazardous path, beset by pitfalls and perils, in which he has carefully to watch every step. He may be sure that the argus-eyed Control Commission is watching him. Any slip, any breach in the spirit or letter of the rules is visited by a graded series of penalties, Party reprimand, demotion, public censure, and, in extreme cases, expulsion.

20. Why Are Communists Expelled from the Party?

In any big mass organization there is a certain percentage of careerists, fools, blockheads, and criminals. So, obviously, there must be some amongst the millions in the Communist Party. Some worm their way into it in spite of all safeguards and vigilance. In others, human nature being what it is, time and circumstances slowly work their corruption. The most zealous become cold or indifferent; the Puritan yearns for the fleshpots; the noblest are poisoned by power; the most self-denying turn to their own self-aggrandizement. The spirit of Communism may have gone out of them but through self-interest or sheer inertia they cling to their red cards of membership. They are "radish Communists," red on the outside but white and decayed within—a drag and deadweight on the Party. Naturally the Party wants to get rid of them.

"Throw out the weak-hearted and wavering!" demanded Lenin on the very eve of the October Revolution. "Reduce the membership and you strengthen the Party." It did so in that critical moment, and has been doing so ever since. The Communists are just as ruthless with themselves as they are with others. Constantly, under the supervision of the Control Commission, there are "cleansings" of the local organs whereby annually two to five per cent are weeded out of the Party. Periodically there are thorough "purges" or house-cleanings of the whole apparatus, as in 1933-1936, when nearly a half million were stricken from the rolls. Narrow is the gate leading into the Party but broad is the way that leads out.

Grounds for Expulsion

"For behavior unbecoming a Communist" members are constantly being ejected from the Party. Under this rubric first of all comes drunkenness. As the use of alcohol is strongly entrenched in the old Russian folkways an occasional lapse may be winked at. But not habitual intoxication, which, like sexual excesses, by undermining one's health, unfits a man for work and discredits the Party. More shameful is any manifestation of contempt for other races or for women—particularly wife-beating, stigmatized as "a relic of the bar-

barous past," but still favored by the old peasants as a method of disciplining their wives.

Almost on a par with this is participation in religious ceremonies, like going to mass or the christening of one's child by the priest or conniving with wife or relatives to do so. Ostentation in dress or living, inciting envy among the less fortunate is a violation of the Communist code of ethics. So is "association with an alien element"— showing too evident a liking for the company of traders, priests, and kulaks, instead of honest proletarians. That is why Communists often hold aloof from foreigners or maintain a certain reserve in dealing with them. As the cardinal Communist sin is living at the expense of one's fellow men, a member who engages in any profit-making enterprise exploiting the labor of others is outside the pale at once.

Other frequent cause for expulsion is abuse of office and authority, arbitrariness or arrogance in the execution of duties, using one's position to bludgeon people into submission—popularly known as "commissaring it" over people. Quite as unpardonable on the other hand is any weakness or capitulation like withdrawal from a village under threats of kulaks, criminals, or bandits, which is "desertion in the face of the enemy." Most reprehensible is the use of power to advance one's personal interests, "to obtain favors from women," to acquire better quarters, or to divert public funds into one's own pocket. Under the last head, offenses rise from petty peculation, like padding one's traveling expenses, to embezzlement in the grand manner, for which many Communists have not only been ejected from the Party, but from the world by way of the firing squad.

Offenses directly against the Party are most summarily and drastically dealt with. For absence without good excuse, or non-payment of dues, members are automatically stricken from the rolls. Likewise, for suppression of facts in the personal history that each member furnishes to the Party, particularly "concealing one's social origin." To be born of priestly or noble stock is not a crime, but it is a crime to hide it. So it is to divulge any secrets of the Party to outsiders. Communists must know how to hold their tongues, and while among themselves they may criticize the Party, they must not in public. Only through the regular Party channels and press may they express their dissent. And they are strictly enjoined from organizing into cliques to advance their own program and "play politics." Any attempt to do so is "factionalism," which, in the eyes of the Party, is the seven deadly sins rolled into one.

It was this that brought the downfall of Trotzky and his Left Opposition with its demand for more "democracy," more drastic measures against the kulaks, and its insistence on "world revolution" as opposed to the policy of building Socialism in the Soviet Union. In clear defiance of the Party statutes he set up a faction with its own program, secret pass-words, and printing press, and over the constituted heads of the Party appealed for outside support. To the world he declared that this was the only way left for him to promote his ideas and principles. But to the Party it was sheer treason, a menace to its very existence. It roused against him the indignation of the masses and lost him the support of most of his own followers. Many of them, at first approving his ideas, became outraged at his tactics, and he was ejected from the Party, and from Russia.

With the same relentlessness the Party shattered the Right Opposition of Rykov and Bukharin, who were calling for a slowing down in the tempo of industrialization. If its adherents were less harshly handled it was because their organization was more nebulous, and, quickly recanting their heresies, they were readmitted into the Party.

In some cases the Party appears high-handed and ruthless in its treatment of the transgressor. More often with patience and forbearance it strives to make him see the light, to confess the error of his ways, and keep him in the ranks. "Expulsion," says Stalin, "is a final and a fatal weapon that must be used only in a hopeless case." Before resorting to it there are first warnings, second warnings, and official reprimands—particularly for one who in weakness has succumbed to the sins of the flesh, to very human failings. It may try to lessen his temptation, to appeal to his shame, pride, honor, chiding and cajoling him in an effort to reform and reclaim him. Vast however as may be the tolerance of the Party for the wayward, there is none for the willful. Whatever leniency may be extended to other offenses, the Party cannot abide anything that savors of insubordination. The stiff-necked rebel, the flouter of discipline soon finds himself outside the camp—an outcast and maybe an exile.

21. What is the Attitude of the Million Outcasts from the Party?

It depends upon the Communist. The very sensitive are overwhelmed with shame and humiliation, and not a few have committed suicide. The zealous sue for reinstatement, often carrying their appeals to the top. Sometimes the charges against them are deemed groundless and they are at once readmitted. More often they are told to demonstrate by loyalty and good works why their petition should be granted. As candidates or "sympathizers," the new category created in 1934, they may start up from the bottom again. The vengeful ones turn against the Party breathing out fire and slaughter, as far as they dare, vilifying it in a way surpassing anything a noble, landlord, or priest can do. Of them it may be said, "Hell hath no malice like a Communist expelled." At the other extreme are the indifferent who accept their lot philosophically. The Party has no use for them! Very well! they have no further concern for it. Quit of their duties and burdens, they are glad to be free men, masters of their lives again. But these are exceptions.

Plight of the Outlawed Leaders. For most Communists expulsion is a bitter grief and affliction. Especially so for those great actors in the revolutionary drama, like Trotzky, now compelled to watch it going on without them. Yesterday on the heights and now cast down from them, they are stripped of office and glory. Particularly is this true of those who once enjoyed great power and whose lust for it grew when deprived of it. Such apparently were Zinoviev, Kamenev and their followers, who, twice expelled from the Party and twice publicly repenting their deeds, were twice reinstated. But their loyalty and that of their fellow conspirators in the "parallel center" was only feigned. They could not reconcile themselves to the leadership of others whom they deemed their inferiors and continued to hold that without world revolution Socialism in the Soviet Union was foredoomed to failure. They counted on a turn in affairs elevating them again to power, and when that did not eventuate, according to their own confessions, they resorted to sabotage, assassination, and plotting with foreign enemies, and in shame and ignominy were led away to execution. For those leaders who are in exile there are some recompenses. There is balm for their wounded pride in the consciousness of being martyrs to their principles. They have passed from the stage but not from the headlines. The eyes of the world are still upon them and by their partisans their names are remembered and their deeds recounted.

Tragedy of the Outcast Rank-and-File. Far more pathetic are the "forgotten men" of the Revolution, the thousands now disowned by the cause for which they hungered, bled, and all but died. First to answer the call to arms, they were the shock-troops, the rough-riders, and daredevils of the Revolution. The armies of Denikin and Wrangel threatening the red capital! With the cry "Proletarians to horse!" night and day they thundered across the steppe to meet the invaders and hurl them into the sea. Bell-ringers giving the signal to the Whites from a church tower! They crawled into the village, up into the belfries, and hanged the bell-ringers with their own ropes. Through the long grim years of civil war and intervention their lives were spent in raids and forays, in desperate hand-to-hand clashes with the enemy. Then came peace.

From carnage and destruction the Revolution turned to reconstruction. Changing fronts it called these men to change with it. From camp and saddle it called them to shop and office; no longer to wield a sword but a pen; not to show lion-like bravery, but ant-like patience. It called them to make a complete revolution in character, temper, habits of life and work. Many of them have done so. Throughout the Soviet land one meets these old warriors, functioning as effectively on the new fronts—education, industry, farming—as they did on the battle fronts. As engineers now building roads instead of barricades. As farm-managers, driving insects from the plague-stricken districts as they once drove out the Whites. As teachers, assaulting the strongholds of village ignorance and superstition as they once did the concrete forts at Perekop.

Others, however, unable to make the inner change are unequal to the new demands laid upon them. Having transformed the world they are unable to transform themselves. Men of deeds and action rather than thought and reflection they were fitted for the heroic exploits of war, but not for the painstaking routine of peace. By their impetuosity, recklessness, and daring they could clear the way for Socialism, but they cannot build it. The very qualities that at an earlier period were assets to the Revolution have now become liabilities. Briefly, the Party records the reasons for their exclusion: "For inability to pass from methods of command to persuasion," "For seeking in drink the stimulus once found in battle," "For failure to qualify for the new tasks of the Revolution." Glorious they were in their day, but their day is gone. As one of them laments in "Azure Cities," "No longer the hoofs of our horses ring over the steppes. The happy days are fled." These outcast soldiers of the rank-and-file are the most poignant tragedies of the Revolution. In peril and danger all they had they gave to the cause, the scars on their bodies bear witness to their devotion, and now they are left to sink into oblivion, unknown, unhonored, and unsung. They don't belong.

But is there no consideration for past services? A little, but not much. Like a republic, a revolution is ungrateful. It devours its own children. It has to. Beset on all sides by enemies and with ever-new crises to grapple with, it adjudges everyone, not by what he has done, but by the acid test of Lenin, "What are you doing now?" It uses its votaries as long as they are of value. But when they cease to serve its purpose, or will not move onward with the onward-moving revolution, it casts them aside.

Filling up the Gaps in the Ranks. While eliminating those who are not adequate to the new tasks, the Party tries to fill their places with those who are. For new tasks it seeks men of a new temper, type, and training. But where can it find them? Not many among the old generation that is passing. The traits and instincts of the old order are too deeply rooted in them to provide good material for the new. However, in lieu of better, the Party makes the best of them. But it places no great reliance on them. It puts its hopes in the new generation, now growing up in Soviet schools, farms, and factories—on its youth more flexible, adaptable, and receptive to new ideas and methods. More specifically it counts upon that section of youth most directly under its tutelage. These are the six million comprising the organization known as the Comsomol, the "reserves" from which the Party will mainly draw its recruits in the future.

22. Who Are the Comsomols?

They are members of the "All-Union Leninist Communist League of Youth," numbering several million from 15 to 30 years of age. They are organized into some 200,000 "cells" or branches in factories, farms, ships, and universities. In structure and by-laws this League resembles the Party, but unlike it the terms of admission are quite easy. Anyone, regardless of class origin, may join on being vouched for by other members as to character and loyalty. He may be expelled for drunkenness, rowdyism, race-prejudice, love of luxury, "passivity," or a "sheerly masculine psychology toward women."

On the members of this League, "the vanguard of the forty million youth of our country," the old revolutionists stake their hopes for the future. While they spent their lives largely in destroying the old order, the task of the new generations is the construction and defense of the new order. They are called upon to be exponents of a new way of living, creators of "the man of tomorrow." As depicted by Postyshev to the Tenth Congress of the Comsomols in 1936, this new man "will be physically healthy, a well-developed, well-rounded personality with a wide circle of interests in life and rich demands upon it. He will be a person of high creative ability and ambitions; not only a consumer of culture, but a creator of it. He will know no distinction between mental and manual labor, a fighter for the complete victory of Socialism throughout the world."

For twenty years the Comsomols have been the faithful allies and reserves of the Party. Critics have pointed to the careerists and timeservers who joined the League to exploit its prestige for their own ends. They have castigated also the most sincere and zealous for being "cocky," "cocksure," "opinionated," "boastful," and "dogmatically intolerant." But no one has ever questioned their enthusiasm and devotion to the Revolution. On all fronts in the civil war thousands perished fighting off the armies of Intervention. In the drive for collectivization they were the scourge of the kulaks, the champions of the new way of farming. In the first years of the Five-Year Plan, they were the ardent leaders of the "shock-brigades" as they are now in the Stakhanov movement.

In every crisis and on every construction front appeared the Comsomols, regardless of danger, hardship, and often hunger. 1,000 volunteered to work in the gold-mines in Siberia; 1,500 to man the stations along the new seaway through the Arctic; 7,000 to build the tractor plant on the steppes near Stalingrad; 36,000 to get the coal out of the lagging Donbas mines and into the furnaces. In every giant project across the whole Eurasian continent the Comsomols have a decisive part—digging the subway in Moscow, erecting steel-mills in the Urals, starting up the new hydro-electric centers in Siberia, and so on out to the Pacific where they are building the city of Comsomol-on-the-Amur.

Now the emphasis shifts from the construction to the "cultural front." To fit themselves for service on its many and ever-extending sectors the Comsomols are now adjured above everything else to "study, study, study." They are called up no longer to regard their League as simply a training school for the Party but as the leader and leaven of the whole Soviet youth. As the rest of this book is an account of institutions, enterprises, and activities, in all of which the Comsomols have a large and vital part, there is no need of detail here. Among those for which they assume a special responsibility are patronage over the Red Navy and Air Fleet; the training of each youth to master some special skill or technique; the liquidation of the last remnants of illiteracy; coaching the hundred million voters in the use of the new ballot; the training of athletes, sharpshooters, pilots, gliders, and parachutists ("We must be a generation of winged people, the best fliers in the world"). To the Comsomols also is assigned tutelage over the fifty million children who "growing up under Socialism have never seen a capitalist and do not know what he looks like." In their special organization, the Pioneers, the Comsomols serve as leaders and scout-masters.

23. Who Are the Young Pioneers and What do They Do?

"The Children's Communist Organization of Young Pioneers in the Name of Comrade Lenin," comprises some 6,000,000 children from ten to sixteen years of age. They are formed in "brigades" of fifty, subdivided into troops or "links" of ten. A brigade is usually attached to a Comsomol unit, one of whose members serves as its leader. To make them "participants and not mere onlookers" in the work of Socialist construction and to secure a proletarian influence, brigades are often centered around factories, or collective farms, but are open to children of all classes. After a period of probation and instruction the boy or girl becomes a member by vote of the brigade and by taking the Solemn Promise.

"I, a Young Pioneer of the Union of Soviet Socialist Republics, in the presence of my comrades, solemnly promise that I shall stand steadfastly for the cause of the working class in its struggle for the liberation of the workers and peasants of the whole world; I shall honestly and constantly carry out the precepts of Ilich [Lenin], the laws and customs of the Young Pioneers."

The Five Laws: The Pioneer is faithful to the cause of the working class and to the precepts of Ilich. The Pioneer is the younger brother and helper of the Comsomol and the Communist. The Pioneer organizes other children and joins them in their life. The Pioneer is a comrade to other Pioneers, and to the workers' and peasants' children of the whole world. The Pioneer strives for knowledge. Knowledge and understanding are the great forces in the struggle for the cause of the workers.

The Five Customs: The Pioneer protects his own health and that of others. He is tolerant and cheerful. He rises early in the morning and does his setting-up exercises. The Pioneer economizes his own time and that of others. He does his task quickly and promptly. The Pioneer is industrious and persevering, knows how to work collectively under any conditions, and finds a way out in all circumstances.

The Pioneer is saving of the people's property, is careful with his books and clothes and the equipment of the workshop. The Pioneer does not swear, smoke, or drink.

To the Pioneer is accorded the use of ceremonies and emblems usually frowned upon by Communists: The red flag badge with sickle and hammer and a camp-fire with three logs symbolizing the Third International. The salute made by raising the open hand above the forehead meaning that above his personal interests the Pioneer puts the working class of the five continents of the world, symbolized by the five fingers. One often sees the red-kerchiefed brigades parading with their flags and drums or hears them shouting out their slogan: *Vsegda gotov!* "Always ready!"

Through the "forepost" in the school, the Pioneer leads in maintaining discipline, in the celebrations, and in editing the "wall-newspaper." He strives to bring fresh air into the home and keep vodka out; to replace an ikon with a picture of Lenin; to keep his father from beating the other children or his mother; or to help his mother to clean out flies, bedbugs, and roaches—and acts generally as a missionary of the new Soviet *mores*. He induces waifs to enter the children's colonies; escorts village comrades to museums and factories in the city; on his summer excursions teaches them new games; wages warfare against crop-destroying pests, undertaking to catch five rats and ten mice annually; collects bones, paper, and scrap-iron for building a tractor. At the brigade meetings supervised by a Comsomol, he reports on his activities and receives counsel and suggestions.

"The Pioneer movement," says Krupskaya, the widow of Lenin, "reaches the children at the age when the personality of the individual is still being formed and promotes their social instincts by developing in them civic habits and social consciousness. It places before the children a wonderful goal—the liberation of the toilers, and the organization of a new order where there will be no division into classes, no oppression, and no exploitation, where all people will live a full and happy life."

24. What is the Rôle and Significance of Lenin?

In shaping the destinies of his country and his cause no leader or statesman in modern times has exerted so powerful an influence. It is far greater than Washington in America, Bismarck in Germany, or Napoleon in France. To grasp this one has only to look around: The Communist Party, and the colossal organizations of youth "in the name of Comrade Lenin"; the "Lenin Corners" in millions of factories, halls, and homes; and the "Lenin Tents" in the camps of the Red Army; the myriads of towns, regions, schools, communes, and children that bear his name; the countless busts and statues cast in bronze, cut in marble, hewn out of wood, and even carved out of ice in the villages of the North; his deeds and wisdom recounted in epic verse and song, or turned into heroic legends by the peoples of the East; his works in million-volume editions, his words engraved on buildings and inscribed on banners.

Insofar as a country can be the projection of the will and mind of a single individual, the Soviet Union is Lenin's. And beyond its borders increasingly is felt the impact of his personality and his teachings—known as "Leninism"—profoundly affecting the minds and movements of all the peoples of the earth. "We may take it for granted," says Bertrand Russell, "that our century will go down in history as the century of Lenin and Einstein, the two men who succeeded in completing a colossal synthetic work."

His Work. Joining in his youth the revolutionary movement against Tsarism, he placed before it a new objective: The complete liberation of mankind from all exploitation and oppression by the overthrow of capitalism, "the blind force which at every step threatens the worker and small business man with sudden destruction and ruin." "Outside of Socialism," he declared, "there is no deliverance of humanity from wars, from the abyss of suffering, torment, prostitution, hunger, and brutalization, from the destruction of millions and millions of human beings." Convinced of the correctness of Marx's and Engels' analysis of society and convinced that the advance of Socialism would be along the lines marked out by them, Lenin became their foremost expositor and protagonist. Freeing Marxism from the rigid dogmatism into which it had degenerated on the one hand and the milk-and-water reformism on the other, he made it into a powerful instrument of political action. In thirty volumes on economics, history, and philosophy, he brought the theory to grip with the living problems of the day, and in countless pamphlets popularized it for the Russian workers.

On them he placed chief reliance for the social revolution and summoned them to prepare for their historic task as destroyers of the old order and builders of the new. For leadership, out of their vanguard, he organized a highly disciplined and devoted body that later grew into the Communist Party. By sheer moral and intellectual force he dominated it and held it uncompromisingly on its path to the Socialist revolution. After decades of intensive training and propaganda, he seized the propitious moment for that Revolution—the night of November 6, 1917—and led it to victory, transforming the former Empire of the Tsars into a Republic of Soviets. In the formation of all policies of the new State—foreign, economic, military, and educational—he was the decisive factor. Not less so in their execution. He determined the strategy of its advances and retreats, initiated the system of design and planning, laid down the principles and charted the course that the Soviet Union should follow in future.

His Character. "Coldly cynical, crassly materialistic, utterly unscrupulous," says John Spargo of Lenin. "An opportunist and an ambitious creature," says the Princess Radziwill. But these vilifiers of Lenin knew him only by hearsay. Quite otherwise is the judgment of those who knew him at first hand. His lifelong opponents—and still more singularly, even most spokesmen of those very classes who were beaten and scourged by Lenin—pay tribute to the terrible sincerity, the intrinsic greatness of this man.

Wherein lies this greatness? "In my opinion," says Gorky, "Lenin was exceptionally great because of his irreconcilable, unquenchable hostility towards the sufferings of humanity, his burning faith that suffering is not an essential and unavoidable part of life, but an abomination which people ought and are able to sweep away." To Romain Rolland, "Lenin was the greatest man of action in our century and at the same time the most selfless." To Bukharin, "It almost seemed an extraordinary sixth sense enabled him to hear the grass growing under the ground and the thoughts in the workers' minds."

With others the stress is laid upon various other qualities of Lenin: His ability to resolve the most abstract and complex problems into simple concrete terms; titanic energy, enabling him to work out in the minutest details all his plans and policies; clarity of vision that made him always know exactly what he was doing and where he was going; readiness to acknowledge blunders and defeat, and to reverse his tactics; contempt for all romanticism, hypocrisy, or phrase-mongering; love of laughter and sense of humor that stood by him in the most trying moments.

Differing as do his friends and colleagues in the characteristics they choose to emphasize, they all agree upon what were the sources of Lenin's power: The complete subjugation of his life to a single purpose, and an inflexible will that drove him on to his goal, as merciless to himself as to others. To paraphrase Heine: He did not have ideas, the Idea had him, and scourged and whipped him into the arena to fight and die for it, whether he would or not.

Lenin's Boyhood. He was born on April 22, 1870, in the Volga city of Simbirsk, now called Ulianovsk, in his honor. For that was his real name—Vladimir Ilich Ulianov. The necessity of eluding the police compelled him, like other revolutionists, to go under various pseudonyms—Ilin, Tulin, Karpov, and the one by which he will always be known, Lenin. His mother, the daughter of a military surgeon, owned a small country estate near Kazan. His father, an inspector of schools, who rose to the rank of active State Counselor was thus a member of the hereditary nobility.

There were six children in the family, three boys and three girls, all of them keenly interested in sports, science, literature, and deeply devoted to their parents and to one another. High-minded and sensitive, they could not help feeling the glaring contrast between their own rich, full life and the slavery of the masses condemned to relentless toil and misery. It roused them to indignant revolt and to seek out a remedy. Convinced that the only escape lay in the overthrow of autocracy, one after another dedicated himself unreservedly to this task.

His Brother Executed. As a student in St. Petersburg, Lenin's eldest brother, the brilliant, versatile Alexander, naturally gravitated towards "The People's Will," an organization of the most militant fearless idealists, aiming to destroy tyranny by destroying the tyrants. Joining a circle of terrorists, he was caught in a plot to assassinate Tsar Alexander III and was hanged with four of his fellow-conspirators on the Schlusselburg gallows. Tragic as was the loss of his beloved brother and mentor, it led Lenin not to revenge but to reflection. He became convinced that as a means of achieving fundamental social change, assaults on high-placed persons, however successful they might be, were utterly futile and sentimental. Or as Disraeli put it, "Assassination never changed the course of history." From henceforth Lenin battled *against* the Social Revolutionaries, the advocates and instigators of assassination—and *for* the Marxists, who, repudiating the method of bomb-and-bullet, were intent on organizing a new party based on mass-action.

It is impossible to exaggerate the far-reaching consequences of Lenin's decisive stand. Not only was it profoundly to affect the course of the working-class movement in Russia, but throughout the whole world. That came 32 years later when Lenin founded the Third Communist International, which unites the Communist Parties in 65 countries of the world. Adhering to the principles laid down by him, it likewise repudiates *in toto* the policy of individual terrorism, as a method of political action.

Turns from Law to Revolution. After graduating with highest honors from the Simbirsk gymnasium, whose headmaster was the father of

Kerensky, Lenin entered the University of Kazan. For taking part in a meeting he was speedily banished to his mother's estate. Pursuing his studies alone, he took the law examinations and was admitted to the bar. Shorter than his career as student was his career as lawyer. After a few cases he gave it up in order to devote all his energies to the Revolution.

For five years—interrupted only by a brief journey to consult with Plekhanov and other leaders abroad—he immersed himself in the life and struggles of the St. Petersburg workers. No matter was too trivial to him. On secretly printed broadsheets he held forth on fines, ventilation, hot water for tea, insulting of women—always showing the social implications of each question and tieing it up with Marxian theory. He wrote leaflets like "Who Are the Friends of the People," read copy on them, organized their distribution in the factories, devised aliases for his fellow-workers, invented codes and ciphers, found short cuts through courtyards to evade the police spies that shadowed them.

Jail and Siberia. In 1895 Lenin was arrested and put in solitary confinement. But this did not stop his activities. Interchange of books was permitted and by a system of dotting single letters in them, he kept in close contact with fellow-prisoners and the world outside. He also devised a method of writing with milk which became legible by dipping in hot tea or exposing to the heat of a candle-flame. In her "Memories of Lenin," Krupskaya says: "To avoid discovery while writing with milk he made little milk-inkpots out of bread. These he popped into his mouth when there was a rattle on the grating." "Today I have eaten six inkpots," ran the postscript to one of his letters. Every letter contained various commissions to be carried out on behalf of the prisoners. Thus, "so-and-so has no visitors—you must find him a 'sweetheart'" or "tell such-and-such a prisoner, through his relatives when they next visit him, to look for a letter in such-and-such a book in the prison library," or "bring so-and-so warm boots."

During his year of imprisonment he wrote several pamphlets; drew up a draft program for the First Congress of the Social Democratic Labor Party, secretly convened in 1898; prepared most of his new book, "The Development of Capitalism in Russia." "It is a pity they let us out so soon," said he jestingly on his release, "I would have liked to do a little more work on the book." For this he had ample time in a little village of Siberia to which he was banished. Thither he was followed by another exile, Nadezhda Krupskaya, who became his wife, secretary, and closest life-long companion.

In their log-hut near the river Yenisei, he finished the book begun in prison, wrote the "Tasks of the Social Democracy," translated into Russian Sidney and Beatrice Webb's work on Trade-unionism and other books, read the classics from Gogol to Goethe, set up a sort of legal clinic for the peasants who from great distances came to him with their troubles. For recreation he joined lustily in the singing of the peasants, romped with their children, went skating or fox-hunting with his Gordon setter, played chess so enthusiastically that he carried on games by correspondence with other exiles and even cried out the next move in his sleep.

At the end of his three years' term in Siberia, forbidden to reside in any big city, university-center, or factory-settlement, he settled in Pskov. But with the eyes of the secret police watching every movement it was too risky to remain in Russia. On a forged passport in 1900 he went abroad.

First Exile Abroad. For five years, under assumed names, he kept moving from city to city. In Munich he wrote his impassioned, "What is to be Done?", pleading for a party of steel-willed conspirators, willing, if need be, to become mere cogs in the revolutionary machine. In London he delved deep into the great library of the British Museum, attended Socialist churches, learned colloquial English from Hyde Park orators, frequently visited the grave of Karl Marx. In Geneva he edited *Iskra* (*The Spark*), which carried at its headmast the motto: "From a spark a flame will rise." He wrote many pamphlets like "To the Village Poor," and through the ports from Persia to Sweden kept a stream of illegal literature flowing into Russia, concealed in double-bottomed trunks and in the bindings of books.

Most important was his part in the historic Second Congress of the Russian Social Democratic Party which began in Brussels and ended in London. In voting on a minor question Lenin's side happened to get a majority, the word for which in Russian is *bolshinstvo*. After this his group came to be known as Bolsheviki, or adherents of the majority, as opposed to the Mensheviki, or members of the minority. Thus, quite fortuitously, these two names came into being. But very fundamental were the points of cleavage. Lenin demanded that workers should have more power in the Party; that it should not compromise or dilly-dally

with the Liberals but seek its allies in the peasantry; that mere sympathizers should not be counted members of the Party but only those
who were ready to burn their bridges behind them and put themselves
body and soul in the fight; that every member be held in strict accounting to a strong centralized leadership. For his irreconcilable position, Lenin was furiously assailed as "autocratic, bureaucratic, sectarian,
pig-headed, suspicious, narrow-minded. . . ." So runs the list of abusive
epithets amusedly noted down by Lenin himself. Unperturbed he stood
adamant.

Officially for a time, until the Prague Conference in 1912, the Social
Democratic Party preserved a semblance of unity. But the wedge splitting the two wings asunder had been already driven deep. Letting the
Mensheviks go their way, Lenin with his handful of Bolsheviks went
his. In the columns of a new paper, *Forward,* he hammered away at
his idea that only a monolithic, iron-disciplined party could function
effectively in a revolution and carry it through to a finish.

The Revolution of 1905. A wave of angry rebellion was sweeping
over the Russian peoples. Faith in the power of the Tsar had been
shattered by the defeat of his army and navy at the hands of the Japanese. Belief in his goodness had been dissipated by the massacre on
"Bloody Sunday," when hundreds coming with ikons and hymns to
beseech the "Little White Father" for redress of wrongs, were shot
down before the Winter Palace. Lenin returned to find the country
paralyzed by strikes, and later a Soviet of workers in the capital. He
fanned the revolutionary flame in the press; addressed a huge meeting
from which the workers emerged tearing up their red shirts for banners; followed closely the armed uprising in Moscow.

This first revolution was abortive. Fortified by foreign loans, the
Tsar savagely crushed the revolt, hanging, shooting, and exiling thousands of leaders. Many in black despair gave themselves up to mysticism, eroticism, and careerism. But not Lenin. To him the events of
1905 were but a prologue to the real, the oncoming revolution. After
a breathing-spell, he proclaimed, the workers having recouped their
forces, would go into a fresh offensive. "For it we must prepare more
tenaciously, more systematically, more persistently."

Second Exile Abroad. In Geneva and Paris Lenin rallied around him
his broken ranks. With funds secured from the Tiflis raid on the State

treasury, he set up the paper *Proletarians* and found new sea-routes to carry it into Russia. To a bigger task, however, he was presently devoting his chief energies. "I am neglecting the paper," he wrote to Gorky, "on account of my passion for philosophy. Today I am studying an empirio-criticist and swearing like a trooper. Tomorrow I shall read another and curse like a bargee." His anger was aroused by their attempts to give an idealistic basis to Marxism. In refutation, he produced "Materialism and Empirio-Criticism," a terrific onslaught on the idealists as anti-revolutionary and reactionary. For like reasons he assailed Lunacharsky's group who were groping after a vague, rarefied religion and seeking to harmonize it with Socialism. "This God-seeking," he wrote ironically, "differs from God-making much as a yellow devil differs from a blue." "Religion is a kind of spiritual intoxicant in which the slaves of capital drown their humanity and blunt their desire for a decent human existence." In opposition to their school at Capri, he set up his own near Paris.

With the same virulence he denounced the "Liquidators" on the right, who would dissolve the illegal organization of the Party, and the "Recallists" on the left, who would withdraw the legally elected Party deputies from the Duma. And it was not only a political struggle that he waged but a moral one. While living on a diet whose main items were horse-flesh and lettuce, he had to inject hope and verve into the poverty-stricken Russian colony harassed by police spies and provocateurs, and swept by epidemics of disease and suicide. His own spirits he revived in libraries, in bicycling, and in the workers' cafés, listening to the revolutionary ballad-singers and humming to himself over and over again, *"Salut, salut à vous!"* a song in praise of a French regiment refusing to fire on strikers.

Then came the news that a Russian regiment had fired on strikers. That was in 1912, when 200 miners were shot down in the Lena goldfields. A wildfire of indignation ran through the land. To be near the area of action Lenin moved into Austria close to the Russian frontier. To consult with him came members of the Bolshevik faction of the Duma. He primed them with ideas, outlined their speeches, poured into the new paper *Pravda* (*Truth*) in St. Petersburg a ceaseless stream of articles, more than forty of which were on the peasant and his rôle in insurrection. Everywhere workers were crowding into the Party. Barricades were thrown up in the streets. Voices were hoarsely calling for the overthrow of autocracy—abundant reasons for the Tsar to seek by the device of war "to substitute national passions for social aspirations." And this he did.

With the declaration of war against Germany the nascent revolution was submerged under a tidal wave of patriotism. Most of the Socialists in Russia, abjuring their high-sounding resolutions against war, lined up behind the government. So they did in other countries. "Treason! Treason to Socialism!" shouted Lenin, when he learned that the powerful German party had really voted support to the Kaiser. In face of the complete debacle of its leaders he proclaimed the end of the Second International, and in the conferences at Kienthal and Zimmerwald, he laid the foundation of a new International—the Third. That was in Switzerland to which he again returned for refuge, after release from arrest as a Tsarist spy. In "Imperialism as the Last Stage of Capitalism," he showed that in the rivalries of capitalist nations for new markets and colonies lay the origins of this War, and of all wars. Denouncing it as a senseless, shameless butchery, he called to the soldiers of all warring nations: "Ground your arms! Turn them against the common enemy, the capitalist governments!" "Convert the imperialist war into war against the war-makers!"

The Revolution of 1917. The Tsar was overthrown. Through the countries of the Allies thousands of exiled revolutionaries hurried back to Russia. But for Lenin, the arch-enemy of the imperialists, there was no visa. Cooped up in Switzerland, he beat against the bars like a tormented animal seeking to escape. Scores of devices, such as flight by airplane, on a falsified passport, or disguised as a deaf-and-dumb Swede, were considered and rejected as unfeasible. At last, sanctioned by an International Committee of Socialists, with his closest comrades, he passed through Germany in a sealed car, followed later by 200 revolutionists of other parties. On his arrival in Petrograd cheering throngs of workers and soldiers lifted him to the top of an armored car, illumined by searchlights, and in triumphal procession he was borne to Bolshevik quarters in the mansion of the Tsar's mistress, the dancer Kshesinskaya. He was astounded by the tremendous ovation.

Not less astounded was everybody by the radical theses that he now advanced: Nationalization of lands, State control of industry and food supplies, merging of all private banks into one national system, immediate cessation of the War, overthrow of Kerensky's government of landlords and capitalists, dictatorship of the proletariat. "All power to the Soviets!" So audacious was his program that many even of his own followers at first recoiled from it. But the Party adopted it, the masses rallied to it, and on their own initiative precipitately rose to support it in a tremendous armed demonstration in July.

But the time was not ripe. Many of the leading Bolsheviks were arrested as "German agents" or, like Lenin, had to seek refuge in haystacks and cellars. From his hiding-place he continued to work at deepening the Revolution, directing its strategy and whipping the wavering Party leaders into line. Characteristically in the midst of manifold activities he found time to write a theoretical book, "The State and Revolution." It stops short with the laconic, "More pleasant and useful than writing about Revolution is the making of one. . . ." That is what he did. Having sensed exactly the right moment for insurrection—the night of November 6—he set it in motion and out of underground emerged into the blazing lights of the Soviet Congress at Smolny. Stepping to the rostrum and stilling the tornado of applause in an unimpassioned matter-of-fact manner, he began: "Comrades, we shall now take up the formation of the Socialist State!"

Premier and Statesman. As President of the Council of People's Commissars, Lenin was now the head of the country in which he had been an alien and outcast for thirty years. Along the new path in which he had started it, he now had to guide it through all the perils and pitfalls of its formative years.

The Germans sought to strangle the new State in its cradle. He made peace with them, "a disgraceful humiliating robber's peace," but through it he obtained a breathing-spell to recoup his forces.

The Counter-Revolutionists tried to decapitate it by assassinating its leader, lodging two bullets in Lenin himself. Against them was loosed the Red Terror of the Revolution, paralyzing their activities.

The Allies encircled the country with a cordon of bayonets and battleships and closed in on it. At the head of the Council of Labor and Defense, Lenin out-generaled them, and, smashing through the cordon of steel, broke the blockade.

The old functionaries and intelligentsia sought to paralyze the new government by refusing their services. With the declaration that "the art of government cannot be gotten out of books," he appealed to the masses! "Try! Make mistakes! Learn how to govern!" and out of the inexperienced and illiterate raised up generals, financiers, and statesmen.

The workers, worn out and demoralized by the long ordeal of civil war and hunger, became listless, lackadaisical, anarchical. With the watchwords, "Order!" "Do not loaf!" "Do not steal!" "Keep strict accounts!" he injected into their ranks a new morale and discipline.

The peasants incensed against the grain levies and War Communism were seething with rebellion. He called for a retreat, a partial return to capitalism, instituting what is known as the New Economic Policy, or NEP, which restored free trading in the markets and placed the smaller enterprises again in private hands.

For this quick shift in policy, as for others, Lenin was called a compromiser and opportunist. But his opportunism was always a compromise with conditions, not with principles. As a master strategist he knew when to drive straight ahead to his goal and when to take a zigzag, veering course, when to fight and when to evade a fight.

Theory Checked by Facts. "Without correct theory," Lenin insisted, "there can be no Revolution, no Socialism." But as a realist he would not make a fetish out of it. "Our doctrine is not a dogma, but a guide to action—not a sacred theory, but a working tool." That was the acid test of any formula. Did it work in a given situation? If it did not, he had the courage to cast it aside, or change it to accord with the facts.

Lenin had a passion for facts. He drew them out of books, statistics, papers, and official documents—best of all out of living documents in flesh-and-blood, eager always to listen to the most lowly and illiterate as well as to the savant. The last time I talked with Lenin was in the Kremlin. In his ante-room, a throng of us had been waiting our turn—waiting long. That was very unusual, because unlike most Russians, Lenin was punctual in his appointments. More than an hour we sat there impatiently cooling our heels, while from the inner office the voice of his visitor went steadily booming along. Finally the door opened and out of it emerged no officer, diplomat, or other high-placed dignitary—but a typical, shaggy-haired peasant in sheepskin coat and bark shoes, such as one meets by the million all over the Russian land. "I beg your pardon," said Lenin, as I entered his office. "This was a peasant from Tambov—a shrewd, old man—and I wanted to get his ideas about debts and collectivization." With the same avidity he gave heed to Volga boatmen and Siberian fur-trappers, to Tula iron-molders and Moscow scrubwomen, to American engineers, British traders, and Chinese revolutionists. The multitude of facts so painstakingly gathered in he carefully weighed, sifted, and synthesized into his plans and program.

Astounding is the amount of work that Lenin crowded into his last three years: He delivered hundreds of addresses and wrote thousands of letters, ranging from high affairs of state to how to sell plows to peasants; joined enthusiastically in the "Saturdayings"—the volunteer giving-up of one's free time to unpaid manual labor—carrying from dawn to dark big beams of timber in a cleaning-up of the Kremlin yard; organized the campaign against typhus and famine while living on a scanty hunger-ration himself; read stacks of books and produced new ones—amongst them an important survey of agrarian conditions in the American Middle West; grappled with all the thorny problems of the Third International as well as the Soviet State; fought long grueling battles against rebels outside the Party and within it. Then suddenly his own body rebelled.

Lenin Dies, "Leninism" Lives On. The rugged, well-knit frame that so long and so well had served as a catapult for his indomitable will and mind, was weakened by the strain of relentless labors and the assassin's bullets it still carried. In 1922 a paralytic stroke laid him low. After a short rest he returned to his post but was compelled again to retire. On January 21, 1924, he died from arteriosclerosis, a breakdown of blood-vessels in the brain. Never was a whole people so deeply grief-stricken. Bonfires were lighted in the streets for the hundreds of thousands waiting in the bitter cold of the long winter nights to file in sorrowing procession past the bier of their beloved leader.

Each year increasingly they pay tribute to him. From all over the Soviet land, from the four corners of the earth, they come to his dark red granite mausoleum in the Red Square of Moscow, backed by the Kremlin wall and the Salvation Tower, now chiming out the "International." Daily, in a long double line, they press forward into the dim-lit interior to pass the glass catafalque where Lenin lies embalmed, clad in a military tunic, the Order of the Red Banner on his breast and his right fist clenched. They come to gaze upon the face of this man, as powerful in repose as he was in life and action.

They come to reaffirm their fidelity to the aims and ideals of the Revolution, to pledge anew their allegiance to the mutual enterprise begun by them together. Among the hundreds of folk tales, legends, and songs created by the Central Asian peoples is this one from the Kirghiz.

> In Moscow, in the great stone city,
> Where the country's chosen lie gathered,
> A hut stands on the square
> And in it Lenin lies.
>
> You who bear a great sorrow
> Which nothing can console
> Come to this hut: Look at Lenin!
> And your sorrow will be carried off like water,
> It will float away like leaves on a stream,
> But a new, quiet sorrow will envelop you
> That he who was the father of his land
> Was stung with the sting of death.
>
> Where shall we look for him now? we cry,
> And the steppe cries with us,
> The moon and stars cry with us,
> They remember Lenin . . . We remember Lenin.
> And neither ourselves nor our grandsons' grandsons
> Ever will forget him . . . Our steppes may choke with weeds
> And tens of Kirghiz generations walk from the earth
> But the last of them will be happy that he goes
> Where Lenin is.

Lenin on Music and Other Subjects

On the Learning of Languages. He not only was eager to learn languages but he wanted others to learn them. In the winter of 1918 from the top of an armored car he addressed a big contingent of Red Guards going off to the front. Then the chairman Podvoisky announced, "An

American to speak to you." As I stepped up on the car, Lenin exclaimed,

"Oh, good. You speak English; allow me to be your interpreter."

"No, I shall speak in Russian," I answered, prompted by some reckless impulse.

Lenin watched me with eyes twinkling as if anticipating entertainment. It was not long in coming. After using up the first run of predigested sentences, I hesitated, and stopped. I had difficulty in getting the language started up again. But no matter what a foreigner does to their tongue, the Russians are polite and charitable. They appreciate the novice's effort, if not his technique. So my speech was punctuated with long periods of applause which gave a breathing spell in which to assemble more words for another short advance. At last however I was quite stopped. Lenin looked up and asked, "What word do you want?" "Enlist," I answered. "*Vstupit,*" he prompted.

Thereafter, whenever I was stuck, he would fling the word up to me and I would catch it and hurl it into the crowd, modified, of course, by my American accent.

"Well, that's a beginning in Russian, at any rate," he said. "But you must keep at it hard! Put an advertisement in the paper asking for exchange lessons as I did in London. Then just read, write, and talk nothing but Russian. Don't talk with Americans—it won't do you any good, anyhow," he added humorously. "Next time I see you I'll give you an examination."

That next time was during the historic Session of the Constituent Assembly as the two factions came to death grips with each other. The delegates shouting battle-cries and pounding the desks, the orators thundering out challenges and threats, and two thousand voices passionately singing the "International" charged the place with electricity. Through it all Lenin sat quite self-composed, sleepy and a bit bored. I slid over to his box, and, recognizing me at once, he asked:

"And how goes the Russian language? Can you understand all these speeches now?"

"There are so many words in Russian," I replied evasively.

"That's just so," he replied, "and the most important word for you is *izoochat,* study. You must go at it systematically. You must break the backbone of a language at the outset. I'll tell you my method of going at it."

In essence, it was this: First, learn all the nouns, learn all the verbs, learn all the adverbs and adjectives; learn all the grammar and rules of syntax; then keep practicing everywhere and upon everybody. As may be seen, Lenin's system was more thoroughgoing than subtle. It was, in short, his system of the conquest of the bourgeoisie applied to the conquest of a language, a merciless application to the job. But he was quite exercised over it.

He leaned over the box with sparkling eyes, and drove his words home with gestures. This greatly incited the curiosity of the onlookers. Most likely they thought Lenin was violently excoriating the crimes of the opposition, divulging the secret plans of the Soviet, or expounding some fine point of revolutionary strategy. In a crisis like this, surely only such themes would be calling forth such energy and animation from the head of the Soviet State and the Revolution. But they were wrong. He was merely expatiating on how to learn a foreign language and enjoying the diversion of a little friendly conversation.

On Tolstoy: "On the one hand we have an author of genius who has produced incomparable pictures of Russian life. Until this nobleman appeared the peasant was unknown in literature; on the other hand, we have the landowner and the fool in Christ. On the one hand he makes a most zealous, direct, and sincere protest against the falsehood and dishonesty of the existing social order; on the other, he produced the Tolstoyans, worn-out, hysterical, pitiable rags of Russian intellectuals, who publicly beat their breasts and cry, 'I am a sinner, a miserable sinner, but I am devoting myself to moral perfection. I no longer eat meat and I feed on rice cutlets. . . .' But what has Europe to compare with Tolstoy? Nothing!"

On Doctors: (A letter to Gorky.) "Dear Friend, what are you up to? You are suffering from over-work, over-fatigue, and neuralgia. Really and truly this is very wrong. It is inadmissible to be ill, to endanger your powers of work and waste state property thereby. The news that you are allowing yourself to be treated by a 'Bolshevik' . . . even if he is an ex-Bolshevik!—makes me profoundly uneasy. Heaven protect us from 'comrades' in general as doctors, but Bolshevik doctors! Comrades are perfect asses as doctors. I assure you, trifling apart, that we should always have ourselves treated by authorities of the first rank. Write often if you are not too lazy."

On Music: "I know nothing more beautiful than Beethoven's 'Appasionata.' It is marvelous, unearthly music. Every time I hear these notes, I think with pride, and perhaps child-like naïveté, that it is wonderful what man can accomplish. But I cannot listen to music too often. It affects your nerves, makes you want to say amiable stupidities and stroke the heads of people who can create such beauty in a filthy hell. But today is not the time to stroke the heads of people. You have to hit them on the head, without mercy, although our ideal is not to use violence against anyone. It is a devilishly hard task!"

On Manners: (Anent a persistent bore.) "Tell him to go to the devil, but tell him *politely.*"

On Style: "Why do you not write ten or twenty lines instead of your usual two or three hundred? Write as simply and clearly as possible—on events which have penetrated into the flesh and blood of the masses."

25. What is the Position of Stalin?

In listing the dictators of today Stalin is usually placed alongside of Hitler and Mussolini. In one respect they are alike. Each of them has been invested with great powers by the ruling class of his country, and with iron will is carrying out its ideals and policies. But who is the ruling class in any country? Those who are economically the strongest. Control of the State lies in the hands of those who own the land, machinery, banks, press, and radio. And in that lies the chief difference between Stalin and the other dictators. In Germany and Italy ownership is largely in the hands of landlords and capitalists, therefore it is in their interests that Hitler and Mussolini "dictate." As ownership in the Soviet Union is in the hands of workers and peasants, it is in their interests that Stalin "dictates."

By no *coup d'état* did Stalin seize the reins of government.

Nor did he arbitrarily arrogate to himself the vast powers he exercises. They were bestowed upon him as secretary of the Communist Party. It is the backing of this dominant, all-pervasive body that gives force to all his activities and utterances. Without it they are nothing. In its name he always speaks. To its councils he defers. Through it he has risen to his high position. By its sanction more and more power has been centered in his office. While it is the Party that made Stalin, he in turn has made the Party, transforming it into a more perfect instrument of action, more disciplined and more unified.

As effectively as Stalin struggled for unity and solidarity in the Party, so he did in the State. That is his outstanding contribution to the science of statecraft. To him is primarily due the Soviets' policy of cultural autonomy and independence toward the 189 peoples and races which stopped their breaking up into separate states and welded them together into a single political-economic entity. The tremendous significance of this is obvious. It secured for the Revolution an immense territory to operate in. But how should it operate? The whole future course of the country—its foreign and domestic policy, education, economics, everything—was determined by Stalin's stand on this hotly debated question.

It was a question of theory: "Can Socialism be built in one country alone?" The legal and doctrinaire Marxists said no. Trotzky and his partisans ridiculed the idea. Without revolutions in other lands, they insisted, it was impossible for Russia to take the Socialist path alone. But Stalin insisted it was "possible, necessary, and inevitable." He had said so in 1917. He reiterated it now, stressing the folly of waiting for revolution abroad that might be ten, twenty years in coming. He used tellingly a last statement of Lenin, "In Russia we have all that is requisite for the building of Socialism." Tirelessly he hammered away on this theme until at last he convinced the Communists it could be done.

Then with his colleagues he showed them the way to do it: By a vast network of factories, steel-plants, and electric-stations lay the industrial basis of the fully socialized society. By merging the millions of tiny holdings into large-scale, mechanized, collective farms, bring agriculture into the orbit of Socialism and convert the individualist peasant into a Socialist.

With these objectives he launched the first Five-Year Plan, a gigantic project covering all phases of life, giving every man, woman, and child a part in it. To its support he rallied the people with the slogan ultimately "to overtake and outstrip the advanced capitalist countries." To steel them to endure the strain and privations it imposed, he imbued them with a sense of the magnitude of the enterprise they were engaged in—made them feel they were creators of a new society, blazing the way for the workers of all lands.

"Will passionately," said Stalin, "and you can achieve anything, overcome everything!" Riding over every obstacle and opposition and driving the First Plan through to completion, he launched the country on a Second and a Third Plan—each a more comprehensive and colossal undertaking.

Stalin's Youth. His real name is Joseph Vissarionovich Djugashvili. Like other revolutionists, he went under various pseudonyms—Koba, David, Chichikov, and the one that so aptly characterizes him, Stalin, meaning "of steel." He was born December 21, 1879, in Gori, a mountain town on the railway leading down to the Black Sea, the son of Vissarion, the shoemaker. His devout mother, Ekaterina, whose other three children had died in infancy, piously dedicated her fourth child to the church. "Soso," she called him, using the Georgian diminutive for Joseph. After years of adversity, during which his father died and his mother earned the family bread with her needle, he entered the Orthodox Seminary in Tiflis.

But instead of a priest he became a revolutionist. Discussing the process of change, he said, "First, one became convinced that existing conditions were wrong and unjust. Then one resolved to do one's best to remedy them. . . . Russian capitalism was the most atrocious and bestial in the world; the government of the Tsar the most corrupt, cruel, and inefficient." The theological school was much like the autocracy it served. In rebellion against its dead formalism, intolerance, and espionage, he turned from the Fathers of the Church to the Fathers of Scientific Socialism. Charged with infecting his fellow students with Marxism, at eighteen years of age he renounced the priesthood to become a bookkeeper by day, a conspirator by night.

While setting up a secret printing-press, he first met Enukidze, who depicts the youthful Stalin in these words, "Brevity, clarity, accuracy, were his distinctive qualities. His natural simple way of behaving and speaking to people, his absolute carelessness of his own private comfort, his inner steadiness and lack of vanity, and the fact that he was already politically educated, made him an authority among the workers who looked upon him as one of themselves. 'Our Soso!' they always called him."

Becomes the "Lenin of the Caucasus." During the round-up following a formidable street demonstration in the center of Tiflis, Stalin fled to Batum. There he organized a branch of the Party and was arrested for fomenting a strike in the Rothschild Mills. After twenty months in prison he was sentenced to three years' exile in Siberia. Escaping after a few weeks, he was back on his home-ground, running the illegal paper, *Fight of the Proletariat.* With the same vigor that he fought the Tsar, he fought the Georgian nationalists, Anarchists, and Mensheviks. For he was now an ardent Bolshevik. Always one by temperament, after intensive study in his prison-cell he had become one by conviction, lining up with Lenin at the start.

From the mountains he carried the campaign to the Caspian Sea, rallying the Moslem oil-workers into study "circles," negotiating a contract with the oil magnates, and turning Baku into a citadel of Bolshevism. Out of it issued the first general strike, an overture to the revolution of 1905, when a fierce partisan warfare raged throughout the Caucasus. The oil fields were fired, the underground press came out in the open, a separate republic was set up in Guria, raids were directed on government institutions, climaxing in the famous Tiflis "expropriation." By bombing in daylight a carriage that under Cossack convoy was carrying funds to the State Bank, 150,000 rubles came into the Party coffers.

In every crisis, most cool and collected in the moments of highest tension, there was Stalin. And there he was not only during the rise of the revolutionary tide, but during the slack days of its recession. For a short time he left Russia to attend the Party congress in Finland—where he first met Lenin face to face—as he did later in Stockholm and London. But he did not linger on. With most of the leaders fleeing abroad for their lives he felt that his place was in Russia. Each time he hurried back to rally and inspirit the workers, to help salvage something out of the wreckage. Through the long black years of terror and reaction he was always in the thick of the struggle.

Hide-and-Seek with the Police. For a decade Stalin lived like a hunted animal hounded by spies, enduring the severest privations and punishments. On Easter Sunday, 1909, with his fellow prisoners, he was forced to run the gauntlet. Many collapsed under the ordeal, but Stalin with head erect and book in hand, defiantly strode between the two rows of soldiers while their rifle-butts beat a tattoo on his head and shoulders. That was in the northern province of Vologda, to which he had been exiled for three years. Escaping after a few months he was back again in Baku. Rearrested as a fugitive from justice he was shipped back to Vologda. Escaping a second time, by Party orders, he took up work in St. Petersburg. A third time captured, a third time he was returned to Vologda, from which a third time he slipped away.

For the ease and agility with which he always wriggled out of his bonds, he vies with Rykov for the title of the "Houdini of the Russian Revolution." It would have been much harder had the gendarmes of the Tsar realized his real identity. He misled them by always changing his name, and, when caught, by passing himself off as a person of no great consequence. Understanding at last how dangerous he was, the next time they caught him, in the winter of 1911, they sent him to Siberia for safe keeping and to cool his revolutionary ardor in those icy wastes. It was a four years' term, of which he served four months. When the snow had melted, he too had vanished. While the police were searching all Russia for their man, he had slipped over the border and was playing chess with Lenin in a café in Cracow. "Here, with us, is a wonderful young Georgian," wrote Lenin to Gorky at this time. "He has collected all the Austrian and other material on the question of nationalities and has settled down to prepare a treatise on the subject." His work, completed in Vienna, appeared as a series in a magazine and later as a book.

Presently Stalin was back again in St. Petersburg directing the publication of the *Star* and *Pravda,* putting militancy into the Duma deputies. But the police knew now the place to look for him, in the center of the movement. There they trapped him in 1913, thanks to the Bolshevik deputy Malinovsky, who was in reality a provocateur. This time he was exiled to a three-house village inside the Polar Circle, with repeated warnings to the governor to keep him there and a special bailiff to watch over him. There he remained a fisherman, hunter, and trapper until the downfall of the Tsar in 1917.

Out of Exile into the Revolution. Plunged suddenly into the vortex of the February Revolution, after long isolation, Stalin was unable at once to orient himself or take up a resolute clear-cut Bolshevik position. "My mistaken viewpoint I shared with the majority of the party," says Stalin, "but surrendered it wholly in April, adopting the theses of Lenin." Henceforth, in support of them, he labored indefatigably in all the key posts he was called to occupy.

By the Soviets he was elected in the summer of 1917 to the *Tsik,* the Central Executive Committee. By the Party he was elected to the new-formed Polit-Bureau and to the management of the five central papers that carried the Bolshevik ferment to the front line trenches and out into the far-off steppes and forests. At the Sixth Congress, as spokesman of Lenin, who was in hiding, he helped to chart the course of the October uprising. In the Committee of Seven, he helped to give it political leadership. In the Committee of Five, he directed the movements of the Red Guards, the storming of the Winter Palace. As Commissar of Nationalities, he put into effect his long worked-out plan of uniting the 189 races and nations by a policy of "cohesion without coercion." As Commissar of Workers' and Peasants' Inspection, he was appointed to cut through the tangles of red tape and bureaucracy that were strangling the State.

Although he was the only Bolshevik heading two Commissariats, each of prime importance, still heavier responsibilities were laid on him. With the Soviets threatened by complete annihilation by the armies of intervention, he was called upon to take on military duties, to transform himself from a civilian into a soldier.

On All Fronts in the Civil War. While Trotzky was Commander-in-Chief of the armies, Stalin was entrusted with the main problems of the "inner defense." As member of the Supreme War Council he initiated some of its most effective strategy. As master-organizer he was transformed into "an expert in cleaning out the stables of the war department," keeping the supplies moving to the fronts, mobilizing the forces in the rear. But he did not long stay in the rear. Whenever a front was cracking up, or a life-and-death struggle was being waged, there was Stalin—tireless, sleepless, nerveless—seeking to infuse his steel will into the panic-stricken, reducing chaos to order.

He took over the defense of Tsaritzyn, the "Red Verdun" on the Volga, and started the flow of grain into the hunger-stricken capital. He injected discipline into the drunken, demoralized army of the Urals and turned their disastrous retreat into an offensive. He overrode the naval experts and, recapturing the "Red Hill" and "Grey Horse" forts, broke up Yudenich's drive on Petrograd. He conceived the idea of sending the famous First Cavalry Army on its thousand-mile raid across the steppes to the rout of the Polish forces. From front to front he was sent by the Supreme War Council, devising new tactics, steadying the wavering lines, crushing out conspiracies behind them, weeding out traitors and incompetents in the staffs, promoting the rank-and-file to high commands . . . extending his already deep insight into men that was to prove invaluable in the new post he was to fill.

Secretary of the Party. To this office he was elected in 1922, and has held it ever since. So solid is his position that the Party disregarded even Lenin's so-called "last testament," in which it is said that his removal was suggested, and has refused to accept his twice-tendered resignation. Nonetheless he has been vitriolically assaulted from all sides. For putting the emphasis on reconstruction at home, he was reviled by the Left Opposition as a "narrow nationalist," a "traitor to the world revolution." For keeping up at all costs the terrific pace of industrialization, he was assailed by the Right Opposition as an "adventurer, hurrying the country into hunger and chaos." In addition to all the abusive epithets used against Lenin, he has been called "an Asiatic despot," "Tammany boss," "unprincipled demagogue," "bureaucratic, unscrupulous, crafty, and cunning."

Over against these diatribes of his enemies may be set down one of the eulogies of the Party press on the occasion of his fiftieth birthday: "In Stalin are combined all those traits inherent in the Leninist Party, in the Soviet proletariat, and in the vanguard of the working class of the world: flaming enthusiasm kept in leash by an iron will; unshakable faith in victory based on a sober Marxian analysis; a proletarian contempt for death; the courage of the Communist who even when tortured remains silent as a grave; the circumspection of a leader conscious of his responsibility for a great cause entrusted to him by his class; the wide outlook of a Leninist theoretician whose mind illuminates the future like a searchlight."

In addition to these qualities stressed by the Party, is one that appeals particularly to the masses. That is the great simplicity of the man in private life and public address. Contrary to accepted notions, the Russian people are swayed far less by flights of oratory than by plain facts. Just as they turned from the spell-binder Kerensky to the logical Lenin, so they did from the brilliant rhetorical Trotzky to the matter-of-fact Stalin whose precise clear-cut speeches are lit up only by a touch of humor or biting satire. Quite as unostentatious is he in dress, bearing, and manner of life. With his wife, the sister of Kaganovich, and the two youngest of his three children, he lives in a modest three-room apartment in the Kremlin, and has a house in the country an hour away from Moscow. With simple, almost ascetic tastes he prefers the classics, enjoys the company of old comrades who, with him, were unswerving in devotion to the cause from the beginning.

Outweighing everything else in enhancing his prestige is the fact that for more than a decade he has skillfully guided the country through perilous waters, sedulously avoiding war, driving steadily onward towards Socialism. Increasingly in Party and people has grown the belief that in the long run the Stalin way is the best way. That is why they not only have kept him so long in this high office, but allowed him to enlarge its scope and prerogatives. To such an extent is this true that to give added force to decrees of State and declarations of policy, they came to be signed jointly by Molotov as Premier of the Soviet Government and by Stalin as Secretary of the Party.

Stalin is a member of the Polit-Bureau and the Presidium of the Third International. In the Soviet Government he has been Commissar of Nationalities, a member of the old Tsik, the Council of

Labor and Defense, the Control Commission, and head of the Committee for Drafting the New Constitution. These offices of State are of very minor importance in comparison with the one he has held in the Party. It is supreme in the country. And as first secretary, Stalin is supreme in the Party.

Stalin Discourses on Americans. "We never forget that America is a capitalist country. But we respect American efficiency in industry, technique, literature, and life. America was a land of free colonizers without landlords or aristocrats. From this fact rises its strong and relatively simple customs in industry. Our worker-managers who have been in America notice at once that characteristic. They note, not without a certain pleasant surprise, that it is hard to distinguish in outer appearance the engineer from the worker. It is quite otherwise in Europe, where in daily life and manners still survive remnants of feudalism, and its arrogant ways are carried into industry, science, and literature."

On Science. "To build one must possess knowledge, one must master science, one must learn. Learn persistently, patiently. Learn from everybody—from your enemies, from your friends, but particularly from your enemies."

On "Russian Laziness." "It is an old and radically mistaken idea that the Russian folk are submissive and lazy. It arose from the days when the Russian landlords went to Paris to squander in idleness the money they had stolen. They were really worthless and without will. But this does not apply to workers and peasants who won and win their living by their own toil. Strange indeed to consider submissive and lazy those who in a short time have made three revolutions, destroyed Tsarism, and are now victoriously building Socialism."

On Lenin. "When I compared him with his brothers-in-arms, it seemed to me that they were a head lower than Lenin, that he was a leader of a higher type, a mountain eagle who knew no fear. Only Lenin was capable of writing of the most confused things with such simplicity, condensation, and daring that each phrase did not speak, it shot. As for me, I am only a follower of Lenin and my aim is to be a worthy follower of him."

On Anti-Semitism. National and racial chauvinism is a relic of man-hating morals characteristic of the period of cannibalism. Anti-Semitism, as the extreme form of racial chauvinism, is the most dangerous relic of cannibalism. Anti-Semitism is of advantage to exploiters as a lightning conductor which enables capitalism to evade the blow of the toilers. Anti-Semitism is dangerous to the toilers as a false path which leads them away from the right road and brings them into the jungles. For this reason, Communists as consistent internationalists cannot help being uncompromising and sworn enemies of anti-Semitism. In the U.S.S.R. anti-Semitism is most severely prosecuted as a phenomenon deeply hostile to the Soviet system. Active anti-Semites are punished under the laws of the U.S.S.R. by death."

26. What is the Chief Evil Afflicting Soviet Institutions?

"Bureaucratism is the parasite that like an octopus fastens itself to the Soviet structure." These words one may see on the walls of Soviet offices, and quite often, sitting at his desk beneath them, a fine old specimen of this bureaucracy blandly practicing all its arts: Making talk a substitute for work. Never doing today what can possibly be put off till tomorrow; endlessly spawning out more *boomagi,* reports, documents, stamps, and seals. With tangles of red tape turning the simplest transaction into an ordeal. In brief, a formal, perfunctory, soulless attitude to one's duties. So ingrained in the Russians is the instinct for bureaucracy that frequently even in their efforts to get rid of it they only create more of it. Are there too many commissions? Very well, appoint a new commission to look into this! Maybe another one to watch out for the first. A hydra-headed monster it grows new heads as the old ones are lopped off.

The devious ways of the bureaucracy has been an unfailing

theme for Russian writers since the days of Gogol's "Inspector General." In Shchedrins' classic tale of the three happy officials one was chief of the Knot-Tying Bureau, one of the Bureau for Untying Knots, and one for the Bureau of Statistics of Tying and Untying Knots. Belinsky called them "a huge corporation of official thieves and plunderers." "Set the most insignificant nonentity to sell tickets at a railway station," wrote Dostoievsky, "and that nonentity will at once feel privileged to look down on you like a Jupiter." In the same tradition their Soviet counterparts are satirized in the tales of Zostchenko and the "Little Golden Calf" of Ilf and Petrov. For while the Revolution made a clean sweep of nobles, landlords, and capitalists, the bureaucrats remain in all their glory.

"Russia," declared Lenin, "is now a Soviet state disfigured by bureaucracy," and characteristically placed part of the blame upon himself and his colleagues. Asking for public trials for people guilty of "disgusting red tape" he wrote half-seriously, "all of us, together with the Commissariat of Justice, should be doubly hanged on rotten rope and I haven't lost hope that some day they will deservedly do it." In like fashion Stalin and Kaganovich keep assailing the "chair warmers," "leaders indulging in speechmaking and soothsaying instead of betaking themselves to their jobs," "departments in which everyone gives orders except those who are too lazy. . . ." For concrete examples one has only to turn to a file of Soviet newspapers or magazines like *Crocodile*. A health department spends so much time, money, and energy on flamboyant anti-fly posters that no means are left to make tanglefoot fly-paper. A trading organization ships French dictionaries to a Siberian tribe unable to read its own language! Another sends silk pajamas to a lumber-camp, along with pails without handles. A factory turns out trousers with different lengths of leg. A consignment of right-footed boots is sent to one village and, to compensate for it, all the left-footed ones go to another. While these are flagrant cases and may even be somewhat exaggerated in order to make them as ridiculous and biting as possible, one does not have to look far to find glaring instances of bureaucratic bungling and ineptitude.

What are the reasons for all this? In the first place, there are the functionaries inherited from the old regime, nurtured in the worst governing traditions in the world. Not only are they versed in all the arts of procrastination, indolence, and evasion, but they often infect the newcomers with them. Secondly, it is due to the deliberate sabotage of counter-revolutionists and disaffected officials seeking to discredit the Soviet power by creating breakdowns, delays, and all kinds of difficulties. The various trials of the engineers reveal how this was done and for those who do not take their confessions at face value, a close survey of the *émigré* press will show how it is still being done. A third reason is the sheer incompetence of persons, without previous experience, thrust into positions that call for expert knowledge and training. It may well be that their thick-headedness and carelessness is more disastrous than venality and sabotage.

Another factor is the inherent complexity of a huge cumbersome apparatus that deals with everything from production of pins to instruction in philosophy. With this is coupled the desire to evade responsibility and the fear of minor officials of deviating in the slightest from set rules, codes, and instructions. They will keep to the letter of the law no matter how they violate its spirit. Back of this are certain traits in the Russian mind with its vague, mystical conception of time and responsibility. It may know that a straight line is the shortest distance between two points, but it cannot bring itself to taking it. Finally there still survives some of that fatalism and passivity in masses for centuries so accustomed to be browbeaten and befooled by bureaucrats that they expect nothing better from them and accept it unprotestingly. Still live the "three horses" on which Russia so long has ridden, *avos, nebos,* and *nichevo,* which may be translated as "Perhaps! So be it," "It doesn't matter," and "Never mind. . . ."

27. What Efforts Are Made to Root Out Bureaucratism and Graft?

To combat these evils there was instituted in 1919 the Commissariat of Workers' and Peasants' Inspection. Its function was to ferret out abuses, bring the guilty to justice, seek to discover the causes, and suggest remedies against their recurrence. It investigated everything from falsification of accounts to the rotting of vegetables in stores, from quality of films to an outbreak of hog-cholera on a State farm, from duplication of stores to the drunkenness of a commissar. In keeping with Lenin's injunction, every effort was made "to secure the direct participation of the masses in this work." Hundreds of offices were opened for any citizen to lodge complaints at any time against any official. Thousands of charges and criticisms were brought into them daily. Tens of thousands of petty autocrats, saboteurs, and embezzlers were brought to justice. There were also many injustices, blunders, and stupidities.

With the aim of obtaining more expertness, judiciousness, and continuity in this work, in 1934 the functions of the Commissariat were transferred to two organs. The Commission of Soviet Control with 60 members now acts to keep a check-up on how decrees and directives are carried out, how each enterprise lives up to the schedules of the Plan and its promises. The Commission of Party Control more specifically scrutinizes the conduct and competence of Communists, especially those in high posts. Members of these bodies have the right to attend conferences and assemblies of all kinds. Without warning they may enter any institution and demand that all books and accounts be put at their disposal. They inquire into everything from fuel-wastage and water-supply to norms of the "Stakhanovites." They call general meetings of employees to air their views on the state of affairs, guaranteeing full immunity to complaints. Working in close collaboration these two commissions serve as powerful agents of correction, audit, and control. Aiding them are the several thousand inspectors of the Labor Unions and all the numerous agencies for enlisting the people generally in the fight against bureaucracy, graft, and corruption.

Among the unique devices for uncovering abuses was the "Light Cavalry." This consisted of detachments of Comsomols, the bane and nightmare of the bureaucrats of all stripes. The possibility of the descent of a squad of these zealous, and usually intolerant, warriors of Communism was a deterrent against lapsing routine and laxity. Even the youngsters had a part in the game, arriving with credentials from the Pioneer Brigades, ready to lend a sympathetic ear to the grievances of office-boy or janitor. While they still operate, more dependence is placed upon less spectacular methods. Most effective is the *Rabselkor* movement by which some four million worker-peasant-Red Army correspondents are keeping a stream of items pouring into the papers. On the basis of their revelations great numbers of the unfit constantly are being warned, demoted, or discharged.

Along with this day-to-day weeding out are the periodical cleansings or purgings called *chistkas*. In the papers or on a red banner strung up before the building, the date of the cleansing is announced and the public invited. Everyone from president or manager to floor-sweeper must appear before a committee of judges to give an account of his conduct and services. There is every reason for making it accurate, for not only is he subject to questions from the tribunal, but from the auditors, acting as a sort of jury. Anyone at any moment may rise to point out an important omission in one's story or remind him that in such-and-such an instance he was high-handed, bullying, irascible, unduly flirtatious, stalling for a bribe.

These *chistkas* are now practically confined to Communists. After handing over their red cards of membership they must stand up and give good reasons why it should be handed back to them. In this way the Party eliminates its careerists, adventurers, violators of party discipline and doctrine, and "radish Communists." Some of the *chistkas* are very serious and even tragic affairs. Others are not unlike a big family conclave in which the shortcomings of members are good-naturedly considered. In one I attended a lot of humor was injected by a clever artist who by cartoons on a big blackboard kept up a running commentary on the proceedings. A typical sleek old bureaucrat dilating on his tireless zeal and devotion to his work promptly appeared on the board as a spotless angel with a halo over his head. Then someone rose to remark he was overbearing with his subordinates, and at a stroke the halo vanished. He was always toadying to his superiors, another said, and a bunch of wing feathers came off. Others pointed out he was late to work, lazy, pompous, supercilious, and the air forthwith filled with flying crayon feathers. Turning about to look at the blackboard, he saw himself in the guise of a poor, plucked, cowering bird, while the room rocked with laughter.

While they are striving to change the habits and outlook of the old personnel, the chief hope is placed on the new generation growing up in the new traditions. From the outset of the Revolution, too, the policy has been to advance workmen as fast as possible into responsible positions. Thus out of the rank-and-file a stream of fresh blood is constantly pouring into the Soviet system. Chosen from the ablest members of the Labor Unions they usually receive a short course of training. Many of the highest posts are now occupied by men and women who a few years ago were steel-workers, weavers, or peasants.

Naturally some do not justify the hopes placed in them, and one may read in the papers of their curious performances and costly blunders. But with zeal and unswerving loyalty to the cause, even these may act as a check upon bureaucratic tendencies. Along with this movement from the bottom up goes one from the top down. Sometimes a fourth or fifth of the office staffs are sent out for active service in the field, and in some cases back to the lathe, the looms, and the tractor. This operates to keep the apparatus from becoming the monopoly of a white-collar class, to break down the barriers between intellectual and manual labor.

What are the results of this long fight waged against bureaucracy?

One still finds petty tyrants lording or rather "commissaring" it over subordinates, offices strangled in red tape, three tea-drinking clerks not doing the work of one. On the other hand, thousands of parallel organizations have been abolished, tens of thousands of superfluous employees eliminated, and there is marked increase in deference and politeness to the public. Most significant are the successes scored in the eradication of graft and bribery. "Grafting isn't popular in Russia because anyone who tries it is shot by a firing-squad," said Colonel Hugh Cooper, engineer of the big projects at Muscle Shoals and across the Dnieper. "If we shot all the grafters in America we would have to reclaim land to get enough room for the graves."

While that was said jocularly and isn't altogether true of America, it certainly was of old Russia where bribery, erected into a system, was a part of almost every transaction. And in new Russia, too, there remain plenty of officials with itching palms, cashiers absconding with trust funds, all sorts of petty thievery, speculations, padding of accounts. But there is much less than formerly, thanks to better ac-counting, closer check-up, and increasing prosperity. This last, in the long run, is the most important factor in the decreasing of graft. With the coming of the classless society and an economy of plenty it is one of the things scheduled to wither away entirely. There will be little or no reason for it when there are enough goods and more than enough to go around.

As to bureaucracy, human nature being what it is, it may well thrive lustily for a long time to come. But human nature changes, the old bureaucrats die off, authority in the economic field is being transferred from the centers to the enterprises themselves, the ap-paratus of government is being simplified by such measures as aboli-tion of food-cards and of restrictions against kulaks, priests, and their children. Great hopes are placed on the effects of the democratic processes advanced by the new Constitution and in the general rise of culture of the whole people, creating a new social conscience, ethic, and intelligence in the ordering of their affairs.

28. What Are the State Holidays, Decorations, Flag, Hymn, and Emblem?

The State emblem is a hammer and sickle on a sun-rayed globe encircled by ears of grain and the closing words of the Communist Manifesto *"Workers of the World, Unite!"* in the eleven languages of the republics. "Thus, the bird of prey, the Tsar's two-headed eagle, is replaced by the symbols of toil and production." During the debates on the new Constitution, it was often argued that the ancient emblems of worker and peasant should now abdicate in favor of a tractor and airplane, but to no avail. The State flag is a red banner with a hammer and sickle in gold in the upper corner near the staff and above them a five-pointed star.

The national anthem, originating in the Paris Commune and sung by revolutionists around the world, is the "International":

> Arise, ye prisoners of starvation!
> Arise, ye wretched of the earth!
> For justice thunders condemnation,
> A better world's in birth.
> No more tradition's chains shall bind you;
> Arise, ye slaves no more in thrall.
> The world shall rise on new foundations.
> You have been naught: you shall be all.

One hears it everywhere—from the bells in the Salvation Tower of the Kremlin, which once chimed out "God Save the Tsar"; from the throats of Red Army regiments and Stakhanov brigades marching out to the mines, the fields, and the forests; at funerals, weddings, and harvest festivals; on all State occasions and holidays.

First of the great official holidays is January 21, *Lenin Memorial Day,* the anniversary of his death. It is carried over into January 22, *Red Sunday,* in memory of the 1905 massacre of the people who came to the Tsar petitioning for redress of grievances and were shot down in the square before the Winter Palace. Following these days of national mourning come May 1-2, a review of the forces of labor; it originated in America and is celebrated as *May* or *International Day* by workers throughout the world. After repeating in unison the Oath of Allegiance, the new contingents of the Red Army lead the huge embannered processions that pour through the gaily festooned streets singing, dancing, and play-acting. The celebrations often last till late in the night. With similar pageantry is celebrated November 7-8, anniversary of the *October Revolution,* each year growing more colorful and spectacular.

In their holidays and festivals the Russians take a particular delight. So do the other Soviet peoples, especially the Georgians, Kazakhs, and all of the Turco-Tatar and Caucasian nations. They are always ready to seize an opportunity for holiday-making, and they have many. Besides the chief anniversaries the calendar is punctuated with other red-letter days all through the year. January 1 is *Udarnik,* or *Shock-Worker's Day,* reviewing the activities of the year in all fields from farming to diplomacy. February 23 is *Red Army Day* with the regiments visiting the factories and children's homes over which they are patrons. March 8 is *International Women's Day* instituted at Copenhagen in 1910. March 12 commemorates the *February Revolution,* the overthrow of the Tsar. March 18 is the *Day of the Paris Commune* which so influenced the Soviet Union that Lenin spoke of it as "standing on the shoulders of the Paris Commune."

April 17 is in memory of the *Lena Gold-Miners* shot down by the Tsar's troops in 1912. May 5 is *Press Day,* celebrating the first illegally printed issue of the Bolshevik organ *Pravda* in 1912. July 7, *International Red Sport Day,* is celebrated by great processions of athletes, demonstrating their solidarity with the workers' sport organizations abroad. August 1 is *Anti-War Day* with a review of events since the outbreak of the World War and the mobilization of forces in the drive for peace. August 18 is *Aviation Day* led by the Society for Chemical and Air Defense, with contests between balloons, dirigibles, gyroplanes, and gliders on every air-field. September 1 is *Youth Day,* another International event on the Red Calendar, with gala parades and demonstrations against War and Fascism. December 5 is *Constitution Day* commemorating the adoption of the new national charter on that date in 1936.

This by no means exhausts the list of holidays. Each of the eleven national republics has days significant to itself and its peoples. Triumphal events, such as the birthday of a great savant, homecoming of the aviators of the ANT-25 from their non-stop flight through the Arctic, are marked by rites of gratitude and rejoicing. And finally there are the old church festivals still tenaciously clung to by the old peasants, the fête-days of the Orthodox saints, Christmas and Easter, usually observed, according to the Julian calendar, thirteen days earlier than in the rest of the world.

Not all these occasions afford a full day's vacation for everybody. Some are only for the people who are particularly concerned, some are celebrated only by half-days, afternoons, or evenings. In any event, however, Soviet citizens enjoy longer and more frequent respites from work than elsewhere. For they have a seven-hour day and a six-day week, which gives them each year 73 instead of 52 full regular rest-days, besides the extra red-letter days. The "right of every citizen to rest," declared by Article 119 of the Soviet Constitution is amply confirmed and supported by the Soviet calendar.

The highest decoration bestowed by the Soviets is the Order of Lenin. Among its recipients are Krupskaya, widow of Lenin; Kollontai, Ambassador to Sweden; Winter, chief engineer of the dam on the Dnieper; George McDowell, the indefatigable American farmer; Izotov, the famous Donbas miner; the Fifty-First Infantry Division that broke through the concrete fortification of the Crimea and shattered the White armies; William Lavcry and Clyde Armistead, the young Americans who helped rescue the Chelyuskin castaways from the drifting ice-floes in the Arctic. For outstanding contributions to the defense of the country the Order of the Red Star is given to civilians as well as military people. To military units and individuals is given the Order of the Red Banner for exploits demanding great courage, endurance, and sacrifice. So signally were these qualities displayed by the seven aviators in saving the Chelyuskin castaways, that a new and high-ranking order, Hero of the Soviet Union, was instituted in their honor.

These decorations are not merely honorific. With them go monetary awards, life pensions, reductions in rent, free use of trams and buses, tickets to any destination twice yearly, and in some cases to any place at any time for the rest of one's life. While lavishing honors upon the brilliant and daring, the Soviet recognizes those services that may be less spectacular but not less valuable. Veterans in all fields of industry who have done yeoman service, and leading "Stakhanovites" who have pushed production up to higher peaks, are given the title of Heroes of Labor, Nobles of Labor. To pre-eminent directors, and factories or farms running far ahead of their quotas, is given the Red Banner of Labor. From the "labor front" for which it was first instituted this order is now extended to scientists, artists, and teachers.

For these "engineers of the mind and spirit," as Stalin calls them, there is also a long list of special awards and distinctions. The highest is People's Artist, conferred on such famous régisseurs as Stanislavsky, Nemirovich-Danchenko, Moskvin and Kachalov. Next comes People's Artist of the Republic followed by Honored Worker in Art or Artist of Merit—titles now held by the cinema producers Shumiatsky and Pudovkin; the creators of a series of films from "Potemkin" to "Bezhin Meadows," Eisenstein and his operator Tisse; the portrait-painter Brodsky, the acrobat-clown and jester Lazarenko. For those excelling in almost any field of endeavor there are badges, medals, and awards— the Badge of Honor, Honored Worker in Science, and so on to Honored Master of Sports, for the best sprinters, skiers, swimmers, gliders, sharp-shooters, discus-hurlers, parachute jumpers. They may be seen heading the columns of athletes in the processions that stream through the cities on the great holidays.

II. Economic Life

II. Economic Life

29. What Are the Natural Resources of the Soviet Union?

Everything concerning the Soviets is subject to bitter debate. To this rule even the natural resources are no exception. "There are more minerals in Montana than in the whole of Russia," declared former President Herbert Hoover to Christopher Morley. "Among the richest in the world, assuring her of a resplendent future as a first-rank industrial nation," asserted the geologist Gubkin. "Among the lowest in the world," retorted a critic, "condemning her to the rôle of a second-rate agricultural state." One reason the subject lent itself to controversy was that the wealth of the country was so much a matter of conjecture. And it still is. With a thousand years of history behind it, with cities and civilizations ancient before America was discovered, half its area remains geologically uncharted. Most of the great Siberian wilderness has not even a good topographic map. Virgin territories, larger than California, are awaiting the pick and drill of the prospector. What riches may be hidden in their depths or even strewn over their surfaces nobody knows.

To the old Russia of woodsmen, peasants, and nomads it was not essential to know them. To the Soviet Union with its program of complete industrialization it is imperative. Under a planned economy, the State must know where are the raw materials on which to base its plans. To this end, the colossal outlay—140 times greater than before the Revolution, and more than all other European countries combined—of funds on geological research. Each year some 20,000 geologists, geophysicists, topographers, soil-experts, hydrologists, botanists, and their aides take to the field. On glaciers and ice-floes, in forests and steppes, from the North Pole to the Pamirs, gleam the white tents and camp-fires of a hundred expeditions engaged in wiping the uncharted white patches from the map. As a result of their labors the pre-War tables of resources are now quite obsolete and useless. The known reserves of gold have increased threefold, coal by fivefold, zinc by eightfold, graphite by tenfold, copper by thirtyfold. The Soviet Union stands first in the world in iron, apatite, timber, and platinum. It has one-third of the total stock of oil, two-thirds of the manganese, three-fourths of the peat, four-fifths of the potash. To these may be added rich finds of sulphur, cyanite, corundum, fluorspar, mica, and wolfram.

As the figures of 1917 are dwarfed by those of 1937, these in turn may be totally eclipsed in a few years or even a few months. For insistently the search goes on, with bulletins coming in from a hundred far-flung fronts. Hills of sulphur are reported from the sandy wastes of Karakum. Quicksilver in the Altai Mountains, along with marbles—yellow, pink, and silver-gray for electro-technics. "Heavy water" in the depths of Lake Baikal. Gold-bearing gravel on the river Anabar, gold mingled with mercury and radium on the Afghan border, and, from the old mines in the Urals, a thirty-pound nugget, the biggest of the century. New fields of oil in the Vale of Ferghana, in Daghestan, and gushers at Lok-Batan spouting a thousand barrels an hour. Pearls and mother-of-pearl in the upper reaches of the river Umba. Aquamarine and beds of topaz—orange, pale blue and smoky green—in the mountains near Mongolia, along with ledges of bismuth, fluorspar, and veins of rare molybdenum—a veritable museum of minerals. In Moscow a deep artesian well taps a sea of brine laden with the potassium salts used in making fertilizers and gunpowder.

Kazakhstan rediscovers a tin-bearing district with diggings dating back to the Bronze Age. A rich strike of silver in Tamerlane's cave in the Valley of Shadimir gives point to ancient legends of hidden treasure in its caverns. Some of the new finds may wait years or decades to be developed. Others, situated precisely at the places where they are most needed, are at once exploited. Limestone in the Urals saves the long hauls to the blast furnaces of Magnitogorsk. Cliffs of rock salt, forty feet high, in

Yakutia are a boon to the fisheries of the Far East. Oil near the Kuzbas rounds out this new metal-power center of Siberia.

Each week brings news of some fresh increment to the collective wealth of the nation—some new field or mine or mineral, the property not of a few but of the whole community, increasing by a mite at least the individual wealth of each citizen. With self-interest adding its stimulus to the innate interest of everybody in the new and exotic, with more than ordinary zest, they hail the announcement of the new discoveries. And with the same avidity that they read about them, they participate in them. Over 2,000 local societies are studying the flora and fauna of their neighborhoods. Children, instructed by the museums in plant and mineral lore, go out to ransack the fields and streams. Brigades of summer excursionists turn over to the institutes sacks of specimens picked up on their treks in the steppes and mountains. Books, plays, and slogans enliven and color the quest for the hidden treasures. The searchers for ores and gems are bidden "to go forth and awaken from their beds the long-sleeping beauties of the earth." The core drills are "the eyes of steel penetrating into the dark recesses of the underworld to spy out their hidden secrets." The waterfalls are "the genies to be tamed by electric dynamos and made the servants of man." With huge territories yet to be explored and with the minds and means of 175 millions of people engaged in exploring them, there is no telling what riches may suddenly come to light. Only in tin, tungsten, cobalt, lithium, and a few other minor minerals is the country comparatively poor and small deposits of these are now being reported. By the most sober appraisal, Stalin's assertion that the Soviet Union has ample resources for building an abundant rounded economy seems fully justified.

Land and Forests

The total area of grazing and meadow land mounts up to 750 million acres. Of arable land there are some 500 million acres, ranging from poor clay and sandy soil to the celebrated "black soil," a rich humus of decomposed Steppe grass reaching in some regions a depth of six feet or more. How new areas are being added by swamp drainage and the irrigation of deserts, what crops are produced, and what new cereals and fruits are developed, are described in the sections following under science and agriculture. (See pages 186-187.)

The forests covering over two billion acres constitute over a fourth of the world's entire stand of timber. From the Volga an evergreen zone of pine, fir, larch, and juniper reaches north to the tundras of the Arctic and across the Siberian plain six thousand miles to the Pacific. Along the fringes of this area of conifers and down to the steppes flourish the lime and the linden, the alder, the ash and the aspen, the close-grained beech, and "the lady of the forest"—the white-gleaming birch—outnumbering all other deciduous trees together. Clothing the steep slopes of the Pamirs and the Caucasus are thick groves of hornbeam, chestnut, tamarisk, ironwood, and pistachio. In the Far East huge stretches of Korean pine, silver fir, and spruce alternate with stands of Sakhalin willow, maple, walnut, and the velvet cork tree while underneath them grow the ginseng roots valued by the Chinese from ancient times for their magical healing properties.

As tremendous as the forests is the rôle they played in the primitive economy of the peasant. Out of them he drew the logs for his house, the moss to caulk it, the branches and twigs to roof it, the fuel to heat it, and even the pitch-pine torches to light it. An easy prey to fire, the village houses went up in flames at the rate of nearly a million a year. But in the forests was material a-plenty for their rebuilding—and for the multitude of things often made by the peasant with nothing more than the cunning of his hands and a hatchet. The outer bark of the birch he turned into buckets, baskets, and boxes. He wove bast shoes from the inner bark of the linden. He bent a sapling of oak into a sleigh runner, a supple maple into an arching yoke to go over his horse's neck. In the same way he got his rake and plow and harrow—picking them out of the forest as an American farmer would from a store. No wonder that old Russia was known as "Wooden Europe"—a country whose people lived in 300,000 wooden villages, paved their cities with wooden blocks, tilled the soil with wooden plows, rode in wagons with wooden axles, and with wooden spoons ate their food from wooden dishes.

Now, leaving behind its age-old economy of wood, the country is passing rapidly into the era of metal. The peasant is becoming a collectivist and a mechanic, and the things he so cunningly fashioned out of trees are more and more being made out of iron and steel, concrete, and porcelain. Industrialization, however, is by no means lessening the demands on the forest. It calls for ever-increasing quantities of timber for telegraph poles, railway sleepers, silos; for everything from mine props to matches, from plywood to pulp for paper print; and for all the distillates of wood—tar, turpentine, alcohol, and acetic acid. Not only must the Soviet forests feed the fast-growing needs at home, but as the wooded areas in most countries are dwindling, more and more they are called upon to supply the markets of the world. So much so that, in the lists of exports from the Soviet Union, timber and its by-products bulk bigger than all of its grains together.

Fortunately the Soviet forests are more than equal to the demands upon them. The annual increment by new growth—some 600 million cubic meters—still exceeds the cutting. Regions bigger than all Germany, still unblazed by the ax, are being charted by air and land surveys and opened up to the loggers. In the Far East the new BAM (Baikal-Amur-Magistral) railway now cuts through the dense wilderness to the Pacific. In the Far West chain-saws and bark-strippers are operating along the new Baltic-White Sea Canal. Out of the *taiga,* the virgin forests of Siberia, rafts now go floating down to new seaports on the Arctic. Steadily the forests are being delivered into the maws of the big sawmills along the banks and the mouths of the rivers. Beside them are rising still bigger furniture, pulpwood, and cellulose plants. With the slogan, "Paper is as essential to culture as metal to industry," they aim by 1939 to turn out a million tons of newsprint and book-paper.

To the Commissariat of Timber is assigned a double task. It has not only to exploit the forests but conserve them. That means treating them not as mines but as a crop. Toward this end the logged-over sections are being replanted with seedlings of pine, linden, and larch or sown with their seeds cast from airplanes. The highroads are being lined with trees for shade, fruit, and fuel. Cultivation of the neglected walnuts, chestnuts, and beechnuts of the Caucasus and Central Asia promises a yearly yield of a half million tons, besides their by-products.

Fur, Feathers, Fish

Furs have always played a big rôle in the economy of Russia. The old boyars paid their debts in furs and hides, and with them the Soviets are paying for about ten per cent of their imports. As vast and variegated as their domains is the fauna which inhabits them—antelopes, badgers, chamois, deer, elk, fitch, glutton, and so on down to the zebus beyond the Caucasus. The celebrated Russian bear comes in white, black, or brown. The peculiar affection of the peasant for the shambling creature is reflected in folk-tales like that of the bear which was befriended by Saint Sergius and followed him about like a dog. In real life they are not quite so amiable. Not long ago in broad daylight they invaded villages of Vologda, killing and carrying off the cattle. Usually the bear reveals his winter den by breath-holes in the snow, for which the hunter stakes out his claim as he would for a mine and at which he awaits the bear's emergence in the spring. While wolves are not so prevalent as one might infer from pictures and stories of Russia, every winter records attacks on lone drivers and skiers, and thousands of hunters take part in the wolf-drives.

The ferocious tigers of the Far East, which play a part in the film "Frontier," are often caught alive in snares, nets, and pits. They now roam the dense thickets of the *taiga* all the way out to the Pacific, frightened from their usual haunts on the Manchurian frontier, say the natives, by the marching troops and the noise of guns. Along with the panthers, jaguars, and leopards of Central Asia, they are the heart's desire of those who hunt for sport or pastime. While their heads and skins make excellent trophies they add little to the national wealth. Nor do the more exotic animals like the ibex, roe-buck, and *ovis poli*—a mountain sheep with huge coiled horns that was hunted by the Roosevelts. The bulk of the income comes from the more ordinary sources. Topping the list are the squirrels with twelve million skins a year. Next come the eight million rabbits furnishing fur enough to cover a fair-sized city. Then the four million minks, martens, and marmots.

Most prized of the foxes are the blue and the polar species often hunted by being driven out upon the ice-covered lakes where they helplessly slide and fall on the glassy surface. Still more coveted are the ermine and the sable, sometimes smoked out of their hiding places in the hollows of trees. Of great value likewise are the moufflons of the Caucasus and the spotted Siberian deer, whose hormone-containing antler-buds are used after the Chinese fashion for healing wounds, stimulating the heart, and increasing sexual potency. While these are comparatively rare, there are great numbers of other unusual animals —the kolinsky, hamster, peschanik, suslik. Huge bales of all these furs and pelts—raw, dressed, and dyed—are shown at the annual fur auctions which attract buyers from all over the world. Alongside of these products of the Soviet forests and steppes are those raised on its farms and ranges—chinchilla, skins of Siberian dogs and ponies, the caracul of Astrakhan and Persian lambs.

Of game birds there are a hundred varieties, ranging from the heath-cock and hazel-hen to the white partridge, pheasant, and white-headed griffon. Wild swans swim on the forest lakes, the tundras are breeding grounds for grebes, white grouse, and eider ducks. From the nests of the eiders, lined with the soft down they pluck from their bodies, comes the finest eider down. Amongst Cossacks and Kazakhs hunting is still carried on as in ancient times, with falcons, goosehawks, and golden eagles taken as fledglings and carefully trained to their tasks.

Much greater than the wealth in wild birds and beasts is that de-rived from the seas and rivers. Of fish there are 310 species of which 38 are found only in Soviet waters. They range in size from the perch to the forty-pound trout of Armenia and the great sturgeons weigh-ing up to two thousand pounds and yielding twenty buckets of black caviar. From the icy waters of Kamchatka comes the giant crab rich in iodine. The Black Sea dolphins supply fats and oils for soaps, glues, and vitamin "D" that is four times as rich as cod-liver oil. The gray, blue, and humpbacked whales yield annually some 5,000 tons of oil, bone spermaceti, and whale meat—canned, salted, and smoked. Seals bask not only on the ice-banks of the Arctic, but on the warm sand-spits of the Caspian which furnish over 100,000 skins a year.

Fishing is being raised from a primitive craft to a science and industry. The spawning and migration of the fish schools along the coast and in the deltas of the big rivers like the Volga are carefully studied and charted. The 130,000 dories, trawlers, seiners, and sealers of the fishing fleet are being steadily motorized and equipped with the latest technique and tackle. Airplanes and radio are used to discover and announce the arrival of the fish schools and to rescue the castaway fishermen on the breaking ice-floes carried out to sea. The whaling flotilla has scout planes to spy out the whales, guns for shooting harpoons loaded with explosives, and devices to keep the whales afloat by pumping air into their carcasses. Herring are trapped by giant seines across the narrow entrances to bays and "locked" in the nets by electric screens created by wires connected to dynamos. Cruising canneries follow the deep-sea fleet to receive the hauls direct from the boats and can them fresh. Counting everything from the tiny anchovy to the big sea-mammals, the catch mounts up to well over a million tons a year.

All this does not mean that the country is a paradise for sportsmen with the spoils of the chase and the rod to be gained without effort. There are regions and seasons when game and fish are scarce or altogether lacking. During a six weeks' river journey in dugouts through the Archangel forests, we saw nothing more exciting than a few squirrels, catfish, and the tracks of a bear. It is because of the bigness of this Eurasian continent that the returns from its wild life are so big, mounting up in the aggregate to over a billion dollars a year. The aim of the Soviets is to double, perhaps triple, this in the not far-off future. Toward this end, aided by the scientific institutes, the million members of the hunters' and fishers' artels, and the ten million amateurs, they have put through the following measures: No hunting during mating and breeding seasons. No killing at any time of nearly extinct animals like beavers, spotted deer, and egrets. Abolishing primitive traps in which one out of every three animals were

eaten by other beasts of prey. The expansion of the old private reserves and royal hunting parks into a network of over five hundred.
Sanctuaries for birds in their migrations, in their summer nesting
grounds along the Arctic littoral, and in their wintering places in the
steppes beyond the Caucasus. A chain of veterinary stations to prevent epidemics in the huge reindeer herds supplying food to the peoples of the North. The allocation of islands for herds of sea-otters,
sea-bears, and sea-beavers. Fish ladders for the passage over dams of
fish on their spawning migrations. Nurseries for the mass-breeding
of raccoons, sables, blue and silver foxes. Experiments in creation of
new and hardy species by crossing the deer and elk, the reindeer with
the caribou, the aurochs and the cow, the zebra and the horse.

Most interesting are the efforts toward a better distribution of fauna.
Into regions well suited to certain animals, transmigration was hin-
dered by the barriers of wide rivers, barren deserts, and high mountains. Hares, because their narrow paws stuck in the soft Ural snow,
and because in the summer they were too busy feeding their young,
never reached the steppes of Eastern Siberia. Certain squirrels, because they could not cross the treeless plains, did not reach the nut-
bearing forests of the Caucasus. To these natural, congenial habitats
they are now being transferred. Fish spawn and fry are being transplanted to distant streams, the Aral Sea, and the lakes of Armenia.
The prolific American muskrat and the beaver are being loosed in
the creeks and marshes. Along with the animals into their new haunts
sometimes are transplanted the plants and small rodents on which
they live. There is even artificial feeding during deep snows and seasons when fodder is scarce. Through these various devices, the Soviet
Union looks forward to a rapid extension of its fish and animal
resources.

Sources of Energy

The Soviets stand second in the world in production and consumption of oil, with reserves of over three billion tons to draw upon. New
deposits are being found all over the land from Shor-Su and the

Salyan steppes to Sakhalin Island. It lies in films upon the forest lakes in the North where it is soaked up in cloths and wrung out by the natives. It oozes in the form of asphalt from the rock fissures in hills along the Volga. It rises in tubings out of the Caspian Sea from the bottom five miles from the shore. In the Emba-Urals it reveals itself in 1,200 dome-like hillocks, like the famous salt-mounds along the Gulf of Mexico, guaranteeing, according to the geologist Gubkin, a future output of twenty-five million tons a year. For the present, however, the old fields of Baku still retain their ascendancy. It was here that the eternal flame fed from underground caverns of gas burned in the Temple of the Fire Worshipers. Here the youthful Stalin served his revolutionary apprenticeship in organizing the oil workers. It was seized right after the Revolution by the armies of the oil imperialists, its oil wells were flooded or set afire, and the twenty-six commissars marched out into the desert and shot. Today, after seventy years, it is still producing more than all other fields combined.

In all fields the former slow wasteful methods are being supplanted by latest technics. Carótage, the use of electric current in prospecting and testing, is extensively employed. Out of the earth, rotary drills and deep-drawing pumps are getting bigger quantities of oil per well and per acre. Out of the crude oil, new cracking-plants and refineries are extracting a bigger variety of products, ranging from ashless coke and paraffin wax to naphtha-soap and lampblack. Transport by barges and tank-cars is giving way to pipe-lines through which the oil is forced by powerful pumps. Through these conduits, it runs north a thousand miles toward Moscow and across the bleak deserts of Kazakhstan to the new centers of Siberia. Over and around the Caucasus it runs to the Black Sea ports where "whalebacks" carry it away to the markets of Britain, the fleets of France and Italy. With a steadily increasing flow an increasing rôle is played by this Soviet "black gold," as it is called, in home and foreign affairs. Alongside these reservoirs of oil are caverns of gas in two forms, "wet" and "dry." They consist chiefly of methane with a mixture of ethane, pentane, and even precious elements like helium. These natural gases are condensed into gasoline or used directly for heat and light. In many cases the bubbling up of mud made by the pressure of escaping gas points to the presence of immense gas chambers in the depths of the earth. In the Caucasus alone the "mud-bubble" region covers thousands of square miles but only a small fraction is as yet being utilized.

Despite the inroads of other fuels, coal is still the primary one. In its three main forms—anthracite, bituminous, and lignite—the Soviets possess well over a trillion tons. This figure may easily be doubled when the enormous Tungus Basin is fully surveyed. New fields are opening in Karaganda where coal can be mined direct from the surface; on Sakhalin Island worked from galleries straight from the seashore; in the Pechora Basin along the Arctic, and a score of other places. Of these, most important is the Kuznetz Basin where an American group headed by Rutgers, Barker, and Bill Haywood of the I.W.W. pioneered in 1921. It contains all types of coal—coking, light, heavy, gas, and sapropelite, rich in coal-tar easily convertible into liquid fuel. But the old Donets Basin still retains its title as the main "coal bin" of the country. Highly mechanized with electric locomotives, pneumatic drills, underground restaurants, and first-aid stations for the miners, it produces more coal than nearly all others combined. It produces the best coal—an anthracite, so low in ash content and so high in energy units that it commands top prices in all markets including New England. It produces increasing amounts of gas by burning the coal in its beds and by piping the gas directly into the factories, a method that lessens labor, dust, and noise. Final and most famous of its products is Stakhanov, the miner who, in increasing fivefold his output by a scientific use of time and tools, initiated the movement bearing his name that swept the country.

Of peat or "green coal" the supply is practically inexhaustible, for like the forests, the peat bogs are constantly renewing themselves. By the old methods it was painfully dug from the marshes, molded into briquets, and slowly dried by sun and wind. New processes are eliminating the back-breaking labor, reducing the drying time from forty to four days, and transforming the raw peat into new forms of fuel—coke, gas, alcohol, and motor oils. Along with oil-shale, schist, and "shungite," it is used more and more for fueling, especially in power-plants and places distant from high-grade combustibles. While peat consumption is fifteen times greater than before the Revolution, less than five per cent of the 150 million acres of bogs is being exploited.

Water, Wind, and Sun Power. Of "white coal"—the energy of flowing, falling waters—the Soviets have well over a fourth of the total world resources. Insistently and eloquently Lenin pointed out the tremendous electric power going to waste in the great rivers of the plains, in the foaming cascades and glacier-fed streams of the mountains, as well as in the discarded low-grade lignite, peat, and slack. Declaring that "with the Soviets, plus electrification, we can build Socialism," in 1921 he launched the project for thirty regional stations. So long did this remain on paper that it was called *electrofiction.* But, soon after the civil war, the big plant on the river Volkhov was completed, first of a long series climaxing in the Dnieproges that outstripped Niagara or Muscle Shoals.

Across the Dnieper, above those islands that once "poured liberty and Cossacks over the Ukraine," now curves a mammoth concrete dam. Converting the swift, turbulent river into an inland lake and flanked by locks cut through solid granite, it realizes the dream of Catherine the Great allowing ships to pass from the Black Sea up to Kiev. Into nine of the biggest turbines in the world—says its chief consulting engineer, Colonel Hugh Cooper—it sluices the force of nine once-raging rapids, extracting from their once-wasted waters the power of 756,000 horses. It supplies the current for a steel, aluminum, coke, and chemical combine covering fourteen square miles and for the new cities and towns rising near them. It sets the huts of the villages around blazing with what the peasants call the "Lenin light." Over high voltage lines it reaches out to turn wheels on distant farms and in the collieries of the Don. Already built or building are big plants all the way from the river Niva, north of the Arctic Circle, to Armenia where the river Zanga pours from a lake a mile above the sea. Biggest of all is the Lower Volga project to generate four times more current than Dnieproges and irrigate ten million acres of arid steppes. This in turn will be dwarfed by the giants that will harness the precipitate Angara, the deep, crystal-clear Siberian river with twelve million horsepower in its racing waters. These last are projects of the Third and Fourth Five-Year Plans. For the present, the output of electric power from all sources is twenty times greater than before the Revolution and second in the world.

"Blue coal" is the name given to the tides that rise and fall in the narrow estuaries of the sea. "Azure coal" to the winds blowing over the steppes. For ages the village windmills with their clumsy wooden sails have been operating the primitive pumps, churns, and millstones for grinding the peasants' grain. They did as long as the winds blew, but stopped when they stopped. How gain freedom from the caprices of the winds and insure a constant supply of power? By transmuting the air currents into electric current and storing it in batteries. Toward this end the Institute of Wind Energy has experimented with towers 500 feet high carrying wings or vanes over 100 feet in diameter. Wind-driven motors capable of generating over 5,000 kilowatts are now operating along the Arctic where the velocity of the winds is highest. Another chain in the Crimea, during periods of strongest winds, will use their excess power to pump sea-water into a huge reservoir. Then in calm weather sluices will be opened, allowing the water to turn the turbines of a hydro-electric station, thus insuring a steady supply of current.

Behind and above these coals of many colors—black, green, white, azure—is the one that creates them all and is the very source of all resources. This is "yellow coal," the heat of solar rays. Power directly from the sun! This is not just a fantastic project of visionary Russians. In Central Asia they are using curved mirrors, like the "sun engines" of Egypt and California, to concentrate heat upon steam boilers. With this and other devices meals are cooked, bath-houses heated, sulphur melted, fresh water distilled from the sea. Of course their value is as yet infinitesimal. They testify rather to the faith of the Soviets in the ability of science to exact tribute from every force in the universe, to subject to the service of man every object from the biggest to the smallest. While the Heliocentric Institute seeks to capture the power of the sun at the other extreme, the Physio-dynamic Institute seeks to release the tremendous power of the atom. Confidently they look forward to the day when, in place of coal, peat, oil, water, and wind, society will have direct access to these more primary limitless sources of energy.

Iron, Copper, Gold, and Other Metals

"Our country," said Kalinin, "needs metal as the steppes beyond the Volga need wheat." Long before the country was in a furor of construction from all quarters came the cry "Metal! More Metal!" But there was no aluminum, tin, or nickel, and in 1920 the output of iron, steel, and copper had sunk to less than one-tenth of the pre-War level. Now it is being doubled, tripled, quadrupled. Steadily Soviet metallurgy advances toward first place in the world from bases assuring it of ample supplies of everything essential.

In reserves of iron, "the bread of industry," the Soviets now hold first place with eleven billion tons. To these may be added the colossal mass of quartzites in what is known as the Kursk Magnetic Anomaly. This is a region south of Moscow, 150 miles long and 30 wide, undershot by a bed of iron ore so large that it exerts a pull on the magnetic needle four times the normal. It also exerts a pull on the cupidity of the Nazi Germans and is one of the prizes they would like to lay hold of by a conquest of Russia. New borings, according to the geologist Gubkin, indicate the presence of not less than 100 billion tons "in all probability doubling the world's supply, deferring by many centuries the menace of a civilization bereft of iron." Much of this ore is deep down and low in content, but there are immense high-grade pockets just beginning to be worked. Of the old smelting centers, most important is the South Ukrainian utilizing the brown iron stones of Kerch and the red iron-rocks of Krivoy Rog. Chief among the new is the gigantic Ural-Kuznetsk combine drawing upon the rich black magnetite of Magnet Mountain and the Siberian West. A third big metal center is to be built in Eastern Siberia developing the recently discovered deposits of this region and, still farther East, another project is to rise along the Bureya River.

Iron ore is but useless heavy rock without other elements to smelt it. Next to coal, most important is *manganese* of which the Soviets have the most and best in the world. About one-third of all used in the United States comes from the Chiatury mines high up in a mountain gorge of the Caucasus where a broad seam runs like a black ribbon just below the snow-clad peaks. Just as essential are certain alloys and rare metals, especially for stainless, rustless, and high-speed steels. Among these are chromium for plating steel, vanadium to render it resilient and niobium to protect it from corrosion. Also antimony for printing-presses, fluorite for glass, tungsten for X-ray electrodes and phonograph needles, molybdenum for filaments in electric lamps. Under the Tsar most of these were imported from abroad. Hence it was said that the only thing Russian in Russian electric bulbs was Russian air. Now they are being mined or made in Soviet laboratories and concentrating plants along with the rare metals cadmium, tantalum, and titanium-gallium used for fire signals, high temperature thermometers, and the treatment of syphilis. Also the new found suromite, labradorite, and indium.

Of the more prosaic but highly essential metals—copper, zinc, and lead—the known deposits have increased from eight to thirty times and production stepped up proportionately. The same is true of mercury and nickel, their annual output rising from practically nothing, under the Tsar, to over a quarter million tons yearly. Still more striking is the increase in aircraft metal, aluminum, in new plants on the rivers Volkhov and Dnieper and around the new found alunite ore of Azerbaijan and the apatite nepheline of the Arctic.

The "Noble Metals." Today as formerly Russia holds first place as a producer of platinum. At one time it was used for coinage and it is said that the peasants in the Urals hunted game with bullets made of platinum. From the same region in 1842 came the celebrated 60 pound nugget of gold found in the ledges of the Mias Valley. Here again in 1935 the spade of the gold-digger Ilya Paltzev struck upon the biggest nugget of the present century. Another famous field stretches along the river Lena where the shooting down of three hundred miners by the Cossacks set off the Revolution of 1905. Another is in Tajikistan whose gold-bearing sands and gravels have been washed by nomads since the days of Genghis Khan. To the old fields are now added new ones in the high Pamirs and the "Celestial Mountains," along the lower reaches of the Volga, near Sotchi in the Caucasian Riviera, in 360 different spots in Kazakhstan. So numerous and widespread are the new finds of gold that it would be simpler to name the regions where it is not being found.

Their development is in the hands of the All-Union Gold Trust headed until 1937 by Serebrovsky, whose name in English means Silver! With 200 two-way radio-stations, with airplanes and new highroads, it is opening up hitherto inaccessible diggings in the *taiga* and tundras. Transport by muleback in summer and sledges in winter gives way to fleets of high-powered trucks and motor boats. Primitive placer mining with wooden sluices and shovels gives way to electric-dredges, rock-crushers, pneumatic drills, and aerial cableways. Huge amalgam and cyanide plants are now treating the ore, although some concentrates are still shipped across the ocean to America. All this mechanization, however, has not eliminated the old-time prospectors although it has done away with most of the hazards and hardships they suffered. Usually miners are organized into artels working in brigades up to a hundred or more, receiving a "grubstake" and a percentage of their findings. Others, as lone wolves, strike out "on their own" to try their luck in the wilderness. After a heavy downpour Siberian natives scour their hill slopes for the shining gold dust washed out by the rain. On off days and holidays thousands of amateurs try washing it out of the gold-bearing sands with pan and shovel. They all add their bit to the half-million regular full-time miners engaged in getting gold out of the Soviet hills and rivers.

In ironic contrast with this zest for gold of present-day Communists is the rôle assigned to it by Lenin in the future world state of Communism. "Then, we shall, I think, use gold for making public lavatories in the streets of the great cities of the world. That would be the most just and graphically edifying use of gold for those generations which have not forgotten that for gold ten million people were massacred and thirty million crippled in the 'Great War of Liberation'! And for the same gold they are no doubt now prepared to murder twenty million and cripple sixty million more in a new war." Quite likely under Communism the noble metal will not be relegated to the ignoble uses depicted in the mordant words of Lenin. It will however be demoted from its present exalted position to one no higher than rightly belongs to it as a malleable, ornamental element. But this is envisioning the distant future. In the present world set-up the Communists are as eager as capitalists to lay hold of the yellow metal. They need it for foreign trade, to stabilize the ruble, and as a war-chest for emergencies. They want all they can get of it and each year they are getting more. With the annual output close to 300,000,000 dollars, by 1939 the Soviet Union expects to take the place of the Transvaal as the first gold-producing country in the world.

Precious, Semi-Precious, and Ordinary Stones

Russia is a land of paradoxes, even in its natural resources. With a great wealth of rare and valuable elements it is at the same time woefully deficient in one prosaic but essential material—good stone for roads and buildings. The great central plains where the big towns and cities are located are almost rockless, and must build with clay, gravel, cement, and bricks. As if to make amends for this dearth of ordinary stone, nature is lavish with gems and decorative stones. "Nowhere else," says Fersman, the foremost mineralogist, "can one find such bright green malachites and deep green nephrites; there are no rivals to our golden-green iridescent chrysolite-chrysoberyls." Most of these come from the Urals, "the jewel box" of the Soviets, just as the Ukraine is their "bread box." Ivan the terrible attributed mystic healing powers to these Ural gems: Its blood-red rubies comforted the heart; sapphires strengthened the eye; emeralds clarified the blood; amber safeguarded the health; while in the Caucasus the water-buffaloes were adorned with bluestones to ward off the evil eye.

In the Urals are many fields of emeralds. The biggest one was discovered on the banks of the Takovaya by a peasant who brought home as playthings for his children some bits of "greenstone" he had found in the roots of a tree blown down by a storm. By such strokes of chance are still being uncovered onyxes and opals, lazurite, woodstone and tiger's-eye. In their finished state the traveler on the Trans-Siberian may view them, sparkling in the shops beside the station in Sverdlovsk. From afar he may see ten thousand of them in the huge five-pointed stars that top the towers of the Kremlin. A mosaic of them over three hundred feet square forms the unique relief map of the Soviet Union commemorating its twentieth anniversary. Its frontiers are marked with topazes and amethysts, its mountains are made of jasper and its forests of jade, the rivers and lakes are inlaid in lapis lazuli, and the new White Sea and Volga canals in aquamarine, while Moscow as the red capital fittingly shines as a five-pointed ruby.

At the State Lapidary Works one may watch the craftsmen with infinite patience engraving gems with tiny sickles and hammers, etching portraits of Lenin on selenite or polishing great vases of jasper that will take ten years to complete. Or, choosing to view them in their natural settings, he may go to the Ilmen Mineral Preserve, an interdicted area in which as in an open book one may read the story of rocks and minerals in the making. Here, amid ledges of slate and granite are massive outcroppings of rhodonite, diorite, and volcanic tufa, pits of black and white agate, mica, porphyry, biotite, needles of tourmaline, and zircon crystals. Over a hundred species in azure, violet, and indigo—all colors of the rainbow imprisoned in stones and lying in the earth-beds that gave them birth. Karelia supplied the dark red diabase for the Lenin Mausoleum and the gray diabase that paves the Red Square in front of it. From Lake Onega came the porphyry for the tomb of Napoleon in Paris as well as the columns of St. Isaac's Cathedral and the Winter Palace. The Crimea produces trass, fulling-clays for soaps and cleansing wool of grease, and the famous Inkerman stone quarried since the days of the Romans. With the Altais and the Caucasus it furnished the marble for the Moscow subway, façading and colonnading it in varied colors from dove-gray to copper-red. From a mile up in the Armenian mountains comes porous, coral-like, rose-tinged, volcanic tufa yielding easily to saw and chisel but highly resistant to the weather.

Other Resources and Lenin's Appeal

While basic elements like coal and iron may be the "bread and meat" of industry, it cannot live on them alone. Nor will the other minerals so far listed suffice to build up a vigorous, full-rounded, full-statured industry. It demands apatite, bismuth, corundum, diatomaceous earth, and so on down the alphabet to the various salts, carbons, and nitrates, essential for fertilizers, dyes, gunpowder, and synthetic rubber. Many of those minerals quite unknown to old Russia have been discovered in deposits unprecedented in size and richness. So rich indeed that they have become the centers of thriving settlements. Beyond the Arctic Circle, where a few years ago reindeer dug the moss and lichens from the snow-covered tundras and their Lapp drivers fought off the hordes of mosquitoes, now stands the city of Kirovsk with over 50,000 inhabitants. It has electricity to light them through the four months' polar night, thousands of cows to give them milk, acres of greenhouses to supply them with vegetables, institutes to educate them, theatres to amuse them. It was apatite, whole mountains of it, that out of the frozen wastes called this great enterprise into being. Shot down in chutes from the high up mines and quarries in hundreds of thousands of tons it goes to fertilize the Russian lands. And with it goes nepheline, titanium, zirconium, and twenty other rare minerals. The same drama is being enacted in scores of places: Around the sylvinite and carnalite potash of Soli-kamsk, with deposits now computed as thrice greater than in all the rest of the world. At Karabugaz Bay utilizing the mirabilite (Glauber's Salts), sometimes cast up on the shores of the Caspian in ribbons a half-mile long. Around the hundred-foot thick salt stratum left by the retreating waters of the ancient Blue Sea of Perm. Beside the plants extracting iodine out of the kelps of the Black and White and Yellow Seas. Near the seams of crystal magnesite in the Jewish autonomous region of Birobijan.

With this recital of Soviet resources one might go on thus for pages, stopping only to note again that even this one-sixth of the earth does not have a plethora of everything. It is relatively poor in tin, tungsten, cadmium, cobalt, and saltpeter. Outside of these and a few other items, new deposits of which may be discovered, the country possesses ample and often enormous stores of all raw materials necessary for the fullest industrialization and chemification, and for agriculture. Up to the time of the Revolution they were for the most part unknown, unsurveyed, or unutilized. Only vaguely did certain persons sense the vast potentialities of the land. "Our country is great and abundant, but there is no order in it" begins the missive said to have been sent by the Russians to the Varangians, a thousand years ago. And some fifty years ago, the contrast between the boundless natural wealth of Russia and its abject cramping poverty impelled the poet Nekrassov to write:

> Thou art so wretched,
> Poor and so pitiful.
> But of rich treasure, full,
> Mighty all-powerful.
> Russia, my Mother!

These words Lenin used as a heading for his article on March 11, 1918, the day the Soviet Government moved from Petrograd to Moscow. As Vernadsky points out, it was a fervent appeal to the people of Russia to utilize its great riches so that Russia should cease to be "wretched and pitiful." "In our natural wealth, in our reserves of human energy, and in our magnificent expanses, now given over to the creative power of the people by the great Revolution, we have all the essentials for the establishment of a truly mighty and powerful Russia." By what means and with what success the Soviets are moving toward this objective under their planning system is told in the following pages.

30. What Are the Five-Year Plans—Their Aims and Scope?

Their aim is to make the best usage of all the nation's resources, human and material, to give the greatest amount of well-being to all the people. They seek to apply the rules of good housekeeping to the whole business of the nation. To do that demands first of all an inventory of what there is in the house. This is the task of the statisticians. They must tell the amount and state of the nation's equipment in the way of mines, factories, and farms. They must furnish the figures on resources, oil, iron, coal, gold, timber, fur, brought up to date by the latest findings. They must show the amount of brains and hands available.

The next question is how all these actual and potential sources of wealth can be transformed into commodities and services. At this point the engineers are called in. They must estimate how much can be expected from the existing farms, plants, and power-houses. What new ones should be added? What is to be the ratio between the "heavy" and "light" industries—between the making of capital and consumers' goods? How are the handi-crafts to be promoted? What new regions shall be developed? All these are primarily economic problems, but not wholly so. For example, a new discovery of minerals near the borders may suggest the building of a huge and valuable factory. It might serve, too, as an example of Soviet progress to the neighboring people across the frontier and incite their admiration. But by the same token it might well incite the cupidity of imperialist in-vaders. Under pretext of preventing the spread of Bolshevism they could easily send their bombing-planes to destroy or capture it. In that case military considerations might outweigh the eco-nomic and political.

Similar complex calculations enter into final decisions in the realm of agriculture. What shall be done with the lands reclaimed by draining the swamps and by irrigating the arid steppes and deserts? What acreage shall be sown to grain in order to assure the population the forty million tons of bread it consumes? How much land shall be allocated to "technical" crops, sugar-beets, flax, sunflowers, and the oils therefrom? What part shall come from the State farms, from the collectives? Along with these immediate questions go the larger issues like the zoning of regions to be devoted to products for which they are particularly adapted: The transformation of the Moscow district into dairy and vegetable raising; the assignment of Turkestan to cotton plantations; the Black Sea littoral to the growing of tea and citrus fruits. These are problems for the agronomists and soil scientists, but not for them alone. They have to be considered in the light of larger policies of State like the campaign for collectivization, the speed in which the contradictions between town and country shall be resolved. On such matters the Communist Party will have a say.

With industry and agriculture vitally dependent upon transport this of course must be closely planned. How can it be made to cope with the ever-growing traffic thrown upon it? How can the rivers be linked up into a great inland water system? What savings can be effected in hauling charges by the transfer from animal to motor traction? Communication with distant regions must be made swifter by the extension of airways for mail, passengers, and freight. Means must be devised for relieving the overburdened railways: by the transformation of coal into electric power at the pit-heads and sending it over wires; by the pumping of oil through pipelines instead of shipping it in tank-cars; by growing frost-resisting wheat around the new cities along the Arctic. With all this goes the building of railways and highways into the virgin wildernesses; the building of new terminals, ports, wharves, lighthouses.

Along with all the building, the plans at every point must consider the builders. They are regarded as something more than "costs of production," not merely as the makers of wealth, but as wealth itself. Since they are the end of all productive activities as well as their source, the plans are consciously and primarily concerned with their welfare and well-being. They aim to deliver to them—and to their wives, children, and invalid fellow-workers—the maximum possible amount of goods and services. First of all, food, clothes, and shelter must be provided for the 175 million people and an additional three million a year. As centers of industry move to the East, millions of people move with them. Plans must be made for housing them in the sixty new Socialist cities rising in the distant steppes and forests; for the collective farmers transferred to the logging-camps in winter; for the staffs manning the radio and fueling stations along the new Arctic seaways. They must include care for their health—the prevention of epidemics like Asiatic cholera, typhus, and scurvy. But they can be efficient workers in farm and factory only to the extent that they are technically skilled and qualified. How many engineers, agronomists, and surveyors shall be trained? But man does not live by bread or machines alone. Besides tending to their material needs, the plans must see to their spiritual and mental needs. That brings in the education of artists, musicians, and teachers; projects for theatres and puppet-shows; projects for parks, stadiums, "green cities."

Thus there are thousands, tens of thousands of projects, all of which are highly desirable. If to build were as easy as to know what were good to be built, then instead of hundreds of blast-furnaces and dams, each Five-Year Plan would bring forth thousands; and theatres, libraries, and hospitals would spring up like mushrooms all over the land. Obviously this is impossible. Plans must be cut to fit their finances. "Where will all the money come from?" That is a constant crucial question. How much may be raised by way of direct taxes on the people? How much by bonds, by levies on profitable industries, by exports? This is where the bankers and expert accountants come in. After canvassing the field they have, for example, 98 billion rubles, the budget for 1937. Of this more than a fourth is ear-marked for new investment. That is a huge sum, but it would have to be ten times greater to do the things that need to be done. How shall this be allocated? The Labor Unions press for a big increase in the insurance funds as well as in wages. Each Commissariat likewise wants a good slice of it. Each republic puts forward its claim for the development of new railways and mines. Every city and town is clamoring for more schools, buses, sewers, clinics. From these rival claimants and the welter of conflicting interests, rigid selections must be made. Which are absolutely essential and imperative now? Which can be postponed for a year, five years, or a decade? Each claim is considered on its own merits and in the light of its contribution to the weal of the nation as a whole. In hotly contested debates, out of the endless weighing of pros and cons, the balancing of economic, political, and military considerations finally emerges the plan. But this is not the end of the matter. It is one thing to set up the plan, another to get it put into action. Otherwise it remains a magnificent set of blue-prints not worth the paper it is printed on.

To put the plan into operation it must have the cooperation of all the Soviet peoples. How enlist their energy and enthusiasm and mobilize every man, woman, and child in its behalf? How get them to think, breathe, and dream in terms of the plan? Toward this end it has already made the plan "theirs" by giving them a part, and a large part, in the making of it. It now seeks further to imbue their consciousness with the significance of the great adventure they are engaged in. Through the press, posters, Labor Unions, clubs, and cinema—it is blazoned as the means for "overtaking and surpassing the advanced countries of the West." It is envisaged as a "declaration of freedom from dependence on foreign powers," "the road from poverty to prosperity," "the way to the classless society of Communism." It is dramatized as a step in the "world revolution" when all the nations of the earth shall be united in one great world-embracing plan. These are the goals which the Soviets seek to attain through each Five-Year Plan, through each of its component parts—the plan for the current year and the quarterly plans into which each in turn is divided.

31. What do the Soviets Seek to Avoid by Planning?

For decades there has been great hue and cry against the evils of a *laissez faire* economy; the alternating cycles of booms and panics; mass unemployment; poverty in an age of potential plenty; production power way ahead of purchasing power; ruthless destruction of resources. Books like Stuart Chase's "Rich Land, Poor Land" and Sears' "Deserts on the March" set forth the astronomical losses arising from a planless, go-as-you-please way of doing things. Through planning, under a system of production for use, the Soviets seek to eliminate or greatly reduce these five main wastages.

Wastage of Natural Resources. In 1909 Theodore Roosevelt began the crusade for conserving America's natural wealth. Public-spirited men have been carrying it on for a quarter of a century. Yet one reads in the report of the National Resources Board to Franklin Roosevelt of the "tragic waste, widespread spoliation, and misuse of natural wealth of the many by the few. . . . Ignorance, inattention, or greed has devastated our heritage almost beyond belief." Coming down to details, it says: "Known supplies of oil, natural gas, and certain metals are sufficient for, at most, a few decades. At the present time in one field enough gas is being blown into the air to supply all domestic consumers in the United States." Out of every four barrels in the ground thanks to the "law of capture," only one gets into the pipelines. For every two tons of coal at the pit-head one ton is left forever irreclaimable in the mines. Forests are cut down three times as fast as they are replanted. Erosion by wind and rain each year renders over 100,000 acres unfit for cultivation. As slight checks upon this private pillage and spoliation there are the public domains—the parks and wildlife preserves, reforestation and power projects. Elsewhere the raping and gutting of the virgin riches of a continent goes steadily on. No ruth or reck for the generations to come. After us the drouths and the deluge! Let posterity look out for itself!

Altogether different is the attitude of the Soviet Union where all the land, forests, and minerals belong to the community. No longer are they objects with which individuals may do as they will in order to extract the maximum profits for themselves. They are the precious assets of the nation to be administered for the benefit of the whole people, not only for those now living but for the generations to come. This is the very soul and essence of Socialism, to think and to plan for the future. Anyone who has lived in the Soviet Union knows how true this is. It conjugates its verbs in the future tense with the ever repeated *boodet*, "will be," so irritating to the foreigner. It endures great strains and privations in the present for the sake of a society of leisure and plenty in the future. And, in the matter of resources, like a far-sighted husbandman, it is concerned not merely in what they will yield today but in conserving them for tomorrow, for dec-ades, and centuries to come. So much concerned that to some extent, at any rate, it holds back the development of the country.

It is the contention of critics that under capitalism the indus-trialization of Russia might go on as fast or even faster than under the Soviets. Conceivably so. But by the same token it would go on with the same reckless riotous squandering of the nation's resources. And thereby the world's supply of natural irreplace-able riches would be that much nearer the point of exhaustion. That this is not happening is due to the October Revolution which by lodging ownership in the nation made possible a broadly planned economy. It applies to them the best science and methods for their orderly, provident, rational development. It digs and pumps from the earth just what is needed and no more. In doing this it rescues these huge reserves of fuel, forest, and metals—if not the first, then the second in the world—from untimely destruction and dissipation. This will redound to the benefit not only of the future citizens of the Soviets of today but of the whole world. On this count alone they may look back to the October Revolution as a red-letter day in the story of man-kind.

The Wastage of Capital in Useless Enterprises. Under *laissez faire,* money flows into those channels that hold forth hopes of biggest and quickest returns. "When the automobile business looks promising," says Stuart Chase, "it goes into new motor-car plants, until before we know it we have twice as many as we need. American shoe fac-tories could turn out 900 million pairs of shoes a year; all we can possibly wear out is about 500 million; all we can buy is 300 million. Nobody ever stops to figure how many shoe-factories are needed or how many automobile plants." The result is a huge loss of building materials, frequent shutdowns, and bankruptcies. Obviously, under a planned system there need be no duplicate plants, competing stores, or parallel railway lines. It can build just those enterprises that are necessary. It can build them close to the sources of raw materials or the markets. And except for repairs and seasonal lay-offs it can keep them steadily running, saving them from idleness or working at half capacity. On the whole the Soviets have done this, despite the outcry from the press and foreign engineers about costly mistakes in the locating and the building of plants. But these are minor wastages of capital and, with the better training of geologists, engineers, and planners, are on the way to being remedied and eradicated.

The Wastage of Man Power. Unemployment ranks first. "The old slave used to complain of compulsory labor, the modern wage slave of compulsory idleness." Normally in capitalist countries millions are out of work, and in crises tens of millions. In the Soviet Union this "arterial hemorrhage" has been stopped. On its colossal building projects there is a place for everyone from ditch-digger to scientist—more jobs than men to fill them. That eliminates not only the wastage of labor power but another real though intangible wastage—the loss in dignity and self-respect in having no place in the social scheme. But how about that future when the building is finished and men are more and more replaced by machines? For that situation Socialist planning has many simple solutions. It can reduce to five or less the number of working hours in a day. It can cut to 200 or less the number of working days in a year. It can raise the age for beginning work to 20, or can cut the age for retiring to 50 or even 40. It can double the demand for teachers by decreasing the number of pupils in a class from 40 to 20.

To these and other like devices, it can readily resort should it face the problem of surplus man-power. Any one of them will easily put new millions to work. The Soviet Union does not have to pour out doles and subsidies to keep armies of able-bodied men in enforced idleness. Nor does it have to support the two idle classes at the extremes of modern society: the indolent rich who live on its roof-gardens and avenues, or the tramps and hoboes who live in its basements and by-ways. The Soviet Constitution says, "Work is the obligation of every citizen capable of working." He who does not work does not eat, or play, or have any standing in the community.

Beside these non-workers is the wastage of those who work to no useful or social purpose. In the field of distribution alone, according to ex-President Herbert Hoover, this mounts up to ten billion dollars a year. Veblen likewise pointed out the colossal waste in the retail traffic "to be canceled out of the community's working efficiency as lag, leak, and friction": Five grocery stores where one would suffice; rival milk companies covering the same route; competing gas stations on the four corners of the street. So far has this gone that almost the same number of persons are now engaged in the distribution of goods as in the making of them. This means many millions of drivers, clerks, canvassers, and promoters working hard without any real gain to society.

In theory a Socialist society does away with all these superfluous middlemen and hangers-on. In practice, thus far at any rate, it has not. Abolished in one form, as Hartley Withers observes, they are apt to return under another name or guise. That this is so is evident in the repeated demands of the Soviet leaders upon the Cooperatives to simplify their apparatus and get rid of the hordes of officials. Equally evident, however, is the elimination of those other hordes of supernumeraries with which capitalist trade is afflicted: There are no armies of specialists in advertising, because it is largely limited to the bare announcement of plays, pictures, and new wares; no high-pressure salesmen breaking down the buyer's resistance to things he neither needs nor wants; no vendors of habit-forming drugs, cure-alls, and like quackeries, because they are not made. There is simply no place for them in the functional society. Nor for commercialized vice, gambling, or child labor. They too are virtually abolished, thereby affecting another tremendous saving in human material and effort.

The Wastages of "Over-production." The word of course is a misnomer. Rarely is there a surplus of what people need, but only of what they can buy. Even in the richest country in the world there is woeful need of more schools, roads, shoes, eggs, fruit, milk. While one end of the Department of Agriculture was reducing the farming area by forty million acres, the other end announced that to feed and clothe and house the American people properly it should be increased that much! But the price-and-profit system did not permit it. Instead of producing more it actually destroyed part of what it produced: Plowing under cotton; dumping coffee into the sea; killing broodsows; burning corn for fuel. These are unthinkable under the planned economy of the Soviets. It enables them to estimate in advance how much of every article the country needs. It enables them to produce— up to the existing capacities of its labor-power, farms, and factories —approximately the amount that is needed. Finally—after setting aside reserves and capital for new enterprises—it can put in the hands of the people the money to buy back all they have produced. By doing this it solves out of hand that problem so baffling to capitalist economists all over the world. *It strikes an even balance between consumption and production.*

This is the most important part of the whole business of planning— the crux of it. By giving the people enough purchasing power there need be no "over-production," because they can consume as much goods as they make and as fast as they make them. That the Soviets have done this no one denies. In their markets the demand for everything is up to and often far ahead of the supply. "So it is for the present," interject the critics, "when goods are scarce. But how about the future when all the plants going full-blast are pouring ever bigger streams of goods into the markets? How will they then deal with this vexing problem of abundance?" To Soviet planners it is no problem at all. Rather it is the devoutly desired end toward which they are striving with might and main. The more goods the better. With every rise in production goes a corresponding rise in wages. This steady increase of income will take care of the increasing output of goods. And in case of a plethora, due to an error in forecasting, a bumper crop, a big catch of fish, a reduction in prices or even a free distribution will easily take care of that. Under a Socialist system, demand can always be made to keep pace with supply. There need never be a "surplus" of man-power or commodities.

Wastage of Technical Knowledge. Marvelous things have been done by science in all realms of life. But they are nothing as to what might be done. "Engineers are convinced," says Leonard, in "Tools of

Tomorrow," "they can design machines to perform any operation no matter how difficult or delicate. All they need is sufficient output to justify the cost of the machine and keep it busy." On a gigantic scale men could be replaced by machines, engines, and dynamos. Hundreds of different types and sizes of window-panes, iron pipes, and tools could be reduced to a few score. Hundreds of new articles could be made from the by-products of coal, wood, and sugar. City smoke could be converted into fertilizers. That these things are not done is due to various reasons—lack of funds for further research; labor opposition; the vested interests of capital in existing enterprises; the buying up of new inventions not to use them but to keep them out of the hands of competitors; the jealous hoarding of trade-secrets and formulas.

In spite of these obstacles, capitalist countries are still making great progress in new skills and technics. Maybe greater, as some critics assert, than in the Soviet Union of today. But not tomorrow, because in the Soviet Union all these obstacles have been swept away. With no private interests to safeguard, no trade-secrets to conceal, no fear on the part of labor of being thrown out of work by machines, the field is wide open to the free, unhindered utilization of all that science can devise. In its planned economy it has the means for steadily reducing the time-lag and wastage in technical knowledge. Consistently, more and more it is doing this.

On the Way to a Wasteless Society

"The appropriation by society of the means of production," said Engels, "will put an end not only to the artificial restraints on production, but also to the positive waste and destruction of productive forces and products which are now the inevitable accompaniment of production reaching its zenith in crises." What he predicted some sixty years ago, today in the Soviet Union has really come to pass. Manifestly social ownership with its system of planning can and does effect tremendous savings in natural and technical resources, capital, and man-power. But by no means has it yet eliminated all the wastage.

Overhead costs and over-staffing of Soviet offices are notorious. The great Dneprostroy was ready long before the plants for utilizing its electric power were finished. The Commissar of Heavy Industry stated that the losses in his field alone mount up into tens of millions. Thousands of tons of grain are lost in the fields or in transit. Fruits and vegetables rot in Soviet stores as well as in American and British. The percentage of spoilage and breakage in factories is even higher. A casual reading of the Soviet press shows that Socialism as well as capitalism has its lamentable wastages. This the Communists do not deny, but they point out a difference. Under capitalist *laissez faire* these wastages are inherent and inevitable. In a planned economy they are incidental and avoidable. They rise in part from flaws in the plans, in part from failure to execute them due to bungling, sabotage, and bureaucracy.

Both of these, the Communists insist, are curable and can be rectified in process of time. Accuracy in planning will come with more experience and an ever-improving technique. Efficiency in executives, engineers, and inspectors will come with better training, rising standards of life, and the increasing initiative and vigilance of the people. Then the immense superiority of Socialist planning will be apparent to all. From a minimum expenditure of energy will come a maximum of wealth and well-being, a wasteless society as is humanly possible.

32. How Did Soviet Planning Begin?

The concept of planning is implicit in Socialism. "With the seizing of the means of production by society," said Engels, "anarchy in social production is replaced by systematic, definite organization." But planning for the Soviets did not rise from the dictum of Marxists. It was forced upon them. They had got rid of the employer but not the functions he and the price system performed. The industries that the Revolution delivered into their hands would not automatically produce goods. Something had to be done. But there was little that could be done in a country ravaged by civil war, pestilence, and famine. In those first desperate years plans were mainly schemes for keeping a few of the factories feebly going and rationing the existing stock of commodities to the soldiers and workers. But peace came and with it the necessity for really producing. For that the Soviets had the apparatus and the premises. To them belonged the big mills and mines, transportation, land, and the banks. But in order to function properly they must be somehow coordinated. They all had to be made to mesh and synchronize. It was either plan or perish.

"Do not be afraid of plans," said Lenin, "without them you will never achieve a regulated economy." Cautiously, step by step, they felt their way in this new uncharted field. For there was no precedent. In 1921 came the first important project—a Ten-Year Plan of Electrification for building thirty power stations containing in embryo the two typical features of Soviet planning, the long-range program and the operating figures for a year.

Next year came one of the red-letter events in Soviet history, the founding of that organ which was to become the directing brain of all the nation's activities. That was the State Planning Commission, Gosplan. It began modestly by checking various programs drawn up by other organs—plans for food and fuel, the sowing campaign, restoration of the famine area. Advancing cautiously step by step, in 1925 it brought the separate plans into a single system known as the Control Figures. They were estimates for the coming year of the output in tons of steel, grain, fish; the outlay in rubles for wages, schools, and hospitals; volume of traffic on trains, boats, and airplanes. To each branch of the national economy was assigned a specific task. Each factory, bank, or institute now knew what was expected of it. Sometimes too little was asked, more often it was too much.

It could not be otherwise. For this was the period known as *NEP,* when there was a "free market" and a considerable amount of trade, small industry, and twenty-five million peasant homesteads were still in private hands. Obviously it was impossible for the control figures to be accurate when there were so many factors over which there was no control. But this changed with the passing of the pre-War level of production and with more of the economic key positions coming into the hands of the State. This gave the Gosplan more solid bases to work from and more reliable statistics to work with in its next undertaking—one of unprecedented scope and daring. That was the drafting of a long-range project for every enterprise in the country and their integration into a unified all-embracing master-plan.

This was the celebrated First Five-Year Plan known as "The Program of Great Works and a Developed Socialist Offensive." In the period between the Octobers of 1928 and 1933 the country was to do these things: 1. Double the output of light industry—shoes, textiles; treble the output of heavy industry—metal, fuel, machines; quadruple the number of electric stations and kilowatt hours; increase labor productivity by 110 per cent and wages by 66 per cent. 2. Transform six million peasant holdings into modernized, mechanized collective farms. 3. Teach 17 million illiterates to read and write; train a new corps of 800 thousand executives, engineers, technicians, scientists. 4. Finance the whole scheme out of its own resources to the extent of 86,000,000,000 rubles. This was the so-called "maximum variant" of the plan, based on the assumption of fair crops and no wars. But even in its "minimum variant"—about 25 per cent lower—so grandiose was the plan and so swift the projected rate of expansion that it was without parallel in the history of nations.

Thus, in concrete, dramatic form, Socialism presented its historic challenge to the countries of capitalism. At first they did not regard it as a challenge, but a fantasy—an effort to hypnotize the Soviet masses with astronomical figures, "an eleventh-hour bid for popular support by a tottering regime." The very idea of this poor backward ne'er-do-well country competing with the strong and mighty was ludicrous, presumptuous. And of all peoples, how could these anarchic, indolent, impractical, undisciplined, music-and-vodka-loving Russians work out a complex plan for an ordered society? And if they did, how could they carry it through! It was dismissed as a "blueprint of the millennium," "a statistician's dream," "a romance of engineering."

Unperturbed, the Soviets went ahead translating their romance and dream into reality. How successfully will be discussed later. Enough so that in a short time abroad, the idea of planning was receiving the sincerest form of flattery. Instead of deriding it, other nations were imitating it. All over the world from Britain to China rose talk of plans and planning and planned economy, the Italian Fascists' corporative state purporting to combine the advantages of Socialism and Capitalism; the Nazis' regimenting of Germany's economic life to military ends, the alphabetical agencies of the New Deal.

Now the tables are reversed and the Communists in turn are the critics. They maintain that you may have a kind of planning under capitalism but not a planned economy. The two terms are contradictions. The aim of Socialist planning is to determine in advance what is to be produced, who shall produce it, and how much of it shall be produced. (Strachey) The essence of capitalism is to leave these three vital questions to the free play of profit and prices. The free, automatic functioning of the market is the antithesis of its ordered control. Production for profit cannot be reconciled with production for use, nor the interests of individual owners with the welfare of society. The attempt to harmonize them leads to endless conflicts, collisions, and confusion. They point out that plans in capitalist countries are hopelessly piecemeal and partial. They are static rather than dynamic. They are largely plans for restriction, not expansion, for retreat, not advance. They do not give free play and "free space" to the economic laws of growth. They are hedged in and hamstrung by property-interests which must be constantly cajoled or coerced. They do not abolish the class struggle between capital and labor but only suppress it. They usually result in contracting rather than expanding economy, in lowering rather than raising standards of living. There may be a species of planning under capitalism, but it is specious. To call it a planned society is a travesty.

To sum up the Communist contentions: It is impossible for a capitalist state effectively to plan because it hasn't the materials to plan with. The crux of the matter lies in this question of ownership. As far as one owns one can plan and no further. Any big business or corporation can and does plan up to the limits of its possessions. The Soviet Union is simply a huge corporation with practically all the mineral wealth, land, industry, banks, transport, trade secrets, and inventions of a sixth of the world vested in its hands. Because it owns everything it can plan everything. The recipe for planning is the same as for cooking a rabbit. First, get the ingredients. That means the transfer of social property from private into public control. In short, to make a plan one must first make a revolution.

33. Who Makes the Plans and How?

At the head of the stupendous task of charting the nation's future activities, is the All-Union Planning Commission or Gosplan, dubbed "the conning-tower," "the board of strategy," of national economy. Into its Moscow headquarters come the projects from planning organs in each of the republics, regions, commissariats; the reports from each trust, artel, and farm as to what it has produced and can produce; how many people are employed; what raw materials, credit, and transport are required. From cooperatives, chain-stores, hotels, cafés, canteens, and kiosks come calculations on consumers' demands. From schools, publishing houses, and studios, come statistics on output and capacity. On the basis of this enormous mass of data, and in keeping with the "General Line" of the Party, the Gosplan formulates the plan for the coming five years. It is the result of the labor of myriads of the best engineers, scientists, and statisticians, the synthesis of thousands and tens of thousands of plans. Even so it is only tentative and provisional. As a draft plan it is now sent out to the country and becomes forthwith the subject of study, discussion, and controversy in every city and village from sub-tropic Batumi to the Arctic.

It is re-examined by the six industrial and agricultural commissariats and translated into more concrete terms and specific measures. Its financial provisions are rechecked by the State Bank and credit bodies. Its projects for developing each economic region are debated by all the local organs with a constant interchange of ideas. Its technical aspects are verified by the Academy of Science to make sure of utilizing the latest inventions, processes, and surveys. Its programs for coal, steel, bread, shoes, cinema-films are threshed out in joint conferences of the corresponding trusts and unions engaged in their production. Its "control fig-ures" for each of the 100,000 mines, mills, and factories are dis-cussed by the shop-committees, brigades, and Stakhanovites of each enterprise and in general meetings of all the workers. They may decide that the schedules are too high or that they are too low, and suggest means of adjusting them. The same thing goes in the artels, schools, farms, fisheries—resulting in hosts of pro-posals, amendments, and suggestions. Thus the work proceeds from above and from below, from the top down and from the bottom up, "a continuous flow of plans in each direction," at every stage and from every angle subjected to a relentless cross-fire of criticism.

By this nation-wide participation in planning is secured that "unanimous consent" emphasized by the Webbs as essential to the workings of democracy. It is not what a few hundred experts think ought to be done but what millions of workers declare can be done, not the fabrication of a small coterie of theoreticians but the pooled wisdom of the whole people. As the slogan puts it, "Millions Make the Plan." In so doing they make it theirs and make themselves responsible for carrying it out. Thus, en-dorsed by the productive men and women of the nation, and, approved by the party, it goes to the Congress of the Soviets to be ratified and legislated into action. If there is a scarcity of workers in some distant region a raise in wages will cause a flow of labor in that direction. If the market is glutted with cer-tain articles, a slash in prices will take them away. It can provide shock-absorbers against deviations from the normal. It can take up the slack here and let it out there. Doing these things depends upon knowing about them in time and swiftly reacting to them. To that end, as component parts of the annual plan, there are the quarterly plans enabling all parts to move forward more evenly and harmoniously.

From all fronts, by mail, messenger, wire, and wireless come weekly and daily reports on the state of affairs. From important sectors like the harvest come hour-by-hour bulletins on the state of weather, the mowing, threshing, and grain deliveries. When they are not forthcoming, special agents and air-brigades go out to investigate on the spot. In keeping with all this information are issued the necessary orders and directives to meet the new situation. Thus, planning is not a sporadic act but goes on all the time. With improving technique reducing the margin of error, it becomes even more effective in registering actual conditions and in making the necessary adaptations to them. While great efforts are made to keep within the outlines of the Plan, in no wise is it a rigid framework or strait-jacket clamped down on the country. It is rather a highly flexible apparatus for guiding and at the same time giving free play to the expanding forces of the nation. In the words of Stalin, "It is not a mere enumeration of figures and tasks but the embodiment of the living and practical activity of millions of people engaged in creating a new life."

In its final form the plan is not final in the sense that it is a hard-and-fast scheme slavishly adhered to at all costs. Unforeseen setbacks and delays are inevitable, so also are unforeseen aids and accelerations. The best laid plans at some point go awry. This was particularly true of the First Five-Year Plan. Some industries fulfilled their quotas in three years. Others fell far behind. Collectivization got out of hand and ran away with itself. The threat of war with Japan necessitated the diversion of great quantities of men and supplies to the Far East. The Second Five-Year Plan held more closely and consistently to its objectives, although the impetus from the Stakhanovite movement did enable several to reach or exceed their control figures in 1936. The Third Five-Year Plan, beginning in 1938, promises to be still more accurate, thanks to better statistics, the almost complete socialization of agriculture, the big reserves of foodstuffs, gold, and trained personnel. It is thus prepared to cope with a natural calamity, a crop failure, the dislocation of labor by a new invention like the cotton-picker, and even the strain of war on the Eastern and Western fronts. But obviously all these coming at once would throw the plan out of gear.

What is true of the Five-Year Plan applies to its component parts, the operating plan for each year. It too may be modified by hitches, break-downs, a bumper harvest, sudden changes in world prices, tastes, and fashions. While it is impossible to foresee all contingencies, it is possible to make adjustments to them.

How the Gosplan is Organized. Appointed by the Council of People's Commissars, it is made up of a chairman and seventy members chosen for distinguished service in other planning bodies throughout the country, or for pre-eminence in technical fields, science, or culture. It is divided into two main groups. The first consists of sixteen departments concerned with mining, timber, foreign trade, housing, culture. The second group is concerned with problems of synthesis, such as district planning, balances and supplies of materials, co-ordination of the various sections, and the verification of fulfillment. In addition there are seven independent sections on defense, labor, communications, and the education of specialists for the planning organs. This education is carried on in schools such as the Molotov All-Union Academy of Planning where over 200 "social engineers" get theory and practice first-hand and in the Institutes of Economic Research in Moscow and Leningrad.

Other auxiliaries of the Gosplan are the Editorial-Publishing Bureau and the Central Administration of National Accounting. With some 4,000 expert statisticians, technicians, and clerks it makes the Gosplan, in the words of the Webbs, "certainly the best equipped, as well as the most extensive permanent machine of statistical inquiry in the world." After pointing out certain defects in the statistics they go on to say, "They command greater credence than the published statistics of any other government, because in the U.S.S.R. they form the basis of all economic and financial action, which, if it were taken on 'cooked figures,' must inevitably result in patent failure."

To gather, correlate, and utilize all these data would be a hopeless task without the thousands of other planning bodies and the whole apparatus of Soviets, Party, Cooperatives, and Labor Unions. In this vast planning organism the Gosplan is only the central brain or coordinating center. "Its function is not to command but to advise, stimulate, and regulate."

34. Did the First Five-Year Plan Succeed and What About the Second and the Third?

The First Plan (*1928-1932*). It was a flexible instrument subject to frequent changes. With the slogan "five years in four," its period was shortened by nine months, and the control figures in many cases revised upwards. In the field of industrialization these advanced goals were surpassed by many enterprises—tractors, machinery, electric equipment. Others, notably metals and railway building, lagged far behind. In the field of collectivization the results exceeded the dreams of the most ardent zealots. From three per cent the socialized sector of farming grew to over sixty per cent, uniting more than 16,000,000 small peasant holdings into large-scale collectives. In the field of education, double the proposed seven billion rubles was invested in schools, the training of a new corps of technicians, engineers, and scientists.

Summing up, Stalin declared that 93.6 per cent of the Plan was fulfilled, accounting for the remainder by the necessity of shipping troops, food, and munitions into the Far East under threat of Japanese invasion. His critics said that this estimate was too optimistic. Admitting giant strides in construction, they pointed out several items on the debit side: shortage of food; slaughter of livestock; devastation wrought by the class-war in the villages; quality of goods sacrificed to quantity; over-emission of currency. Altogether they maintain that only to the extent of some 80 or 70 or 60 per cent was the Plan realized. But this dispute is now rather academic and futile.

The essential fact is that the First Five-Year Plan telescoped into a few years the development that in most other countries has taken decades. It increased the Soviet's share in the world's industrial output from four per cent to fourteen per cent lifting it from fifth to second place. (*London Economist*) It covered the land with foundries, mills, elevators, power-trestles, silos, and tractor-stations. Still more significant is the fact that all this was done by a backward country out of its own resources. Unlike America, which in its great era of expansion built its transcontinental railways and industries with the aid of loans from abroad, and, unlike Europe, receiving billions of American dollars for post-War reconstruction, the Soviet Union was compelled to find its new capital at home. It had to lift itself by its own bootstraps.

It is often said that the Plan changed the face of the Russian land. To the most casual observer that was perfectly obvious. Not so obvious and not appearing in any of its charts and figures was another important thing that it did. *It changed the character of the Russian people*. It placed before them a definite goal on which to focus their minds and energies. It brought forth for peace-time construction the fervor and sacrifices hitherto manifested only in times of war. It taught them to steel their wills, to discipline their habits, to work intensively. It infused into them the feeling that they were not at the mercy of blind economic forces, but masters of their own destinies. Not in all the people by any means. But in all the active, organizing ones, the builders and dreamers. With faith in themselves, in the efficacy of planning, and in their power to direct the march of history they went forward to the next and greater undertaking.

The Second Five-Year Plan (1933-1937)

"In this," said Stalin, "the ardor for new construction must be supplemented by the ardor for mastering the new plants and new technique." However, it called for not less construction than the First, but vastly more. So much indeed that to the press abroad it was "staggering," "stupendous," "breath-taking"—but not "incredible." From 50 billion rubles, in 1933 the amount of new investment was to rise to 133 billions in 1937, the total basic capital from 85 to 195 billions.

Among the new projects were 178 coal mines, 93 oil-cracking plants, 95 electric stations, 45 blast furnaces, 38 big silk, linen, and woolen mills. Culling thus from the bulky volume of control figures one might go on wearily for pages with statistics on transport, education, and housing. As they are set down under the next forty questions dealing with these subjects, there is no point in restating them here. It is enough to note the Plans' outstanding features.

The Second Plan shifted the emphasis to consumers' goods and services. While the yearly output of heavy industry was to increase by 14.5 per cent, the rate of growth for light industry rose to 18.5 per cent. Formerly the main energies went into the making of machines. Now the machines were to make commodities. By 1937 they were to turn out 32 meters of textiles for each person as against 3 meters before the War. They were to double the output of articles like glass, hardware, and shoes. Likewise, through intensive agriculture, the value of farm products was to be doubled. The aim was not only more food, but a better, more varied diet. To this end there were a multitude of projects for the processing, packing, and preserving of foodstuffs. Hundreds of sanitary abattoirs, bakeries, canneries, scores of plants for refining sugar, extracting flax and sunflower oils, the crisping of cornflakes.

Quite as important in improving the general health and stamina of the people were the tens of thousands of public baths and washhouses, crèches, clinics, and first-aid stations, and the extension of rest homes and resorts so that by 1937 over two million would be holidaying in them. A similar expansion in schools, institutes, night-and-day universities was to increase the number of students to 36 million. In hand with this main sector of the cultural front went a similar advance on the two-score minor ones: The doubling of clubs, reading-huts, and Lenin "corners"; a seven-fold increase in the output of pianos; a complex of pulp and paper mills relieving the printing presses from their prolonged "starvation ration" by feeding them a million tons a year.

The Second Plan accelerated the movement of people and industry toward the East. From the old centers they were rapidly gravitating to the new virgin farm lands, to the sources of water-power and raw materials. Instead of shipping cotton a thousand miles to Ivanovo, it began to be woven near the fields where it grows. For this purpose the Plan allocated to Central Asia ten huge cotton mills with over a million spindles. Four out of its five new trunklines were built beyond the Urals. Over half of its capital outlay went into the large coal and iron combines and the new Socialist cities of Siberia. This created for the Soviet Union a new industrial heart far enough from the frontiers as to be secure from attack by air-raiding enemies. At the same time it raised its prestige in the Orient and the whole cultural life of its own backward races—the Uzbeks, Yakuts, Tajiks, Tungus.

The basic political task of the Second Plan was "the liquidation of capitalist elements and of classes generally." This meant an end to private profit-making, the complete socialization of trade, industry, and farming. Every shop, store, mine, mill, and movie was to be run by the State and cooperative organizations. All handicraftsmen, so far as possible, were to be united in artels and the last of the tiny peasant holdings merged into large-scale collectives. With tractors, scientific farming, and division of labor, they were to be organized like factories for the production of grain, milk, and vegetables. "In its social form agriculture will become identical with industry; farm labor will become a variety of industrial labor." In general the plan aimed "to overcome the survivals of capitalism in economy and in the mentality of the people." "To accomplish the latter," as Molotov sagely observed, "it will take a whole series of Five-Year Plans."

While the Second Plan got under way rather slowly, its tempo was accelerated by two very auspicious factors that enabled it to come through with flying colors. It began with a food shortage caused by drought and resistance to collectivization, but, thanks to good harvests, the bread-cards were abolished in 1935, followed by a steadily increasing stream of all kinds of farm products coming into the markets. It began with a lag in several branches of industry, but, thanks to the impetus of the Stakhanov movement, many of them reached or exceeded their quotas in four years. Among these were the merchant marine, railway cars, engines, sugar, synthetic rubber, and so on down a long list including bicycles, window-glass, and gramophone records.

Third Five-Year Plan (1938-1942)

With this begins the building of the eight dams and electric stations on the river Angara flowing out of Lake Baikal, with an estimated capacity of nine million kilowatts. The development of this East Siberian region into a great power-and-metal center utilizing the newly discovered deposits of iron ore, aluminum, lime, manganese, tin, tungsten, and the thick seams of Cheremkhov coking coal lying almost on the surface. Attainment of first place in the world in production of gold. Expansion of the highways and waterways, along with the double-tracking and electrification of railways. Wide extension of the airlines including regular service with America along the 10,000 mile route flown by Levanevsky—Moscow, Cape Schmidt, Nome, Fairbanks, Seattle, San Francisco—or perhaps by a still shorter route directly over the North Pole. Cultivation of the lands reclaimed by the huge Volga irrigation project and the general intensification of agriculture with emphasis on further mechanization, crop-rotation, fertilization, and the specialization of regions.

With the problem of supplying the people with such staple necessities as food, clothes, and shoes, partly solved by the Second Five-Year Plan, the Third promises to increase their quality and quantity and to begin to satisfy the colossal demand for the comforts and amenities of life—radios, bicycles, pianos. Concerted efforts will be made to remedy the almost critical situation on the "housing front" and barring war, which would divert the allocated supplies away to the battle-fronts, there will be a decided betterment in living quarters. This will be accompanied by a general expansion of all institutions for the promotion of cultural, scientific, and athletic activities. Education is to be made compulsory up to eighteen years of age. And under the aegis of the new Constitution begins the march forward to achieve "the most advanced democracy in the world."

The Major Motive in the Three Plans

There is no sharp dividing line between them. They organically merge into one another as parts of one dynamic process. Each, however, shows a certain difference in emphasis. The First stressed the building of giant plants, the Second the mastering of their technique, and with the Third will come the fuller utilization and enjoyment of their products. According to another simplified scheme, the dominant note in the three plans are respectively: industrialization; goods for consumers; the expansion of leisure, culture, arts, and sciences. Obviously these are very arbitrary and artificial rubrics. Each plan necessarily concerns itself with industrialization, with consumers' goods, and with science and arts. Above all, with industrialization. That is the theme song that runs through all three plans and will in others to follow.

The huge *combinats* of the Urals and Siberia, begun in the First and growing into giants in the Second, will be expanding into super-giants in the Third. But there must be a whole race of them rising up throughout the land. Colossal construction must be still more colossal, if the Soviets are to do what they have set out to do—build the Socialist society of plenty over one-sixth of the world for the 200,000,000 people it will contain a few years hence. In the field of transport alone this calls for literally millions of bridges, tunnels, terminals, wharves, airports, ships, engines, autos, institutes, clubs, clinics. In most other fields the needs are not less pressing. Toward this goal, then, during the next decades a good part of the Soviets' minds and energies will be directed—to build as much as they can and as fast as they can.

35. Why do the Soviets Stress and Speed Up Industrialization?

To lift this agrarian land out of its poverty and backwardness and bring it into line with the foremost industrial nations of the world. "We are from 50 to 100 years behind the advanced countries," said Stalin in 1931. "We must run through this distance in ten years. Either we do this or they will crush us." Hence the popular slogan, "To overtake and surpass America." At present in national income, mechanical power, and industrial output, America is far away in the lead. In a series of Five-Year Plans, the Soviets aim to close the gap—under forced draft to reach the level of America.

To provide through large-scale abundant production the basis for the future Communist society. The economy of plenty will give every man all requisites for his creature and cultural well-being. The shift from muscles to machines will give him the leisure and strength to enjoy them to the full. At the same time, through the mutual dependence and discipline it enforces, large industry prepares the citizen for the future society. "Through socialized work to the social man."

To free the country from dependence on other nations. Because Tsarist Russia was non-industrial, it imported most of its machines, medicines, chemicals, and agricultural implements. From this necessity Soviet Russia aims to liberate itself by producing these things at home. This does not imply that it champions the Fascist doctrine of national self-sufficiency. On the contrary, it envisages a world-plan in which each country specializes in the products for which it is most fitted and delivers them to the places most needed. This, of course, is a vision of the future. For the present, it faces the fact that it is a lone Socialist state encircled by hostile capitalist powers. At any time they may again impose a boycott and blockade cutting off supplies vital to its existence. To avert such a catastrophe, it makes great sacrifices in order to bring to completion every essential industry. For example, it might be twice cheaper for the Soviet Union to buy airplane engines abroad. But suddenly there might be a blockade and it would not be able to buy them at all. Therefore it willingly shoulders the extra loss involved in learning to build them at home.

To fortify the country against war. It is impossible to exaggerate the fear of assault from a coalition of hostile powers pervading all peoples in the Soviet Union, although it possesses the largest army in the world and enormous reserve of man-power. So did old Russia, but it repeatedly went down to defeat because it was woefully lacking in transport and technique. These defects the Soviet Union determined to remedy at all costs. By rapid industrialization it set out to prepare to hold its own in the future war of airplanes, tanks, and gases.

"The history of old Russia," said Stalin to a conference of Soviet industrialists in 1931, "is the history of defeats due to backwardness. She was beaten by the Mongol khans. She was beaten by the Turkish beys. She was beaten by the Swedish feudal barons. She was beaten by the Polish-Lithuanian squires. She was beaten by the Anglo-French capitalists. She was beaten by the Japanese barons. All beat her for her backwardness—military, cultural, governmental, industrial, agricultural. She was beaten because to beat her was profitable and it could be done with impunity. Do you remember the words of the pre-revolutionary poet: 'You are both poor and abundant, you are both powerful and helpless, Mother Russia!' These words of the old poet were well known to those gentlemen. They beat her saying: 'You are abundant—so we can enrich ourselves at your expense.' They beat her saying: 'You are poor and helpless—so you can be beaten and plundered with impunity.' Such is the law of capitalism—to beat the backward and weak. The jungle law of capitalism. You are backward, you are weak, so you are wrong, hence you can be beaten and enslaved."

Some five years after that conference on industrialization Stalin was speaking in quite another vein to new graduates of the Military

Academies: "You know, comrades, that we received as a heritage from old times a technically backward and semi-impoverished country. A country ruined by four years of imperialist war, again ruined by three years of civil war. A country with a semi-literate population, with low technique, with isolated oases of industry submerged amid a sea of extremely petty peasant economy. This is the kind of a country we received as a heritage from the past. Our task was to switch it over from the rails of medievalism and darkness to the rails of modern industry and machine-equipped agriculture. A serious and difficult task, as you well know. The problem stood thus: Either we solve this in the shortest possible time and strengthen Socialism, or we do not solve it and our country loses its independence and becomes an object of the game between the imperialist powers.

"It was imperative for us to create a first-class industry. To do this we had to make sacrifices and resort to the strictest economy in food, in schools, in textiles—in everything. There was no other path and on it we went confidently and impetuously. Now everyone admits we have a first-class industry, a powerful mechanized agriculture, a transportation system that is developing and on the upgrade, an organized and splendidly equipped Red Army." To its excellent morale and fighting spirit is now added the fullest mechanization, motorization, and chemification. No longer is the Soviet Union a backward nation—"a country with rich natural resources and a poor army." Thanks to industrialization, it no longer needs to fear the fate of China, India, Ethiopia. "Out of its weakness and unpreparedness it has become a powerful nation fully able to defend itself, ready for all eventualities."

36. How Are the Industries of the State Organized and Run?

Most of the 61,000 large-scale enterprises are ranged under the six Commissariats—Timber, Food, Heavy, Light, Defense and Local Industries. Each of these is subdivided into "administrations" which are just what their name implies. Thus Heavy Industry has thirty-three administrations—coal, oil, machinery, power, and so forth. Under Light Industry are textiles, footgear, furniture, glass. On these commissars and administrators, the Soviet "captains of industry," devolve tremendous responsibilities. With them go equally tremendous powers and opportunities. They stand in the position of proprietors of the lands, factories, and resources under their control, or they may be compared to boards of directors with vastly larger scope to their authority and activities. They outline general policies, allot capital, fix prices and wage scales, decide crucial problems like the grouping of enterprises around a source of raw material or a center of energy. Finally they appoint the heads of the several hundred Trusts and Combines.

The function of the Trust is to organize in the field the actual work of production. Uniting all enterprises of a similar kind, they are usually "horizontal" in structure. Pumping the crude oil from the ground through its own pipe-lines to its own refineries, the Grozny Oil Trust converts it into gasoline and kerosene and delivers it to the filling stations and the consumer. A number of plants are sometimes associated to form a Combine which is usually "vertical." Utilizing the residues of one process as the raw material for another, the big Bobriki Chemical Combine manufactures nitrates, fertilizers, ammonia, dyestuffs, drugs, and ceramics. But there is no rigidity in these arrangements. Old trusts are being dissolved and new ones created. On the principle that "the best is that which works best," enterprises are transferred from one trust or combine to another. With the trend toward decentralization others are handed over to the Commissariat of Local Industries.

In this highly flexible industrial set-up, these midway organs are simply the means for carrying out the directives of the higher organs. While there is a great variety in forms of the trusts and combines, their functions are quite definite. They are responsible for all the properties transferred into their keeping, which gives them legal status and financial autonomy. They carry out the building programs of the planning bodies and relay back their own recommendations. They see to the purchase of raw materials and the sale of the finished goods, in some cases through their own stores. They make contracts with the Labor Unions as to wages, hours, and working conditions. They settle disputes arising between different enterprises in the same trust, carrying their own claims for damages and breaches of contract against other trusts into the regular courts. They establish the research institutes and schools for the training of technicians and foremen. Finally, they appoint the managers.

The tasks of the manager of a Soviet mine, mill, cannon-works, fishery, or cheese-factory are similar to those in similar positions in other countries. His job is to cut costs, reduce overhead, raise the output of labor, increase the quantity and quality of goods. Along with better goods he is supposed also to turn out better men—more resourceful, technically trained, and qualified to fill the posts in his own enterprise and in the hundreds of new ones opening throughout the country. With this in view, a big Soviet factory has its schools, night "university," newspapers, crèches, clinics, insurance, and sport-fields. In the proper functioning of these institutions as well as the factory the Soviet director is directly concerned. But if his obligations are many and varied, so are the means for carrying them out. One of his aides is the Plant Committee, elected by all the workers in each enterprise to improve conditions, enforce discipline, and raise production. Another is the Communist "cell" or branch, to raise the morale of the workers, instill in them the idea that the factory "belongs to all," and hold it up to the plans. Representatives of these two bodies, together with the director, constitute the "red triangle" of factory control.

The aim of the director is to secure the fullest cooperation of these two powerful allies. That is the test of his ability and upon it depends the success or failure of the enterprise. While all three have definite and important places in the scheme, the chief responsibility in the last few years has been increasingly shifted to the director. In the final reckoning it is he who must answer for all that transpires. Consequently to him has been given great power, authority, and prestige. With them, if he acquits himself creditably, go much the same honors and awards that are bestowed upon leading scientists, authors, and artists.

37. What is the Rôle of the Workshops and Handicrafts Cooperatively Owned and Run by Their Members?

In the field of industry, alongside of the 75,000 chief enterprises owned and operated by the State, exists another system of quite independent and self-governing enterprises, about 25,000 in number. They go under the name of Producers' Cooperatives, Integral Cooperatives, Artels, and Collectives. Each is composed of from five to a hundred or more members and in a few cases runs up to five thousand. In them over 3,000,000 persons are engaged in the making of all kinds of wares from pearl-buttons to barges and boilers, from crude wooden wagon wheels to exquisite laces and embroideries. They operate brick-yards, lime-kilns, glass-plants, distilleries, canneries, bakeries. They send semi-finished goods to the State factories or take from them products to finish. They render all kinds of services from house-building to tailoring, and the carrying of baggage at airports, wharves, and depots. A chain of 7,500 repair shops mends books, shoes, samovars, sewing machines, and musical instruments. Half the total catch of fish comes from the Fishermen's Collectives and most of the furs from the artels of Trappers and Hunters in Siberia. There are artels of Leather-Tanners, Charcoal-Burners, Knitters and Weavers, and Toy Makers; Associations of Sculptors and Painters with their own ateliers, of Writers publishing their books on their own presses.

In distinction from the State industries, in the cooperative or artel, ownership of workshops and tools is vested in its members, and the management instead of being appointed from above is directly elected and controlled by them. In place of regular wages and salaries, the income derived from the sale of goods or services is divided among the members according to work performed. Several local artels in the same line of production often join in a "union" to facilitate the purchase of raw materials and the sale of their wares to the State agencies or through their own stores, booths, or stalls in the bazaar. That also is a function of the "regional council," composed of delegates from all the artels of every kind in a given region. This council in turn sends delegates to the All-Union Council whose president advises with the Planning Commission and other high State organs about credits, supplies, and the rôle of the cooperatives in the national economy.

That it is a big rôle is attested by their annual output, already amounting to some twelve billion rubles and growing larger every year. They have their own health service with clinics, rest-homes, skiing-stations. They direct their own trade schools for the training of apprentices, higher technicums, colleges, research institutes, and in Leningrad an imposing "Palace of Culture." They administer their own insurance funds, and through the artels for retraining "invalids of war and of industry," they enable the partially disabled again to take part in life and add a bit to their pensions.

Over all these activities of the Cooperatives the control of the State and even their own councils is strictly limited. The function of the higher organs is largely to advise, correlate, and aid in planning, accounting, and auditing. Great pains are taken to preserve the fullest autonomy of each enterprise, allowing its members to manage their own affairs in their own way. This answers the nature and needs of those individuals to whom the regime or routine of the State factories is uncongenial. If one does not like that kind of life he may join his fellows in one of these self-governing enterprises, determining their own rules and working conditions. Or, if one is such a sheer individualist that he prefers to go "on his own," there is nothing to prevent him. Tens, if not hundreds, of thousands of craftsmen in their homes are making articles out of waste metals and wood, leather, ivory, bone, and birchbark. But, with a growing socialist mentality and the obvious advantages of associated effort, they are rapidly uniting in artels and cooperatives.

Art and Handicraft Artels

The artels and cooperatives of today are the outgrowth of the old *kustarni* or cottage trades existing in the Russian villages from times immemorial. Millions of peasants, especially during the long winters, were engaged in turning out all sorts of wares amounting to a third of the national output. Organized along capitalist lines, they were notoriously exploited and "sweated" by middlemen, and suffered a catastrophic decline during the Revolution. At first, intent on building up big factories and mass production the Soviets gave scant attention to these little enterprises. But with growing appreciation of the extent and value of the contributions of these small units they were revived, reformed on socialist lines, and incorporated in the national economy. Of particular interest to foreigners are certain villages specializing in articles of an artistic nature, the secrets and skills of their making handed down from generation to generation. In them often is revealed a high order of talent—imagination, fantasy, a deep sensitiveness to line and color. New processes are being invented and new shops built with modern lathes and drills, powered and lighted with electricity. But one still finds old, shaggy, sheepskin-clad mujiks working away with a few crude tools in their straw-thatched log huts, turning out articles of real beauty.

Out of bluish-white walrus tusks and mammoth ivory dug from the frozen tundras, the natives of Archangel carve brooches, bracelets, goblets, and sets of chessmen in novel designs. Instead of knights, bishops, and kings, man and his allies, the dog and reindeer, are arrayed against their enemies, the wolf, the wood-devil, and winter. Or the Red Armies advance across the board to give battle to the Whites. Out of camel hair and the down of goats the women of Orenburg make large shawls, so fine and spider-web like in texture that they can be drawn through a finger ring. From the forests about Gorky on the Volga come millions of candlesticks, plates, spoons, and tableware of almost feathery lightness—the Khokhloma ware. Made of birch and linden, the leads and oil with which they are covered are transformed in kilns into glistening gold, silver, red and green lacquers—durable and heat-resisting.

The ancient monastery town of Zagorsk and its satellite villages are renowned for their wooden toys. Favorites of the Russians are the screwed, nested, and collapsible dolls in graduated sizes fitting one into the other, quaint animals and grotesque human figures in which the peasant-carvers take a satirical fling at greedy bureaucrats and priests. To these are now added ingenious toys with blocks, pulleys, and levers reflecting the advent of the Machine Age. Zvenigorod and sixty other centers produce guitars and strumming balalaikas, along with the accordion, favorite instruments of rural Russia. From the semi-precious mines of the Urals come articles of jade and jasper, hornstone, moonstone, lapis lazuli. From Viatka come one-piece boxes for cigarettes made out of Karelian birch and burls—growths on tree-trunks, roots, and branches. From Gogol's countryside come glazed vases, jugs, and bowls baked by the Ukrainian potters in brick-lined holes in the earth. Riazan and Vologda are celebrated for their laces with fir-trees, stars, and rivulets as motifs. A score of provinces produce home-spun linens and towelings embroidered with the frost-flowers from the winter window-panes and the red rooster of the barnyard, along with mythical birds of the ancient Slavs, or other symbols coming down from the misty past.

The assurance to each nationality of its own language and culture has given a great impetus to the folk arts and crafts of the non-Slavic peoples. Over 200,000 women are engaged in the weaving of oriental rugs, mostly on hand looms and with an increasing use of vegetable dyes extracted from nuts, grasses, and leaves. While there are many new patterns they cling to the old motifs—the Tree of Life, the branching palm, the serpent, the "Solarski Rose," symbol of abstract beauty coming down from antiquity. Most famed are the velvety maroon and ivory brocades and rugs of the Turcomans, the long and short naps of Armenia and Azerbaijan in deep blues, reds, and golden yellow. They have up to 39,000 knots to the square foot and long use only serves to add to their luster.

The Uzbeks love their flashing raw-silk robes but the old turbans are giving way to gay colored skull-caps and the Eastern veil to scarves and the three-cornered red kerchief of the Pioneers. From the Volga Tatars come burnished and enameled buttons and buckles along with rainbow leather boots sewn out of a hundred pieces. From the mountains of the Caucasus come curved silvered daggers, horse trappings, and jewelry embossed in gold and black. And from the Mansi, fur and bead tapestries depicting reindeer racing and the hunting of seals.

"Palekh Artel of Ancient Painting"

Palekh, a village in the forests of Vladimir, 200 miles from Moscow and 26 miles from the nearest railway station, was a center for the making of ikons, painted images of the Virgin and saints. The annual sale of thousands dropped to almost nothing after the Revolution. But with an impulse to create after returning from the War, the peasants sought for a new medium for expressing themselves. With brushes from the tip-hairs of squirrel tails and a few colors, supplemented by the juice of barks and roots emulsified in egg yolk and kvas, they began painting on wood, metal, and finally on boxes of papier-mâché. Coated with oils, in the kitchen ovens along with the black bread and cabbage-soup they were baked twenty times and polished a hundred times.

Out of these experiments were evolved the Palekh lacquers of today —exquisite miniature paintings, Byzantine in form, Italian in coloring, Russian in feeling. They received the highest awards at the Paris Art Expositions and were acclaimed by connoisseurs as rivaling the best old Japanese and Chinese lacquers. Stylized in form and with a great deal of symbolism, they depict hunting and harvest scenes, fairy tales and legends like the "Fire Bird," the "Fisherman and the Fish," poems of Nekrasov and Gorky, episodes out of the civil war like the "March of Chapayev and His Men," exploits of the heroes of the Arctic and the Stakhanov movement. Striking out into new fields they are producing frescoes for theatres, panels, monumental paintings on porcelain, and illustrations for rare books. From the sure, steady hands of seventy-year-old Ivan Mikhailovich Bakhanov, laying on his colors so cunningly that they shine forth deeply luminous like mother-of-pearl come illustrations for the poems of Pushkin. The high-strung gifted Galikov, father of seven children, produces an illuminated manuscript of the "Song of Prince Igor's Army." The young Zinoviev inheriting his father's talent for the finest miniatures tells the story of man and the earth in a series of paintings.

The original little group of seven pioneers has now grown into an Artel of over a hundred. It has a large edifice housing the kilns, a common room with a huge samovar around which gather the members for debates, discussions, songs, and stories; an Art School for the training of peasant youth, and studios in which the student apprentices work under the guidance of the older masters. In many ways the Artel revives the system of the medieval guilds. After three years' study the apprentice goes before the committee of seven "masters" and on the basis of exponents submitted may be elected to the coveted rank of master. It summons others before it for reprimands for negligence or willfulness, censures even a master "for increasing his output at the expense of his art," for "tendency to imitation in his scroll-work." Appeals against its decisions or any other dispute may be carried to the general meeting of the Artel, to the regional council, or even to Moscow. But almost never have the rulings of the old masters been disputed.

Each month the finished lacquers are brought to a Commission of three elected by the members to be classified as first, second, or third with corresponding remuneration. Paintings of exceptional merit are given special awards. But seldom do even the best masters receive over four ·hundred rubles a month. After certain taxes and levies about a fourth of the net profits of the Artel is set aside as reserve capital in the bank. The remainder goes to the upkeep of the new museum, "red corners," and crèche, for the purchase of magazines and books, to loan funds for members building a house, buying a cow or bicycle, into excursions to Moscow museums and galleries and distant places like Armenia to study the old paintings so strikingly like their own.

In the vanguard of community life, the Artel sponsored the establishment of a large *Embroidery Artel* for women. It encouraged the revival of folk arts in Mstera and other neighboring villages. It aided in the formation of the Palekh Kolhoz, uniting the two hundred separate farms into a single agricultural collective to which most of the painters belong, taking part in its plowing, planting, and reaping. On finding that this heavy field work unsteadied their painting-hands they secured early allocation of a tractor and other machines to lighten their labors. But still much of the work is done with the old plows, sickles and scythes. So it was at any rate during my last sojourn to Palekh when the advantages of collective over individual farming were still a matter of question and controversy.

Fortunately that summer the prospects for a good harvest were promising. Round about the village rolled the billowing crops, light-green seas of flax, dark-green seas of vetch, and over the hills in the distance, wide stretches light golden with the ripening oats and winter rye. Over the fallow field like a huge locust crawled the chugging tractor. Wagons laden with last late fragrant hay came creaking up from the meadow by the river. A band of singing girls with sickles went trooping over the hill to the first gathering of the harvest. All very idyllic were it not for human nature. For human nature, with all its sorry traits, functions in the best regulated collectives. And so it did in Palekh: Carelessness—overworking the horses until they were worn out; laziness—some members did not want to work at all; malice—some enemy set fire to the spring rye-rick and six thousand sheaves of straw went up in flames. And on top of all this, just when the fields were ripe for the big harvest, a cold wind with heavy rain flailing the crops, threatened to flatten them low. Deluges of rain, day after day. Then a sudden let-up in the downpour. But no telling when it would begin again; any delay would be catastrophic. Like a tocsin through the village echoed the cry, "The harvest is in danger!"

It was heard in the homes and the women laid aside their tasks. It sounded in the schools and the children put aside their books. It was echoed in the Artel and the painters laid down their brushes and picked up their scythes. With forty curved steel blades flashing above their heads they looked like a phalanx of ancient swordsmen advancing into combat. At their head as brigadier marched Bakhanov, sinewy and clear-eyed, despite his years. A master artist, but a real mujik too, with a keen knowledge and love of labor in the fields. That was why he had been chosen brigadier with these five fields of alfalfa to be cut.

The first field he assigned to the apprentices. Then with a wide stroke he slashed into the second, handling his scythe with the same swift precision that he did his brush. One by one, a few steps behind, the other masters followed. Swiftly the green stalks went toppling down before the steady swinging of the steel blades as the twenty scythemen with machine-like rhythm moved diagonally down the field. Faster and faster went the pace. It set the muscles tense beneath bared arms and brought the sweat to their faces. It raised water-blisters on the hands of Galikov, unaccustomed to such friction. But with the spirit of those long-lanced warriors on charging horses that he loves to paint he kept grimly going ahead. So did all the twenty masters.

And so did all the four and twenty apprentices over in the first field. In the Artel all day, all year long, the masters taught them how to handle the brush. It was their turn now. In the strength and pride of their youth they show their elders how to handle a scythe. Relentlessly they drove ahead, striving to be first to finish their field. But the two forces were evenly matched and it ended in a draw. A pause to rest, to smoke, and to crack a few peas from their pods. Then into the next two fields urging each other on with taunt and jest and banter. Another short pause and joining forces for the fifth field they finished it off together. Now at ease they looked down the long high-piled winnows with the smooth-shaven lanes of stubble running between. A rich crop, and it is all reaped and ready for the wagons. The danger of a fodder-famine was over. That threat to the Kolhoz was liquidated.

In masters and apprentices was that feeling of solidarity in those who have toiled together, merging their strength in a common cause. Now homeward bound, with the sunset gleaming on their scythes lifted high above their heads, they were merging their voices together, singing in unison. Songs of far away and long ago, jovial rollicking songs, and finally songs of the Red Army and the Revolution. To me Russian melodies under the wide Russian sky, poured out by resonant Russian voices rolling out across the fields and forests, are always fascinating. This night from the throats of these painter-singers they were singularly pulse-quickening. For they were taking part in another act of vast significance. In the struggle for preserving the old folk arts and carrying them on to new heights they had wrought valiantly. Now they were doing yeoman service on another front on which all the forces of the nation were engaged—the drive for collectivization, for victory over age-old hunger, poverty, and backwardness. In their little sector they were demonstrating the superiority of collective over individual farming, carrying on the processes initiated by the Revolution in 1917. The scythes in the hands of the Red mowers were as truly weapons of the Revolution as the bayonets of the Red Guards I saw on the night of November seventh glistening in the light of the Winter Palace they were besieging.

38. What Are the Chief Forms of Socialized Farming?

The big State farms called *Sovhozes* are owned and run by the government. Of these there are about 10,000 engaged in the raising of grain, flax, cotton, and hemp; the breeding of horses, sheep, or reindeer; the cultivation of soy-beans, medicinal herbs, rubber plants, flowers for perfume, oils of mint, anise, and geranium. Like the big factories operated by the various Commissariats for Industry, these big farms are mostly operated by a special Commissariat of Grain and Livestock Farms with some under the Commissariats of Agriculture and Food. Under these in turn are the trusts or combines such as Grain, Tea, Sugar, Sheep, grouping together the separate farms, ranches, or plantations which specialize in these products. On each the manager is appointed; and everyone, from doctor to tractorist, watchman, shepherd, and wolf-killer, works for wages and is organized into unions.

At the outset some of these farms, such as the Gigant "grain factory," embraced hundreds of thousands of acres with huge fleets of combines, batteries of search-lights for night work, radios sending orders to the harvesters encamped for weeks in the distant fields, airplanes bringing them medicines, magazines, and entertainers. Carried away by the idea of sheer bigness, it was freely predicted that all agriculture would be absorbed by these giant enterprises. But unfortunately while they grew bigger they did not always grow better. They often proved altogether too unwieldy for efficient operation. Hence the decision to cut down their area, to split them up into smaller units, and in some cases to hand them over in whole or part to the *Kolhozes*.

The *kolhozes,* cooperative self-governing associations of farmers, are far and away the biggest and most important sector of agriculture. To them belong over one billion acres, about four-fifths of all the arable and grazing lands. Most of them are organized in artels, of which there are about 250,000. Each is composed of from a dozen to a thousand households, and bear such names as "Lenin's Will," "No Surrender," "May Morning," "First Ray of Communism." Their status is similar to the artels of industry, jointly owned and run by their members, to whom, after the deduction of certain levies and taxes, belong the fruits of their labors.

Supposing 130 peasants unite their separate holdings of about ten acres each to make a farm of 1,300 acres, the average size of an artel today. To it as a corporate body is now given the use of this land "forever" and it may not be reduced, sold, or rented. Besides this communal land each member has an individual plot for his house, garden, orchard, cow, poultry, and bee-hives. As in an industrial artel, authority is vested in the "general meeting" which elects a chairman, a board of managers, and auditors. It confirms the plans for seeding, reaping, building, and swamp-draining; accepts or expels members; decides on the division of income; votes funds for books, papers, radio, the care of invalids and orphans. In long and often stormy sessions are settled the questions that keep coming up: The penalizing of a member caught illicitly distilling "moonshine" in the woods; organizing a gala leave-taking for the young recruits off to the Red Army; harvesting all through the night in order to win over a rival artel against whom they are pitted in Socialist competition.

Besides the artel there are two other types of kolhozes. In the Partnership, *tovarischestvo,* the land is plowed and cultivated in common, but only the land. Everything else, draft animals, cattle, and tools, remains as before the private property of the members. Most of these rudimentary forms of collectives have evolved into artels, some of which have in turn evolved into a still higher form of cooperative effort, the *commune.* In this the members retain only a few personal possessions. Everything else is socialized—homes, gardens, poultry, as well as land, horses, cattle, and implements. With a common dining-hall, nursery, and living quarters whenever possible, the communal life reaches its highest state of development. But there are comparatively few of this kind of kolhoz—less than one in a hundred—and they play a negligible rôle in the total economy. The basic accepted type is the artel, and on it the Soviets are staking the agricultural future of the country.

The case for collectivization is stated by Thomas D. Campbell, Montana "wheat king," former adviser of the Soviets. "Russia is solving the age-old agrarian problem by consolidating little farms into big ones and applying industrial methods. To solve the problem in America we likewise must have large farms. I do not mean communized farms as in Russia but mergered farms created by farmers pooling their land and becoming shareholders in a large corporation instead of trying to carry on as small farmers. The farm which is not big enough to be an economic unit cannot carry on successfully. If four 160-acre Iowa corn farms were united under competent management they could be tilled with virtually the machinery and equipment of one and be successful!"

39. What Were the Aims in Collectivization of the Land?

In merging the millions of peasant holdings into large-scale farms operated by modern methods and machinery the Soviets sought to achieve three things:

First, to insure adequate supplies of food to the cities, cotton and flax to the factories, and grain for export. Productivity of the land in old Russia was notoriously low; the yield per acre was almost the smallest in the world. This was mainly due to the prevailing system by which the village land was divided into three fields which in turn were subdivided into the good and bad, the meadow-land and hill-land, the far and near. To each peasant was allotted a share in each section, so that his "farm" consisted of tiny strips or plots in ten to fifty different places. From above the country looked like a crazy-quilt of onion beds. It is hard to conceive of a system so absurdly wasteful and unproductive.

These conditions were only aggravated by the Revolution. Having driven out the landlords, the peasants annexed the great estates, realizing their dreams cherished for centuries. But their only program about the land was to get it. For its rational use and cultivation they had no plan. The chief use they had for the Bolsheviks was to legalize its seizure and to defend it against the White armies of the former landlords. The Bolshevik Land Decree of November, 1917, magnificently proclaimed: "The lands of the crown, the monasteries, and the landlords are hereby declared the property of the nation forever." As a matter of record 90 per cent of it was appropriated by the peasants and divided among themselves. This greatly increased the small holdings. From 16 million of tiny many-field "farms" in 1913, the number rose to over 25 million in 1928. Many were carved out of the big farms and estates—the very ones that had once, under expert managers, been the chief source of grain for the market. As a result, the marketed grain in 1928 was but a little more than half the pre-War level and the yield per acre of all crops had declined by a fourth. To increase it, it was imperative to use machines, disc-plows, harrows, and reapers. But these could be operated efficiently only on large tracts of land. By converting the tiny holdings into big unbroken collectives the Soviets chose the only way out.

Another aim of collectivization was to release the peasant from his age-old bondage to the soil. With the crudest implements he was compelled to toil like a slave. His wooden plow scarcely more than scratched the surface of the earth. Out of a crib he scattered the seed by hand, much of it to be picked up by crows and ravens. Bent double all day, he reaped the rye and oats with a sickle, and threshed them out with a flail. In scoopfuls he flung them above his head to be winnowed by the wind, the heavy grains falling to the earth, the light chaff blowing away. Picturesque to the outsider, but grueling and body-racking to the peasant. With every man, woman, and child toiling from before dawn until after dark, the harvest well deserved the name the peasants gave it, "the suffering season," *stradnaya pora*. By machinery the Soviet sought to liberate the people from this inhuman strain and free the reserves of labor-power in the village for industry.

In our village of Saburova, 70 miles from Moscow, the progressive peasants formed an artel for renting a tractor for the threshing season. With instinctive dread of the new, the old women in particular were against it. "A device of Satan," they went about mumbling, "it smells of the devil!" A week later their worst suspicions were confirmed. Into the village came the clanking monster snorting like a devil, shooting smoke and fumes out of its belly, smelling like ten devils. Into their huts ran the old crones, crossing themselves in holy fear, and crying, "The Antichrist is coming!"

But presently the tractor, belted up to the thrasher, was working with the energy of a hundred devils. Into its hopper went the russet sheaves, out of its chutes a stream of golden grain and flying straw, piling up in stacks that rose like herds of large brown elephants above the roofs, threshing in a day as much as the back-breaking flail did in a month. No more rubbing of aching joints and limbs. No more kinks in their spines. But standing erect now with wonder in their eyes and gratitude in their hearts, the old crones looked upon the tractor, not as an Antichrist, but a Messiah. And as it went chugging along the road to the next village they stood waving it good-by, "Good-by! *golubushka,* little dove!" "Come to us again" "How sweet to lay our burdens upon the iron shoulders of the little child of Jesus." "Little child of Lenin!" put in a young Communist reprovingly.

Finally by collectivization they sought to resolve the age-old conflict between city and village by bringing agriculture along with industry into the orbit of Socialism. "We cannot for long," said Stalin, "base the Soviet power on two foundations: on large-scale unified Socialist industry, and on our most divided small peasant farming." Even though political power and all strategic positions might be in the hands of the proletariat, the tens of millions of peasant proprietors were capitalists in embryo, ready at any time, in the words of Prince Mirsky, "to renew the insidious attack on the industrial citadel of Communism. Without collectivization the Soviet Union would be a Socialist giant of steel on petty bourgeois legs of clay."

As America could not remain "half-slave and half-free," the Soviet Union could not continue half-socialist, half-capitalist. With the aim of creating a homogeneous organism, Socialist from head to foot, it embarked on its most audacious enterprise: The supplanting of the ancient primitive agriculture and implements in one-sixth of the world with a new system based upon the latest science and technique; the transformation of over a hundred million property-minded peasants into collectivists and Socialists. In 1928 began in earnest "the march of the battalions of Socialism into the last stronghold of the old individualist, capitalist anarchy."

40. How Did the Soviets Get the Peasants into the Collective Farms?

By every device they strove to convince the peasants that the only hope of escape from their present plight and poverty lay in a new way—in collectivization. As early as 1918 they organized big State farms, *Sovhozes,* to serve as examples of good farming. Soon after came the formation of the *Kolhozes,* associations of the peasants themselves for the joint tillage of the soil and the sharing of its products. But the villages as a whole were reluctant to enter them. It was not easy to overcome that deep-rooted conservatism and inertia reflected in their saying, "As things were they needs must be. As our fathers plowed, so plow we."

With the opening of the "Socialist Offensive" in 1928 the government sought to get the masses into them. By a series of measures making it still more difficult and hazardous to carry on as individual farmers it sought to make them abandon their old ways. On the other hand, to lure them into embracing the new way, it granted corresponding exemptions and privileges to the collectives: tractors, machines, seeds, instructors, fertilizers, nurseries for children, first claim on clothes, boots. All these advantages were promised the peasants on joining the kolhozes. And one thing more: deliverance from bondage to the kulak, literally a "fist."

The kulak was usually the most prosperous farmer in a

village, his wealth augmented by being also the local shark, usurer, or speculator. "Of all the human monsters I ever met on my travels," says Dr. E. J. Dillon, thirty years resident in Russia, "I cannot recall any so malignant and odious as the Russian kulak." If that is too sweeping an indictment undoubtedly the kulak was quite generally envied, feared, and hated. Beginning in 1928 he was slated for the same fate as the big landlords, his "complete liquidation as a class." He was debarred from the kolhozes as a parasite who had exploited his fellow men; as an individualist who by every instinct and in every fiber of his being was anti-social; as a capitalist, who, for all his fair words, pretense, and pleas to the contrary, must be the enemy of collectivization. Upon him were now laid the heaviest taxes and disabilities. With his holdings in whole or in part confiscated, forbidden to rent other lands, and deprived of a vote he was virtually turned into an outlaw. To escape being branded as kulaks, the peasants hastened in droves to enroll themselves in the collectives.

War with the Kulaks

Fighting for their very existence the kulaks resisted by every means. Where threats and force might not avail to destroy collectives, they sought to discredit them by trickery and cunning. Now insinuating their way into the collectives, they damaged machines, sowed confusion by mismanagement, and generally sabotaged from the inside so that many of the new farms fell to pieces. Now telling peasants that "in the kolhozes the government will give you everything," they instigated them to wholesale butchery of cattle and horses, to cut down fruit trees, to sell everything—even the iron from their roofs, and to enter empty-handed. Now subsidizing beggars to go about asking alms, saying, "We were once prosperous peasants brought to hunger and rags in the Volga collectives." And always playing upon fears and credulity with fantastic tales that in the end, along with everything else, the women too would be collectivized, their children taken from them and put into barracks; that all collectivists would be compelled to eat out of one big kettle and sleep under one big blanket a hundred yards long.

Moreover, they said in the collectives one forfeited his hopes for happiness not only in this world, but in the next. To help in this propaganda the kulaks mobilized the reactionary priests on their side, and they in turn mobilized the heavenly powers. The Mother-of-God appeared on the bell-tower of Boskova to announce that Antichrist had broken from his chains, and, raging over the earth, was stamping his seal on all who joined the collectives. In Tolvin the kolhoz president was killed by a cross falling from the skies, on which was written, "Beware of entering the collectives; the end of the world is at hand." Far and wide these rumors spread throughout the countryside. And while the tides of antireligion ran strong in Russia, signs and portents like these were still potent enough to rouse fears and hates and incite to furious resistance, particularly the women. In bands they went parading before the local Soviets defiantly chanting:

> Cut off our hands, chop off our nose!
> But you can't make us join your damn kolhoz!

For all this the kulaks paid dearly. The chief offenders and wreckers were denounced by their neighbors. New lists were drawn up by the poor and middle peasants. In thousands the kulaks were marched to the stations where under Ogpu guards they were deported to the lumber-camps in the North and new settlements in the far-away steppes and tundras. This in turn brought those who remained up in arms with ax and knife and sawed-off shotguns. In scores the Communist officials perished—waylaid in ambush, clubbed to death, or hacked to pieces. And, throughout the land, the "red cock was set to crowing"—that is, the torch was applied to barns and houses of the collectives, the skies reddened by flames from burning hayricks and granaries.

According to the plan some twenty per cent of the small individual farms were to be united in the collectives. But so irresistible was the first drive that over half the peasants were swept into them. The abuses and excesses with which this was accompanied brought from Stalin the famous article of March 2, 1930, "Dizziness from Success." He pointed out that by zealots, intoxicated with the idea of creating Communism in one jump, large numbers had been forced into the new farms against their will, middle peasants had been hounded like kulaks. He declared that joining or remaining in the collectives must henceforth be a voluntary act. The result was a stampede of millions back to the old way of farming, but the class war went on unabated. So serious was it that two whole intransigent Cossack villages in the Kuban were exiled to Siberia. In some cases ordinary peasants for fighting against the collectives were branded by their neighbors as kulaks and suffered their fate. In many regions opposition took the form of passive resistance. The fields went unsown or unweeded, crops were ungathered or left to rot on the ground to be eaten by mice and gophers. In the wake of this followed what has been controversially called the "acute food shortage" and the "famine" of 1932. In any case undoubtedly many perished of hunger and disease.

Victory for the Collectives

The kulaks were only partially to blame for the recalcitrance of certain sections of the peasantry. It rose also from the fact that so many of the first collectives were dismal failures. That was due to poor management, to the attempt to form communes in which everything was socialized, and to sheer village inertia and backwardness. As a peasant himself put it, "Yesterday I was a mujik; today I am a 'collectivist.' I have changed my name, but have I changed my nature?" "I want things for myself and I want them now." To this old peasant nature the collectives now made concessions in a new Constitution. To satisfy his cravings for possessions it allowed him his own garden, poultry, and cow. To counteract his natural apathy and listlessness it established piece-work systems, so that if he worked little he ate little. To stir him with the incentive of immediate rewards it gave him advances against the proceeds of the harvest. And finally it allowed him to sell his surplus products on the open markets.

The government came to the aid of the collectives with various measures. Among these was the dispatch of the "Twenty-five Thousands" hand-picked volunteers to organize, instruct, edit papers, and raise the morale in general. Most effective was the establishment of a chain of Machine-Tractor Stations, centers for supplying the countryside with the best kinds of plows, reapers, threshers, and motor-lorries. Also with technical staffs teaching the peasants how to drive and run them; accountants assisting in the keeping of books and tallies; soil experts planning the rotation of crops, snow and rain conservation, fertilizers. Payments for these services were made in kind, according to the size of the harvest. From 158 stations in 1930 the number grew to 2,660 in 1933. Thanks to them and favoring weather there was a bumper crop that autumn. "One good harvest year in Russia," said Catherine the Great, "atones for five bad ones." This one of 1933, bringing in almost 90 million tons, was an all-time record. It was followed by harvests nearly as good in 1934, 1935, and 1936 in spite of droughts and other setbacks.

Victory for the collectives, in the last analysis, was due not to the fact that they were backed by the coercive powers and propaganda of the State, formidable as they were. It was because on their side vastly more formidably were arrayed the machines, the forces of science and technique, in league with nature herself. This was most vividly brought home to me early in the struggle. It was in the summer of 1931, on an exploring expedition into new regions. With me went three American Senators, Wheeler of Montana, Barkley of Kentucky, and Cutting of New Mexico. In high spirits we set forth on an August morning into the rolling plains of Vladimir. But it was more of an adventure than we had bargained for.

So rough were the roads that we were battered, pitched and tossed about like cargoes in a heavy sea, and our ramshackle cars broke down. Under a broiling sun the Senators hauled them out of muck-holes, pushed them up long hills, and poured endless buckets of water into the radiators leaking at every seam. So primitive were our lodgings that out of the wooden walls swarmed regiments of bedbugs, assaulting the representatives of American capitalism with peculiar zest and fury. The Senators fought back all through the night, but it was a losing battle, and now in the veins of these Vladimir insects runs a strain of the best Harvard and Kentucky blood. So far from the beaten track did we stray that the natives gazed wonder-struck at the sight of Americans in the flesh, and the old women violently crossing themselves fled to their houses crying out that we were Anti-christs. But we had our reward for our troubles.

Here in these remote fastnesses into which mischance had led us we came face to face with the new kolhozes. In Russian and German we talked with their members, drank the milk that they pressed on us, and found out that, unlike most of the first collectives, these were really flourishing. As yet they were few in number, like islands iso-lated in a sea of peasant individualism. More striking then was the contrast between the old way of tilling the soil and the new. On the one hand were the pitifully narrow strips and tiny plots of the in-dividual peasant; on the other, the compact, unbroken expanses of the kolhozes sweeping away to the horizon. In one field the women bent double reaping the rye with a sickle; in the next a mower sliced it down in clean wide swathes like a clipper clicking over a horse. Here a peasant with his wife and children beating out the grain with flails winnowing it with the wind; over there a collective thresher with a stream of grain flowing from its chute, and the flying straw piling up into stacks.

Side by side stood the two rival systems of farming, yet ages apart. A turn of the head, and, from primitive methods and instruments little changed since the dawn of history, the eye leaped hundreds of centuries to the modern mechanized order of the collectives. And with it went one's sympathies and convictions. About the outcome of the contest between the two ways there could be no doubt. On the face of the earth was written the superiority of the collectives, in the rich stands of full-eared grain, and their big herds of grazing cattle. It was written too on the faces of the collectivists, in the satisfaction of their common toil together, their release from isolation and inse-curity in a fellowship of mutual aid and dependence.

41. How is Work on a Collective Farm Carried On?

That depends upon its size, locality, and what it specializes in. From little artels engaged in gardening to bigger ones in sunflowers and sugar-beets they run up to tens of thousands of acres in the artels for breeding of sheep and cattle. A typical artel is one engaged in the growing of cereals, flax, cotton, hops. Some are well equipped, but most of them look to the Machine-Tractor Stations for tractors, gang-plows, combines, flax-pullers, potato-diggers, and big trucks. Their operation and all the field labor of the artel is done by its members. They are assigned to "brigades" of five to fifty, to each of which is allotted a specific task. To fix responsibility, each is charged with the cultivation of a definite section of land the season through. Others are assigned to the care of the artel's herds, horses, oxen, or camels.

At the head of each brigade is a leader appointed by the managers. On him—or her, for over 125,000 women are heading brigades—devolves the task of getting the workers into the fields or stables, directing their day-to-day activities, and, most important, seeing that they perform them properly. That is the crux of the whole matter. How get each man to give the best that is in him? How prevent Ivan shifting the burden onto Nikolai and Nikolai in turn onto Pavel or Pasha? This is done by making one's income depend on the quantity and quality of work he performs. To this end there are seven categories with definite norms for each reckoned in so-called "work-days," according to the amount of skill and energy required. Thus the binding of a certain number of sheafs may count as one "work-day," the services of a water boy as a half, of a first-class tractor-driver as two. For those running ahead of the norms set by the artel there are bonuses; for those falling behind, deductions. In this way the self-interest of the individual is made to serve the common interest of all. The more each member exerts himself the bigger are the crops, income, and prestige of the whole artel. On this plan the work goes on through the cycle of the seasons from planting time till the harvest is gathered in, threshed, delivered, or stored for the winter.

Now comes the division of the harvest, the casting up of the accounts for the year. First is the part that goes to the State for taxes, usually in the form of deliveries of grain, flax, and meat at low fixed prices. Then the payment, also in kind, for the services of the Machine-Tractor Station. That leaves about two-thirds for the artel to dispose of. After setting aside seed and fodder for the coming year, the general meeting allocates certain sums for building a new silo, crèche, or "laboratory hut"; for buying a blooded bull, stallion or ram; for crop insurance; and other funds. The rest is divided among the members according to the number of "work-days" to their credit. A big family may receive a ton or more of grain as well as its quota of potatoes, meat, butter, and wool.

In addition to his share in the joint products of the artel each member has all the income from his own garden, cow, poultry, rabbits, berries, and bees. The amount of this depends on how well and diligently he tends to his ground plot and animals. It also depends upon the locality; for, instead of fixing the same amount of land or cattle for each person, the statutes are flexibly adapted to the kind of husbandry. In those districts where there is little or no tillage of the soil, each homestead may own up to 8 camels, 10 cows, 150 sheep or goats. These, together with its share from the general income fund, may be consumed by the family, sold in the bazaars, or otherwise disposed of as it sees fit. The claim for the artel is that it combines the benefits of social cooperation with the free play of individual initiative and enterprise.

Problems and Prospects of the Collectives

While some are efficiently managed, most of them show plenty of room for improvement. There are big wastages in every process, from the sowing of mildewed seed in the spring to the careless storing of the grain in rat-infested granaries. Thousands of cattle are plague-stricken or lost on the ranges through sheer negligence. There are malcontents, wastrels, hot-heads, and malingerers. For human nature continues to function in the best regulated kolhozes. How deal with the old peasants cunningly sparing their strength on the common fields in order to have the more for their own individual ones? Or with the young shirkers seeking to escape from the sweat and dust of outdoor labor into some soft job with a pen in the office? In the solution of these and other questions the collectives will be engaged for years and decades to come. But they are quite minor alongside of those that already have been overcome. Thanks to collectivization the cities and factories are now assured of foodstuffs, fibers, and oils. There are ample reserves for the Red Army, enough for a short year or a calamity, enough to promise a steady rise in the level of living.

Admitting all this, the critics point to some twenty years hence when there will be a quarter billion people to support. They shake their heads dourly over "pressure of population," diminishing returns, acid and exhausted soils. In rejoinder the Soviets point to great territories still untouched by the plow. In Central Asia there are over 100 million acres of virgin lands, while huge irrigation projects are beginning to sluice the waters of the Volga, Manich, and other rivers into once arid steppes now covered with thriving kolhozes. In the Far North where, formerly, the summers were considered too brief for farming, thanks to the shortening of the growing season through "vernalization"—the partial germinating of seeds before planting—and the shortening of the harvesting season through quick reaping, great areas are now being brought under cultivation. In the old regions, too, land reclamation goes on by means of drainage-canals, swamp-plows, stumping, and scrub-cutting machines.

Even if there were no new lands to cultivate, the yield could be greatly increased by intensive cultivation of the old. The chief problem in Russia is not to get more soil but to get more out of the soil. It calls for better prepared ground beds and clean sorted seeds to put into them. It calls for more fertilizers, trainloads of which are now coming daily from the apatite mountains on the White Sea. It calls for utilization of all the findings of science from those of the Academy of Science, down to the kolhozes' own little laboratory huts. Thanks to these measures, the yield per acre in some regions has been doubled. It would not be a tremendous exploit to do likewise in many regions and it may well be done in the not far distant future. For the present, Stalin asks for an increase of a billion and a half *poods* (36 pounds) raising the total output to seven or eight billion by 1940. That seems a modest enough request in the light of the present steady trend upward.

So manifest are the advantages of collectivization that many who once bitterly fought it are now its ardent champions. That includes thousands of former kulaks who are now enfranchised and received as full-righted members in the artels. Besides the benefits of big scale scientific farming, they offer satisfactions for many old, deep-rooted instincts and yearnings. Among these is the profound attachment to the earth which in some Russian peasants amounts to a passion. Instead of being a seasonal worker, or even a well-paid expert on a State farm, he much prefers the artel where he has his own place on the soil. And a secure place, for under no circumstances can it be sold, leased, or mortgaged. No longer is he compelled to see his land slipping away piece by piece to pay his taxes or his debts to the kulak. No longer is he paralyzed by a natural calamity, a steppe fire, hot winds blowing in from the desert to wither the crops, or armies of locusts flying up from the South to devour them.

Thanks to science and collectivization, most of these scourges are on their way out. When they do come, when a drought or early frost blights the crops or pestilences fall upon the cattle, the insurance funds covering almost every conceivable risk come to the rescue. Gone are the old days when the peasants crouched terror-stricken before the "acts of God." Gone, in all likelihood forever, are the old famines which periodically decimated the villages. Gone or fast going is the darkness, ignorance, and superstition in which they were steeped. Into the once "deaf" corners of the country, the collectives are bringing schools of all kinds, books, radio, theatres, cinema, organizing hundreds of thousands of dramatic, dancing, singing, and sport "circles." And quite as important they are bringing the people the leisure and energy to enjoy them.

Seldom if ever are those last items listed in the achievements of the kolhozes. But to the once so heavy-laden, hard-driven peasants, especially the women, they stand high up on, if not at the head of, the list. Even if the collectives did not produce more bread they would be justified in that they are releasing multitudes of human beings from inhuman labors and strains, opening the way for them into the new worlds of science and culture. No longer is the peasant, as he was wont to say, "lower than grass, quieter than water." In place of the old *mujik,* cap in hand, bowing low before the master, is a new type, standing erect, looking straight into one's eyes, confident of his own worth and powers. Such fundamental changes in outlook and character, Lenin declared, would take generations to accomplish. But at so fast a pace is it proceeding that already in the summer of 1936 *Izvestia* declared that "this transformation of the once backward, downtrodden peasant stands as the greatest achievement of Socialism."

42. What is the Condition of the Railways, Waterways, Airways and Roads?

Old Russia was a land of magnificent distances but with miserable means of communication. In normal times lack of transport was a heavy handicap. In crises it was tragic. In the World War great armies stood defenseless at the front while the junctions were clogged with munitions and supplies. In the famines millions perished of hunger while mountains of grain were rotting in Siberia. Regularly the spring thaws and autumn rains turned the roads into seas of mud completely isolating 100,000 villages.

All these evils were aggravated by the long years of civil war and intervention, which were fought mainly along the railway lines, and played havoc with them. Over 7,600 bridges were blown up, 100,000 miles of telegraph wires torn down. Green wood under the boilers ruined the locomotives. In vast "cemeteries," along with dead cars, they stood on the sidings. The trains, in the colorful words of Charles Crane, consisted of "splintered match-boxes drawn by battered samovars over two ribbons of rust." More than half the trackage was out of commission and half the shipping. On the Kama alone 300 steamers were burned or scuttled. So rickety were the few score airplanes that they were known as "flying coffins."

In sharp contrast with that dark past is the present. In the number of civilian and military planes, the Soviets now bid for first place among the nations of the world. The railways to their former 36,600 miles have added some 25,000 more. They carry four times the pre-War tonnage of freight, six times the number of passengers. The river fleet and merchant marine is expanding. Motor plants are turning out 300,000 cars and tractors a year. This is good as far as it goes. But it doesn't go far in one-sixth of the world. Transport till recently was the weakest link in the Soviet economic chain—in the words of Premier Molotov, "the tightest of places." Masses of materials piled up at the junctions and wharves. Mills closed or slowed down for lack of them. Travelers waited hours, even days, to find a place on the trains. Street-cars were packed like sardines, only as a cynic remarks, "sardines do not cling to the outside of their cans, while Soviet citizens must cling to their trams." This was an intolerable situation. Old agrarian Russia might muddle along with a crippled primitive transport, but modern industrialized Russia cannot. Everything depends on it. Colossal new resources may be discovered, but they are not assets until they are brought to the centers. Great plants are "white elephants" without a steady stream of cars. The 1,500,000 Red Armyists are fully effective only if they can be rapidly shifted from one front to another.

The Soviets are at last vigorously grappling with this stu-

pendous problem. In 1935, Stalin's right-hand man, the indefatigable Kaganovich, builder of the Moscow subway, was appointed Commissar of Railways, and in the course of two years
the 50,000 daily carloadings were almost doubled. The Second
Five-Year Plan allocated 27 billion rubles to transport. It reno-
vated the old railways, built 9,000 miles of new ones, double-
tracked the Trans-Siberian. It increased the number of telegraph
stations to 25,000 as against 6,000 in 1913. It finished three big connecting canals, linking up the rivers and seas into an inland water
system on which big ships may pass from city to city and out to
the ocean. It lengthened the airways to 50,000 miles. It opened up
250 new street-car, auto, and trolley-bus lines. It constructed eight
great macadamized roads such as the two strategically important
military highways from Moscow to Kiev and Minsk, and the one
leading to gold-bearing regions beyond the Amur. Among the
colossal works of the Third Five-Year Plan are the completing
of the Volga-Don and the Manich Canals, uniting the Black
Sea with the Caspian. But it will take a whole series of plans
to cover the country with a traffic web equal to all its demands.

Railways

"Give us better rail service!" cried Voroshilov to the Seventh Congress. "It is the Red Army's blood brother." From other Commissars similar appeals, warnings, and exhortations have been voiced
again and again. Carloadings lagged far behind the quota set by the
First Five-Year Plan, and in the first years of the Second. Trains were
made up, switched, run, and unloaded with inexcusable slowness.
Cars were "dead-headed" empty back to the loading points or held up
on sidings to be used as store-houses. In 1935 the number of accidents,
counting everything from serious rail breakages to appalling wrecks,
ran into the tens of thousands.

Many rail troubles were due to poor discipline—drunkenness, being
asleep at the switch or the throttle, and errors in signaling. But more

could be charged to the railways themselves. They were simply inadequate to the terrific strain imposed upon them by an ever-swelling volume of traffic. That was the crux of the report made by Ralph Budd, former President of the Great Northern Railway after a 20,000-mile trip of inspection. As the Soviets face the same problem of long hauls as in America, he suggested that its system should be adopted. Along these lines a basic reorganization is being effected. Light rails and bridges are being replaced with heavy ones. Sleepers are increased in number, chemically-treated, and strongly ballasted. Low-powered engines are replaced with high-powered ones—for passengers, the "J S" named after Joseph Stalin and for freight the "F D," after Felix Dzerzhinsky, the deceased head of the Cheka who always delivered the cars to the Hoover Famine Relief. The "S O," named after Sergo Ordjonikidze, instead of ejecting the exhaust steam into the air, condenses it into water to be used over and over again, a great advantage on the long runs through arid deserts of Central Asia. Low-tonnage cars give way to big gondolas, refrigerators, and tanks; hand brakes to automatic couplings; signaling by whistles and lantern-swinging to semaphores. The twists and turns by which the roads cork-screwed their way into towns are straightened out. "Bottle-necks"—crossovers and one-track bridges—and steep grades are eliminated. The mountain and suburban lines are being electrified.

As imperative as rehabilitating the old lines is the construction of new ones. With an area more than twice as great as the United States, the Soviet Union has less than a fourth of the trackage. Often grain and timber must be hauled tens and even hundreds of miles to a loading-point. In some regions it is a full two months' journey on foot or horseback to the nearest station. Virgin untracked wildernesses —some of them five times bigger than England! How long will it take for railways to open them up? Several new lines are already doing this. A very important one is the Turk-Sib which, by supplying Siberian wheat and lumber to Turkestan, allows it to specialize in the growing of those sub-tropical crops for which it is peculiarly fitted—cotton, rice, and rubber. Another is the Moscow-Donbas, coal-carrying line pouring fuel into the industrial zones of the center and the North. The first, built under the direction of William Shatoff of the American I.W.W., is over 1,000 miles in length. The second, completed in 1936, is 700 miles long.

They are dwarfed by a whole array of projects for the coming Five-Year Plans. Biggest of all is the Great Northern Way, charted to run across the two continents of Europe and Asia straight to the Pacific. So intrigued was Lenin by its stupendous possibilities that even in the midst of the life-and-death struggle of the Revolution he discoursed on it with enthusiasm: "Look at the map of Russia! To the North of Vologda . . . and Tomsk lie immense areas, patriarchal, half-savage and in some places wholly savage, in which scores of civilized states could be built up." That is the aim of this grandiose plan once offered by Lenin as a concession to foreigners, and now undertaken by the Soviets themselves. A new line from the upper end of Lake Baikal to the Amur river known as the *BAM* is already finished. Into the markets it will bring the products of this vast region rich in forests, furs, and precious metals. And in the event of the cutting of the old Trans-Siberian by the Japanese, this new line, which parallels it at the safe distance of hundreds of miles to the North, will carry food and munitions to the Red Armies fighting in the East.

The first surprise to the traveler arriving in the Soviet borders is to find that the cars are larger. That comes from the wider span between the rails. Instead of the standard 4 feet 8½ inches, they are 5 feet apart. This, it is said, is due to military considerations—to prevent German soldiers riding straight into the country. But it may be that the first Russian engineers blundered by taking the distance from the outside of the rails instead of the inside. Whether the broader gauge came from intent or mistake, it redounds to the benefit of the traveler by giving him roomier coaches. They are built on the European plan with corridors on the side and are of two kinds: "Soft," which eases the journey with cushioned seats, and "Hard," which exactly describes it. The wooden benches have extra backs which are swung up on hinges to form upper berths. Above them is a third tier for luggage. On local trains these too usually have their occupants. At every stop fresh hordes jam their way in, laden with rope-bound baskets, bags, bedding, and boxes, without which no Russian seems ever able to leave home. Windows are usually so tightly sealed that the car arrives at its destination with much the same air that it starts with.

Conditions are generally better on the through trains, as all seats in both kinds of cars are reserved. Each "Soft" car has its own porter furnishing bedding, towels, and tea. In the "Hard" cars these articles may be obtained though not always so readily. But the seasoned traveler, who wants really to understand the country, prefers to travel this way. He will have to fend for himself, sleep doubled up on a hard board, and join in the general scramble at each big station to fill his teakettle at the hot water tank. But his reward is a contact with the people he can get in no other way. He meets enthusiastic young Comsomols setting out for some big construction project in the Siberian wilderness; old bourgeoisie whispering about the terrors of life under a dictatorship; peasants hotly debating the relative merits of tractors, camels, and horses; grizzled old Tatars with high cheek-bones spreading their prayer-rugs in the corridor, indifferent to the banging, swinging train; red-kerchiefed farm women arguing the pros and cons of abortion; Red Army men going home to help in the harvesting; Stakhanovites bound for rest-homes in the Crimea or Caucasus. If one cares for none of this, he may travel *de luxe* in the International *wagon-lits* which constitute a super-class. If he can get accommodations on the new trains running to the Soviet Riviera, he will find real bedrooms, baths, a children's room with toys and games, a library, and a cocktail bar.

Among the new provisions for the convenience of the public are rest rooms and crèches in the big stations where mothers may leave their children to be bathed and fed by competent nurses and attendants. Also staffs of doctors and translators to aid the traveling Buriats, Uzbeks, Gypsies. Among the experiments in new types of transport is the "aero-train" consisting of two Zeppelin-shaped cars suspended from a single-rail track, and the "sphero-train" with its stream-lined cars running on huge motorized ball-bearings in a grooved track. But these devices belong to the future. Of importance now is the success of the railways in handling the enormous traffic and in pushing new lines to the industrial centers. Of significance politically is the rebuilding of the great bridge over the Dniester—blown up during the Revolution to prevent the advance of Bolshevism—and the resumption of train service with Rumania. The "North Express" cuts the running time from Moscow to Paris by fifteen hours. Most significant of all is the project for the strategic railway over the Carpathian mountains to Czechoslovakia.

Waterways

With these "roads that run" the Soviets are richly endowed. Of the nine largest rivers in the world, four are in Siberia. The steamer route on the Irtish and the Ob is longer than from Liverpool to New York. But for the most part sluggish and emptying into the Arctic, these rivers are as yet commercially insignificant compared to the Volga. Running through the heart of the old Russian land, this artery with its thousand tributary rivers and lakes forms one of the greatest water systems in the world. Unfortunately the Volga empties into the land-locked Caspian with no outlet to the oceans. Fortunately, at one point in its course, it flows only a short distance from the river Don, and all that is needed is a 70-kilometer canal to unite the two rivers. This was one of the dreams of Tsar Peter and Catherine the Great. Now this canal is being dug and presently Volga steamers, towed by tractors through its 13 locks, will sail down to the Black Sea and into the Atlantic.

By another project over an artificial lake uniting the headwaters of the Kama and the Pechora, they will sail North to the Arctic. By still another, lifting them over the Ural mountains to join the Tom and Tobol, they will enter the great river system of Siberia. And there are still more grandiose plans for the future. But to turn from them to what the Second Five-Year Plan actually accomplished. The Dnieper whose swiftest rapids were eliminated by the great dam was opened to sea-going ships. The Baltic-White Sea Canal was dug through to Archangel, shortening the stormy seventeen-day voyage around Norway, to six days by way of the quiet forests and fenlands of Karelia; South from Ivanako on the upper reaches of the Volga, armies of dredgers and dynamiters razing 124 villages and forcing rivers into new channels, constructed an 80-mile canal, supplying Moscow with a billion gallons of water a day and transforming it into an inland port. By 1940, through the elimination of silted channels and sandbars, the illumination of fairways and the building of sluices, flood-gates and dams, 80,000 miles of waterways will be navigable day and night for deep-draft vessels. The blast of their sirens will be heard in the heart of the Soviet capital as they set forth to the principal cities of the Soviet Union, to the five Russian seas, and the oceans beyond.

The expansion of maritime shipping, begun in the Second Five-Year Plan, is to increase geometrically in the Third. Capital construction is going on from semi-tropic Batumi to Murmansk, which is the most northerly port and at the same time ice-free the year round. Over a billion rubles is now being expended in deepening harbors, building jetties, lighthouses, ore- and oil-loading wharves. Upon the Black Sea and from Hamburg and London to Leningrad regular Soviet lines are in operation. Timber-carriers, no longer confining their visits to Archangel, follow the Northern Sea Route to the new ports at the mouth of the Arctic rivers. Big freighters go through to Vladivostok. The Far East has its "marine express." While the tonnage of the Soviet merchant fleet counts less than five per cent in the world total it is rapidly growing and over half of Soviet sea-borne freight is now carried under the Sickle and Hammer.

The Soviets are now building their own liners and tankers up to 12,000 tons. The shipyards are turning out all kinds of craft from electric-boats and "river trams" to powerful ice-breakers like the *Krassin* that rescued the Nobile expedition. For studying of the Polar regions a non-magnetic ship has been designed, its iron parts replaced with copper, bronze, and aluminum in order to eliminate any pull on the compass. From the bottom of seas and rivers, "the graveyard" of hundreds of ships sunken in the civil war, the Salvage Trust has raised many by fastening pontoons, filling them with air, and lifting them to the top. Most Soviet-built ships have A-1 rating at Lloyd's. They are reasonably clean and comfortable, but, like all forms of Soviet transport, generally overcrowded. The "Old Man" of the ship is frequently a young man and sometimes a woman. A spirit of camaraderie between officers and crew does not seem to preclude a discipline that is effective.

Airways

A fast-growing network of airlines is annihilating the barriers of space and linking the far reaches of the land with the center. Most of the trunk lines from Moscow to Tiflis, to Tashkent, to Alma-Ata, are up to 3,000 miles in length. From Minsk by way of Vladivostok to Kamchatka, it is 8,000 miles—twice the distance from London to India. From 70 hours by water or 12 by rail, the journey from Moscow to Gorky has been cut to 4 by airplane. Similar reduction has been effected in travel time between all the principal cities within the Soviet borders and beyond. Regularly the swift liners of the air set forth to Berlin, to Paris, to Praha, to Persia, and over the high peaks of the Pamirs into Afghanistan. The capacity of the airways carrying in 1936 some 165,000 passengers, 35,000 tons of mail and freight is to be more than doubled in the Third Five-Year Plan. Even now the Soviets have one of the largest air fleets in the world, all home built except for some of the engines.

"Soviet planes, both in construction and performance, are up to American standards," says Thomas Morgan, President of the Curtiss-Wright Corporation. "The institutions and shops for research and study are equal in quality and far surpass in size anything abroad . . . because they have the whole resources of the State at their disposal. Engineers and designers have an opportunity for experimental work that no private company could afford." From this has come a vast variety of aircraft designed to meet Russian conditions: Polar planes with engines that will operate freely at 40 degrees below zero; amphibians with retractable gears and wings, capable of alighting on land, water, snow, or ice; dirigibles, rigid, semi-rigid, and non-rigid, to be used on the route connecting the cities of Central Asia; "sky-trains," consisting of a "locomotive" plane towing three to seven passenger or freight-laden gliders which can be uncoupled and go gliding down to the earth.

Of regular planes there are a series of types usually constructed of stainless steel and welded by electricity. They range in size from the diminutive "sky-fleas" and the Stal-2, called the "Ford of the Sky," to the Ant-14, powered by five engines and carrying 36 passengers. The new twelve-passenger Ant-35 maintains a cruising speed of 225 miles an hour. Biggest monoplane in the Soviet Union—and in the world—was the *Maxim Gorky* which crashed in 1935. Equipped for blind flying in fog and darkness, and driven by eight motors, it could cruise for 1,500 miles without refueling. It carried a broadcasting set, movies, photo-laboratory, and a rotary press for turning out 8,000 two-page leaflets an hour. Dubbed the "flying printshop," it went on propaganda campaigns from town to town sending down its "voice from the sky" through a loud-speaker and showering leaflets on its way. Immediately after the crash began a campaign for building another by popular subscription. So enthusiastic was the response that sixteen of these air giants are being built, each of them driven by six engines of 7,000 more horsepower and with cabins for 70 passengers.

In the employment of specialized planes in such fields as forestry and agriculture the Soviets are easily first in the world. Hydroplanes are used for the swift transport of living "fish-seed" to the fishless inland lakes. Ski-shod planes maintain winter service with the ice-bound ports of Siberia, bringing out valuable furs to the market. Ambulance planes hurry the fever-stricken and wounded from remote places to the hospitals. In the far-off steppes and forests the natives crouch in terror before the monstrous "dragon-flies" suddenly swooping down on them from the sky, "the birds with iron beaks and flapless wings." They may be the scouting planes of distant flights of scientific expeditions. Or surveying planes with cameras charting the routes of new roads over the mountains. Or "malaria" planes spraying the breeding-nests of mosquitoes with arsenic. Or gas planes raising barrages against the locust armies swarming up from the South to ravage the crops. Or rescue planes such as saved the American aviator Mattern, stranded in the North and brought the body of Eielson to Alaska. Flying high in the Arctic, airplanes spy out the dark spots on the ice, the resting places of the seal herds—and, through the open channels, guide ships to them. Flying low in the Kuban, they sprinkle the rice swamps with seed.

This method of sowing from the air is being extended to other seeds that do not demand insertion in the soil or evenness in cast. Thus sown with the drought-resisting sand oats, stretches of arid deserts from the Volga down to Kazakhstan are being turned into green pastures; the grazing meadows on the mountains enriched with new grasses—alfalfa, timothy, and clover. In the grain regions, where wet fields hitherto held back the early planting, rye and wheat sprayed from "seeder"-planes, sinks into the soft muddy ground to benefit by the moisture once sucked away by sun and wind. With a sowing spray 65-feet wide, flying at a speed of 60 miles an hour, a plane can seed 1,200 acres in a day and in some cases the harvest yield is ten per cent above normal. However this method of sowing grains from the air is as yet largely experimental.

"Through the air to the conquest of nature and all the enemies of man." With this objective the Institute of Aerodynamics pushes its researches into ever new fields. For the frost-endangered zones it has tried spreading smoke clouds over orchards and gardens. For the drouth-stricken areas it experiments in bringing rain from the skies. For the flood-stricken regions there is a project to prevent the spring inundations that follow the sudden thawing of snow. Aircraft would anticipate the action of the spring sun by sprinkling the mountain snows with black coal dust to attract the sun's heat and with salt to further aid in the melting. Instead of coming with a rush, the waters would then come gradually and under control.

But, from these somewhat fantastic visions of the future, to return again to actual accomplishments: Planes are used for forest survey-ing and patrol over 40 million acres of land; for control of devastat-ing steppe fires by laying in front of them obstructive zones of flame-killing chemicals like caustic soda; for hurrying fodder to cattle, sud-denly blizzard-bound on the ranges; for dropping tents and supplies to mountain-climbers and to victims of earthquakes and floods; for rushing matrices of the Moscow *Pravda* and *Izvestia* to other cities so that these papers can appear in the provinces on the same day they do in the capital. Every winter they come to the rescue of fisher-men swept out to sea as they did to the Chelyuskin castaways on the drifting ice-floes of the Arctic.

The intense popular interest in aviation is attested by the scores of schools for training amateur airmen, the 160 Air Clubs, 2,000 gliding "circles," and a half-million children engaged in aircraft modeling. Parachute-jumping is a mass sport with some 500 "circles" and over 1,000 high towers for training novices. To the air festivals come squadrons of planes, autogiros, glider "air-trains," balloons, and dirigibles. After the tail spins, loop-the-loops, and side-slips of the stunting aviators, follow battleplanes forming against the blue the letters USSR and five-rayed stars, or scattering on the crowds "bombs" of flowers and "gas" clouds of perfumes. From other planes, musicians playing on their instruments and dogs trained for military service, come floating down in parachute baskets. Then diving into space go a hundred dark figures changing to white, red, and yellow as their multi-colored parachutes open behind them and come drifting down to earth. Among the world records in high altitude and delayed jumping are those of six women leaping from planes four and a half miles high. To them is given much the same acclaim as the famous aviators Levanevsky, Molokov, Kokkinaki, Vodopyanov, Chkalov. Those who have flown a million kilometers are called "millionaires" of the air and decorated with the Order of the Red Banner.

Likewise in the realm of "pure" science Soviet aviation has scored considerable successes. A sky-rocket is designed to travel 2,200 feet a second and, on reaching its "ceiling" 20 miles high, to release and send back the scientific instruments it carries. The stratostat *USSR* climbed to 60,332 feet and another that crashed in landing attained an altitude of 70,000 feet. Further flights will continue to explore the possibilities of super-speed air routes in the stratosphere. But while the Soviet Union soars bravely in the air, it limps badly on its roads.

Roads

"What in all the world," asked the eminent historian Kluchevsky, "could be more dilatory or tortuous than the Russian road?" True, under the Tsar there were a few first-class *chaussées,* the excellent military roads leading over the Caucasus, and remnants of the Great Stone Way over which the hordes of Genghis Khan advanced on Europe. But these are brilliant exceptions. "The real curse of the land," says Grinko, "is its roads." A chief reason for this is the scarcity of stone. Out of a total of 2,000,000 miles, not five per cent are hard-surfaced. The rest, consisting largely of ruts, pitfalls, muck-holes, and mires, are fearfully and wonderfully made. Rather, they are self-made

—mere tracks picked out along the higher, drier places by the first driver to venture forth after the spring floods, or, if he is drunk, by the horse. They go zigzagging through meadows, tunnel into dense forests, lose themselves in bogs and quagmires, bob up again in a rye-field. As the peasants cynically remark, "You may travel on them forty days, but you won't get anywhere."

Like his other afflictions, the peasant takes his roads philosophically. "*Nichevo*," he says. "Why worry? They will be all right in winter." And they are. The deep snow makes smooth and easy-going the worst-rutted roads, their routes now marked out by branches torn from the trees. The heavy frosts transform the rivers and streams into boulevards macadamized with ice, along which caravans of camels and horses travel into the farthest reaches of the land. Most of the peasants' vehicles were very primitive. The runners of his sledges were wooden, the wagons wooden-axled, clumsy and exhausting to horses and oxen. From animal transport the Soviets are turning now to motor transport. Increasingly gasoline and electricity are furnishing the energy once derived from grass and oats.

In the output of tractors the Soviets stand first in the world but they have only about a million automobiles as against over twenty million in America. The Stalin Works is now turning out 70,000 cars annually and is to more than double its output in the Third Five-Year Plan. The Gorky plant modeled after the Ford plant in River Rouge is to increase its production to over 300,000 cars a year. But where are the roads to run them on? To this query the Russian rejoinder is that autos came first in America, then roads. To direct their building is one of the functions of the Commissariat of Internal Affairs which utilizes large numbers of prisoners it has in its keeping. Over 200 schools are training road-builders, drivers, and mechanics. New types of vehicles are being tried out on grueling test runs, like the one from Moscow through the Kara Kum desert to the Pamir mountains and back again.

Among the new devices are trucks with generators for converting wood into gas, invaluable where the great forests furnish an abundance of fuel. The half-track autos, built for the deep sands of the desert, run on two rubber tracks, laid down like "caterpillars," by rollers. These swift "mechanized camels of the desert," as they are called, may in time entirely replace the slow-moving caravans on the ancient trade routes of the South. As they operate as well on snow and ice-fields of the Arctic, along with the new aero- and auto-sledges, they may also drive out the reindeer and dog teams from the frozen regions of the North.

Since the foreign tourist seldom visits these far places, he does not lament their passing. But he does regret the passing from the cities of the old *izvoschik,* in huge padded and skirted greatcoat, perched high on a tiny sleigh, or rattling over the cobblestones in his rickety swaying cab. He was an intrinsic part of the old Russian life— humorous, good-natured, a lover of vodka, haggling a half hour over a ruble, spicing his jests with those rich mother-oaths of which he was a great connoisseur. Now he is rapidly disappearing from the scene. From 10,000 in pre-Revolution Moscow, their number has dwindled to a few score. A similar change is going on all over the land. Taxis and trolley-buses are in the ascendant. Cobblestones give way to asphalt. The few cities under the Tsar with street-car service, mostly horse-drawn cars, have grown to more than sixty. Auto-buses have penetrated into the ancient walled cities of Asia and into the mountains beyond. Instead of climbing for days with ox-carts and water buffaloes the Tajiks and Caucasians now shoot up to their homes in the hills in a few hours. To the foreigner this is not so picturesque and exotic. But it is to the natives—also it is more comfortable and exhilarating.

43. What is the Rôle of Science in Developing the Economic Life of the Country?

"Science is the servant and handmaid of industry." "If the arts are impressed into the service of Socialism how much more should science be directed to that end." "We are facing the fortress of science and at all costs we must capture it." (Stalin) "Science is the savior of humanity." These citations show the Soviet conception of the functions of science. Like everything else in the country it is assigned a definite part in building the new society. Just as the Labor Unions are to mobilize the forces of labor, science is to mobilize the forces of nature and to harness them for the well-being of man. So it does, one remarks, in other countries. In the Soviet Union it is done more consciously, on a vaster scale and in a highly organized manner.

To begin with, the directing brain of all scientific work in the country—the All-Union Academy of Science—is a part of the State apparatus. It is attached to the Council of People's Commissars, and, in order to make the alliance as close as possible, it is now located in Moscow. To house it there is now rising near the Lenin Hills an imposing complex of laboratories with a fire-proof library for eight million volumes. This center serves as consultant, clearing-house, and court of appeals. It receives and correlates the reports from the Academies of Science in White Russia, Georgia, Armenia, and other republics. It coordinates the activities of the 50,000 workers in science and the network of research institutes and stations, the mere cataloguing of which runs into pages: Arctic, Artificial Rain, Agro-Soil, Aerodynamics; Brains, Bees, Beans, Botanical; Chemical, Camels, Ceramics, City Planning; and so on down the alphabet to X-ray, "Yarovization," Zoological. To list them all one would have to run through the alphabet forty-six times. Most of them are adjuncts of specific industries and trusts carrying on research in their behalf. Engaged in the solution of urgent problems of the present, they are predominantly utilitarian. "As the Marxist studies society with the aim of affecting it, he studies science with the aim of utilizing it." This in no way precludes concern for abstract and abstruse research, the fruits of which may not be tangible until twenty, fifty, or a hundred years hence. In evidence thereof is the work of Frumkin in chemistry, Joffe in physics, Pavlov in physiology, Muller in genetics.

To the Communists there is no valid distinction between pure and applied science. All knowledge, every secret wrested from nature can be made use of, sooner or later. As fast as feasible new discoveries are tested in practice, often on a huge scale. Thus theory is closely related to life and linked up with reality. Venerable mathematicians are consulted on the designing of supertankers, high-speed steels, and high-tension wires. To its botanists, historians, sociologists, philosophers, orientologists, the formerly somewhat ivory-towered Academy of Science adds some twenty eminent engineers and technicians. Thus, in the words of Karpinsky, who was its president for twenty years, "Socialist construction and science become component parts of a single whole." By airplanes it sends expeditions to the far reaches of the land, by sledges into the Arctic wastes, by camel caravans into the Southern deserts, by balloons into heights of the stratosphere, by submarines to survey the bottoms of the seas. On big building projects such as dams, it establishes its own observation quarters. Geologists watch out for traces of minerals in the borings and blastings; archaeologists for clues to the historic past of the region before it is flooded with water. In the Volga city of Uglich great care is taken to preserve the thousand-year-old monuments of Russian architecture, and where that is impossible exact models are made before they are inundated.

From the wide-flung network of bases and branches reports are constantly relayed to headquarters. It analyzes and classifies the incoming data, fills in the gaps, strives to avoid lag and overlapping. Most important of all, unless some weighty reason of state intervenes, it makes the newly acquired facts accessible to all. This can be done freely because the socialization of property eliminates fears of rival concerns stealing new ideas and inventions and exploiting them to their own profit. With no monopolies or private interests to safeguard, there are no secrets to be confined in laboratories, no patents to be locked up in corporation vaults, no barriers to the free circulation of findings. This is an inestimable boon to the scientist. No longer need he work in isolation nor in ignorance of what others are doing. He can know exactly what his colleagues are doing in every field and can call on them for assistance. This is in keeping with the demands of modern research for concerted effort. Doubtless in the past great discoveries have been made by brilliant individuals. But even geniuses like Einstein and Edison were heavily indebted to the work of hosts of investigators, their contemporaries as well as their predecessors. This will be more so in the future. With the increasing complexity of problems the great triumphs will be achieved through the synthesis of many minds. This is secured by the Soviet system of planning in which science, like everything else, is planned. It makes for unified effort, the concentration of many specialists on a single problem, the collaboration of the whole corps of scientific workers.

To this is added the collaboration of the whole people. Just as the Communists assiduously seek to enlist the interest and enthusiasm of the masses in statecraft and construction, so they do in matters of research, invention, and exploration. Chiseled on the façade of the Moscow University is the legend, "Science to the Toilers." To this end even the most eminent savants visit the factories to lecture on hydrodynamics or the splitting of the atom, and work together with the Stakhanovites in improving technical processes. The Academy of Science goes on visiting sessions to big industrial centers like the Urals and the oil city of Baku. In tens of thousands the workers crowd into its public meetings. In hundreds of thousands they study the rudiments of science in "circles" in clubs, the Red Army, and collectives. In the new Socialist cities almost every block has a special room fitted out with test tubes, chemicals, and retorts. In the villages, "laboratory cottages" aid the farmers in testing the seeds of grains and weeds, poisons for field pests, the breeding of plants and animals. The Societies of Young Naturalists train the youth in the use of simple instruments—the drill, compass, and barometer. Thus, besides the fifty thousand to whom science is a vocation, there are millions to whom it is an avocation.

In these ways is being carried into effect that "alliance between labor and science," proclaimed by Lenin the first days of the Revolution. It was not just a democratic gesture, but rose from his deep faith in the creative power of the masses. And it has been justified. From the workers each year come tens of thousands of suggestions and inventions. From their journeys to the glaciers, deserts, and forests, vacationists bring back useful plants and minerals. New ideas are coming even out of the Children's Technical Station where the talents of the future generation of scientists are stimulated by contacts with the leading engineers, agronomists, and chemists of the community. In turn these scientific tutors of the people—not excluding the eminent academicians—are their beneficiaries. They in turn come in contact with new ideas, materials, and problems—fresh angles of looking at things which lift them out of their accustomed grooves. Out of the rank-and-file rise up gifted men pouring new blood into the world of science.

Wide vistas open out to Soviet science, thanks to this cooperation of the masses, the unified system, the almost limitless funds at its disposal, and the vast terrain it has to operate in. Over against these advantages outside critics set a great minus—"Soviet science is put in the procrustean bed of Marxian methods." To the Communists that is emphatically not a minus but a great plus. To them Marxism is the perfect instrument for science, the dialectical method—dynamic rather than static and mechanistic—the fundamentally correct one. The references to "red biology," "red physics," "red astronomy" do not imply that somehow under Socialism science is subjected and obedient to different laws than elsewhere. They serve rather to emphasize the organic relationship between the work of the scientists and the continuously evolving society; to keep them aware of their unique position and tremendous powers to effect changes, affect environment and so accelerate the processes of evolution; to remind them of the human and social responsibility laid upon them even in their most abstract studies and experiments. In vindication of the methods pursued by Soviet scientists they can point to an imposing array of solid achievements, especially in the realm of practice and technics.

How Soviet Scientists Obtained Rubber—Natural and Synthetic

In 1931 Stalin said, "We have every natural resource in our country but rubber." At the same time there was a large and fast-increasing demand for it. Industry was using ever greater amounts of rubber for belts and tubing. Transportation was shifting from wooden wagons and ox-carts to pneumatic-tired autos and trucks. The markets were clamoring for more rubber for raincoats, footgear, sanitary and contraceptive devices. In tens of thousands of tons the Soviets were importing it from abroad. This not only put a heavy burden upon the exchequer, but in event of war or blockade placed the country in a most precarious position. To remedy this state of affairs the scientists were called in and commissioned to produce rubber—to grow it, to make it, to devise some substitute for it.

They found that gutta-percha trees would flourish well along the sub-tropic coast of the Black Sea. But this area was already allocated to citrus-groves, tea plantations, gardens, and villas. A more hardy plant was needed, one that could withstand the rigorous climate of the North. They experimented with different kinds of goldenrod procured from the Edison Studios in New Jersey. From Mexico they brought in thirty species of guayula, one of which proved to be fully adaptable. Searching for some plant still more resistant to cold and pests, Soviet scientists turned to their own country. Someone suggested a shrub called *hondrilla* growing somewhere in the sandy wastes and mountains of Kazakhstan. Thither they went and found the nomads chewing a gummy substance. It was not the plant they were searching for, but another called *tau-sagiz* containing rubber in the form of threads in its roots. Other explorers brought back *kok-sagiz* and *krim-sagiz,* a sort of dandelion from the vine-covered slopes of the Crimea, secreting a milky fluid which on drying coagulates into a rubber. Altogether the various expeditions collected over sixteen hundred plants, three hundred of which are latex-bearing and six of real commercial value. Fully acclimated, some of these plants hitherto unmentioned in any botanical book may now be seen in large plantations extending from Turkmenia up to the environs of Leningrad. To these may be added the nine-million acres of sunflower plantations, if the effort to utilize the elastic gum in their stalks proves profitable.

Besides natural rubber, great successes have been scored in the making of *synthetic rubber*. At first it was fabricated solely out of alcohol derived from potatoes. With an already colossal consumption of potatoes for food, starch, and vodka, their supplies are limited. But there are almost no limits to the peat-bogs of Russia. Turning to them the experimenters perfected a process for distilling alcohol from peat. Encouraged by these successes, they reached into other fields. If synthetic rubber could be made out of alcohol, why not from other substances? To this problem the Institute of Chemistry addressed itself and devised a cheap and satisfactory method of obtaining it from acetylene, derived in turn from a mixture of limestone and coal. Next they found ways of extracting it out of the waste gases of oil-refineries, then from the by-product of coking-ovens.

Continuously the search goes on for new substances. Each year they are improving the processes, getting more rubber out of less raw material. Each year they are making it more viscous, tensile, rupture-proof, and acid resisting. In tens of thousands of tons, synthetic rubber is now being produced in big plants in Yaroslavl, Krasnodar, Kremenchug, Kazan, and other places. It is being manufactured into all sorts of articles from children's toys to corrugated tires that stand up to the tests of the severest mountain and desert runs. And it is still a youthful industry, not yet ten years of age, while its 600 engineers and researchers average less than thirty. Even so they are brilliantly fulfilling the task assigned them. In their factories they are producing a rubber in some of its qualities superior to that grown in the fields, and at half the cost. They have already saved tens of millions of gold rubles in imports and freed the Soviet Union from its perilous dependence on other countries.

Other Achievements, Projects, and Institutes

The extraction of agar-agar from Arctic sea-weeds, of alcohol and sugar from discarded straw and sawdust. Reduction in the seasoning-time of tobacco from twelve months to six weeks by a process of artificial fermentation instead of natural curing. Freezing of beets so they can be stored without losing their sugar content, enabling refineries to operate the year round. Accelerating the smelting of iron by introducing oxygen blasts into furnaces. Obtaining cheap sulphur from the fumes liberated in smelting copper ores, and of radium concentrates from the waters of the Caspian Sea. Finding of the new mineral, "aurismidrid," composed of gold, osmium, and iridium; of "lovchoritt" with properties of radium. Discovery that the upper air strata of the Arctic are warmer and calmer than in temperate zones; of subterranean waters in ancient sand-drifted valleys of the arid deserts.

Invention of the atomic "divining-rod" which detects the presence of oil in the earth by its extreme sensitivity to escaping gas; of an instrument for detecting the "voice of the sea," those inaudible sound-waves made by wind and water, enabling sailors to prepare for oncoming storms; of a lighter-than-glass celluloid for hot-houses, capable of withstanding heavy rains, hail, and winds. Reviving to life grasses, insects and eggs dug out of the frozen soil of the Ice Age. Combating the virus causing paper decay and the disintegration of documents in the archives. Growing roses of all colors, including green and blue. Fabrication of "acrichin" to replace quinine in treating malaria; of composition materials to replace expensive ivory, mahogany, and tropical resin in the making of telephones, pianos, and precision instruments.

Thus from all the far-flung scientific "fronts" constantly are being reported achievements of inestimable value along with those rejected as worthless and chimerical. Like the bulletins of new natural resources from the exploring expeditions, almost daily there is the announcement of some new process or discovery coming in from the thousands of institutes, laboratories, and farm-centers. Some of these are small and of local importance. Others are colossal and world-ramifying such as the Institute of Plant Industry directed by the famous botanist-geneticist, Vavilov, and the Academy of Agricultural Science with its 200 zonal stations and 1,600 contact points. Their expeditions ranging from the Caucasus to the Andes and Himalayas have assembled 4,400 specimens of flax, 11,000 of beans, 14,000 of barley, and 31,000 of wheat, including the two parent strains—the 42-chromosome wheat of Afghanistan and the 28-chromosome of Ethiopia. "Anyone wanting to make a special study of cereals," says Julian Huxley, "must come to Leningrad, for the collection is by far the largest in existence."

Out of this enormous array of seeds and plants—by growing them in greenhouses, artificially reproducing the hot winds of the steppes or the cold of the tundras, and in the open fields of the collectives— are being selected the kinds most suitable to Soviet soil and climate. With this goes ceaseless experimentation in the creation of new varieties, more resistant to frost, drought, fungus, and pests. Crossing wheat with couch-grass produces a sturdy perennial with ears that hold the grain when shaken by the reaping machines. Vernalization, or *yarovisation*—the incubating of partially-moistened seeds before sowing—results in the early maturing and reaping of crops—a great boon in a country where summers are short. Thanks to all this harvests are growing bigger and better. Cotton moves up from the warm regions in which it once was confined. Around the Arctic Circle flourish not only the cereals but potatoes and other vegetables.

In pushing plant-growing into the North, the pioneer was Michurin who toiled away in his garden almost unrecognized until discovered by Lenin in 1922. "We must not wait for the favors of nature," he said. "We must wrest them from her." By hybridization of remote strains, he produced 300 hardy new berries, nuts, vegetables, and succulent fruits—plums as big as duck-eggs, currants the size of marbles, cherries in clusters like grapes. The pride of his heart was a peach-tree which by cross-breeding with a wild almond developed such Spartan qualities that it flourishes at 50 degrees below zero. In the city and institute of horticulture now bearing his name the work of this "Soviet Burbank" in plant mutation is carried on by a host of successors.

While they are adapting vegetation to the climate, the Institute of Experimental Meteorology seeks to adapt the climate to vegetation. It has caused rain to fall in Ashkhabad, the dryest spot in the country, by sprinkling passing clouds with chemicals from airplanes. Thick low-lying mists have been generated for the blanketing of sub-tropic crops threatened by frost. Another weather-changing scheme on a colossal scale emanates from the Institute of Oceanography. It is the damming of the narrows between Sakhalin Island and the Siberian mainland in order to deflect the cold Japanese current into the Pacific and raise the temperature of the whole Far East region. But such projects for altering the climate of a continent, like the general utilization of synthetic weather, belong to the far distant future. So far the most notable advances in this realm have been made along less spectacular lines: by the creation of lakes and water-basins in the arid steppes and deserts and of wooded zones serving as barriers to the parching winds of the South; by moisture-conserving devices like "checkerboarding" the fields—clearing the snow from alternate patches so that the waters, instead of quickly running off in the spring thaw, are held back and sink into the earth; through improvement in the technique of weather forecasting, which aids in the timing of planting, reaping, and the migrations of flocks and herds to the grass plains and mountains.

In the field of animal husbandry there are some 260 institutes and stations. At the Askania Nova Game Preserve, covering 80,000 acres, extensive work goes on in acclimatization and hybridization. The crossing of the zubro-bison with the gray Ukrainian cows results in doubling the yield of milk. The crossing of the Astrakhan and Romanoff sheep produces three lambs instead of one a year. By the injection of certain chemicals into sheep much longer wool is obtained in a much shorter time than by the old method of shearing. Pigs are fattened through artificial anemia produced by bleeding. The quantity of eggs from hens and milk from cows and goats is increased by feeding them lysates. The keeping of bees is being introduced into the sub-Polar regions where under the long summer daylight the river meadows break forth in a riot of flowers. Most valuable to the country as a whole is the artificial impregnation of cattle and horses with the spermatozoa of pure bred males. Carried in test tubes to the remotest regions, it is effecting a noticeable improvement in the quality of livestock everywhere.

The chief stations of the Institute of Seismology are located in the four special earthquake areas—the Caucasus, Turkestan, Lake Baikal, and the island of Sakhalin. Besides observing "pure" earthquakes and the recording of shocks by radio it designs quake-proof houses and schools. It measures the effects of blasting in mines and quarries and of traffic vibrations on buildings and bridges. It registers the air-waves from cannonading which leads to the detection of the location of big guns. It conducts gravimetric surveying with instruments delicately sensitized to the slightest change in gravity, revealing the presence of mineral lodes and the strange changes in gravitation in the Caucasus, presumably caused by shifting of enormous masses of matter in the depths of the earth.

One may mention the work of Gurevich in mitogenetic rays radiated by plants and living organisms, capable of stimulating the growth of others; the work of Skobeltyzn on cosmic rays; of Alkhanov and others on the positron, X-ray and photoelectricity. Quite obvious are the functions of the Institute of the Steppes, the Institute for Training Dogs, the Institute of Radium, of Fuel, of Fisheries, Flax, and Hemp, Silk-Worms. But to deal with all of them even sketchily would require a whole book. In fact, while confining himself largely to the institutes attached to the Commissariat of Heavy Industry, J. G. Crowther in "Soviet Science" has produced a large-sized volume. Pointing out that individuals and groups are given laboratories and facilities to carry out investigations in their chosen fields, he goes on to state that "planning is not conceived as merely an efficient system of issuing orders to a corps of scientists. One of its objects is to enable gifted persons to persevere and develop to the utmost their ideas and skill."

In connection with the Third Five-Year Plan to the Academy of Science are assigned the following ten key problems:

To establish scientific methods of prospecting for minerals, especially tin, rare metals, and oil so as to reduce blind prospecting to a minimum.

To create a unified electric power system with high voltage transmission.

To extend the exploitation of the gas resources.

To study new types of fuel for internal combustion engines.

To rationalize technological processes in chemistry and metallurgy.

To give a scientific basis for fulfilling the task set by Stalin of increasing the grain harvest to 8 million *poods*—130 million metric tons—annually.

To give a scientific basis for the development of animal husbandry and fisheries.

To develop telemechanics—long distance control of machinery—and extend automatic processes in industry and transport.

To establish a scientific method for drawing the balance sheet of the national economy from the point of view of both economics and technique.

To study the history of the peoples of the U.S.S.R., especially the former subject nationalities.

44. What Are the Functions of the Labor Unions?

As an organic part of the Soviet system, they do not have to fight for "recognition." On the contrary, all the influence of the State is exerted to get every worker into them. The Labor Code compels all enterprises to deal directly and solely with the Unions. The best buildings, from the old columned Hall of the Nobles in Moscow to the new steel-and-glass structures in the Far East, are assigned to their use. The Union card brings preference and privileges in the form of places in rest homes, entry into parks and clubs, free legal advice.

The result is the biggest organization of labor in the world. While less than a fifth of wage and salary earners are enrolled in the craft unions of America, more than nine-tenths are enrolled in the industrial unions of the Soviets. There is a Union of Workers in the Gold and Platinum Industry, in Precision Instrument Enterprises, in the Heavy Engineering Industry. Likewise there is one Union embracing all persons engaged in Forestry and Rafting, on Fur and Poultry Farms, on Tea and Sub-tropic Plantations, in the Arctic, in Cinema studios, in Book-stores, and so on through a list of about 170 Unions, enrolling some 25,000,000 members.

As far back as 1922, Lenin described the function of the Unions. They were to be a training-school for Communism—"a school of association, a school of solidarity, a school of defense of their own interests, a school of management, a school of administration." That was the task given the Labor Unions to do. And they did it. For more than a decade they drilled and educated the millions who poured into them with the aim of preparing them to direct all their own affairs. By 1933 the time was deemed ripe for them to do so. The Commissariat of Labor was abolished outright, and all its functions were handed over to the Unions.

The Unions themselves now draft the laws and regulations about working conditions. They appoint the inspectors who see that the measures for health and safety are carried through. They enforce the contracts between themselves and the management. They administer the eight-billion-ruble fund insuring themselves against accident, illness, and old age. Finally, on the planning boards, they help determine what part of the national income shall come to them in wages. In return for these prerogatives the Unions assume certain obligations. Chief of these is the raising of the general level of production. On this, as Lenin and the other leaders after him so often repeated, depends the triumph of the new social order. "As feudalism gave way to capitalism, because it created a higher productivity of labor, so in turn capitalism must give way to socialism because it will create a still higher productivity." For achieving this the responsibility must rest primarily upon the workers themselves. In effect, the State says to them, "If you want more goods, make more." To this end the Unions are organized, and in the Labor Code that is precisely what they are called—Productive Unions.

At the same time the Unions have not renounced their protective and fighting functions. They are not, as critics contend, simply organs for regimenting the workers so they will passively carry out the policies of the State. They take an active and continuous part in the creation of these policies as well as in the execution of them. In the determination of the wage-fund, how much is necessary for the several industries and Unions? What shall be the proportion between cash wages and "socialized wages"—cultural and medical services, rest homes, clubs, insurance? How much shall go to the hand- and bench-workers, machinists, gold-diggers, the tenders of looms and lathes? How much to the brain- and desk-workers—the accountants, book-keepers, clerks, typists? How shall the collective contracts with the trusts and combines be drawn up and enforced? What rates shall be fixed for piece-work, overtime, night work? All these are the subject of heated debates, clashes, and conflicts.

At the same time there are all sorts of boards, councils, and commissions for the adjustment of differences. If there is a juris-dictional dispute between Unions it is usually settled by the Central Committee of all the Unions. If a protest arises against a dismissal or piece-rates, it comes before a joint conciliation board of employees and employer. If that fails, it goes to an arbitration commission. If that fails, it goes to a higher one. Beyond that a strike is theoretically possible. But, that practically never occurs because the workers know that they would be striking against themselves. They know their welfare and income, in the last analysis, depends upon the aggregate amount of wealth in the country, and on that alone. Therefore their struggle in the main is *not for greater share in production, but for a greater production in which to share.* That is the chief difference between Soviet Labor Unions and those in other lands. With the slogan, "Eyes on Production," they strive by every means to raise the output of labor through their Production Conferences, Shock-Brigades, and "Stakhanovites."

45. What is the Cause of the Low Productivity of the Russians—and Its Cure?

The output under the Tsars, and for a long time under the Soviets, was appallingly low. The peasant got from the soil almost the poorest crops in the world, while the efficiency of the Russian worker was about a quarter of that of the French or British. Of course there were exceptions, but as late as 1930

General Haskell was saying, "I estimated that on every construction job there were twice as many persons as would be on a similar American project, and even then it required twice as long to finish." Such observations are not confined to outsiders. More often and more caustically the Soviet leaders themselves are pointing them out. The building chief Ginsberg demonstrated with charts that the output of Russian quarry and structural workers was way below Western levels. In his 1936 address to the directors of heavy industries, Ordjonikidze compared a certain American plant with a Soviet plant which was quite as well equipped. "With a third the number of workers they have an output three times higher than ours. Don't boast, Comrades. If you want to surpass America you must make a study of this America. At the present time, if you please, labor productivity over there is twice as high as in our country."

A primary cause of low Soviet output has been the tremendous influx of untrained labor into the industries. During 1928-32 they absorbed 12,500,000 new workers, two-thirds of whom came from the steppes and villages. Not in a day or a year could peasants and nomads be transformed into mechanics. To begin with, unlike Americans, they had no predilection for work in itself. "Work is not a bear," says an old adage; "it will not run away to the forest." This attitude in the peasants came in part from centuries of exploitation. Why should they work hard when so much of the fruits of their labor was taken by the landlords and tax-gatherers? It was due also to the long winters which enforced long periods of idleness and to the ninety Saint-days and fêtes of the church, in which the peasant considered it his duty to loaf and get drunk. This does not imply that at times he could not exert himself prodigiously, especially in plowtime and harvest. But industry cannot run on sporadic efforts. It demands steady sustained effort all day long and all the year round. It calls for entirely different qualities from those ingrained in the peasant through life in the fields. Small wonder that he could not at once adapt himself to the routine and exacting demands of the shut-in mines and factories. Accustomed to regulate his comings and goings by the sun, it irked him to punch a time-clock and follow the screech of a whistle.

Rebelling against these restraints, he wandered off, not only to seek a better job or food, but to gain a respite, to see new places. The result was a colossal turnover of labor, rising in some plants to a hundred per cent or more, and reaching its zenith in the spring. Then, in answer to the age-old elemental pull of the soil, came a mass exodus to the villages.

Even those who took readily to the factories could not at once master the strange new contrivances that filled them. Accustomed to the primitive ox-cart, the plow, and the sickle, the peasant had suddenly to adjust himself to the swift tempo, complexity, and precision of the machine. Instead of wooden axles with as much as a two-inch play, he had to handle metal lathes demanding accuracy down to the thousandth part of an inch. Instead of a go-as-you-please existence in which he stopped his horse to smoke or talk to a neighbor, he had now to keep up with a never-stopping conveyor belt. Instead of living by the rule of thumb he found himself in an assembly room where the right tool had to be in the right place at the right moment. No wonder the newcomers often stood in awestruck bewilderment before the array of rods, pistons, and belts. But if they were lacking in knowledge they were not lacking in curiosity. With childlike naïveté they wanted to know "what made the wheels go round," and often stalled them. They wanted to know how hard the trip-hammer would hit, and cracked it. They wanted to see how fast the engine would run, and smashed it. Having mastered one machine they often were eager to try another. This inquisitive nature was promise of future inventions, and has resulted in many. But it has been costly for the new plants, taking a heavy toll in stoppage, spoilage, and breakage.

Out of these facts, foreigners, especially the Germans, have waxed sarcastic over the mechanical ineptness and stupidity of the Russian masses, their congenital unfitness to build an industrial civilization. That, of course, was simply the expression of race superiority. The peasants could not operate the machines for the simple reason that they were not brought up with them. Even so, they have sometimes shown a remarkable aptitude. Such an instance was cited to me just after the Revolution by Rodzianko, the old President of the Tsar's Duma. To his estate had come a French engineer to install a complicated pump. Try as he would he could not make it go, and in despair he went off to telegraph Paris for instructions. On coming back, the old mujik who had been helping him asked, "Will Your Excellency allow me to try to put it together?" The Frenchman smiled his assent, and with the greatest confidence the mujik proceeded to set it up. To the astonishment of all, it ran. To the query why he had been so sure he could do it, he replied, "When you went out, I tried it my own way and the devil ran all right. But I took it apart again because I feared Your Excellency would be angry."

As to the skill and competence of the old guard of mechanics, foreign engineers have paid whole-hearted tribute. "Like the Russian soldier, there is no better worker in the world if he is rightly led." Unfortunately that leadership was woefully lacking during the first years of construction. Thousands of the best Communist engineers, technicians, and foremen perished in the Revolution. I knew sixteen of these well, half of whom had been technically trained in America. They were at once idealists and stern realists, the incarnation of the dynamic spirit of the Revolution. Springing from the masses and whole-mindedly sharing their hopes and dreams, they were eminently fitted to act as their tutors, instructors, and guides. They would have worked for the new order as valiantly as they fought for it. But they all perished, fighting the Allied armies of intervention, assassinated by the Whites, or dying of typhus and cholera. It was a holocaust of the most capable keymen of industry. Another large group, comprising some of the best of the old engineers, ran away from the Revolution. Many who remained, embittered by the restrictions imposed upon them by the Soviets, and resenting the control of the factories by the workers, held themselves aristocratically aloof and disdainful. The workers in turn, distrusting their integrity, were prone to carry on long arguments rather than carry out their orders. They resented being taught by those who really didn't care to teach.

Nevertheless there were not a few managers, engineers, and foremen who loyally, painstakingly, and successfully sought to impart their knowledge and skill to the new workers. But if the number had been tenfold greater it would have been inadequate to instruct and drill the millions of raw recruits thronging into industry.

With all these handicaps the Soviets had to contend in their double task of expanding industries swiftly and at the same time training the men to run them.

Transforming Green Peasants into Seasoned Workers

In building some of the giant new plants many speed records were broken. In 1928 camels and bullocks were plowing the brown steppes beyond Stalingrad. Two years later the land was covered with miles of glass and concrete structures with a capacity for 50,000 tractors a year. Still faster time was made in building the tractor plant at Kharkov. "Of all the jobs I ever did none required so much construction in a single year," said Leon Swajian, chief engineer from Ford's plant at River Rouge. "In America we did not build giant factories all at once—it meant tying up too much capital. But in the U.S.S.R., with government financing and no other plants from which to buy spare parts, the whole plant had to be built at once, and swiftly. It was really the wonderful enthusiasm of the Ukrainians that did it. Out of Kharkov, seven miles away, came the volunteers by train, bus, and afoot. Girls, women, policemen, pioneer children, and professors, up to 2,000 every day, gave their free days to do unpaid work. We used them for digging, loading, and carting away debris—for which we could never have found sufficient labor otherwise."

Though enthusiasm might build tractor plants, it took more than that to run them. So Stalingrad discovered, when out of the quiet fields it called the peasants into its clanging factory. They came bringing their wives, children, and samovars with them—likewise the slow habits and moods inbred in their minds and bodies by centuries of life on the land. As a result there was much spoiling of materials, smashing of expensive machines, and, instead of a hundred tractors a day—one, and a bad one at that.

What seemed to foreign experts an insoluble problem, the Communists and the Labor Unions chose to treat as "growing pains"—an inevitable accompaniment of development—and they mobilized all forces to heal the breaches. To attach the worker to the plant, he would be asked to pledge to stick to his job for the duration of the Five-Year Plan or at least for a year. The perpetual rover flitting from one place to another was branded a "grasshopper," and a picture of that insect was affixed to his Union card. Norms of output were fixed, with premiums, and bonuses for exceeding them. To create the feeling that they were all joint owners of the plant, there were mass-meetings and conferences in which everyone from water-boy up to Red Director threshed out their common problems together. A technical school was established with 1,200 youths alternating a day of instruction with a day of shop-work, and 2,500 more receiving short courses in engineering. By scores of devices the factory papers raised the general morale of the workers, stimulated their best efforts, awed them with cartoons of the "camel." The camels, to be driven from the fields by the tractors, naturally appeared rejoicing and kicking up their heels when the stream of tractors stopped or faltered. Upon the doors of the shops that fell behind their schedule was hung a laughing camel, which could be transferred to another laggard department only by stepping up to full production. Soon they were all stepping up. From one to ten to fifty the output slowly, steadily climbed to a hundred forty-four tractors a day.

The days of the camel were over. This "museum of machines," as foreigners dubbed the plant, had become a first-class going concern. The mujiks, or at any rate the sons of the mujiks, were transformed into mechanics. This Volga city that once rallied the revolting serfs into the rebel armies of Stephan, Razin, and Pugachev, was now drilling descendants of those serfs into disciplined armies of industry and sending them out to other fronts. To the opening of the new tractor plant in Kharkov they gave three thousand workers who had mastered the new processes of production. To improving these processes they began to contribute their own suggestions and inventions.

"Saturdayings," "Shock-Brigades," and the "Stakhanov" Movement

From time to time have arisen movements for greater productivity, capturing the imagination and enthusiasm of the whole nation and creating new forms and methods of labor. Significantly, they were not initiated from above but rose spontaneously out of the masses themselves. First were the "Saturdayings" that began during the civil war when the railwaymen of Kazan voluntarily gave extra hours to put disabled engines and tracks in order. With incredible swiftness the idea took hold and presently machinists, weavers, Red Armyists, clerks, and typists everywhere were donating their holidays to perform the most difficult and menial tasks. (See page 268.) Lenin, himself a participant, hailed the movement as "the beginning of a revolution which is more difficult, more essential, more radical, and more decisive than the overthrow of the bourgeoisie because it will mean a victory over our own mediocrity, lack of discipline, petit bourgeois egoism, over those habits which accursed capitalism has left as a heritage to the worker and peasant. When this victory will be fortified, then and only then will a new Socialist discipline be created."

A big stride toward this Socialist self-discipline was the "Shock Brigade" movement. It began in 1928 when a squad of Leningrad Comsomols volunteered to increase its output by pledging not to miss a day, not to let its machines lie idle a minute. It instigated others to form a similar brigade, which, having set a new record, challenged the first one to beat it. The terms of the contest were set down in black and white. The contract was solemnly signed by the two parties and the race was on. The idea took hold and within two years 5,000,000 members were enrolled in 250,000 brigades of various kinds: Cost-Accounting Brigades, pledged to reduce overhead, to hold strictly to the norms in the use of oil and fuel; High-Standard Brigades, pledged to improve the quality of output; Chain or Cycle-Production Brigades, pledged to bring some product through all processes from start to finish; Towing Brigades, going out to aid the sectors lagging behind. The essence of this movement in the simple words of the famous shock-miner Izotov was "to work well and teach others how to do so."

The next big movement for raising production was "Stakhanovism," characterized by Molotov as "a combination of shock-brigade work with the mastery of technique." It started in 1935 in the Don Basin where the output of the miners was less than half that of the American. It was not that they did not have first-class tools, but they did not use them effectively or organize their work rationally. The individual coal-driller did everything, stopping his pneumatic hammer frequently to fetch props, clear away the debris, load the coal, shore up the veins. By dividing the last tasks among the several members of a brigade one miner was left to keep the drill incessantly in action. This man was the one-time peasant Alexey Stakhanov. The results of the first day were phenomenal. Instead of 7 tons each member turned out 35, a fivefold increase in production. The story of the exploit was flashed throughout the country and straightway the name of Stakhanov was in the headlines of 12,000 papers and on the lips of 100 million people. "What a coal-digger has done a forgeman can do," declared Busygin of the Gorky Auto Plant. By organizing an uninterrupted flow of materials and by reducing strains and motions to a minimum, instead of 674 crankshafts a shift, he was turning out 1,146 and soon there were scores of "Busyginites."

"What men have done, women can do," said Vinogradova, "the young Juno of the Ivanovo textile mills," Straightway with her strong-legged, nimble-fingered helpers, she jumped the 24 looms they were tending to 144, and presently there were hundreds of "Vinogradovites." "What factory-workers have done, farm workers can do," said Marya Demchenko, a digger of sugar-beets in the Ukraine. With her brigade, she weeded the fields nine times, poured water onto the parched soil, and kept fires blazing through the night to attract the moth pests into the flames. So heartily did the beets respond to this unaccustomed care that instead of the usual 13 tons an acre she harvested more than 50 tons and some of her colleagues did even better. "Never have I seen such women," said Stalin when they came up to Moscow to receive medals, awards, and the close attention of those who wanted to learn how it was done.

Against the champions and zealots of Stakhanovism were arrayed its enemies and skeptics. There were loud protests from the experts as they saw the old norms they had so "scientifically" set now badly shattered and discarded. Some of them stoutly insisted that the new ones were impossible and sought to sabotage them. The anti-Soviet critics who once said the Five-Year Plan was a myth now stigmatized Stakhanovism as a psychosis. The émigré press wailed over "the new slavery for the Russian people." There were outcries against "speed-up" and even assaults upon the new record-breakers, but the movement swept steadily onward. One after another the first high records were exceeded. Oil-drillers, engine-drivers, gold-diggers, aviators, and sales-girls declared themselves Stakhanovites. A magazine, "The Stakhanovite," was established and from Stakhanov technical courses came Masters of Socialist Labor. Whole enterprises set out to excel themselves on special Stakhanov "days," "five days," and "decades," and finally 1936 was declared a Stakhanov year for the whole country.

In essence the Stakhanov movement is rationalization, or "common-sense" in the utilization of tools and time. "It is simply a better division of labor," explains Kofanov, the champion bricklayer of the Ukraine. "Instead of each man going through the motions of preparing mortar, picking up bricks, and so on, he is united into a 'link' of three. One man prepares the mortar, the next picks up bricks and hands them to the third, who does nothing but lay them as fast as they are fed to him." Each "link" consists of one skilled, one semi-skilled, and one unskilled worker, with the earnings divided at the ratio of 5-3-2. It is apparent that this is analogous to those devices for obtaining the maximum output in the shortest time with the least outlay of energy, such as have long existed elsewhere. Most heatedly, however, do the Communists disclaim that it is simply the taking over of the efficiency systems of Taylor and Ford, whose "intent and significance," says the official journal Bolshevik, "is a striving to transform the worker into an automaton, a blind tool, a living cog in a fast-moving machine creating profits for the capitalists. Stakhanovite methods mean scientific use of all the available power of modern advanced Socialist technique, combined with a well-thought-out approach to labor by the workers themselves."

As a result of the Stakhanov movement, many new and important processes have been devised and, in certain cases, notably in shoe-stitching, world-records were established. But in general the Stakhanov movement means the lifting of the old Russian norms up to Western levels through the mastery of technique. To do that is no mean achievement for a country which, as Stalin said, was "a hundred years behind."

While the first furor over Stakhanovism dies away, its effects remain permanent and far-reaching. By stepping up production levels all around, it is bringing a big increase to the wealth of the nation and consequently to every citizen. It demonstrates that, in the double task of building factories and at the same time training the men to run them, the Soviets were eminently successful. It destroys the old canard about the inherent unfitness of Russians for industry by showing that five million peasants had assimilated in a few years the skills and technics accumulated in decades by the West. It renews the confidence so often expressed by Lenin in the reserves of talent, inventiveness, and enthusiasm of the masses. The Labor Unions are well adapted in spirit and structure for nurturing and developing these reserves.

46. How Are the Labor Unions Organized and Run?

Instead of being organized along craft lines, Soviet Unions most nearly resemble what are known in the West as industrial unions, now ardently championed by John L. Lewis of the C.I.O. "One industry, one union," "One undertaking, one union." In a Soviet steel plant the Union local comprises all who have any part in the making of steel. By all is meant all. It includes the engineers, puddlers, roller-men, sweepers—everyone from gate-keepers and samovar-servers to director. In a hospital the Union likewise comprises the janitors, nurses, orderlies, ward doctors, surgeons—everybody up to head physician. Besides these Unions, doctors, engineers, and architects have their own particular associations, clubs, and journals dealing specifically with their own professional problems and interests. But that is something else. In the economic field regardless of race, age, sex, income, position, or qualification, all are united in one big Union.

At stated intervals the workers in each enterprise come together in a "general meeting" to consider all matters vital to their welfare. They hear the reports of the director, delegates, and representatives, vote to approve or condemn their activities. They discuss the record of the enterprise, its relations to others in the same field, and to the life of the country as a whole. They debate—often very hotly—the pending collective agreement as to wages, piece-work rates, rules, and holidays. In brief, they are the parliament of an enterprise which in a big one is composed of thousands of members. But even in a small one this "general meeting" is too unwieldy to deal effectively with all the problems that are constantly arising. So it elects an executive body which in institutions is called the Local Committee, *Mestkom,* and in industries the Plant Committee, *Zavkom.* It is composed of from three to fifty persons, its chief officers receiving their regular wages while serving.

This committee is the "voice of the workers" in all relations with the management and, with it and the Communist "cell," constitutes the "red triangle" of plant control. It inducts the newcomer into the life of the plant and helps determine his job, his grading, and his pay. It distributes to each man his "wage-book," and collects the Union dues—about one per cent of his earnings. It organizes the work of the shock-brigades and Stakhanovites, elicits new ideas, suggestions, and inventions. It checks up on the fulfillment of the contract; hears complaints against managers, foremen, and fellow-workers; directs the "comradely courts" for the adjusting of petty disputes. It appoints the worker-aides to the labor, technical, and sanitary inspectors; the leaders of the clubs, sports, and choral-societies; the editors of the shop and wall newspaper. Assisting it are several sub-committees: Wage-Conflict, Culture, Labor Protection, International Workers

Aid, and the very important one on Production which discusses how to raise norms, cut overhead, stop waste, and the vital intriguing problem of finding under Socialism new incentives in place of the old.

These Plant and Local Committees, some 200,000 in number, are the basic units of the great Labor Union pyramid. It is built up by a series of councils, rising vertically to the Central Committee at the head of each of the 170 Unions. It is laced together laterally by another ascending series of councils, reaching out horizontally through the districts, regions, and republics to unite the Unions in one sort of enterprise with all those in others. At the apex stands the All-Union Congress of about 1,500 delegates meeting triennially and vesting its authority between sessions in a council of 170 members. It is this body that helps decide how much goes into the national wage-fund, and so powerful is it that its representatives sit in most of the high State organs and no decree pertaining to labor is issued without its approval. To keep all this Union apparatus properly functioning there are tens of thousands of presidents, secretaries, organizers, instructors, and inspectors, paid at about the same rate as highly skilled workers. Aiding them are over two million "activists," contributing their unpaid services to the Union's manifold activities.

Five Main Activities of the Unions

The main objective of the Unions is to raise the general level of production. Hand in hand with that goes the task of raising the general level of the producers. An economy of abundance, without which there can be no thought of Communism, depends upon a nation of workers who are highly skilled, alert, resourceful, intelligent, healthy, and happy. Toward this goal the Unions are advancing along five lines.

Reducing Hours and Raising Wages. Under the Soviets' six-day week, five days of work are followed by a day of rest. The working-day is the shortest in the world, seven hours. This is further reduced for those who work in hot or damp places, under compressed air, or amid noxious gases, or who are subject to poisoning by felt, lead, or phosphorus. The aim is to make the six-hour day universal. It is already that for office-workers and underground miners. Those who work in specially dangerous places have a four-hour day. The regular fortnight vacation with full pay is extended to a month for apprentices and workers in harmful, hazardous trades. The increase in wages depends upon, and keeps pace with, the increase in production. That is the means by which the Soviet achieves the solution of the twin problems of unemployment and "overproduction." As fast as the workers put goods on the markets the money goes into their hands to take them off the markets. The amount each individual gets depends upon his skill and energy. It runs from about a hundred rubles a month to a thousand or more for the highest qualified. The rates for piece-work, overtime, and night work are set forth in detail in the collective agreement signed by the Union and the manager, and all provisions must come up at least to the standards laid down by the Labor Code, or they are void. The enforcement of these measures is the function of the "labor inspectors" appointed by the Unions and subject to their recall. They have the right to enter any enterprise day or night, demand the books, check up the accounts, and bring violators into the courts.

Guarding Against Accidents, Poisons, and Fatigue. As most accidents occur in the last hours of work the constant shortening of the Soviet work-day has greatly decreased them. But they are still numerous enough among the newcomers from the villages who do not know the dangers of monkeying with the buzz-saw or punch-press. Hence the "Safety First" campaign and devices for making machines fool-proof by guards, wire nets, and "electric-eyes" registering the approach of a hand to the danger zone of a machine and stopping it immediately. Goggles, masks, and respirators are widely used to protect the workers against sparks, burns, dust, and gas-fumes. To keep them wide awake and alert many factories have fifteen-minute gymnastic periods in which the machines are stilled while everyone goes through setting-up exercises.

Frequently these new ideas and devices are suggested by the workers themselves. Others originate in the institutes for Labor Hygiene and Protection, conducting experiments and research in every field: The designing of machines enabling operators to attain the maximum of force, accuracy, and speed with the least expenditure of energy. The immunity or susceptibility of the various types to occupational strains and ailments. The effects of mental and physical fatigue in generating toxic poison. The weights that women can be permitted to lift without injury. The use of the "auto-audion"—a sound-measuring device for selecting persons for the "noisy professions," boilermakers, riveters, sand-blasters, and artilleryists. Studies in the deftness and size of hands most suitable for different trades such as sewing and shoe-stitching. Inventions like "hydrox," a water-cartridge for fireless blasting, that eliminates dynamite and danger of explosion in gaseous mines. The value of exercise, sports, travels, and physiotherapy in the restoration of energy as compared to inactive rest, idleness, or sleep.

Out of the institutes the new ideas and appliances are taken into the factories and fields which serve as huge mass-scale laboratories for testing and trying them out. After demonstrating their merits, with the Unions assenting, they become part of the rules and practice of the industry. To see that all these regulations for making labor safer, easier, and healthier are lived up to is the duty of the corps of the "technical inspectors" appointed by the Unions.

Better Housing, Food, and Health. Steadily the shacks around the old factories are giving way to modern cottages and tenements. The temporary barracks of the new plants are being replaced by apartment blocks, rather bleak but comfortable. Mud-holes like Gorlovka are transformed into model mine settlements, with one old earth-floored home enclosed in glass as a relic of the old regime. But for the new regime proper housing of the millions of land and factory workers will long be a vexing problem. To cope with it every enterprise must allot a percentage of its profits to a building fund which may be augmented by State grants, amounting sometimes to millions of rubles for plants topping the Red List of Honor. In planning and construction the Unions have an important part, as well as in the assignment of quarters to tenants, the number of rooms, and the rents to be paid.

The matter of food is likewise of vital concern. Sustained labor demands a sustaining diet. Of that the workers were by no means assured while the drive for collectivization was in full swing. So the factories and Unions went out and organized their own dairy, poultry, pig, and rabbit farms. They allocated to individuals small garden plots and seeds for raising their own vegetables and berries. The Workers' Supply made direct contact with the farms for delivery of grain and potatoes. Although industries are now assured of a steady flow of foodstuffs, as of raw materials, they continue to retain some of these methods of self-supply. The plot cultivators cling to their gardens out of sheer joy in tilling the soil as well as for their produce. The system of communal feeding is rapidly eliminating the old lunch baskets and tin buckets of the workers. In dining halls, sometimes spacious and well-appointed, they receive their meals at cost price or less. In quality it varies from dishes so tasteless that even the peasants protest to elaborate menus satisfying the most fastidious Stakhanovite palates. In some places underground canteens, lighted, heated, and ventilated by electricity, cater to the miners; "factory-kitchens" send out hot meals to homes, relieving women of part of their household drudgery; big restaurants often have special diet tables for those suffering from stomach, lung, or kidney disorders or seeking to prevent them.

On this principle of preventing rather than curing disease the whole medical-sanitary service of the mills, mines, and farms is conducted. Necessarily there are first-aid stations for accidents, hospitals for quarantine cases, and polyclinics for treating the general run of ailments. But the emphasis is on keeping the workers in a state of health, fit and functioning all the time. To this end there is a corps of Union-appointed sanitary inspectors supervising the bath-houses, laundries, drains, lavatories, toilets, and instructing the newcomers from the village in the right use of them. There are periodical examinations of workers—with blood-counts, urine tests, and records of each case as complete in the best clinics as in the Life Extension Institutes of America. To the Unions belong a chain of rest homes, medical springs, bathing beaches, and skiing stations reaching from the sub-tropics to the Arctic. In these resorts over two million members spend their annual vacations, their summer and winter holidays.

Education, Authorship, Sports, and Recreation. A leading rôle is played by the Unions in the elaborate network of schools that are closely linked up with industry. There are night and day "universities" open to workers in off-hours, free days, and holidays; vocational schools for apprentices working part time and receiving wages while studying; technical courses of the Commissariats for the training of engineers and directors; the three Stakhanov courses—the primary preparing for the State technical examinations, the middle for those who have passed them, and the advanced leading to Masters of Socialist Labor. Through all these and new courses that are constantly being added the millions are becoming masters of the machines that are being placed in their hands.

They are becoming likewise masters of the social meaning and significance of the machines. For workers' education does not confine itself to utilitarian subjects, but includes the "humanities." There are classes in music, Marxism, English, and "circles" on every subject from astronomy to zoology. Highly favored are the literary "evenings" devoted to the discussion of plays, poems, and novels, the old classics and the new. The participants are encouraged not only to read and to criticize, but to create. In simple, terse, colloquial language two thousand worker-authors have published their experiences and ideas about tractors, the Revolution, gold-digging, vodka. Tens of thousands contributed to the monumental "History of Plants and Factories."

The center of these activities is the club, often called the Labor Temple, or Palace of Culture. Usually it is a spacious building with halls for lectures, concerts, and movies; rooms for radio, dancing, chess, and needlework. Often there is a laboratory with test-tubes, chemicals, and retorts for amateurs; always a library, and a reading room where people are really reading. The Unions themselves publish several national dailies, scores of plant newspapers, thousands of shop organs and weeklies and tens of thousands of broadsheets and "wall-papers," dealing with the intimate life of the factory, exalting the local heroes of labor, lampooning the loafers and wasters. Adjacent to the club are fields for tennis, football, volley-ball, basket-ball, parachute jumping. Small wonder then that every Soviet worker is a clubman. "He can spend his whole life in and around a factory," says Anna Louise Strong, "and have all his social and recreational needs tended to."

Social Insurance forms a large and increasing part of the Soviet worker's "socialized wages"—those goods and services which he receives gratis and in the aggregate adds over 40 per cent to his regular wages. The amount and uses of these insurance funds which are administered in their entirety by the Unions are set forth in the next section.

47. How Are the People Insured Against Illness, Accident, Old Age, Unemployment?

Mostly through the Labor Unions, which constitute the biggest insurance company in the world. Just as every member is assured of a living while he works, so he is when for some reason he cannot work. So comprehensive is the system that it protects him and his dependents against all the exigencies of life from the cradle to the grave. Indeed, while he is still in his mother's womb it concerns itself with his well-being. With the watch-words, "Every child has the right to be well born," it gives his mother eight weeks' respite with full pay before delivery and the same free time afterwards. It furnishes him a baby's layette, a nine months' allowance for extra milk and clothing, and a crèche with nurses to tend him. It helps to support the parks and summer camps for him to play in, the dining-rooms to lunch in; the schools from kindergarten to technical college to study in; and, if he shows talent, grants him a monthly stipend or scholarship.

From the first day he enters the office, factory, or mine as an apprentice, through maturity and old age, some provision is made for every contingency. If he falls ill or is injured he gets free treatment with part or full wages from the moment of disability until he gets back to his job. If he is quarantined or must stay home to tend a sick wife or child he is paid for it. If he needs serious, prolonged care he may be sent to one of the 500 rest and convalescent homes on the sun-drenched shores of the Crimea or Caucasus with free transportation to and fro. If he is only run-down or ailing, after the day's work he may go to a "night sanitarium" for proper diet, bath, bed, and breakfast —until he is up to the mark again. If he is transferred to a far-away job or loses time in a labor dispute, he gets paid for that. If he loses an eye or a limb, he receives free, artificial ones and an invalid's pension.

An old-age pension of half to two-thirds his regular wages comes to him at 60, if he has worked for 25 years; it comes to him at 50, if he is engaged in an unhealthy, underground, or hazardous trade. (For women the retiring age is 55 after 20 years' service.) When he dies, he is assured of a decent burial with all funeral expenses taken care of. And he does not have to worry about the fate of his family and needy survivors for the insurance benefits are extended to them. The amount of benefits depends largely on one's service-record—where, how long and how well he has worked. Most favored are members of shock-brigades, Stakhanovites, and veterans of labor, on the principle that those who contribute most to the upbuilding of the country deserve most. At the same time the actual needs of the recipients are taken into account. As the needs of the dependents of the breadwinner are the same whether he dies or disappears, in either case they are pensioned. As the slightly disabled may continue work or be retrained in another trade, they receive a pension of a third, a half, or two-thirds their former income. The totally disabled, the blind, paralyzed, bedridden, who may require a nurse or attendant, get a hundred per cent. Because they need more they receive more. But this principle does not apply to those whose disabilities were brought on by drunkenness.

In most cases despite the colossal size of insurance funds in the aggregate, the benefits paid directly to any one individual are far from being munificent. But they grow with the growing wealth of the country. Insured against every hazard and mishap, Soviet workers are liberated not only from want but from the haunting corrosive dread and fear of want. That was the aim of the program drawn up by Lenin at the Prague Congress of the Bolsheviks, five years before the Revolution. On November 12, 1917, five days after the Revolution, he announced that it should be forthwith put into operation. It long remained practically a dead letter because of civil war, famine, and general poverty. But with peace and growing prosperity, it was galvanized into life and made applicable to the workers for hire in ever increasing numbers. Now on similar lines the other sections of the population are developing their own systems of security.

The 250,000 collective farms—with their buildings, crops, and livestock already insured against fire, frost, hail, and drought by the Department of State Insurance of the Commissariat of Finance—have their own measures of providing for widows and orphans and are extending them to their other members. The artels of hunters, charcoal-burners, goldsmiths, and lacquer-painters are doing likewise for their five million owner-producers. There are tens of thousands of mutual aid societies helping to tide their members over a temporary adversity, to buy a cow, to pay a fine, or take an extra holiday. Life pensions and special grants from the state treasury go to eminent explorers, scientists, and artists; to the families of old Russian musicians, authors, and generals; to the veterans of the Revolution, including those who were non-Bolsheviks; and even to foreigners as in the case of the two American mechanics who helped in the air rescue of the Arctic castaways. A few years hence, barring war or a major catastrophe, the then 200 million Soviet peoples will enjoy the same full coverage against the risks of life as those in the Unions.

A distinctive feature of Soviet insurance is that the costs are entirely borne by the employer. *The funds come not through deduction from wages or salaries but out of the enterprises themselves.* Each enterprise pays over a sum ranging from 10 to 20 per cent of its pay roll into the bank. If it is remiss in doing so, its other deposits may be attached. Beside collecting their funds each workers' organization is the sole agent for disbursing them. In this it is aided by a corps of volunteer "delegates" in close touch with the daily life of their fellow workers. With the motto "Help is twice help when it is timely," the money is paid directly to the recipients through 250,000 offices in the mills, factories, and State farms, at the moment and point when it is most needed. Invalids and pensioners usually receive their checks by mail. While every need is fairly covered, one notes the absence of that item that bulks so big in insurance schemes in capitalist countries. There is no provision whatever for unemployment benefits.

The excellent reason for that is that there are no unemployed. The Socialist system avoids caring for the jobless by providing every able-bodied person with a job. That permits all insurance funds to be devoted to the sick, the crippled, the infirm—and to the means for reducing, as far as possible, the number of them. Better avoid an accident than pay compensation after one; better good food, air, and cleanliness than illness and epidemics; better rest homes and holidays than premature old age; better constant employment than out-of-work relief; not palliatives and poultices, but prevention! That is why a large and increasing portion of the budget goes to safety campaigns, sanitation, solariums, dietetic kitchens, sports, excursions, and other means for raising the general health and stamina. In the last analysis economic security rests upon a secure economic system. From that standpoint all the organs for upbuilding it and the Red Army that defends it may be regarded as insurance agents.

48. How Are the People Clothed and Fed?

In the villages, Consumers' Cooperatives are the most important source of supplies. As the government aimed to get every worker into the Labor Unions, it sought to get every citizen, except the disfranchised, into the Cooperatives. As a result, with over sixty million members, they are second biggest of the four mass "pyramids" in the country. At the top stands the Central Union, *Centrosoyuz,* which trains managers, advances credits, arranges fairs and exhibits, supervises chain restaurants and schools for cooks, imports tea and chocolate. It obtains goods from the farms, the trusts, its own plants and trading-posts all over the world from the forests of Siberia to New York's Fifth Avenue—doing a yearly volume of business of over 25 billion rubles. It distributes its goods through 30,000 societies which operate over 200,000 stores, shops, and stalls, selling everything from pins to pianos, carving-knives to caviar—when they have them. The cost of joining a Cooperative is from a third to two-thirds of a month's income paid in installments.

The other big and fast-growing distributing agency are the stores of the State. Most of them are under the Commissariat of Home Trade which in 1935 took over all the cooperative shops in the cities. Others are run by the Commissariats of Food, Light, and Local Industry, and the artels. They sell direct to the public the products of their own canneries, creameries, fishing-fleets, abattoirs, and orchards. Hence the far-flung system of chain stores, specializing in bread, fruit, groceries, furniture, sport-goods; also the huge emporiums with scores of departments and a turnover up to a million rubles a day. They bring producer in closer contact with consumer, and in competition with the Cooperatives they help to improve the quality of the goods and speed up the service. Toward the same end functions another system which may be regarded as a survival, or a development of the old "closed" Cooperatives that once served the needs of a special clientele. These are the Workers' Supply Departments of the big factories and railways which obtain cereals, vegetables, and meats directly from the farms or from their own truck-gardens, hot-houses, dairies, and piggeries.

Fairs, Bazaars, and Markets. With their milling crowds, their jumbles of stalls, cattle, wagons, or sledges, their horse-traders, mountebanks, Russian Punch and Judy shows, they were color-ful features of life under the Tsar. They still flourish, especially in the provinces, before the big holidays of May and October. Here alongside the booths of the State, Cooperatives, and Collec-tive farms, the private traders are making their last stand: Peas-ants vending their cabbages, cucumbers, and calves; housewives their pasties, chickens, and sunflower-seeds; craftsmen the prod-ucts of their own hands from wooden-buttons to wagon wheels; old bourgeois ladies pathetically hawking remnants of their past glory, tawdry trinkets and gewgaws, lovely laces and ikons; speculators, with one eye out for the police, illicitly selling their "bootlegged" goods. In these markets, full of noise and color and motion, the people give vent to their age-old passion for trading, often haggling for hours over a ruble or two. Sallies of wit and satire mingle with shouting of offers and counter-offers, the loud hand-clasps sealing a bargain. But there are not many "bargains." Every seller charges all the traffic will bear. And it bears a lot. For the buyers come hither eager for the goods they can't find elsewhere and they must have at the mo-ment. Not untrue were the tales told by returning travelers about a fabulous sky-rocketing of prices—eggs at a ruble apiece and boots at 200 a pair! The public pays for wares that are scarce, and pays through the nose. However, all these transactions amount to but a tiny fraction of the total turnover in trade. The fraction grows tinier every day. In due time the State and Co-operative agencies will be doing it all. There will be a single system of trading units—open to all consumers and with all goods at uniform stable prices.

"Learn to Trade," said Lenin. A count of all stores, shops, and stalls mounts up to the impressive figure of half a million. More

impressive to the visitor, till recently at any rate, were the queues standing in front of them. Long lines of people patiently waiting for meat, kerosene, newspapers, soap—often waiting for hours. The chief cause of this was the emphasis, particularly during the First Five-Year Plan, on the production of machines. Unfortunately people could not eat machines, clothe themselves with kilowatts, or sleep in blast-furnaces.

Unfortunately, too, the peasants before entering the collectives, slaughtered their animals in wholesale fashion, inflicting a dearth of meat, wool, and leather long to be felt. This shortage of goods was aggravated by incompetent personnel and bad distribution. Warehouses were choked while store-shelves were empty. Train-loads of fruits and vegetables spoiled in transit. It sometimes took fifty days to ship stuff fifty miles from Moscow. Fur coats and felt boots arrived in midsummer; light clothes in the dead of winter; rural stores received consignments of cosmetics and lip-sticks, instead of crowbars and nails.

In short, the Communists did not readily take to Lenin's dictum about trading. They tended rather to hold aloof, and bizarrely enough, like the landed aristocracy of old England, looked down on business with a certain hauteur and disdain. From past associations it carried the odor of cheating and exploiting, the sin of sins in the Communist decalogue. From the barricades they might fitly turn to something big like diplomacy or the building of blast-furnaces. But how could they descend to engage in business and barter like vulgar merchants or hucksters! Ridiculing this attitude as "snobbish" and "supercilious," Stalin pointed out its baneful results. It has afflicted the Cooperatives in particular with an unusual amount of bureaucracy, red-tape, embezzlements, mismanagement, and muddling. But these things are passing.

An Insatiable Market. The Soviets are now tackling the business of merchandising with vigor. Even the Commissar of Heavy Industry once turned from his steel-mills to discourse on how to sell cucumbers. The cash register replaces the Chinese abacus, a wooden rack on which the clerks still add up accounts by brown, red, and black buttons strung on wires. The Third Five-Year Plan proposes to more than double the supply of commodities. The ration-card, the "closed" stores and restaurants, are practically abolished. A swelling stream of foodstuffs, textiles, pots, pans, and footgear pours into the markets. But the insistent clamor for goods continues. A great vacuum created by the long years of war and goods-famine waits to be filled. Go into the hinterland and see the hundred million peasants in need of so many things deemed essential to the Westerner. This, one may say, is likewise true of the coolies and ryots in the countless villages of China and India. But there is this profound difference: The Soviet masses are acutely conscious, articulate, and aggressive about their needs. And they are out to satisfy them. This is the fruit of twenty years of revolution, agitation, and ferment.

Access to palaces and manor-houses has opened their eyes to the existence of things never dreamed of before. Education by radio, press, and movies has created new tastes and desires. Constant reiteration that the workers are "the salt of the earth," creators of all the riches of the world, makes them feel that they have a right to them all. And finally, in response to the doctrine, "Not in any next world, but only in this world here can you enjoy the good things of life," comes the cry, "Very well, give them to us! Give us lots of them! Give them to us now."

No longer do the Communists complain about the "accursed wantlessness" of the masses. They want everything and they want it in a hurry. Tractors in place of wooden plows. Clothes instead of sheepskins! Apartments instead of single rooms! Electric lamps instead of oil and tallow-dips! Leather boots instead of bark sandals! And it is not only the basic necessities that they are demanding but a share in the comforts, luxuries, and graces of life. Supplies increase but demand is always far ahead of them. It is a seller's market. No advertising campaigns need be waged. There is no sales resistance to break down. At the doors of the marts stand millions of buyers, and in their hands billions of rubles to buy with.

What the Soviet Peoples Eat and Drink

Bread is the Staff of Life. The old economy was based primarily on bread. "Bread-plowing" is the old Russian word for agriculture, "bread-worker" is another term for peasant, "bread-and-salt," *khleb-sol,* means hospitality. With these symbols of life borne on a trencher, the old nobles greeted the Tsars and with them today the peasants in the back villages welcome the Soviet leaders. The importance of bread in the past is attested by hundreds of proverbs. "Without bread the palace is a prison; with bread it is Paradise even under a pine-tree." "Bread turns the table into an altar." How important it is under the Soviets is shown in the decree abolishing the bread-card on January 1, 1935. To offset the rise in bread prices, wages were correspondingly boosted 10 per cent, adding 4 billion rubles to the pay rolls.

Whatever else the peasant may forego, he cannot do without bread. Spread the table with the most tempting dishes, but if there is no bread watch his eyes go hungrily hunting about for it. Give him a few loaves and, light of heart, he fares forth on long journeys on the steppes and forests. Mostly it is made of rye, very aromatic in the baking, and issuing from the oven in big black loaves. White bread is relished by the peasants, but until recently that was a delicacy reserved for feast days. Buckwheat is used as a porridge or as browned grits, *kasha.* The predominance of cereal in the diet is conducive to full rounded figures abounding in curves. The Russians like their women that way. In the old "Domostroi," on which the family life was based, there are detailed instructions on how to make and keep the women fat and buxom. Upon the slim, straight-lined American girls visiting the village of Saburova, where I lived, the peasants gazed wonderingly—but not with delight. Moved to compassion for American men, they asked, "How can they possibly keep warm in winter, with such bony creatures?" They saw no health or use or beauty in them. A real woman should be well-padded, radiating heat and strength. For these qualities nothing better than good black bread.

Soup and Samovars. After bread comes soup, generally made from cabbage with a little meat, if the peasant was lucky enough to get it. It is sucked into the mouth with a deal of noise, thereby, as the peasant stoutly maintains, adding to its taste and flavor. His other mainstay is the potato, euphemistically called "the goose that Columbus brought from America." He likes garlic and onions including their tops beaten up into a rich green cream. Above all vegetables, most prized is the cucumber, devoured with great gusto—raw, salted, or pickled. Thus, besides starch, the peasant has his own due share of vitamins. And always more than his share of liquids.

The consumption of tea, a term loosely applied to many substances, is enormous. Highly preferred is real tea, which still comes by the old caravan routes from China. Some 50 million pounds a year are grown in the sub-tropic plantations of the Caucasus, which are now being rapidly expanded. Sometimes the tea is pressed into bricks as hard as flint from which pieces are hacked with a knife or hatchet. It is steeped in a china-pot on top of the samovar, "self-boiler," a big urn of shining brass or nickel with a central tube for burning charcoal. Through a spigot the boiling water, drawn into glasses and flavored with the tea, is usually sipped through a bit of sugar adroitly held between the teeth. Delighting in their samovar, the Russians jocularly boast of it as the one great "machine" they invented. With its glowing coals and pleasant bubbling it forms a sort of hearthside around which the family gathers its guests to drink and talk for hours. Often it goes with them on their travels to be set up on trains, boat-decks, and in the fields among the harvesters. They must have their tea-machine even if, often enough, they haven't real tea to go with it. In that case they resort to carrots, roots, or birch-buds, anything imparting to hot water an amber color.

Whenever forced to forego the genuine article, the peasants have somehow always contrived to find something in place of it. As a substitute for butter, they used vegetable oil pressed from the seeds of sunflowers, hemp, or flax. As a substitute for tobacco they used an acrid plant, *makhorka,* rolled in a strip of newspaper, its fumes smelling like a burning dump-heap. In lieu of that they smoked crushed hornets' nests, burdock-leaves, or nettles, "anything to prick our lungs and warm our noses." As a substitute for vodka, the potent drink in which periodically they forgot their poverty and sorrows, they distilled their own "moonshine"—less palatable, but more powerful.

Monotonous, unalluring, and often scanty was the fare of the masses. But their metabolism was excellent. The amount of energy and endurance they managed to extract out of their limited diet has been a marvel to foreigners. And it still is. For, under the Soviet, as formerly, the standbys continue to be bread, soup, and a few vegetables. Of these staples, thanks to the food-crises, they have not always been certain. That was the reason for the ration-card. At low, fixed prices it assured the basic necessities, first to the workers in essential industries; then to engineers, teachers, and scientists, the chief builders of the future; and to the children, the inheritors of the future, it gave first claim on milk, eggs, and butter.

Mushrooms, Game, Fish, and Appetizers. Supplementing this minimum fare are a number of edibles, largesse of the streams, the steppes, and the forests, to be had for the taking. Springing up in the damp woods and pastures are a hundred species of mushrooms of which the peasant is a real connoisseur. He calls them by name: Oaken, Under the Aspen-Tree, Butter, Little-Red-Cap, and scores of other apt, fanciful names. He weaves them into his songs, folklore, and soothsaying. He dries and strings them to season his soups, eats them fresh, pickled, and marinated. As great as his zest in eating them is his pleasure in picking them. On holidays, Kalinin, basket in hand, goes questing for them in the same haunts he knew as a boy. Lenin, too, was an ardent mushroomer, hunting them all day long in spite of rain and mosquitoes. Nature is less generous with nuts, although there are lots of hazel-bushes, and pine nuts in thousands of tons come from the cone-bearing trees of the North. The ground beneath them is carpeted with the pale pink cloudberry, while the bogs are reddened with the *klukva,* a kind of cranberry. Along with garden berries and currants, they are made into jam and preserves which the Russians like with or in their tea. Game-birds range in size from hazel-hens to the wild turkeys of the Caucasus, weighing up to 50 pounds. While the Soviet citizen gets less beef, pork, and mutton than the Westerner, he gets far more grouse, pheasant, plover, and partridge—also more venison and bear-meat. Most favored by the Moslems is horse-flesh or choice cuts of the sweetish meat of the camel. Most favored by the natives of the Arctic are the milk and blood of reindeer, and birds' eggs from the huge flocks nesting there in summer.

Besides these animal proteins, derived from the land, are those drawn from the rivers and seas. The catch of fish and shell-fish runs over a million tons a year. For the most part out of icy waters, they are firm and toothsome. Highly rated are the sandre, the salmon, and above all the sterlet, pronounced by epicures the "king of fish." Surpassing them all in manifold uses is the sturgeon which is often of gigantic size. Its pearl-gray eggs are renowned over the world as the best caviar. Its gelatinous spinal cord is used to thicken soups; its head to make chowders; its flesh boiled, broiled, baked, or sliced in semi-raw state, or smoked, forms one of the famous *zakuski,* appetizers. First place among appetizers is held by the common herring, garnished with parsley and onions. Apples, pears, and plums are relatively scarce; oranges and lemons still scarcer, though the citrus-groves of the Caucasus are rapidly expanding. Many fruits are inferior in size, and spotty, but melons and grapes from the southland are abundant and luscious.

Fine Cookery, Wines, and Vodka. Most of the foods so far listed—some of them subtle and delicious—are the direct simple products of nature. Besides these are the more elaborate dishes coming down from the old Russian past. The pages of writers from Gogol to Chekhov are filled with curious exotic concoctions, fearfully and wonderfully made, with tales of amazing gastronomic feats performed by the merchants and nobles of old. There were gourmands in those days. Also gourmets with palates trained to finesse and fragrance in foods, and master-chefs to cater to them. The old culinary arts still survive, appearing in all their glory at State banquets and collations for diplomats. If ordinary mortals have no access to these feasts, there are compensations in the regular cuisine, savory, succulent, and satisfying. The average citizen is getting a taste of them now and will have more in the future, thanks to the sharp curtailment in exports of luxuries such as crab-meat, caviar, candies, and mushrooms.

Among the many super-soups, whole meals in themselves, the favorite is *borsch* made out of beet-root, seasoned with dill and bayleaf. It comes to the table a steaming blood-red liquid, turning a deep mottled pink with a spoonful or two of thick sour cream. Out of its coral depths one forks up a sausage-link, kidney of lamb, slice of ham, gizzard of goose or duck. In old merchant fashion it is eaten with a big cloth tucked in the neck with much lip-smacking and other sounds evincing delight and surprise. With the soups go *pirogi,* brown pasties with a filling of chopped cabbage, raisins, or cheese, anything the dough can be handily wrapped about. The Russians have a peculiar affection for pancakes, the very thought of which starts up in the *émigré* a nostalgic longing for his homeland. These *blini,* as they are called, are converted into desserts by a sprinkling of sugar and rolling them around a dab of jelly or jam. Even cottage-cheese is deliciously transformed into cakes, *sirniki,* and into miniature dumplings, *vareniki.*

While the Russian takes his tea weak, he likes his vodka strong. Ordinarily it is clear and colorless, but there are special grades like the amber-tinted *zubrovka* with the sweet taste of buffalo-grass from which it gets its name. Vodka is usually swallowed at a gulp and, with an alcoholic content of 40 per cent and higher, provides a maximum amount of exhilaration in a minimum amount of liquid. At the other extreme is five per cent beer, which in the words of Wicksteed, the authority on Soviet liquors, "possesses the disadvantages of both English and German beer and the merits of neither." Cordials and brandies are distilled from cherries, ashberries, prunes, and peppermint. Cognac and a sparkling champagne well received in Europe come from the valleys of the Caucasus. Also light, dry wines, bottled after two years' ageing in the wood. A heavy dessert wine is made after an old formula of the monks of Athos. Vintages under famous foreign labels, Port, Madeira, Muscat, Tokay, come from the great cellars of the Crimea. From the vineyards of Moldavia comes Chablis, introduced by French colonists settling there under Catherine the Great.

Revolution on the "Food Front"

Slowly the production of food is being transferred from homes to factories. All over the land are being built huge mechanized bakeries, refrigerating-plants, packing-houses and canneries, with daily showers and fresh linen for the operators. As private profit is eliminated there is no incentive to the use of harmful adulterants, dyes, and chemicals. "One of our tasks is to reconstruct the food habits of Soviet citizens," says Mikoyan, the Commissar of Food. "We must not surrender to the old custom of living on cabbage-soup and *kasha.*" New articles are constantly appearing on the markets—soy-bean milk, the bottled juices of currants, rhubarb, and carrots, coffee and cocoa tablets. Soft-drink factories are putting out new beverages to wean the people from vodka. The era of the tin-can has arrived, creating new tastes, breaking down old food prejudices. Even the peasants are taking to pork-and-beans, to corn and corn-flakes, hitherto scorned as "food for cattle." Vitaminized products are supplied to the Red Army and to regions affected with scurvy and rickets. Mealtimes are becoming more regular. Instead of being rather helter-skelter, according to the speed of the housewife or the caprices of the stomach, they are now determined by the whistle of the factory, the hands of the clock.

However, the great changes are not in what and when the Soviet peoples eat, but where. Like Americans, they are dining less at home and more and more in public places. The influx of women into industries necessitates their release from bondage to the stove and the table. Hundreds of huge "kitchen factories" prepare meals to be served on the premises, to be sent out in bulk to mills and offices, or carried home in containers. Over 30,000 restaurants, dining halls, and cafés are operated by the Communal Feeding Trust and the Cooperatives. Over 80 million hot meals are served daily to employees of most enterprises at cost price or less, as well as to children in schools. Catering to the general public are cafeterias, quick-lunch and "hot-dog" stands, while restaurants with music and gypsy troups are now open till midnight and after. There are sporadic crusades against Soviet waiters demeaning themselves by the taking of tips, especially in the hotels catering to foreigners, but not often are tips refused.

About the quality of food and service the complaints in the press are long, loud, and bitter. These are in part due to bad management, in part to rising standards of taste and living. Said a Communist to a crowd of peasants, "Let the Soviets put bread in your mouths and you will cry for them to put butter on it!" "Yes," they retorted, "and if we cry loud enough, we may get not only butter but a bit of cheese or caviar." The common man is standing up to demand his share in the good things of life, even if they are not always so good for his health. In addition to his black bread, he wants white wheaten bread, pancakes, and pastries. Besides red caviar, the eggs of the sal-mon, tough-skinned like tiny balls of gutta-percha, he wants the glossy black and pearl gray kind from the sturgeon. Instead of plain boiled water, he wants it sparkling in bottles from the mineral springs of the Caucasus. Instead of home-brewed *kvass,* made from mildly fermented berries or bread, he wants the "real stuff," with alcohol in it. Instead of weed tobacco, he wants the genuine with nicotine in it. Instead of packing home his groceries on his back, he wants them delivered. Some of these things he has already tasted and the ap-petite grows with the eating.

Clothes and the Vanities of Life

The visitor's first impression of the street throngs is—lack of style and color. Occasionally there is some jaunty Caucasian in skirted-coat with silvered dagger at the belt, or the flashing raw silk robes of a man from Turkestan. But the tone in general is rather drab and dreary, a distinct disappointment to one who has seen the gay flam-boyant costumes of the *Chauve Souris* and the Russian opera, and ex-pects to see all the people clad in them. The same lament was voiced in Murray's Guide Book a hundred years ago. One should not con-clude that these gay costumes are non-existent. Away from the beaten track they still survive in all their pristine splendor. On holidays in the forest villages of Archangel I have seen the women emerging from their log-huts in all their ancient dazzling regalia. Arrayed in gowns of shimmering silk, crowned with the crimson pearl-sown head-dress, and with long rainbow ribbons streaming from their hair, they were gorgeous as *boyarinas* of the sixteenth century. Still prevalent are the flowered shawls, and the green and scarlet kerchiefs bound about the head. But with the advent of the machine the bright sarafans, bodices, and rich embroidered linens are distinctly in the discard.

"Why don't you wear your old native costumes?" I asked a bevy of kolhoz girls in short machine-made dresses and high French heels. "They are so much more quaint and colorful!" "And why don't you wear your old native American costume?" retorted one of the girls home from school in Moscow. "Painted bodies like your Indians and feathers down your back. Also quaint and colorful!" Except for masquerades the Soviet girl would no more put on her mother's old ornate gowns than would an American girl a crinoline or Mother Hubbard. With a few sighs of regret for the old picturesque raiments so swiftly passing are mingled greater sighs of relief. Relief not only from the tedious labor of weaving and washing them, but from the burden of wearing them. Release, from heavy skirts dragging the ground, into a feeling of lightness and freedom. Escape, from a few dresses lasting a life-time, into the variety and novelty of a wardrobe that the flimsier machine fabrics afford and compel.

Less sweeping is the change in men's apparel. They still wear the belted blouse or the old *rubashka* with banded cross-stitch collar, tied about the waist so that the end falls outside the trousers. A more elaborate smock is called the *tolstovka* after the great Russian writer. Leather-jackets are popular, as are the military tunics such as Stalin wears. Instead of hats most men affect the peaked cap of the worker, while students favor the Tatar's multi-colored skull-cap such as Gorky wore. Everybody hankers after a pair of high-top, full-dress boots, but the Red Army has first claim on them. Millions of peasants still shuffle about in bast-sandals, woven from the inner bark of the linden-tree, although there has been a five-fold increase in the output of shoes and galoshes.

Winter Garments. These are the products of centuries of battling against the Arctic cold. First line of defense is the *shuba,* a long coat of sheepskin or broadcloth collared with fur and heavily wadded with baton. The rôle it plays in the life of the Russian and the sacrifices he will undergo to get one was told by Gogol in "The Cloak," a hundred years ago. And it is quite as true today. In this greatcoat, topped with a shaggy cap of fur or caracul, he looks to the oncoming winter complacently, even with delight.

The first leaf-fall and the peasants, men, women, and children, draw on their *valenki,* seamless boots of pounded felt so soft-padding that the noise of footfalls dies from the village streets. The first hard frosts bring out the *tulups,* gigantic hooded mantles, fortifying their owners so well against the elements that they actually suffer less than the people in more southern climes. Completely muffling them from crown to sole they blot out all semblance of the human figure. With just a peep-hole for the eyes and the warm breath shooting out like jets of steam into the icy air, they resemble herds of big brown or cinnamon bears waddling down the road. Unfortunately they provide warm sanctuaries not only for their owners, but sometimes for hosts of other inmates, tiny and pestiferous. An old English chronicle records the arrival at the court of Queen Elizabeth of long-bearded emissaries from Moscow, "clad in fur and ermine, dropping pearls and lice." Now into these insect-lairs an exterminating war is carried on with fumes and chemicals. Modern methods for curing and tanning are being introduced. But in the main, the old garb, so admirably adapted to ward off the long and bitter winter siege, remains essentially the same as before.

A New Regard for Dress. That is the most significant change on the "clothes front." The long prevailing shabbiness was largely due to necessity, the dearth and shoddiness of materials. But it was also in part an affectation. In revolt against the bourgeois, even their ways, customs, and speech were scorned and tabooed. Fine clothes were bourgeois. Therefore, away with them! Among the extremists grew up a cult of slovenly attire and rude manners. These were the hallmarks of the true proletarian. True, there were young Communists who brashly flaunted white collars and neckties, and girls who wistfully fingered the fashion magazines that were smuggled across the frontier. But their Marxism was suspect. They were looked upon as light-minded and frivolous. Concerned with such trivialities how could they be really devoted to the big things of the Revolution!

Such attitudes are now ridiculed and derided. As the collective farmers are exhorted to become well-to-do, so are people to become well-dressed. From total absorption in the Five-Year Plans they are turning to the finesses of life. The women are becoming "style-conscious." Wax figures, gowned in the new rayon silks and satins, are revolving in the shop windows. Newspapers feature "What the Well-Dressed Soviet Woman Will Wear." Clothing trusts exhibit their new models and invite the public to criticize. They do so with a vengeance. They complain that there are too many blacks, dull browns, and grays. They complain that the textiles are too monotonous, too heavy, too thin, too fragile. They complain that the ready-made suits fit only the normal person. "Evidently the Soviet citizen who presumes to be tall or short is doomed to go naked," remarks one satirist. "Too dowdy! made on the motif of a sack tied in the middle," says another. "Too Parisian!" gibes a third. "They have forgotten that our peasant women have hips and breasts." "They try to make them look like petty bourgeois women at their worst."

The Soviet artists are called in to design new forms for the new conditions. One school, out for an utter break with the past, insists that the old costumes be entirely relegated to the museums. Others demand that some of their distinctive features—cross-stitch, lace, and tucking—be embodied in the new styles. The debate goes on in the usual manner—with citations from Marx, and much theorizing about the class-rôle of dress in the past and the present. Also with speculations as to its future under Communism. "When clothes are no longer an index of one's bank account or social position," said Lunacharsky, "there will be sharper divisions than hitherto between working clothes, sport-wear, and festive garb. The last will, perhaps, be even brighter than ever, because of the greater joy in living, and a holiday crowd will be more what Robespierre called it: 'a spectator and a spectacle in one.'"

By this criterion the Soviet peoples are still far from Communism. But they are on the way. Special work-clothes for mechanics and miners are copied from American overalls and jumpers. The youth, turned athletic, are stripping down to knickers, trunks, and shorts—so new and so scandalous to the old women of the villages that they looked upon these first near-nudists as "Antichrists" and chased them with pitchforks. On the other hand they are blossoming out in bathing-suits, again affronting the feelings of propriety of their forebears who always swam naked and unashamed. Best of all, the innate love of color of the Russians is again in the ascendant. For "red," they had the same root-word as for "beautiful." When they wanted to tell a girl she was lovely they called her *krasnaya devitsa*, "little *red* girl." When they wanted a fitting name for the great plaza before the Kremlin they called it—centuries before the Revolution— Red Square, *Krasnaya Plostchad*. On holidays or in harvest times the peasants put on their red shirt-blouses and the women their red kerchiefs, and looked like scarlet poppies against the green background of the woods and meadows. This flair for red and all vivid colors is again asserting itself. The somber days of toil and sacrifice for the Five-Year Plans are passing. The dividends are beginning to come in, the people feel relaxed, light-hearted, and gay about it, and they want their dress to express their feelings.

Cosmetics and Coiffures. Under the caption "The Return of Venus," a Soviet paper discourses on the value of beauty in dress and in person. It bids the women "make themselves attractive and luring"— a rather needless injunction. Russian women always knew how to heighten their charms. They always had a predilection for cosmetics. Even the peasant girls knew the secrets of make-up and made no secret of it. Lacking talcum, they powdered their faces with flour, their already ruddy cheeks they further reddened with beet-juice, and in lieu of cold cream they applied real cream or fat to their skins. More adept and long-practiced in these arts were their Moslem sisters who carried them to perfection. In staining their nails the women of the West are doing what the girls of Tatary have been doing for centuries. On the bleak steppes I have seen them trooping to a festival with hennaed nails, penciled brows, and blackened eyelashes—in toilettes and coquetry not inferior to ladies of the court. Held somewhat in abeyance by the Revolution, rouge, lip-stick, and perfumes are again in the ascendant.

Almost as numerous as book-stores are hairdressing salons, with long queues of patrons before holidays. Bobbed hair is favored by the women. Men like theirs rather close cropped or shaved off altogether in summer. The celebrated beard of the Russian has almost disappeared. In cartoons he is still bristled with whiskers, but in real life very rarely. Far more whiskers are to be found in a convention of Western bankers than in an assembly of Bolsheviks. True, among the old Believers, the patriarchs, robed in long flowing *caftans* and with virgin-beards that fall to their bosoms, still look like Druids of old. Against the wearing of beards Peter the Great waged a furious campaign but in vain. Desperately the Russians clung to them, holding that "man, made in the image of God, was made with a beard," and without it would be barred from Paradise. Now in these back villages the clippers, the shears, and the razor are assaulting the last strongholds of hair. What the stern edicts of the Tsar could not do is being done by the machine, totally transforming the faces of the people as well as of the land.

49. How Are the People Housed?

Rather badly, as the visitor reports it. Nearly four million people crammed into the city of Moscow built for half that number. From crowded public halls and cafés, on crowded trams they return to their still more crowded homes. Construction has a long way to go before it wipes out all the congested areas. Five families in an apartment with one lavatory and a single cooking-range. Housewives humorously calling the table their dining-salon, the book-shelf their library, the couch their bedroom, the oil-stove their kitchen, and the sink their bathroom. (Friedman) Divorced couples, unable to find separate quarters, living on in the same one as before! Professors, at their home work-desks, with a baby's crib beside it! In the villages families of five to fifteen persons huddled in little straw-thatched huts usually swarming with insects and often with lambs, chickens, and calves brought in from the winter storms. These are facts. Beside them should be set down another fact of which the reporter usually is ignorant or which he omits: *Bad as housing*

*conditions at the present may be, for the overwhelming majority
they are better than in the past.*

Under the old regime most workers were condemned to the
unpaved, unlit, unsewered outskirts of the town. They lived in
ramshackle wooden shanties, in tiny cubicles of tenements swarming like rabbit-warrens, in basements, attics, and dug-outs. "Upward of ninety per cent of people alive in Russia today," says
Duranty, "were born and brought up in one small room, in conditions of squalor and poverty almost inconceivable to all save
a fraction of native born Americans." To multitudes even one
room was unattainable. They rented "sleeping-corners," improvised beds out of tables and trunks, or slept in their day-clothes
stretched on the floor. Even in Moscow in the factory-barracks,
consisting of one big hall, a hundred families carried on all their
domestic functions from eating and washing to the conceiving
and rearing of children. Some of these wretched quarters are
preserved intact in all their ugliness as historic relics of the recent
past. As the palaces are used as museums "to show the luxurious
life of the nobles in the days of the Tsar," in the same way these
dingy hovels serve "to show the sordid lot of the workers under
the yoke of autocracy."

To move out of dark cellars and slums even into a single decent
room is to make a step up in the world. Millions of workers did
this during the first years of the Revolution. Millions more are
now moving up into the luxury of whole apartments. Big blocks
of them are rising in the suburbs, in new settlements, and in the
urban centers on top of the old structures—one to four stories
added to those that will stand them. They are built by factories,
by the cities, and by the people themselves united in Housing
Cooperatives. To service these buildings with water, light, and
central heating a special department of the Municipal Soviet is
devoted. With the slogan, "Turn the gray cities green!" the boulevards, squares, and avenues are being replanted with trees and
shrubbery. Useless arches, towers, and churches are being replaced with parks and playgrounds to put "lungs" into the

congested centers. Sixty new Socialist cities are springing up like the boom towns of the West, but, unlike them, planned in every detail from sun-bathing roofs to flower-gardens.

In all its new housing, utility, and cultural projects the Second Five-Year Plan invested 32 billion rubles. As the general staff in this "warfare for more air, sunlight, and living-space" there are the thousands of architects of the Academy of Communal Planning and other institutes. With their field maps and blue-prints, brigades of engineers are directing armies of masons, carpenters, electricians, plumbers, and riveters. To the construction fronts are moving whole forests of timbers, rivers of cement, mountains of tile and glass, millions of tons of steel, pipes and wiring. Nevertheless for a long time housing will be "the gravest of problems." (Grinko) Fast and furiously the Soviets are building. But hard at the heels of the builders presses the birth-rate. Into the houses it brings some six million new babies each year while the death-rate takes only about half that number away. Thus to the already colossal task of improving the living-quarters of some 175 million citizens each year is added the problem of finding accommodations for three million new ones.

Building and Renting

The enterprise that gives a man a job is supposed to give him a place to live in. Consequently about half the apartment-blocks are erected by industry and transport. The space allotted an employee depends upon the kind of work he does, and the size of his family. The "sanitary norm," the minimum for decent good living, is set at nine square meters a person. Till recently he counted himself lucky with the "crisis norm" of six square meters. Rents are decidedly cheap because in computing the total amount of rent to be collected from a building no account is taken of its value or that of the land it occupies. It is determined solely by the cost of amortization and upkeep —repairs, janitor service, and heating. This sum is apportioned to each of the tenants according to the size of his quarters and the size of his income. The less one's wages, the less he pays for each square foot. By and large about 10 per cent of a Soviet worker's budget goes for rent as against 20 or 30 per cent in other countries.

Cooperative Apartments, Courts, and Communes. To encourage the people to build their own homes the Soviet subsidizes the Housing Cooperatives. Twenty-five members may form a Cooperative though some of them are composed of a hundred or more. The shareholders subscribe 10 per cent of the cost of the building, the other 90 per cent comes from the State as a long-time loan at a low rate of interest. Groups with common activities are offered every facility for the construction of special dwellings adapted to their specific needs. Hence the new type of Houses for Artists, Writers, and Engineers.

In most large houses the residents elect a Committee of Management known as the *Domkom,* as powerful in its domain as the *Fabkom* in the factory. Its functions extend from assignment of quarters to the catching of rats, disposal of garbage, and finding out why the janitor gets so little heat out of so much coal. Before a "Comradely Court," chosen likewise by the residents, come violators of the house rules and order; window-breaking boys; pilferers of door-knobs and electric-bulbs; women littering sunflower husks over the halls or filling them with samovar smoke; roistering parties dancing and vodka-drinking late into the night. By way of reprimands, small fines, and exhortations, this informal court seeks to cajole offenders into a more social behavior, to educate them to live aright in communal houses. In some of them, well-equipped with buffets, nurseries, reading-rooms, lounges, gymnasiums, and playgrounds bringing the residents freely and frequently together, the community spirit is highly developed. It had its highest expression in the Communes of the New Way of Life. (*Byt*)

Privately-Owned Homes and Servants. The vast majority of people, however, have no desire to live in one big family. They want to live privately or in the bosom of their own family. Great numbers have no desire even to live in big multiple-family houses. They prefer the old individual one-family dwelling. These are now being extensively built, especially by the Stakhanovites with their big wages. In tens of thousands, a huge combine on the Volga is turning them out ready-made from door-sill to roof beams to be transported in sections to their sites. As a matter of fact, most families in the Soviet Union have a whole house to themselves. For in the villages, and that is where a hundred million still live, the peasant still holds to his one-story cottage. It is privately built and privately-owned. The cooperative member, too, owns his apartment and may bequeath it to his children. The occupant of a city-owned flat has a tenure on it that amounts almost to ownership. He may be fired from his job but only with difficulty can he be ejected from his lodging. Thus paradoxically in Communist Russia more people "own" their houses than in capitalist America.

Another paradox, reversing the expected, is that there seem to be more domestic servants in Russia than in America. The reason for this is that so many housewives have gone into public life. So much energy must be spent to make up for the lack of most of those labor-saving appliances common to the West, so much time is lost in lugging things home from stores, that servants are almost indispensable. But they are increasingly difficult to have and to hold. Under the old regime they usually slept on the floor. Now they demand a bed. Formerly they worked for a pittance all hours of the day and night, at the beck of the mistress. Now their own Union of Household Employees sets the scales of hours, wages, and welfare and calls high-handed, nagging employers to account and rebuke. Formerly they were content to drudge away in the kitchen all their lives. Now in a few months the girl from the village revolts against the confines of the home, and follows her mistress into the freer life of the office or factory. This naturally gives added impetus to the erection of more and more communal buildings. For women cannot carry the double burden of wage-earning and housekeeping in the old way. They are demanding more public dining-halls to relieve them from bondage to the kitchen, more laundries to release them from slavery to the wash-tub, more crèches to relieve them from constant care of the children. Incidentally these new enterprises along with the multiplicity of clubs, theatres, and stadiums are relieving the pressure of housing space. Like the ancient Greeks, Soviet citizens increasingly do a great deal of their living in public—in forums, sport-fields, and the open air. Houses do not have to be so large for people who spend so much of their time outside of them.

Furniture and Toilets. Despite their public activities Russians have a strong affection for their home—a place for their belongings, their books, and their friends—however small it may be. Often enough the interiors are rather bleak and barren, or they may be afflicted with a mid-Victorian atmosphere verging on the gaudy. The innate artistry of the Russians manifested in so many other realms somehow fails to assert itself in their homes. And from the American standpoint they are lacking in comforts. Instead of "There's Not a Bathing-Suit in Russia," Will Rogers might more correctly have entitled his book "There's Not a Rocking-Chair in Russia." As for good beds with sleep-inviting mattresses, they are also scarce. But somehow most Soviet peoples can sleep anywhere, an ability inherited perhaps from nomadic days. Numbers of them likewise seem to be able to get along well enough with a few hours' sleep. Tables, chairs, and cupboards are as a rule more utilitarian than decorative. "I hate Russian-made furniture," says one of Turgeniev's characters. "Russians know how to grow long beards, but not to make furniture. It is cheap, but rotten." The same plaint is echoed in the press today, although many new models and designs are being put on the market. Besides factory-made articles, there are great quantities of handicraft utensils, and tableware, most of them excellent in design and color. From the Khokhlomsky district come millions of wooden spoons, bowls, and vases, beautifully lacquered in vermilion, red, gold, and black. From the new houses the ikon-corners and cases are disappearing. The mild-eyed saints, holding forth promises of a heavenly Paradise in the world to come, are being replaced by portraits of Marx, Lenin, Stalin, Voroshilov, Blucher—the militant Bolsheviks summoning to struggle for a good society in this world.

Many apartments have dumb-waiters and gas-rings, electric irons, tea-pots, and toasters—a source of marvel and delight to the newcomers from the village. Often they are out of order and broken. This is due not only to carelessness, but to curiosity—the same passion for novelty and experimentation that damages machines in the factories. The instructions on the automatic-lift explicitly limits the number of passengers to three. "But why not four, or five?" ask the new peasant lodgers. They try it with the result that everybody has to climb the stairs for a week. They want to find out whether the toilet will carry off newspapers or garbage, with the result that to find its location one has only to follow one's nose. Hence the justifiable plaint of new-arriving foreigners—that lavatories often proclaim their presence at from 10 to 20 yards. Old-timers recalling the days when they did so from 100 to 200 yards gratefully note the advance on this sector of the cultural front. To revolutionize age-old habits in matters of sanitation, bathing, and ventilation takes more time than a day or a decade. But already these modern mechanized dwellings have greatly changed the practices of millions. Among the peasant occupants, who until recently had never even heard of plumbing and electricity, a tremendous transformation has been wrought. More tremendous it appears to anyone knowing the primitive conditions under which they once lived—and tens of millions are still living—in the villages.

Peasant Households

According to an old saying, "The air is good in the country because the peasants use so little of it." Certainly in their old log huts, swarming with children and often with animals, and with windows hermetically sealed most of the year, they used little of it. And there was little to use—for, in contrast to the vastness of the country, the houses were miserably small. In this realm the Revolution came as a godsend. While the first fruits of it in the cities was to cramp the people up into tighter quarters, in the villages it greatly increased the number of houses, and their size. With all the forces of the Soviets engaged in the civil war, the peasants could not be kept out of the forests. While the cannons roared away on the fronts, the axes steadily thudded away in the rear on the new houses rising in hundreds of thousands. Hence the saying, "Admire the mujik's new *izba,* but do not ask where he got the logs!" He got them out of the unguarded forests—for a few paper rubles or for nothing at all.

Bigger Houses and Stoves. While the opportunity for the getting of timber was good he got lots of it. The new houses therefore were bigger, better, and with more window space. "We want now to live in the light." He built them in much the same fashion as did his ancestors centuries ago and as the pioneers built their cabins in the West. And so he is building them today with unsquared logs, dovetailed at the ends, and caulked with moss, tow, or mud. He thatches the roof with straw, banks up the walls with earth; and, with double windows, he makes his house like his garments of fur and wool, thick ramparts against the biting winds and frosts. The more warmth outside his body, the less heat he has to create from within it by the consuming of food. That is why the stove, a pile of white-washed bricks, is so big and important.

The nearer one moves towards the Arctic, the bigger the stove grows until it fills a third or more of the room. In keeping with the space it occupies is the rôle it plays in the life and ritual of the family. It has its place of honor even in the ancient cycle of the wedding-week. In a forest village of Archangel I have seen it dressed up with a fresh coat of lime to receive the farewell of the bride. Arrayed in a gay embroidered gown, she half-sang, half-chanted a litany of thanksgiving for all its services. And well she might. On its broad top she had been born, and there she had slept and played as a child. In its deep hot oven she had been laid when sick, to cure her colds and cramps, sweating them away. Out of that oven she had drawn the big loaves of black bread and pots of steaming soup. In its draughty chimney she had listened to "Grandfather *Domovoi,*" the house-spirit, groaning and moaning away on windy nights, while she read into his mutterings answers to her troubling questions and problems. Through the long years from babyhood to bridehood it had been giver of life, companion of her joys and sorrows. For all this she gave thanks, then bowing low said a tearful good-by as to an old and faithful friend.

Outside, rude sheds for the horse and cattle, a sheep-fold, a granary, and a sty for pigs form together with the house a compound, usually a quagmire. Into this courtyard one enters by a huge high-arched gate, the pride of the peasant. To make it as imposing as possible he ornaments it with scrolls, fret-work, and carving on its doors—or on the projecting roof-beam—a conventional flower, a horse's head, or one of the birds of Slavic mythology. Out of the village well the women draw water by means of a rope wound on a roller or a sweep rising above the house tops like a giant one-legged crane. The "refrigerator" is a pit dug deep in the earth in which the winter's ice packed with sawdust or swaddled in straw lasts well through the heat of summer.

Baths and Bed-bugs. Last, but by no means least, is the bath-house built on the stream that usually runs at the back of his garden. It is a primitive shack with wooden benches, basins, and barrels, a collection of stones and a fire-box for heating them. From gourdfuls of water, flung on the fiery stones, burst scalding blasts of steam to the delight, and sometimes the stupefaction, of the bather stretched full length on the wooden shelves. After a parboiling he scrubs his body with a mat of linden fiber and beats it with a besom of green birch-twigs until it is a glowing red all over. Then out of this torrid heat, with characteristic passion for extremes, he often plunges headlong into the icy waters of the creek or a snowbank. Every week he goes joyfully through this ordeal of steam, sweat, and flagellation, emerging from it one of the cleanest persons in the world. About the same ritual, but in a milder form, is followed in the big bath-houses in the cities, which are just replica on a bigger scale of those in the country. Inasmuch as in the typical village almost every family owns its own bath-house, there are far more of them in Russia than in any other nation in the world.

All this in no wise accords with the general assumption that the Russian masses are unclean, unkempt, and ridden with pests. True they often appear so, and sometimes they are. But it is not to inclination that this is due but largely to adverse conditions beyond their control. Against them the women especially carry on a valiant battle for cleanliness, but too often a losing one. How, for example, can people without paint or varnish keep vermin out of wooden houses with their countless cracks and crevices affording them millions of warm safe places to nest and breed and multiply? Against them the family wages guerilla warfare with boiling water, by leading ants in to devour them, or by decamping in midwinter to the house of a neighbor after opening windows and doors to freeze them to death. But on the hair and wool of the animals they quickly come back again. Fortunately towards them the peasant has developed a high degree of immunity and tolerant philosophy, maintaining that the lively rustling cockroaches are good company and the bed-bugs have a therapeutic value—leeching only the bad blood out of one's veins.

New Life, New Dwellings. Gradually modern structures are replacing the ancient straw-thatched, log-built *izbas.* They may be picturesque but they are unsanitary, uncomfortable, and easily inflammable. The romantics who loudest lament their passing would not want to live in them. The peasants likewise are beginning to prefer the new fire- and insect-proof houses—poured out of concrete, tile-roofed, or slated, sided with slabs pressed out of peat, diatomaceous earth, reeds, and the by-products of flax. The collectives are working out their own type of buildings adapted to their needs. New agrarian towns are being built with tall silos, power-trestles, and smoke-stacks. All over the Soviet land they are rising—in the white-plastered hamlets of the Ukrainians, alongside the sun-baked clay-huts of Uzbekistan, and in the Caucasus around the granite *aouls* of the mountaineers. Slowly under the impact of industrialization the whole aspect of the countryside is changing. But, very slowly, for building material is scarce, the land is big, and there are some 300,000 villages in it. Still prominent on the Russian landscape are the brown and gray weathered huts, huddling close to the earth and each other as if in mutual protection from the wolves and storms.

50. What Incentives to Work Has the Soviet Citizen?

The basic incentive is to get a living. Article 12 of the new Constitution reads, "Work in the U.S.S.R. is the duty of every able-bodied citizen, according to the principle: 'He who does not work, neither shall he eat.'" The kind of living one gets depends on how hard and well one works. The diligent farmer gets more than the easy going; the skilled mechanic more than the pick-and-shovel laborer; the fast brick-layer more than the slow one;

the talented author more than the ungifted one; the scholarship student with high marks more than the laggard. In most enterprises the graduated scale runs from 150 up to 500 rubles a month—still higher for foremen, managers, and directors. Does not this differential wage violate the Socialist doctrine of equality of income?

There is no such doctrine, says Stalin, stigmatizing the advocates of it as "levelers," "ascetics," "petty bourgeois," "Utopian," "un-Marxian." Under full-fledged Communism there may be the equality that Bernard Shaw insists upon, or something akin to it. But even the Communist ideal, "From each according to his ability, to each according to his needs," does not imply exactly the same income for everybody for the obvious reason that the needs of different people are different. The sick and crippled may require more than the strong; the scientist engaged in intensive research more than the clerk in a store. Certainly in this period of Socialism there is no equality of income in the Soviet Union. This is in keeping with the Socialist principle of compensating everyone according to his labor. Particularly in the present situation the country wants goods, goods, and still more goods! Therefore it offers the greater rewards to those who produce the most and the best.

"We shall pay fifty thousand rubles to a specialist," said Lenin, "if we can save thereby." Prizes and premiums for suggestions and inventions provide an incentive to work intelligently and creatively. Payment by piece-work—in existence despite the general impression to the contrary for over a decade—provides the stimulus to work intensively. Bonuses for good work provide a similar stimulus to day workers. Norms of labor are set on time jobs and if one does five days' work in four he gets paid for five. The best shock-workers and Stakhanovites get not only glory, but tangible returns in the shape of automobiles, scholarships, name-plates on seats in the opera, or even cruises to Europe. The collective farmer draws out of the harvest, according to the amount and kind of labor he puts into it. Clerks and managers of stores sometimes receive a percentage of the turn-over. As in other countries there is an extra reward for extra effort—"the more work, the more wages." If one wants more, he must show he deserves more.

However, one must guard against overstressing this old economic incentive to work. While it operates under the Soviets, there are many factors that lessen its importance. Neither one's standing in the community nor one's welfare depends so much upon one's income. Moderate exertion assures a person of the primary needs and comforts of life and an elaborate system of social insurance provides for its exigencies. By doubling his income one does not necessarily double the amount of goods and services he gets. Most certainly not the honor in which he is held. It is true that the able-bodied and able-minded may and often do earn big incomes while the royalties of popular authors and artists are sometimes munificent. But let them presume to live easy on their accumulations and they are distinctly in disfavor. Persons drawing the big prizes in the State Bond lotteries generally donated a good part of their winnings to one of the numerous causes or societies in need of support. All the royalties from "We Salute You! Spain," played in a hundred theatres, were handed over by its author, Afinogenov, to the funds for aiding the Spanish Loyalists. In the Soviet Union the sheerly acquisitive person is frowned upon and ostracized. Making money is not making good. For these reasons, the monetary motive is much less a driving-force than in capitalist countries. But how about another old motive—the desire for power?

The craving for place and power plays its part in impelling men to exert themselves. To some, mastery and domination of one's fellows is the supreme satisfaction of life. They enjoy power. They like to sit in the seats of the mighty, to make important decisions, to give orders, to control the destinies of others. The Revolution has not exorcised these desires from the hearts of the people. Calvin B. Hoover goes so far as to say, "The energy in the capitalist world which finds expression in the struggle for wealth, for social position, and for the comforts of life, in Soviet Russia is canalized into the struggle for power." But this again is an overstatement.

The Soviet *mores* are all against the aggressive, ruthless careerist and climber. As vehemently as they condemn the greed for riches, they condemn the lust for power. So much so that the one who has it seeks to dissemble it by all means. But it is hard to do so. The Control Commissions are closely watching his movements. The Party comes down with heavy hand upon anyone exploiting his position to his own gain or glory. The public will not long abide the vaunting official who "commissars it" over them. It is quick to discern the self-seeking sham or pretender and has means of humbling him in the press, the "wall-paper," and the "purgings." This does not mean that the masses are a churlish lot, looking with jaundiced eyes upon men of superior strength and talents. On the contrary, they greatly admire them. In all the history of Russia no leader had such power as Lenin and no one was so loved by the people. His word to them was law. His every wish a command. With the profoundest respect for the man of brains and force and action, they readily grant him tremendous powers. But he must use them not to his own vantage and glory, but for the common good. Then only will he receive what all men desire—honor, gratitude, and homage.

Another and growing incentive to action is to win the approval and respect of one's fellows. Enthusiastically the Soviet public pays tribute to those who perform feats of strength and valor and cunning. It exults over the exploits of the balloonists climbing up into the high reaches of the stratosphere, the pilots of the Ant-25 making a non-stop flight of 5,825 miles through the uncharted Arctic, the explorers of the Pamirs hewing a path through the ice-bound peaks. For them the cheers and accolades of an admiring state and people. But there is nothing unique in this. In other lands they do likewise. The unique thing is that the Soviet Union does not reserve its honors for the spectacular and daring. It bestows them as lavishly upon those who serve well along the more humble, prosaic ways of life. As it acclaims Molokov for his rescue of the Chelyuskin castaways from the drifting ice-floe, so it hails the coal-miner Stakhanov for digging more tons of "black gold" than any man in the country. As it names a city after the great botanist, Michurin, to commemorate his exploits in the breeding of plants, so it names a new ship "Blacksmith Lesov" to celebrate Lesov's exploits in swinging a sledge-hammer.

With the slogan, "Let the nation know its heroes of toil," it broadcasts the names of the leading metalists, miners, weavers, oil-drillers. It headlines the records of the foremost bricklayers, bakers, glass-blowers. A big marble plaque in Moscow emblazons the names of the best collective farmers. An avenue of bronze statues glorifies the best shock-workers in the country. If one cannot achieve that All-Union distinction, he may aspire to be a "Hero of Toil" in his own republic, region, or town. If that is beyond his strength or skill, he may at least see himself posted up on the "Red Board of Honor," or the list of Stakhanovites, which hang in every shop as a daily record of those who have labored faithfully and well. Alongside them may stand the "Black Board of Dishonor," with the names of slackers, drones, and malingerers. If a man will not exert himself to win the plaudits of his fellows, he may bestir himself enough to avoid their jibes and censure.

As powerful a motive as pride is the sense of shame. Paralleling the ingenious devices for commending the faithful are those for condemning the faithless! On one hand there are gala nights when to the strains of the "International" the winners of medals and citations march to the rostrum to receive their awards; on the other hand the "Shame-Booths" built like vodka bottles from which guzzlers and loafers must collect their pay. On one hand there are "Windows of Renown" exhibiting to passers-by busts and portraits of those who have stopped gaps, repaired breaks, and prevented breakdowns; on the other hand "Chairs of Disgrace" in the dining-halls for the machine-wreckers, fuel-wasters, and spoilers of goods. For managers pushing their factories to the front there are torchlight processions with banners proclaiming their triumphs and a fanfare of trumpets; for those criminally falling down on their duties, "Black Parades" with coffins behind bands playing a funeral dirge. For enterprises that keep themselves spick and span, clean, and tidy, there is the All-Union "Red List"; for the dirty, disorderly ones, the "Black List." For loyal yeoman service there are badges, the Order of Lenin, and the Red Flag; for laggards there are the satirical decorations bestowed by their fellow-workers, such as the "Order of the Laughing Camel," the "Snail," and the "Tortoise."

Thus, the choice is presented to every man. By his own will he can classify himself. He can have what he wants. Naturally everyone wants a place on the Red Board, the Order of Lenin, a torchlight procession. These are the things that spell success and distinction and give one standing in the community. Men will strive for whatever does that. In primitive society it may be scalps. In capitalist society, money. In Soviet society it is increasingly public recognition and decorations. The Soviets have not changed this old incentive to action—the desire to be known as men of skill, prowess, and ability. But they have changed the symbols thereof, greatly increased their numbers, and made the winning of them possible to the masses.

To the old incentives to work the Soviets have added a new and more distinctive one in the feeling of ownership. This, one may demur, is not altogether new. In the capitalist world attempts have been made to enlist the interest of workers by giving them a small share in the profits. But in the Soviet world all the profits, in the last analysis, go to the workers and to them only. None of the surplus product of their labor is diverted into the pockets of private owners to support an alien class in luxury or idleness. All of it goes into the public pool, and ultimately returns to the community in the form of more commodities, schools, parks, rest homes, theatres.

The Soviet worker knows that every value he creates ultimately redounds to the benefit of himself, his own kind and class. The influence of this is far-reaching. It invests his labor with a social meaning in that not only he himself but all his fellow toilers benefit from his exertions. It induces him to keep them up to the mark, for by the same token all suffer from the shortcomings of one. It changes his attitude toward the fast worker from suspicion to trust. Instead of regarding him as the bosses' fool or knave for working himself and his fellows out of a job, he respects him for adding to the common fund. The more that goes into it the more for each to share.

To Stalin, so important is this consciousness of ownership, that in his talk to the American Labor Delegation he placed it first in the list of incentives. All workers, of course, do not have it. It is particularly lacking in the newcomer from the village. He enters the factory with the individualistic idea of "each man for himself," "grab the most and give the least." But gradually a change is wrought in his attitude. He discovers that in working for himself he is necessarily working for others. He finds that the factory is not an alien thing aloof and apart from his life. Constantly he feels that it is *his* shop, *his* factory. Slowly the idea lays hold of him. He begins to identify himself with it. Its interests become his interests. "The most astounding feature of industrial life under the Soviets," says the American engineer Rukeyser, in "Working for the Soviets," "was the fanatical pride of all workers from the head-director down to the lowliest mop. The system had indeed made it their plant."

From that, the social horizons may easily widen out to *their* industry, *their* country, to *their* fellow-workers throughout the world. To one who really feels that, it imparts a new zest and meaning to life. No longer is he engaged simply in getting a living for himself but in giving a living to others. No longer is he merely toiling for a place in the sun but to make the sun shine on all. He is now a part of something vastly bigger than himself.

A final incentive, impelling the Soviet citizen to work, is the feeling of being engaged in a great venture—the building of a new world. Ceaselessly it is drilled into him that he is a soldier in the cause of Communism—the liberator from poverty, ignorance, and war, the forger of a new society of freedom and justice. This concept is not a monopoly of the Russians. In some degree it has been implicit in followers of other great movements—Crusaders, Cromwellians, and early Christians. Always it has haunted the minds of the poets and philosophers like Blake, who swore not to cease from fight until he had "built Jerusalem on England's green and shining land." In Russia this vision of the great seers has been brought out of the clouds and given definite form and content. It has laid hold of a large company of practical men with an understanding of social laws and forces and with a scientific program for directing them to the remaking of society. With it the ragged, hungry Red Guards went forth to triumph on a score of fronts. And with it today the armies of builders are toiling away on a hundred far-flung fronts.

There in the Ural mines is Peter Petrovich, a tireless, sleepless miracle of a man, sixteen hours a day on the job, doing the work of three men. Tell him to stop, to rest, or he will drop dead in his tracks. "And what if I do?" he laughs. "Then I will have a long

rest and over my grave they may say, 'Here lies Engineer Peter
Petrovich who died at his post doing his duty for the cause.'" Far
off in the Archangel forest I saw Popov, the little surgeon, all day
long dealing with fractures, hysteria, and fevers in a province as big
as Belgium. Then a smallpox epidemic sent long lines of bare-armed
lumberjacks into his log-cabin where he stood late into the night,
scuffing away the skin with a lancet. So casual, so matter-of-fact—a
hero of labor, but never thinking he was heroic. There were the two
lads I saw in a Volga village with clenched fists before a portrait
of Lenin dedicating themselves to Communism. All day they dragged
a sledge through the villages, gathering gifts of rye and cabbages
from the peasants to build a "Lenin Corner," then entering the all-
night clubs to drive out drink and rowdyism with games and reading.
Serious, but not taking themselves too seriously, they won their way
with humor and good-fellowship.

This spirit one finds in most unexpected places—in the foreman
who looks like a hard-fisted labor-driving boss; the gaunt woman
heading a collective farm; a teacher in the Siberian forest. At once
dreamers and hard workers, idealists and stern realists. Day after day,
year after year, at the grim humdrum task of lifting, enlightening,
energizing the backward masses. Conscripts of the dream to build
the world anew! It is this that kept the Russians going through dark
and perilous days, doing so many things deemed impossible. It helped
them to overcome tremendous obstacles, to endure incredible hardships and privations. Because of it they were driven to deeds that
were truly heroic and magnificent. And by the same token it has
driven them at times to do things that were harsh and cruel. Unspar-
ing of themselves, they have not been sparing of others. In pursuit
of an ideal, ruthlessly they have swept aside those who stood in its
way, the means justified to their mind by the great goal toward which
they were driving.

Call this social passion, or call it religion—as Bernard Shaw did to
Stalin's amusement—it is a factor that must be reckoned with. One
may see the new Socialist cities, the new schools and stadiums, and
all the giants of the Five-Year Plans, but if he misses this it is like
"going to the circus and not seeing the elephant." Yet it is easy enough
to miss. Communists do not wear their hearts on their sleeves. Those
possessed by a social vision are not given to talking about it. It is an

intangible thing not set down in diagrams, charts, and figures. That is the reason the casual visitor and economist have so often been led astray. That is the reason their oft-repeated predictions of Soviet collapse have come to naught. They have left this out of their calculations, priding themselves on being realists. But this is very much of a reality—this ideal which created the Revolution and at the same time was created by it.

On the Red Square thousands of Comsomols chant in unison:

> We are building a new world,
> We are building the world anew!

How many are really affected by this? How much of a factor is it in their lives? Doubtless with very few is it a dominant incentive. On the other hand, probably very few are wholly untouched by it. For no one is completely an egoist as no one is altogether an altruist. What it is that moves a man to action no one can tell, not even the man himself. Usually the individual, self-regarding motives are uppermost. But occasionally, at any rate, the social, other-regarding ones are in the ascendant. At times people will do for others even that which they would not do for themselves. Of this the Communists see many evidences and on their increase they count for the future.

Mass Incentives—Socialist Competition and Mutual Aid

Men think, feel, and are moved to action not only as individuals, but as groups. This is particularly true in the Soviet Union with its emphasis on class consciousness and solidarity. More original and striking than the incentives for individuals are those means for rousing the initiative and energy of the masses which the Communists have devised. Rather they have for the most part emerged spontaneously out of the masses themselves. Chief among these are the Shock Brigade and Stakhanovite movements. (See page 220.)

Entire factories declare themselves to be "Shock" or "Stakhanovite" factories. So do mines, farms, ships, and schools, challenging each other to beat old records, to make new ones, to lift them as high or higher than in America. Blast-furnace challenges blast-furnace to an iron-smelting contest. The dam construction gang on the right bank of a river pits itself against the gang on the left bank while electric lights flash back and forth which is ahead. The same device was used by Colonel Goethals in digging the Panama Canal. He pitted the army engineers on the Atlantic against the civilian engineers on the Pacific, and published the records of the steam-shovels. In the Soviet Union this group emulation goes on in every sphere from subway digging to the dressing of shop windows. Theatre challenges theatre to produce the most artistic revolutionary play. Cooks engage to make tastier meals if the charwoman will sweep the floors cleaner. Children covenant with their parents never to play truant from school if they in turn never play truant from the factory. They promise to attain 100 per cent in their lessons if their vodka-drinking fathers stay 100 per cent sober on their jobs. Congresses of the best workers—the most eminent shock miners, metalists, weavers—meet to consider their achievements and pledge to surpass their past. In comic relief, congresses of the worst workers—the most eminent "shock" loafers, guzzlers, and wasters—meeting to consider their failings, promise to reform and mend their ways.

Thus the spirit of rivalry is transferred from the fields of sport into every realm of workaday life. And it is carried on with all those devices used in games and contests with the aim of producing better team-work and morale: Banners to wave over the contenders; battle cries to rally them—"Fight for the honor of our steel-mill"; cheers, decorations, trophies for the victors and sometimes rewards more tangible and material. Evidently then, under Socialism, as Lenin said, "Competition is not destroyed, but, on the contrary, for the first time it is applied on a really wide mass-scale." At the same time it is being raised to a higher level on a different plane. That is why the old word for competition, *konkurs,* with its connotations of selfish struggle for oneself is now replaced by another, *sorevnovaniye,* friendly contest or emulation. As Stalin explains it, "The old capitalist competition says: 'Devil take the hindmost.' Socialist contest says: 'Help the ones behind to catch up to you so all may take part in the general advance.'" This is precisely what the victorious shock-brigades do. After beating their rivals they render them first-aid, searching out the reasons for failure, and applying the remedies. This is known as the "social-tug," a towing-expedition to pull the lagging ones up into line and inspiring them to keep the pace.

Another way through which this instinct for mutual aid finds outlet is the "chef-movement"—older groups becoming the patrons of younger, weaker ones. A factory adopted a village, bringing it tractor-menders, sorted seeds, a football, or a bust of Lenin, the "yeast of the new life." A grand opera adopts a Seamen's Club, sending it singers, musicians, and ballet dancers, while, at the same time, it is on the lookout for gifted voices and players, bringing them under its tutelage. A college assumes patronage over a Red Army regiment which in turn becomes patron to a band of Pioneers. "Communism," said Lenin, "begins at the point where men work not for their immediate gain but for the common interest of all."

The highest expression of this is found in the "Saturdayings," *Subbotniks,* or "Sundayings," so-called because the participants give up their normal rest day to cope with some emergency. (See page 220.) A trainload of fruit or vegetables is in danger of spoiling, a sudden winter blizzard ties up traffic, a construction job must be rushed to a finish—the call goes out for all good citizens to come to the aid of their country. They come in droves, turning their holiday into a workday—clerks and conductors, printers, postmen, and Pioneers, housewives and high officials like Kaganovich. Over a million helped carry timbers into the Moscow subway and rocks and dirt out of it. Tens of engines and airplanes are each year donated to the nation as the fruits of labor on off-days and overtime. These "Saturdayings" resemble the old American building and snow-clearing "bees" when everyone joined hands to raise a neighbor's barn or dig out a drifted road. And they have much of the same fun and festive spirit. Bands or accordions accompany the "Saturdayers" to their tasks; there are songs, banter and laughter, while they are at them.

Lenin, who took part in the first "Saturdayings," saw in them an augury of how work will be done under Communism. Out of joy in a big job well done grows sheer delight in the sense of creation. "Constructiveness," said William James, "is a genuine and irresistible instinct in man as in the bees or beaver." In Marx's words, "Work is the natural activity of man." Stalin speaks of "a radical change in man's attitude toward labor transforming it from the shameful and heavy burden it once was considered to be into a thing of glory and honor." In the good society envisioned by the Communist all the old and new incentives—gaining a living, power, honors, the sense of ownership, even working for the common good—will play a minor rôle in spurring men on. Men will work simply because they like working—out of joy in self-expression, out of sheer pleasure in the play of one's muscles and the exercise of one's brain. "They will paint for an age at a sitting and never get tired at all." That is true of some even now. What is already manifest in a few, the Communists maintain, is potential in all. Once humanity is liberated from concern over the necessities of life, then, in the words of Engels, "work will become the first necessity of being." Then the tremendous capacities, long latent in mankind, will unfold and blossom forth in ways undreamed of.

51. Where Does All the Money Come From— and Go To?

Back of all big things in the Soviet Union stands the budget. In 1937 it was 98 billion rubles. At the official rate of exchange about 19 billion dollars—more than that of the United States and Great Britain combined. Behind this looms the still bigger Financial Plan, "recording in red and black all receipts and all expenses in all branches of the nation's business." But let the experts lose themselves in the mazes of that gigantic balance-sheet. The budget itself is enough to grapple with.

Why is the Soviet budget so large? It includes the cost for the upkeep of the State, army, courts, and schools just as do those of other countries. But where they leave off the Soviet budget begins. Its big task is to provide the capital for a colossal fast-expanding economy. It must find the means to bring thousands of infant enterprises into being, to nurture hundreds of others to full maturity, and to satisfy the appetites of the ever-growing giants of industry. To pass from figures of speech to actual figures: In addition to spending some 58 billions for current expenses, the Commissar of Finance has the task of producing 40 billions to invest in transport, industry, and farming.

Each year the Soviet government raises a similar fund for investment, increasing it, if expedient, as the national income increases. In doing this it ends the old debate as to whether capital could be accumulated in a Socialist state. Its opponents said it would not, could not, be done. Only under capitalism, they insisted, out of a surplus in the hands of individuals, could come the wealth to be used in making new wealth. In a Socialist society people would not save as they would refuse to stint themselves now in order to live more abundantly later. They would not emulate the planful bee but the carefree butterfly, preferring to enjoy the food and drink and clothes of the present rather than build up the machines for producing more of these things in the future.

To these contentions the Soviet budget is a final and effective refutation. It shows that each year under Socialism a third of the national income has been saved. This has been done in an impoverished country by a naturally spendthrift people consenting to forego the luxuries and comforts of life and oftentimes its very necessities. "To build blast-furnaces, we have gone without boots and butter." "To put belts on machines we have tightened our own belts."

Indeed, to make the primary accumulation of capital without aid from abroad, this sacrifice was necessary. The mills and power plants now covering the country are all owned by the people. However, it is not only this aspect of Soviet economy that makes it different from other countries. There is another and more important distinction. Soviet capital is invested according to the Plan and appears in the budget as non-repayable grants to new industry and agriculture. By this method the annual sums credited to the national economy for the Volga-Don Canal, railways, rolling-mills, airplanes, and subways get into circulation without becoming a huge private debt. Expanding productive en-

terprise does not mean simultaneously building a vast debt structure that may interrupt production as it does elsewhere. It is just
as though the State were sole stockholder of a new business bought
outright. Capital in the Soviet Union does not lie idle in the banks,
is not exported to foreign countries for a high return, nor does it
get into the hands of a small, powerful group. It is this control of
credit in the Soviet set-up which accounts for much of the success
in solving unemployment, eliminating cycles and steadily raising
the standard of living. How has the Soviet managed to accumulate this capital? By what devices does it provide for a budget of
nearly a hundred billion rubles and steadily growing bigger each
year?

How the Budget is Raised

Revenue from the "Socialized Economy." The great bulk, 90 per
cent, is derived from the State-owned industries and trade. It comes
mainly from the Turnover Tax, akin to the sales-tax. It is collected,
however, not directly from the consumer, but at the point where the
goods are made. Beginning at 2 per cent on basic products, such as
coal and tractors, the rates rise to 12 per cent on food-stuffs like flour
and cheese, to 20 per cent on footwear and textiles. These are doubled
on luxury articles like cigarettes and cosmetics and, as a deterrent to
the use of alcohol, 88 per cent is levied on vodka, cognac, and liqueurs
—which is really an excise tax.

After handing over these large sums most enterprises still show a
surplus. Who gets this? In theory all these profits, too, belong to the
State as it is the sole owner. It elects, however, to take only a share
in the profits of each concern, ranging from 10 to 80 per cent. The
rest is used for future expansion and housing, for clubs and stadiums,
for bonuses and prizes to the managing staff and shock-brigades,
acting thus as a stimulus to efficiency.

Revenues from the People. From direct taxes the receipts are relatively small and decreasing. But they have been of great importance politically. They served to squeeze out the non-Socialist elements by laying on them the heaviest load.

The Agricultural Tax consists of a levy of three per cent on the gross income from arable land, meadows, vineyards, cattle, sheep, horses, mules, or camels. Sometimes in order to encourage the planting of hemp, mustard, kenaf, sugar-beets, or soy-beans, half rates are laid on these special crops or they may be exempted from any tax whatsoever. An Income Tax is collected from persons earning more than 140 rubles a month. Beginning at 80 copecks, it mounts to 35 per cent on salaries and wages above 500 rubles and is deducted monthly. Exempted from tax are Red Army men and commanders, pensioners, veterans of the civil war, and "heroes of labor." The amount paid by others depends not only on what one earns, but how and where he earns it. It favors literary workers, scientists, and artists, exacting 1 per cent on incomes up to 1,000 rubles a month and rising to 20 per cent on 20,000 and 38 per cent in excess of that. It deals leniently with actors, cooperative artisans, physicians, and inventors—their tax ranging from 2 per cent on the first 1,000 to about 50 per cent after 24,000 rubles a month.

The Inheritance Tax is steeply graduated, but there is no actual limitation on the amount of the property which can be inherited. In England death duties take 50 per cent of all fortunes over 2,000,000 pounds. The Soviets take 90 per cent of any amount over half a million rubles. One may not dispose of his property exactly as he pleases. Formerly it could be willed only to surviving wife or husband, parents, children, and grandchildren, or to persons incapable of self-support who have been dependent on the deceased for a year or more. Under the new Constitution the right of inheritance is considerably broadened. Exceeding the receipts from incomes and inheritance is a special surtax for housing and cultural purposes. Altogether these direct taxes on the people bring into the treasury less than three per cent of the total receipts.

Mass Loans bring in about 5 billion rubles a year. Their purposes are indicated by their names: "Loan of Industrialization," "Third Year of the Second Five-Year Plan," and so forth. They are floated in a win-the-war spirit—the war against Soviet poverty, backwardness, and defenselessness. Vivid posters of the long bayoneted Red Army guarding arrays of smoke-belching mills summon the workers to subscribe at least a month's wages, usually paid in installments. So strong is the pressure, assert foreign critics, that it amounts to compulsion. But there are other cogent reasons for the popularity of these bonds: They bear interest at about four per cent. They are tax-free, may be borrowed upon up to 30 per cent of their value, and are redeemable in cases of dire need like fire or prolonged illness. They appeal to the old gambling spirit of the Russians, with lottery features a part of some issues. On stated occasions called "Bondholders' Day," public drawings are held in the chief cities attended by great crowds to hear the calling of the lucky numbers as they are drawn from the revolving drums. All these loans are now consolidated into one issue amounting to 19 billion rubles.

The question arises, "Will not this interest on bonds and savings create a new class of *rentiers* and coupon-clippers?" In rejoinder the Communists point out that there were in 1936 some 55 million sub-scribers among whom large holders can hardly be more than a hand-ful. Also the whole Soviet psychology is against the acquisition of wealth enough to live without working. So much so that the winners of big prizes in the lotteries almost always hand over to orphanages, libraries, or sport-fields a good part of their takings. To buyers of Soviet bonds in foreign countries, both principal and interest are paid in dollars, pounds, or francs. The rate of exchange is based on a fixed quantity of gold so that holders are insured against fluctuations in foreign moneys.

Not much is obtained from Duties on Exports, nor on Imports although they reach fantastic heights on luxury articles like coffee and silk. There is a Stamp-Tax on wills, bequests, depositions, bills of lading, deeds of sales, and the mass of documents, intrinsic to the old Russian roundabout system of doing things. A fight against this red-tape is part of the campaign against the bureaucrats. But it is hard for them to renounce their old methods or for the people to give up their faith in the greater value of papers with an imposing array of stamps and seals. How vital they were is reflected in the old saying, "A Russian citizen is composed of three things: a body, a soul, and a passport." How numerous they still are is shown by a glimpse into a Soviet office, or into the pockets of a citizen bulging with membership books, applications, affidavits, and petitions. To most of these must be affixed a stamp costing from a few copecks to several rubles. There is also a steady income from notary fees, harbor levies, pilotage, and light-house dues, duties on trade-marks, patents, and hunting licenses.

Besides the enormous size of the budget another striking feature is that it is balanced. Instead of the usual deficit, the Soviet exchequer has a handsome surplus. In 1936 receipts exceeded expenditures by 1,700,000,000 rubles. In contrast to most capitalist countries the budget of the Reds is not in the red.

How the Budget is Spent

Every page in this book is an account of activities which have their sources primarily in the budget. It is enough, then, to indicate in percentages the way it is apportioned.

As the "socialized sector" provides about 90 per cent of the revenue, so in turn it receives the lion's share of the disbursements. But why go through the motions of taking from trade and industry with one hand and giving to them with the other? Why maintain an army of officials to do this? In order that the State may carry out its economic strategy, directing its resources to the points where they are most needed at the moment. Thus, in the First Five-Year Plan, heavy industries were nurtured on the tribute taken from the light industries. If the quick development of an air-fleet, a Northern Sea Route, a rubber plantation, is deemed imperative, then into these channels the necessary funds are diverted. Altogether about two-fifths of the budget goes to financing the national economy.

How is the remainder of the budget spent? Less than 2 per cent is used for administrative purposes. In spite of the huge apparatus of State and the outcry against the "plague of bureaucrats," this is a small sum. One reason for this is that the fabulous salaries of the old regime have been done away with. The armed forces absorb about 20 per cent, which again is not large considering the size of the army and the air fleet. Critics say it would be much larger if it included the costs of the munition-plants. But these probably would be offset by the huge sums invested by the Red Army in its educational system. About 18 per cent is assigned to social and cultural activities, schools, universities, science. About 8 per cent goes to the health service, hospitals, rest-homes, veterinary-points, the fight against epidemics. About 3 per cent goes to the state police, courts, prisons and rehabilitation colonies. About 6 per cent is set aside for the banks, the reserve, and emergency funds.

In sharp contrast to most budgets is the small amount for service on debts and loans. About 3 per cent is paid out for interest on State Bonds and that goes largely into the pockets of the wide masses. Very little, likewise, goes to pay for past wars, and nothing to support the unemployed because there are none. That is why it is called a "living budget." It is mostly poured into productive channels—into new industries, farms, education, science, and the arts, quickening and enriching the economic and cultural life.

52. What is the Rôle of Money, Banks, and Credits?

As is evident, there is money in the Soviet Union, and lots of it—12 billion rubles. It pays wages, sells goods, buys tickets for trains and theatres. Likewise there are lots of banks—more than 50 thousand counting all branches. They cash checks, float loans, and grant credits. Is not this just like any other system of finance? Apparently it is in technique. But in reality there is a great difference. The rôle that money plays in the Soviet scheme is one of the things that makes the new civilization.

"It has now become the orthodox thing to say . . . that Soviet money is not money in the capitalist sense at all, since it does not obey the same rules and laws." (Calvin B. Hoover) It is for domestic purposes only, the export and import of it being strictly forbidden. It is a "managed" currency, so that fluctuations do not directly affect the price-level as that in turn is controlled. Its purchasing power depends on who has it and where it is spent. It is being shorn of its power to exploit others, as profit-making in private fields is almost gone. It does not primarily make for security as people look more and more to society for that. Possession in itself does not confer distinction; on the contrary, the moneyed man is an outcast, the "money-face" is fast vanishing.

Not less striking are the differences in the banks. They do not trade in money seeking the most profitable loans, but are primarily agents for redistributing the national income. They advance certain great sums to industry that draw no interest and are never repaid. They grant credits to the seller, rather than the buyer, abolishing thus the bill of exchange. They settle accounts between Combines, Collectives, and Cooperatives without resorting to legal tender, but by a system of debit and credit entries. When a tractor plant buys a million rubles of steel, that sum is deducted from its account and added to that of the Steel Combine. This practice is similar to the use of checks in America and through it more than 80 per cent of transactions are effected.

Ultimately, all business will be done by this direct transfer of credits on the books of the banks. When it reaches a full 100 per cent then present financial institutions, along with the State, may "wither away" and the transition to the moneyless society of Communism may be completed. Then, instead of rubles, the unit of measure and exchange may be "labor-hours" and the banks will be transformed into simple clearing-houses, offices of record and account. In the words of Lenin, "Good book-keeping and control pave the way to Socialism." But this is a vision of the future. "The dialectic of our progress," says Finance Commissar Grinko, "lies in the fact that the better we organize our finances on a sound basis, the sooner will we finish the building up of our Socialist order and the sooner will we be able to throw money into the scrap-bag of history." For the present, then, the Soviets are using banks, credits, and currency in their own peculiar way. Money is still performing its four functions: As a medium of exchange, a standard of deferred payment, a means of storing wealth, and a unit of account between enter-prises.

Money, Gold, and Commodities

On April 1, 1935, there was nearly eight billion rubles in circulation. About half of this was in Bank Notes, or *Chervontzy,* of 10 gold rubles each. These were backed by 858 millions in gold bars and coins, 7 millions in other precious metals, and 35 millions in stable foreign moneys. This aggregated about 784 million gold dollars. This reserve was built up from almost nothing, inasmuch as the gold stocks of the Tsars were spent during the Revolution or carried abroad by fleeing Whites. Slowly, the new reserves have been accumulated, mainly by the direct mining of gold, silver, and platinum by the State.

There is gold, however, not only in the hills of Russia, but in its hoardings. Like India, it is an old country, and for centuries a part of the inflowing gold has been salted away in jars, pots, boots, and iron-bound boxes. To lure this treasure from its hiding place, the Soviets opened the Torgsin, a chain-store system in which goods were sold only for gold or its equivalent. In some 1,400 places it tapped this underground reservoir, bringing steadily into the State-coffers a golden stream of old rubles of the Tsar, British pounds, rings, brooches, and bracelets. Up to the closing of Torgsin in 1936 it brought in 270 million gold rubles ($235,000,000), a part of which came from foreign remittances.

With this fast increase in the metal reserve has gone a faster expansion in trade and industry, and with it the need for more currency. Hence, the issue of "unsecured" Treasury Notes, of 1, 3, and 5 rubles, supposed not to exceed the Bank Notes in circulation. The difference between the two forms is largely technical. Both are really inconvertible into gold as the Soviet Government clings to its reserves as tightly as does the British and the American. Both have the same value as legal tender. Both are sold on the market at the same rate of exchange—five rubles for one dollar.

The Soviets have always denied the existence of any such thing as "inflation" or "fiat money." "How can it possibly be asserted that our currency represents no value?" asked Stalin. "Is it not a fact that with it we built Magnitostroy and Dnieprostroy, the Stalingrad and Kharkov Works, thousands of State farms, hundreds of thousands of collective farms? What determines the stability of Soviet currency? Of course, not simply the gold reserves, *but the tremendous quantities of commodities in the hands of the State marketed at fixed prices.* Who can deny that such a backing, which exists only in the U.S.S.R., constitutes a more genuine security than any reserves of gold?"

Capitalist economists, however, assert there was a marked inflation in the Soviet Union during the early period of capital construction. The ruble in retail trade did not buy nearly as much in 1934 as it bought in 1930. This was due to the shortage of consumption goods arising from emphasis on the building of machines, tractors, steel mills, and power plants. As there were not enough goods for the people to buy, a part of the money paid them in wages remained unspent in their pockets. But as the government had to keep on paying wages it had to keep on issuing currency. To prevent prices from skyrocketing, the Soviets instituted a system of "closed" stores in which limited quotas of goods were sold to workers at low fixed prices. However, in the "open" markets which handled a small part of the total trade, prices rose to great heights. But in general instead of rapidly mounting prices, the usual index of inflation where prices are not fixed as they were in Russia, there was this scarcity of commodities. At any rate, it occurred in the construction of values and not in their destruction as is usually the case.

The corner was turned in 1934 when the supply of commodities began to increase rapidly. By a series of decrees to the State Bank was given almost absolute power over industry by the strictest allocation of credits, which kept the emission of currency from getting out of hand and running away with itself. In the hands of the government were the means necessary for controlling its finances and it vigorously applied them. The temporary rise in the cost of living following the abolition of food cards and rationing in 1935 was a normal process of adjustment in reaching an equilibrium between goods and money.

This is the salient fact about Soviet money: The value of the ruble is determined primarily by the volume of goods in the country. Now with increasing quantities of goods coming into the market the value of the ruble is increasing. Barring war or some major catastrophe the process will go steadily on. With a supply of food and commodities equal to all demands there will be a stable currency and the purchasing power of the ruble will rise to the world level or above it.

Banks, Credit and Savings

The nerve-center of the financial system is the State Bank, *Gosbank,* with some 2,800 branches. 1. It is the bank of issue, printing the paper money and minting the coins—about a half billion in silver, copper, and bronze. 2. It floats the government loans. 3. It holds the reserves of precious metals and foreign currencies. In its vaults are the celebrated crown jewels, displayed on special occasions to the delight of visitors. 4. It receives the taxes and other revenues through its own network of branches and those of other credit organs. As its aides in this work of bringing the billions into the keeping of this national treasury there are seven thousand inspectors. 5. It grants all the short-term credits running from two weeks up to ninety days. This assignment of working capital is a vital matter—too little and industry is strangled, too much and there is no incentive to cut cost. In the past managers relying on the bounties of the State have come to it for funds to make up all arrears. Now the bank holds them to strict accounting, granting credits only as they live up to their contracts and as their use is accompanied by the scheduled production and delivery of goods. If the goods are not forthcoming, if the credits are used for other purposes than for which they were allotted, further credits are stopped while a thorough investigation is made. In this way an exact and continuous check up on the functioning of every enterprise is carried on. A council of Forty, headed by the Commissar of Finance, outlines the bank's policies and chooses the seven members of its Board of Directors. Interest charges and commissions more than pay its expenses, particularly as its growth has been phenomenal, increasing its transactions twenty fold in the last decade. Of its profits, half goes to the government and half to increase its capital.

The funnels through which pass the allocations from the budget are the Long-Term Credit Banks. Chief of these is the Prombank, which advances more money to new industries and electrification than any bank in the world. It goes in the form of loans for as long as forty years or in the form of subventions—non-repayable, non-interest bearing subsidies granted out of the budget and recognized as national surplus or savings being spent for the common good. Thus, enterprises come into being unhandicapped by a pyramiding debt owed to some person or class. The initial capital is given outright. In return the Prombank in behalf of the State receives a percentage of the profits of each enterprise, a portion of the funds for depreciation, interest on funds used for machinery and extension, and, most important of all, the right of rigid supervision and inspection. To do this effectively it opens branches on the big construction jobs. It sets up their bookkeeping, audits accounts, prevents over-staffing, and, like the State Bank, it makes their finances depend on how they keep up to the mark set by the plans. "We grant you the money. Now let us see what you are doing with it." In this realm Commissar of Finance Grinko calls for the utmost "Bolshevik vigilance," a term often used interchangeably with "American efficiency." Through this "control by the ruble," as it is called, financial discipline is maintained over the huge complex of industries and they are kept in line with the Plan.

There are three other banks extending long-term credits in specialized fields. The Agricultural Bank finances farming in everything from seeds to tractors. The Bank of Municipal Economy and Housing provides for public utilities, schools, theatres, and apartments. The Commercial Bank finances the capital construction of cooperative organisations, the system of chain stores and "kitchen-factories," the artels of hunters and trappers, the art and handicraft guilds, making samovars, lace, lacquer, and woodware. The Bank of Foreign Trade finances imports and exports. Outside the Soviet borders purchases and sales are made with foreign currency, and by outright payments in gold of which they have ever larger amounts, thanks to the fast increasing output of the mines.

Savings Banks. Under full Communism individual thrift may well disappear as there will be no motive for saving in a society of plenty. But there is now. Even though the worker is insured against illness, accidents, and old age, he may want to lay by something extra for a rainy day or a holiday. The State too, pressed for funds for its Five-Year Plans, wants every copeck it can lay hands upon. Therefore, to encourage savings, it offers many inducements. It pays 3 per cent to individuals, and about half that to organizations. Or if clients prefer, instead of receiving interest, they can draw lottery prizes in money. It exempts interest on savings accounts from the income tax, all deposits from the tax on inheritance, and all correspondence thereon from the stamp-tax. It opens up banks at easily accessible places in mills, schools, village reading-rooms—more than 60 thousand of them. The average deposit is about 225 rubles but there are more than 15 millions of them. This enables the government to mobilize out of funds that otherwise might be idle, enough to build a score of giant farms and factories, relieving also, by that much, the pressure on the market for consumers' goods. By a single order on a Savings Bank, a citizen may pay his bills for food, shelter, light, and heat. Thus they serve as training schools, preparing the masses for the future moneyless society.

53. Will the Machine and Industrialization Under the Soviets Standardize People, Create Conflict Between Classes, and Lower Aesthetic Values?

"No," reply the Communists, if they stop to discuss the question at all. "Machines! More Machines!" is the cry that goes up all over the Soviet land bent on the fullest industrialization. Against it one dissenting poet rises to declare, "I prefer to behold the steppes sown not with steel and nails, but with flowers; to see a peasant embracing a peasantess and not a tractor!" To the Communists that is the nostalgia of a sick befuddled mind, sheer nonsense and insanity. So is Spengler's prophecy of a time when "man will blot the machine from his memory and create

a new world in which nothing of this devil's technique is left."
For such views the Communists have only smiles or contempt.
Not because they are unaware of the indictment against the
machine: "It turns men into automatons." "It takes a machine
to run a machine." "The drone of the motors, the clang of the
trip-hammer drowns the voice of the nightingale." "In the wake
of industrialization follow bitter exploitation, strife, and disillusion."

All these evils, insist the Communists, are inherent not in the
machine but in its ownership. To exorcise them it is only necessary to establish social ownership of the machine. Then, instead
of running for private profit it will run for the service and en-
richment of all. Instead of dividing people into warring classes,
into owners and workers, it will unite them into one great family
of toilers, promoting good-will and fellowship among all men.
"There is more of brotherhood in asphalt and electricity," said
Chekhov, "than in all the preachings of Tolstoy." The same idea
is reflected in an address of the Soviet Academy of Science to
their colleagues throughout the world. After a recital of achievements in planning, discoveries of natural resources and building
of giant industries, it goes on to say, "We are raising the material
level of the masses. But we do not in the least desire to build
a soulless civilization like the machine civilization of America
where the toiler is an accounting unit, an appendage of the mechanical system. On the contrary we are building a perfected
technical basis for a society where the human being is the master
of the system, an instrument for releasing him from excessive
toil, and a basis for the blossoming out of a comradely society."
Instead of blighting the spirit of song and poetry, in emancipat-
ing man from drudgery and poverty, the machine will give him
the leisure and means to create and enjoy the arts as never before.

But everywhere in the world, insist the critics of the machine, as
mechanical powers increase, artistic powers have decreased. They
point to industrial America, where the spirit of music seems to fade

from the immigrant Mexicans, Slavs, and Italians—certainly from their children. They point to the handicraftsmen, the Minnesingers, and the morris dancers of old England, disappearing with the advent of the machine; the loss and dissipation of the moral and aesthetic values drawn from centuries of contact with nature and the soil. What the machine has done to other peoples, they argue, it will do to the Russians.

In rejoinder to this the Communists point out how the machine came to England. It came under the Manchester economy, the *laissez-faire* doctrine that forbade any interference with its free operations. From the village green it swept the people into the factories to toil unlimited hours under ghastly conditions. It drove women out of the open air to work naked in the mines, out of the asylums it took the orphans to chain them to the wheels till they dropped. It left them stunted in mind and body and out of their lives drained the feeling of joy and beauty. (Elizabeth Barrett Browning's "The Cry of the Children")

But that isn't the way the machine is coming to Russia. Into Russia it comes under a Socialist economy that curbs and controls it, that protects the workers by a close network of social legislation and makes the machine the servant, not the master, of men. Take a concrete instance: the new cement mill across the Moscow River from Saburovo. To it flock the peasants from all the villages about. Out of it they pour when the whistle blows, not drooping and exhausted but with energy enough to till their own fields and time enough for banter, fun, and laughter. Through the village streets parade the youth singing "Vanka Tanka" and the "Bells of Novgorod," all the old folk-songs of the far away and long ago and the new songs of the machine, the Red Army, and the Revolution. And often until midnight the village greens resound to the soft thudding of feet dancing to the strains of the accordion and balalaika.

Into this countryside the machine has come, and, so far at any rate, with no devastating results. Upon their cement mill the worker-peasants look, not as an alien ruthless thing, but rather as a friend, enriching their lives. It is the home of people working with machines and not of machines served by human beings. In part it belongs to them, and in conference with the managers they share in its direction.

Through their Labor Unions conditions of labor are fixed: A seven-hour working day, a six-hour day for the rock loaders; a five-hour day for grinders and stokers working in heat and dust. Every worker receives full pay for a fortnight's vacation—a month for apprentices. There is a free clinic; a dispensary; a club for concerts; cinema; theatre; and library.

In the light of these extensive provisions guarding the health and welfare of the worker, Lillian Wald observed some years ago that "while America has the highest production and the lowest social protection, Russia has the highest social protection and the lowest production." Maybe Russia's low production in part was due to these liberal measures. But that is in keeping with Socialist ideals and theory. The mill must be concerned not only with the production of cement, but with the whole life and well-being of its workers—physical, mental, and cultural. And the workers, conversely, through their Labor Unions are concerned not only with their own welfare but with the increase of production. Under the Soviet system the two are dialectically related to each other.

Pointing out in 1934 that during the first period of construction "our emphasis was one-sidedly placed on machines," Stalin went on to declare that "henceforth it must be put on the men who master and run them." Says A. C. Pigou, "To have enshrined in the actual policy of a great country the doctrine that it is life, not machinery, that matters in the end; that the supreme commodity is man himself; that the approaches to civilization should be free to all, and not the privileges of a few, is to have made a unique contribution to history. Here has been lit a candle that will not go out."

III. Social Life

54. What is the Status of Women Under the Soviets?

"The Soviet Union has not left a stone unturned in all the laws that formerly held women in subjection," said Lenin in 1920. "With pride and without exaggeration we can state that this is the only country in the world where women enjoy full equal rights with men." Women comprised a fifth of the membership of the last All-Union Congress of Soviets. Five hundred thousand are elected as deputies to the local Soviets with several thousand acting as presidents and secretaries. A fourth of the judges and lay judges are women. Along with a ceaseless campaign to bring more women into administrative posts and into the professions, every effort is made to fit them for their new tasks. More than half the students in the medical schools are women; in the engineering schools—civil, mining, and electrical —a third are women. Several hundred have attained distinction as farm managers and directors of plants. A thousand have been awarded the Order of the Red Banner or some other Soviet decoration for their achievements in the arts and sciences or for personal courage and heroism. Four million train regularly in parachute, gliding, gas-mask, aviation, rifle, sport and physical culture "circles." Among the graduates of the military academies are several who have attained the rank of general.

"For full emancipation of women and to ensure their real equality with men," declared Lenin, "it is necessary for them to participate in general productive labor. In place of a few hundred women, millions and millions all over the land must take part in it." Today there are eight million women wage-earners, a large proportion of whom are engaged in industry and transport as aviators, sailors, stevedores, locomotive engineers, watch-makers, iron molders, miners, carpenters.

"In building the AMO auto plant," says the American engineer, C. M. Peter, "most of the mortar was mixed by women, and carried in loads on their shoulders up ladders and runways while the walls rose rapidly under the deft hands of the women brick-layers. The work was not only done quickly but was treated as a game with a constant exchange of jokes and banter. Certainly there was no forced labor on the part of these happy, efficient women doing their bit for the Five-Year Plan. Nor in the capable corps installing the sash glass and window frames in the fac-tories. Nor among the women operators of machines, trucks, and tractors whom I observed in many parts of the Soviet Union."

With equal pay for equal work, the same status for married women as for single, and the rapid annihilation of all sex-taboos, the Soviet Union puts into operation the ideas of the most ad-vanced feminists. Nowhere is there a trace of sex discrimination, unless certain protective laws based on the physiological differ-ences of women may be thus construed. Under eighteen they must not do heavy lifting and the norm for women loaders is half that for men. Women on tread-machines or tension jobs are allowed two days off a month. Pregnant or nursing mothers may not work as conductors or stokers. The coercion of a woman into sexual intercourse through threats or intimidation, or by force of her financial dependence on a man, or employment by him, is a criminal offense.

Fight Against the Old Folkways—Polygamy, Wife-Beating

"In the legal field," said Lenin, "we have done everything to put women on an equal basis with men. But that is only the beginning." The real struggle is to bring public opinion up to the level of the laws, to liberate women from the tyranny of the folkways—especially among most of the non-Slavic races.

Immediately after the Revolution, polygamy, wife-purchase, and the stealing of brides were interdicted by law. But in masked form these practices persisted and the Moslem woman continued to carry the "veil," a heavy, hideous, horse-hair shroud, completely enveloping the whole figure. She was so habituated to it, that, in exposing even her face, she felt the same sense of nakedness that the Western woman might feel in exposing her body. To men, its removal meant violation of all holy traditions, brazen defiance of the laws of Allah. Upon it, nevertheless, as the badge of woman's inferiority, a furious assault was begun. The cry, "Unveil! Unveil!" rose in the bazaars of Samarkand and Bokhara and before the mosque in the far-off mountain *aouls.* Hundreds of the pioneers who dared to discard it were cast out of their homes, raped, tortured, and slain. Out of this came a series of mass-unveilings, with ten thousand women in one day casting their shrouds into bonfires. In other places the symbol of woman's servitude was the *berek,* a tiny bonnet with silver coins perched on the forehead. Amidst thunderous applause great assemblies, demonstratively throwing away the ancient headdress, are replacing them with silk kerchiefs of Soviet red.

No longer do Mohammedan women regard the silence and obedience enjoined on them by the Prophet as their chief virtues. They want a place in the new world rising around them and a part in the making of it. This drive for emancipation rouses against them all the age-old forces of superstition and reaction. They find out that freedom is not given to anyone, but must be taken. Powerful aids in the taking of it are the breakdown of the feudal order under the impact of industrialization, and the zealous espousal of the aims and ideas of the Revolution by the younger Moslems, and intensive education through their own clubs and co-operatives. From chattels and harem slaves, the women of the Middle East are being rapidly transformed into citizens with full rights.

In the Russian villages, the doctrine of woman's essential inferiority to man was not so deeply entrenched. But that it was there is attested by hundreds of proverbs: "A woman's hair is long, but her brain is short." "Walls built by women do not rise high." "Towns built by women do not endure long." "All women are Eve's kin; from them issues every sin." As against the rib theory of the creation of woman, the peasants had their own version—still more derogatory and humorous. Having extracted the rib from man's side, God was holding it before fashioning it into a woman. Just then a dog snatched it from his hands and started to run away with it. Reaching out, God seized the dog by the tail. But the dog tore loose, leaving his tail in God's hand. So as not to lose time, God made the best of the situation, and, in lieu of the man's rib, used the dog's tail to make Eve. According to the canons of the church, woman was essentially an "unclean" creature, forbidden to touch the holy altar lest she defile it, and, after childbirth, compelled to undergo a ritual of cleansing.

In the old *Domostroi,* the rules for the management of the household composed by the priest Silvester, the injunction to chastise their wives is solemnly laid upon all good husbands. In this domain of Christian ethics, the old mujik acquitted himself with zeal and fervor. Wife-beating was his favorite indoor sport and winter pastime, an outlet for surplus energy, a ready relief for pent-up emotions. In low spirits he beat her, and when he felt good he beat her out of sheer excess of joy. He beat her when the cow was lost; and maybe when it was found again. He beat her when he was drunk; and when he was sober a few blows in passing would do no harm—on the contrary, they served to keep order in the home, to restore health to the soul, and to assure his wife of his continuing love. However bizarre and fantastic this may seem, its truth is attested by scores of proverbs from "Hit your wife harder, the soup will be tastier," to "Love your wife like your soul, *dooshoo;* thrash her like a pear-tree, *grooshoo.*" And, not only to the mujik, but to the wife too, chastisement was the evidence of a deep affection: "Behold how he loves me!" sings the matron in a folk song, as she recounts her welts and bruises.

No longer, however. The collective farms and the women's organizations with millions of "delegates" in local and national conferences, are creating a new, capable, and confident type of woman—and new folkways. When the new ways are not powerful enough to stay the hand of the wife-beater, the law steps in. To the older peasant, interference with his age-old prerogatives as head of the house is an outrage, the shattering of the very foundations of society. It is one more count in his long list of grievances against the Revolution.

I heard these threshed out at length by a group of patriarchs in Yelshanko, a village that lies fifteen miles over the hills from the Volga town where we lived. The old men were sitting on the long bench in front of the Elder's house, listening with ire and indignation to the story of Ivan Petrovich, a visitor from another village:

"On St. John's Day I went to market with a load of grain, sold it for twenty rubles, bought a bottle of vodka, and drank it. On the way home the rest of the money dropped out of my pocket, or some devil picked it—God only knows. Naturally I felt bad and began to thrash my wife. Out of the house she ran and came back with two Communists. May the palsy shake them to pieces! The stupid Red devils took me off to jail. Would you believe it?"

No one did. So Ivan Petrovich repeated the story, adding that hitherto his wife had been a good wife. "It was the Women's Conference that put evil into her head."

"Arrested for beating your own wife?" asked one peasant incredulously, in a manner implying that if you can't beat your wife whom *can* you beat?

"My own wife," reiterated Ivan Petrovich, grimly.

"But not according to law!" put in the Elder, seeing in this merely an arbitrary act of the local authorities.

"According to law—to Moscow Soviet law. The judge read it out of a book."

A dazed silence fell upon the patriarchs. The arrest of their fellow *mujik* for chastising his own wife in his own house was an outrage, sheer lawlessness in the guise of the law. Where now was the sanctity of the home, the unity and integrity of the family? It was this that particularly disturbed the Elder. "A man and his wife are one," he declared with moral profundity. "Did they arrest her too?"

While the elders stubbornly hold to the old ways, the youth are ardent champions of the new. I witnessed a bitter clash between the two generations on another trip to Yelshanko with the Communist organizer, Bolshakov. To a general meeting of the villagers he explained the plans for the coming elections, and that the Soviets aimed at a ninety per cent participation of women in them. This brought the elders up in arms with dour shaking of heads and fists and with grunts of disapproval. The essence of all political wisdom and statecraft, to them, was voiced by the trading *kulak,* Abrozov, in the words, "A woman is a woman, and has no place in politics." To this oft-repeated declaration, the graybeards responded with long and vociferous applause. Longer and louder were the protests from the younger, beardless section whose exasperation found vent in the words of one of the Comsomols:

"A woman is a woman," he repeated mockingly. "So a horse is a horse, a sheep is a sheep, and an old man is an old man—when he isn't a fool. But what of all that? How does it prevent a woman taking part in the elections?"

The elders, as they do all over the world, brought forward the home, the children, the kitchen. To this argument, the Comsomol sarcastically retorted:

"Why don't you remember that when the grain is to be harvested? Or the hay cut in the meadow several versts away? Or the wheat driven fifteen versts to market? Then the women seem to be able to spare the necessary time from home. And if they can stand three or four hours in church, why can't they give one hour to vote?"

Steadily, under these onslaughts from the new generation and the new ways of life and work on the Collectives, age-old customs and prejudices break down and disappear. In Yelshanko village today, women are not only voters but brigadiers, Stakhanovites, secretaries, party organizers, and delegates to the big congresses.

New Problems for Women and Their Solutions

New laws, new folkways, new opportunities for women. But how use and enjoy them to the full when they are tied down to the dull routine and treadmill of the household? "The actual building of the new society," said Lenin, "will begin only when women are freed from petty, dreary, and futile drudgery. Housework, in itself, is utterly inconsequential and stultifying. . . ." This is doubly true in the cities where crowded quarters and the dearth of modern appliances turn housekeeping into an ordeal. Not less so in the villages where the burdens of field-work, added to housework, make the women prematurely old and exhausted.

The full liberation of woman required not only the creation of a new public opinion as to her worth and character, but new public kitchens, dining-halls, laundries, and nurseries; and, in the villages, Machine-Tractor stations giving women time and energy for study and development. This is going ahead on a stupendous scale, accelerating the mass-movement of women out of the kitchen into school, office, and factory. As someone has said, Stalin is exerting as much effort to get woman out of the kitchen as Hitler is to get them back into it. "Woman, the co-worker in Socialist construction, is taking the place of woman the household drudge, woman the slave."

With a few exceptions, however—Krupskaya; Yakovleva, Russian Commissar of Finance; Kollontai, Ambassador to Sweden—the highest posts in the Soviets are not held by women. In industry, too, they fill the less skilled positions, with the result that despite equal pay for equal work, the average woman's wage is less than the man's. But Soviet women are on the way to add economic equality to their present political, social, cultural, and sex equality.

No longer beset by the question of marriage or a career, girls give the same thought and preparation to selecting their life-work as do boys. They expect to marry, just as boys do. It is not a matter of either/or—but both. Even if a woman slows up on her outside work, as she must often do when her children are small, the interruption is regarded as temporary and does not mean a complete break. However, this program, carried out on a vast scale, is presenting certain new problems, particularly among the most advanced women whose professions call for long years of preparation and a definite location in which to function—or mobility of action.

Should some shift or promotion call for the separation of husband and wife, the question arises whether she should refuse the position or he should find a new job where she is to be. Is a life work or a life marriage more important? What if he won't change his work? Shall they just be together on vacations? Or shall they be divorced and perhaps remarry elsewhere? Questions such as these are arising and are settled according to the circumstances and temperaments of the people involved. With the present trend toward closer family ties, every effort is now being made by the Soviets to keep husband and wife together. But public opinion does not demand that the woman invariably follow her husband or do all the sacrificing.

There is social approval for her activity. She still carries a double job, which impels the conferences of women to demand that more be done to equalize the responsibilities for the home and the children. But the tendency is forward to new solutions and adaptations, not backward. A woman's prestige is primarily dependent on her own

position, not her husband's. Many have jobs superior in authority
and income to those of the men they have married. Their homes are
run on the pooled salaries of both. Going to their work in the morning, they leave apartments to the care of a servant or someone who
comes in by the half day or hour. The children go to the crèche or
school where they have their meals and recreation, as well as studies.
In fact, a woman's seven-hour work-day is over and she is home
again before the children return. Recent comments by Soviet leaders,
that more time should be given the family, emphasize not the institution of the family as such but the possibility of using the growing
leisure for this richest of all human relations.

55. How Are Marriages Made in the Soviet Union?

The law recognizes two kinds: *Registered Marriages,* in which
a couple pays three rubles to the nearest office of *Zags,* the Bureau
of Vital Statistics, and, after answering a few questions about
health, previous marriages, and children, is formally united in
wedlock. Husband and wife may each retain his own name or
take the other's name, or an entirely new name may be assumed
by the family. The wife is free to choose her own profession, and
if one of the couple changes residence the other need not follow.
All property acquired after marriage is jointly owned. They are
jointly responsible for the support of their children and the upkeep of the household. Marriage is forbidden to those under
eighteen years and to the mentally defective and diseased. A citizen may not marry a relative in direct line of descent, or a half-
brother or -sister. Examination is given free at the clinics and any
concealment is severely penalized.

Unregistered or Common-Law Marriages have the same standing as registered marriages and may be recorded as of any prior
date desired. Registration is encouraged as it simplifies property

adjustments and care of the children in case of divorce. The law is explicit in defining what constitutes this *de facto* marriage: "Living together, declaration of marital relations before third parties . . . , the fact that both have contributed to household expenses." A casual sexual connection is not a marriage, but a child born of such a union has the same legal and social standing as any other, the same claim to support by both parents.

The Socialist Family and Children

From the beginning of the Revolution the status and functions of the family under Socialism were bitterly debated. "The main kernel of society is the family," declared Lunacharsky. "Whether there will be a free family without a head, or whether the family will break up entirely, we do not decide in advance. Individual differences will not be eliminated in a Socialist society, nor do we strive for that, and quite probably there will be different forms of the family." From this position the theories of Soviet leaders ranged from the extremes of Kollontai on the left, who was an advocate of the state assuming most of its functions, to the stern moralists on the right, who would make the family well-nigh indissoluble.

Undoubtedly the old family is disintegrating under the effects of the economic independence of women, the decline in religion, and the socialization of the functions of the home. On the other hand, there is the cohesive power of love and children, and the mutual obligations of its members which are certainly not lessened. Not only are parents responsible for their children, but children reaching their majority are held responsible for the support of needy parents and step-parents. Grandparents must care for grandchildren when parents have died or disappeared, and vice versa; older brothers and sisters for younger ones, in case of necessity. But most of the old props of the family are gone, and the family survives through the power of mutual love, common work, and children to hold it together. Says *Pravda,* "Love is the whole foundation of the Socialist family. Without it that family cannot exist. Young Communists must be capable of this noble feeling."

With this exaltation of love go admonitions to those who would take lightly the responsibilities ensuing from it. "Get together, young people, and separate at your will," said Semashko, former Commissar of Health. "But do not forget your little children. If you do, then we shall drag you by the ear into the sun of the people's court." With their deep love and solicitude for children, the overwhelming majority of Russians are not in need of this admonition. But taking no chances, the law strives to set up safeguards at every point. In case of divorce a mother receives one-fourth of the father's income for the support of a child until it is eighteen, and vice versa, in those rare cases where the custody of the child is given the father. For two children, a third of the earnings may be assigned; for three or more, fifty per cent. To facilitate the collection of this alimony the facts are recorded on one's union-card and paid directly by the factory or office where the man works. The same regulations apply in the dissolution of unregistered *de facto* marriages, and also when children are born of a casual union. The man, designated at the *Zags* bureau as the father, is served notice, and, if no suit is brought in denial, is registered as such. Every baby is legitimate; it has two parents and is entitled to the care and support of both.

Upon the mother as the giver of life and the home-maker primarily devolves the nurture and upbringing of the children. But in a country where the women often are engaged in outside work and social activities, she—and her children—are in need of every assistance. To this end there is increasing emphasis upon the responsibilities, as well as the privileges and joys, of fatherhood. "People who think the Socialist revolution, having deposed the father from his former unrestricted authority over his wife and children, has also relieved him of the duties of the family are under bourgeois illusions. 'Father' is an honorable title in the Soviet Union, but the Soviet family is not a bank account in which regular deposits signify merit. The Soviet child has a right to claim his true father as an educator and friend. It is only when the father brings up the new builders of Socialism that he can feel himself a worthy citizen of the fatherland." —*Pravda.*

56. How Are People Divorced?

Marriage, being a voluntary partnership, may be terminated at the will of either party. When both husband and wife desire a divorce, they simply file notice in person at the *Zags* bureau, and within a month the marriage is dissolved. When only one party files notice, the other must make an appearance and be personally apprised of the procedure. This does away with the famous "postcard" divorce which was found to be uncertain and involved complications if a letter miscarried, as it sometimes did.

No reasons for separation need be given. No red tape, no lawyers, no washing of dirty linen in public—provided, of course, the couple have come to an amicable settlement of their affairs. Each party has a claim to an equal share of the property acquired during marriage, a claim to the other's support for a limited time in case of sickness or unemployment, an equal obligation to support the children. If there is a dispute over these matters, it is settled in the courts.

Easy divorce is based on the principle that coercion of any kind is a violation of the very spirit of marriage, that nothing should compel people to live together who wish to be apart. This does not mean that divorces were ever encouraged. On the contrary, even the official *Zags* bureau generally attempted to effect reconciliation, and often succeeded. But there were too many divorces; as against 18 per hundred marriages in the United States in 1935 there were 38 in the Soviet Union. Too many were taking advantage of the liberal provisions of the code to further their own sheerly egoistic aims and caprices: There were Don Juans lightly assuming ties and lightly casting them off, with a dozen or more divorces to their record; ladies seeking to lure high-placed men into alliances in order to attach a third of their salaries for some other father's child; professional divorcees making the divorce-mill grind out a good income in the form of alimony from many men.

The rousing of public opinion against these and similar abuses has been followed by more drastic laws and measures, especially against sheer sexual exploitation. The railway worker, Kvyat-kovsky, had long sought to persuade the nineteen-year-old daughter of the station-guard to live with him. She finally consented to enter into a regular marriage and they were registered as man and wife. Shortly afterwards he filed notice of his divorce from her. The court, holding that Kvyatkovsky's only object was to have sexual relations with his wife and then abandon her, found him guilty of seduction by fraud and gave him two years in prison. The courts likewise stepped in as effectively to put a stop to the notorious "summer brides," strong peasant girls married by kulaks in the spring only to be divorced when the hard work of the harvesting was over. That came to an abrupt end when these short-term wives were allowed half of the harvest. A further deterrent to over-hasty separations is a tax of 50 rubles on the first divorce, 150 for the second, and 300 for subsequent ones.

The Soviet press takes pains to explain that these measures aim at more stable relationships and in no way imply a return to the "old bourgeois family or Philistine morals." While recognizing the abuses of comparatively easy divorce and seeking to correct them, it regards its evils as more than over-balanced by its benefits.

57. What is the Attitude Toward Sex?

The single standard. Sex is a subject of public discussion like any other matter. Men and women placed in the same sleeping compartments on trains and visiting one another freely in private rooms. No chaperons. No fetish made of chastity. Adultery, unmentioned in the criminal code. No such thing as an illegitimate child. No privileges and liberties, permitted to men, are denied to women. The legalization of birth control.

Is not all this conducive to license and laxity? In theory, perhaps yes. In practice, no. At any rate, the general impression is that Russians are vastly less preoccupied with sex than in the West. For this there are many reasons. "The peasant masses," says Hindus, "have ever regarded sex with undisguised frankness, without that sense of curiosity, mystery, horror, and sin with which Puritanism and chivalry have invested it." Before the West ever heard of night clubs, old Russia had half a million *Keli*—cottages rented by the peasant girls in which, without losing their virginity, they sang and danced and often slept together with the village youth until morning. This is the Slavic equivalent of "bundling," which was once practiced in New England, and through it young people often found their mates. Such institutions and practices, like mixed bathing without costumes, continuing to some extent in the present, have long accustomed Russian men and women to mingling together with a singular unconsciousness of sex.

Besides this absence of inhibitions, there is a more Spartan attitude towards life, and there are fewer rich foods and luxuries to stimulate the body. Nor is the imagination incited by erotic suggestion in plays, pictures, or stories. Instead of sex intrigue there is the romance and adventure of building a new world. There is enough in this to absorb the interests and energies of youth—and moral obloquy falls upon him who dissipates his powers in self-indulgence!

Apart from the biological implications of sex, there is exaltation of its social and aesthetic significance. True, there have been fulminations in the press against excesses and promiscuity. "Does the normal man drink from the same glass from which a dozen others have drunk?" (Lenin) True, there are still crimes of passion. Although the green-eyed monster, jealousy, as a "bourgeois" emotion should have been exorcised from the human heart by the Revolution, one notices no great diminution in its ravages. And it must be noted that the law defends the right of the wife to refuse her husband's embraces in case of illness, pregnancy, or his drunkenness. Nevertheless, on the whole, sex relations themselves are private affairs left to the judgment and conscience of the individual. But the State vigorously concerns itself and intervenes in behalf of children.

Sex Offenses and Prostitution

These are dealt with in the statutes as crimes against the life, health, liberty, and dignity of a person. Corruption of minors, violence of any kind against children or those of the mental age of children, are placed almost on the same footing as murder. Seduction is severely penalized, as is the crime of infecting another with venereal disease or of promoting prostitution.

In Moscow under the old regime there were 15,000 women carrying the "yellow ticket" as the badge of their profession. At present prostitutes are not registered, but their number is comparatively small. They make their appearance on the big construction jobs where thousands of men are congregated. And in the cities there are still some sophisticated professionals, known as the "valuta girls," specializing in the solicitation of foreigners for money, silk stockings, and cosmetics. Mostly, however, they are peasant girls drifting in from the villages who are unable to adjust themselves, and who in bewilderment have taken to the streets. They soon find their way to the *Prophylactoria* which provide medical care, classes in reading, music, games, and training in some trade. All this is offered without stigma or taint of charity. The girl becomes at once a member of the toiling community. Instead of being treated as a "case," everything is done to nurture in the girl the sense of her worth as a human being, her value to society. "She is made to feel," wrote the American psychiatrist, Frankwood Williams, "that she is the only one who thinks she is unimportant and no good; that she not only has a place in the scheme of things but that she is wanted, in fact, needed, in that place; that friendship, marriage, children, leadership are all possible for her if she will but take her place. And this is no hoax, but is actually true." True, also, there are relapses into the old ways.

Some girls are nymphomaniacs; some do return to the streets. But the great majority are fully reclaimed, gladly visiting the institutions in which they once resided, aiding the morale of doctors, nurses, and others.

The *Prophylactoria* thus play an important rôle, but general economic factors, such as the abolition of unemployment and the possibility of early marriage, are the fundamental causes of the decline of prostitution in the Soviet Union.

58. What About Birth Control and Abortion?

Subject to supply, all kinds of contraceptives are freely obtainable. In the clinics people are instructed as to their use, especially as a means of effecting the proper spacing of children. In 1920 the old ban on abortions was removed. At the same time it was declared to be a temporary measure to continue "as long as the moral heritage of the past and hard economic conditions of the present force women to undergo the operation." Special hospitals were opened with competent doctors and nurses to perform the operation. Provisions were made for at least three days' rest and convalescence. Everything was done with a minimum of expense or danger to the patient. Unfortunately recourse to abortions was excessive. The card catalogue showed that many women had ten, twelve, or even fifteen operations. Evidently they preferred them to preventive measures. But abortions caused susceptibility to disease, nervous disorders, abnormal conception, and sterility. This roused Soviet leaders and doctors to deep concern over the health and stamina of the nation.

To counteract the evil, a Commission for the Study of Contraception and Combating of Abortion was formed. A campaign against abortion was waged by posters, pamphlets, radio, and cinema. After nation-wide debates and discussions in 1936 the law was revised. It permits an operation only when a woman's health demands it, or in the case of hereditary disease. It punishes with two years in prison anyone compelling or inducing a woman to undergo an operation. It penalizes with imprisonment up to three years anyone who performs it illicitly or under unsanitary conditions. Finally, it provides a "social reprimand" for the woman who goes through such an abortion; and, in case of repetition, a fine of 300 rubles. Many of the abortion hospitals are now turned into maternity homes and crèches. A network of new homes extending from the tea plantations of Batumi to the reindeer stations of the Arctic is being opened. In them the latest scientific methods for "painless childbirth" are increasingly utilized. The funds for assisting mothers and children are increased to over two billion rubles. All the economic reasons leading to abortions are being remedied as far as possible.

Abortion was legalized originally to lessen the illness and mortality resulting from clandestine, criminal, and unsanitary operations. This, at least, was accomplished. In 1935 there was less than one fatality in 10,000 cases. By the estimate of the gynecologist, Dr. Frederick Taussig, there are 681,600 abortions annually in the United States, causing 10,000 maternal deaths. There is reason to think that in Europe the facts are not so very different. Certainly in old Russia the activities of the "angel-makers" were widespread and disastrous.

Still more disastrous would have been the results, observes Dr. Eric Matsner, President of the American Birth Control League, were it not that "the average Russian woman developed an extraordinary immunity to the ordinary strains of bacteria." In the villages especially the methods were most unsanitary, crude, and often barbaric. Against them the Soviets carried on a campaign through the Collectives, schools, and courts. In Pine-Tar Village, I witnessed the trial of one of the village practitioners, a wrinkled old *babka,* or midwife. With her was her "surgical outfit" consisting of dried carrots, wires, spindles, and other sharp instruments used in procuring an abortion. Picking up a rusted knitting-needle used in her last case, the judge asked:

"Where did you keep this needle?"

"On the ikon-shelf behind Saint Nicholas, the Wonder-Worker."

"Did you ever disinfect it before using?"

"Sometimes I sprinkled it with holy water," declared the old crone to whom holy water, so powerful in driving off devils, must necessarily be a specific against diseases.

When she promised to cease her operations, the judge made her sentence conditional, and went on to explain to the peasants the Soviet position: "We hold that the right to bear a child or not rests with the woman. If she wills not to, she doesn't have to run the risk of being crippled or killed by ignorant *babkas* like this. Let her go to the district hospital where it will be done by skilled physicians— that is, if she is too ill to bear a child, or has too many children, or is in dire necessity."

These three reasons were accepted in the consultation clinics as justifying an abortion. But before it was sanctioned by the committee of three—gynecologist, representative of the Health Commissariat, and secretary—an effort was made to persuade the applicant to have the baby and not an abortion. If she was unmarried, the committee helped find the father and in any case assured her of support.

In the new decrees it is this point that is emphasized. The measures providing for the maintenance of children by the father are more stringent. Employers are forbidden to discharge expectant mothers and must give them lighter work without reduction in pay. To aid mothers of large families the law provides for an annual allowance of 2,000 rubles on birth of the seventh and each subsequent child. But so rapid is the increase in the birth rate and so big is the drain on these funds that this law is in process of modification. In general, however, the provisions for the care of all mothers and children are greatly expanded. The four months' maternity vacation with full pay for factory working women is extended to all women in offices and institutions. Also free hospitalization. Not only has each child the right to be well born, but to be well fed. On registry of birth, he receives a layette and to his mother goes an allowance of 10 rubles a month during nursing and weaning. After his first years, he enters the circles, playgrounds, and summer-camps, which provide for his care and nurture while his mother is busy. The aim of all this is to do away with abortion by doing away with its causes. There is no reason why Soviet men and women should not have all the children they want if they want them.

In the past, in spite of easy abortion and difficult conditions of life, they wanted children, and they had them. Every year saw the arrival of 6,000,000 Bolshevik babies giving a net annual increase of over three millions to the population. Very striking is the increase in some of the 188 former subject races and nationalities who seemed doomed to extinction. Along the Arctic tundras the Nentsi, dwindling 71 per cent in the thirty-year period up to 1925, have grown by more than five per cent since then. An even greater growth is taking place amongst the formerly fast-dying race of the Voguls. The birth rate for the whole country is already 44 per thousand of the population, as against 22 in the United States and 18 in France and Germany.

It is very likely that there will be a further upswing in the birth-rate as a result of the new measures and steadily improving conditions. That is precisely and frankly what the Communists are aiming at. "And so are the Fascists and all the military-minded!" cynically observes the outsider. "They, too, want to be assured of ample reserves of soldiers to fight their battles in the oncoming war." Quite obviously the Soviets do anticipate war, "a coalition of capitalist powers against the Socialist Fatherland," and indefatigably they are preparing for it. But even now their man power is so great that not half of the recruits eligible for military service are called to the colors. Moreover, this war they visualize is a matter of the near, not a far-off, future. By the time the Soviet babies of today are grown and able to carry a gun, they are confident that it will be quite unnecessary for them to do so. By that time they believe a world-wide federation of nations will be established, and with it the abolition of war.

This conviction is reflected in Communist doctrine, writing, and speeches, and is deeply imbedded in the minds of the people. Most certainly it was the motivating power in the capable intelligent woman at the head of the work for invalids, mothers, and children in the Bauman district of Moscow. A graduate from the Tsar's prisons, a fighter on the barricades, a trusted revolutionist, she was assigned this important post with all its complex, nerve-racking problems. All day I watched her allotting places in nurseries and maternity-wards; collecting alimonies from deserting husbands; finding quarters in this congested section for big families steadily growing bigger; smoothing out differences between quarreling young couples; allaying the fears of nervous, expectant mothers. Around her big office were a score of ailing, crying, and crippled children and into it poured a continuous stream of mothers with infants in arms, in carriages, and in the offing. Looking at the scene was enough to drive one distracted.

"Too many babies," I muttered.

"Too many what?" she asked as if not believing her ears.

"Babies!" I repeated, falteringly. "Wouldn't it be better to have fewer of them?"

"If your mother had thought that, where would you be?" she said. Then, as if forgiving me for being the benighted foreigner I was, she went on to explain briefly and simply so that even a wayfaring writer, though a fool, might not err therein.

"Ever since I was a girl of eighteen, I fought for Communism. Now in not so many years we will be having it. Under it life will be rich and full and joyous. The more people there are to enjoy this happiness, the more happiness there will be in the world."

Naïve, visionary, ingenuous as this may sound to the outsider, to this servant of the Revolution and to legions of her comrades, it is the actuating principle of their lives. It proffers, too, something new in reasons for viewing with approbation a large and growing birth-rate. To the old concepts of more children for the church and the glory of God, or for the sake of the State and its future armies, is now added this new one of the Communists: They want more children to enjoy the fullness of life in the new society which is coming. With great zest they cite Lenin's caustic onslaught on neo-Malthusianism—"this tendency of the Philistine couple, pigeon-brained and selfish, who murmur fearfully, 'May God help us to keep body and soul together, as for children, it is best to be without them.'"

Whole-heartedly and devoutly the Soviets want children, better children, and more of them. With regions as big as England crying aloud for people to fill them, they have ample room for the oncoming generations. With the famous botanist-geneticist, Vavilov, promising a five-fold increase in the productivity of the land through scientific farming, they will be able to feed them. With an energetic nation-wide assault on the vexatious problem of housing, they will be able to shelter them. With a system of social security providing for all the exigencies of life from the cradle to the grave, Soviet men and women are delivered from most of the anxieties about having a child and his future. His proper birth, his schooling, and a place for him in the social scheme are provided for. Why not have the baby?

59. What Are the Soviets Doing to Combat Disease and Promote Health?

"Only a strong and intelligent people can build Socialism." Ill health like illiteracy is not a private affair of the individual to be indulged in as he sees fit. It is harmful not only to the person suffering but to the community of which he is a member. As vitally concerned with the people's health as with their education, the Soviet seeks to provide them freely with one as with the other. This is State medicine with a vengeance. All hospitals, rest-homes, and drugstores are socialized. Ninety-eight per cent of the doctors, nurses, and orderlies are civil servants. Nearly all medical students are supported in their five-year courses out of the State funds.

To prevent disease is better than to cure it. This idea is implicit in the name of the People's Commissariat for Protection of the Public Health. The Commissariat strikes, first of all, at the sources of the frightful epidemics which have always ravaged Russia: Against the black plague, by flying squadrons to exterminate the rats and gophers infested with the pestilential fleas. Against typhus, by destroying the "dirty louse that threatens to conquer Socialism" (Lenin). Against cholera, by quarantining the boats in which it comes stealing up the Volga. Against malaria, by draining the mosquito-breeding swamps.

It supervises the work of the sanatoria in some six hundred health resorts, "the repair-shops of the workers." Among them are the resorts located at the carbonated springs in the Caucasus, the medicinal sand and mud baths of the Sea of Azov, the gypsum and "peat-silt" centers around Moscow, the Koumiss establishments—with their milk from mares grazing on the steppes. From the sub-tropics, they reach beyond the Polar Circle where the germ-free Arctic air is inimical to head colds and pneumonia and where broken bones mend more rapidly. It cooperates with the Red Cross and Red Crescent societies comprising more than a million volunteer members—and together they organize the "medical defense" of the country, give instruction in first-aid to the victims of accidents and gas attacks, mobilize forces and funds for regions stricken by earthquakes and floods.

It directs the experimentation and investigation in the Research Institutes, thirty of them in Moscow alone—Tropical Diseases, Control of Serums and Vaccines, Hydrotherapy, Aviation Medicine, Public Feeding. In the Psychiatric Hospital cinema-therapy is used for the quieting of epileptics and the hypnotizing of alcoholics. In the hundred laboratories and clinics now being built for the Institute of Experimental Medicine physicians may test and apply every hypothetical cure from ultra short-wave radiotherapy to the emergency transfusion of canned blood taken from dead and living persons. Its expeditions investigate the longevity of Caucasian mountaineers who not infrequently live well over the century mark, the use of snake-venoms in the treatment of malignant tumors, the rôle of flies and fishes in spreading intestinal worms, and salvage from folk medicine whatever good there is hidden in its weird formulas.

It carries to the people an insistent propaganda on the rudiments of medicine and hygiene: Through consultation clinics, hostels, and dispensaries, stressing the causes rather than the symptoms of disease. In big museums like that of Motherhood and Childhood with its slogan, "The basis of health is laid in infancy," its model rooms and beds, proper food in wax specimens. In little "sanitation-corners," with vivid posters against the scourge of flies and the Russian habit of sleeping with windows sealed tight. In "mock-trials" in which the tuberculosis germ is haled before a court, charged with manslaughter.

It takes an active part in actually changing the conditions under which the people must work and live. After every diagnosis in the big polyclinics, a nurse visits the patient's home to report on the environment and recommend improvements. Doctors can press reform of any condition that menaces the general well-being of the public. It is part of their function to keep a vigilant eye on the healthy as well as the sick. Factory and food inspection, the prevention of industrial accidents and occupational diseases, are measures pursued to a certain extent in all civilized countries. Under the Soviets, where the State carries the cost of illness and finds it cheaper to keep its citizens fit, there is an added stimulus to extend the scope of these services. Thus in laying out the new cities or remodeling the old, physicians are on the Planning Commissions to select sites that are healthy, to insist on space between houses, proper drainage, clean water, parks, and sport fields. Over 5,000 have been specifically trained and assigned to the physical culture "circles" and clubs.

Finally the Commissariat of Health organizes and staffs the chain of medical centers for the actual care of the sick. It aims ultimately to provide every big collective farm, fishery, factory and mill with a unit of doctors and nurses paid for out of State and insurance funds. Large factories have hospitals of their own. Each city district of a certain size has its central polyclinic with special departments which reinforce and assist the smaller units. All medical services including X-rays, blood-tests, surgery, obstetrics, dentistry, and drugs are practically free. Any sick person may send for a doctor from his factory or farm or from the polyclinic of his district. He may choose whom he will and change if he is dissatisfied. He may even ask a physician from some other section to call during his free time, but this constitutes private practice and must be paid for. Within these limits, he has the benefits of a staff of specialists, treatment in the hospital, full wages while ill, and, if necessary, convalescence in one of the many rest homes.

All these efforts—together with the leisure brought by the seven-hour day and the sense of security from the comprehensive system of social insurance—are visibly raising the standards of the nation, psychically and physically. "In the health field," exclaims a Soviet enthusiast, "we do not have to overtake and surpass America! We have already done so." If that is not altogether true, at any rate, great strides have been made in that direction. From 26,000 physicians in 1913 the number has increased four-fold to over 100,000. The pre-War death rate of 27 in a thousand has dropped to 18, and infant mortality from 360 to 130. But Soviet medicine has still a long way to go, for infant mortality in America is 60 in a thousand and the general death rate is 11 in a thousand. (For the status and incomes of members of the medical personnel see pages 452-453.)

Folk Medicine and Faith Healing

Like all primitive people the peasants had their own system of cures, some of them not without therapeutic value. In their bath-huts and kitchen ovens all kinds of colds were sweated out with blasts of steam from hearth-stones that had been heated white and then drenched with water. Into swarming ant-hills rheumatics thrust their ailing limbs, and, as long as they could bear the pain, let the formic acid pour into them. In cholera epidemics the villages were encircled with bonfires and no one was allowed to enter without passing through their disinfecting fumes. Faith in the magic powers of a candle burning before an ikon was universal. But it must be the proper ikon. For the heavenly powers were organized like a medical faculty, the calendar of the church listing each saint according to his specialty: Saint Konon specialized in smallpox, Saint Ipatia in barrenness, John the Baptist in trachoma.

There were likewise living saints possessing miraculous powers of healing. Such was the Moslem Ishan, near Kvalinsk, a fat and courtly personage who while other mortals slept held celestial converse with the prophet Elijah himself. He was deeply revered by all the Tatars, especially the patriarchal family of the Kayuvas, one time camel-traders and tea merchants. Halima, the fair-haired daughter of the house, without her parents' knowledge, by reading pamphlets about Mohammedanism "being the opium of the people," had become a member of the Comsomols. Thanks to her good offices we were frequent guests at the table of the Kayuvas and were apprised of many strange practices and rites that otherwise would have been concealed from us as infidels and unbelievers. The coming of the Ishan, announced by sentinels riding in from outposts on the hills, was the high point in the Feast of Ramadan. After prayers in the wooden mosque, he was followed by throngs of the faithful pressing the hem of his robes to their eyes and tying up in kerchiefs the earth he had trod upon.

After feasting at the Kayuvas grandfather Sadir, slowly repeating the ninety-nine names of Allah, poured water over the Ishan's hands, carefully catching every drop in a big brass basin. This was later decanted into bottles to be used as a lotion for red eyes and trachoma. To Halima, the Ishan gave a lock of his white hair as an amulet against concupiscence, Bolshevism, and other wiles of the Shatan devil. For her mother he blessed three cakes of soap as a specific against the evil eye and pangs of child-birth. Finally, as recompense to the poorer devotees crowded in the courtyard, the Ishan's apparel was carried out that they might touch the things that had touched the holy man. In ecstasy they stroked his robes, rubbed his fez along their rheumatic joints, licked his cane, and even the polish on his boots. In the glory that the Ishan came he rode away, taking with him many costly presents and leaving with the givers an array of magic medicaments against almost any ailments that might afflict them.

The use of the old pagan incantations, survivals of the ancient nature worship of the Slavs, is still widespread in the back villages. Here is one against toothache:

Young moon, golden horn, where have you been?
Beyond the seas, over the mountains, over the dark forests.

What have you seen?
I saw God's slave, Nikolai, his teeth aching on the right side,
Let them become mute! Harder than stone!
Let them ache no more till the end of his life!
Amen! Amen! Amen!

That this spell, thrice repeated by a wizard, will cure a toothache most peasants still believe. And, as they believe firmly, it often does. Most of the remedies, however, were not only futile but often cruel and atrocious. The cure for high fever was to lay the patient in the snow and let the cold wind "blow the heat out of the body." The specific for fits and convulsions was to beat the hapless victims with clubs "to chase out the devil." In the pharmacopoeia of medicine of the village *baba* were included worm-juices, dried bat-wings, snake-skins, and powdered bird-hearts—their curative powers rated according to their rankness of taste and smell.

Against these ancient superstitions and soothsayers the Soviets wage a relentless warfare. Thousands of clinics and dispensaries have been opened in the rural districts—tens of thousands of crèches and summer kindergartens. With medical movies, posters, and placards the Collectives have become lighthouses illuminating the darkness of village life. Sanitary exhibits traveling by boat, reindeer sleigh, and camel caravan are penetrating into the farthest corners of the land. It is not easy, however, to change the minds and habits of a hundred million people, with stubborn tenacity clinging to the old ways, fearful of the new. Doctors coming into the villages to disinfect the waters against typhoid were until recently assaulted as "poisoners of the wells." Many babies are still soothed with a "pacifier" made of a morsel of black bread chewed in anyone's mouth and tied with a rag. But with the steady increase of doctors, midwives, and nurses, faith in the old remedies and practices is dying out. (See page 342.)

"Anti-Social" Diseases

Among the peasants the habits of eating from a common bowl, drinking out of one vodka bottle, and kissing the sacred images has been conducive to the spread of syphilis. As an inheritance from the old regime there are not a few "snub-nosed" villages in which the whole population has been so long infected it has built up a kind of immunity. Among certain non-Slavic tribes to whom it was often brought by demobilized soldiers it has been more virulent and destructive. To the old folk-practitioners syphilis was not more serious than a cold and they believed that it could be cured by passing it on to another, preferably a virgin.

To combat this scourge there are venereal expeditions carrying salvarsan and bismuth into the afflicted districts; day-and-night prophylactic stations at the big centers, terminals, and river wharves; 200 well-staffed dispensaries. Treatment is free and the patient is known by a serial number instead of his name, although the physician tries to obtain consent to visit the home to see if other members are infected. Article 155 of the Criminal Code provides six months' imprisonment for "knowingly placing a person in danger of venereal infection." At the marriage bureaus the bride and groom are pointedly asked whether they have exchanged certificates of health. As a result of all these measures the cases of gonorrhea and syphilis have been reduced over 50 per cent and are so rapidly decreasing that Semashko, former Commissar of Health, looks forward to a not far distant "future when venereal diseases will be completely eradicated."

In the campaign against tuberculosis all the usual devices are employed, even tag-days, the "Day of the Proletarian Daisy." Also, some unusual ones, like the part-time sanitarium which affords incipient cases the benefits of medical treatment and rest without interruption of work. Coming directly from office or factory to the sanitarium— usually a former mansion with well-lighted rooms and spacious gardens—the patient receives a bath, fresh clothes, and rests. After a simple nourishing meal there is another rest period, followed by music, games, calisthenics, and visits from the family. Then to bed in rooms with open windows. After breakfast the patient returns to his work. Excellent results are obtained by this system of curing and convalescing on the job. There are similar institutes for children of low vitality living in very crowded quarters. After the day spent in school or at home, they come to the sanitarium at five o'clock, remaining till eight in the morning under much the same regime as their elders. For chronic cases there are permanent schools in the pine forests. Thanks to these and other measures, Moscow's pre-War tubercular death-rate of twenty-two in 10,000 inhabitants has dropped to less than ten. (For industrial medicine see pages 226-228.)

Unique methods are used in the narcotic dispensaries dealing with addicts of cocaine, morphine, and tobacco, as well as alcohol. Instead of a psychiatric disease alcoholism is classed along with tuberculosis and syphilis as an "anti-social" disease. In the treatment of insanity and mental and nervous disorders emphasis is placed upon the curative value of useful, congenial work. As Frankwood Williams said, "the psychiatrist does see patients but that is not his primary function. His function is to see that the factory, the school, or whatever the institution, is so conducted as to be conducive to mental health." The partial elimination of their social causes—worries arising from economic insecurity, inhibitions from false ideas about sex, and morbid religious fears—has already brought about a marked decrease in these diseases. In the future good society, most of these ailments with which humanity has been afflicted are "to wither away" and disappear. Out of normal natural conditions will emerge a people sound of mind and body. One means to that end is their wide participation in outdoor life and physical culture.

Sports, Health, and the Life-Span

"The chief pastimes of the Russians," notes a pre-Revolutionary traveler, "are singing, dancing, chess-playing, interminable conversation, broiling themselves red in steam-baths, and swallowing prodigious quantities of tea and vodka." In all these arts the Russians of today still maintain a high degree of proficiency. In the chess-playing "circles" alone there are 900,000 members, the last news of tournaments are cried in the streets, the names of the victors flashed over the country. In congratulating Botvinnik, the co-winner of the International Chess Tournament in Nottingham, Lord Derby said, "I am particularly glad at the victory of the Soviet champion. Victory to any other player means only a personal triumph whereas in your case it means the triumph of the mass chess movement of the Soviet Union."

To these old favorite indoor sports is now added a great enthusiasm for all sorts of outdoor ones, from mass parachute-jumping to tennis, sun-bathing, baseball, and even golf. Hundreds of thousands follow the horse races; cheer themselves hoarse at the Turkish-Soviet football matches; watch the sprinters, divers, pole-vaulters, and discus-throwers in the All-Union Spartakiads of Sport and the Water Festivals. They exult over the breaking of world records in weight-lifting, long-distance swimming, sharp-shooting. The experts meet in competitions from fly-casting for distance and accuracy to the ancient "grappling" bouts of the Caucasus carried on to the music of the *zurni*. Polo was introduced by ex-Ambassador Bullitt, with the explanation that polo is not aristocratic in origin but a game first invented by nomad horsemen of the steppe. The honorary title "Master of Sports" is conferred on the running Znamensky brothers, Georg and Serafim—also the "Human Dolphin" Malin, the speed-skater Melnikov.

More significant than the exploits of star athletes is that the whole population is increasingly taking part in some form of sport or exercise. To meet their needs there are some 1,500 skiing stations, boating and swimming clubs, 2,500 gymnasiums, 4,500 stadiums and playing-fields, 60,000 "circles" with over 10,000,000 members. Of these a fourth have passed the first grade tests of the GTO, "Ready for Labor and Defense." To obtain its badge one must know the rudiments of first aid, sanitation, and hygiene and reach certain norms in thirteen different sports such as archery, balancing on a log, chinning, rope-climbing. Qualifications for the first grade include the 3-mile run, 25-mile walk with gas mask or rifle, 35-foot ski-jump; proficiency in some game like volley ball, hand-ball, or ice hockey; adeptness in the art of self-defense—wrestling, boxing, or jujutsu; also rating as a shock worker on one's job.

The aim is not professionalism but an all-round development—sureness of eye, steady nerves, dexterity, and endurance; the creation of a citizenry adequately prepared to serve the country as it builds and to defend it when attacked. That is why the government adds its support to the widespread and almost passionate interest of the masses in physical training. It is going on everywhere and at all times, not only on vacations and off-days but during working hours. In some factories the machines are stilled a few minutes for everybody to go through breathing, stretching, or setting-up drills. In certain occupations special exercises are instituted to counteract fatigue and improve the general stamina and morale. The peasants likewise are going in for sports and gymnastics. All the big collectives have their stadiums, courts, and grounds for basket-ball and *gorodki,* an old-time village game of skittles. Thanks to the liberation from ceaseless drudgery effected by the machine even in harvest season there are interludes for games and dancing.

"A rest home is good for the tired, a sanitarium is good for invalids, but a healthy person needs first and foremost change of impressions as well as occupation. Who will assert that one gets better rest remaining always in the same place than traveling on a bicycle, in a boat, by horseback, or climbing the ice-covered peaks of the great ranges?" Thus speaks the Commissar of Justice Krylenko, an ardent pedestrian, hunter, and alpinist. To promote these expeditions is the function of the Society of Proletarian Tours and Excursions, which operates a gridiron of bases, camps, and shelters. Under its auspices hundreds now make the perilous ascent of Elbrus and Kazbek each summer. Thousands set forth on month-long treks into the dense *taiga* forests of Siberia, the rolling steppes and grasslands of the south. Tens of thousands enter the great marathons, cyclists using the roads, skiers the snows, and canoeists the network of waterways from Lake Baikal to the Dnieper. Hundreds of thousands participate in the cross-country runs, a fifth of them women harriers. Millions take hiking trips of a few hours or days to new dam sites, collectives, and the country homes of writers and scientists. To prevent zealots, especially the youngsters, from overtaxing their strength, the Commissariat of Health prescribes certain rules and norms. Children must not exceed ten miles a day and must alternate each hour of walking with a period of relaxation, each day of hard exertion with a full day of rest.

Coordinating these far-flung activities is the All-Union Physical Culture and Sports Committee on which sit representatives of the Commissariats. Research is carried on in eight special institutes; the training of instructors, coaches, umpires, and referees in 30 technicums. From all sides goes up the cry for more leaders, doctors, camps, stadiums, and apparatus. Already apparent are the effects of this nation-wide enthusiasm for sports, the open air, and a better physique. Along with socialized medicine and rising standards of life, it is slowly transforming the Soviet people. The old lethargic, passive, indolent Russian is disappearing. A new type is coming on, sinewy, active, hard of muscle, and tanned by the sun. The recruits to the Red Army show an increase in weight, chest measure, and stature over those of five years ago. The life span is steadily lengthening, already adding six years to the age of men and eight to women. The Soviets are well on their way towards a more robust, vigorous, virile race.

60. How do the Soviets Deal with the Liquor Problem?

The Russians were always heavy drinkers. According to the old historians when Vladimir in the ninth century was choosing a new religion for the pagan Slavs, he rejected outright the Moslem faith because it forbade the use of intoxicants. In Gogol's famous novel of the seventeenth century, the old Cossack, Taras Bulba, discourses eloquently on the "two sciences of war and drinking." The chronicles record that after drinking to Patriarch Nikon, "the wine-cups were placed inverted on their heads to show they had drunk his health complete." More recently it was a custom after each toast to dash the glasses to the floor until it was covered with the crackling fragments.

Among all classes liquor was indispensable to every ceremonial —at weddings and funerals, name-days and christenings, to speed the traveler on his way, to welcome him home again. Following the law that the coldest countries create the strongest drinks the favorite of the Russians is vodka, a distillate from wheat, rye, fruit, potatoes, or ordinary sugar, 40 per cent and upwards in strength. For the peasant, the stronger the better. He drank not for its taste or as a tonic, but for intoxication, for escape from his misery and woe in utter oblivion. "The mujik staggers but he is not drunk," goes an old saying. "When two men hold him up and another works his legs he is half-drunk. When he lies in the gutter, a crow pecking at his eyes, and he doesn't feel it, then only is he drunk." There was rarely a church holiday that he did not achieve this stupefaction, and with him often his sons and the priest. So it was said: "The village riots in drunkenness that the Tsar may be rich." For vodka was a monopoly of the State bringing colossal revenues into the treasury.

Then the Great War, and by *ukase* of the Tsar prohibition was proclaimed throughout the vast empire and continued by the Soviet. It was effective as long as the ten million peasant soldiers were at the front. But with their return home came a return of their ancient thirst. To drink and to get drunk, the mujiks held, was an inalienable right and they had no intention of renouncing it. If the Soviet wouldn't supply them with vodka they would do it themselves. Presently out of the village forests blue smoke was rising from the home-made stills of the moon-shiners, and again the mujiks were dancing drunken down the streets. Tens of thousands of moonshiners were fined or imprisoned or sent into exile. Hundreds of thousands of stills were confiscated by the Soviet militia. But all efforts were futile. Unable to cope with the elemental demand, in 1925 the Soviet capitulated and re-established the trade in vodka.

The Drive for Temperance

Not only do peasants continue to drink but so do workers. Although Lenin declared "the proletariat does not need the stimulus of alcohol," it has not thrown off the old habits and practices, deep-rooted in the folkways. Workers still go direct from the pay-desk to the pot-house. Peat-bog diggers go on prolonged sprees like lumberjacks. Drunkenness is one of the chief causes for expulsion from the Party. "Are we to drink up the fruits of the Revolution?" shriek the newspapers. "Shall we turn Workers' Clubs into drunkards' dens?" This is the

Bolshevik way of focusing attention on an evil by painting it in lurid colors—too lurid. For drunkenness is much less frequent than before the Revolution. According to the official report of Molotov, the consumption of vodka, amounting in 1913 to over nine quarts per person, in 1931 had dropped to exactly one-half of that, and decreased steadily each year. To make it still less is the object of a steady, insistent campaign carried on by scientific education as to its ill effects on mind and body and by appeals to the pride, shame, and common sense of the people. As slogans put it, "Alcohol is our enemy!" "Inebriation is incompatible with industrialization!"

The sale of spirits is prohibited on State holidays. Dry zones are established around factories. In health resorts, and, in districts where a large majority are against the vodka-shops, they are closed; also in those Northern and Siberian regions whose primitive peoples formerly were dying out from its ravages. Each of the several million young Pioneers pledges himself not to use tobacco or alcohol. With songs and banners children's crusades march to the factories securing promises from their elders not to drink. Those who have lost time through drunkenness are sometimes obliged to collect their pay from "shame booths," huge vodka bottles ten feet tall with wooden drunkards' heads for corks. There is a steady increase in the number of total abstainers. Even in the wine-valleys of the Caucasus, there is a Young Men's Temperance Society. It limits its members to a bottle a day! But this is such a defiance of the ancestral codes and customs that the old patriarchs sadly lament "the decay of morals and drinking" in the rising generation.

Nevertheless, as in other lands, one sees quite often an intoxicated man wildly zigzagging through the street or blissfully lying down in it. In Russia he is not carted away to jail but to a "sobering-up" institute. After a bath he is put to bed. On waking up in the morning he receives a glass of tea and a bill for five rubles, two of which go to the militia as a fine. If he is short of cash he is sent home to get it. Confirmed drunkards are treated in the Alcoholic Hospitals which employ psychiatry and hypnotism along with the usual medical therapy. With this goes a fundamental re-education, the pleasant surroundings of a club, and work in carpentry, shoe-repairing, or an outside factory. Gradually the hours of work are increased until the patient is entered on the regular pay roll. All the time wages are paid to the family out of the social insurance funds as in other cases of illness.

So few are the cases of chronic alcoholism among women that the hospital for treating them is now closed. This is credited to the sharp reduction in prostitution and the general participation of women in public life. While the Soviet utilizes all modern methods to cure its excessive drinkers, the emphasis is on removing the causes that produce them. It relies, in the main, on a steady rise in the economic, social, and cultural level. In the words of a pamphlet of the Anti-Narcotic Society: "The only hope for the complete elimination of alcohol as a subtitute for happiness is an elimination of the harsh exterior conditions and inner conflicts of life which is the goal of Communism."

61. Are the Church and Religion Persecuted in the Soviet Union?

"The church is separated from the State." Thus begins the famous decree of January 23, 1918, dissolving the thousand-year-old bonds between the government of Russia and the Orthodox Church. The great estates belonging to the church and monasteries already had been nationalized. Now the church was divorced from education, and the parochial schools incorporated in the general system. The edifices were declared "the property of the people" and their free use granted to religious societies. These are defined as "groups of believers not under eighteen years of age and numbering not less than twenty persons who unite for the satisfaction of their religious needs." If unable to maintain them properly, their premises revert to the State.

Along with the Tsar's gendarmes, bankers, merchants, and manufacturers, the clergy of all faiths were disfranchised. No Orthodox or Catholic priest, Protestant minister, Mohammedan mullah, Buddhist lama or Pagan shaman was allowed to take part in Soviet elections. Still further restrictions were imposed by a later decree in 1929. They were forbidden to serve more than two parishes, or to give religious instruction to groups of children under eighteen years of age. Churches were obliged to confine themselves to worship and not engage in social and cultural activities—clubs, guilds, cooperatives. Severe as were these regulations, they were not as drastic as the Spanish order for the expulsion of all Jesuits, or the Mexican law limiting the number of priests to one in 50,000 of the population. On such a basis there would be less than 4,000 priests in the Soviets, instead of more than seven times that number today.

While there were, and still are, legions of the clergy, they have labored under increasing disabilities as the conflict between the new order and the church, bulwark of the old, grew more bitter. Numbers of bishops and priests were exiled or executed on charges of counter-revolutionary activity. Many religious societies could not pay the heavy taxes levied upon them. They could obtain little paper for publishing Bibles and hymnbooks and often were boycotted by the printer's Unions when they did. Science was exalted and in the schools took the place formerly held by religion. The great festivals and saints' days no longer were legal holidays. Sunday disappeared from the calendar with the advent of the six-day and continuous working week. In the large cities the ringing of church bells was forbidden and bells were melted up to make tractors.

Many of these restrictions still remain in force. Others are rescinded or let fall in abeyance as the country grows stable and prosperous and the danger of the church as a center of reaction and counter-revolution dies away. Most significant is the change in the political status of the clergy made by Article 135 of the new Constitution whereby "every citizen has the right to elect and be elected irrespective of his race, his religion, his social origin, and past activity." This confers on all the hitherto disfranchised priests, mullahs, and ministers the right to participate in Soviet elections, an act justified by Kalinin to protesting workers on the grounds that "priests taking part in social affairs would become social-minded." The old bell-ringers are also coming into their own, and many famous carillons, now restored at considerable expense by the Soviets, once more ring out over the Russian land. Mocking or jeering at beliefs is forbidden and zealots ostentatiously manifesting their contempt of religion are summarily punished and jailed.

In December, 1936, the comic opera "Titans" was taken from the boards and its author Demian Bedny was vitriolically assailed for his false and frivolous picture of the historic baptism of the Russians in the river at Kiev. Said *Pravda,* "It is well known that the Christianizing of Rus was one of the principal factors in bringing the Slavs closer to Byzantium and later to the countries of higher culture in the West. It is well known that the clergy played a considerable rôle in promoting literacy throughout Kiev, Rus, in fostering book learning and the study of languages. The first translations of foreign books, including secular books, were made in connection with the conversion of the Slavs to Christianity." In this appraisal is reflected a much more fair and judicial attitude towards religion than has hitherto prevailed in the Communist press. But while such changes are significant, they do not greatly alter the position of the church. It is shorn of all its former pomp and privileges. Its ancient powers and prestige are gone. The social pressure which in other countries induces people to go to church operates in the Soviet Union to keep them away. Organized religion is still in retreat and on the defensive.

62. What Are the Causes of the Antagonism of the Revolution to the Church?

The hostility and antagonism of the church to the Revolution. In the Orthodox Church the autocracy found its most faithful servant and ally, always ready to use its tremendous powers against every movement for the liberation of the masses. Acting as the spiritual police and gendarmerie of the Tsar, the priests used secrets ferreted out in the confessional to trap and destroy the leaders of the Revolution. Under the notorious Pobedonostzev, High Procurator of the Holy Synod, over 10,000 school teachers suspected of sympathizing with the Revolution were imprisoned or sent into exile. Crosses and ikons sanctioned the execution of rebels and headed the procession of the pogromists entering the Jewish quarters to slay, pillage, and burn.

Hostility of the church was not confined to political rebels. With the same ruthlessness it persecuted dissent in other forms and through the centuries it fell upon non-conforming faiths with fire and sword. Five million Old Believers were declared a menace to the State and put outside the law. Their treasures were confiscated, their monasteries broken up, their asylums and divinity schools closed. Seals were put upon their altars, and their clergy forbidden to perform their offices. Their children were declared bastards and torn from their parents. Hundreds of thousands fled to the distant forests and wastes of the empire. With like vindictiveness the Orthodox Church pursued even those social and ethical reformers who sought to show the peasants a better way of life. The solemn ceremony of their cursing was enacted every year. Clad in gorgeous vestments the Archbishop appeared upon the altar steps crying out three times, "Cursed be Leo Nikolaevich Tolstoy!" the choir thrice responding with the antiphonal "Amen." Not only were individuals put under this anathema, but whole groups.

After the Revolution the church's antagonism became even

more bitter. At a critical moment in the struggle the entire Bol-shevik Party was officially declared excommunicate and outcast from the church: "That which you do is verily a Satanic deed," thundered the Patriarch Tikhon on January 19, 1918. "For it you are condemned to hell fire in the future life and to awful curses by coming generations in the present life. We adjure all you faithful children of the Orthodox Church not to enter into any kind of association with these monsters of the human race." In the *Sobor* that enthusiastically received this message from the head of the church, prelates rose up to declare that "the only salvation for the Russian people is a wise Orthodox Russian Tsar." In the civil war that raged through Russia in 1919-20, as in Spain in 1936, churches secreted arms and munitions of the reactionary anti-revolutionary forces. "Regiments of the Holy Virgin" were organized, and "Battalions of Jesus," composed largely of priests, fought against the Red Armies. Pealing bells and *Te Deums* welcomed back the White Armies of the generals and landlords returning to restore the old order.

During the great Volga famine of 1921, the summons of the Patriarch, to resist "by all means available" the requisitioning of the surplus treasures of the church in aid of the starving resulted in riots and bloodshed. True, these acts a few years later were repudiated by the reformed "Living Church" and the Patriarch recanted his words and deeds. Nevertheless, high-placed ecclesi-astics at home and abroad continued to plot for the overthrow of the Soviets. And until this day the church, sometimes against its will, often serves as a rallying center for elements hostile to the workers' government. "A class rising into power," wrote Professor Walter Rauschenbush, author of "Christianity and the Social Crisis," "cherishes those institutions and organizations that aided in the long struggle upwards." The records of the church in Russia fail to reveal any weighty reasons why the victorious working class should nurture towards it feelings of regard or tenderness.

As the abettor of ignorance and superstition, the church was an obstacle to social and moral progress. As an indictment of the church the revolutionists point to the old Russian village. It took the peasants' money to build magnificent temples and allowed them to live in straw-thatched huts—miserable, overcrowded, and unsanitary. It mesmerized them with mystic rites, with bells and incense, while 70 per cent were unable to read or write. It gave them ikons to pray to in misfortune—a saint for every sickness from toothache to tuberculosis—and left them to the ravages of plagues and disasters, a third of the children dying before one year. It began the great church festivals with imposing pomp and ceremony and let the people continue them wallowing in drunkenness for days—and often the priests with them.

Not only did the church do little or nothing to deliver the peasant from his miseries, darkness, and ignorance, but the effect of its teachings—submission, passive resignation, and contentment with one's lot—was to paralyze his will, to leave him without desire to deliver himself. His inbred fatalism and conservatism further strengthened by religion was especially disastrous to agriculture. Ludicrously primitive and unproductive as were the peasants' methods, what point in trying to change them, argued the peasants, when all things were in the hands of God? Angrily they rose up to resist and persecute as infidels the few advocating new ways in farming. Such a pioneer was the peasant Yarkov whom I frequently visited in Seltzo village sixty miles out of Moscow. He was extraordinarily well read and far-seeing, the kind of peasant that inspired Tolstoy to say, "We intelligentsia should sit at their feet and learn their wisdom and ways." While he had never seen Tolstoy, his teachings had led Yarkov to do away with his ikons, an act that brought down upon him the deep suspicion of the other villagers.

When Yarkov sought to show the way to bigger harvests by the rotation of crops, they turned upon him. "So you are more clever than God?" they shouted in scorn and fury. "If it pleases God, He can make crops rise up from stones. If it displeases Him, there will be no crops at all. You can't outwit God. You can't get around Him!" When he tried to persuade them to abandon the antiquated three-field system they retorted: "God in three persons! The land in three fields. So it always was, so it needs must be."

With these ideas deep-rooted in them the peasants spurned the new methods of agriculture urged by the agronomists, and stubbornly clung to the practices prescribed by the church. Instead of spraying the insect-infested fields with chemicals they marched around them in solemn procession with waving banners and crosses. Instead of running irrigation ditches into the drought-stricken areas they sprinkled them with holy water. Instead of turning to the veterinary to aid the cattle stricken with plague they summoned the priest with the ikons.

These beliefs in the efficacy of spells, rites, and incantations fostered by the Orthodox Church stood as a barrier to all agricultural progress. Not less detrimental were the teachings of the mosque, the synagogue, and other religious bodies, excepting some of the more progressive rationalist sects.

A third reason for the antagonism to church and religion is that they are regarded as both inimical and unnecessary to a Communist society. In one terse phrase is summed up the indictment: "Religion is opium for the people." The "Handbook for the Red Army" thus amplifies the charge: "By preaching the divine right of rulers, nonresistance to evil, and abetting superstitions of every kind, religion darkens and stupefies the minds of the masses, shackles their powers, and renders them submissive to the rule and merciless exploitation of their masters. In the Imperialist War the churches and clergy of all lands consecrated and blessed the armies sent out to slay and pillage in the interests of capitalism." Under the old order, Communists would not deny that religion did perform certain functions. It salved the consciences of the warmakers and exploiters by granting them absolution for sins and indulgences. It induced the exploited to bear patiently their hardships and sufferings by holding before them the glories of the world to come. Into another mystic world they might escape from their present miseries, uncertainties, and fears.

To the revolutionist these evils for the most part are destined to disappear with the coming of the classless society of Communism. With the abolition of exploitation and crasser forms of injustice man will no longer be hounded by the sense of guilt and sin. In solidarity with his fellows in a community of equals he will no longer be stricken by loneliness and isolation. With freedom and means to live out life to the fullest he will no longer feel thwarted and frustrated. Depending upon science and himself rather than on prayers and propitiations of the supernatural, man will for the first time realize the tremendous potentialities in him. Under these conditions the Communists assert there will be little or no necessity for the antidotes, compensations, and escapes offered by religion. Rather they regard religion, in any of its present organized forms at any rate, as an impediment to the onward march of humanity. Therefore they are seeking to prevent it from resuming its ascendancy over the minds of the people.

63. How Was the Campaign Against Religion Carried On?

Along with "freedom to perform religious rites" Article 124 of the Constitution states that "freedom of anti-religious propaganda is recognized for all citizens." The chief agency in this has been a voluntary organization called the League of Militant Atheists aiming at "dethroning the heavenly tsars as we have the earthly ones." At the height of its militancy in 1932 it counted 65,000 groups or "cells" enrolling 5,500,000 members. Headed by the indefatigable Yaroslavsky and numbers of former priests, its activities once ranged from the translation of scientific works like Fraser's "Golden Bough" to inducing stores not to handle Easter-egg dyes, Christmas trees, or *Kosher* food; from the founding of schools and seminars for the training of agitators to the staging of plays, reviews, and burlesques on religion; from the conducting of public debates with the clergy to campaigns against the ringing of church bells, the drinking of vodka, the use of ikons and relics to ward off diseases.

In furtherance of its aims the League published thousands of books, pamphlets, posters, and periodicals. For the masses there was a weekly paper and a magazine, each called *Bezbozhnik*, The Godless, or Man Without a God; for students, the *Anti-Religious Worker*. On the principle that one tractor was more effective in breaking down superstitions and taboos than a ton of pamphlets, it helped to supply tractors and machines to the Collectives. With funds raised from subscriptions it presented the Red Army with an airplane, a tank, and a submarine, each named "The Atheist." In the face of these prodigious efforts and their apparent success it is interesting to note that the preachers of atheism are beset with much the same problems and setbacks as the preachers of religion. At their congresses there are frequent complaints about the apathy of fellow atheists, the unqualified personnel, "anyone who can do nothing else is considered all right for anti-religious work"; "the light-minded attitude of people toward the serious problem of life and society"; "the tenacity with which they cling to their old habits and ways" . . . and of late a great falling off in members and funds has compelled the closing down of publications.

Most effective in exposing the crass superstitions fostered or countenanced by the church are the anti-religious museums. Most of them are former monasteries and cathedrals now displaying what are termed "exhibits of a past civilization," among which are an amazing collection of relics and amulets; hundreds of nails from the true cross, tears from the eyes of the Virgin, milk from her breast, ikons miraculously shedding blood. In a Suzdal cathedral I was shown a blonde lock of hair belonging to the Mother of God, an ear-bone of her mother, Anne, wood from the cradle of Jesus, a wisdom tooth of Moses, the thumb-nail of Isaiah—some sixty relics in all.

Still more unique are the remains of the saints. The Orthodox Russian Church maintained that the text, "Thou shalt not suffer thine holy one to see corruption," was not a figure of speech but a fact. The reward for holiness in life was the preservation of the body incorruptible in death, which age could not wither nor time decay. Sometimes this actually occurred. Bodies were naturally embalmed in the chalk or lime soil in which they were buried. This was hailed as evidence of God's favor. The body was placed in a casket, swaddled in silks and silver, with a tiny portion of hand or brow exposed for the devout to kiss. From far and wide came the pilgrims to see the miracle and leave their offerings of gold and silver and copper. Every cathedral and monastery, naturally, yearned for such a saint. When they could not find one they sometimes made one in effigy. How this was done was revealed by opening the tombs in the presence of doctors, the clergy, and representatives of the State. In them instead of the uncorrupted bodies of the saints were exposed moldering skeletons and bones; sticks of wood wound with cloth and cotton wool, covered with wax and artfully colored; figures made with stays and skirts and ladies' stockings.

Besides relics in the anti-religious museums are diagrams showing the colossal revenues of the church, the princely incomes of the archbishops and metropolitans, the six million acres of richest land held by the monasteries. Charts and documents graphically present the history of religion with emphasis on the evils of clericalism and the holy inquisition. Wax figures and sculptures dramatize the persecution of Bruno and Galileo. The evolutionary theory of the origin of man is opposed to the Adam and Eve story. A huge swinging pendulum demonstrates that the earth really revolves on its axis. To a modernist and liberal in religion there is little or nothing particularly anti-religious about these museums. Nor for that matter is there in most of the publications and pamphlets of the League of Militant Atheists. They explain the origin of hail and lightning, the superiority of fertilizers over spells and incantations as a means to better crops, the danger of spreading infectious diseases from hundreds kissing the same ikon. Or they explain, as it was still necessary to do in 1936 in order to keep the peasants from fleeing panic-stricken to the churches, that the eclipse is not a portent of war or some monster swallowing the sun. In other countries this literature would be generally classified as educational. But so obscurantist and unscientific were the teachings of the Orthodox Church, the mosques, the synagogues, and the fundamentalist sects of Russia that the simple presentation of a modernist view of the world becomes an assault on religion.

64. What Have Been the Results in the Closing of Churches and Loss of Faith?

Hardest hit has been the Orthodox State Church. "It acquired pomp, power, riches," said Archbishop Vedensky, "but lost its soul." Cut off from government support, it lost its revenue also. Of the 54,000 Orthodox churches about one-half have been forced to suspend. They have been handed over to other denominations or converted into museums, clubs, Houses of Culture, warehouses, or restaurants. The pilgrimages to the famous wonder-working shrines have almost ceased. The great companies of monks and nuns have shrunk to a handful serving mostly as curators of the former monasteries, nunneries, and hermitages.

Similar inroads have been made on the Jewish and Moslem faiths with the consequent closing of thousands of mosques and synagogues. The actual losses of the Roman Catholics are not large as they comprise but a small percentage of the population. They have steadily decreased as have the other smaller bodies— Buddhists, Shamanists, and nature-and-fire worshipers. Only the Protestant sects have shown much vigor and vitality in resisting the tides of infidelity sweeping the land. Some have actually increased since the Revolution the number of their parishes, ministers, and members, while the *Bapsomol,* Baptist Union of Youth, enrolled at one time more than a million young people. But these sectarians, fundamentalists in theology, clinging to a literal interpretation of the Bible and an outworn cosmology, cannot long appeal to the rising generation trained in the natural and social sciences.

Religion and the Peasants

While the Russian intelligentsia, scientists, writers, educators, and students, were to a considerable extent agnostics, the Russian mujik was always considered deeply religious, the pillar and bulwark of the church. From the days of Dostoievsky to Stephen Graham he has been pictured as a seeker after God, the Christ-like soul in whom was manifest all the Christian virtues. Events have shown that this is just another legend and have raised the query as to whether the mujik was ever truly Christian at all. Was not his Orthodox Faith simply his old paganism and nature-worship dressed up in Christian forms? Were not the saints to whom he prayed just the old Slavic deities with new names but the same functions? Veles, the heathen god of cattle, re-baptized, became Saint Vlas, protector of his cows and horses. Perun, the ancient god of storms, was transformed into Elijah thundering through the skies in his chariot, the lightning flashing from the flying wheels.

The peasant had scarcely heard of the Sermon on the Mount, and his theological attainments are reflected in his naming the members of the Trinity as "The Savior, the Mother of God, and Nicholas, the Wonder-Worker." To him religion was largely a mass of mysterious rites with a secret magical power of averting evil in this world and securing felicity in the next. So lightly rooted, small wonder that before the fierce blasts of the Revolution it so rapidly wilted and crumbled away. And like his reputed loyalty to the Little White Father, the Tsar, his devotion to Mother Church has turned out to be very much of a myth.

Very few candles now burn in the wayside shrines, the churches are often in disrepair, and in the peasants' houses the somber ikons of the saints are being replaced by portraits of Lenin and Stalin and gay posters of the Five-Year Plans. True, at Easter time, ancient festival of the returning sun, the churches are overflowing. Amid clouds of incense, the priests, in gorgeous vestments and golden crowns, intone the impressive litany of the Orthodox Church. In many villages more children are christened than in similar rural districts in America. In solemn procession ikons and crosses are carried around the fields to drive away the insect pests and drought. Priests and people participate together in elections to the Soviets. Synagogues are open in cities where they were hitherto non-existent. From the minarets comes the cry, "There is no god but Allah," and at the Feast of Ramadan the faithful Moslem hosts bow toward Mecca. From remote districts come reports of "revivals of religion," incarnations of Jesus, and the appearance of the Mother of God. The sectarians still hold the allegiance of multitudes.

Despite such facts one cannot escape the conclusion that the church, the mosque, and the synagogue are in process of disintegration, that the ancient pieties are fading away. As Dr. Walter Van Kirk of the Federal Council of Churches of Christ in America observes, "Organized religion in the land of the Soviets is on the way out." The interests, energies, and loyalties it formerly absorbed are being directed into new channels.

65. What is Taking the Place of Religion in the Soviet Union?

"The satisfactions offered by religion can be found by man in the social passions engendered by devotion to a cause," said Rousseau. Certainly this is true of the leaders of Communism. It was no church or creed that inspired and sustained them in their long years of struggle. Socialism and the Revolution were the be-all and the end-all of their lives. That was all they had and it was enough.

Feeling no need for religion in themselves the Communists saw no need for it in others. Give man the vision of a new world without poverty or oppression. Let him lose himself completely in the struggle to achieve it. Let him explore the universe, enriching himself and mankind with the wonders of science and the beauty of art. Let him understand that in humanity his noblest deeds and thoughts and aspirations go on forever. Thus may one find the true meaning of life, the fulfillment and satisfaction of his deepest desires.

That this is the experience of multitudes, particularly the youth, there is no gainsaying. The idea of Communism captures the imagination and loyalties of millions and gives new purpose and meaning to life. From the lives of the saints they turn to the heroes of the Revolution, who, for their convictions, unflinchingly endured prison, exile, torture, and death. In the chants and songs of the Revolution they find the same inspiration their fathers found in the ancient hymns and litanies of the church, and in their embannered parades the pageantry of the processions of the cross. In the theatre, cinema, and radios, untainted by commercialism, they absorb the new emergent ethics, ideology, and culture. There seems to be little consciousness of any void or vacuum in their lives.

In every realm the appeals and ministrations of the church are being supplanted by those of Communism. "Thrice is a man wonderful," says the Russian proverb, "at birth, marriage, and death." As the church sought to make these events significant with its ceremonies, so have the Communists with their "red weddings," "red funerals," and "red christenings."

In place of the old rite of baptism developed a new one called "Octobering." Under the sponsorship of a factory or Collective, amid gay banners and music and speeches, the child was dedicated to the aims and ideals of the Revolution that began in October. The parents pledged themselves to bring him up in the true Communist doctrine. The Pioneers promised to be his guardian, and when grown up enlist him in their ranks. He was presented with a cake of soap as symbol of the new way of hygiene and health, and with a copy of Marx or the Communist Manifesto "that with his young teeth he should early learn to gnaw the hard granite of social science."

Most unique of all was the name he received. While the Soviet almanacs continued to print the old favorites, Pavel, Nikolai, Ilya, alongside these names of the Orthodox Saints it offered the new revolutionary ones, Spartacus, Marat, Engels. To parents who would entice the spirit of the great seers and pioneers, it suggested Hugo, Darwin, Robertowen. As evidence that Soviet Republics are not ungrateful there was Nansen, the friend of children in the great famine. Obviously there was one name that every Communist desired for his son. It is likewise obvious that every boy could not be called after Vladimir Lenin. Fortunately ingenious variations were hit upon. Combining name and surname produced Vladlen and Vilen, and by spelling Lenin backward, Ninel. Zarya (Dawn), Naooka (Science), and Razoom (Reason) attested the faith in the era of light and knowledge to be inaugurated by Communism. Others, not so sure of its speedy coming, and seeing hardships and struggle ahead, chose for their offspring Sila (Strength), Volya (Will), or Barricada. Rem was an acrostic for Revolution, electrification, and Moscow, Diamata for Dialectical Materialism, Yupee for Young Pioneer, Cominterna for Communist International, Profinterna for Trade Union International.

Of late these new names are much less often bestowed upon children and the "Octobering" rite is disappearing. There is also much criticism as to the inadequacy of the ceremonies and conduct of the red weddings and red funerals. They are not as dramatic or solemn or festive as the occasion calls for. But the intention is to invest them with the significance and meaning for the new social order, as religion did in the old. That brings up the question as to whether Communism itself is a religion. In support of this contention it is pointed out that it has its great teachers and prophets in Marx, Engels, and Lenin. It has its saints and martyrs in those who died for the cause, paying honor to their memories in speeches and music and rituals of silence. It has its authoritative writings and doctrines, and manifests all the intolerance of a new vital faith. It holds out promises of a glorious life in a future society of joy and abundance. It demands and receives from its followers whole-hearted devotion, obedience, and sacrifices. It has invincible belief in its rightness and ultimate triumph. And so on down a long list of parallels and analogies. But all these do not make Communism a religion except on the basis of some very broad definition like the "giving of the best there is in a man to the best he knows."

The Communists themselves scornfully disavow all attempts to call their movement religious. They reject the supernatural and every theory that explains life and society in the terms of creative activity of some outside spiritual form or power whether it be personal deity or abstract idea. (Counts) They regard religion as a by-product and reflex of economic factors utilized as an instrument for the exploitation of one class by another. With the abolition of exploitation in a classless society, religion is destined to wither away and disappear. As to its future under the Soviets one may well turn to the most qualified authority, Julius F. Hecker, one-time professor in the Moscow Theological Academy. "Step by step, in place of the abandoned cults and traditions, the new life creates its own social and cultural forms. We see, therefore, no reason why the former institutions of organized religion should not disappear altogether and be replaced by something new, a higher synthesis in form and content of the obscure cults and ideologies of the past. . . .

"The former anti-religious agitator, gradually and hardly conscious of the change, is now turning to the functions of teacher and ethical instructor. From the ranks of the more active enthusiasts, students are recruited, trained in the history and psychology of religion and in the fundamentals of Communist philosophy. These young men, by temper and qualification, under different circumstances would probably have chosen the study of theology and entered the service of the church, but in the new social order they pursue a function similar to teachers of Communist ideology. Trained for this activity, they are forming certain mental habits which partially unfit them for any other work, and for that reason they will probably stay on in this profession for the rest of their active lives. While at present their message remains largely a critique of religion, the needs of life call more and more for the positive presentation of a theory of life and action. In this manner there develops a new institution of professional men to teach the ways of the good life in the Communist social order."

66. What Are the Aims and Instruments of Soviet Education and Propaganda?

Their aim is to give an understanding of Socialism to the 175 million peoples of the Union; to generate in them an enthusiasm for the building of it; to replace the old individualistic traits and outlook on the world with social, collective ones; to prepare the oncoming generation for the future society of Communism. "In a word," queries the critic, "to make Communists out of everybody?" "Precisely," reply the Communists. "Without the co-operative mind and spirit how can one live in a cooperative society?" To this end every institution in the country is utilized. They are all instruments of Soviet education, not only these that are specifically cultural, but the political and economic ones. They are all schools in which the people "learn by doing."

The Soviets are schools of government in which 1,300,000 deputies are learning to rule by ruling. The courts are schools of law, in which tens of thousands of "lay-judges" are learning to judge by judging. The giant plants are schools of industry in which the peasants are learning to work with machines and one another. The Labor Unions are schools of discipline and administration. And so on to the more specific field of education. This is called the "third front" and it again is a very wide-reaching one. It consists not merely of the formal school system reaching from crèches to university but also of the theatres, cinema, museums, libraries, art galleries. The press and radio are also important agencies in this drive for the re-education of 175 million people. They are all integral parts of one tremendous movement which aims to mold a new type of citizen and to fire him with zeal for the classless society of Communism "whose fundamental principle is the full and free development of every individual." (Marx) "In behalf of this burning, public faith," says John Dewey, "propaganda and education are more than confounded. They are identified."

67. What is the System of Schools and Universities?

"A school for every person and every person in school!" That goal has not yet been realized, but the Soviets have gone a long way toward it. In 670 institutions of university standing there are a half million students, living mostly on stipends or scholarships. Two million young people are in high-schools and technicums, twenty-eight million in the lower grades. Teaching goes on in 75 languages. There are schools for Armenians, Bashkirs, Chinese, Digorians, English, French, Gypsies, and so on down the alphabet to the Zyrians. The aim is to give every child its native tongue and culture. Sledge-schools follow the reindeer herds of the Nentsi over the Arctic snow-fields to the new feeding grounds. Yurt-schools, with their frames of staves and felt packed on camels, accompany the Uzbek nomads to their new camps on the steppes. Tent-schools are set up for families of seasonal workers—the cotton pickers and the harvesters of fruit and grain.

There are Forest-schools for frail and ailing children, with windows opening into the pines and birches. Schools for clever and gifted children like the Musical Treasure-Chest of Odessa, turning out competent composers and directors and real virtuosos on the piano, cello, and harp. There are schools for the backward and delinquent, schools for the deaf, dumb, and blind.

Schooling is in no wise a monopoly of the youth; nor is it confined to the regular system run by the State. Alongside of it rise up other systems conducted by and inside the Party, Labor Unions, and the Red Army; some form of educational effort is an intrinsic part of the activities of every big enterprise. They range from simple "circles" in drawing or physics to Scholastic-Combines, like that of the Dynamo Plant with extensive courses in the various technics and thousands of employees in them. There are the Schools for Illiterates in which 70 millions have been taught to read or write, and often by those who have just learned to do so themselves. At the other extreme are the Seminars in Sciences grappling with the most complex questions under the tutelage of eminent academicians.

There are Radio-schools broadcasting cycles of lectures, each one complete in itself, so the casual listener may profit thereby; Home-study groups taking courses by mail; Workers' Faculties, Trade-schools, Night and Day "Universities." So one might go on at length, drearily cataloguing the schools. In them nearly a million teachers are at work. Upon them the Soviets are spending eighteen billion rubles, tenfold more than under the Tsar. As the allotment grows with each increase in the national income, the network grows more embracing. From eight to fourteen years of age education is already compulsory. In the Third Five-Year Plan the aim is to make it so for everyone up to eighteen.

Many of these schools are crude and primitive. On the frontiers they are mere log-cabins or mud-plastered huts. In the crowded centers they are run in shifts. Scholastic standards are often low, and the teaching staffs incompetent. There is usually a dearth of text-books, paper, and pencils. But there is never a lack of avidity to learn. On every side is evident this zest for knowledge: The eagerness with which the children await the opening of the school year; the inability of the presses to keep up with the demands in spite of editions running into millions; the crowds around book-stalls and thronging lecture-halls to listen to the most abstruse discussions; the heads buried in books and pamphlets on the tram-cars. Lenin enjoined the rising generation to do three things: Study, study, study. That injunction the whole nation has taken to heart as if striving in a few years to make up for the centuries of ignorance. Fully a fourth of the people in the Soviet Union are studying away at something. More are enrolled in its schools, colleges, and institutes, according to the U. S. Bureau of Education, than in any other country in the world.

The aim of the schools is to enable the rising generation to take its rightful place in the new society that is forming. Hence the stress on social science which occupies the place in the new school that religion held in the old. The youth must understand the social mechanism—its wheels, cogs, belts, and dynamos. More than that they must know how to build it. For that is the historic task to which they are called. Therefore the schools are "polytechnical." To the regular curriculum is added training in the basic skills and technics, the principles of energy, the organization of industry, the why and wherefore of human labor. To make this real and vital the children are brought into close contact with the actual processes of production.

"Every factory, mill, and electric-station," said Lenin, "should be a place of education." To this end each school is linked up with some enterprise which acts as its chef or patron. The workers enter into its life, donating text-books and tools, helping in its workshop or laboratory, explaining the use of blue-prints and charts, even serving as instructors. The further one goes up the educational ladder, the closer the tie-up with industry. So close that the technical colleges are no longer under the Commissariat of Education. The whole training of specialists is in the hands of the Commissariats that later will employ them. The Commissariat of Health educates its physicians and nurses; Heavy Industry runs 115 institutes for the training of engineers and electricians; Agriculture, 56 schools for agronomists; Timber trains its foresters; Finance, its bankers.

Still more to the point, these specialists are being trained at the places where the actual work is being done. Why build an electric laboratory in Moscow when there is such a big one already operating on the dam by the Dnieper? And still bigger ones are to be built in the Third Five-Year Plan by the Volga and Angara. Nearby these power-plants the new institutes are now being located. So they are close to the banks, the hospitals, the farms, and the forests. In this way theory goes hand in hand with practice. Periods of study alternate with actual work in the field. What the student learns out of books today, he may test out in a bank or a blast-furnace tomorrow. Instead of being abrupt, the transition from academic life into the work-a-day world is gradual and easy. Thus the function of the schools is two-fold: *To explain society to its builders, and at the same time to initiate them into it.*

Pointing out that the emphasis on industrialization is apt to give visitors a wrong impression of the educational aim, Beatrice King in "Changing Man" goes on to say, "Right through Soviet education runs the refrain of the development of the whole human being. That means development, emotional, artistic, social—in a word, cultural as well as technical. Just as in our schools, the curriculum does not allow much time for the arts.Then, said the Soviet educationalists, it must be supplemented out of school. This is being done with a fervor and enthusiasm, and on a scale, that must be unique in the world. There is a passionate belief that every child must be provided with beauty, with the opportunities for creative self-expression through every known form of activity."

An Ever-changing School

Reports about Soviet education are confusing and conflicting. It could not be otherwise. It has constantly changed in response to the demands made upon it by a changing society. In the first days there was an absolute break with the past. "Behold, I make all things new!" said the Revolution. It certainly did that to the schools, turning them upside down and inside out. To counteract the influence of the teachers inherited from the old regime, the schools were made self-governing. The children drew up their own rules, directed their own "circles," planned their own studies. To discover more effective ways of instruction, they tried out all innovations—Dalton plan, project method, brigade, and complex system. They focused on some one theme like the village street or the budget, letting the pupils pick up reading, writing, and arithmetic by the way. To bring the children close to life and labor they worked stated hours in the fields and factories. They went on excursions to distant regions, paying their way by speeches, singing, and plays. To destroy the monopoly on higher education held by the sons of the nobles, merchants, and priests, the doors of the universities were flung open to workers and peasants without examination.

In these new schools the youth received a training quite different from their fathers. Absorbing the ideas and spirit of the Revolution, they were more social-minded, freer from the prejudices of race and nationality, far better versed in civics, economics, and politics. They could hold forth eloquently and at length on the class struggle, the evils of capitalism, and the meaning of Marxism. But alas! while even the children might prattle glibly of politics, they could not spell correctly. (Krupskaya) They might know that New York was the center of finance capital, but they did not know where it was. (Fischer) The schools turned out excellent Marxists, but poor engineers. (Kalinin) This was an intolerable situation.

With the country entering the stage of gigantic construction, there was an acute need for good engineers and technicians, for highly disciplined brains and hands. To meet these exacting demands came a series of decrees drastically reforming the schools: The authority of the teachers was restored; history, geography, and mathematics became formal studies; definite lessons and work schedules were established; the pupil's progress was tested by marks and examinations. This was hailed abroad as a retreat to the old system of pedagogy. But quite wrongly. The Soviets still stand firmly by Lenin's rejection of "the old text-book school, the school of drill and mechanical learning, the leading of the mind with a welter of facts—nine-tenths useless and one-tenth harmful."

In the schools of today are incorporated the best features of the first decade of the Revolution. The pupils still have a voice in the affairs of the school, sitting with the teachers on the school council and helping to enforce discipline. They still go on excursions, the new decree prescribing "three visits to electric-stations, factories, or farms." The schools still hold to the principle that the best way to learn about life is by participating in life. While guarding against overloading the pupils with social duties as Octobrists, Pioneers, and Comsomols, they allow them to take part in the life of the community. They still emphasize group solidarity and the responsibility of each for all. The forward students coach and coax the lagging ones to gain better marks in order to win higher standing for the whole school or class. They put even greater stress upon technical knowledge, especially of electricity. As Communism is to be the age of electricity, it calls for "the mastery of it as applied to industry, to chemistry, and to the U.S.S.R."

Are the Soviet schools conservative or progressive? George S. Counts says they are neither. They are Socialist. They are servants of the Revolution, changing in response to its changing needs and demands. At each new stage in the development of the country, they are called to new tasks. In the first period it was to break the hold of old established institutions like the church molding the youth along personal individualistic lines. They were called upon to imbue them with the new revolutionary ideas—to produce rebels, iconoclasts, fighters. And they did it. In the period beginning with the "Socialist Offensive" in 1928 their chief task has been to train the personnel for building hundreds of thousands of new mills, factories, and farms. They were called upon to turn out armies of technicians, engineers, geologists, chemists, inventors. This they did, and are doing.

In due time—with the rounding out of the great works of construction at the end of the Third Five-Year Plan, or the Fourth, or Fifth—will come the next stage, when the people will enter fully into the fruits of their labor. Then the great emphasis will be upon the humanities, the enjoyment of arts and nature. The chief task of the schools will be to nurture "engineers of the mind and spirit," specialists in the art of living together and the graces of life. They will be called upon to produce legions of musicians, architects, poets, painters, philosophers. The extent to which they are now doing this is an earnest of what will be in the coming society of leisure and abundance.

Only to a small degree do the schools affect society. They are rather a reflex of the world outside them. The kind of society determines the kind of schools. So much is implied by John Dewey when he says, "Only in a society based upon the cooperation principle can the ideals of educational reformers be adequately carried into operation."

Pre-School Training

Lenin repeatedly called for the release of mothers from the constant care of their children. The entrance of millions of women into public life makes it a necessity. Already some 10 million are provided for by the Soviet system of nurseries, kindergartens, playgrounds, child-centers, summer and winter colonies. Quarters are usually furnished by the big offices, farms, and factories; nurses and doctors by the Commissariat of Health; teachers by the Commissariat of Education.

Up to four years of age children may be taken to crèches. There are Day and Night crèches, where mothers may leave their children on the way to work; Evening crèches for mothers going to meetings or theatres; University crèches for student mothers while in their class rooms and libraries; Seasonal crèches when the harvest mobilizes everyone to work in the fields; Twenty-four Hour crèches in the parks and railway stations. Usually the one who brings in the child undresses it and hands it naked to the nurse, who, after a bath or sponging, places it in a crib or playroom. If it is a breast-fed infant, the mother returns at stated intervals to nurse it. The others receive two light breakfasts, a dinner, and "tea." They are daily examined by a doctor, records of weight and temperature are kept, and blood-tests are taken yearly. The object of the crèche is not only to give proper care to the children but to teach the mothers to do so. This is badly needed in a country where peasant women sometimes suckle their offspring up to three years of age, and, among the aboriginal tribes of the North, up to ten!

Against such practices a continuous campaign is waged by talks and discussions, by visits to the Institutes of Mother and Child, by vivid posters and slogans: "A clean child is a healthy child!" "Open the windows!" "Do not kiss the baby!" "Do not disturb a child while he plays, or he will disturb you while you work!" Nurses or teachers call fortnightly in the home to advise about food, bedding, and books. This does not rouse the resentment that it does in most countries for the women are eager to learn the new ways of living. And they are rapidly doing so. Infant mortality has been cut in half, and the level of health and hygiene has appreciably risen.

Crèches are not only nurseries but training-schools for the children. Taking the children at their most formative period they seek to educate them in correct habits of mind and body, and prevent the forming of wrong ones that will have to be broken in later life. (Alice Withrow Field) There are separate rooms for infants, for creepers and crawlers, and for the three-year-olds. The children are divided into groups of ten and training goes on under the watchword: "Do not do anything for a child that a child can do for itself." To teach self-control as soon as possible they are taught to hold crayons and pencils, to pour water from one jar to another without spilling it. To make them self-sufficient they hang up their own clothes, clear the table after eating, put away their playthings. To stimulate a co-operative spirit they help one another to dress and undress. With circling games and building-blocks so big that it requires two or more to handle them they learn the value of collective effort. To orient them to the world, they learn in the cities how to cross busy streets, and on the farms how to tend rabbits and chickens. To insure rest and solitude, there is a room to which a child may go when tired, or when he wants to be by himself.

About the same ideas and regime are followed in the kindergarten for ages from four to seven: To prevent contagion, street-clothes are changed to school-clothes; heads are usually close-cropped or shaven; each child has its own glass, toothbrush, soap, and towel. Though it is called the "bookless school," there are plenty of books—gay-colored books, books with pictures of Lenin as a child, story-books to be read aloud by the teacher about the lives of children in far away lands. While fairy tales are no longer taboo, those that deal with the actual work-a-day world are favored. "Just as a child brought up only on cereals will not be healthy, so one brought up on the pap of meaningless stories will not develop a strong and creative imagination." To do that the children are encouraged to create their own stories and games, and to make their own toys. They model birds and cattle from papier-mâché and potatoes. Out of tin cans, boxwood, and wire, they build ships, airplanes, and tractors. They learn what makes the wheels go round not only in the machines but in the life of the community. They observe its activities and even have a part in them. "Every child is a little builder of Socialism!" In caring for one chick or gathering up old iron, they, too, do their bit for the

Five-Year Plan. Even the littlest ones know that the work of five of them is equivalent to the work of one man.

One must not get too roseate a picture of the pre-schools. Many of them are bleak and primitive. In the villages they are frequently dilapidated, unscreened, and infested with flies. Even so, they are a big advance over the past when the women toiled from dawn to dark in the fields, leaving their children to shift for themselves. Another misconception is that somehow the pre-schools are intended "to break up the home." On the contrary, they proclaim, "There is no substitute for a mother's milk or a mother's love." They do not supplant the home but supplement it. Together they collaborate to assure the children the proper food, clothes, and training. Their common concern is to give the future builders of the new society the right start in life. The verdict of foreign observers is that they are highly successful in doing so. Soviet youngsters on the whole are a happy and healthy lot—sturdily built, bronzed by the sun and wind. They are resourceful, self-reliant, ready for responsibilities. If anything they are perhaps a bit too serious and solemn. But they are at home in the world. They emerge out of the kindergarten, by way of the so-called "zero" class, prepared for the next step in life.

Elementary and Secondary Schools

Under this head are included the primary school, the so-called Seven-Year School, and the Ten-Year School which functions as yet in only the more progressive regions but is slated to become the one universal type carrying its pupils up through all grades from eight to eighteen years of age. Beginning with the three R's, the children pass on to the formal study of geography, drawing, history, physics. The aim of these schools, in the words of Krupskaya, is an "all-round training." "As our children are to become not only workers but owners and directors of industry, this school must give them wide horizons. It must equip them for a world of rapid change—ready to work in a mill or organize a collective farm, at the bench one day, a commissar the next. It should be a comprehensive education leading to a specialty." To this end the schools are on a "polytechnical" basis. By that is meant a grasp of basic principles and skills underlying production and their relations to society. The experience of the child broadens to take in the first elements of energy—the wind-mill and the wind-motor; the first consideration of the machine as it serves the purpose of transportation—locomotive, airplane, auto, and steamer; the first conception of industry—handicraft in the school and shop compared with mass production of factories and farms.

The Five-Year Plan comes into the schools in the persons of engineers fresh from the building fronts. In the Centers of Art, Technic, and Agronomy the pupils come under the tutelage of the best local electricians, draftsmen, tractorists, painters, and musicians. In excursions to plants and farms they see how theories work out in practice. In Moscow they may visit the Planetarium with its big revolving dome, showing the movements of stars and planets, or the House of Wonders, displaying the latest achievements in physics, geology, and chemistry. By this kind of education the Soviets are preparing for the decades of stupendous construction lying before them. It is imperative for their future citizens to understand the fundamentals of science and technic. It is essential, too, in a country of 189 different peoples, for them to understand one another. Hence the stress on the learning of languages. Besides his native tongue, every child must study at least one other. Among the minor nationalities it is usually Russian. Thus the vast country is assured of a common medium of communication. Most widely known of the Western languages are German, English, and French in the order named.

Increasing attention is given to the physical and social well-being of the youth. Sports are coming into their own. At least one hot meal a day is provided at nominal price or gratis. The new decrees warn against overtaxing the pupils with outside tasks. Teachers must not assign work for vacation times. Homes that cannot provide a separate room for their children are exhorted to find them at least a "study-corner." The active interest and co-operation of parents in schools is enlisted. They sit on its councils and carry its problems into their clubs and meetings where debates on the upbringing of children are now the order of the day. Here is the report of a Kiev worker, A. M. Dobrovolsky, before the Communist branch in his plant:

"My son, Volodya, is in the eighth class. He makes good progress in his studies. He is of course a Pioneer. Recently he was elected monitor. A short while ago he made application to join the Comsomol. I hold that every person who is getting on in years should make a point of telling his children about life in the old days. That will help him to understand the class-struggle. I, for example, often tell Volodya about my own boyhood. He is very fond of hearing about it, and I have a thing or two to tell him. 'Compare my boyhood with yours,' I say to him. 'Do you realize how fortunate you are?'

"What else do I do for my son? I subscribed to *Pioneer Pravda* for him. Now I subscribe for *Comsomol Pravda* because he is growing big. I recently bought him 12 copy-books, three jars of India ink, and good paper because he is very fond of drawing. Of course my wife and I know that there are lots of things that we have left undone. We haven't bought him a radio set, but we shall get him one soon. . . ." After Dobrovolsky's report questions were asked. What songs did Volodya know and which did he like best? When was he last at the doctor's for general examination? What pictures had he seen lately? Dobrovolsky confessed he could not answer, for which he was criticized in the subsequent discussion participated in by eight of his fellow-workers.

At the end of the meeting a resolution was adopted stating that the interest he and his wife took in their boy's work was "satisfactory." "However," the resolution continued, "we consider it abnormal that Volodya goes late to bed and gets up late, that he does not clean his teeth regularly, spends too little time in the fresh air, and does not read enough works of literature." The meeting instructed Dobrovolsky to correct these defects, recommending that Volodya should read the works of Pushkin, Nekrassov, Gogol as well as Sholokhov's "Seeds of Tomorrow" and Furmanov's "Chapayev." The resolution also provided that he should take his son to a doctor to be examined. Finally, "for his good work in school Volodya is awarded a supply of oil paints by the factory."

The results of Soviet education are reflected in the aims and longings of the youth. In response to the old familiar question, "What do you want to be?" there are the answers, "a great writer like Gorky," "a composer of music like Miaskovsky." Most of them, however, show that their minds are fired by science and the conquest of nature. One boy says, "I want to be an agronomist, to increase the harvest yield three times and turn out the best seeds in the world."

Another says, "I want to be an engineer because the country needs them; I want to give it a learned man." Prophetic of the new world is the lad who announced, "I want to invent a rocket machine and fly in airless, interplanetary spaces." Even the girls say "an aviator," "a radio engineer," "a chemist." For these specialties they take the next step up on the educational ladder, provided their marks are generally "good."

Technicums, Higher Technical Colleges, and Universities

Students completing the full span of the so-called Ten-Year School, are prepared to enter the colleges. As already noted, however, in many places the three upper grades of the Complete Secondary School have not as yet been provided. But every district has vocational three- or four-year technicums which train directly for work of one kind or another. For most young people who are not book-minded or are keen to get into active work, training in a technicum is sufficient. There are several kinds from which to choose—agricultural, pedagogical, medical, art, socio-economic, transport, commercial. From such schools the youth emerge as specialists with middle qualifications— assistant draftsmen, mechanics, agronomists, assistant teachers, nurses, or typists. They step into a job and join a Union. Others do this on leaving the elementary grades, but may prepare themselves later, if they choose, for more skilled work or even for college in the part-time factory school, or in the *Rabfac*. Many students after a period of work in which they show their ability are delegated by their Unions to go on with their training, and voted a stipend or scholarship.

In the new institutes built and supported by the farm and industrial commissariats are trained the engineers, experts, and specialists in various technics. Many of them, as already noted, are located in the basic industrial regions—mining in the Donbas, oil in Baku, textiles in Ivanovo and Turkmenia. The Polytechnic Institute at Leningrad has ten faculties, while the one in Moscow in its engineering department enrolls over two thousand students and is affiliated with thirty factories. These affiliates are an important part of the system. Through them the broad general knowledge of scientific principles and technical processes, begun in the elementary grades, is completed by actual participation in productive work. After the first year, for every three months of theory there are two months of practice, which necessitates extending some of the courses up to six years.

Qualified engineers and professors not infrequently give the lectures in the factory as well as in the classroom, and practical experience comes from actual labor with hydraulic pumps, Diesel engines, precision instruments, hot and cold metals. A student in the Institute of Transport along with his mathematics, history, economics, and chemistry, engages in signaling, switching engines, and making up timetables. The student-architect must pass his period of apprenticeship in all stages of actual building, from laying bricks and mixing cement to acting as an assistant foreman. The aim is a first-hand contact with all problems from manual labor up to management. The graduate must spend the first five years in the field, rather than in offices or administrative posts. Despite the efforts exerted to get everyone into active service an increasing percentage of students continue in postgraduate work. Even here the idea of learning by doing is carried out as often the "aspirants" work as assistants and collaborators in the institutes connected with the Academy of Science.

Besides the great array of technical colleges are those specializing in the humanities—history, languages, and arts. The famous old seats of learning are now used largely for the training of professors, scientists, and research workers. For those intending to make public work and politics their profession, there are the higher Party schools and universities engaged in studying the problems of the evolving Socialist society. As a matter of fact in all schools from the Institutes of the Theatre and Cinema to the Planning and Military Academies much stress is placed upon social sciences.

In all institutions life follows much the same pattern. To a large extent student bodies are self-governing. Through their elected committees they organize their dining halls, living quarters, and outside activities—such as editing papers and directing art, literary, and technical "circles" in clubs and on collective farms. Since the Soviet Union has "gone athletic" there are now several thousand students' skating, skiing, parachute-jumping, and rifle clubs. But in general the life of the Soviet undergraduate is quite different from campus life in England or America.

"In what does the difference lie?" I asked a girl graduate of the University of Moscow, who for a few years had investigated colleges and libraries abroad in America.

"In one way," she replied, "you are infinitely better off. You are far ahead of us in grounds, buildings, and equipment. They are well-kept, clean, and orderly while too often ours are not. In the second place you have better methods of pedagogy and better pedagogues. Too often we complain that our professors do not know how to teach us. And they complain that we do not understand what they are teaching, that we were not properly drilled and disciplined before we came up to the university. And it's all very true. The lower school didn't have the time or the means and there were too many of us suddenly wanting an education. Before the Revolution there were only 150,000 in our universities, now there are a half million and more. To provide for them as adequately as yours will take ten years or longer."

"But in the students themselves, in their general outlook and attitude, do you notice any difference there?"

"Ours," she replied, "seem to have a clearer idea of what it is all about. They are more sure of what it is that they want to learn, and what they are going to do when they learn it. They are more interested, animated, eager, aware. What shall I say? More full of life and living. And while we are more serious about life than your young people, at the same time we are less worried. We are more serious for a lot of reasons, one of these is that we get our stipends from the State, and we feel it is our duty to make every day and moment count. We are less worried because instead of hunting for a job after graduating, we know that there are two, three, or a dozen jobs hunting for us. We are needed." (For the status and income of teachers see pages 451-452.)

68. What is the Function of the Soviet Press?

Not to make money or entertain the reader, but to inform him and stimulate his interest and zeal in Communism. This is done in the peculiar Russian manner, by way of long, erudite editorials, detailed reports from the various "fronts," and interminable statistics. The opening of a new blooming-mill or battery of coke-ovens is often first-page news. A fourth of an issue may be given over to an abstruse discussion on Marxism. Chess problems occupy more space than do cross-word puzzles abroad. To the average foreigner they are dry and colorless. There are no big display advertisements; no playing up of sex, racy night-life, and scandals; no special sections devoted to comics, sporting events, or the stock exchange; no "society" news, unless the deeds and pictures of Stakhanovites, women tractorists, and parachute jumpers come under that rubric; no sensational stories of crime and passion, unless they serve to point a moral.

The chief relief from facts, figures, theory, and exhortation is found in the articles on art, science, and foreign affairs, topical verses on themes of the day, or witty feuilletons with a sting or a laugh. While these lighter and "human interest" features are on the increase, to the average outsider the Soviet papers still seem dull and monotonous. But not to the Russians. With such avidity do they turn to them that they queue up in front of the news-stands; big editions are sold out as fast as they come off the press, and the Moscow dailies have more subscribers than they can handle.

Only shortage of paper prevents the Soviet press from being the largest in the world. Even so, its growth is phenomenal. The 859 papers before the Great War have expanded to over 12,000, an increase of more than tenfold in number and about twentyfold in circulation. With a similar growth in the output of magazines, instead of one periodical for every fifty persons, as under the Tsar, there is now one for every three persons. And sometimes up to a hundred readers to a copy, thanks to out-loud reading to groups at rest-hours in the harvest-fields, Red Army camps, and factories. And as they listen they understand, no matter to what race or nation they belong. For already, types are cast and papers are published in over 60 languages. In one region alone, the Caucasus, there are 240 organs in the three major tongues, Georgian, Tiurkic, and Armenian; a score more in the minor ones, Avar, Assyrian, Greek, German, Tat, Tatar, Talysh; and thirty in Russian.

The Soviets are fast on the way to realizing their goal: "For every people its own paper in its own language." At the same time they are seeking to make them *of* and *by* the people. Every effort is made to get them to take active part in their work. "A paper will be strong and vital," said Lenin, "when the five men of letters directing it are supplemented by 500 or 5,000 labor correspondents, workers who are not professional writers." "Why," asked *Pravda,* "should we send reporters to the village to write about you peasants? Write about yourselves. Never mind if you are semi-literate and must use capital letters or 'chicken-marks.' Start that way and you may end a columnist. But don't send in such items as 'Ivan beat up Manka' or 'A new well has been dug on Petrov's farm.' Write about things that have a social significance: All that you see in nature or life that gives joy or pain to your heart; all our successes and all our sad failures. Proletarians and peasants, to pen and ink!"

In response to this rose the Rabselkor, the "Worker-Peasant Correspondent" movement. So strong the urge to self-expression that it quickly enrolled two million volunteers. Their ranks are now swelled by three million more of "Army," "Air," "Child," and "Photo" correspondents, sending a steady stream of contributions to the papers. Even the smallest gets not less than a hundred items a month, while big ones like the *Peasants' Gazette* receive over a hundred thousand, necessitating a large staff of experts to sift and classify them. Besides bringing a huge grist of news into the printing presses from all corners of the land, these letters are invaluable for other reasons. They serve as a barometer of public sentiment, reflecting the temper of the masses and guiding the leaders in the making of new laws and the "Party Line." They reveal hidden talents which are fostered in circles, conferences, and special journals, from which have emerged some of the best Soviet writers, cartoonists, and authors of today. Finally, they uncover a multitude of abuses—arrogance of officials, arson of kulaks, sabotage of bureaucrats—for which service many lay correspondents have paid with their lives.

This steady drumfire of criticism from the rank-and-file has brought low a multitude of grafters, careerists, and loafers—including a good bagful of editors. No matter how highly placed, their derelictions do not escape the watchful eyes of these writing plebs. The editor's duty is to give heed to every complaint, no matter from what quarter it comes; to investigate it or hand it over to the proper authorities for investigation; and to follow it through to the end. If he fails, being willfully negligent or careless, he does so at his peril. For the writing masses regard the press as they do the schools, the mines, and the factories, as belonging to them. From their editors they expect just what in other lands the owning magnates and bankers expect from their editors, ready and quick response to their wishes. Thanks to their caustic pens, hundreds of Soviet editors have lost their posts, 50,000 officials have been demoted or jailed, and over 10,000 Communists expelled from the Party.

It is evident then that the Soviet press is much more than a purveyor of news. In the words of Lenin, it is the "collective organizer" of the life of the nation, an instrument for mobilizing the people's mind and energies for concrete tasks. On all major issues it presents a solid, unserried front. Occasionally its columns are open to hot discussions on moot questions of the day. But when the debate is closed, or any crisis arises, every organ, from the biggest in Moscow down to the tiniest sheet in a mountain village, speaks in a single voice. Sometimes it is the voice of praise, self-congratulation, and approbation. They break forth in jubilation over the building of the subway, an artistic film, the conquest of the stratosphere, the finding of a new frost-resisting wheat, the outpouring of funds in aid of the Spanish workers.

At other times it is the voice of lamentation, of scorn or ridicule poured out upon Soviet sins and shortcomings: The breaches in the Five-Year Plan; the cupidity and stupidity of bureaucrats; the ignorance and incompetence of Communists; the neglect of children by their Don Juan fathers; the bombast and boastings of orators covering ugly facts with phrases, "uttering windy words but doing nothing." Rich pickings here for enemies seeking material on Soviet follies and blundering. But in lieu of an opposition press, this "self-criticism" is imperative. Sometimes it reaches the point of self-castigation. While this "strongest, sharpest weapon of the Revoluton," as Stalin calls the Soviet press, is used against its external foes—the Nazis, Fascists, and war-mongering imperialists—more often it is turned against itself, that is, against its mistakes and failures. *But never against the ideal and goal of Communism, and rarely against the general policies for attaining them.*

The Official Organs of Moscow

The lead and tone for the whole Soviet press is set by the capital. *Izvestia, News,* is the mouthpiece of the Soviet Government. *Pravda, Truth,* the spokesman of the Communist Party. Playing on their names the witticists say, "There is no truth in News and no news in Truth." Usually they consist of six or eight pages, but as they are bigger in format than Western papers and practically devoid of advertising, they contain much solid reading matter. Too solid, stolid, and austere for the casual reader. Editorials often run up into two columns or more. Reports of shock-brigades, of journalists traveling out to farms and factories to improve technique and whip up production are complex but highly condensed. Stories and despatches coming in from bureaus of the Tass News Agency at home and abroad, at the rate of a million words a week, are usually stripped down to the barest essential facts. But in spite of limited space there is always room for science and culture, and whole pages are devoted to honoring their great savants: The hundredth anniversary of Goethe's death; the three hundredth of the birth of Spinoza; the thousandth birthday of the Persian poet, Firdusi. Not less generous are the tributes to the living. There are columns of articles and telegrams of congratulation to Bernard Shaw arriving in Moscow to celebrate his seventy-fifth birthday; to Maxim Litvinov, decorated with the Order of Lenin on his sixtieth birthday; to Romain Rolland.

As the official medium of the government, *Izvestia* sets forth foreign policies, prints and comments on the new decrees and directives. It has been doing this continuously since the day after the fall of the Tsar. But to *Pravda* is accorded the distinction of being the mother of all revolutionary papers. May fifth is "Press Day" throughout the country in celebration of its founding on that date in 1912. Then it was often raided by the police, its issues confiscated, its editors jailed, and even its subscription-list used as the basis of arrest and exile. Now it is ensconced in a handsome, modern plant and throughout the country are scores of local *Pravdas* proudly bearing the same name.

Each of these two great papers has a circulation well over 1,500,000 which could easily be doubled were it not for a dearth of newsprint and ink. So insistent is the demand that distant places used to wait days and weeks for their coming. Later, by sending matrices of their pages by rail or airplane, they were printed and appeared on the streets of other cities a day or a few hours later. Now, thanks to the telephone transmitting negatives of their contents by wire, they read the same papers almost at the same time as the capital.

As almost every Union, Cooperative, and Commissariat has its official organ, over a hundred are published in Moscow, about twenty of which are dailies. *The Red Star* reflects the life and interests of the Army, *The Whistle* of the railway men, *Communist Enlightenment* of the teachers, *Comsomol Pravda* of the youth movement. Biggest of all papers is the *Peasants' Gazette,* which publishes fifteen regional editions. By organizing, teaching, or working in the fields for three months in the year, members of its staff keep close touch with the every-day needs of the village. Over 20,000 delegates from all over the land bring their plaints and petitions to its offices, and its legal departments handle over 100,000 cases a year. Simplest amongst the big galaxy of papers for the masses is *For Those Beginning to Read,* edited by the Cossack woman, Kravchenko. Printed in big type, lines, and colors, it is not only excellent for semi-literates, but for foreigners starting to learn Russian. Besides these papers in

Russian there are scores in the strange new Soviet languages. Also in languages of the West, like the *Moscow Daily News, Journal de Moscou.*

Local, Factory, and Traveling Press

All republics, regions, and cities have their own official organs. Some like the *Eastern Dawn* of Tiflis, mirroring the life and customs of the mountain peoples, are very lively. Generally, however, they are smaller replicas of those at the center. More unique and original are the 7,000 papers of the mines, factories, and farms. Their first concern is bigger and better output. But, as the life of the Soviet citizen centers about the place he works in, they deal with every question: With the care of engines and dynamos, and the proper care and raising of children; with the cleaning out of loafers and saboteurs, and the cleaning up of bachelors' quarters. The paper of the Kharkov Hammer and Sickle Plant sent a questionnaire to about a thousand employees as to how they spent their leisure on a certain day, March 21, 1936. The replies showed that 550 went to the cinema, 145 to the theatre, 25 to museums, 300 read some fiction, 14 books by foreign authors in the original, and *all* read the speech of Litvinov at the League of Nations.

Some of these organs, like *Bolshevik Steel* and *Produce Tractors* are dailies, printing up to 20,000 copies, and issuing extras called "lightnings." Some have elaborate weekly supplements, like that of the Stalin Auto Works' *Overtake and Surpass,* out of which has evolved a scientific monthly, a literary magazine, and an illustrated journal of satire. The plant prides itself in its output of poets, humorists, and cartoonists, as well as in its output of cars. No lack of opportunity for anyone with the itch to write, to draw, to moralize. For in the big combines besides the main "house organ," there are special papers for each big shop, department, and brigade.

Not only in the big farms and factories, but wherever in the Soviet Union men go forth to work, to play, to drill or to fight, there go the printing-presses. During the Revolution they accompanied the artillery to the battlefronts, so that propaganda as well as shrapnel did its part in destroying the enemy. Now, on an immensely bigger scale, they are playing an important part on all the construction fronts. Often they arrive at the new dam or mill site before the excavators —editors are not less essential than engineers. With daily and hourly bulletins they spur the builders of bridges and blast-furnaces.

From "agit trains" they pour out messages to the crowds at the wayside stops. From "agit planes" they rain down flyers on the fields during the sowing and harvesting campaigns. On Arctic icebreakers they print the last radioed news for the natives along the Great Northern Route. By boats and sledges they are carried to the workers in the reindeer-ranges, the forests and fisheries; by camel caravans to the cattle and sheep-raising nomads of the steppes. With these traveling presses, ready to go into action anywhere at a moment's notice, the Soviets are ready for any situation.

"Wall" and "Living" Newspapers

Wall newspapers are exactly what the name implies—broadsheets of news and pictures, posted upon walls and doors of factories, offices, or anywhere that crowds gather or pass by. Usually they are typed or hand-written "one-copy" papers, appearing daily, weekly, or at odd times. One might call them glorified bulletin-boards, but they are much more than that. They have their elected editors, regular correspondents and artists, and call on everyone to bring in suggestions, complaints, compliments, challenges, grievances. And they get them in sheaves—serious reports, lighter skits and lampoons, mocking ditties and caricatures. If conscience is "the still small voice that tells us someone may be looking" then these wall-papers are the collective conscience of the plant telling everyone from the Red director to floor-sweeper about his shortcomings: "Although the spinner Marya is six months here from the village, she can't read a word and doesn't want to learn. She is a blot on the textile mill." "Comrade Malkin is such an ardent revolutionist that even his nose is red. He gets it out of a vodka bottle." "Shock-brigader Plootkin is usually late in starting his lathe. But he makes up for it by always being first in the dining hall."

Still more caustic are the prison wall-sheets. As the editors are selected by the inmates and contributions may be unsigned, everyone feels free to vent his grievances, to say what he thinks about anything. Congratulations to the supervisor for providing better meals and bedding alternate with charges of ill-temper and favoritism. In one issue some prefects are praised for teaching the illiterates to read, others are censured for loafing and card-playing. "In room 44 the art of abuse is highly developed and the barber excels all the rest. He thinks out new swear-words every day and apparently has no intention of stopping. He proudly says, 'I was born with oaths. I shall die with oaths, and with oaths I shall be buried!' If he doesn't reform, let the comrades' court take him in hand."

So popular are the wall-papers that since the first one appeared in a Red Army camp in the civil war they have grown to a million. One sees them stuck upon trees by the lumberjacks, on derricks of oil-wells, on mine pillars a half-mile deep under ground, on barges and timber-rafts floating down the Siberian rivers. On gala occasions they come out and in every crisis and emergency. A few hours after the crew of the sinking ship, Chelyuskin, escaped to a drifting ice-floe, appeared *No Surrender* as the organ of these castaways in the Arctic. In the early days of the Revolution when the masses were illiterate there were "Living Newspapers"—troupes of actors, musicians, and acrobats presenting the daily paper complete from leading article to local news in the form of speeches, pantomime, songs, and dances. There is a new device called the "Talking Newspaper" using the "electric-eye" to reproduce sounds recorded on a ribbon of photo paper, which enables the public to listen to speeches and concerts two hours long, anywhere and anytime it chooses. Finally, as an ally of the press in raising the morale and self-initiative of the people there are the placards and posters in which simple messages and slogans are driven home by graphic images.

69. What is the Part Played by Radio?

In its drive "for the conquest of the air" the Soviet Union includes the radio as well as aviation. It enrolls millions of members in a volunteer society, "Friends of the Radio." It stages radio festivals with thirty nationalities participating and broadcasts in sixty languages. It sends out "agit planes" talking from the skies through giant loud-speakers audible for fifteen miles. It stands first in the world in the power of its broadcasting stations, with several of a hundred kilowatts or more. From the antennae mast of its biggest 500-kilowatt one it flashes messages direct to America, raising protest from border states against "jamming the air." But with a sixth of the world to cover and comparatively weak in other means of communication, the Soviet Union is determined to be strong in the air. To its seventy main stations it is adding thousands of smaller ones, forming a grid of wireless reaching to the farthest frontiers of the country and binding them ever closer to Moscow. The most isolated far-off regions may hear the bells in the Kremlin tower striking at noon or midnight and playing the "International."

In the matter of news, weather forecasts, and gymnastics, Soviet programs are not unlike those of America. But there is no ballyhooing of toothpastes, pain-killers, and cure-alls, and more time is given to education of all kinds. In cycles on physics or biology, each lecture is complete itself and all are united into a rounded course with book lists and directions for experiments. Often there are two versions, one popular and one for the technically trained. Plays also are given in full or in a simpler, condensed form preserving the basic plot and characters. Besides readings from the classics, living authors often recite their own poems and stories.

A good speaker who has something to say, and is saying it, is not cut short in the middle of a sentence and may even go over his allotted time. This seems a bit ludicrous to Westerners accustomed to the split-second in the timing of broadcasts. But it has decided advantages in the realm of music. There is no butchering of great compositions in order to dovetail with commercial programs. "It is quite the regular thing," says Albert Coates, director of symphony orchestras in New York, London, and Moscow, "to broadcast all the concert and not a small part of it, as we do here in the United States. As all the people are passionate lovers of music, and as so far there are less than three million receiving-sets, they gather about the loud speakers even if they have to stand for hours in the snow." The repertoires range from "The Magic Flute" by Mozart, Wagner's "Valkyrie," Berlioz's "Requiem" to the old and new folk songs of the Russians. From "Boris Godunov" and the "Arctic Symphony" by Vasilenko to the weird melodies of the mountaineers and the nomads of the East. Including orchestra, military band, soloists, choir, and players on native instruments, the number of musicians in a big studio often runs up to three hundred.

Special hours are devoted to the Red Army, to the Collectives, to the resting workers at midday and midnight, to the dwellers in the night-bound Arctic. Usually two hours are given to the children's program with its "Pioneers' Bonfire," its "Reading Room" presenting the scientific fantasies of Wells and Jules Verne, dramatizations of Andersen's "Fairy Tales" and the "Arabian Nights" and excerpts from Gorky, Dickens, Dos Passos, Sinclair. In the "Club of Curious-Minded Children" they travel with a professor who "knows it all," has been everywhere, and talks about anything. They listen to explorers and inventors over the microphone telling of their own exploits; they hear how Pioneer Yurkin built a "fly-dynamo," so small that it goes into a match-box; how eleven-year-old Olga presented a bouquet of flowers to Stalin on the Red Square and stood beside him to review the Sports Parade. Fan letters come pouring in from the far-flung radio audiences with comments and drawings of favorite "air characters," some of them artistic enough to find a place in the art museums.

From all sources a big station receives up to a thousand letters a day, all of which are typed, classified, and answered by a large staff, mostly volunteers doing this job as part of their "social work." If the letter is of interest to the public at large, it is read and discussed over the wireless. If it is personal—a request to find a fleeing wife or husband, to get back a room or a job from which one feels he is unjustly ousted—it is handed over to the legal section for investigation. This huge correspondence makes the radio, like the press, an excellent barometer of public sentiment. It is invaluable to the government in revealing what the masses think about the new laws and policies, and to the radio staff in telling it what bores or pleases them in its broadcasts. As another means to this end its members go out on the street to listen to the comments of the crowds clustering around loud speakers or to meetings in schools and factories to elicit first-hand opinions and suggestions. These may appear as symposiums in the radio papers, and aid in fashioning programs. If "Millions make the Five-Year Plans," then tens of millions make the radio programs.

10,000 Wireless Sub-Stations

In 1930 a Communist official was pointing out to a group of peasants the advantages of installing a receiving-set with a loud speaker in their village. "If you do so, then no longer will I have to come and tell you what Stalin and Kalinin are saying in Moscow. You will be able to hear for yourselves!" "Very good, little dove!" interjected an old mujik. "We will be hearing what they are saying in Moscow. But will the new machine talk backwards? Will Stalin and Kalinin be able to hear what we are saying in our village?" While even now only a few peasants may talk back to the capital, there are millions talking to each other, thanks to the thousands of local short-wave stations now set up on the big farms and factories, in logging-camps, fisheries, saw-mills, and gold-diggings, in a huge grid of wireless reaching from the summit of Mount Kazbek to the Bering Strait. Some are mere sub-stations for relaying the programs from the centers. But most of them have their own "studios," usually primitive and dingy, but priding themselves on their local talent, sometimes not without reason. In close touch with the needs of the communities around them, in a few short years they have come to play an important part in organizing their daily life and activities.

In a big plant there may be a hundred or more loud speakers in the shop, yards, boiler, and engine rooms. Through them streams the local news—accidents, breakdowns, humorous incidents, along with setting-up exercises, music, songs, and plays from the factory "art-brigades." Most important and interesting are the five-minute talks of the workers, listened to not without trepidation on the part of foremen and managers. For, though the speeches are limited in length, they are not in content. The speaker has the right to say what he thinks and sometimes he says it with vinegar and gall. Attempts to suppress or persecute him for exposing of evils has frequently roused a whole plant in indignant protest. On the whole it is constructive criticism, pleas for cleaner drinking water, better lighting, plans for quicker routing of materials, the saving of oils and fuel.

On a big Collective the wireless is becoming as integral a part of the equipment as its schools, silos, or tractors. It informs its members and the nearby villages of the market prices of everything, from milk to mushrooms, and what to get ready for the next big fair or bazaar. It announces the arrival of a delegation of journalists or artists from Moscow and calls everyone to assembly. It warns of a coming blizzard, a sortie of wolf-packs from the forests, a threatening epidemic of measles or typhus. It sends out an S.O.S. for all hands to rescue teams caught in a sudden break-up of ice on the river or to raise a smoke-screen of burning brush against armies of grasshoppers flying up from the South.

From the first plowing and planting through the whole cycle of seasons, it plays an important part in field-work, especially as it hastens to its great dénouement in the harvest. Then everything moves at high speed and tension. For as the peasant says, "The day feeds the year." Time is the essence of the harvest and the radio is the means of saving an incalculable amount of it. Often a brigade of reapers or echelon of tractors carries a portable receiving-set. It flashes the orders of the farm director to the men camped in the far-off fields for a fortnight or longer. It notifies them of the despatch of trucks with supplies and aid to victims of sunstroke and accidents. It coordinates the movements of the combines reaping along a twenty-mile front. It tells them to stop cutting because of an impending rainstorm or to cut swiftly all through the night to save the grain from a sweeping steppe fire.

In the Arctic a fast-growing chain of stations is reaching out from the mainland ever closer to the Pole. Upon it depends the welfare of all the inhabitants scattered over the frozen wastes of the North. It directs the big ice-breakers convoying the ships through the fog and icebergs of the new Northern Sea Route. It replaces the magic spells of the shamans and medicine men in the daily life of the Eskimos, Nentsi, and Enverks. To it their hunters now turn for news about the location of the herds of seals and otters, the treks of reindeer and caribou to the new moss-pastures. It brings to the farthest ice-and-night-bound outpost the music and gaiety of Moscow, and keeps in touch with remotest settlements, uniting them all into one big Polar community. The doctor at lone Cape Hope radios that he is powerless to help the wife of Yegorov suffering in the pangs of child labor for 36 hours. Fortunately Dixon Island has a first-class obstetrician and all other stations are stilled while he tells what should be done and exactly how to do it. Three hours later Yegorov himself announces the glad news of the birth of a son. All Polar stations again swing into action: "Welcome to our new citizen of the Arctic!" "What is his name?" "How is his mother doing?" "Congratulations to the parents and all the Cape Hope colony!"

But the good offices of these radio stations are not confined to the Arctic dwellers. By immediate broadcasting the forecasts of the Arctic meteorological stations they are of immense service to the whole country. For "weather is made in the Arctic." It is the starting-point of the cyclonic storms sweeping down over the vast plains of Russia, burying roads under sleet and snow, paralyzing traffic, spreading death and destruction in its wake. Forewarned, to some extent, the people can fortify themselves against their ravages. Or, again, if observations point to a comparatively rainless year, they can take measures to ward off its evils by conserving moisture in the soil, the planting of drouth-resisting crops.

It is proposed to use the radio to keep the locomotive engineer in touch with the rear end of the train! Radio is used in signaling from "radio probes" and balloon ascents in the stratosphere, in conducting chess-tournaments between isolated settlements in the tundras and mountains. Reaching out into ever new fields the radio is becoming a more vital factor in the daily life and economy of the 189 peoples of the country, a powerful instrument in creating national unity and solidarity.

70. What Happened to the Art Treasures in the Revolution?

Only an infinitesimal amount were lost or destroyed, thanks to the attitude of the people and the indefatigable efforts of the eminent Bolshevik critic and savant, Lunacharsky. So distraught was he over the reported demolition of the famous Basil Cathedral during the first days of the Revolution that he became ill and took to his bed. Lenin went to see him and made him the head of a special commission for protecting and preserving the cultural inheritance of the past. To it was delegated great power, even to the shooting of vandals and looters. Experts were sent all over the land to ferret out and to inventory every object of art, imposing severe penalties for concealment. Pictures and sculpture were rescued from the burning manor-houses, the rarest ones placed in the central galleries, the others in hundreds of new ones opened in the provinces. Almost everything of artistic value was preserved, including most of the hated statues of Tsars and the double-headed eagles.

Not only were the treasures saved from the assaults of marauders, thieves, and iconoclasts, but great efforts and means have continually been put forth to save them from the ravages of frost, rain, moths, and microbes. That is the task of such organizations as the Bureau for the Restoration of Historical Monuments, with its large staff of historians, architects, chemists, and needle-workers. Frayed-out tapestries, tattered banners, and war standards in hundreds of pieces, become whole again under the deft hands of these experts. The crumbling away of ancient churches, mosques, and towers is arrested by iron girders, by waxing, and even by roofing them with glass. The plasters and whitewash with which ignorant monks covered old walls and paintings are painstakingly scraped away, revealing beautiful ikons and frescoes hidden for centuries. The huge grotesque *Babas,* "Stone Mothers," on hillocks in the steppes are brought under cover.

Important finds are being made by archaeologists, the Academy of Science sending out over 100 expeditions a year. From the Caucasus come hoards of golden coins of the ancient Khans and Caliphs, and out of excavations for the Moscow subway a clay jar of silver monies of the early Tsars. In a hunters' camp of the end of the Ice Age are unearthed huge flint axes and figures carved out of mammoth tusks. Drawings in red pigment of battle scenes are found on cliffs of the Crimea. From the bed of a dried-up sea in Kazakhstan come pterodactyls and, from the Hungry Steppe, giant maropauses that lived fifteen million years ago. From burial mounds of the Altais are exhumed the skeletons of gold-ornamented warriors, horses in silver bridles and trappings, a woman wrapped in a red silk shroud. The tombs and caves of the Crimea, its "dead cities," and those buried beneath the waves continue to yield up rich remains of the culture of the Greeks and Romans, and of their predecessors, the Scyths and Cimmerians. Thanks to all these acquisitions, the value of the Soviets' treasuries of art and archaeology, in spite of the sale of some famous paintings, is much greater than before the Revolution.

To the immense scale, thoroughness, and enthusiasm with which this work of restoration and expansion is carried on by the Soviets, increasing recognition is given by competent critics. "I had looked forward to great things," says Sir Martin Conway of the British Museum in "Art Treasures of Soviet Russia," "but I was utterly unprepared for the phantasmagoria of riches that greeted my eyes. As I look back these sparkle and shine in my memory: Incredible quantities of jewels and masses of plate measured by tons rather than by numbers, galleries of porcelains and 75,000 pieces for which rooms cannot be found; great vases, tables, and even walls of lapis lazuli and malachite, carpeted floors by the acres, ikons by the thousands, upwards of 20,000 pictures, endless suites of furniture; antiques of all periods including 10,000 objects of gold yielded up from the soil of South Russia; vestments and robes heavy with pearls, chalices, and crystal cups, libraries of illuminated manuscripts and books in golden bindings. That such a mass of treasure should have passed through the chaos of an unparalleled Revolution is indeed remarkable. Their escape from theft or destruction seems almost miraculous.

"Some losses there must have been, but they were trifling. Clearly the psychology of the Russian masses must have been very different from the revolutionary French. . . . It was far otherwise in 1789. Where is the treasure of St. Denis, of Rheims, or of Chartres? Hardly any of the work of French goldsmiths of the eighteenth century escaped the melting-pot. Ruin overtook the great abbeys and many of the noblest examples of medieval architecture were leveled to the ground. In Russia, nothing of the kind has happened. The monasteries—so far from being injured, their paintings, vestments, jewels, and embroideries have been carefully gathered together and many of them saved from the progressive decay they were suffering. They are better cared for by the Soviets than they were by the monks."

71. How Are Museums and Art Galleries Used?

As an integral part of the cultural system from the start they received a generous share of "that extravagant budget for public education," which Lunacharsky declared should be "the pride and glory of the nation." Says Professor Arthur Upham Pope, Director of the American Institute of Persian Art, "The Oriental Staff of the Hermitage comprises thirty scholars, far more than the most richly endowed institution in any other country. With amazement Western savants have recently realized that in the Soviet Union there are not less than a hundred specialists in Iranian culture alone." More significant than such tributes from eminent connoisseurs and aesthetes is the wide utilization of the museums and galleries by the masses. With the same zeal and care the Soviets exercised in preserving and expanding the art treasures, they have addressed themselves to a second task—to rouse the people's consciousness of the rich heritage which is theirs.

"Only by acquiring the accumulated culture of mankind can you hope to become a Communist," declare the posters, listing the special excursions to the museums. Not satisfied with making them highly accessible and attractive, the Soviets also advertise them and promote their visitation on a tremendous scale. Into the Moscow museums alone are admitted more than three millions each year. In delegations they come—men from the farm, from the forge, and the mill, children and women and Red Armyists—following a guide through the labyrinths of art and history, bringing back to their 200,000 "art circles" their ideas and impressions, to analyze, argue, and discuss. With the slogan, "Art for the Masses," traveling museums carry exhibits directly to the factories, the collective farms, and far-away villages.

New Museums and New Methods

The Soviets declare war on the static conception of museums as "temples of art," mere repositories of valuable objects. Instead of "cemeteries of past beauty" through which the visitor wandered often sadly bored and bewildered, it seeks to make them tell a consecutive story, to make them as interesting and dynamic as life. The Leningrad Hermitage with its ten thousand Scythian-Sassanian golden antiques; the Tretyakov Gallery with its assemblage of Russian paintings, old and new; the Museum of Western Art with its priceless Picassos, Cézannes, Van Goghs, and Renoirs, also its Lozowicks, Gellerts, and Groppers—all these famous old institutions have been enlarged and vivified by introducing the "complex method." Instead of starring beautiful vases, coins, or sculptures, the aim is to show them in relation to the life of the artist and the society that produced them. Instead of hanging pictures alone in one room, often there are added sculpture, furniture, and decorations of the period, seeking to reconstruct the general atmosphere.

So many new museums have been created that it is almost hopeless to attempt even a casual visit to them all. In his travels from Georgia to the upper reaches of the Yenisei, Alfred Salmony reports finding them everywhere, even in the remotest villages. Counting the 87 existing before the Revolution, Moscow now has 212, ranging from the Museum of "Life in the Forties" to the Exhibition of the Communist International, from that of the old Imperial Army of the Tsar to that of the Red Army and Fleet. There are museums of the most variegated subjects: Ikons, Aerodynamics, Children's Playthings, Peasant Handicrafts, Theatre, Communal Economy, a "Palace" of the History of the Earth. Museums of the writers, Chekhov and Tolstoy and Hertzen. A magnificent one to Lenin, of course, and another for the anarchist Prince Kropotkin. Even a museum in the name of Vassily the Blessed, the gorgeous "pineapple" church on the Red Square, built by Ivan the Terrible. Many buildings like this one have been kept intact with all their belongings and converted into museums to show the life of rulers and classes now passed away.

Exactly as the Tsar left them, the rooms in his palace near Leningrad are preserved today, affording an insight into his intimate life and his bad taste in books and pictures. In the sumptuous Sheremetev Museum the luxury of nobles and landlords is revealed to the descendants of their serfs now padding over its waxed parquet floors in sandaled feet. The town of Zvenigorod is shown as a typical city of the feudal era. In the Novodevichy Nunnery are preserved the habits and paraphernalia of the monastic orders, a few ancient nuns serving to exhibit, and as exhibits.

From contemplation of these practically extinct classes one may turn to study the rising one in the Museums of the Revolution. Here are graphic pictures of the first strikes and peasant uprisings: Iron-cages in which rebels were displayed to the populace, the prison shackles that chained them, the cat-o'-three-tails that flogged them; a hammer engraved with the two-headed eagle with which serfs were sold from the auction-block; the mirror in which was hidden the famous Bolshevik manifesto smuggled into Russia, and secret messages rolled up in cylinders and baked into loaves of bread; diaries written by revolutionists in the "stone sacks" of Schlusselburg and other Bastiles of the Tsar; rude homemade bombs, underground printing presses, red flags that floated from the barricades. Through them is told the story of the long struggle against autocracy, ending with the triumph of October. Sometimes it is told in bitter irony as in these venomous lines engraved beneath Troubetskoy's squat, ponderous statue of Alexander III standing in the Square of Insurrection in Leningrad.

> My father and my son, wearing the crown,
> Were by the executioner struck down,
> But my shame's posthumous; an iron joke,
> I stand a lasting scarecrow for the folk.

Everything is utilized—even the Museums of Ethnology, of Porcelain, and Painting—to point a moral and adorn a tale. The tale is the oppression of the people under the old order. The moral—strive with all your might to build the new order.

72. Do the Arts Serve as Instruments of Propaganda?

Yes, and they always have, insist the Communists. All art has been class art and will be until the classless society arises. The absolute freedom of the artist is an illusion because "one cannot live in a society and be free from that society." (Lenin) An individual cannot help but absorb the ideas and aspirations of his environment and only rarely and by heroic effort does he break away from its influence. Consciously or unconsciously, he tends to reflect the point of view and interests of the ruling class, the one from which he mainly derives his living. Therefore, literature, music, the theatre, hitherto serving mainly to portray, comfort, and glorify the dominant nobles, clergy, and bourgeoisie should now perform the same service for the new ruling class, the workers and peasants. They should strive to awaken in them a joyous attitude toward life and labor, to give them consciousness and pride in their historic mission and enhearten them in the struggle for the new order.

This was the purpose of the new proletarian art which the Communists set out to create. At the outset, in the first gusty days of the Revolution, control was in the hands of the extremists. Those were the halcyon days of the Suprematists and Constructivists, the flamboyant decorations of the agitation-trains, the monstrous cubist canvases on the public squares, blank paintings of nothing done in one color, symphonic assemblies of factory whistles and sirens. Everything new—however ugly, bizarre, and incomprehensible—was acclaimed as truly revolutionary; all the past was contemptuously condemned and rejected. "But why," interjected Lenin, "turn away from real beauty just because it is old? Why worship the new as a god to be obeyed, just because it is new? This is nonsense, sheer nonsense."

From these first extravagances came a reaction. Like the treasures in the museums, all the masterpieces of literature, drama, and music were made accessible except those blatantly counterrevolutionary, salacious, or mystical. The new artists were exhorted to turn to the classics and master the old forms before seeking to transcend them. A long debate was carried on between rival schools and clashing factions as to the forms of the new art. This is now settled in favor of Socialist realism which rejects formalism on the one hand and crude naturalism on the other hand. As to its contents, let the artist depict what he please. But public opinion frowns upon sex intrigue, crime, and Bohemianism, all mawkish and petty lyricism about flowers and princesses. It looks askance upon any idealization of the past, any sentimentalizing over pastoral life or people forever feeling the pulses of their sick souls. It scorns or pities the artists who stand arrogantly or elegantly aloof from the storms and struggles of life. Out of studios and ivory towers it calls the "workers with the pen, brush, camera, and chisel" to join their fellows in remaking the world. It calls them to enter the factories, the fields, and the forests, to reflect in art what they find in reality.

At this juncture the hostile critic remarks that apparently Soviet artists find mainly the crass, material, and earthy. They dismiss an exhibit of Soviet pictures as so much propaganda for more tractors, blast-furnaces, and machines. But that is not the spirit in which the painters conceived them or the public looks at them. A tractor is not simply an instrument for plowing the earth, but for releasing man from his age-old bondage to the soil, ignorance, and superstition; a blast-furnace is not merely a device for smelting ore into iron but for the welding of men and nations together by wires and rails and "lifting them on wings of steel to the sun." Both are symbols of something far greater than themselves. Thus they are used by the painters, poets, and dramatists, and thus they are understood by the revolutionary masses. They have a common language of communication, because they have the same aims and interests. As a matter of fact, great numbers of artists are avowed, and ardent, Communists. About half the Union of Writers are Party members and most of the others stand on the same platform with them. They did not have to be cajoled or coerced into writing about tractors, blast-furnaces, or "Stakhanovism." Bent on industrialization these were the objects which engaged the energies of the Revolution. And, because artists were organically a part of it, these objects likewise engaged them.

Now the Revolution moves on to a new stage, concentrating less upon machines and more upon men. So do the artists. The new emphasis on the individual is reflected in novels and dramas of personal and family relations, the return of the poets to the universal and eternal themes of life, love, and death. People are portrayed as the products of their environment and, at the same time, by reacting on it, as the means of creating new social forces, new patterns of life. Better living conditions and the general rise of culture under the Soviets will beget in the course of time a more tolerant attitude even toward their enemies. Instead of the stock villains in the piece the bourgeois already are beginning to appear as brave men and idealists. In the film "Chapayev" the columns of Whites, with rolling drums and death's-head flag flying, advance against the machine-guns, utterly indifferent to death. In glowing colors on screen and canvas, in brighter dress, gayer comedies, exuberant dances, and triumphant songs will be reflected the new joy and optimism of a people abounding in energy and faith in the future.

To give a coherent picture of the past, of the new Socialist man and the new society in the making is the aim of the Soviet artist. Not only to depict this rapidly changing life but to do so in such a manner as to make his work a factor in the changing of it. That is the gist of what is meant by Socialist realism. It is distinguished from the individualistic realism of Joyce by an understanding of the direction in which the world is going. It is concerned not only with what was and is but with what is to be, and how to bring it into being.

Art is not a closed preserve for the professionals. "Art," said Lenin, "belongs to the people. It ought to extend with deep roots into the very thick of the broad toiling masses. It ought to be intelligible to these masses and loved by them. And it ought to unify the feeling, thought, and will of these masses, and elevate them. It ought to arouse and develop artists among them." To this concept of art the Soviets are dedicated and they are seeking by every means to make it an integral, vital part of the daily life of the people. One sees on the curtain of village theatres the oft-quoted words, "To live without work is robbery; to work without art is barbarism." The walls of workers' clubs are hung with pictures often of real merit.

In summer the city theatres pack up their trunks and load their scenery into cars to tour the provinces, the Red Army camps, the farms, and the fishing fleets. Choir-masters lead the mass-singing of lumberjacks, miners, and stevedores. Renowned ballerinas like Geltser appear on the construction fronts. The best conductors sometimes direct the orchestra of a factory or bring their own with them. Said the first violinist to Albert Coates after a stormy encore, "Congratulations! They like you and they are the metal workers. The metal workers are a very critical lot." In questionnaires the audiences are solicited to record their reactions to the contents and quality of the performances. In tens of thousands of dramatic and literary "circles" and classes in musical listening, the sense of aesthetic appreciation is being cultivated. The aim of all this is to make the masses not mere onlookers and auditors, but active creators of the new art and culture, to stimulate into self-expression their own native talents.

Witness to the vigor and versatility of those talents are the sagas, *bilini,* the endless epic songs reciting the exploits of the half-mythical heroes of old, passed on from generation to generation; the exuberant folk dances on a thousand village greens with the strumming balalaikas ever clanging and improvising melodies; the wealth of color and imagery in the embroideries wrought out by the women in the long winter nights; the fables and wisdom-proverbs racy of the soil. From this rich storehouse the great artists from Glinka to Tolstoy freely borrowed their themes, motifs, and stories. In Leningrad province alone some 2,000 groups of farmers take part in the gigantic "Festivals of Art" with their "flax" dances, ensembles of shepherds' horns and reeds, enactment of ancient rites and ceremonies. "A people reveals its soul in its folklore," said Gorky. To the old folklore is now being added thousands of new tales, songs, and fantasies about the Revolution, Lenin, the airplane. This mass of oral material, the series of "Histories of the Civil War and of Factories" from the pens of the workers and fighters themselves, the collective volumes like "Tales of the High Hill" written by a hundred miners, and "Tales of the White Sea Coast" by hunters and fishermen of the North show the reserves of power in this gifted Russian folk. Not less striking are the talents displayed by some of the former subject races whose long-suppressed arts, now sedulously fostered and encouraged, are experiencing a renaissance.

In times past, through the transcendent power of an idea, individuals and groups have been welded together and impelled to achievements bigger than themselves. By this community spirit great things like the medieval cathedrals have been conceived and created.

In the Soviet Union this community spirit is again manifest on a colossal scale. A hundred and eighty-nine peoples and races, animated and unified by a common purpose, are thinking and toiling together for the building of a good society. The attainment of a good society in which men have learned the arts of living together would in itself be the supreme artistic achievement. But even the striving for it evokes creative impulses in the masses, profoundly influencing the drama, painting, music, and literature. It may well be that nothing of great merit has yet been produced. But till now the chief energies of the people have been devoted to the making of the Revolution, and in defending it. Twenty years is a short time for the flowering of the arts. But the ground has been broken and the seeds planted.

73. Who Writes Soviet Books and Who Reads Them?

Men of letters have always been highly revered in Russia. This is true in spite of the fact that under the Tsars almost every great writer—Pushkin, Lermontov, Shevchenko, Dostoievsky, Tolstoy —was jailed, excommunicated, or sent into exile. Under the Soviets the literary man holds an exalted place in the minds and affections of the people. Triumphal arches were erected in honor of Gorky's homecoming from Italy. On his fortieth jubilee his name was given to a big city, an academy, an air squadron, to countless streets, schools, and factories. Since his death the peoples in sorrow and gratitude pay tribute to his memory, in great assemblies from the Black Sea to the Pacific.

From the far corners of the land delegations bring greetings to the Congress of Writers in Moscow. Thousands stand for hours in the cold to get a glimpse of their favorite authors. The newspapers devote solid pages to the centenaries of Dostoievsky, Gogol, Goethe. The State allots a million rubles for the first complete uncensored edition of Tolstoy in ninety volumes. The program for the anniversary of Pushkin included the restoration of the places where he lived, the broadcasting of his poems, the staging and filming of twenty of his stories and fairy tales, the publication of an eighteen-volume de luxe edition of his works, a six-volume popular collection, a nine-volume pocket edition, an exhaustive encyclopedia for which museums, archives, and attics have been scoured. Even the foreign classics from Homer to Maupassant and Mark Twain are read with such avidity that the presses cannot keep up with the demand.

Not less insistent is the demand for literature of the Revolution and life today. Very little of this has been furnished by the older generation of Russian writers. In their youth they made a god of the people, but when, in the Revolution, the dark masses rose with all the wrath and thunder of a god, these writers could see in their revolt only horror and madness. There were some exceptions, like Briusov, who cried out:

> Love this mass, though it be vulgar,
> Love it, though it savage seem.
> Love its curses, love its anger,
> But above all, love its dream.

Also Blok, who in "The Twelve" put Christ at the head of a roistering group of Red Guards, and Alexei Tolstoy, Serafimovich, and the surgeon Veresayev. Most of the older writers, however, fled abroad or lapsed into silence.

Upon a new generation devolved the task of creating a new literature, with the extremists at first in the saddle. The Futurists filled their work with the idiom of the street, café, and gutter. The Imagists shouted: "Destroy the old syntax and grammar. Down with the verb and the preposition! Turn the word and the world upside down!" This, they insisted, was truly proletarian. But they found small favor with the masses who turned from these new stylists to those who wrote simply, straightforwardly, of their lives and hopes and struggles. Or they read the "fellow-travelers," those gifted non-Communist writers who accepted the Revolution and "traveled" with it, the Pilnyaks and Ivanovs, rooted in the great literary traditions.

Their works were vehemently denounced as bourgeois by the ultra-radicals who demanded that the powerful social weapon of literature should be exclusively in the hands of militant revolutionists. For a long time they had the whip-hand in *Rapp*, the Russian Association of Proletarian Writers, trying to make every artist conform to its dogmas. It was dissolved by the Party on April 23, 1932, with a declaration against the literary dictatorship of any faction, which left the forms of art to be determined by free competition between all schools while the masses acted as jury. To sharpen their critical faculties cycles of literary lectures and discussions are organized throughout the land. In Moscow alone hundreds of "evenings" are devoted to Romain Rolland, Feuchtwanger, Sinclair, Dos Passos; thousands to Tolstoy, Gorky, Pushkin. But the masses talk not only about authors but to them. In person they appear in the clubs to hear what is said about their latest works. A factory becomes the patron of the poet Bezimensky. Literary shock-brigaders go out to work on the Collectives. For "how can one write about life without taking part in it?"

Never is it quiet on the literary front. "Quiet Flows the Don," first of a trilogy by the young Cossack Sholokhov is stigmatized as plagiarism, then hailed as a masterpiece. A new luminary flames up in the public eye and fades away as a "one-book" author. The peasant lyricist Essenin, husband of Isadora Duncan, and Mayakovsky, "poet of the posters," commit suicide. Tatar or Armenian writers, vainglorious in their new-found nationalism, are rebuked for chauvinism. Demian Bedny, the most popular of poets, is publicly warned by critics that he is getting "old in his style." His libretto for "Titans" is condemned as a foolish caricature and perversion of Russian history. The "Communist conceit" of young proletarians is held up to ridicule. Critics assail certain writers as "formalists," and Koltsov in turn assails the critics with caustic irony. Others are condemned for living smugly and indolently on the returns from their past works and too aloof from the struggle. Outcries are raised against the too generous scale of royalties. No one is immune from criticism. Even Gorky, "the grandfather of all proletarian writers," in his day came in for a drubbing.

Out of ceaseless ferment and fighting emerges the new literature. It uses a new imagery—steel, brass, concrete, derricks, and triphammers. In place of mystics and Hamlets, tormenting their souls, it depicts strong-willed men of action, battling for the welfare of humanity. The peasant "God-bearer" becomes the bearer of the collectivist idea. The hero is he who puts dead factory wheels into motion, makes two blades of grass grow where one grew before, storms the stratosphere, conquers the Arctic.

Exultant and triumphant as this new literature is, it is not stultified by indiscriminate eulogy of the new order. "Write the truth," said Stalin to a group of authors. "The truth about the Soviet Union cannot be sweet like candy or polished and shiny like a Tula samovar." It is a literature of realism, not merely the chanting of hosannas to the Revolution but recording likewise its tragic failures and defects. In Sholokhov's "Seeds of Tomorrow," a story of the collectivization of the land among the fiery Don Cossacks, kulak, peasant, bureaucrat, and Bolshevik are drawn with scrupulous honesty. The challenge to the property instinct makes the deep drama of this book. Fiercely it burns in the breasts of the prosperous farmers who are driven by it to conspire, sabotage and murder. It comes out even in the Bolshevik factory worker sent out by the Party, and stirs the middling Cossack, who was first to bring his horses to the collective farm, to confess, "I'm sick with longing for my property. I'm sick at heart for my bullocks. When I pass by the stalls and other men's horses are standing there, they mean nothing to me. But when I reach my own horse and glance at his clipped left ear and his back with the black stripe running right to his tail, I begin to choke and then he seems dearer than my own wife." Vividly and truthfully is portrayed the long bitter struggle for the new

way of life on the land with all its attendant cruelties and tragedies.

In "Humus" Seifulina shows the village Bolshevik raping the
teacher and killing the doctor. "Moon from the Right Shoulder"
is an almost unrelieved picture of the arrogance, egoism, and
eroticism of a section of Soviet youth. In "A Single Breath"
Ehrenbourg depicts a young Communist as a scoundrel pursuing
his career. In "The Birth of an Era" by the blind and paralyzed Nikolai Ostrovsky, who died in 1936, a group of Comsomols
are shown recoiling from the inhuman tasks imposed on them
and giving up their red cards of membership. In a score of
novels appears the civil war veteran conquering the whole world
of enemies but unable to conquer himself, lapsing into bribery,
soft living, and debauchery. All that is dark and sad and ugly
is here, reflecting life as it is. At the same time with boundless
faith in the future the new literature sets out to organize that
life, to mold it nearer to the Communists' desire. That is one
reason why to Westerners it seems largely propagandistic and
evangelical; it is too alien to their desires and concepts of life and
they are too distant from the struggle. Another excellent reason
is that so far Soviet writers have produced very little in any way
comparable with the great Russian masters of the past.

Publishers, Censors, Books by the Billion

As significant as the success of the Soviets in teaching the masses
to read is the creation in them of a voracious appetite for reading.
In the effort to satisfy it there have been issued since the Revolution
in 106 languages over 6 billion books among which are 12 million
copies of the works of Tolstoy and 32 million of Gorky's books. For
the Pushkin centennial a total of 8,150,000 volumes of poems, stories,
and fairy tales of the great national poet were printed. Counting
everything from pamphlets to encyclopedias, there are forty-five thousand new titles each year, considerably exceeding that of any other

country. The quality of paper, however, is usually inferior, and, like the French "yellowbacks," they are mostly unbound. In sharp contrast to the general run of printing are the exquisite editions of the classics—Sophocles, Rabelais, Anatole France, the Persian poets, "Paradise Lost," the sayings of Genghis Khan and Tamerlane. They are put out by the Academia with engravings and color plates by leading artists including the peasant lacquer-painters of Palekh.

On the inside cover of each Soviet book are stated (a) the number of copies in the edition; (b) the size of the book computed by "lists" of 40,000 letters, on the basis of which authors' royalties are paid; (c) the number of the permit of the "political editor" or censor. The aim of censorship is to prevent the circulation of anything deemed "counter-revolutionary," obscene, trivial, or tending to incite racial animosity or crime. Sometimes it is very strict and even puritanical, again it is liberal enough to publish Joyce and "Lady Chatterly's Lover." But no book that seems to the censor hostile to Soviet ideology will be accepted. Obviously his verdict depends upon his interpretation of it. As in the case of the publisher's editor in other countries, it is determined by his individual outlook, dogmatism, temperament, humor. What one censor heartily approves, another may summarily reject. In the latter case the author may choose to argue it out with the objecting censor or take his manuscript to another publisher with a less exacting censor.

Fortunately there are now scores of publishing centers. In keeping with the trend to decentralization, no longer is the aim to concentrate the making of books in one colossal State Publishing House, the "Ogiz." While it is still the biggest, there are others under the Commissariat of Education as well as those run by the Red Army, Labor Unions, Cooperatives, and Writers' Federations. A considerable amount of fiction first appears serially in the magazines. Among the 1,800 Soviet periodicals are several devoted to literature, pre-eminent among which are "Red Virgin Soil," *Krasnaya Nov* and "New World," *Novy Mir*. Much larger than "Harper's" or "The Fortnightly" they are known as the "thick" journals. The critics have their say in the "Literary Survey"; the humorists, satirists, and short story writers in "Crocodile," "Projector," "Little Fire," "Red Cornfield."

Altogether some 25 million books of poetry, plays, and novels are printed annually. Most of the best Soviet sellers have been translated into English, and some are listed in the bibliography at the end of this volume. Through them the Western readers may obtain an excellent insight into Soviet life and literature. The Soviet reader in turn gains his view of Western life and literature through the works of Sinclair, Dreiser, Anderson, Dos Passos, Hemingway, Lewis, Gold, Barbusse, Gide, Wells, Huxley, Mann. In Russian translations they often appear in editions running up to 50,000 copies and over.

Great interest is centered in the Children's Publishing House, its half-million editions of their beloved Soviet authors Chukovsky and Marshak and translations of English favorites from "Robinson Crusoe" to "Black Beauty" and "Huckleberry Finn." Till recently mythical tales of kings, queens, elves, and fairies were practically taboo on the principle that they took children into an unreal dream world, teaching them to depend on luck or the caprices of unseen powers instead of cultivating their own powers and self-reliance. Besides, is not the story of how a field of flax is transformed into garments just as fascinating as a frog suddenly changed into a princess? Isn't it quite as wonderful to read how oil, "the black blood of the earth," sends life and light and energy coursing through the arteries of trade and industry?

So, at any rate, it was long maintained. And there is no denying the charm and glamour with which the incidents and objects of everyday life are invested in the new books for children—"Snow from the Sky," "The Minnow and the Whale," "Mischa in Moscow," "How the Subway Was Built." Read the excellent translations by Beatrice Kinkead of "Black on White," the story of the alphabet, paper, and printing, "Turning Night into Day," the story of light, and "What Time is It?" which tells how stars, sun, rooster's crow, sand, and water-glasses told time for man until clocks were invented. They are by Ilin, well known abroad for his "New Russia's Primer" and "Men and Mountains." Even eminent academicians are called to write for the children—Vavilov to explain "The Technique of Light," Molchanov, "The History of the Calendar."

In shouting colors and vivid pictures they flood bookstalls and stores which are as omnipresent in the Soviet Union as ice-cream stands in America. Not only are they a delight to the youngsters but to their elders, offering a respite from the heavy, somber tone prevailing in the social-economic treatises. They range from simple pamphlets about Stakhanovism to the "Memoirs of Colonel House," or Sidney and Beatrice Webb's "Soviet Communism: a New Civilization?" while the works of Lenin and Stalin come pouring from the presses at the rate of over ten million volumes a year.

Libraries for Everybody

To the Central Book Chamber go fifty copies of each publication —some for deposit, the rest to big libraries at home and abroad. Among the biggest libraries in the world are the Lenin Memorial in Moscow and Saltikov-Shchedrin in Leningrad, each with about six million volumes and six hundred employees. There are also libraries in the Ukraine and Armenia with over a million books. "The Egyptian Pharaohs raised colossal stone pyramids to commemorate the dust of monarchs. But we, our Revolution, will build living pyramids of human thought and aspiration." These were the words of Lenin to his secretary, Bonch-Bruevich, commissioned to scour the country and salvage from the ravages of civil war every rare book, manuscript, letter, autograph. A million of them are now housed in the new Literary Museum of Moscow.

Among the treasures in the great centers are gold-covered missals studded with rubics, emeralds, and pearls: mammoth Bibles encased in onyx, sardonyx, agate, and aquamarine; the tiniest book in the world, "Krylov's Fables," printed in diamond type on pages the size of a postage stamp; parchments of the three-thousand-year-old "Book of the Dead," the newly discovered Sogdian manuscripts on skin, wood, and birch bark; William Russell's "Reporte of a bloudie and terrible Masacre in the Citty of Mosco in 1607"; the prayer-book of Mary Stuart in her own handwriting; the first European account of Ethiopia by the Jesuit Father Francisco Lobo; the Phonetic Archives preserving on victrola-discs old sagas, music, and sayings in scores of strange dialects; originals of edicts signed by Robespierre; letters of Washington, Lincoln, and Darwin; Voltaire's own library of 7,000 volumes; a collection of 230 hand-written Chinese classics recently presented by the government of China; the sealed War-time memoirs of Romain Rolland.

While attending to the interests of the bibliophile, research student, and scholar, the main effort and energies of the Soviets went into the establishment of general libraries, putting books into the hands of the masses of peasants, workers, and soldiers. Among many ingenious devices in the campaign to teach a hundred million to read was a series of gay-colored posters, extolling the virtues and joys of reading. One of them entitled "A True Friend" depicts two peasant lads gazing wonder-struck at a huge half-open book out of which march armor-clad knights, kings, giraffes, pythons, airplanes. Along the margin runs this story told in small print and pictures:

"Ivan was idling, reading no books, taking to no occupation. Life was a bore to him, the days dragged on endlessly, he didn't know what to do with himself! But then he met his friend Pavel to whom he complained that life was a bore. Pavel said, 'If you like, I shall introduce you to a friend of mine. Then life will become a joy and you will be a new man. A whole day will pass with the swiftness of a single minute.'

" 'Introduce me to him,' said Ivan.

" 'Good! Come to see me on Sunday.'

"On Sunday Ivan went to see Pavel. 'Here is my friend,' said Pavel, 'a book. It will acquaint you with everything; it will tell you what people are living on the earth, as well as what people lived here millions of years ago; you will learn what is taking place on the surface of the earth, as well as under the surface and in the sky. Your friend, the book, will teach you how to live life fully and be helpful to others. You will never be bored again. It will change you so that you will no longer know yourself. It will give you a hundred eyes, the strength of a giant, the wisdom of a sage!' "

Now that the masses are literate, the problem is not to awaken an interest in books, but to satisfy the enormous, insatiable demand for them. In directing and cultivating the minds and tastes of these legions of new readers the libraries undertake the most varied activities. They instruct the neophytes in the use of catalogues and the right care of books. They organize "circles" for oral reading of simple stories for the semi-literate and of classics for the advanced. They conduct contests as to who reads the most and the best books, with prizes to the victors. They broadcast talks on the contents of books, and, in shops and offices, set up question-and-answer boards on literary topics. They invite local authors to discuss and defend their new poems, novels, and plays, and obtain rank-and-file opinions on new manuscripts sent in from the publishing houses. Through Book Lovers Councils and Friends of the Library they gain the assistance of hosts of volunteers.

Training the personnel for all these tasks goes on in seventy special library schools, technicums, and institutes, which turn out several thousand graduates a year. Even so, there are not enough to staff the great and fast-growing network of libraries. Extensive systems are operated by the Red Army, Labor Unions, and Commissariats. Big plants, beside their main book stacks, have a dozen shop libraries and scores of circulating ones. There are Blind Libraries printed by the Braille system of raised letters and Sound Libraries with records and phonofilms of important speeches, folk-songs, and musical classes. Altogether some 6,000 libraries are specializing in technics and science, 3,000 are catering to children, 43,000 to the general reader, and 20,000 migratory libraries are carrying books and magazines by wagon to the harvest fields, by sledge to the logging camps, by camels to the nomad herdsmen and shepherds of the steppes.

To consolidate these myriads of units into a single modern unified system is a colossal task pioneered by Henriette Derman of the Congressional Library in Washington, Harriet Eddy of the University of California, Anna Kravchenko, and Nina Vanikov. The aim is complete cataloguing, in some cases both in Cyrillic and Latin characters; open shelves where anyone can browse as he wishes; an inter-library exchange making any book available to any person in any part of the country. There is a long way to go before realizing these ideals. Staffs are inadequate, rural libraries sometimes consist of a few hundred badly worn volumes, buildings are often primitive, the equipment archaic. But books by the hundreds of millions are getting into the hands of the people. They come to them through the libraries, the thousands of book-stores, book-stalls, and vendors in parks, farms, railway and machine-tractor stations, "Red corners," the lobbies of cinema houses. Says Bennett A. Cerf, head of the Modern Library, in "Publisher's Weekly," "The market is there waiting to snap up editions of a hundred thousand and more, the distributing machinery is amazingly good, and the governmental check prevents the publication of trash that might ruin the whole picture."

74. What Are the Soviets Doing in the Theatre and Cinema?

"No people," said the venerable producer-actor, Stanislavsky, "so passionately loves a spectacle as the Russians." And no people is so amply provided with them. Bread at times they have been compelled to do without, but never without circuses, plays, pageants, operas. Wars, insurrections, famines, and epidemics ravaged the land, but the theatres went on, hardly missing a single performance. Into them surged masses of rough-clad, wonder-eyed workers, soldiers, and peasants. Outside waited still bigger throngs clamoring to enter. Everywhere new theatres were hastily improvised to meet the demands of this new play-hungry public. From 240 regular theatres the number has grown to nearly 600. There are also some 5,000 non-professional theatres run by clubs and collectives, countless amateur groups and circles. With dramas going on in sixty languages, new theatres are being built all over the land.

They are as integral a part of the Five-Year Plans as their dams, airways, steel-mills, and power-houses. Into them go the same zeal, pride, and devotion. And the dramas enacted on their stages are reflections of the colossal drama going on outside—the struggle against wreckers, bureaucrats, and spies, the clash of forces around the building of some industrial giant, the triumph of science over the powers of darkness and superstition of the village, the conquest of the Arctic and the defense of the country against the Fascist plotters. It is a theatre of present-day life, of history in the making. And it is a powerful factor in the making of this history. It gives to the masses a concept of the grandeur of the enterprise in which they are engaged, rousing their initiative and enthusiasm for it.

From the beginning of the Revolution these were the demands placed upon the old theatre by the Communists. They were determined that this powerful instrument, organizing the thoughts as well as the emotions of the masses, should serve the interests not of reaction but the Revolution. But when the old personnel, bound by temperament or tradition, would not or could not comply with these demands the Revolution went out and created its own theatre. Rather it rose spontaneously out of the elemental need of the insurgent masses to give vent to the new ideas and aspirations that had laid hold of them. Out of the stuff of their daily lives they wrought plays and staged them in cellars, storehouses, and barracks, in the open fields between battles on the war-front. As in the festivals of the French Revolution, on the streets were re-enacted historic scenes like the Storming of the Winter Palace with over 6,000 participating. With no past to break with, these people-actors had no traditions to conserve. They had only to find the best means of expressing themselves. This they did in complete disregard of all the conventions and artifices of the past, creating a new style, technique, and type of actor. These were best seen and still are today when the old repertory is presented in the theatre of that indefatigable pioneer, dreamer, and Red Armyist, Meyerhold.

It hardly looked like a theatre at all. Instead of sylvan backdrops and drawing room sets there were scaffolds, pulleys, pistons, cylinders, and belts shifted about in full view of the lighted auditorium. Curtains and footlights were stripped away, the orchestra-pit boarded over. Gone was every barrier dividing the stage from the audience so that one could scarcely discern where the one ended or the other began, or distinguish spectators from the players. Out of the audience, actors and firing troops stormed onto the stage which spilled them back again to mingle once more with the audience. Irresistibly drawn into the action the spectators came to feel they were looking not at a picture of life but at life itself, that they were not mere passive onlookers at some great event but themselves participants in it. Out of their seats spontaneously they rose to cheer the cinema slogans flashed on walls and ceiling, to voice anew their fealty to the Socialist "fatherland." So they did in all the complex system of revolutionary theatres directed by Trade Unions, Red Army, and the *Tram*—young workers who toil by day and act by night. Instead of a closed preserve for professionals, these theatres were forums for the people themselves, playgrounds in which they could laugh at the follies and vanities of the old order—and their own. In them not the star actor, not the individual, but the mass usually held the center of the stage. They were training grounds for those histrionic talents with which the Russians are so richly endowed, and out of them developed some thirty regular theatres.

Alongside of this revolutionary theatre of the Left stood the old theatres of the Right and Center whose brilliant galaxy of directors, playwrights, and actors had put Russia in the forefront of the theatrical world in the past. Against them the Revolution kept up a constant drum-fire of criticism. At the same time it was fearful of losing any of the values of this rich theatrical heritage. Paradoxically then, while with one hand it assaulted them, with the other hand it poured money into them. It railed at the sentimentality and ideology of their old bourgeois plays but went to see "Uncle Vanya," "The Cherry Orchard," and "Boris Godunov." It assaulted the ballet as a decadent art form but lavishly subsidized their training schools. It called them "fossils" and "museums of theatrical antiquities," but allowed them to go on playing the old classics in the old manner.

Not altogether in the old manner, however. Even without any direct pressure the old theatres could not remain unchanged in a changing world. Into them swept a current of ideas from the new revolutionary theatre profoundly affecting not only their repertoires but their stage-craft and acting. In turn these old theatres affected the new by maintaining their lofty traditions—

their minute attention to details, perfection of ensemble, the superb finish of their acting. They helped the new theatre to slough off its crudities, excrescences, slapdash manner, to raise its standards to meet the ever more critical tastes of the new playgoing public.

Out of this interaction has grown a unified national theatre, comprising all the theatres of Russia—Left, Right, and Center. "It is not a theatre made up of a number of separate and un-related bits, like the theatre of England, America, or France," says Huntly Carter. "It forms an organism, every part of which has a function, whilst all parts function as one." It can draw costumes, plays, designs, and librettos out of central property houses. It can turn to 76 training-schools of the Drama, Ballet, Bio-Mechanics for the right expert or actor it is needing. From a hundred thousand members in the Unions of Art Workers it may select directors, musicians, hairdressers, circus-saddlers, painters, carpenters, scene-shifters. In rehearsing a play years, instead of weeks or months, may be taken to bring it to perfec-tion. In presenting it there is always an audience with enthu-siasm unbounded.

"These folk make a habit of theatre-going," says Norris Houghton in "Moscow Rehearsals," "but never does it lose its excitement for them. Many times they remind one of a football crowd in America. They sit forward on the edges of their seats, sometimes almost fall off them in their excitement; they laugh loudly, they weep copiously, they applaud vigorously. When the performance is over, they run down to the footlights to cheer their favorites by name. When the audience in America and England goes to the theatre, it sits back with a sort of an 'all right, you show me' attitude, waiting to be amused, waiting for the actor to come to it. Not so in Moscow. There the audience reaches out to the stage, it goes more than halfway to meet the actor; the artist comes more than halfway to meet the audience, and in that something-more-than-one-hundred-per-cent which is engendered lies the greatness of the Soviet theatre. . . . It has risen to a peak because the people of Russia put it there."

The Soviet theatre however is not without its restrictions. It cannot stage any plays deemed inimical to the interests of the Revolution or public morals. All plays come before the Chief Repertory Committee which serves not merely as censor but as general consultant and guide both to playwright and theatre. But, though this new unified theatre has to keep an eye on the censor, it does not have constantly to consider the box-office. It can call upon State funds to help in staging new costly productions and to make up some of its deficits which in the past have amounted to as much as thirty million rubles a year. "In Russia," says Eugene O'Neill, "commercialism does not throttle the theatre, nor tradition blind it. There men get a chance. New ideas are tried out and there is a real renaissance of the theatre."

To the playgoer is presented a well-nigh unlimited choice in acting, repertory, and stagecraft. Wide use is made of revolving and sloping stages while in some theatres an altogether new place is found for the stage. Instead of being at one end it forms a circle about the spectators, while for Okhlopkhov's theatre there is a plan for swivel-chairs so they may swing about to follow the acting. In the Realistic Theatre the position is reversed: the stage is in the center with the audience forming a circle about it. In the new Meyerhold Theatre in place of a stage there is an arena surrounded by tiers in the form of a stadium from which may be seen the actors entering from small rooms at one side of the arena and the properties rising up on elevators from below. Wide ramps will allow automobiles and holiday processions to enter from the streets and pass right through the theatre. In the new theatre in Erevan, Armenia, the floors of the three revolving stages are divided into cubes which can be mechanically raised to form all sorts of steps, platforms and pyramids.

In acting one may choose the realism of the Art Theatre with its vowel emphasis, its actors identifying themselves so completely with their parts as to forget they are on the stage. He can compare that with Tairov's "Kamerny," in which the actor is not allowed for a moment to forget that he is on the stage. He can still see the athlete-acrobats trained by Meyerhold to such mastery of themselves that they do not depend on words, but cutting out whole sections of dialogue rely upon gestures and pantomime to convey the meaning. Or in the "Jewish Kamerny," whose former director Granovsky was one of the "Big Five" producers, he may observe the perfect unity in speech and movement of the whole ensemble, every word suited to the action and the action to the word.

In theme and contents the Soviet theatre runs the whole gamut of life—past, present, and future. From its wide-ranging repertoires one may select according to his predilections. If one's interest centers in the Revolution he may see it in all its aspects upon the stage: In "Bread," the war to the death against the kulaks in the village; in "Tempo," the orgiastic fury of reconstruction; in "Roar China!" the hopes of the Communists for the rising of the coolies against the imperialists in the East; in "We Salute You, Spain!" the fierce struggle of that country against the Fascist forces. Even the Art Theatre alternates its introspective, psychological studies like "Tsar Feodor" or "Dead Souls" with turbulent dramas of action like "The Armored Train," with Siberian peasants shouting and shooting across the footlights. More subtle and sophisticated is Bulgakov's "Days of the Turbins" in which the Whites are depicted as brave men and idealists. "Aristocrats" by Pogodin shows the regeneration of criminals in building the White Sea Canal. "Umka, the White Bear" shows the impact of the new culture upon the primitive tribes in the Arctic. In Afinogenov's "Fear" the pure scientist, at first fearing the Revolution, is converted into an ardent champion and co-worker. In Korneichuk's "Platon Krechet" are depicted the ethical problems of a Soviet surgeon and his struggle with bureaucrats. Scores of these new plays make their debut every season, more than enough to provide a theatrical diet exclusively of them if one likes that sort of thing.

On the other hand should one's taste run to old plays he can gratify it with anything from Shakespeare's "King Lear" to Tolstoy's "Resurrection." In the last decade most of the classics—Aristophanes, Ben Jonson, Cervantes, Machiavelli, Lope de Vega, Schiller, Sophocles, Racine—have been staged, but not always in the classic manner. In the Vakhtangov Theatre a brand new Hamlet appeared upon the boards—not a mad, melancholy neurotic, grieving over his father's death, but a robust, scheming politician intent upon getting the king's crown for himself. In its own likeness each epoch creates its Hamlet and, logically enough, in this case he was made in the Marxian image. "We English-speaking audiences," says Edmund Wilson, "should look silly complaining of the damage done to Shakespeare by the Soviets when we have ourselves been tolerating for two centuries adaptations which bowdlerize him, sentimentalize him, and make hash of him."

Later this Soviet Hamlet was roundly condemned by the critics and removed from the boards for being untrue. Turning toward Socialist realism, the theatre is now interpreting the classics in keeping with the age in which they were written on the principle that only by presenting the past as it really was can people understand the dialectical significance of history. However with a few slight changes "The Golden Cock" of Rimsky-Korsakov is transformed into a satire upon absolutism, "Pickwick Papers" is served up in modern Soviet style, "Egyptian Nights" is a composite of the Cleopatra plays of Bernard Shaw, Shakespeare, and Pushkin. If these innovations are shocking one may take refuge in the old academic Little Theatre and see the old dramas played much as they were fifty years ago, and with distinction.

Instead of many plays one may prefer through many theatres to pursue a single play, like Gogol's "Inspector General," which one may have in any version from the naturalism of Stanislavsky to the constructivism of Meyerhold. It is the impostor theme, an exposé of petty grafting rascals, a satire against bureaucrats, as pointed today as when it first set Russians into gales of laughter a century ago. Even more widely staged was Gorky's "Yegor Bulychev," in which the old merchant foresees the crash of his world and dies cursing God while his daughter turns to the new life. Still another by Gorky which depicts the decay of a class and an epoch, is "Dostigayev," a nice jolly merchant who tries to meet the inevitable by ingratiating himself with the revolutionists.

The Opera

Moscow alone has four companies staging operas as various as the old Russian favorites like "Prince Igor" and "Queen of Spades," Western classics like "Faust," "Carmen," and "The Barber of Seville," new Soviet productions like "Quiet Flows the Don" and Shaporin's "The Decembrists" which depicts the abortive revolution of 1825 of the officers, nobles, and poets against the first Tsar Nicholas. Better soloists one may hear in New York, London, or Paris, but star singers cannot make an opera. It is the spirit, the élan of the entire company, the perfect coordination of lights, voices, settings, orchestra, such as is achieved in the Great State Theatre with its 2,190 members and decades of training and tradition to draw upon. "I never heard opera until I heard this company," says Leopold Stokowski. "If any part is outstanding it is the great chorus composed exclusively of artists. One hears the mass chorus and yet hears the individual singers. And each one is an actor. They are acting all the time. The great chorus moves back and forth along the stage never relaxing. Nothing can compare with it. You look back across the audience and find them breathlessly still, enthralled. They have floated out of themselves."

"Acting all the time." This is the effect of Stanislavsky and Nemirovich-Danchenko upon the opera. No longer a glorified concert, sound for sound's sake, it is an extension of the actor's art into the realm of rhythm. Old librettos have been scrapped. Hoary conventions are gone. Costumes and colors become expressions of musical tone and the musical idea is more powerfully revealed by emphasis on psychological content. (Markov) Choruses are no longer mere supers. Sometimes, as in "Lysistrata," the chorus becomes the principal *dramatis persona*. Sometimes it is removed from the stage action and entrusted with the rôle of author and observer as in "Carmen," or again it may be used as in "Lady Macbeth of Mtzensk" to express a final synthesis —the voice of the suffering Russian people of a hundred years ago cries aloud in the last chorus of the prisoners in chains on their way to Siberia. In light operas the Russians have never excelled. But now, in keeping with the growing demand for sheer amusement, more attention is paid to musical comedies and gay operettas.

Plays for All Peoples, Tastes, and Ages

Thanks to the cultural renaissance of the former subject races, there are over 250 national theatres playing in 60 different languages. Even the Tatars, Kazakhs, and Uzbeks have their national operas. In some of their productions the Georgian Rustaveli, the White Russian Dramatic, and the Ukrainian Shevchenko hold their own with the leading theatres of Moscow and Leningrad. Their repertoires include foreign plays like O'Neill's "The Hairy Ape," the old Armenian classic "Pepo," and modern themes about the liberation of Moslem women from the veil or the tractor driving the camel from the desert. Great pains are taken to make them accurate in costume, dancing, and music. Aiding thus in the revival of national feeling and pride, they are at the same time powerful factors in wakening interest and understanding of the different peoples in each other.

The schools likewise use this method of teaching social life and history by acting it. Out of this and the work of enthusiastic directors like Natalie Satz have grown over a hundred Children's Theatres. In some the actors are adults, in others, with child actors as well as child ushers and attendants, one may see performances little inferior to those of their elders. Close observation of the audience is kept by psychologists, studying the reactions of the children in tears, laughter, applause, and recording them afterwards in appropriate charts and graphs. At the point where little Eva in "Uncle Tom's Cabin" dies to the accompaniment of soft weeping music the tear-graph shoots up swiftly to an extremely high point. Too great a strain on the emotions, say the psychologists. Cut out the music and bring down the graph! Take the tremolo out of Uncle Tom's voice!

Other foreign favorites are "Hiawatha," "Robin Hood," and "Tom Sawyer," whose exploits are as great a joy to Soviet boys as to American. Still more mirth-provoking are the antics of their own Petrushka, Little Peter, the Russian Punch of the Marionette Theatres and Puppet Shows set up in city parks and village greens. Petrushka has become a revolutionist—a rambunctious, rollicking Red, cracking the heads of kulaks, bureaucrats, and Fascists, as he drones out ditties about the Five-Year Plan. The Blue Blouses took their name from the blue denim usually worn by these traveling troupes of rhymesters, dancers, and acrobats. With a minimum of stage properties, using the backs and fronts of the same costumes they presented exuberant skits on topics of the day. The Blue Blouses and the Living News-papers (see p. 357) have practically disappeared as a result of the growth of literacy and the network of theatres and amateur groups throughout the country. There are thousands on the collective farms of which 150 have a professional status, sending their brigades of actors into the fields during the planting and harvesting seasons.

For the circus the Russians have always had a particular flair. Out of the West, Peter the Great imported not only skilled artisans and scientists to act as mentors and teachers for his subjects, but rope-walkers, jugglers, and clowns. The Russian Barnum of today is Krasovsky, head of an organization operating 130 circuses, not travel-ing tents of canvas but amphitheatres of stone and steel. Their arenas are big enough to hold cavalcades of camels and bareback riders, or flooded with water to float a ship or tropic island. Favorite items on the programs: the breath-catching feats of the flying trapezists; camel riding; the droll antics of "Mishka," best beloved animal of the Russian folk, and his fellow bears; the "Court Jesters to His Majesty, the People," the tumbling clowns and satiric tomfools hurling their quips at the bourgeois, bureaucrats, and blundering Bolsheviks. The Soviets take their circus seriously, too, supporting a Circus Institute which gives a three-year course in theory and technique with studies ranging from physics to lion-taming, from Marxian dialectics to sword-swallowing.

To list briefly some other forms and aspects of the Soviet world of play and drama: The dozens of studios, satellites around the big theatres serving as tryout grounds for new methods and ideas. The Theatre of Improvisation in which the actors in the first years made up their lines as they went along. A theatre for deaf-mutes that bears the name Palace of Silence. A traveling Gypsy Theatre for these long-wandering nomads now settling down in the Collectives. The Theatre of Folk Art presents wandering minstrels of the Caucasus, Oirot hunters playing on fifes for enticing deer, Cossack choruses in their picturesque caracul caps, blue caftans, and red-striped trousers, shep-herds imitating bird-calls, tap-dancers, singers of the latest limericks

and of the oldest runes and ballads, a symphony orchestra composed
of scientists, doctors, and engineers. On its stage each year appear
some 10,000 performers from all nationalities and walks of life "asking
no mercy from the critics on the grounds that we are amateurs."

There are also mass carnivals like the World of Fairy Tales and
Legends and Golden Flames, the story of fire starting with the first
spark struck by primitive man and ending with a display of "fiery
fountains." Finally, the festive processions of May Day and November,
lasting from dawn till nightfall with a million people participating.
Each year these spectacles grow more colorful, musical, and dramatic,
incorporating features from the pageants of the Middle Ages and
the outdoor dramas of Greeks. "In Russia," says Fülop-Miller, "there
is an astonishing impulse and enthusiasm for the theatre such as can
only be paralleled in the ancient world." Says Lee Simonson, "For the
artist all roads once led to Rome, yesterday to Paris. Today, for the
artist in the theatre, whether actor, director, or designer, the road
leads to Moscow and the theatres of the U.S.S.R."

The Cinema

"An empty futile amusement," said the last of the Tsars.
"Only an abnormal person would put this vulgar circus on a
par with art." Against this stands Lenin's declaration, "For us
the cinema is the most important of the arts." So important has
it become that leading men of letters are now scenarists. Eminent
academicians supervise the making of films about the ways of
nerves, stars, and atoms. The State College of Cinematography
gives a four-year course under the tutelage of outstanding directors, cameramen, and scenarists. A chain of studios extends from
Leningrad with its "Cinema City" to semi-nomadic Tajikistan.
Along the vine-clad coast of the Crimea with its picturesque
ruins, palaces of the Tsar and two score races with their ancient
costumes, music, and dancing, the "Soviet Hollywood" is building. In some forty-five thousand theatres ranging from the city

cinema palaces to the hutments in steppes and forests over two billions each year are gazing on the silver screen. The International Exhibit at Venice awarded the Soviets the coveted Silver Cup "for the high merit and originality of their films."

To its high place among the industries and arts the Soviet cinema has grown from rude beginnings. Casting off all traditions the first directors like Vertov "broke down the walls of the studio and took their cameras into the streets, the fields, and factories." The first films were calls to action carried by the agitation trains to the battle fronts and villages. Some were merely glorified newsreels. Others were unique in their angle-shots, use of symbolism, and *montage*—the skillful weaving together of many episodes with rapid cross- and back-cutting to show the interplay of time and events. Abroad no attention was paid to the new paths the Soviet cinema was blazing until the appearance of "Potemkin," "a rugged, savagely breath-taking document," recording the historic revolt of the Black Sea Fleet at Odessa. At once it was hailed as a masterpiece and its director, architect Eisenstein, was pronounced the "Michelangelo of the celluloid." This was followed by "Ten Days That Shook the World," a huge canvas crowded with masses of soldiers and sailors, rebelling against war, hunger, treachery, and showing their triumph in the revolution of October. Then "Old and New," an epic of the soil in which the chief characters, as Eisenstein points out, "are a milkmaid, a bull, and a milk-separator."

In these great screen dramas attention was always centered on the peasant-worker masses—their fears and bewilderments, their hates and hopes and dreams. The masses rather than individuals were the heroes, and, by the consensus of critics, superbly played up to the leading rôle in which they were cast. One forgot they were actors. And they were not. Instead of professionals, often people without any training whatsoever were central figures. Straight out of the streets, fields, and factories were picked the types that were wanted. Many never saw a movie camera until they were put in front of one and told to be themselves. That was the secret of their good acting. They were simply re-enacting oft-repeated scenes out of their own lives. On the other hand, the chemist-director Pudovkin preferred regular actors and put more stress on the rôle of the individual. Among his outstanding films are "Mother," adapted from Gorky's novel, "Storm Over Asia," the awakening of the descendants of Genghis Khan from centuries of sleep; and "The End of St. Petersburg" with its contrasting of speculators on the bourse frenzied with joy as war-stocks go shooting upward and regiments of hungry, horror-stricken soldiers driven out to die in the trenches. The individual was used as spokesman of the masses, rising up to express its feelings, to formulate its will in a word or gesture. In the same monumental style the Ukrainian director, Dovzhenko, produced "Arsenal" and "The Soil." Although these are all silent films, most of them still stand as classics of the cinema world.

There followed a period of comparative stagnation and mediocrity. This was due to the paralyzing influence of the ultra-leftists on all the arts, the dearth of good raw film, and troubles with the new technique of sound. With the overcoming of these obstacles and just when critics were saying the Soviet cinema had spent itself, it began to create again with vigor and versatility. The first sound film was Ekk's "Road to Life," a story of the wild, homeless waifs and their regeneration through useful labor. From Vertov, master of the documentary film, came "Three Songs About Lenin"—the thanksgiving of Asiatic women to him for liberation from their age-old woes and bondage, the lamentation of the people from the deserts to the seas when he dies, the final song of joy and triumph, "If Lenin could only see our country now!" From Trauberg came "Son of Mongolia," the first Soviet sound film in an Eastern language. Against a background of gathering war clouds, a shepherd of the Mongolian Republic enters Inner Mongolia where he falls afoul of the Japanese militarists and is sentenced to die as a revolutionist. He escapes and returns home politically literate, freed of superstitions, and ready to help in the struggle of his people. In "Frontier," Dovzhenko pictures the founding of a new "air city" on the shores of the Pacific where the forest guards and hunters defend their territory against Japanese wreckers.

A milestone was "Chapayev," a faithful portrayal of this impetuous warm-hearted man who headed a band of partisan fighters near the Volga. Hardly able to read or write, he is a born leader of men. He sings with them; gives them lessons in tactics with potatoes, a pipe, and a mixing bowl; rules them with an iron hand. Despite its tragic climax, the killing of Chapayev by the Whites while he is swimming a river, in it the Soviet people re-live the glory and pathos of their recent past. Over three million in Moscow alone went to see it. Its directors, the Vassilyev brothers, at once became household names all over the land. To them and their staff were given the highest decorations and awards. Georgians demanded a like epic of their insurgent leader Arsen; the Ukrainians of their partisan hero Shchors; children pleaded for a Chapayev of their own. It also inspired the filming of two famed insurrectionists—the seventeenth-century Cossack Stephan Razin, and eighteenth-century Pugachev, executed after leading a peasant revolt. The Vassilyev brothers turned to "Far East" picturing Japanese intervention in the early years of the Revolution. "Peter the Great" is a screen adaptation of the novel by Alexey Tolstoy and "Prisoners" of the play by Pogodin about the rehabilitation of convicts in the camps of the North. "Revolutionists," directed by Vera Stroyeva, depicts the feelings of the masses before and after the massacre at the Winter Palace. "Three Women" is an epic of young girls working with the Red Cross troops at the front.

The popularity of these films shows that the Soviet public is not tired of revolution and reconstruction. They like these old themes. They like the new genre of comedies, fantasies, and adventure, focusing on the individual as a facet of the mass. They like anything provided it is good cinema. Increasingly they are getting it. Plots are more closely woven. Characters are less stereotyped, schematic, and abstract, not used simply to point a Socialist moral or adorn a Bolshevik tale. They are presented as they really are, products of their economic-social environment. Shock-workers sometimes appearing as cowards and careerists, the bourgeois as loyal to their ideals and their class. And they are shown not only in their social relations, but grappling with the personal problems of love, life, and death. At the same time the Soviet cinema of today holds fast to the best features

of its past. It is highly realistic. It displays the same superb handling
of mass scenes. It builds its stories around the idea and not the actor.
Above all it is purposive. "We can build a subway in two years," says
the director of "Peasants," Ermler, "but how sadly lacking in culture
are those who build it! Our cinema must aim to develop a new proletarian nobility to depict the new Socialist man in the making and
educate the emotions."

Educational and Children's Films

While most films aim to be educational, five studios are specializing
in health, science, and technics. There are some 300 films covering
the whole field of industry, from watch-making to oil-drilling, from
gem-cutting to the harpooning of whales. Courses of sound films in
color are replacing the old text-books in teaching drivers of autos,
airplanes, and gliders. Workers wishing to increase their output can see
just how the leading Stakhanovites reach their high norms by making
best use of their time and energy. Peasants learn from the screen how
to fight fires, eradicate bed-bugs and cockroaches, care for rabbits
and horses. Doctors and nurses observe in slow-motion pictures the
technique of complex operations, the behavior of alcoholics and
epileptics in a fit, and how to do field service at the battle fronts.
Campaigns against alcohol, abortion, and syphilis are waged with
films in some cases too shockingly realistic for Westerners.

In "Treasures of a Sunken Ship" one may watch the deep-sea
divers at their salvaging work under water; in "Searching for Rare
Elements" the work of exploring expeditions is presented; in "The
Higher Nervous System" the reflexes of dogs, monkeys, and humans;
in "The Mechanism of Normal Birth" the rotary movement of the
foetus in the womb. A series of scientific "shorts" opens up the won-
der-world of the blood-stream, the beating of the heart, the evolution
of flowers into fruit, the formation of crystals. From the firm ground
of science there are leaps into the realm of fantasy, as in "Cosmic
Rays," depicting the flight of an "astroplane" to the moon with a
Pioneer as stowaway. To make it technically correct, and convincing,

the advice of engineers, astronomers, and airplane builders was constantly sought.

While most pictures are for movie goers of all ages a fifth are specifically designed for children. Among the most popular are "Captain Grant's Children" after Jules Verne, Pushkin's "Tale About the Fisherman and the Fish," and "The Quartette," based on Krylov's fable of a monkey, a goat, an ass, and a bear. In the animated cartoons, instead of a Mickey Mouse, their favorite animal, the hedgehog, is the hero. Over ten thousand schools have their own projection apparatus. Gay carnivals open the juvenile cinema festivals that are held in the collective farms as well as in the chief centers. Eisenstein's "Bezhin Meadows" is dedicated to the memory of the ten-year-old Pavlik Morosov who was killed by kulaks.

In the puppet film, "The New Gulliver," the hero is a boy moving like a giant among the hosts of tiny wooden dolls. At a Pioneer camp in the Crimea, Petya while reading Swift's classic falls asleep and dreams he is shipwrecked on the coast of Lilliputia. The tiny citizens of the kingdom chain the "man-mountain" and the fire-brigade sprays water into his mouth without waking him. Tractors then tow him to the king, who gallops up to his face on horseback and tickles his nose with his scepter. Petya's sneeze sends the king flying. At a celebration in his honor he inquires for the absent workers and in alarm the Lilliputians seek to divert his interest by putting on a musical program. Petya breaks into a Pioneer song which he hears echoed by the unseen workers underground. A revolution follows in which Petya drags the royal fleet away from the workers, and the king is overthrown. The making of "The New Gulliver" called for 3,000 dolls, some with a hundred different face and lip expressions; new sound devices for the shrill voices, music, and noises of the Lilliputians; and special trick photography to combine the marionettes with a live, normal boy.

With similar devices its director Ptushko made "Morning Star," depicting an airship driven by atomic energy to the planet Venus in a search for uranium ore. Another animated feature is Pushkin's "Tale of the Priest and His Worker Balda." "In contrast to American films of this kind," says its director Tsekhanovsky, "we like to depict people in a satirical aspect."

How Soviet Pictures Are Made

In preparing a scenario, or "kino drama," a director usually collaborates with the scenarist, or "kino dramatist." More and more authors are learning the technique of writing for the screen. Babel wrote the script for his "Land of the Sun"; Leo Rubenstein for his "Path of the Samurai"; a whole galaxy of writers for Tolstoy's "War and Peace" and for the Pushkin centennial film, "Youth of the Poet," and his "Queen of Spades." After its completion the script goes to a committee to pass upon its artistic merits, its political soundness, and social value. If the film deals with industry or the land, delegations of workers or peasants may be called in to say what they think about it. If it is a children's picture, like "Broken Shoes," it is discussed by parents, teachers, and the youngsters themselves. If it is a costume picture, like "Peter the First," historians are consulted in order that the coronation and battle scenes may be accurate in every detail. Cinematograph specialists were sent abroad to supervise its French version. Whenever possible, historical pictures are made where the events occurred as in the case of "Chapayev." A troupe does not merely go on location, but lives there for a season. With the Red Army it shares the life in camps or barracks and carries on discussions about the story to be filmed. This mutual contact gives the main actors the feeling and spirit of the men, and the men in turn an intelligent understanding of the drama in which they are to participate.

From the studio the film is often sent back for their comments and corrections. They may even be invited to the preview, joining in the assaults or, as is more likely, stoutly rising to its defense. And it needs defenders. For criticism is usually caustic and grilling, and even the best films are subject to a raking cross-fire. And it goes on long after they have made their debut. "In 'The Soil,'" said Gorky, "Dovzhenko gave us much of the earth but little of the force of Rubens, and he had to resort to sculpture-like immobility." Gorky also arraigned "Peasants" for "its gross ignorance of peasants. To show them stuffing down dumplings in the sweat of their brow is ridiculous. And to have peasants who know the value of bread, as we do not, throw it out of the windows! That is impossible." The veteran director Kuleshev says that "Accordion" is done "in the spirit of an Easter postcard or a Russian Punch and Judy show." "If it is," retorts Lars Moen, "then what the Soviet cinema needs is a more liberal dose of that spirit," and goes on to accuse the critic of "artistic biliousness and jealousy."

These conclaves on the cinema evoke a lively interest in all layers of the population. They aim to spur the director to better work, to raise the taste and discrimination of the public, and give it an understanding of the meaning of the great new films. This education goes on constantly in the press, on the radio, and even in the foyers of the theatre where a lecturer holds forth upon the new feature that is showing. However, if one is surfeited with instruction he does not have to listen to it. He may dance to the music of a good orchestra, refresh himself with tea or sandwiches, read the current magazines or papers, browse through the new novels or plays on the bookshelves, play chess or checkers in a game room. That's the reason the foyers are so spacious. They are built to accommodate the throngs of early comers or late arrivals. For the rule of the regular theatres holds good in the cinema. The doors are closed after the show begins and no one is allowed to enter until the next one. Besides preventing noise and interruptions, it is of advantage to the director. It assures him that his picture will be viewed as he meant it to be, not piecemeal but as a complete artistic entity. Never is a picture touted as the "most spectacular," "breath-taking," or "hair-raising." If it has any merits it is assured of a long run with houses everywhere packed with appreciative and often rapturously enthusiastic spectators.

Films In and Out of Russia

Most of the pictures listed above have been shown abroad. Also the "Youth of Maxim"; "We Are from Kronstadt," depicting the Baltic Fleet battling the interventionists; and the musical satire "Moscow Laughs," in which a herdsman inadvertently finds himself conducting a symphony orchestra. Films of the nationalities are increasingly popular, outstanding among which is the musical "Gypsies," showing the decline of the despotic patriarchs with the youth turning from a nomadic life into the new security offered by the collectives. One of the pioneers of national themes was Lucita Squier, author of the Tatar film, "The Mullah's Third Wife." Incidentally, the Soviet films which have enjoyed the greatest success at home are the ones most loudly acclaimed by foreign critics and movie-goers. They like them though they criticize them for being rather plotless, lacking in "continuity," starkly realistic. Another charge is that they are laden with Communist propaganda. That is precisely the indictment the Soviets bring against foreign films brought into their country—they are laden with capitalist propaganda. They exalt the virtues of money-getting, rewarding the hero with "the girl, the motor car, and the million." They inculcate false ideals by stressing the career of the individual regardless of his relation to society. They pander to the baser instincts by throwing a glamor about criminals, suicides, and libertines. "In its spiritual content bourgeois films reek with the rankness of decay."

Nevertheless, the Soviet public throngs to see them, curious to observe the life and peoples in that strange world beyond its frontiers. They laugh over the antics of Harold Lloyd and Charlie Chaplin, especially in "Modern Times." In the Moscow Film Festival of 1935 high tribute was paid to the directing of King Vidor, Alfred Green, Rouben Mamoulian, Jack Conway, John Ford. The second award went to the French picture, "The Last Billionaire," the third award to Walt Disney for his "Mickey Mouse" and "Silly Symphonies."

To the technical finish and craftsmanship of foreign films the Russians are always paying tribute. They envy too the superb equipment of the studios swiftly turning out one big picture after another. In Russia it is quite different. Life there is now moving faster than the films. Often it takes two years to produce one, so it is out-of-date before it is completed. That is why Shumiatsky, head of the Russian cinema, took his colleagues with him to Hollywood—to learn about speed and efficiency. Another reason was to promote that cinema internationalism which began with the interchange of the first silent films, and which received a setback as a common medium of communication with the advent of the "talkies." In the past, by simply translating captions, people of any race or nationality could enjoy any picture no matter what country it came from, but this method is not so successful with talking pictures although the gist of the dialogue is now superimposed on the films. A few Soviet pictures are now shown abroad with sound in English, French, Swedish, while a few imported ones are heard in the Russian language, as in the case of "Invisible Man," and "On the Roofs of Paris."

A third device is the one used in the Soviet picture, "Peter the First," made with French and Russian versions. Many Soviet directors are emphasizing the sound film instead of the "talking." Natural sounds, they say, may be as emotional, expressive, and rich as words. Combined with right *montage* and *"typage"*—defined by Eisenstein as "presenting each new figure at first sight so sharply and completely that his future use may be as a known element"—aural images and visual symbols may be as effective as the spoken word in telling a story. This is but one of many fields in which the Soviet cinema is searching out new methods and technique. Paying tribute to its force and vitality, Cecil DeMille says, "This Soviet spirit of experimental-ism, the life blood of any art, stimulates us to more daring experiments with our own ideas."

75. What Are the Soviets Doing in Music, Ballet, and Folk-Dancing?

Hailed abroad as typical of the new music are works like Mosolov's "Soviet Iron Foundry." Russians, however, have no predilection for noise and dissonance. Like the "Song of the Volga Boatman," this was more often heard in America than in Russia. In general, a spirit of conservatism prevails in the realm of music. The classics are still very much in the ascendancy. The old composers, for the most part mystics, aesthetes, and romantics unable to change in the changing world, have contrib-uted little to the creation of new forms. The singer Chaliapin and many of the best musicians—Stravinsky, Rachmaninov, Glazunov—fled abroad.

The first impact of the Revolution was felt in the mass narratives and marching songs of the masses. They were simple and popular in style, the initial expression of the struggle in terms of music. Then came a series of bizarre, raucous "factory rhapsodies," "work-shop symphonies," and "tractor oratorios." The people, however, did not like them and the conservatives denounced them for their "opportunism" and "pandering to the mob." But for a long time as in *Rapp* so in *Rampam* (Russian Association of Proletarian Musicians) the extremists were in the saddle. Against them were arrayed such veterans as Ippolitov-Ivanov, friend of the "mighty group," Borodin, Rimsky-Korsakov, Moussorgsky. "Very well," said Ippolitov-Ivanov, "let them write for the people. Let them call it revolutionary, proletarian, or anything, but first they must understand the people and know how to write good music. As for myself, I have always been with the people, so am I now." To his famous "Caucasian Sketches" he added the "Voroshilov March" and "Last Barricades" and united around him the more gifted young composers like Shebalin and Shostakovich. While growing up with the Revolution they drew upon the old technique and traditions of Russian music to express the content of the new life.

On every hand is manifest the people's interest and love of music. In the winter concerts great ovations go now to the Russian director, now to the Ukrainian, with one still more tremendous for guest conductors like Coates or Fried. The philharmonic orchestras and academic choirs of Leningrad and Moscow continue their old rivalries. From all the Soviet republics the best amateur musicians and dancers come up to compete in the Moscow Olympiads of Music. A factory orchestra alternates with a Gypsy troupe with guitars and tambourines; a quartette of miners from the Urals with performers on primitive instruments like the ancient Russian *gusli,* a zither with twenty-six strings, or the plaintive two-stringed *ghijak* of the Turcomans; a shepherds' trio playing on reeds or cow-horns with performers on the newly invented "sonar" and "emiriton." Unions of railway and forest workers are becoming famous for their choruses. The cities echo to the singing of the Red Army on horse or foot or in their motor-lorries lurching through the streets. Sources of fresh inspiration are being sought in the old melodies rendered by peasant voices. In the deep forests of the North, the hunters of folk music are still gleaning motifs and fragments of song from the dying race of *bilini* singers and recording them on phonograms. The old topical ditties, *chastushki,* with the end of each verse begetting another, are turned into musical dialogues on themes of the day, humorous and satirical. Among non-Slavic races, especially the Jews and Armenians, a musical renaissance is in progress.

"Heroic," "simple," "monumental" are terms in which the new music is conceived. To its creation a generation of young composers, wholeheartedly accepting the new order, are devoting their talents.

Among the well-known compositions are the "March of Budenny," Knipper's "Cavalry March" and "Higher and Higher" depicting the flight of a squadron of airplanes. Also continually played, whistled or sung are "Field, Dear Little Field," Shostakovich's "Morning Met Us with Coldness" and other popular pieces from new operas and cinema. Abandoning old themes for the concrete symbols of a new age Miaskovsky calls his Twelfth Symphony the "Kolhoz." It depicts the darkness and despair of the old village, ending in the dance song of harvest and the joy of free labor. In Steinberg's Fourth, known as the "Turksib Symphony," constructive forces are arrayed against the sands and mountains of the desert and against the inertia of the nomad Kazakhs with their weird, wild songs. They call the train a "devil's chariot," and the music in the finale expresses this mixture of fantastic imaginative awe of the people with the promise of new achievement and triumph as the engine makes its first run over the iron rails. Gnessin's "Triumph of the Revolution" is based on Essenin's poem:

> If the sun be in league with our oppressors
> We shall pull him down with our bayonets.
> If the moon be a friend of the dark powers
> We shall stone him down from the sky.
> We shall scatter the clouds, clear the path.
> We shall attach the earth to the rainbow.
> Let Mother Earth rejoice with us in freedom.

With mass-songs and solos Zhivotov's cycle, "In the West," depicts the war in the trenches, the call to revolt, the onward march of the people. Young Knipper is known for his "Red Army Symphony," "Cities and Years," and his opera "North Wind," which tells the story of the shooting of the twenty-six Commissars in the sands of Central Asia. His contemporary, Shebalin, has written the "Lenin Oratorio." The works of the thirty-year-old Shostakovich have been played by Stokowski in Philadelphia and other cities. To his credit are the "May Day" and "October" symphonies for full orchestra and chorus of several hundred voices; the athletic ballet, "The Golden Nose"; and "Lady Macbeth of Mtzensk," first of a cycle of four operas depicting the lot of women under the old and new regimes. In his studio, among pictures of the great composers, a bust of Lenin, and a Stalin calendar, he discourses on a new era in music:

"There can be no music without an ideology. The old composers, whether they knew it or not, were upholding a political theory—for the most part bolstering the rule of the upper classes. Only Beethoven was a forerunner of the revolutionary movement. It is true Wagner is played a great deal in Russia today. But we hear him in the same spirit as we go to a museum to study the forms of the old regime. As revolutionists, we have a different conception of music. Lenin himself said: 'Music is a means of unifying broad masses of people.' Not a leader of masses, perhaps, but certainly an organizing force. For music has the power of stirring specific emotions.

"Chaikovsky's Sixth Symphony produces a feeling of despair. Beethoven's Third awakens one to the joy of struggle. On the other hand, Scriabin's music tends to an unhealthy eroticism, to mysticism, passivity, and escape from the realities of life. Not that the Soviets are always joyous or supposed to be. But good music lifts and heartens and lightens people for work or effort. It may be tragic, but it must be strong. It is no longer an end in itself, but a vital weapon in the struggle. Because of this, Soviet music will probably develop along different lines from any the world has known. There must be a change! After all, we have entered a new epoch and history shows that every age creates its own language. Precisely what form this development in music will take, I cannot say, any more than I can say what the idioms of speech will be fifty years from now. The notes will be the same." (Reported by Rose Lee in the *New York Times*.)

In 1936, an article, "Noise Instead of Music," launched a barrage of criticism against Shostakovich for his "muddle of sounds," "formalist tricks," crude naturalism, and travesties on Soviet life. So furious was the onslaught that Joseph Wood Krutch pictured him as being "cast out into utter darkness" and "sitting amid the ruins of his reputation." But this is overstressing an episode in the battle constantly going on in all the arts, in the struggle to find the forms and themes adequate to express the new epoch. As for Shostakovich, his music continues to be played and he is commissioned to write new librettos.

Ballet and Folk Dancing

The Russians are wont to lament their backwardness in dancing. But they are doing lots of it. There are dance "circles" in parks, mills, skating-rinks, schools, even in the House of Scientists. Some two million members are participating in "plastic," folk, national, and social dancing. The Western foxtrot, Charleston, and tango, once branded as arch-bourgeois and sexually inciting, are in great vogue. The old Kremlin walls resound again to the music of the waltz, polka, and mazurka. The Commissar of War orders his officers to perfect themselves in the graces and arts of the ball-room. To the Olympiads of Dance and Music come scores of ensembles and hundreds of soloists. A wasp-waisted Georgian in the "dagger dance" moves slowly as he drives the silvered knives into the earth, then, pulling them out and holding them between his teeth, breaks into a wild and furious pace. The Ukrainians, now in a squat position with quick leg flings to the front, then upright and rotating like revolving pillars, finish their famous *Hopak* in a whirlwind of leaping, flying bodies. Eskimos pantomime episodes in the hunting of the Polar bear and the walrus. Tatars, to the plaintive Eastern music, do their symbolic dances ending with the *emenia,* a light rippling movement of the head. To the strains of the accordion and the rat-tat-tat of wooden spoons a group of villagers go through the lively figures of the *Yablochka.*

One of the oldest rural pastimes is the *Khorovod,* a choral dance with play-acting which stems from a pagan rite of the ancient Slavs—solar magic or the circling dance around a wooden idol. I have seen it in the village of Palekh where the peasant lacquer-painters, clasping and unclasping hands, bowing and kneeling, enacted an hour-long dance-drama of courtship, marriage, the comedies and sorrows of family life. Segments of it may be seen in the round and semi-marches of the village choirs. With the preservation of these old forms goes a search for new elements and themes. The machine, the shock-worker, along with the capitalist, the bureaucrat, and the drunkard, are depicted in dances, "grotesque," "revolutionary," "satirical." Out of the calisthenics and drills of the physical culturists are evolving athletic dances with thousands clad in snow-white jerseys waving red scarfs in the Isadora Duncan manner. Out of the gymnastic exercises for special groups in offices and factories may well come new kinds of trade and occupational dances. In the "Silk-Dance" the Uzbek girls depict the feeding of silkworms, the unwinding of cocoons, spinning and weaving the cloth, and the final exultation over the glistening fabric. Experiments in new dance idioms and technique are carried on in special studios to which innovators go for counsel and criticism. While little new or significant has yet emerged, everywhere the people are dancing.

Along with all democratic forms of the dance the classic ballet likewise is flourishing. In the first flush of the Revolution it, too, was stigmatized as a decadent bourgeois art that had no place in the proletarian State. But to no effect. The pirouetting, fairy-like figures still go sweeping across the stage, delighting the new audiences of workers as they once did the aristocrats. One night they appear in old favorites like "Swan Lake" and the "Little Hump-backed Horse," the next in the new ballets introducing new freedom of movement, miming, and even acrobatics. First among new productions of the Moscow Bolshoi is "Red Poppy," wherein a Chinese girl is shot for saving her Bolshevik lover from the imperialists. It is praised by some critics for its gaiety and spontaneity, denounced by others for transforming the ballet into a circus. "Flames of Paris" is the story of a court ballerina who goes over to the side of the people in the French Revolution. The "Three Fat Men" are shown trustifying all the coal, land and iron of Fairyland. "Clear Brook," with Shostakovich's brilliant music, pictures life on the Collectives by choreographic methods rather than pantomime. "Partisans," depicting the war of the Reds and Whites in the Caucasus, has a colorful pageant of its many tribes and races. "Lost Illusions" is based on Balzac's novel of the same name. More important still are Leningrad's "Fountain of Bachchisarai," and "Esmeralda," in new settings and with the best solo dancers in the country.

Altogether there are some 2,600 professional ballet dancers and several hundred pupils in the ballet schools. As they give not only physical and artistic training but a rounded education, places in them are eagerly sought and highly prized. One afternoon while we were sitting around the samovar in the house of Boris Sokolov, director of the Museum of the Peoples, there entered a courtly handsome boy introduced by his mother as Mitya, their only son. "And what is Mitya going to do in life?" I asked. "We have dedicated Mitya to the ballet," said the father, and in his voice was the pride and piety of an old New Englander speaking of his son going into the ministry. If the artists take their profession seriously, so do the people. The names of solo dancers like Sylvia Chen, Messerer, and Mey are widely known throughout the country. The leading ballerinas, Ulanova, Semeonova, Lipishinskaya, are looked upon almost as heroines and greeted with ovations. The aged Geltser, with a grace and suppleness in her sixty-year-old body that a girl of sixteen might well envy, tells of leaving the gorgeous gold-and-red opera house in the capital to dance in the bare wooden theatres of the construction camps in Siberia. "I have performed before the sophisticated and exacting audiences of the Metropolitan in New York and Covent Garden in London. I have appeared in Paris, Rome, and Berlin. But how compare these tours with the response of the weather-tanned builders of a new life in the wilderness? From their rude benches they follow each movement with rapt attention and make the wooden walls shake with the thunder of their applause."

Attesting to the early interest of the Russians in dancing are the murals on the Cathedral in Kiev dated 1071. Dancing was first introduced into the court by Tsar Alexis. Tsarina Anna would slap the face of a courtier who failed to keep time to the music. Peter the Great took part in the dances and compelled his boyars by *ukase* to do so. The ballet imported from Italy reached its zenith in Russia under Imperial patronage and the direction of the great masters like Fokine. Meanwhile the peasants, independent of any impetus from abroad, were creating their own dances full of vigor, fire, and imagination. So absorbed were they in these "wanton pastimes" that the Church anathematized them and pictured horrible fiends dragging the mimes and buffoon dancers down to hell. But it could no more suppress them than singing and vodka-drinking on holidays. Neither could the fulminations against dancing on the part of the Bolsheviks in their ultra-Puritan days. They may have stilled the feet in the town, but not in the villages. "To these children of the soil, dancing and singing is natural as breathing," says a critic about the Russian peasants at the 1936 Dance Festival in London.

In the village of Saburova every Saturday night sixty or seventy youths would pass singing beneath our window. Then came dull muffled sounds of thudding feet on the earth, the crowd dancing till midnight or morning. Beside the old forms and patterns they were constantly inventing new ones. It was creative dancing. Usually these new figures burst forth in competitions in which the most agile matched their skill against each other. Now it was the ferryman pitted against the head of the Comsomols; now the shepherd against the watchman's son. Most hotly waged was the contest precipitated by the arrival of Alexsey Grigorivitch, a peasant boy from a Volga village near Saratov, who was now a student of engineering. To him, a Party member who sojourned in a village a week or even a day without leaving in it some Communist idea or impression, was a Communist in name only. It seemed to him that our Saburova youth were too engrossed in pastimes, especially in dancing. A bit shocking to find such a state of affairs so close to Moscow. He would remedy it by discussions on politics, economics, the future of Russia. But how get them to listen? By meeting them on their own ground and beating them. By dancing them down. Through the dance to Communism!

In our yard he set to work limbering up his legs and brushing up on all the regular steps, adding to them a sort of fandango picked up from a Cossack roommate. Joining the promenade, he made himself generally agreeable, sharing his sunflower seeds with the girls, whirling them about in the waltz and *Cracovac*. Then the musicians sounded the notes of the *Barina,* calling for the competitive dance. "Did Alexsey know the Barina?" Alexsey said he did, and, if they had a good dancer, bring him on. Accepting the challenge, a message was sent to summon their best man, Kolya, the shepherd. Across the fields he came, cracking his thirty-foot cattle-whip like a cannon, emerging out of the dark a lithe, sinewy lad in a red blouse, with the light of battle in his eyes.

"Saburova against Saratov!" cried the crowd, and straightway inside a big circle ringed about with eager, expectant onlookers, the two contestants faced each other, bowing. The accordion and balalaika players, sitting on a log, struck up the Barina. The shepherd stepping inside the circle executed a fling and a stamp and beckoned to his Saratov rival. Alexsey curtsied and followed. Then the shepherd, and so alternating. It was a contest of art and endurance, each one cunningly using his simplest figures at first, holding the intricate, difficult ones in reserve. Now with bodies bending and swaying, then rigid and tense like steel. Now arms above the head, then waving or folded across the breast. Now with snapping fingers, clicking like castanets; now slapping legs or soles of boots. Now in full stature, erect; then close to earth in the hip-and-knee dance of the Ukraine. Thus for an hour the rivals went reeling, capering, prancing, swirling around the circle. After forty rounds my recollections of the first were blurred. Too great a strain upon the memory. But not for the score of Barina experts around the ringside, as connoisseurs critically reviewing each figure, as judges on the lookout for repetitions.

Once there were cries of "Default, *Doloi.*" That was when their own champion seemed to be repeating himself. Recovering, Kolya did a dervish whirl and rat-tat-tat on his boot-soles that brought a burst of applause. So, with swinging legs and whirling arms, the supple bodies shot back and forth, up and down, round and round. Another half-hour. Still no sign of fatigue in either rival. With a perpetual carefree smile Alexsey sought to convey to his antagonist that he was just beginning. And by a placid, indifferent countenance, Kolya indicated that, as for him, why, he could keep this up until morning. By the end of the second hour it was apparently heavy going for Kolya, the Saburovite. He was panting and wiping his sleeve across his brow. Alexsey, taking this as a sign of the long hoped for collapse, in dashing style let loose his Cossack dances and wild fandango. That should break the morale of his now drooping, tired opponent. But the canny shepherd wasn't tired at all. That brow-mopping was only a ruse to discover the resources of his adversary. Now he knew, and launched forth into a series of figures learned from the Tatars in the cement-mill across the river, seven in succession, his muscles tense and vibrant as a steel spring. Alexsey, having shot his bolt, was in despair. Vainly he ransacked his memory for other figures. His repertoire was exhausted, and so was he. Throwing up his hand, he acknowledged defeat.

Though Alexsey lost, he won. For he was a good loser. First to congratulate Kolya, to hoist him on the shoulders of the admiring crowd and carry him round and round, a victor in the arena. Very pleasing to the Saburovites, this sportsmanship of their Saratov visitor. Besides, hadn't he given them the best contest of the season and almost danced their champion down? He too was lifted up and carried round amid the plaudits of the crowd. The next night began his discussions upon economics and the future of Russia. Through the dance to Communism!

Through Communism to the dance. The coming society of leisure and plenty promises a race abounding in health and vitality. Out of sheer physical energy, if nothing more, they will seek expression in sports dances, in exuberant rhythmic movement. Already this is manifest in the tremendous growth and popularity of the dance circles, the Olympiads, and the festal holiday processions. Marching through the Red Square the athletes form into wheeling circles, five-pointed stars, sickles and hammers. A group of Caucasians break into the weird *Lezghinka* goaded to a maddening tempo by the hand claps and cries of "Tosh!" "Tosh!" from the spectators. A troupe of Gypsies follow with tambourines and tinkling bracelets. A hundred children with waving streamers stamp through the measures of the *Snow-Bird*. A fanfare of trumpets and the ballet ensemble from the "Flame of Paris" performs the mass-dance of the *Carmagnole*. Along the boulevards Merry Petrushka plays his pranks to the delight of all ages. On raised platforms crowds of youth dance through the night to the strains of fifty bands and orchestras.

Here my mind flashes back to the grim days of the October Revolution and John Reed in one of his flights of fantasy talking about going to Kharkov to be Commissar of Art and Amusement. "And what would you do?" I queried. "First of all, I'd put joy into the people. Get up great pageants. Drown the city in red flags and banners. And once, maybe twice a month, put on a gorgeous all-night carnival. Fireworks, plays, and orchestras in all the squares, and everybody dancing to the music." Reed knew that the hungry cities were on half ration, the mines flooded, bandits scourging the villages. But he felt that if he could only get all the people out on the streets singing and dancing till morning, somehow the Revolution would be saved! After all he was only a bit ahead of his time. Now before the granite boulder that marks his grave on the Red Square his idea is taking shape in this mass pageant of music and dancing that each year grows more colorful, colossal, spectacular.

76. What New Developments in Soviet Painting, Sculpture, and Architecture?

More than any other of the arts the new architecture has reflected the influence of the Constructivists with their insistence on utility and a complete break with the past. In violent contrast to the old buildings with their pillars, cupolas, and ornaments stand the severe straight lines of the new. At first sight they are too austere and forbidding. Rectangular and unrelieved by any decoration, the Lenin Institute to some critics looks like a huge packing case. Too stark against the winter sky appear the bleak gray cliffs of the State Building in Kharkov. Built of steel, concrete, and with a liberal use of glass these new structures are well-lighted and spacious. And whether it be library or laundry it usually has the merit of being suited to the purposes for which it is intended. This is modern "functionalism," the word that Soviet architects at first always stressed, relying on fitness or function to give the edifice whatever beauty it may possess. The British architect, Williams-Ellis, found in them "a vigorous freshness, a welcome absence of fuss and nonsense, and, as a consequence, a complete absence of vulgarity. A touch of genius could lift this into the realm of real architecture."

In some cases this has already been attained, notably in Lenin's Mausoleum by Schussev, in certain Houses of Culture and in the designs of Fomin, the Vesnin brothers, Serafimov, Modirnov, Ginsburg. Their projects are losing the grim severity of the first emergency construction. Materials are becoming more plentiful. Technical skill is increasing. It is now possible to add, to utility, comfort and beauty in the buildings where the people live, play, and work. "We must no longer regard factories as boxes for machines," says Nikolaiev, "but as places where men spend a good part of their day. We must make them cheerful and attractive with skylights, swimming pools, alcoves for greenery, and in time we will embellish them with frescoes and statues." The Congress of Architects urges more use of the rich heritage of the past and suggests that the intricate scroll and fretwork with which the old peasants gaily decorated their eaves and shutters be incorporated in the new collective village. More color, a bolder use of glass and metal, daring ensembles of buildings approaching the monumental, indicate the trend in urban development. Whatever lyric quality the new architecture may achieve, it is bound to be quite different from the strident proud assault of the New York skyline.

The very fact that architects must plan for the needs of the whole people gives to them a new social significance and creates for them a wide and responsive audience. Witness the popularity of exhibits; the acclaim to the men who designed the subway stations; the passionate debates on the planning of new towns and plants; the assaults against bare "cubist monstrosities" on the one hand and the ornate "pseudoclassicism" on the other; the actor's interest in adaptations of the theatre to bring them in closer contact with their audiences; the clamor for assembly halls of every kind and size to meet the demands of a people perpetually going to meetings, conferences, and congresses. Even the peasants are aware that there is an Academy of Architecture and from distant villages send their delegates for consultation. In a society where the most flattering epithet is to be called a "builder of Socialism," the architects are engaged in literally building the outer shell of the new order. They must coordinate the activities of engineers and technicians with scientists and plastic artists. They must design the details of doorways and window-jambs, the layout of parks and esplanades and whole new cities.

The City Planning Institute with its 1,200 members has elaborate projects for the complete transformations of the older cities. Instead of a maze of narrow streets the new Moscow, pivoting on Yofan's colossal Palace of the Soviets, 113 feet taller than the Empire State Building, is to become a metropolis of magnificent squares and boulevards. With industry invading the Soviet East, the ancient, squat,

dusty towns are being rebuilt on modern lines without losing altogether their oriental atmosphere. But it will be a long and difficult
task to bring order and good living into the anarchically grown, congested centers. From them the inhabitants may find temporary escape
for a day, a week, or a fortnight into the "Green Cities" for rest and
recreation that are building on the outskirts.

From the sixty new Socialist cities now springing up around the
new industries their citizens will not want to escape. Built for the
most part on virgin steppes and wildernesses, they are wide and spacious. But while they cover large areas they are not large cities. For
the Soviet holds that "megalopolis" is a disease of capitalist civilization,
and it is against piling people on top of one another in big towns as
it is against isolating them in the country. Avoiding these two evils,
the model cities seek to combine the advantages and neighborliness
of an urban life with an abundance of fresh air, sunshine, and freedom of rural life. The layout of the city depends in part on the character of the region and the school of planners. Some are advocates of the
ribbon system along an arterial highway. Others of the radial, the
angular, or the checkerboard. All are agreed upon the division of the
cities into three zones—industrial, living, and agricultural—separated
from each other by wide belts of trees and shrubbery. The first is occupied by the factories, power plants, research institutes. Distant enough
to be free from its noise and fumes is the second zone, with its resi-
dences, schools, stores, theatre, playgrounds. Beyond this lies the farming area with its orchards and dairies and perhaps the crematorium,
stadium, or yacht club on the river.

While adhering to this general zoning scheme, there is much debate
and experiment on other matters like the size and type of living quarters. Some champion "garden city" dwellings. But it takes too much
space to house a whole city in separate cottages. Others are for block
squares with an open court in the center. But that does not permit
the sun to shine in all rooms. This trouble is alleviated by separate
narrow buildings extending along the march of the sun. Then there
is the question of laundries, kitchen, factories, crèches. Shall they be
located in the apartment houses or elsewhere? Shall every big house
have its own auditorium? Are solarium and gymnasium adjuncts of
home life or club life?

In the laying out of these cities, unhampered by considerations of space and property interests, the new engineer-architects have full scope for the application of their creative talents. In their construction, however, they are handicapped by the necessity for speed, lack of skilled craftsmen, the use of green sapwood instead of seasoned hardwood, resulting in a lot of jerry-building, often a too bare and box-like look. (Orjonikidze once called Magnitogorsk a "pig-stye.") However, as time and means permit they are to be replaced with more finished and permanent structures. With their admirable plans and magnificent vistas these cities should become as beautiful as they are utilitarian.

Painting and Sculpture

Except for the early ikons the Russians have achieved no great distinction in these arts. They have produced a Repin, a Troubetskoy, a Verestchagin but they have none of the great names of the French or Italians. Half a century ago the "Travelers" intent on speeding the day of liberation from the Tsar depicted the venality of officials, the greediness of priests, the tragic lot of the peasants, the ugliness and brutality of war. In traveling exhibits they carried their narrative paintings to the people, and in the galleries where they hang today they are still centers of wonder-eyed throngs of workers and peasants. In sharp contrast stood the "Decadents," described by Lozowick as "outspoken individualists who held that art is only debased by preoccupation with social, moral, or other problems, and that aesthetic pleasure is the beginning and end of creative activity." They turned to gay and exotic themes, court life, fairy tales, and oriental legends.

Pre-eminent among other groups were the Futurists, contemptuous of all the old forms and vehemently assailing them. Seizing the opportunity offered by the Revolution they declared that, as the Soviets had broken with the past to create a new state, so the Futurists had broken with the past to create a new art. Proclaiming themselves the troubadours of the new epoch they demanded complete hegemony in their field and got it. But as in the other arts, the extremes to which they went provoked a reaction. The workers protested that the huge cubist canvases on the squares were entirely incomprehensible to them and even the horses shied at them. Lenin branded some of the monuments hastily erected as "futurist scarecrows." When the stylized head of Perovkaya was unveiled, the horrified crowd loudly demanded its removal. Equally outraged were the Anarchists by the mad figure of their leader Bakunin, and being men of deeds they forthwith smashed it to pieces.

While indifferent or hostile to these bizarre compositions the people were deeply gripped by the work of the graphic artists like Deny, Malyutin, Moor. The whole story of the Revolution unfolds itself in the hundreds of posters that came from their hands. Some made their headquarters in the Telegraph Agency illustrating the daily dispatches with trenchant cartoons. Others accompanying the armies were cited for military decorations "for valiantly fighting on the fronts with brush and pencil." In laughter-provoking caricatures, in stinging lampoons, they assailed the traitors, satirized the weaklings, rallied the people to war against the invaders and then to the tasks of reconstruction. If art is something that serves to unify the thought and will of the masses, then in spite of much crudity, harshness, and exaggeration their works were truly art.

Strikingly enough it was this militant group, forging their way up out of the vortex of the struggle, that formed the "Association of Easel Artists." Not less striking is their pronouncement upon the hotly-waged debate as to what is revolutionary art: It consists neither in eccentric attempts at novelty, nor in proletarian themes, but in a new creative attitude on the part of the artist toward society, plus the finest possible technique. "Revolutionary art is good art." As to themes let the Soviet artist paint, chisel, draw, or engrave what he pleases. But because he identifies himself with the society and people about him it pleases him to be interested in the things that are interesting them. One in mind and aim with the workers, engineers, and teachers, he reproduces in art what they are producing in actuality. That is the reason for so many tractors, giant plants, sun-bronzed athletes, crèches of happy children. But there is no taboo on still lifes, landscapes, or nudes. Konchalovsky, painting only these subjects even in the heyday of the "leftists," enjoys the title of People's Artist and all the emoluments that go with it. This is not to imply that there are no restrictions whatever. To avoid the perpetration of artistic monstrosities there is a commission of artists to pass upon the merits of every fresco, painting, or monument. Obviously, too, nothing will be accepted for public display or reproduction that smacks of counter-revolution. But with the growing tolerance and breadth of interpretation, few if any Soviet artists feel themselves cramped or constrained. Steadily the Soviets are moving towards that state of affairs in which "every artist can claim the right to create freely according to his ideal." (Lenin)

The inner impulse of the Soviet artists to create is further stimulated by the tremendous demand for his creations. Scores of expeditions into far away places—the Arctic, the deserts, and the mountains—commission artists to record their exploits with brush, pencil, and camera. Hundreds of square miles of walls in clubs and palaces of culture are waiting to be adorned with frescoes or hung with pictures. Thousands of new theatres, terminals, and embankments have plans for decorative sculpture and bas relief. The Palace of Soviets alone calls for five hundred statues. Even the vestibules of the subway are being embellished with plastic design. Factories order oil portraits and chiseled heads of their shock-workers. Art posters, book jackets, exquisite editions of the classics call for legions of engravers, illustrators, makers of wood-cuts, dry points, brush and pen-and-ink drawings. The gigantic processions of May Day and October summon the artists to transform the million marchers with massed flags and the rivers of crimson banners into a gorgeous pageant, a mosaic of a million living pieces in motion.

To help the artist to find his place and part in this maze of projects there are the various unions and associations. To conserve his time and energies there are Cooperatives providing paints, brushes, and marbles, foundries for casting, agencies for disposing of his works. To uncover and encourage new talent there are hosts of amateur art "circles," schools and brigades for mutual counsel and experimenting on new lines. Gone is the old idea of the artist working in isolation, aloof and apart from his fellows and the surging life around him. Fast vanishing, likewise, is the idea of each of the arts going its own way regardless of one another. A synthesis of the arts is being sought, especially of those that are closely related, each one impregnating and enriching the other without losing any of its specific qualities. No longer do the architects complete their plans for a new building or a new city and then hand it over to the plastic and pictorial artists to embellish. By working together from the outset so much greater are the chances for harmony. Hence, beside the separate congress of architects, sculptors, and painters, increasingly there are joint conferences of them all.

Monuments and Sculpture

"In his 'City of the Sun,'" said Lenin in 1918, "Campanella speaks of the frescoes on the walls of his imaginary city. They were to serve as vivid lessons in science and history, awaken the civic consciousness of the youth, and be a vital part in their education. Not a bad idea at all, it seems to me. . . . Unfortunately our climate is hardly suitable for those frescoes dreamed of by Campanella. What I have in mind is something I call propaganda by monuments—busts and full-length figures of the forerunners of Socialism, the leading lights in philosophy, science, and art. Also trenchant inscriptions of their principles, and concise accounts of great events on walls or specially erected pediments. Please do not think I have my heart set on marble, granite, or gold lettering. We must be modest for the present." Forthwith Lenin's proposal was carried out. While the Red Armies were fighting on seventeen fronts, the Red sculptors were busily erecting monuments in plaster and concrete in the rear. Some were so bad they were taken down soon after unveiling. Others like those of Robespierre and Volodarsky, the impassioned tribune of the people, were blown up by counter-revolutionists. The best of this period, Matveyev's statue of Marx, stands in front of the old Smolny Institute in Leningrad. Sinaisky's Lasalle was also deemed worthy of preservation and recast in bronze.

Now with the material bases for art growing more strong and assured the ideas of Lenin are beginning to be carried into effect on a grand scale. On the new avenues of Moscow marble plaques will record the deeds of the men after whom they are named. The façades of State buildings, fountains, and plazas will be decorated with friezes and statues. Already there are myriads of Lenins ranging from small busts to the projected sixty-foot figures that will crown the Palace of Soviets. Andreyev alone did over 250 studies of Lenin modeling him from life as he wrote, spoke, or sat at ease. One of the best images is that by Shadr which stands on the power dam of the swift-flowing river above Tiflis. Manizer's monument to Shevchenko portrays the peasants under serfdom, revolt against the Tsar, and final liberation, in fifteen bronzes rising in a spiral towards the towering figure of the great serf poet and hero of the Ukrainians. Chaikov constructs figures of iron-workers that are cast in iron and placed perhaps in the iron foundry. In his Football Players and Parachutists he reveals a new conception of motion, mass, and space. Yefimov's animals, Falcon and Rooster, are molded in copper by being beaten from within.

Most of these sculptors are quite young and a large number are women, whose work is often more bold, virile, and robust than that of the men. Sara Lebedeva is attracted by the rhythm and cadences of the human body. Vera Mukhina casts her figures in bronze. Beatrissa Sandomirskaya "hews her peasant men and women from birch, oak, and lime." She collaborates with Yakerson who depends for his effects as much on the grain patterns and gnarls in the wood as on the strokes of his knife or chisel. (Chen I-Wan) Thus continues the ancient craft of woodcarving in which Russians have always been adept. In spite of the new materials—alloy, glass, cement, papier-mâché—wood is still a favorite medium. Some of the figures erected on special occasions, or in honor of national heroes and Stakhanovites, are of gigantic stature. Unlike an easel picture, nobody could possibly want to own or have them in one's home. But they can be enjoyed by the multitudes and serve to emphasize the joint ownership of art.

Frescoes, Paintings, Wood-Engravings

Like the other arts, Soviet painting moves forward under the aegis of Socialist realism. Eschewing formalism and stylization, on the other hand it seeks to avoid the mere copying of things. "Don't give us colored photographs," wrote the Stalingrad workers to the artists, "but something that will make us see more clearly into the life around us." In general it cannot be said that Soviet paintings live up to this injunction. The big canvases of Brodsky, "Shooting of the 26 Commissars" and "Second Congress of the Comintern," incorporating hundreds of portraits of the participants, and the stupendous panorama of the "Capture of Perekop by the Red Army," are magnificent as factual records, but they are hardly interpretations of life. For that, one must turn to compositions like "Mother and Bathing Girls" of Deyneka, to the new industrial landscapes of Krimyov, or the dramatic psychological studies like "Cross-Questioning the Communists." In such paintings, particularly those from the brushes of the new generation, is manifest the ability to seize the essence of social experience, to illumine and clarify it.

"This new Soviet art," says Christian Brinton, "is richly affirmative and human. It does not seek to perpetuate that legacy of restless, dominant individualism which descends to the modern world from imperial Rome. It is more akin to the communal spirit of the Greeks to whom artistic appreciation and expression were a social necessity." This is evident not only in the Russians but in the former subject peoples, now that all barriers to national self-expression have been swept away. No longer are Tatars and Mongols restrained by the Mohammedan taboos against portraying the human figure. Out of the Caucasus come new compositions, revealing cross-currents of primitive folk art of the mountains, Persian miniature painting, the rich traditions of ancient Armenia. On lacquered paintings in tempora the old ikon villages unite the Byzantine style to the most modern themes, now grimy and realistic, now very gay and fanciful. The trend toward the monumental is reflected in the decorations of the Moscow Subway and the two big exhibitions in celebration of the Soviets' twentieth anniversary sponsored by the Commissariats of Heavy Industry and Defense.

While still showing strongly the influence of the French, Soviet painting is seeking to become more self-sufficient and independent, to make greater use of the legacy of the past. Among the many fields for study are the frescoes on the oldest churches, in order to discover the secret of their weather-withstanding qualities. But the subjects of the new wall-paintings are not saints and patriarchs in aureoles of gold. They are the people in everyday life, such as appear in the Museum of Mother and Child, done by the versatile Favorsky. In the House of Models he divides the ceiling into ten panels in pastel yellows and browns, depicting May Day in town and country, arts, sports. Around them run ornamental friezes of flowers, fruit, and familiar domestic objects like shopping-baskets and sewing-machines. Favorsky is also a designer of back-drops and settings for theatres; an engraver of portraits, celebrated for his woodcuts of Dostoievsky and Dante; an illustrator of books, as enthusiastic over a cover of a horse-manual for peasants as over a de luxe edition of Anatole France which he composes in all details from format and typography to end-pieces. As a sort of Soviet da Vinci, at home he is surrounded by a circle of admiring pupils, and in exhibits abroad repeatedly is awarded first prizes.

Everywhere there is a renaissance of the pictorial and graphic arts, "national in form and socialist in content." In wood-engravings Kravchenko memorializes the big dam on the Dnieper, or "Stradivarius in His Workshop," or does a series of grotesque characters out of Gogol and Dickens. Gerassimov illustrates the poem "Who Can Be Happy and Free in Russia?" in water colors, while his colleague Rodinov in the same highly realistic style draws landscapes in India ink. The social irony of Lebedev flashes out in the "Streets of the Revolution" and the children's book, "Petrushka." Yefimov and the trio known as the "Kukriniksy," a *nom de plume* made up of the first syllables of their names, are famous as cartoonists. The Soviets may lag far behind in painting, but in the graphic arts they are well up in the forefront. (For conditions of life and incomes of artists, authors, and composers see pages 449-450.)

77. How do the Soviets Treat the Criminal?

It depends on whether he is a political offender or an ordinary criminal. The latter is treated as a sick man who through his own weakness and insanitary social conditions has succumbed to a disease. The one concern of the State is to cure him. Meantime he must be kept from infecting others, not "punished" but "withdrawn from circulation." Like a patient afflicted with mumps or typhus, he is put in quarantine and kept there until convalescent, fit to take his place again in society. To the Communist he is simply the victim of a faulty social organization, not a criminal but a social defective.

In this viewpoint the Communists are at one with the instinctive feelings of the broad Russian masses. The peasants never spoke of criminals, the word does not even exist in their vocabulary. They were simply "the unfortunates," *neschastniye,* those who had suffered the mischance of being caught and very likely had done only what they might have done themselves. Always their hearts went out to them with pity and compassion—and with bread. True, these same peasants, infuriated, might beat to death the horse-thief, or the miscreant who fired the village. But these were in outbursts of sudden rage against the destroyers of their lives or livelihood—never in cold blood, deliberately. The court records show almost universally the peasants on the side of the ones entangled in the meshes of the law. Even against their own interests voting for acquittal, pleading for mercy, probing into the past for extenuating circumstances—often cunningly inventing them.

"To know all is to forgive all." And still more profoundly the peasants, informed not by books or formal philosophy but by the vaster knowledge of the heart, acted on the principle "to know all is to know there is nothing to forgive." Nothing to do but to understand and help the wrong-doer and try to bring him back into the fellowship of labor. Maybe to chide, rebuke, and constrain him, but never to shun him as an outcast.

This is precisely the spirit and method of Soviet penology, which regards the offender as one temporarily gone wrong and aims only to set him right again. Because he has broken the rules of the game of life is no reason why he should be broken, needlessly humiliated, and punished. No element of torture or needless suffering, no lowering of human dignity adjures the Criminal Code. Some sixty per cent are not imprisoned at all. For the others no prison garb, handcuffs, or fetters. No physical chastisement or flogging. No life imprisonment taking the heart out of a man.

With Warden Lawes of Sing Sing the Soviets believe that, as a deterrent of crime, long term sentences are "sublimely ridiculous." The death penalty may be inflicted for high treason, counter-revolutionary activities, theft of collective property or armed robbery in which someone is killed. But no one can be sent to prison for life. Ten years is the limit even for murder, on the theory that, if a man cannot be reformed in ten years, he cannot be reformed at all. Generally this maximum is cut to seven or five by good conduct, which also brings constantly increasing liberties, as the prisoner shows himself fitted to use them. First, friends may visit him in confinement, later his privileges are extended to allow visiting them in their homes, overnight, and going unattended on errands in the town. From the strict "isolator" he is promoted to a house of correction or "rehabilitation colony" where most of the warden's duties are taken over by the inmates. They draw up their own rules, run their own courts, enforce their own discipline, organize their own classes and sports, and even enjoy a fortnight vacation, or a longer one, if they want to go home and help in the harvest.

It is the same sort of self-government that is practiced in the schools and has the same objective—to prepare for life by participation in life, and that means—in work. First, in the special prison factories where wages are from twenty to fifty per cent of the regular rates and are given to the family; then, in factories in the outside world, from which the prisoner returns at night. Constantly the restrictions are lightened until, imperceptibly, the distinctions between the two worlds fade away and the one-time prisoner finds himself a working member of society, a free full-righted citizen.

In a word, the Soviets incorporate in their penal system all the ideas of progressive prison reformers, or, as their critics would say, "all the sentimental notions of soft-headed people for pampering and coddling the criminal." Only the Soviets consider their methods very hard-headed, practical, scientific. If they stress methods of kindness and re-education rather than coercion, it is because the latter are so futile. As Dostoievsky wrote in "The House of the Dead," out of his terrible ordeal in a Siberian convict prison sixty years ago: "Neither penitentiary, nor the hulks, nor any system of hard labor ever had any results except to develop in the men a thirst for forbidden pleasures, a profound hatred, and revenge. They never cured a criminal."

But the Soviets are intent at all costs on curing criminals. Not so much on humanitarian grounds as on economic. They want every man to be a productive unit, to pull his weight in the boat. They have found that humaneness is the best way to salvage criminals, to transform defectives into effectives. In proof of this, they point out that less than twenty per cent are "recidivists" or repeaters as against twice that number in capitalist countries. They maintain too that there has been a reduction of fully one-third in the number of crimes committed. Undoubtedly this is in part due to the Soviet penal system. But it is also due to the

Soviet economic system in which everyone is assured of a job. There is a place for every man in the Five-Year Plans which provides not only a task for his hands to do but a big idea that appeals to his imagination and sense of adventure.

Rehabilitation Colonies and Convict Camps

A Mecca for visitors is the Bolshevo Labor Commune founded by the Gay-Pay-Oo in a pine woods near Moscow. It started in 1924 with the famine waifs or "wild boys"—sneak-thieves, pickpockets, and drug addicts, such as one sees in the Soviet movie, "The Road to Life." From a colony of thirteen boys it has grown to 5,000 boys, men, women, and girls, living under a regime quite the reverse of the old penal colonies.

"Because we could not behave ourselves," the old convicts were wont to say sardonically, "we had to pass down Green Street," a euphemism for the lithe green switches, in the hands of two lines of soldiers, lashing their bare backs as they ran the gauntlet. The new colony has its Green Street, the wide forests and fields to roam in, the river Moscow and its grassy slopes for sun and water bathing. No walls or bars, no guards or keepers, and, after the first year, almost uncurbed freedom. "Because we would not sow or reap," said the old convicts dolefully, "now we must pound stones." In this new colony likewise all must labor. Not, however, at stone-pounding or in jute-mills, but in the making of sport goods and footgear. This was their own choice, and they are now engaged in turning out shoes, skis, skates, sleds, footballs, boxing-gloves, and rackets.

Self-discipline through self-government. Joy in work. Fullness of life. Everything so far as possible that pertains to a normal human being. If they like, they can marry—and with the consent of the council many do—fellow-inmates or peasant girls from the villages around. And that, in Russia, means babies, kindergartens, schools. In reality the whole colony is a vast school. So attached to it do many become that on "graduation" they prefer to stay close by, away from the town and temptation. They join the large settlement with its own farms and factories growing up around it. Others, about eight per cent, do not wait for graduation but run away. These "departures" do not weigh heavily on the director. "If they follow the paths of crime again they will be caught, and if they take the road to life, honest living, what more can we ask for?" On similar lines are conducted many other industrial and farming colonies such as the very athletic Kungur Commune in the Urals where a thousand former thieves, swindlers, and safecrackers now proudly sport the coveted badge of the G.T.O.—Prepared for Labor and Defense.

The universal, unstinted praise for these "open" colonies is not extended to the so-called "closed" colonies, especially the construction camps in Siberia and the North. With the drive for collectivization in 1928 into them were sent hordes of kulaks evicted from the farms, in addition to the general run of criminals, bandits, embezzlers, smugglers, prostitutes, pickpockets. The privations endured by the whole country during the first Five-Year Plan were probably intensified in these camps. At any rate gruesome tales have been told about conditions by released or escaping inmates: Big contingents arriving in the bleak, barren wastes without adequate provision to receive them; epidemics, and a terrible shortage of food, clothes, and medicine; children dying like flies; cruelties inflicted by guards so brutal and sadistic that they were shot.

In contrast to these dark pictures stand the eulogies of writers like Gorky and Tolstoy to the success in rehabilitating the exiles engaged in the big construction projects. Biggest was the Baltic-White Sea Canal, a series of dikes, dams, ditches, and flood-gates through 147 miles of Karelian swamps and forests, built almost in its entirety by the prisoners themselves. Only a few higher posts were held by state officials. The three chief engineers were "wreckers" but they did not wreck this enterprise. The crews were composed of thieves, desperados, and counter-revolutionists, many of whom at first flatly refused to work. But the job won and changed them. They could not help being infected by its spirit and magnitude. Robbers soon found blasting granite as intriguing as safe-blowing. Bandits became as expert in tree-felling as in looting and cutting down people. Thousands of old-time convicts enrolled in the brigades of shock-workers. And so zealously did they work that they completed the canal in the record time of two years. In reclaiming the wilderness they reclaimed themselves. As a reward for loyalty and heroism, fifteen were decorated with the Order of the Red Banner, 300 received scholarships for study in schools and colleges, 12,000 were liberated, and 59,000 had their sentences reduced.

As to numbers in these camps, which are usually run by the Commissariat of Home Affairs, estimates run up to a million or more. The peak was reached at the height of the drive for collectivization. Since then tens of thousands of kulaks have been reinstated into full civil rights and hosts of others have been granted amnesty. So effective is the work of these camps both in the building of big projects and in the rebuilding of men that, along with the "open" industrial and farming colonies, they are rapidly replacing the old prisons. Out of 468 central prisons, inherited from the old regime, all but 123 have been closed. Many were of the antiquated type with cell-blocks poorly ventilated and infested with vermin. But the Soviet is not building "good prisons" to replace them. That is one kind of structure entirely omitted from the Five-Year Plans. Though it faces plenty of crime, it is not building any new prisons at all. It is concentrating its energies, as Krylenko says, "to eliminate the primary causes of criminality, to rebuild society upon a Communist basis where crime will no longer be produced."

Political Crimes and the Death Penalty

In contrast with the Soviets' policy of mercy and forbearance in dealing with crime in general is its harsh severity toward political crimes—plots aiming at the overthrow of the State, or endangering its security. As all clemency vanishes in the tolerant, mild-mannered peasants when they catch the incendiary who burns down the village, so it does in the Soviets when they lay hold of the incendiary who tries to burn down the whole social edifice. Ten years for the murderer of a fellow-man! *Rastrel!* Death by shooting, for the man who tries to murder the whole State!

It was not always so. At first, capital punishment was abolished, but in the throes of intervention and civil war it was re-established as a special measure in the fight "against counter-revolution, speculation, and banditry." It has been extended to other crimes as the Soviets were confronted with situations that seemed to threaten the foundations of the social order. In 1926, when a wave of rowdyism was sweeping the land, six "hooligans" were shot for assaulting a girl. In 1930, when the currency was menaced by collapse, four speculators were shot for the hoarding of silver coins. With transportation imperiled by sabotage and criminal negligence, four railwaymen were executed for causing a wreck that cost 70 lives. When collectivization was imperiled by wholesale thievery and arson, death was made a permissive penalty for pillagers and incendiaries.

Foreigners are perplexed by the severity of the Soviets in dealing with persons stealing from a collective, factory, or school, in contrast to the mildness towards those who steal from an individual. The explanation is found in the words of the decree, "Public property is sacred and inviolable." For the masses, especially those nurtured under the old regime, this is a new concept. To the peasants for centuries the State was an alien thing and everything belonging to it a legitimate field for plunder. To the counter-revolutionists the Soviet state is a hateful thing, which cannot be fought in the open but may be covertly weakened by sabotage, by squandering or embezzling its funds. Still others, now that all avenues to personal gain in private trade and industry are closed, instinctively turn to the public domains to enrich themselves. Obviously such attitudes are particularly dangerous in a society where so much property is public. If the new society is to survive, its enemies must at all costs be rooted out and replaced by a new ethic and conscience. The Soviets are seeking to do this by re-education, exhortation, and compulsion. In his oath of allegiance the Red Armyist pledges "to safeguard the property of the nation as the apple of his eye." "The thief taking the property of the public is as bad as the spy or traitor, if not worse." (Stalin) "He who steals from the commonwealth steals from all." These concepts are constantly iterated in the press and the schools, and are driven home by applying, or at any rate making it legal to apply, "the maximum measure of social defense" to transgressors. Particularly is this measure directed against Communists recreant to their trust. Because of the high obligations they have assumed, acts, which might be looked upon in others as simple misdemeanors, become with them monstrous political crimes.

All these are emergency measures and in the aggregate concern a relatively small number of persons. Even in the case of declared counter-revolutionists, not one per cent are executed. With full confession and recantation, they often get off with a term of imprisonment. Such was the case of the Mensheviks in 1931 who were convicted of fomenting kulak uprisings and conspiring with foreign groups. In the case of Ramzin and eight other engineers confessing to the "wrecking" and sabotage of military industries, the death-sentence was commuted; later these men were freed and now hold positions of importance and honor. Customary sentences range from loss of civil rights to confiscation of property and "exile." Exile covers anything from Siberia to the "minus six"—forbidding residence in the six principal cities, Moscow, Leningrad, Kharkov, Kiev, Odessa, or Rostov. Often less than ten months of a ten-year term are really served, and anniversary amnesties are frequent and sweeping.

Against bandits likewise the Soviet employs other means than bullets. In the Caucasus many patriots, to avenge the conquest of their land by the Tsar, became highwaymen, robbing travelers and slaying officials on the highroads through the mountains. Entering their *aouls* the agents of the Gay-Pay-Oo said: "Your country no longer belongs to Russia. No longer is there any excuse for political banditry. The Caucasus is now a free Soviet Republic. Take your place in it as an honest citizen. Give up your weapons and receive in return land and work." Scores of them have done so.

Nevertheless, over against the lofty ideals first enunciated by the Revolution and the professed principle of the Soviets that their sole concern is the redemption of the criminal, the death penalty continues to exist for political and economic "treason." This is distinctly a step backward. In face of this relapse, even that stalwart implacable Communist, the Commissar of Justice, Krylenko, is impelled to offer a justification: "This punishment is applied to those who offer no hope of reform, to the class enemies whose whole activity has been directed against the Revolution, or to those who have so far broken with society that it is impossible to adjust them to it. But according to our law the death penalty is a temporary measure against the gravest crimes, against those who menace the very basis of the proletarian state; and it is applied only as a measure of exceptional defense pending its complete abolition." The last phrase is a citation from Article 21 of the Criminal Code.

With the country delivered from its war psychosis—the fear of impending assault from hostile powers without and class-enemies within —it is assumed that all politicals will be regarded and treated by the Soviets as are the other 95 per cent of criminals; simply as erring individuals to be reformed, as citizens whose lives and interests are to be carefully guarded in the courts.

What Was the Gay-Pay-Oo?

The political-military police entrusted with the task of protecting the State from counter-revolution, espionage and all crimes striking directly at the State's existence. Hence its name, United State Political Administration—*Obyedinennoye Gosudarstvennoye Politicheskoye Upravleniye* (O.G.P.U.). To foreigners it was the "three-letter organization" and generally it was called by its three last Russian initials G.P.U., pronounced *Gay-Pay-Oo,* and pronounced reverently: with pride and affection by its friends to whom it was "the resolute watch-dog of the Revolution," "the glorious colleague of the Red Army in defense of the workers and peasants"; with hate and shuddering by its enemies to whom it was "the avenging hand of the Bolsheviks," "the terror that walks by night." This last expression referred to the time of arrests—usually after midnight when the person was at home and in bed.

In this, as in other tactics, the Gay-Pay-Oo followed the formidable old *Cheka,* the Extraordinary Commission that after Allied intervention and the attempted assassination of Lenin loosed against the White Terror of the counter-revolution the Red Terror of the Revolution. The Gay-Pay-Oo was the lineal descendant of that grim ruthless organization but with more restricted powers. It made arrests at its own discretion but had to report them to the *Tsik,* the Central Executive Committee. It tried and condemned persons—those it did not hand over to the courts—but it had to allow appeals over its decisions, in writing or by telephone, to the State Procurator. It inflicted the death penalty but not without the approval of the *Tsik.*

As to the number of executions no exact figures are available. To the American Labor Delegation, Menzhinsky, head of the Gay-Pay-Oo, announced that in the five years, 1922-1927, 1,500 were shot by its own order or that of the courts. This in itself would not account for the dread its name inspired. There were other factors: the lightning speed with which it often struck; the dragnet arrests of suspects in moments of crisis and political tension; the atmosphere of mystery and secrecy with which its acts were shrouded; the lurid tales about its cork-lined execution chamber on the Lubyanka, or Dzerzhinsky Square as it is now called. All this conspired to instill into all anti-Soviet elements a feeling akin to terror. To protests against this, the reply was "Thank God it does! So much the better! It saves them from committing treason and saves us from executing them for it."

To the American Labor Delegation in 1927, Stalin said: "The Gay-Pay-Oo is a punitive organ. It is more or less analogous to the Committee of Public Safety during the great French Revolution. It punishes chiefly spies, conspirators, terrorists, bandits, speculators, and forgers. It is a sort of political court martial for protecting the interests of the Revolution against the attacks of the counter-revolutionary bourgeoisie and its agents. It hits these enemies with severe and certain blows. It is the unsheathed sword of the proletariat. No wonder that the bourgeoisie have a fierce hatred for the Gay-Pay-Oo. All kinds of fairy tales and slanders about it are fabricated. The workers, however, respect it.

"People preach mildness and propose to abolish the Gay-Pay-Oo. But can anyone give us the guarantee that when it is abolished the capitalists of all countries will cease to organize and finance the conspirators, terrorists, incendiaries, and bomb-throwers? To disarm the Revolution without the guarantee that the enemies of the Revolution are also disarmed, would that not be madness? Would that not be a crime against the working class? We are a state surrounded by capitalist states. And our internal enemies are not isolated individuals. They are connected with the capitalists abroad by a thousand threads. No, Comrades, we do not want to repeat the mistakes of the Paris Communards. The Gay-Pay-Oo is necessary for the Revolution and will continue to exist to the terror of the enemies of the proletariat."

This military political police does continue to exist, although it is under a different name and the range of its activities are sharply curtailed. Just as the Cheka was abolished in 1922 and its place taken by the Gay-Pay-Oo with diminished powers, so in turn the Gay-Pay-Oo in 1934 was abolished and in its place was instituted the Department of Public Security under the Commissariat of Home Affairs. From it was taken the power of pronouncing the death penalty, though it retained the right of investigation, making arrests and sending persons into exile up to a term of five years.

Now, according to Chapter 9 of the new Constitution, "Citizens of the U.S.S.R. are insured the inviolability of person. No one may be subjected to arrest except by decision of the court or with the sanction of a State Attorney (Prosecutor)." In effect, this Chapter, with its many guarantees, ranging from freedom of speech, press, and assembly to "the inviolability of homes and secrecy of correspondence" is a new Bill of Rights. How fully and how quickly it will be carried out in actual practice depends again upon a number of factors chief of which is war.

78. How Are the People's Courts Conducted?

No legal niceties or hair-splitting. No flowing gowns, wigs or other regalia. No solemn oath. No strict rules of evidence. No impassioned pleas to a jury.

The procedure is as simple and unpretentious as the bare room in Kvalinsk on the Volga in which sits one of the People's Courts. In these courts are heard over 80 per cent of all cases throughout the land. This one is typical of them all. It has no flag or coat-of-arms, only a dais with a faded red-clothed table for the judges, a big portrait of Lenin, rough wooden benches crowded with spectators drawn by the intense interest of Russians in the dramatic. Out of *Pravda* a woman is slowly reading aloud about that ever all-absorbing topic, the harvest outlook; an old man strokes a cat sunning itself on a window-sill; a peasant hands a half-smoked cigarette to one of the defendants, a forlorn frightened lad of eighteen; someone hums the melancholy refrain of a Volga song.

Clang goes a bell! Everybody rises as the three judges take their places at the table. In the center sits the presiding judge, sometimes called the permanent or professional judge. Formerly chosen by the local Soviet, the People's Judge is now elected directly for a period of three years by the voters of the district. This one, Khonĭn, was a Tolstoyan, who enthusiastically embraced the Revolution, fought valorously as a cavalryman in its defense and from the saddle was drafted directly into service in the courts. With deep sincerity, never-failing humor, and a natural flair for the law fortified by two years of special study, he holds the respect of the entire community.

On either side of him sit the two "lay-judges" or "co-judges." This is a distinctive feature of the Soviet system though it is not entirely unique. In the county courts of the state of Vermont there used to be two "side-judges"—laymen chosen by the community for their character and common sense—who served as advisers to the professional judges. In the Soviet courts these lay-judges after a short session are replaced by others. The aim is to keep the courts vitalized by direct participation of the people, ever responsive to their ideas and the changing "revolutionary conscience." They are not mere jurymen, but actual judges.

One of them, a beaming red-kerchiefed peasant woman, a successful crusader against the moonshine stills in her village, is a bit uneasy in her new rôle, but resolute. The other, a brawny coatless stevedore, has shown some legal acumen as a member of the "law circle" in the Rivermen's Club. In preliminary conferences with the permanent judge, both have been instructed in the application of the law to the special cases on the docket. After twelve days on the bench, their places will be taken by other "lay judges," while they return to their regular tasks, the stevedore to his wharf and the loading of ships, the woman to reaping the fields.

Today they are full-fledged magistrates invested with the same powers as the permanent judge in conducting the case and determining the verdict, even in deciding questions of law as well as fact. While almost always deferring to his superior knowledge they may out-vote and overrule him. But this rarely happens.

All are in their places. At side tables sit the girl clerk of the court and the brusque prosecutor; on "the bench of the accused" the dejected 18-year-old Petrov. The other defendant in the case, Razumov, a man of 30, is brought in by two militiamen with drawn sabers. Although the Soviet papers rail against this as "needless humiliation," a futile, brutal holdover from the old regime, it strangely persisted here.

"Do you challenge any member of this court?" asks the presiding judge.

"No!"

"Do you have confidence in the judges to give you a fair trial?"

"Yes!"

The formal "act of accusation" is read to the two defendants by the prosecutor. They are charged with swindling the Co-operative store out of cloth valued at one hundred rubles. From the office they stole a stamp and after making a good copy of it smuggled it back again. With the forged one they stamped a sales-slip, received the goods, and sold them to a "fence." On the second attempt, Petrov, the younger, was caught red-handed in the act and put on parole. Razumov ran away to another town and a month later was arrested.

"Guilty," mumbles Petrov.

"Not guilty," declares Razumov, at the same time announcing that he will avail himself of his legal right not to testify, and that he has his own advocate. He might, in the usual way, have chosen one from the regular College of Defenders attached to the courts. But he prefers to have his own private counsel of which there is still a very small and fast-dwindling number. Thereby he prejudices his case with the woman judge who, like all peasants, is singularly unmoved by the pleas or eloquence of a "hired" lawyer. To them it is something bought and paid for, not much different from bribing a judge. The courts likewise look askance upon these private attorneys, who for the most part are former members of the old Tsar's bar. They are scarcely more than tolerated by the courts. With suave voices and elegant, though now somewhat threadbare dress, they strike a jarring note amid the simple-mannered, rough-bloused, and booted proletarians. More alien still is the old spirit they bring with them. Instead of falling in with the Soviet conception of the court as a forum with all parties co-operating in a straightforward search for the truth, they are still prone to regard the court as an arena, a battleground of wits, with much sparring for points, quibbling over words and technicalities.

Sometimes this is useful even in the People's Court. Soviet law is complex enough for an adroit lawyer to find loopholes through which he may drag his client, and a show of erudition may well impress judges of simple minds, untutored in the law.

But not these judges or prosecutor. Rapidly they proceed to develop the case. Through witnesses it is clearly established that, while Razumov did not himself forge the stamp or dispose of the goods, his undoubtedly were the brains that conceived the plot. By playing upon the weakness and poverty of Petrov, he used him as a tool for carrying it out.

The prosecutor demands six months' sentence for Petrov, and three years for Razumov as a socially dangerous character, "a class enemy of the workers and peasants." For proof he delves into Razumov's past and digs up a lot of damning facts: His father, a vodka-distiller, fought with the Whites against the Red Army; he himself intrigued his way into the Comsomols but was expelled under suspicion of speculating in rubles; he was implicated in the mistreatment of a girl but he ran away.

"But his past has nothing to do with the case," protests Razumov's advocate. "It is entirely irrelevant. The only question is whether he committed the felony with which he is charged. May I refer to the Code of 1864?"

"And may I refer to the Revolution of 1917?" puts in the stevedore co-judge, mildly sarcastic. "It threw overboard the old code and most of its ideas. It has made everything relevant. It is concerned not only with the crime in itself but in what lay behind it and led up to it, all the causes and circumstances—social, economic, and political. Particularly the last. We want to find out if it was motivated by enmity to the Soviet or its institutions. That is a prime factor in determining the degree of guilt, the penalties to be imposed. In the courts of the Revolution everything is relevant, nothing is ruled out." The stevedore is repeating the lessons learned in his "law circle" at the Rivermen's Club. Nonchalantly he flicks the ashes from his cigarette, evidently enjoying to the full this chance to reprove a bourgeois advocate.

"Of course," smiles the advocate ingratiatingly, "I accept and support the Revolution." Though the stevedore does not say "Gad! you'd better!" his look implies it.

The prosecutor also comes in for a reprimand. His animus against Razumov—all too apparent—is a violation of the Soviet conception of a trial as an impartial inquiry into all the facts in order to come to a just conclusion. Indeed it is called not a trial but a "judicial inquiry," and even the prosecutor is presumed to maintain a purely judicial attitude. His duty is not merely to convict but to present everything *for* as well as *against* the accused. This he has not done. While stressing all the adverse in Razumov's record he has passed over in silence one fact favorable to him, his services in salvaging a Soviet tugboat from a flood on the Volga.

"Why did you omit that?" asks the judge.

"Didn't consider it important," says the prosecutor, lamely.

Taking courage from the tea brought in by an attendant, the woman co-judge turns to Petrov with a few queries. At first the boy is quite dumb-stricken, but her kindly ways coax out of him a few faltering replies: "We left our village after my father died in the famine." "My mother had four children to find bread for." "For a long time we had only rye and bark and roots to eat." "I was hungry when I stole the goods."

The judges retire to an adjoining room, the law specifying they must be absolutely alone in preparing the verdict. Meantime the spectators are drawing up their own verdict, hotly arguing in groups every aspect of the trial that grows into a general free-for-all debate. Twenty minutes. The bell clangs, and again all stand to hear the reading of the verdict. It is a clear résumé of the factual aspects followed by the sentences: Razumov—two years "deprived of liberty," Petrov—four months. "But, taking into consideration his peasant origin, his youth, and dire poverty, his sentence is suspended."

On grounds of bias in the prosecutor against Razumov, his advocate announces an appeal on cassation to the higher court. This, the next step upon the judicial ladder, is the Provincial or Regional Court.

The Provincial or Regional Court as a Court of Review examines cases from the People's Court for errors in law or flagrantly unjust decisions. Finding them it does not itself re-try the case, but remands it to the People's Court. Cases are brought before it (a) by way of cassation—on complaint of any party that rules have been violated or interests infringed, (b) by way of supervision—on its own motion it may demand the records of any case at any stage. "This procedure is constantly invoked," says the English jurist Pritt, "and leads directly to correcting wrong verdicts and indirectly to greater efficiency and vigilance." As a Court of Original Jurisdiction it tries grave offenses—premeditated killing, rape, corruption of minors, banditry, instigations of mass disorders, incitations of race or religious animosity. In its decisions it is guided by the "social consequences of the act rather than the moral culpability of the individual." It declares it "socially unnecessary" to imprison a mother of 21 who, horror-stricken at discovering the father of her child is a syphilitic, has drowned her six-weeks-old baby. Wide in its discretionary powers, swift and resolute in action, like the revolutionary tribunals of which it is a descendant, this Regional Court is known as the "strong judicial fist." Above it stands:

The Supreme Court of the Republic. It issues instructions, disbars advocates, interprets the precise meaning of the Land, Labor, Civil, and Criminal Codes, passes on the constitutionality of legislative acts, and tries important cases like espionage. It is responsible for and controls all courts below it, examines, and passes on their acts by its own initiative. In turn it is controlled by the court at the very top of the judicial ladder,

The Supreme Court of the U.S.S.R., consisting of a president, deputy, and thirty judges. It has power of supervision over the verdicts of the Supreme Courts of the eleven Republics. It has cassational jurisdiction over the decisions of the military courts of the Red Army. Through its plenum it explains and interprets the laws and decrees. It adjudicates disputes between the republics and exercises criminal jurisdiction in cases that involve officials high in the state or army. Decisions are made by majority vote. To its Military Collegium, composed of six judges, is given the power of life or death in those cases formerly handled by the Gay-Pay-Oo. Before it come those accused of treason to the state which may involve the death sentence. Nikolaiev, the assassin of the Leningrad leader Kirov, and his thirteen fellow conspirators were tried and condemned by this division of the Supreme Court in 1935. Shortly afterwards, Zinoviev, Kamenev, and other members of the "Moscow Center" were tried for encouraging the assassination, but in the opinion of the court, while they had morally aided the plotters, they were not directly implicated in the plot and they were sentenced to terms in prison. In 1936 the members of this group were again brought to trial and on the basis of new evidence and their own confessions that they had "planned and directed the murder of Kirov as well as assaults on other Soviet leaders," they were condemned to be shot. On the basis of this testimony and further evidence that there were other participants in a Trotzkyist plot to seize the State power, in 1937 Radek, Piatakov and others were charged with high treason and after confessing to planning a campaign of terrorism and sabotage in collusion with Fascist agents, were sentenced to death or imprisonment.

The final authority in all matters, judicial as well as legislative and executive, is the All-Union Supreme Council. When it is not sitting, power is vested in its Presidium of forty-four members. It interprets the law, issues decrees, exercises the right of pardon. Daily in a large chamber in Moscow one may see its chairman or one of his deputies receiving a long line of petitioners with appeals against sentences of the courts, hearing complaints, and granting releases from prison or exile. This Presidium submits all legislative proposals to the Supreme Court, asks and receives from it legal advice, but in the last analysis the Supreme Council determines the validity of all its acts.

Like all other institutions the courts are instruments for carrying out the general policy of the government. While the judges of the People's Courts are elected directly by the people, all the judges of the Provincial and Regional Courts, as well as the Supreme Courts of the Republics and of the Union, are appointed by the corresponding Soviet organs for a term of five years. However, to prevent the judicial apparatus from being wholly dependent upon those organs which it must in turn supervise, tremendous power is lodged in the Procuracy—headed by the State Attorney or Prosecutor of the U.S.S.R. appointed by the Supreme Council for a term of seven years.

This State Attorney in the words of Article 113 of the Constitution is charged with "the highest supervision of the strict observance of the laws by all Commissariats and institutions under them, as well as by individual officials and citizens. . . ." He appoints the State Attorneys of the various republics, autonomous regions, and provinces for a term of five years. Their authority is as far-reaching as their duties. They inquire into the legality of the acts of all Soviets, trusts, and Labor Unions, raise protests and institute proceedings against violations. They receive complaints, written or oral, of citizens seeking redress— over half a million a year. They conduct the preliminary fact-finding investigation in all cases. They look for errors of law or miscarriage of justice in trials and on their own initiative carry them on cassation to a higher court. They see that no one is unlawfully held in custody, that sentences are properly executed, and inspect prisons and "colonies," hearing petitions and plaints.

Each of the eleven constituent republics has its own Commissariat of Justice. Its function is to organize the courts, codify legislation, train lawyers, and make provision for the whole judicial apparatus. At the head of the Russian Commissariat stands the impetuous, electric, tense, illiberal, uncompromising, skull-shaven Krylenko, first commander of the revolutionary armies, declaring: "For us only such courts as will always and under all conditions guarantee the defense of the workers and peasants."

New Justice for Old

In contrast to the administration of justice under the Tsars stands justice under the Soviets. In the first place it is—or was up till the adoption of the new Constitution in 1936—*class justice.* The celebrated code of 1864 was on the whole liberal and tolerant. If, as interpreted by the old courts, it became a bulwark to conserve the privileges of nobles and bourgeoisie, at any rate it proclaimed the principle of the equality of all before the law. The Soviet codes for twenty years did not. They made no pretense of abstract, impartial justice. Avowedly the scales were weighted in favor of the once exploited and now ruling class, the workers and peasants. Frankly, openly, the Soviet courts were used as instruments in their behalf.

True, the Supreme Court reminded judges that this class attitude consists not in convicting the bourgeois and kulak, and acquitting the worker and poor peasant, but in a clear understanding of "the social danger in the act committed by the citizen brought to trial." Still the courts always found—and still find—more social danger in a crime committed by a bourgeois than by a proletarian—unless he is a Communist. Fortunate is the defendant who can say, "My mother came from the loom, my father from the wooden plow."

It is honest. "In the court-room are deft hands and deep pockets," "A gift to the judge, the case is decided," are old peasant sayings. The giving of bribes was erected into a system, so universal, so taken for granted that, as Beaulieu remarks in his classic study, "The Empire of the Tsars and the Russians," "The peasant deemed that judge righteous who took with both hands from both sides and sold his decision to neither." In the Soviet courts this has been practically eliminated. Whatever their failings they cannot be accused of graft or corruption. True, there have been instances when bandits and counter-revolutionists, intriguing their way into the Communist party, have dominated the courts and used them to terrorize and lay tribute on a whole region. True also that the Revolution has not cured all judges of the itching palm. But it has made it extremely dangerous to stretch it forth. Besides, there are few individuals or interests rich enough to place in it enough to make it worth while to take the risk. That is the chief reason why the plague of bribery and venality that infested the old courts has now practically disappeared. It is not that the Revolution has magically made judges incorruptible, but that there are few to corrupt them.

It is speedy. Litigation under the Tsars was notoriously dilatory. The classic story is that of a nurse brought to trial for deserting the infant she was tending. Wearily from instance to instance the case dragged on through the courts. But at last the decision—she must return to her charge. He was now 22 years of age and an officer in the Hussars! On the principle that "justice delayed is justice denied," half the cases are now completed within a month. In the Moscow district 80 per cent are finished in a fortnight.

This has been achieved by the abolition of old Russian technicalities and red tape which still strangle and gum up so many Soviet institutions. But not the courts. Another reason for swiftness is the thoroughness of the "preliminary inquiry," carried on prior to the trial. As in the French system the investigator exhaustively cross-examines the accused and all witnesses for and against, takes their depositions, and makes complete summary of the case. In fact it is he who decides whether there is a case. With all the data before it, the court can proceed rapidly with the trial or "judicial inquiry," which is simply an open public rehearing of all the facts in the presence of all the parties.

In this final stage the inquiry continues quite informally with the aim of getting at the truth as quickly as possible and from whatever source it may come. To this end judges, prosecutors and even outsiders often interrupt the proceedings with leading questions, comments and speeches. So may the defendant who can challenge any witness at any time, deny or withdraw his previous testimony and is always assured of a long last word. This is the practice not only in the People's Court but in all the courts including the Supreme Court of the Union. That is one reason why the Terrorist Trotzkyist trials with their by-play, confessions, and repentances were so perplexing to the British and Americans accustomed to a quite different procedure in their own courts.

It is inexpensive. Under the old regime long delays and large fees made litigation almost prohibitive to the poor. "Don't go into the courts," the old proverb warned the peasant, "the bast shoes you sue for will cost more than leather boots." No longer need expenses

deter the poor man from taking his case into the courts. He may have
the services of an advocate from the College of Defenders without
any payment at all. Other citizens pay according to a definite schedule
of fees adjusted to their income. The state also provides Legal Consultation Clinics, which like Health Clinics are open to all citizens in
trouble. They are attached to the courts, clubs, newspapers, recreation
parks, and the radio-centers with scores of lawyers on their staffs. In
them one may obtain advice on any problem, from how to find a fleeing husband to how to stop a noisy all-night accordion player in a
neighboring room. First-aid stations in legal affairs.

It is simple and comprehensible. Of the popular concept of law
under the Tsar, the great jurist Nastyrev wrote: "In the eyes of the
peasant, law is something terrible, mysterious, inscrutable, in the name
of which the government terrorizes, abuses, and mutilates, whips out
arrears in taxes, exiles to Siberia, disembowels corpses, pulls down
houses, kills stock, drafts into the army." Most of these things the
Soviets continue to do. But with great pains, by every means, they
strive to state the reasons, the why and wherefore; to make the law
perfectly clear and within the grasp of all; to envisage it not as a rigid
code, arbitrarily superimposed from above, but as rules of life drawn
up by the people themselves. It is no small undertaking to re-educate
175 million people in a new concept of the law and radically change
their whole attitude toward it. To do this the Soviets are working
along three lines:

1. By an insistent propaganda seeking to train the people *in an
understanding of the law*. To this end there are thousands of "legal
circles" alongside of the drama, science, and other circles in the clubs
and Collectives. A series of pamphlets, "Get to Know the Soviet Laws"
instruct the various sections of the population, particularly women, in
their rights and how to stand up for them. "Exemplary" trials are
held in great halls and theatres with movie cameras recording the big
moments and radios carrying speeches and testimony direct to the
people. And, most important in a land of a hundred languages, is
Article 110 of the Constitution, which declares that persons who do
not know the language of the republic or region "have the right to
address the court in their own tongue" and be fully informed about
the case through an interpreter.

2. By collaboration of the people *in the making of the law*. As "revolutionary expedient law," it changes quickly with the changing situation, but usually after long consultation with the public. Countless meetings were held all over the land, even in the remotest villages, before the Family-Marriage Code was promulgated. Forty million copies of the 1936 draft Constitution were printed and so intense was the interest in this new basic law of the nation that in some half million conferences thirty-six million citizens assembled for debate and discussion which was often carried on till late in the night. From them came 154,000 proposals for amendments of which of course only a few were embodied in the final text. Likewise, there were many amendments offered to the 1936 law prohibiting abortions and scores of letters and speeches caustically criticizing it appeared in the press. Although it was enacted into law, if in the course of time the public at large becomes convinced that its evils outweigh its good, doubtless it will be changed in response to popular demand.

3. Through the widest participation of the masses *in executing the laws,* under the slogan "judicial service—the duty of every toiler!" Besides the lay judges on the bench there are the "social prosecutors" delegated by organizations to present their views in a case or defend some public interest. In this way hundreds of thousands have a direct part in the administration of justice. More still in the unique institutions that lie outside the regular courts. These are the "Comradely Courts" attached to almost every organization and bringing to trial fellow-members for petty offenses involving no criminal responsibility. In a factory a mechanic is haled before this court for allowing his loom to rust. He is condemned for "wanton cruelty to a machine," and damages up to 50 rubles are assessed. In a Collective, a manager is tried for failing to produce the quota of eggs; he receives a public reprimand. In a jail a prisoner is tried by the inmates for exceeding his "leave of absence"; he is fined 10 rubles. In an apartment house a boy is tried by his peers for mistreating a cat; he is declared a "class-enemy of animals" and excluded two weeks from the playground.

Besides blame and condemnation the Comradely Courts distribute praise and commendation. Like the village "chambers of reconciliation," they seek to cajole the erring ones into a more social behavior, to induce them to settle their problems in the light of the collective mind and conscience of their fellows. Bare and unimpressive in surroundings and lacking in formality, they are not lacking in a certain dignity imparted by the spirit of moral earnestness and friendliness pervading them. They are civic training schools in which millions are learning not only the rudiments of law but the "rules of social life known for centuries, repeated for thousands of years in all sermons which eventually they will become accustomed to observe without force, without constraint, without subjection, without the special apparatus of compulsion which is called the State." (Lenin)

In that happy distant future, envisaged by the Communists, when the State withers away and with it the whole judicial apparatus, it may be that in Comradely Courts people will adjust those differences that may still arise in the most smooth-running Utopia.

79. What Are the Incomes and Status of the Soviet Brain Workers—Artists, Doctors, Teachers, Engineers?

As insistent as the demand for commodities is the demand for brains, skill, and intelligence. While in most countries there is a surplus of intellectuals, in the Soviet Union there is a shortage. Thanks to a swiftly expanding economy, instead of a dozen candidates for every vacancy, there are a dozen vacancies for every candidate. Exploration of the Arctic, the stratosphere, and the depths of the earth call for phalanxes of navigators, chemists, scientists. The building of industrial giants, the digging of ship and drainage canals, slum-clearance, the planning of new Socialist cities call for armies of architects, surveyors, engineers. Universal education, the creation of alphabets, grammars, and text-books for fifty-eight new languages, the salvaging of old monuments, folklore, and music, demand ever new levies of teachers, linguists, ethnographers, archaeologists. It is quite the same in every field from the medical to the military. Every year creates thousands, if not tens of thousands of openings.

To find the people qualified to fill all these posts is a serious problem. It will be solved when the hosts of the new generation now training in the institutes and universities come into action. "Already," says *Izvestia,* "our new proletarian intelligentsia is growing up and consolidating itself in all fields from engineering to philosophy." But it will be some years yet before there are enough of them. Meanwhile, the Soviet Union makes shift with men, promoted straight from the ranks or rushed through short emergency courses, who are often more zealous than competent. It calls to its aid engineers and experts from America, England, and Germany, often paying them gilt-edged salaries. It utilizes as best it can, the specialists inherited from the old regime, many of whom, from the start, have given loyal yeomen service. Like the dean of Russian music, Ippolitov-Ivanov who exclaimed, "When I die let them write over my grave: 'Here lies the most fortunate of men,'" some of them have found in the Revolution a new meaning and fullness to life. Others, hating and sabotaging it and bitterly resentful of the suspicions and discriminations against them, have been half-hearted or hostile. But this is past history. With the removal of the old disabilities and the passing of "bourgeois-baiting," they are reconciled to the Revolution. "Now that the intelligentsia has turned to our side," says Stalin, "our task is to accord them the utmost attention and solicitude."

To men of brains and genius the Soviet Union offers the greatest opportunities. If they can accept its aims and program all things are theirs: A sixth of the world to work in; immense resources to work with; the plaudits of a grateful public and government. Witness the honors and ovations given to writers like Gorky, scientists like Pavlov, artists like Stanislavsky; Michurin, the botanist; the explorer Schmidt; Rossinsky, "the grandfather of Soviet aviation"; the old Tsarist officer Kamenev. With these honors go substantial awards in the shape of special grants, houses, pensions to themselves and their families. These benefices are not confined to the outstanding luminaries. The services of all professional men and white-collar workers are increasingly recognized and rewarded. Of the dividends now coming in from the Five-Year Plans they are getting their share—perhaps more than their share.

In general, the income of the brain-workers, except in cases of popular writers and great engineers, is rather modest. But on the other hand it is assured. If one has small hope of a munificent income, on the other hand he is not haunted by fears of having no income at all. Nor does he have to worry about the exigencies and mishaps of life—illness, accidents, expenses of child-birth, and burials. A comprehensive system of social insurance takes care of all that. He enjoys the manifold privileges of the great clubs in which the life of each profession is centered. From the old mansions in which they were first located they are moving into new and often palatial buildings, equipped with buffets, lounges, gymnasiums, solariums, libraries, and reading-rooms with specialized journals of which over a thousand are published. At his disposal likewise are summer and winter vacation resorts on the coast of the Crimea and the Caucasus, floating rest-houses on the Volga, homes for veteran scientists and actors.

Engineers, Technicians, Inventors

"Technique during the period of reconstruction decides everything." This slogan has been thus amended by Stalin: "Technique without men is dead. It is time to state plainly that while formerly our emphasis was onesidedly placed upon machines, henceforth it must be put on the men who master and run them." This demands a greater concern for their interests and well-being. They must be cultivated "as carefully and attentively as a gardener grows a favorite fruit-tree." They must be promoted, transferred to new positions if they are misfits, prompted to higher skill by higher wages. In these ways the Soviets seek to create a new type of engineer, foreman, draftsman—a new spirit and attitude.

The old Russian engineer was usually well-educated and erudite. He was strong on theories but weak in applying them. Frequently, too, he had a feeling of caste and superiority, symbolized by the inevitable paralyzing portfolio under his arm. Instead of showing the workers how to repair a broken-down machine he was prone to write a long report about it. In sharp contrast with this aristocratic tradition are the democratic ways of the engineer from America. In greasy overalls and rolled-up sleeves he goes down into mine-pit or fire-box to grapple first-hand with an emergency. He mingles freely with the men on the job, taking his share of the strains and stresses, the sweat and smoke. It is this spirit and attitude that the Soviet leaders seek to inculcate in the new corps coming on. In their training, theory is closely united with practice. A few months of study in school alternates with a like period of work in the field. Thus, instead of being laboratory- and office-minded, they become mill- and factory-minded. Sometimes they are sent abroad to study Western methods or purchase machines. Their monthly salaries run from a few hundred rubles for a novice up into thousands for talented veterans.

Anyone with a bright idea may join one of the thousand branches of the Society of Inventors providing the novice with laboratories for experiments, study rooms, and advisers. Each of the commissariats has its Commission on Inventions, and as authors' titles or patents are granted they are registered with the State Planning Commission. Mills and mines have their Inventors' Brigades whose members jointly contribute to the solution of vexing problems. A unique institution for arousing interest and initiative is the *Signal Post* which points out defects and needs in machines and technique and calls for remedies. Another is the *Loan of Ideas* printed like regular bonds and paid for, not with money, but with ideas. They run from simple ways of saving oil or fuel to complex schemes for utilizing by-products. The more valuable the idea the more bonds. They are not only honorific to their owner but negotiable. He may exchange them for a technical library, a trip to the Caucasus, treatment in a sanitarium.

As a result of these ingenious devices with their stimulus to creative endeavor, each year brings forth some 25,000 inventions, and over a half million suggestions and proposals. Many of them, of course, are fantastic and useless. None, however, may be dismissed out of hand. For each written proposal the plant-director must give a receipt and one has the right to be present when its merits are discussed. If rejected, a written reason must be given. If accepted, the inventor or rationalizer is entitled to a portion of the annual savings effected by his idea. From thirty per cent on savings up to 500 rubles it tapers down to two per cent on savings up to 1,000,000, plus a small premium. In no case does anyone receive less than a hundred rubles, nor more than a hundred thousand. The rights and interests of inventors are fully protected by the law. Patents are granted for 15 years with the proviso that they be brought into use within three years. If one chooses, he receives simply an *Inventors' Certificate* which confers various privileges—more housing space, a regular pension, a chance to devote himself exclusively to research. Sometimes an outright money payment is made. An award of 100,000 rubles went to chemists Amsamov and Kalkovsky for their process of extracting cyanide from coke. A like sum went to the fitter Lensky for an apparatus for testing pneumatic hammers.

"Engineers of the Mind and Spirit"

Such is the term used by Stalin for the molders and makers of public opinion and morale, the artists and writers. In building Socialism, their work with pen and brush and camera is as highly valued as that of their confreres with compass and blue-prints. As the Soviet Union issues some 45,000 new titles a year, it is particularly a paradise for *authors*. Payment is based on the size of the manuscript as measured by "sheets," about 8,000 words, for which one receives from 150 rubles to 1,000 rubles on editions of 3,000 depending on the author's popularity and character of his work. On succeeding editions he receives sixty per cent of the original rate. About a third or half these rates are paid to *translators* of foreign books into Russian. *Journalists* receive a stated salary of 300-1,000 rubles a month, which is usually augmented by extra articles. *Playwrights* and *scenarists* usually get a lump sum for their scripts and librettos. After this come the royalties which run from three to six per cent of the box-office receipts from all cinema houses and theatres.

As the number of performances of popular plays and pictures runs up into thousands and the sale of books into millions, the royalties of leading authors and playwrights, likewise of cinema *directors* and music *composers,* frequently amount to tens of thousands of rubles a year. And they may receive them year after year, as long as their works are successful, for copyright is held by the author as long as he lives and by his heirs for fifteen years after his death. To enforce these rights is one of the functions of the Union of Writers which has sections in all the republics. It publishes a score of periodicals, organizes courses for training new writers, runs clubs in the cities, Houses for Creative Work and Rest in the country, sport-fields, ski-stations, Cooperatives. Besides dues, there are special funds coming directly from the state or from a fixed levy on playhouses and publishers, amounting annually to over ten million rubles. This provides subsidies to beginners who show signs of promise, special grants to the sick and the needy, and—to authors of ten years' standing who have become incapacitated or have reached their fiftieth birthday—a pension equal to their average income for three years previous.

On similar lines is organized the life of workers in the graphic and plastic arts, in music, cinema, and the theatre. There are some 50,000 *actors* with monthly salaries of 500 rubles and up depending on abilities, the type of theatre to which they are attached, and its location. Several thousand *engravers* and *illustrators* are engaged by the publishers of books, charts, placards, and posters at a few hundred rubles a month. *Painters* and *sculptors* usually contract with some organization to furnish from two to five paintings, statues, or drawings a year, receiving in return a minimum of 300 rubles a month. These sums are doubled if they go out to make a pictorial record of some expedition to the Pamirs, the Arctic, or the building of an industrial giant. Reproductions are often made in myriads of copies, the artist usually retaining the original with the right to sell it to a club, museum, or individual.

To those holding the honorific titles, "Peoples' Artist," or "Honored Artist" go monthly pensions running up to hundreds of rubles. The annual income from various sources of such outstanding ones as Gardin, Gliere, Ermler, Shostakovich, the playwrights Afinogenov and Kirshon, often amounts to 100,000 rubles and more. But there is nothing unique in that. In any country the geniuses—or at any rate the popular idols—usually do rather well by themselves. The noteworthy thing about the Soviet Union is the effort to do well by anybody and everybody who has the impulse to create. Gone is the old romantic notion of the artist starving in attic or basement. Instead of Bohemian quarters there are Artists' Communities like the one in Moscow—a garden city with a field for sports, a lake for swimming, pergolas for rest and outdoor work. Besides individual studios there are studios for working on monumental statues and canvases; ateliers for plotting out murals and frescoes; shops for textile designers, for makers of emblems and banners. There are hundreds of art and handicraft artels through which apprentices may rise up to become masters in lacquer, enamel, filigree, ivory. All kinds of facilities for all sorts of artists. Assured of a small income, enough at least to free them from the acute material worries of life, they may go ahead and develop whatever talents they possess.

Teachers, Professors, and Scientists

In sharp contrast to the privileged lot of the artist has been that of the teacher. Eloquently Lenin demanded that "the people's teacher be placed upon such a level as he never attained and never could attain in a bourgeois society. Undeviatingly and persistently we must work for his spiritual uplifting and on his general training for his truly lofty vocation." So far as material welfare is concerned that long remained but the expression of a pious hope. During the early years of the Revolution the teachers not only suffered mentally in their efforts to adapt themselves to the cataclysmic changes in education, but actual physical privations. Now the Soviets are proceeding systematically toward the goal set by Lenin. But they still have a long way to go.

Salaries range from 150 to 700 rubles a month, depending upon qualifications, length of service, kind of school, and its locality. Rates are higher for teachers of problem children or the blind, and for those serving in isolated settlements or the Far East. Usually living quarters are rent free, which, with sick and pension benefits and such perquisites as books post free in the villages, means an addition of about forty per cent to one's basic salary. Besides annual vacations of at least two months, teachers are granted leaves of absence periodically with full pay in order to attend special training courses. Chief grounds for dismissal are striking or slapping a child, opposition to progressive ideas, or conclusive evidence of anti-Soviet activities. Cases are decided by a commission made up of representatives from the Teachers' Union, the school, and the local departments of education and labor. From its decision the ousted teacher may appeal to the courts, and, if reinstated, receive payment for lost time. But this question of losing one's job or not finding one is largely academic in a country where a fourth of the people are in schools of one kind or other. Counting all teachers from crèches and kindergartens up to libraries and universities, the number of pedagogues is approximately a million and the aim is to add a half million more.

The monthly salaries of *professors* in institutes and academies runs from 500 to 1,000 rubles which makes a fair income, especially when they hold two or more positions as many do. Even in the nightmare years of civil war and famine, the *scientists* were singled out for special care and attention. At Lenin's behest, they were given extra rations of food, and, out of the meager resources of the struggling State, all means possible to carry on their work. "The Russians seem to regard a scientist as a sort of superman," says Professor Walter B. Cannon of Harvard University. "It is not merely a question of courtesy, but of respect and admiration that is perfectly startling to a humble professor." Workers delight in electing eminent geologists, physicists, and botanists to honorary membership in their societies. Distinguished scientists are recognized by the granting of generous awards, decorations, and premiums. And not infrequently an eminent academician wakes up on his birthday to read in the press telegrams of congratulations and announcements that a scholarship or even an institute or street has been named after him.

Doctors, Dentists, Health Officers

Like the teachers, all through life they get their income directly from the State—stipends while in training, fixed regular salaries when practicing, and pensions on retiring. Aiming at a tenfold growth in the medical personnel the six main pre-War medical schools have been enlarged and increased to fifty, most of which are attached to hospitals. Besides general practitioners, surgeons, and dentists, in keeping with the emphasis on prevention of disease, much attention is paid to the training of epidemiologists, sanitary inspectors, dietitians. On finishing the five-year course, the graduates, over half of whom are women, are usually required to spend their first five years in rural districts where there is still a great dearth of doctors.

In the towns and cities most all are members of the staff of hospitals, polyclinics, and dispensaries. Some are eye or ear specialists, gynecologists, hydro- and electro-therapists, psychiatrists. Others receive the daily run of patients usually limited to a norm of six per hour. Still others are visiting physicians called by telephone or messenger to attend cases in homes and victims of accident, responding sometimes, according to complaints in the press, none too promptly. Hours are limited to six per day which is reduced to four for workers in X-ray and radium. One day in five they enjoy complete cessation from duties. Salaries range from 300 to 800 rubles a month, depending upon the position one holds and the community in which he is located. *Assistants, midwives, nurses,* and *pharmacists* receive 150-350 rubles a month. From 20 to 50 per cent is added to these rates for those serving in hazardous posts, insane asylums, the Far East, and the Arctic. In order to refresh their knowledge, all doctors are required every third year to re-enter the schools for three to six months of post-graduate study, the expenses of those from rural and remote regions being borne by the State.

What about private patients? Most physicians have ample time on their off days and off hours to carry on a private practice and some ten per cent of them do so. But it is difficult to compete with the excellent equipment and the almost gratuitous services of State institutions constantly being improved and expanded. Medicine, partly socialized in other countries, in the Soviet Union has been logically pushed in all its branches to complete socialization and with it is bound up the weal and woe of the physician. One advantage it gives him is release from the distractions of running an office, collecting bills, winning the good graces of the wealthy. A young doctor does not spend years working up a paying practice, anxiously sitting in his waiting-room waiting for patients. From the start he has them in abundance, so many that sometimes he cannot give each individual the full personal attention he might desire. That is one drawback. Another is that unless he is another Metchnikov, he must renounce all hopes to those glittering rewards of enormous fees that come to specialists in other countries.

On the other hand the Soviet medical man is assured for life of a steady income and one that grows larger year by year. He is assured too of every opportunity to improve his skill and knowledge in the hundreds of research institutes, laboratories, and seminars open to all. Other compensations are his, less tangible but not less real. With the monetary motive eliminated from his relations with patients, altogether regardless of fees, he can give each one his best services. That enhances both his professional self-respect and the respect in which he is held by the public. As a social servant, working primarily not for his private gain but for the common good, upon him converges the esteem and gratitude of State and people. They have good reasons for being grateful. In a single decade the cholera and typhus plagues that ravaged old Russia have been practically eliminated; most of the soothsayers with their malodorous medicines, spells, and incantations have been driven from the villages; the incidence of tuberculosis, trachoma, and venereal diseases greatly reduced; the infant mortality rate cut in half; the general health and stamina of the whole population visibly raised. Anyone may well take pride in belonging to a corps with these achievements to its credit. To the new socially minded generation of doctors particularly it is a source of satisfaction.

Lawyers, Merchants, Bankers, Chiefs

The status of government officials from chiefs of local bureaus to the heads of Commissariats is similar to those holding corresponding posts in other countries. Most of the higher offices are held by members of the Communist Party, whose tests, prior to and after admission, may be regarded as the equivalent of civil service examinations, only more searching and severe. The salaries of Labor Union functionaries are about the same as those of highly skilled machinists and Stakhanovites.

On passing the prescribed examinations, *lawyers* are admitted to the Bar, the College of Defenders. Fees are collected from litigants commensurate with their incomes, which do not go directly to the attorney who handles the case but to the so-called "Collective" or association to which he belongs. This in turn pays him a fixed salary running up to a thousand rubles a month or more depending on length of service and ability. Many attorneys are attached to Labor Unions, newspapers, and other institutions which render legal advice to citizens free of charge. There are still lawyers carrying on private practice. *Judges* of the People's Courts are elected directly by the people while members of the higher courts are appointed by the Supreme Councils of the Union, republics, regions, or provinces.

Under the Soviets all persons engaged in trade, commerce, and finance are salaried employees. In that respect their position is not so different from what it is coming to be in other countries as individual enterprise increasingly gives way to collective. The individual shopkeeper is being transformed into a manager of a chain-store or a clerk in a big emporium; the private banker into a functionary in some branch or local unit of a banking system. Instead of owning their means of livelihood the middle classes are becoming dependent on some corporation in which they are hired men. In the Soviet Union this natural evolution towards a collectivist order has been completed. Like the industries, all stores, banks, hotels, restaurants belong to the State, the Cooperatives, or Unions. The men who run them draw monthly salaries ranging from a few hundred rubles in minor posts to thousands for the non-Communist specialist in finance and trade. In some cases these incomes are augmented by bonuses, awards, premiums. In essence the status of these red bankers, merchants, accountants, and inspectors is analogous to those working for big concerns abroad. The one big difference lies in the matter of ownership. In capitalist countries it is vested largely in a small group of stockholders. In the Soviet Union it is vested in the community, with all surpluses redounding to the benefit of all.

IV. Foreign Relations

80. What is the Third Communist International— the Comintern?

It is the Home Office or Central Bureau for the Communist Parties of the world. These parties were not created by fiat of Moscow, but spontaneously came into being in each country after the Great War. They were formed by radical workers, intellectuals, and left-wing Socialists who felt the time had come for a new political lineup. Thus in nearly every country arose a militant Marxist party called Communist, altogether sixty-five of them. There are big parties like the Czechoslovakian and small ones like the British. There are legal parties like the French with seventy-two members in the Chamber of Deputies; "Underground" ones like the German with thousands of its members in concentration camps. One party is already in power, the Russian. Another is fighting for it with machine guns and bayonets, the Chinese. Thus they differ greatly in size and status, in problems they face and tactics they employ. But they all pursue a common aim, the establishment of the new order of Socialism in place of the old order of Capitalism.

They all felt the need of a common meeting-ground—a center for discussion, mutual counsel, and aid. This is the purpose of the Comintern, magniloquently called "The General Staff of the World Revolution." The supreme body is the World-Congress composing about 500 delegates from all over the globe. In the long intervals between sessions authority is vested in an Executive Committee of 46 members. Into its headquarters in Moscow pours a stream of reports and statistics on trade, wages, strikes, lockouts, elections. From these it gauges the rise or fall of the revolutionary tide—the condition and prospect of the parties. It coordinates their activities, gives directives, hears complaints, acts as critic, mentor, and guide. It enforces a strict discipline and may expel individuals, groups, and even whole parties presuming to violate it. From its decisions appeals may be taken to the congress. Work is carried on through various Commissions on Women, Nationalities, Agriculture.

Where does the Comintern get its funds? About ten per cent from the sale of publications and donations. The rest from dues paid in by the 65 component parties, each contributing according to its size, with the weaker ones exempted. The last budget shows collections from 3,148,000 members with total receipts of about one million dollars. About half went for office and routine expenses, the rest to the subsidy of party papers and publications and the upkeep of training-schools.

Why Called the Third International?

It was the third time workers have organized themselves on a world-wide scale. The *First International* was founded in London in 1864. To its opening meeting came British and French workers, Italian exiles drilling to fight for Mazzini, Poles eager to protest the Tsar's bloody repressions, and a German group headed by a certain scholar, Dr. Karl Marx. He summoned the workers to revolutionize the whole social order; drafted the constitution that opens with the ringing words, "The emancipation of the workers must be achieved by the workers themselves;" wrote the letter hailing Abraham Lincoln as the great liberator. The response of Lincoln brought publicity to the First International, which, although it did not accept all the theses of the revolutionary "Communist Manifesto" written by Marx and Engels, played an important rôle in creating a sense of solidarity among the rising working classes of the different countries, and in leading them in their struggles. It backed the English trade unionists in their efforts to stop the importation of strike breakers; advocated state ownership of mines, land, and transport; declared for a general strike against war. Disheartened by the collapse of the Paris Commune in 1871 and disrupted by the bitter Socialist-Anarchist debates between Marx and Bakunin, it withdrew to New York and flickered out in 1876.

The *Second International* was founded in 1889 and still exists with headquarters at Brussels. It is a loose organization of parties like the reformist Labour Party of England, the Socialists of France and America. Their ultimate aim is the same as the Communists', the abolition of capitalism. They believe that this can be done by winning over the majority of electors to the Socialist program. They often collaborate with bourgeois parties and have held the premiership in England, Germany, Belgium, Sweden. At the same time, by transcending national frontiers and creating the sense of solidarity between the workers of the world, they hoped to prevent war. That hope crashed in 1914 when the leaders in France and Germany rallied to support their governments. Lenin denounced them as traitors to Socialism, for leading the workers into the trenches to kill one another instead of rousing them to a mass-strike for peace. He pronounced the Second International dead. With Swiss and Italian Socialists, he helped organize the conferences at Kienthal and Zimmerwald where he called for no compromise or opportunism. With others like-minded he formed the so-called Zimmerwald Left under the slogans, "Transform the imperialist war into civil war," and "Through the class-struggle to the conquest of power."

This group may be regarded as the beginning of the *Third Communist International*. It was not formally established until March 2-6, 1919, when the first of its seven world-Congresses assembled in Moscow. Paying tribute to the work of its predecessors in bringing the concept of the Socialist revolution to the masses, it set forth a new technique and strategy. These were in effect the methods that led to triumph in Russia, formulated into a militant program of action, an "International of Deeds." Affiliated with it are a number of auxiliary bodies: The International League of Communist Youth; The International Labor Defense, which aids revolutionists in court and prison and their families; The Red Trade Union International which once set up its own unions in opposition to the old line unions but is now cooperating and merging with them.

Aims and Tenets of the Comintern

In its own words, as set forth in its program, "it aims to replace world Capitalism by world Communism, thus abolishing the private ownership of the means of production and with it the selfish lust for profits, exploitation of man by man, all inequalities based on sex, religion, and nationality; devastating crises and still more devastating wars." Historically, this is inevitable because "Capitalism is planless, anarchic, and disintegrating, an intolerable hindrance to mankind, threatening to degrade and destroy it. In its last stages, Imperialism, the rival powers racing for markets and raw materials impose their yoke upon backward races and colonies by methods of blood, iron, and starvation. At one pole it creates a handful of magnates and parasites who live by clipping coupons, at the other a gigantic mass of exploited and discontented proletarians."

Thus "Capitalism musters the army of its own grave-diggers." But they must be rightly led. "Hence the necessity in every country of a compact Communist Party consisting of the most active and courageous members of the working-class, closely linked up with the masses." It must lead them "to the conquest of power. But this does not mean peacefully capturing the ready-made bourgeois state machinery by means of a majority." The Comintern vehemently assails the Second International for misleading the people into thinking this possible. Faced with extinction the bourgeoisie will not abide by the rules of its own parliamentary game. "To safeguard its property and domination it will resort to every means of violence." Hence "Fascism, a terroristic dictatorship by big capital, whose principal aim is to destroy the labor vanguard." This in turn compels the workers to use force. But it must not take the form of terroristic acts against individuals, or untimely futile uprisings. While waiting for a revolutionary situation to ripen they must go on organizing, agitating, "defending their fatherland, the U.S.S.R." Then, seizing a propitious moment like war, when a country is in a state of collapse as was the case in Russia in 1917, they are to move forward in armed insurrection, "replacing the dictatorship of capitalists with a dictatorship of the proletariat—a transitional form of government that ends in the stateless, classless society of Communism."

Said Stalin to H. G. Wells: "You are wrong if you think Communists are enamoured of violence. They do not in the least idealize methods of violence. They would be very pleased to drop them if the ruling-class agreed to give way to the working-class. But they do not want to be taken by surprise. They cannot count on the old world peacefully departing from the stage. History teaches that up to now not a single class has voluntarily made way for another class. They see the old order violently defending itself, and that is why the Communists say to the working-class: Answer violence with violence. Do all you can to prevent the old dying order from crushing you."

Questions of War and Propaganda

The Comintern wants the Social Revolution. It believes that its coming will be accelerated by an imperialist war piling more misery upon the masses and ultimately driving them to revolt. Out of it will emerge a whole galaxy of Communist states. Yet paradoxically the Communists are doing everything they can to prevent war—because of the sufferings it would inflict on the masses and the difficulties of building a new civilization on its ruins. In the first place they furiously agitate against the war-makers, unmasking the intrigues of diplomats, the plots of the armament rings. In the second place they serve notice on governments that the moment they start a war of aggression they will do all they can to overthrow them. They will incite the workers to strike, to sabotage, to turn their guns against the generals. This threat acts as a healthy deterrent on rulers and statesmen inclined to bellicosity. They may be less ready to declare a war that may bring their own downfall or death-warrant. However the Communists are not pacifists and may well support a defensive war of a democratic country against Fascist aggression or a war for the liberation of oppressed nationalities. Incidentally if the Comintern in any wise promotes the idea and spirit of revolution amongst the masses, to that extent it is a factor for peace between nations. This brings up the moot question of propaganda. What does it do?

"Propaganda doesn't do anything," said Stalin to Walter Duranty. "Constitutions and systems are changed by natural causes, not by talk or books. In the old days the Tsars blamed the French or German Socialists for importing Socialism into Russia, forgetting that the conditions of life and not propaganda determine the course of events. Now I suppose they are making the same mistake in the United States when they say we are re-exporting Socialism to Europe." Stalin re-iterated this in his 1936 interview with Roy Howard. "Each country, if it so desires, will make its own revolution. If no such desire exists, no revolution will occur. Exported revolution is nonsense." The same viewpoint was expressed by Senator Cutting, "Revolutions cannot be imported. They grow. If revolution should ever come to this country of ours it will be because of our own failure to meet our own prob-lems. It will have no relation whatever to foreign propaganda." Again and more specifically in the words of Senator Borah, "We have 10 million men and women unemployed, seeking something to do. Mass production continues to pile up goods in the sight of those whose purchasing power is daily diminishing. What has Communism to do with that? It is these conditions that are disturbing our peace, not Russian propaganda." On the other hand there are still those who look upon Communism as a contagious disease, like smallpox or typhus, carried into other countries by outside agents and infecting them with its bacilli. And they regard the Soviet government as its bounden ally and accomplice.

Relations Between Soviet Government and Comintern

Moscow maintains that the two organizations are entirely distinct and independent. Its enemies deride this as a legal fiction. Aiming to hold the Soviets to account for the acts and utterances of the Comin-tern they insist that the two bodies are organically related. Following are the four contentions on which this is based and the rejoinders that are offered:

1. *The Soviet Government harbors the Comintern and refuses to expel it from Moscow.* The rejoinder to this is that the United States once harbored for a time the First International. England likewise harbored the Second (Socialist) International when it was in bad odor, refusing to expel it from London. Furthermore it ill behooves govern-ments to ask the Soviet Union to expel the Comintern when they permit their own Communist Parties to function. As America of yore, so the Soviet Union today offers a refuge to revolutionists of all lands

and of all colors. According to Article 129 of the new Constitution, "The U.S.S.R. grants the right of asylum to foreign citizens persecuted for defending the interests of the toilers or for their scientific activity or for their struggle for national liberation." While welcoming Syndicalists, Anarchists, Socialists, it certainly will not refuse to give asylum to Communists and their headquarters, the Comintern. There are excellent reasons for transferring it to some other capital, but, since none of them want it, it remains in Moscow. But it is absurd to state that because it exists in the same city with the Soviet government they are therefore indissolubly connected. The Italian government and the Vatican, which unites the Catholic churches in the 65 countries of the world, are both centered in Rome. They have similar ideas about property, ethics, and marriage and at times work together in harmony. But no one argues that therefore the two bodies are coterminous and identical. Certainly not on the mere grounds that their buildings are in close proximity.

2. *It is asserted that the Soviet Government subsidizes the Comintern.* The reply is that not a single copeck goes to the Comintern. It doesn't even give money to its own Communist Party which is in control. The income of the Comintern is derived solely from its 65 component parties, and is comparatively trifling—about one million dollars a year.

3. *It is asserted that the two bodies have an "interlocking directorate."* Leaders occupying positions in the Soviet Government like Stalin and Zhdanov are also officials of the Comintern. The rejoinder is that the Belgian premier, Vandervelde, and the English prime minister, MacDonald, were high officials in the Second International, but no one thought of holding Belgium or England responsible for its activities. Why, then, should the Soviet Union be charged with the activities of the Third International?

4. *It is asserted that the two bodies pursue the same aims and policies.* The reply is that the Soviet government is concerned exclusively with the internal affairs of its own country and does not interfere with others. Hence the functions and activities of the two bodies are quite different and at times diametrically opposite. The Comintern furiously denounced the Kellogg Pact; the Soviet Union was the first state in the world to ratify it. The Comintern rages against all monarchs and potentates; the Soviet Government gave to King Amanullah a grandiose

reception. The Comintern carries on relentless warfare against the Fascist regimes, assailing Hitler and Mussolini as "butchers" and "sadists"; the Soviet Government, on the contrary, maintains diplomatic relations with them, and officially takes no notice of the persecution of foreign revolutionists.

On these four points a bitter debate has been waged for a decade. It still flares up occasionally as it did in 1935 in the interchange of notes, after the Seventh Congress, between the United States and the Soviet Government. Washington maintained that the non-propaganda pledge of the Litvinov agreement had been violated. Moscow, by a sharp refusal to accept the protest, again put itself on record as taking no responsibility for the Comintern. But rarely now do foreign statesmen attempt to bait the Soviets with the Comintern's activities. One reason for this is the feeling that it has been relegated into the background, that its fires and fangs have been drawn, that "it has degenerated into a mere bureau for the defense of the Soviet Union." "It is in a state of total eclipse," says Florinsky. The followers of Trotzky would create in place of it a Fourth International—"one that is really revolutionary."

Of all meetings of the Comintern the Seventh Congress was by far the most moderate and conciliatory. It gave to each of the 65 Communist Parties greater freedom and autonomy in the conduct of its affairs. It advocated a "united front" with all liberal movements in the struggle against Fascism. It even went so far as to advise the workers in any country to support their ruling class in a war waged for independence from imperial exploitation or in defense of the Soviet Union. However, George Dimitrov, hero of the Reichstag fire trial and now head of the Comintern, resolutely asserted that cooperation on certain issues means no abandonment of fundamental beliefs. Closing the congress, he said, "Comrades, war is coming. It will smash Europe to pieces, and you must be ready to pick up those pieces." Such fiery manifestoes, critics maintain, are for home consumption—full of sound and fury, signifying nothing. But there are those to whom the Comintern is still a menace and nightmare; they still attribute to it some occult power to conjure up insurrection by fiat of Moscow. They still charge that through it the Soviet Union is striving to overthrow other governments.

81. Does the Soviet Union Seek to Overthrow Other Governments?

At one time it did. That was when other governments by armies, battleships, and blockade were trying to overthrow it. It fought back with every weapon at its command. It rained pamphlets upon the German troops, calling them to dethrone the Kaiser. It backed the short-lived Soviet republics of Hungary and Bavaria. It turned the defensive war against Poland into an offensive and drove its armies up to the gates of Warsaw. It radioed its "To All!" appeals to workers abroad to stop the shipment of war munitions against the Soviets. It used the Comintern and every available agency to rouse the masses against their rulers. The contest ended in a stalemate. In the words of Lenin, "The Allies did not succeed in crushing us and we did not succeed in overthrowing them."

A way had to be found for capitalist and socialist states to live together on the same planet. One constant source of friction was the Comintern which continued to send forth its fiery proclamations. "Suppress it," said the Allies to the Soviet Government. "Drive it off your soil and we shall recognize you." The Soviets replied by disclaiming any responsibility whatever for the acts of the Comintern: "The Soviet Government is one thing; the Comintern quite another." On this distinction the Soviets insisted and won out. The Comintern continues to remain in Moscow. The Soviets are recognized by all the great powers.

On its part the Soviet Government solemnly binds itself not to engage in propaganda against other states. It gives assurance that its ambassadors, consuls, and trade agents will not abuse their diplomatic privileges and immunities. It enjoins them to give no aid to the Communists of the countries to which they are assigned, to have no connection or dealings with them. It pledges itself not to intervene in any way in case of revolution or counter-revolution in another country and insists on the feasibility of the "peaceful coexistence and collaboration of two different social-economic systems."

These guarantees do not mean that the Russian Communists have lost faith in World Revolution. They hold that Socialism alone can solve the problems of war, unemployment, strife between races and classes. They look forward to the ultimate establishment of a World Union of Socialist Republics. As in its youth the United States rejoiced to see other nations go Republican, so the Soviet Union would rejoice to see other nations go Soviet. It believes that ultimately all of them will do so. But it is making no overt or covert acts to help them. Its energies are concentrated on building Socialism in its own domains, hoping it will serve as an example to others. Obviously this will not be furthered by provoking other governments to ill-will and resentment. These things it seeks to avoid by "a policy of cultivating peace and friendly trading relations with all nations." (Stalin)

82. Why do the Soviets Make Peace the Cornerstone of Their Foreign Policy?

They rose to power with the slogan "Peace to the World" written on their banners. On the morning after the Revolution, November 8, 1917, they issued the celebrated decree calling on "all warring peoples to conclude a just and democratic peace." Since then in over a hundred notes, protests, and appeals the Soviet Union has waged a resolute struggle for peace. It was first to ratify the Kellogg Pact outlawing war as an instrument of national policy. It fought for the abolition of all armed forces at Geneva, and, when its plan was rejected, stood ready to discuss any scheme for reduction. It joined the League of Nations, in complete reversal of its former attitude, because now it was "anti-war" and "pro-peace." It has signed Treaties of Friendship, Neutrality, and Non-Aggression with a score of nations. It has kept its temper in the face of a series of provocative acts that might rightly be deemed insults to its honor—the British raid on Arcos, the assassination of its envoys in Lausanne and Warsaw, the arrests and killings of its railway officials in the Far East, the provocative assaults of Hitler and his fellow Nazis. By every means it has sought to avoid a conflict, as if actuated by the idea that there never was a good war or a bad peace. Three good reasons for this:

The Soviets want peace because their peoples have suffered so much from war. In the Great War 2,700,000 Russians were killed, 5,000,000 wounded. Then for three years more the fighting went on all over the land. The ravages of it are still evident in blown-up bridges, burned-down villages, the scars on millions of bodies of survivors. No people feel more profoundly the folly and criminality of war. No people so strip it of romance and glamour. Formidable as the Red Army may be, it does not glorify war. Posters proclaim it as the scourge of the human race, a threat to civilization. Cinemas depict the hunger, disease, and terror that follow in its wake. Museums exhibit its atrocities such as the "human glove," the hand immersed in boiling water until the whole skin comes off in one piece.

These horrors and privations the Soviet people want to escape. They want also to find an escape for their fellow-toilers in other lands, those who will be driven first into the bloody shambles. Their strong feeling of solidarity and internationalism impels them to that. That is why they acclaim with enthusiasm every speech and move for peace throughout the world. Behind it is the will of 175 million people. Reflecting their deepest desires and yearnings it rallies the support of even those otherwise hostile or indifferent to the Soviets. Unfortunately, humane and pacific sentiments are not enough to prevent war. They can be swept aside and even converted into furious national passions, if the rulers of the state or those who control them deem it to their interests to make war. Much more significant than this loathing of war is that there are no economic motives impelling the Soviets to war.

The Soviets want peace because they need none of the things that may be gotten by war. They do not need more territory. With half of Europe and half of Asia they already have one-sixth of all there is in the world, room enough for their population for generations to come even though it increases at its present rate of 10,000 a day. More raw materials? The Soviets already have untold quantities of oil, coal, iron, gold—ample supplies for its industries for decades, centuries to come. Investments and concessions in other lands? These are practically non-existent because the Soviets have no private capitalists with surplus monies to export, they have abundant uses for all the capital they can raise at home, and abroad they have no extra-territorial privileges to be safeguarded by marines. Outside markets for their products? They already have an enormous domestic demand, and a social-economic system that makes it ever expanding. Consumption can always keep pace with production for as fast as the wares are made the money goes into the hands of the people for purchasing them. That gives the Soviet Union an insatiable market at home absorbing goods like a sponge. Why then should it set out to acquire abroad what it already has in abundance? Besides the absence of any of these economic motives propelling a nation into war, there is one tremendous reason for avoiding it.

The Soviets want peace in order to go on with the colossal tasks of construction. Into the building of Socialism are going all their resources and energies. To divert them suddenly into channels of destruction would be a set-back. Even the threat of conflict with Japan necessitating the despatch of troops, munitions, and food to that region threw the first Five-Year Plan out of gear. What havoc would be wrought by actual war! That is why the Soviets are so anxious to avoid it. That is why peace is as much an obsession as the Five-Year Plan. The one is dependent on the other. They must have peace to go on building their blast-furnaces, power-plants, airlines, schools, roads, theatres, hospitals.

"But when all the building is finished," interject the alarmists, "what then?" Having become a giant will not the Soviets act like a giant? To them the Soviet policy of peace is merely temporary and tactical. It is NEP on the international field—a breathing-spell for gathering strength in order later to resume the Communist offensive. Then Litvinov and his diplomats will be retired in favor of Voroshilov and his warriors. Then the "Red Hordes" will come sweeping over the frontiers bringing carnage and revolution to Europe. Calling this a phantasy, "an atavistic bogey of Attila, Tamerlane, or the Turks," Duranty points out how utterly alien it is to every idea and principle of the Soviets. Much as they would like to see Socialist revolutions in other lands, they know that they cannot be superimposed by an outside force but must rise organically out of the people themselves.

Stalin said to Roy Howard, "If you think that the people of the Soviet Union have any desire themselves, and moreover, by force, to alter the face of surrounding states you are badly mistaken. Naturally they desire that the face of surrounding states should change but this is the business of those states themselves." As often said, "Revolutions cannot be carried abroad in suit-cases." Much less do the Soviets believe they can be carried on the bayonets of the Red Army. In evidence thereof are their reiterated offers to destroy those bayonets, to scrap all tanks, bombing-planes, and battleships.

Peace by Disarmament

The first proposal of the Soviets to disarm was made when their envoys first appeared on the international arena—at Genoa in 1922. Others followed. Nevertheless it was a thunderbolt to the world when four years later Litvinov presented to Geneva his plan for "immediate, complete, and general disarmament." It demanded "the dissolution of all land, sea, and air forces," destruction of all cannons, fortresses, warships; abolition of military service, budgets, and war ministries; "prohibition of patents on all kinds of weapons, removing the incentive to their invention," and so on to the last of the fourteen points, which makes any advocating or preparing for war "a grave crime against the state." Anticipating that this would be denounced as Bolshevik propaganda, Litvinov said, "It is propaganda. Propaganda for peace. And where is there a better place for it than at a disarmament conference?"

In essence the Soviet idea was that "the only way to disarm is to disarm." It was to be done at once—in a year. If that were impossible, then by gradual steps over a period of four years. It was coldly received, ruled out as "too simple," and rejected. A later project for partial but still drastic arms reduction followed, to be likewise met with rebuff. At Geneva in 1935 Litvinov said, "To many it may seem paradoxical that I am again raising the question of total disarmament when the most modest attempts at partial reduction have failed. My answer is that I always contested the thesis that total disarmament is Utopian while partial disarmament is easily realizable. On the contrary the utmost difficulty is presented by partial and the least difficulty by total disarmament, given the will to do it. If what has seemed feasible has proved Utopian, let us try whether what seemed Utopian will not prove feasible." Unable for the time being to obtain this best, he resorted to the second best. He made two proposals to promote peace. He recommended turning the dying Disarmament Conference into a Permanent Peace Conference where issues affecting the security of all could be decided, and advocated the conclusion of non-aggression and mutual assistance pacts among the nations.

Peace by Pacts and Treaties

To the Soviets the existing compacts seemed largely "dead documents without any content." They were too vague, indefinite, and "had no teeth in them." For many years now the Soviet Union has been forging its own "chain of peace." First came the Non-Aggression Pact, a bilateral agreement binding each party not to enter into any coalition or boycott against the other, to refrain from all acts of hostility—military, political, financial—over a period of time, usually five years. The Mutual Assistance Treaty went much farther and pledged actual aid and assistance in case of an attack by an aggressor. But what constitutes an act of aggression? This was made clear by the Litvinov Declaration of 1935. Section one defines the aggressor as that state which first invades, bombards, or blockades the coast of another country, with or without a declaration of war.

More significant and original is Section two: "No consideration whatever of a political, strategic, or economic nature"—such as the desire to exploit natural riches, to protect investments—"can be accepted as justifying aggression." To stop up every loophole for evasion it stipulates that there can be no pretext for an attack on any of the following grounds: The backwardness of a given country; alleged mal-administration; possible danger to life or property of foreign residents; revolutionary or counter-revolutionary movements, civil war, disorders, or strikes; rupture of diplomatic or economic relations; repudiation of debts; limitation of immigration; infringement of diplomatic privileges; and so on, through fifteen points to the last in the list, "frontier incidents." "These basic principles," said Litvinov, guaranteeing the inviolability of frontiers and the non-interference of any state in the affairs of another, "would be a Charter of the Freedom of Nations." With minor alterations they were adopted by the Security Committee of the Conference.

These pacts of mutual assistance are a logical outgrowth of the League itself under whose Covenant every nation is pledged to respect the sovereignty and territorial integrity of every other nation. But what actually happens if an aggressor violates the borders of a neighbor? Has the League an army to punish the offender, or protect the weak? By a treaty of mutual assistance in which two or more powers agree to rush military and financial aid to one another in case of attack by an aggressor, nations do promptly for one another what the League would do were it in command of an armed force. It gives the spirit of the Covenant instant military expression by relying on the self-interest of those nations most nearly involved in a conflict. Any reorganization of the League of Nations to make it more precise and effective in guaranteeing the security and equality of nations, must be along these lines, thinks Litvinov.

Locarno was the first pact of mutual assistance. It was an effort on the part of France, Germany, Belgium, England, and Italy to make membership in the League mean something in a military sense. The agreements which the Soviets have ratified with France, Czechoslovakia, and Outer Mongolia are only an extension of this principle, but the principle has not been applied widely enough as yet. All regions should be protected by interlocking pacts to be adequately insured against war. "Peace is indivisible," Litvinov has said repeatedly in advocating this new security system to supplement and strengthen the League. He might just as well have said, "War is indivisible." For it is hardly probable any conflict can be localized. All keep the peace, or else all go to war.

83. What Are the Soviets' Relations with the 65 Countries of the World?

Most of them have accorded full *de jure* recognition. The red hammer-and-sickle flag of the Soviet Union flies in all the great capitals. In the League of Nations' Council it is one of the four major powers now occupying permanent seats. In all the world conferences, from Red Cross to Opium and Epidemics, it speaks in the name of 175,000,000 people. It stands as a great power with a balanced budget, a huge air fleet, and 1,500,000 men under arms.

This present status sharply contrasts with that of fifteen years ago. Then it was outside the pale, an Ishmaelite and an outlaw among the nations. Then its leaders were "hirelings of the Kaiser," "crime-mad lunatics intent upon the destruction of civilization," "nationalizers of women." Then the great powers combined to crush the new Soviet republic in Russia, as in 1789 they had the new democratic republic France. They closed in with a million-bayoneted ring of steel seeking to strangle it in its infancy. They placed an embargo upon ships entering Soviet ports, cut off communication by post, telegraph, and radio.

Through war, blockade, and boycott the Allies sought these objectives: To replace the Soviets with a government more amenable to their dictates; to re-establish the Eastern front by drawing Russia back into the war; to stop the publication of the secret treaties, unmasking the "war for democracy" as a war of imperialists; to eradicate the plague-spot of Bolshevism spreading its contagion through the world; to take advantage of the weakness of Russia in order to parcel it out into spheres of influence— "after killing the bear, to divide up the carcass." But intervention failed to achieve any of these aims.

Debts and Propaganda. Intervention also left unsolved these two major problems around which have centered stormy debates in negotiations for the resumption of normal relations. On the propaganda issue most governments have followed the 1925 declaration of Poland's Foreign Minister Skryznski, "I distinguish between the Comintern and the Soviet Government." But they are on the vigilant lookout for Soviet words or deeds that savor of propaganda. To these the Soviets themselves are little inclined. Intent on the stupendous task of reconstruction, their energies are devoted to carrying through the revolution at home, not in fomenting it in other lands.

Likewise through mutual gives and takes they are ready to come to terms on the question of debts. The Soviets still uphold the validity of the decrees annulling the Imperial loans and nationalizing the property of foreigners. They remind the bankers of Paris and London that as early as 1905 they were warned that, as their loans to the Tsar would be used to suppress the on-coming revolution, they would not be repaid. They point out that revolutionary France proclaiming "the sovereignty of peoples is not bound by the treaties of tyrants" also repudiated her national debt. They cite from the American Constitution that "any debt or obligation incurred in the aid of insurrection or rebellion against the United States shall be held illegal and void."

Nevertheless the Soviets stand ready to pay on condition that other nations recognize counter-claims for damages inflicted on Russia by their armies. Repeatedly the Soviets proposed to settle a part of the old pre-War debts by paying a higher than normal rate of interest on new loans, but these offers were never accepted. Many claims like those of the General Electric Company have been erased by direct negotiations. Without abandoning their principles the Soviets have been able to adjust their differences with other states and clear the ground for collaboration.

League of Nations. "We are not doctrinaires," said Litvinov. In foreign, as in domestic affairs, the Soviets pride themselves on pursuing a realistic policy—now firm, now flexible. "Chameleon-like" their enemies call it. As circumstances change they have not hesitated to change their attitude, or even to reverse it. For fifteen years they inveighed against the League of Nations as perpe-trators of the injustices of the Treaty of Versailles. They de-nounced it as "the league of capitalists against the nations," "a wasp's-nest of international intrigue," "an alliance of world bandits against the proletariat." Then, suddenly, in 1934 they came in as a full-fledged member. An immediate reason for this face-about was the withdrawal of Japan and Germany, the two nations most menacing to the peace of the world and to the Soviets. "The fact," said Stalin, "that bellicose nations with ag-gressive designs cannot stay in the League is one of the best proofs of its worth."

The League is now composed mainly of powers whose self-interests, for the present at any rate, are in the preservation of peace. That is precisely what the Soviet Union above all desires. It does not justify the Versailles treaty. It still condemns the exist-ing frontiers as iniquitous but it holds that attempts to rectify them by force instead of agreement would be a greater iniquity. Therefore in spite of "its colossal defects" it joined the League, although it might be "only the tiniest bump to hinder the drive toward war." The growing strength and prestige of the Soviet Union was the chief factor in bringing about its entrance into this commonalty of nations. Likewise in the establishment of normal relations with each separate country.

The Four Big European Powers

Although Great Britain was one of the prime movers in forming the coalition against the new Socialist State, it was first of the Allies to accord recognition. Relations between the two countries, however, for a decade were anything but harmonious. Always the British lion has been suspicious of the Russian bear. More so when the bear, turned Bolshevik, started up fresh apprehensions for the safety of the Empire. To the old fear of the Cossacks, riding down over the Khyber Pass into India, was added a greater fear of the effects of Communist ferment on the restless masses in the colonies, China, and at home. This was reflected in the fury and fulminations of the Tory "die-hards." "The Bolsheviks," gibed Balfour, "have found an excellent way for making the rich poor, but not for making the poor rich." "A junta of assassins and plunderers!" cried Churchill.

The vindictiveness of words was matched by deeds. In the general elections of 1924 they loosed the last-minute "Zinoviev letter," purporting to be instructions from Moscow on how to incite the British army and navy to mutiny. In 1927, incensed by activities in China and the money sent by Soviet Labor Unions to the striking British miners, they raided Arcos, the Soviet trading agency, and broke off diplomatic relations. In 1932, retaliating for the arrest of the six Metro-Vickers engineers, accused of sabotage, they placed an embargo on Russian imports.

Fortunately for the Soviets, England, as Disraeli remarked, is a country inhabited by two nations—the rich and the poor. So the Conservatives have not had it all their own way. While spokesmen of the owning-class pursued a policy of abuse and ultimatum, it was countered by a diametrically opposite one from the working-classes. In every crisis they have manifested a spirit of solidarity and conciliation. They fought against intervention through the powerful "Hands Off Russia" committee. They forced recognition of the Soviets, the resumption of trade and diplomatic relations each time they were severed. They hailed the Soviets' entry into the League of Nations as "the decisive factor in realization of its basic aims, the organization of peace." Peace, too, is what the Conservatives now ardently desire for the sake of the trade and safety of the British Empire. That is menaced most of all by the armaments and ambitions of Germany, Japan, and Italy. So, logically though reluctantly, there is a British orientation toward Moscow, evidenced in the granting of a government loan and in the negotiations for a Naval Treaty. Many leaders advocate still closer co-operation. Brailsford even conjures up the vision of a future federation consisting of Socialist Britain and Communist Russia extending from Land's End to Vladivostok, "assisting one another on the economic field as no other pair of powers could do, and, if no wisdom or patience or offer of arbitration can stave off war, again on land and sea they are complementary."

France's long enmity against the Bolsheviks rose in part from the "gigantic desertion" of the Russian armies, a blow to her security, and in part to Bolshevik repudiation of debts, the loss of her gilt-edged securities. She had loaned to the Tsar over a billion dollars, the savings of French peasants aiding in the suppression of Russian peasants. She had invested over 300 million dollars in Ukrainian mines, munition-plants, railways. Twice these claims were on the verge of settlement when the old hostility got the upper hand. It expressed itself in France's allowing White *émigrés* to train and drill on French soil, in attempts to wean Germany away from the Soviets, in her backing of Polish designs.

This anti-Soviet policy suddenly changed with the advent of the Nazis. Frightened by the specter of a Germany rapidly rearming itself, France sought a stronger counter-weight in the East than Poland. Could not the spirit of the old *entente cordiale* with Russia again be called into being? Following former Premier Herriot to Moscow, flew Cot the Minister of Aviation. He found the Soviets possessed of an excellent air fleet and factories for turning out ten planes a week. "Here," says Brailsford, "was an ally with all the moral qualifications for entry into the League of Nations. She can bomb with the best."

To smooth the way into the League France did everything possible.

Once within and bound by its covenant, the French Chamber of Deputies on March 6, 1936, ratified a pact of mutual assistance with the Soviets. Declaring it was a violation of the spirit of Locarno, Germany marched her troops into the Rhineland. "The pact was signed in the absence of Germany," protested Flandin, "with regret for her absence and in the hope of her eventual adherence." Later, France's ally, Czechoslovakia signed a similar pact which amounts to a defensive alliance.

The contracting parties pledge to respect existing frontiers, to refrain from fighting one another, and to render every assistance to the country invaded by an aggressor. This does not apply unless borders have actually been crossed by enemy forces, nor is France obliged to assist if the Soviets are attacked by Japan. Besides military advice and weapons, France is sending Soviet Russia technicians and engineers to strengthen the weakest spot in its economic-military system—transportation. They are paid for not by bonds, as in former times, but by shipments of Soviet metals and oil for the French fleet. Thanks to this and other factors, such as the interchange of artists and scientists, this once implacable foe of the Soviets is being transformed into a friend and ally.

With Germany also there has come about a complete reversal in Soviet relations. In this case, instead of a warming-up, there has been a cooling-down. At the end of the Great War the fact that both nations were treated as outcasts and pariahs drew them together. They startled the world by signing the Treaty of Rapallo. They carried on a lively trade with large German long-term credits. They presented a common front against most of the moves on the European chessboard.

Then came the rise of the Nazis to power. Although outraged by the ruthless repression of German Communists, the Soviets, observing their pledge not to meddle in internal affairs, did not protest. But they could not ignore the ominous declarations of the Nazi leaders: "The new Reich," said Hitler, "must march on the way once trod by the Teutonic Knights in order that the German sword may win sod for the German plow and daily bread for the nation." Not only did the Nazis specify how they would get their new domains but where. They intended to carve them out of the Soviet Union. "Let the Russians turn to the East," exclaimed Adviser Rosenberg, "there is no room for them in Europe," while Minister Hugenberg demanded of the London Economic Conference, "more room for the Germans." The Soviets' answer to all this was the proffer of a pact of mutual assistance, thus placing the Nazis on the horns of a dilemma. If they signed they must renounce their dreams of conquest and expansion. If they did not sign they could not complain of measures to counter their aggressiveness, nor of "hostile encirclement."

They did not sign and the belligerent attitude of the Nazis increased with alarming rapidity. At the Nuremberg conclave in the autumn of 1936, Hitler again startled the world by saying: "We are not in the fortunate position of the Bolshevik Jews. If we had the mineral wealth of the Urals and the grainfields of the Ukraine, then Germany would be swimming in plenty!" Jockeying for position, Berlin proposed to London and Paris a 25-year guarantee for peace in the West, but refused to make any such arrangements in the East. On the contrary, posing as the champion of civilization against Bolshevik chaos and barbarism it concocted the so-called anti-Communist Pact with Japan and invited other countries to join the crusade. But the pact is generally considered to be a military alliance of the chief Fascist powers directed against Russia.

One of these powers is Italy. From 1923 to 1936 the attitude of this first Fascist state toward the first Socialist state was correct and ever cordial. "I recognize the Soviets," Mussolini announced to his parliament in the fall of 1923. On these words Italy based her claim to be first of the Allies to accord recognition, though it was not done formally until February 7, 1924, five days after England. Among the motives driving Italy to this step was macaroni. The best sort is made from the gluten wheat of the Ukraine. Then there was the good silk woven from the cocoons of Central Asia, an artificial kind made from the cellulose of timber. Still more impelling was Italy's need for oil for its fleet, iron and coal for its factories. All are easily obtainable by the all-water route from the Black Sea ports. Thanks to these economic bonds and the fact that there were no ancient hates, no debts, nor territorial disputes, relations between Italy and the Soviets were close and almost friendly. This all changed when Mussolini began his invasion of Abyssinia. While reasserting at Geneva, "their high respect and ardent sympathy for the Italian people; their interest in strengthening existing political, economic and cultural relations," the Soviets at the same time strongly advocated and put into effect sanctions against Italy. Later they bitterly denounced military intervention in Spain which further incensed Mussolini and brought forth furious blasts of denunciation against the Red menace.

The Small States of Europe

Most of the lesser European nations follow the lead of the Great Powers of which they are satellites. In Soviet affairs Belgium and the Little Entente—Czechoslovakia, Rumania, and Yugoslavia—have usually taken their cue from France. Now fearful of Hitler's domination of Central Europe, the accord with Austria and the territorial ambitions of Hungary, Czechoslovakia and Rumania are reaching out to the Soviet Union as their natural protector or ally. That is the reason for Czechoslovakia's treaty of mutual assistance and its closer connection with Russia by means of the projected railway over the Carpathians to be built by Rumania.

Sweden broke the Allies' blockade against Soviet gold. Norway is grateful for rescues of its sailors by Russian trawlers in the Arctic seas, reciprocating the yeoman services rendered by the explorer Nansen to the Volga famine victims in 1921. Norwegian vessels are extensively engaged in carrying the ocean freight of the Soviet Union and in seal-hunting along its coasts. The Soviets in turn are allowed to develop the coal mines in the Norwegian island of Spitzbergen. When the Soviets have a surplus harvest, Holland likewise reaps a harvest of guldens by the transit of grain through its port at Rotterdam into Central Europe. But even after the Soviets' entrance into the League of Nations it stubbornly held off from recognition. So did Portugal and Switzerland. With the latter the Soviets have long been at loggerheads. Only after it agreed to compensate the family of Vorovsky, the Soviets' envoy who was assassinated at Lausanne, would they send their delegates to the League of Nations. When at last they came to enter it, the premier of the little country rose to a vitriolic assault on the Soviet giant as the enemy of God and civilization.

Relations with Spain have changed as the regime swung from right to left. In August, 1936, amid exploding bombs from rebel airplanes the first Soviet envoy opened the embassy in Madrid. As the civil war grew more intense, threatening to bring on a general European conflict, the Soviets and twenty-four other nations bound themselves to non-intervention in Spain. After protests against the flagrant violations of this pact by Italy, Germany, and Portugal, Moscow shipped supplies to the legitimate Spanish government as well as contributions of food and clothes and medicines from the Soviet workers to the beleaguered Loyalists.

There is nothing absolute or fixed in diplomacy. Small nations quickly alter their policy as they move into the orbits of the big ones. Those with long-range objectives change their methods of attaining them. Even the Vatican, not relinquishing its hope of bringing the millions of Orthodox Russians into the Catholic fold, has divided counsels. While the Italian Archbishop Signori, seeking a rapprochement with the Soviets, was clinking his wine-glass with Chicherin in Genoa, the intransigent American, Father Walsh, was crossing swords with the Bolsheviks in Moscow. In his 1936 Christmas message Pope Pius vehemently denounced the works of Bolshevism thereby giving moral aid to the Fascist forces. As none of the small states listed above, except Rumania, touch the Soviet frontiers, that in itself lessens the rôle they play. Of much more serious concern to Moscow are relations with its immediate neighbors.

The Six States on the Western Border

Barring the way to the rest of Europe are Rumania, Poland, and the four Baltic States. All six are carved, in whole or part, out of former Russian territory and four of them are not averse to more of it. The Fascists in Finland have laid claim to the adjacent land of Karelia, partly inhabited by her kinsmen. The Fascists of Estonia would like to enlarge her borders to include the ancient city of "Lord Novgorod." The chauvinists of Poland dream of a "Greater Poland from sea to sea," that is, from the Black Sea to the Baltic, adding more Ukrainians to the four million already restless under Polish rule. However, she has a non-aggression pact with the Soviets and is closely linked up with France by a renewal of the old alliance in the autumn of 1936 and by big loans. Rumania wants only to retain the fruitful vine-growing Bessarabia, seized by her armies in 1918. Her rights to this rich province the Soviets have never recognized. They marked it on their maps as their own. They clung to Queen Marie's two jewel chests, the gold and archives sent for safekeeping to Moscow during the Great War. But on entering the League, Litvinov gave Rumania assurance that his government would not raise the question of Bessarabia. This is usually interpreted as being tantamount to a surrender of the Soviets' claims to the country. In addition they sent back the archives and the jewels. Most friendly is Lithuania, grateful for the Soviets' refusal to recognize Polish seizure of its capital, Vilna.

It was these border states that formed the famous *cordon sanitaire* against the "Red Peril." Were they united today their combined forces would again be a serious threat to the Soviets. Such an alliance, Poland, with its deep-rooted antipathy toward old Russia, long and zealously sought to achieve. But in vain. Rivalry and suspicion of each other has been more powerful than the bogey of "Red Imperialism," the fear that Russia would try to bring them under its yoke again. This fear the Soviet Union has quieted by repeated assurances as to their independence, by the benefits of its transit trade, and a permanent policy of good will. If it has not converted all these neighbors into friends, it has at least pledged them to keep the peace by pacts of neutrality and non-aggression now signed by all of them.

In the Baltic States the agents of Hitler have been working hard to draw these countries into the Nazi orbit. But they are decidedly against being made to serve as a base for an assault by German armies on the Soviets and along with the Scandinavian countries seem to be moving toward closer relations with Moscow. This tendency was accelerated by the defeat of the reactionary Nationalists in the 1937 elections in Finland and the elevation to the presidency of Kyosti Kallio who is committed to rapprochement with the Soviets. In furtherance of the good "neighbor" policy there is an interchange of friendly visits between high officials of the Soviets and these border countries.

The Soviets and the Orient

To the people of Asia, the revolution in Russia was an earthquake shaking them out of age-old submission and lethargy. On the heels of the fall of the Tsar came the Bolsheviks' complete renunciation of his policies. They declared the old treaties "torn up and void," canceled all special privileges and concessions, "restored the properties ravenously seized by the Russian bourgeoisie."

From gendarme and exploiter of the peoples of the East, Russia was suddenly transformed into protector and champion of their lost liberties. Like wildfire the news swept from the Dardanelles to the Pacific, kindling nationalist hopes and ambitions. Freed from the fetters of one imperialist power why not from all of them? With the rally-cry "Asia for the Asiatics," 1,891 delegates from 37 nationalities assembled in Baku to swear on their uplifted swords and daggers a Holy War against the imperialists. That was in 1920. Since then, less dramatically, but not less powerfully, the Orient has felt the impact and influence of the Revolution. It is to be found everywhere—in the unveiling of Moslem women, in the legends of "The Great Lenin" recited by story-tellers in the bazaars, in the stubborn campaign of the Red Armies of China.

No other people are so fitted to deal with the brown and yellow races as the Russians. Over half their territory lies in Asia and to it they are bound by ties of tradition, religion, and the blood-stream. "I too am an Asiatic," said Stalin in welcoming Enver Pasha. The welcome of Moscow has been extended to thousands of students from the Orient, to its generals and savants, its kings and coolies. Absorbing the ideas of the Revolution and fired by its spirit, most of them have returned to their peoples as its apostles and missionaries. And, as the masses of the East listen to the doctrine of Communism, across the Soviet frontier they look at its deeds. They see their own kinsmen, often of the same Buddhist or Moslem faith, freed from the feudal yoke of the beys, the sheiks, and the khans. They see irrigation canals driving drought from the desert, electricity driving darkness from the villages. They see the vast spaces being threaded by highroads and railroads, and dotted with schools, crèches, and hospitals. They see

Communism as the bringer of freedom—not in the abstract intellectual formulas of the West that mean nothing to them, but in concrete tangible forms—freedom from exploitation by beys and khans, from epidemics of typhus and cholera, from hopeless poverty and back-breaking toil. The imperialists may rail against propaganda, the Soviets may renounce it, but it cannot be stopped. The stories of Soviet achievements, borne across the frontiers by every trader, shepherd, and newspaper, act like a ferment upon the already stirring masses of Asia, who constitute half the peoples of the world.

The Near East and China

Events in Russia had immediate repercussions in the Levant. Out of the ruins of the Ottoman Empire rose the new republic of Turkey under the leadership of Mustapha Kemal Ataturk. Declaring that "Turkey must cease to be a land of sheiks and dervishes," after the Soviet pattern he separated Church and State, outlawed polygamy, introduced the Latin alphabet, abolished the fez and the veil. To Moscow he appealed for support and got it. It sent him military advice and munitions to fight off the invasion of Greece. It backed up its famous Proclamation of December 7, 1917, "Constantinople (now Istanbul) must remain in the hands of the Mohammedans." It handed over Kars and other territory amounting in all to 7,780 square miles. It loans its money and engineers for the building of factories and in its own factories trains the Turks to run theirs. It sends its highest envoys and Commissars to celebrate anniversaries of the Turkish Republic. "Look hard at these Russians," said Kemal, introducing Voroshilov and his staff, to his own officers. "They may one day be your leaders in war." If war comes the Soviets are in an excellent strategic position thanks to the Dardanelles agreement which makes Turkey again master of the Straits. While other nations are strictly limited in the war tonnage they may send into the Black Sea, Soviet Russia may send her entire fleet through the Straits into the Mediterranean in peace time and during a defensive war. Thus it advances towards realizing the long-cherished dream of finding ice-free outlets into the world.

For the control of Iran (Persia) and Afghanistan, a tug-of-war went on for a century between the lion and the bear. To Britain they were indispensable as buffer states for the protection of India. To Russia they were steps in the drive toward a warm water port. While Britain entrenched herself in the oil-fields of Iran, the Tsar moved down from the North, building roads, docks, electric-stations, and loaning money secured by revenues from the customs, posts, and telegraph. The Revolution put a stop to the Russian advance. By one stroke of the Soviet pen all debts were annulled and all banks and concessions returned to the Persian people.

Having no properties to deed to the Afghan peoples, the Soviets, as a token of good will, handed over a slice of their territory. In a letter to the new reforming king, Amanullah, Lenin denounced Britain as "the most rapacious imperialist government on earth," and hailed him as the deliverer of all Moslems from their oppressors. After winning his fight for independence, Amanullah set out to modernize his country after the manner of Moscow. But he went too fast. Women's rights and schools for girls were an affront to the Moslem priests. Instigated by foreign agents the backward tribes rose in revolt and established a more conservative regime. However, with an airline linking Moscow with Kabul, the capital of Afghanistan, and its merchants enjoying the special trading privileges offered these countries of the Near and Middle East, relations are close and cordial.

Further along lies the Chinese province of Sinkiang too distant to be effectively ruled from Nanking. Stimulated by the building of the Turksib Railway close to its borders, trade has rapidly increased with the Soviet Union, all but superseding that carried by caravan over 2,000 miles from Chinese ports. In 1934 the faction favoring Moscow came to power and there are more Soviet consulates in Sinkiang than in England and the United States together. Nanking watches with apprehension lest this province proclaim its independence, as did Tannu-Tuva and Outer Mongolia. As large as the United States west of the Mississippi, these two People's Republics are inhabited by a million herdsmen, mostly descendants of those warriors who once terrorized Europe and conquered Asia for Kublai Khan. Later they were allies of the Manchu rulers of China. But they were never conquered by the Chinese, and, with the fall of the Manchus, in 1911 asserted their autonomy. In this separatist movement they turned north to Tsarist Russia for support and granted many concessions in return for aid and recognition.

During the Revolution, Red and White partisans as well as Chinese interventionists fought on their soil. At last the marauding bands of Whites were driven off by Moscow which aided in the building of schools, air lines, and a reorganized army; sent in a corps of veterinaries to stop the ravages of the dreadful plague that for centuries had decimated the cattle; and acquired a virtual monopoly of the trade in wool and hides. While signing with Outer Mongolia a treaty of mutual assistance, the Soviet Union assured China that it in no wise contemplated the annexation of it. What will happen if the Japanese, pushing west from their bases in Inner Mongolia, attempt to seize this vast territory so strategically important for the Soviets? To that question, put by Roy Howard to Stalin, the answer was, "We will fight."

Relations with China were established by the Sino-Soviet treaty of 1924. In that history-making document Moscow relinquished its share in the Boxer indemnity; restored all properties except its share in the Chinese Eastern Railway which it retained by request of the Chinese themselves; renounced all extra-territorial privileges like the right of Russians to be tried in their own courts instead of the Chinese. Thus the Soviet Union was the first great power to sign with China a treaty based on equality. It was also the first to send to China, in the person of Karakhan, a full-fledged ambassador, all other countries being represented by diplomats of a lower rating.

The arrival of the new Soviet envoy was greeted with fireworks, banquets, and ardent declarations of friendship. Soon after Borodin was invited to become High Advisor to the Kuomintang. To Americans who wanted to know his real name, its leader Sun Yat-sen replied, "His name is Lafayette. He came to aid us in our struggle." The struggle was for a modernized, unified China, freed from vassalage to the Western powers—not for Communism. For that China was not ready as Borodin saw clearly. Aided by his staff, the Chinese cleaned up the city of Canton, organized unions of peasants and coolies, loosed the British strangle-hold on commerce at the port of Hong Kong, built up schools and a fighting army that carried the new revolutionary ideas into the North. These measures were too radical for the big Chinese merchants, landlords, and generals. Getting control of the Kuomintang, they bloodily suppressed the left wing, broke with the Russians, raided their embassy and consulates.

The severed relations were resumed but they are none too cordial. The rulers of Nanking and the seaboard cities were averse to the close ties with the Soviets always advocated by Sun Yat-sen and again stressed in the letter he wrote to Moscow just before his death: "Bidding you farewell, I hope the day will come when the Soviet Union will find in a powerful China a brother and an ally, and both will work hand in hand for the liberation of nations." Such an alliance, rejected by the war lords and upper classes, may be realized by the revolutionary Chinese masses and students. Already with their Red Armies, they have risen to power in the six provinces containing 40 million people and known as Soviet China.

The Soviets and America

The first contacts with America were established by the fur-hunters venturing ever further East after the seals and otters. While today Russia is sending thousands of furs to America, 150 years ago, curiously enough, Russia was taking millions of furs from America. Crossing the Bering Strait the seal-hunters pushed their way steadily down to the Farallon Islands off San Francisco where Sir Francis Drake records seeing them as early as in 1580. In 1806 Rezanov, the handsome envoy of the Tsar, appeared before the Spanish Governor of California. Obtaining supplies for his starving colony in Alaska, and for himself betrothal to the governor's beautiful daughter, Concepción, he sailed away. The long awaiting of her lover's return is the theme of a Bret Harte poem that ends with her learning thirty-six years later that he was killed on his journey back to St. Petersburg.

Meanwhile, the Russians above San Francisco founded a colony at Fort Ross where one may still see the stockade, officers' quarters, and chapel topped by its three-barred cross. Through trading, fishing, and ship-building, they so entrenched themselves along the Pacific that the Tsar called it a "closed Russian sea." In protest the United States in 1823 proclaimed the Monroe Doctrine warning European powers that,

"We should consider any attempt to extend their system to any portion of this hemisphere as dangerous to our peace and safety." The Tsar heard and gave heed out of a desire to maintain the friendly relations so recently established.

At first the Russian autocracy, horrified by the republican regime set up by the American revolution, would have nothing to do with it. It was a denial of the divine right of rulers, a dangerous experiment, and doomed to failure. Why recognize it? So the Great Catherine thought when she refused to receive Francis Dana, the first envoy appointed to Russia by Congress. That hostile attitude was stubbornly maintained for 33 years, while the United States steadily grew in power and prestige. Forced at last to reconcile herself to the existence of the new republic, Russia in 1809 received its first Minister. He was John Quincy Adams, who skillfully cultivated cordial relations between the two nations differing so widely in structure and culture. In course of time, these ripened into a warm tradition of friendship. A firm commercial basis was given to that friendship by the Treaty of 1832 made "In the name of the Most Holy and Indivisible Trinity." It was further strengthened by a series of acts of good will at critical junctures. In the Crimean War the sympathies of America were on the side of the Russian armies, fighting against the British. In the Civil War, when the British blockade was threatened, the North was heartened by Russian squadrons sailing into New York and San Francisco. In 1867 Russia gave up Alaska, derisively called an "ice-box," which returned, for the 7,200,000 dollars paid for it, 400,000,000 dollars in gold dug from its frozen soil. While President Theodore Roosevelt definitely supported the Japanese in the war with Russia, in the Peace of Portsmouth he prevailed upon them to mitigate the harsh terms imposed upon the defeated Russians.

Meantime, millions of Russian immigrants were pouring into America. Their tales of oppression, Jewish pogroms, and Kennan's exposure of the exile system stirred revulsion and protest. Dead, or fast dying, was the traditional friendship between the two nations, when suddenly the Tsar was overthrown and it sprang into new life again. Even after the advent of the Bolsheviks to power the United States continued to render invaluable services. It staunchly defended the territorial integrity of Russia. It insisted upon Japan's evacuating its troops from Siberia and the island of Sakhalin. It sent over 66 million dollars' worth of supplies during the famine of 1921, saving countless victims from death by starvation and plague, "making for America a unique place in the hearts of millions of Russian people." (H. H. Fisher)

While helping in this way "the great and generous Russian people," the United States would officially have nothing to do with the Soviet Government and added its troops to those of the interventionists trying to overthrow it. It was a denial of the rights of property, an experiment that was dangerous, and doomed to failure. Why recognize it? So, in effect, argued Wilson and Colby in refusing to receive Ludwig Martens, the first envoy from the Soviets. This hostile attitude was stubbornly maintained for sixteen years while steadily the Soviet Union grew in power and prestige. At last, reconciling itself to the existence of the Soviet system, in 1934 the United States received its first ambassador, Alexander Troyanovsky. This was history repeating itself. Russia had been last to recognize the new democratic state in America. Now in turn America was the last of the great powers to recognize the new Socialist state in Russia. Among the many reasons leading to this step were trade; cooperation in science and exploration; a counter-move to Japanese aggression in the East. "The most impelling motive," says President Franklin Roosevelt, "was the desire of both countries for peace and for strengthening the peaceful purposes of the civilized world." The expectations in certain quarters that recognition would be immediately followed by a big increase in trade were not realized. With the resignation of William C. Bullitt in 1936, Joseph E. Davies was appointed American ambassador in Moscow.

Almost a decade before recognition by the United States, Kollontai was received as the Soviets' plenipotentiary to Mexico. But relations were broken off in 1930 and are not likely to be resumed so long as Mexico gives asylum to Trotzky. Some trading is carried on with the twenty countries of Latin America, but it amounts to little because of the tension that was created by raids on Soviet agencies. With Uruguay, whose charges of propaganda were sarcastically refuted by Litvinov before the League of Nations, came a rupture in 1936. Canada long maintained a policy of aloofness, conducting a campaign against Soviet exports competing with its own timber, pulpwood, and asbestos in the world markets, but in 1937 full commercial relations were established.

84. How is Trade Carried on with Other Countries?

As all diplomatic relations are directed by the Commissariat of Foreign Affairs so all commercial intercourse with the outside world is in the hands of the Commissariat of Foreign Trade. With full control over the volume and character of goods entering and leaving the country, this Commissariat's function is to strike a balance between the needs for foreign goods and the exportable surplus, keeping the whole business in line and in gear with the general economic plan.

The actual transaction of business is delegated to some thirty State-owned trusts or syndicates. They have their agents abroad but usually negotiations are carried on with foreign firms by mail, cable, or their representatives coming to Moscow. "Exportles" sells lumber, pulpwood, plywood, veneers. "Mashinoimport" buys engines, ships, gold-dredges, pumps, hoisting and drilling equipment. Other trusts specialize in all sorts of products from vodka, caviar, sausage-casings, ginseng and licorice root to furs, Oriental rugs, manganese and semi-precious stones of the Urals. Still others are devoted exclusively to trade with Sinkiang, Mongolia, and Afghanistan. To facilitate the work of these organizations abroad are Soviet Trade Missions such as "Arcos" in England and "Amtorg" in America, organized on the basis of the laws of these countries. Their function is to furnish information, regulate the conditions of contracts, inspect purchased goods, expedite the sending of representatives of foreign firms to Moscow, the placing of advertisements in Soviet journals, and so on.

Through this apparatus is put into effect the Monopoly of Foreign Trade that was instituted by the decree of April, 1918, signed by Lenin and Stalin. As the "first line defense and shield" of Soviet economy, its function is to see that nothing goes out of the country which is urgently needed at home and nothing comes in that does not conform to the general plan of development.

In the era of restoration of industry this Monopoly of Foreign Trade prevented the Soviet market from being flooded with outside goods and the much needed capital from being sucked out of the country. During the first Five-Year Plan, it clamped down the lid on the import of consumers' and luxury goods, enabling the Soviets to obtain the metals, machines and technicians so essential to its great program of construction. At present, while somewhat relaxing restrictions, its aim in general is to maintain a favorable balance of payments in order to secure reserves of foreign currencies, which the Soviets are adding to their reserves of grain and gold against the exigencies of a war.

These are some of the accomplishments of the Soviet system in which all the enterprises in a sixth of the world are welded into one and carry on their trading operations as a single unit. This enables them to buy in mass where goods are cheapest, from mutually competing firms. It enables them to make up losses sustained in one field by profits in another. It enables them also, to exert pressure on recalcitrant countries by transferring trade to those that are friendly or diverting traffic through other ports. But the advantages, however, are not all one-sided. Thanks to the Soviet system, foreign firms do not have to worry whether their clients will become bankrupt, insolvent or repudiate their obligations. They deal with corporations organized and backed by all the resources of the Soviet State and which in the course of transacting over five billion dollars' worth of business have not defaulted on a single penny. They meet their bills punctually and where favorable credits are not forthcoming prefer to pay cash.

On the basis of this record, the Soviets are no longer satisfied nor content with anything but the best trading arrangements. In the words of former Assistant Secretary of State Raymond Moley: "They used to beg for credit and pay exorbitant interest. Now they demand the kind of terms ordinarily extended to the big customer who never has failed to meet a bill when due and often anticipated due dates. They used to buy wherever they could get accommodation; now they are in a position to shop for quality and for preferred treatment." This independent position is a reflex of the economic strength of the country, the successes scored in building up a well-rounded industry. This is shown in the statistics of foreign trade. While a few years ago three-fourths of Soviet exports were agricultural in origin and only one-fourth industrial, now the figures are reversed. So far and so swiftly has industrialization progressed that the Soviets now declare that they can put through the gigantic third Five-Year Plan with very few imports, and, if necessary, with practically none at all.

This declaration, however, does not imply that, like the Nazi spokesmen, they are committed to a policy of national self-sufficiency or autarchy. On the contrary, Soviet leaders from Rosengoltz, Commissar of Foreign Trade, to Mezhlauk, the new Commissar of Heavy Industry, are definitely against isolation, and are strong advocates of economic cooperation with all nations. They realize that their own advance will be accelerated by closer ties with the progressive industrial countries. They can still utilize a tremendous amount of tools, machines, and technical services. They cite history to show that an expanding internal market, a rising standard of living, and a rising rate of production are great stimulants to trading. And finally they want this trade in order "to cement friendly relations with other countries and actively assist the policy of peace," but they want it on terms of equality and the basis of mutual interest.

Examples of the various ways in which trading with the Soviets is or may be carried on may be listed as follows: The agreement with the United States to purchase at least 30 million dollars' worth of goods annually in return for most favored nation treatment on tariffs. The extension of a ten million pounds' credit guaranteed by the British government. The Czechoslovakian five-year loan, the money to be used entirely for purchases in that country. The joining of international quota arrangements for fixing prices and regulating the sales of commodities on the world market. Contracts for technical and engineering services such as were made with Ford, Colonel Hugh Cooper, Albert Kahn, Freyn and McKee.

85. How Large and Effective Are the Armed Forces—the Red Army, Navy, and Air Fleet?

In numbers they are one of the most formidable fighting forces in the world. But victory, especially in modern wars, does not necessarily go to the nation that puts the most troops in the field. If it did, then in the Great War the fourteen million Russian soldiers, in the words of their old saying, might have "swamped the enemy simply by throwing our caps at them." If sheer size counted, the gigantic military machine of the Tsar would have crushed the Germans completely. But it did not. Instead of driving relentlessly forward, the celebrated Russian "steam-roller" went into reverse, and, rolling steadily backward, broke into pieces. In Lenin's trenchant words, "the masses of peasant soldiers with their legs voted against the war by running away." Losing faith in the Tsar and his generals, lacking in morale, munitions, technique, and transport, they would not, could not, fight.

The Soviets are not making the Tsar's grievous mistake of relying on numbers. At the same time on all citizens is laid "the obligation of defending the fatherland of the workers." Under the Soviets danger, like everything else, is socialized. Every able-bodied male on reaching the age of nineteen is called to the colors. That means each year some 1,800,000 report to the recruiting stations. Approximately a third of these are selected for full-time, intensive training in the regular forces. Villagers who constitute the vast majority are usually assigned to two years' service in the infantry; Cossacks, Caucasian mountaineers, and nomad horsemen to three years in the cavalry; mechanics to the same term in the artillery or air fleet; fishermen and bargemen to the navy for five years. Certain quotas are assigned to the special detachments of the Commissariat of Home Affairs for guarding the frontiers, the railways, and camps for prisoners. Thus annually some 600,000 are taken out of civil life to devote themselves wholly to training in one of the various branches of the military forces.

What becomes of the rest of each year's enormous class that is liable to service? From five to ten per cent are rejected as physically unfit, defective in sight, hearing, or stature. Others are exempted on special grounds, such as being the sole support of their families. Up till 1937 the sons of kulaks, priests, and private traders were disbarred as alien, unreliable elements, "unworthy of the proletarian honor of bearing arms." They paid a special tax and might serve in trench-digging battalions, the ambulance corps, and food commissaries.

That discrimination is now abolished by Article 132 of the new Constitution which declares that "universal liability to military service is the law." The only exceptions are members of certain religious sects conscientiously objecting to war, who are usually sent into the non-combat units. Refusing to have anything whatsoever to do with fighting their fellowmen, they may fight forest-fires, floods, and epidemics. All the rest of the recruits go into the Territorial Army, organized on a militia basis like the National Guard of America. They receive about eight months' training, spread over a period of five years at times and places interfering as little as possible with the normal course of their lives. Workers drill close to their factories; peasants in the fall after the harvest is gathered in; students during their summer vacation.

Besides the Red Army regulars and the territorials there are scores of auxiliary and volunteer forces. There are the Factory and Labor Union Brigades, clad in leather caps and jackets, carrying rifles slung over the shoulders, hunter style. A million are wearers of the "Ready for Labor and Defense" badge, qualifying for it by passing tests such as map-reading, grenade throwing, scaling barricades, skiing seven miles, running 100 meters in fourteen seconds, swimming 50 meters with a gun. A million more are "Voroshilov Marksmen" of the first grade, scoring 84 hits out of a hundred, shooting at a distance of 50 meters from a small-bore rifle. A fair quota of these are women and girls, for their activities are not limited to the Red Cross and Red Crescent Societies. They are trained to operate field telephones, to guard bridges, to be sharpshooters and machine-gunners. The young Pioneers, likewise, have their place in the scheme, being trained as scouts to search out the enemy or signal his approach by foot, horse, auto, or airplane. Even the little children are taught to deliver messages, creeping along the hedges "as quietly as kittens." As Voroshilov and others often say, "Our soldiers are the whole of the Soviet peoples." To these are added likewise most of the Soviet animals. Every spring there is a registration of every horse in the country useful for cavalry or transport. Certain breeds of dogs are included in the inventory, in fact everything available for military purposes from camels to carrier-pigeons.

Much of this heads up in the Air and Chemical Defense League, *Osoaviakhim,* with some 15 million members, and branches in almost every big office, school, farm, and mill. It conducts "Defense Week" with drills in the use of gas-masks, bomb-proof cellars, subways, and other hide-outs. It organizes rehearsals against night air raids, when the approach of enemy planes is announced by whistle and radio, and every lamp, bulb, and cigarette light is extinguished and wet blankets are hung over the doors. It supplies the "House of Defense" in the villages with guns, guides, and instructors. It erects high towers from which the parachutists take their first lessons in jumping. Out of the enormous funds collected by dues, lotteries, and popular subscriptions it presents planes, tanks, and dirigibles to the army. The Red Army, turn about, lends its rifle-ranges and flying-fields to these volunteer societies. It camps and marches side by side with their battalions in the fall maneuvers. It acts as first aid in emergencies—unloading cars with perishable goods, cleaning up the debris in mill yards, bringing in the harvest endangered by floods or insect pests.

Constantly the Red Armyists participate in civilian life just as the civilians do in military life. With no hard-and-fast separating line, they mesh and merge one into the other. The soldier is now a civilian, the civilian now a soldier. It is a nation of 175 millions under arms. The Red Army is simply the first-line defense, the part that is better trained, more mobile, and ready for action.

Difference Between the Army of the Tsar and of the Soviets

Under the old regime the youth shrank from their conscript years with fear and misgivings. They had good reasons to do so. It meant three to seven years of hardship and humiliation. The officers bullied, intimidated, and used them as lackeys. The code (Sections 98-103) forbade them to travel on boats and trains except third-class, to eat in any but inferior restaurants, to ride on the inside of trams, to smoke in public places without asking leave of an officer. At every step they were rigidly bound by rules—for the slightest infraction of which they might have to run the gauntlet or "stand under the rifle," stock-still for two hours under a load of 72 pounds of sand in the knapsack. While just before the World War corporal punishment was forbidden, officers in rage did not hesitate to give a soldier "a fist in the face" or call him a "fool" to which he might only reply, "Quite so, Your Nobility!" The aim of all this was "to show the soldier his place" and to keep him there. That place was at the bottom of the social ladder. Treated as an inferior he came to act like an inferior. The word "soldier," *soldat,* was an epithet of opprobrium, and doorways bore the sign, "No admittance to soldiers!"

With conditions of service so harsh and dismal in the army of the Tsar, no wonder many sought to evade it. They did so by bribery, by running away to America, by rendering themselves physically unfit. In any village one may still hear strange stories of how they emaciated their bodies by fasting, chewed tea to double the heart-beat, mutilated their trigger-fingers, jumped off high places to damage a leg or an arm. Of course only a few resorted to such bizarre and heroic measures. In general they accepted the inevitable. Knowing they had to go, they made the best of it.

Like all important events in peasant life the departure of the recruits had its own ceremonies—a cycle of songs, dances, and feasting lasting a week and culminating in a series of farewells. First, the Farewell to the Relatives—the boys, from noon till midnight, driving fast and furiously to godfathers, grandfathers, uncles, and aunts. Then, on the village green, the Farewell to the Girls. Facing north with a long and loud "Ah-oo! Ah-oo!" they shouted, "Good-by, girls! We're off to the war!" and so to the south, the east, and west, "Girls, good-by, good-by!" Next morning the Farewell to Home, with mothers wailing, "O, my son, my fair young falcon! From your warm nest they are driving you into the cold, cruel world!" Thus to the Final Leave-Taking when the recruits slowly moved out of the village in the center of a swarming crowd—younger brothers galloping around on horseback, old men bestowing their blessings, sisters and sweethearts their last embraces, mothers sobbing and moaning.

With the Russian flair for the dramatic some of this sorrow was simulated. To a few recruits, at least, going away meant a new world of life and adventure. To most of them, however, and to their families, it was a calamity. Though they tried hard to be festive, through all this ritual ran a minor note. The songs were dirge-like and melancholy; or sometimes they verged on the obscene. The feasting often turned into orgies of dissipation. Out of vodka flowing like water came fighting, sex excesses, rowdyism, and remorse.

In the back villages one may still find survivals of these old ceremonies. But the spirit has gone out of them. The young recruits may still sing the old songs of lamentation at going away, but the girls, knowing most of them are eager to go, only tease and laugh at them. They still would like to go on a spree, swaggering about as young braves, but public opinion is against it. On the hoardings may appear placards like this: *Down with the Shameful Old Customs!*

New Recruits! Into the Tsar's army your brothers went protesting against the old discipline of blows and beatings. In drunkenness and bravado they sought to drown their grief. Now you consciously go into the Red Army, a school of warriors for the toilers. Down with cursing and ribald songs! Forward to the new life opening before you—a life of cleanliness, comradeship, and culture of mind and body! Be worthy of your high calling.

It is hardly necessary to exhort and admonish the conscripts in that fashion any longer. They are fully aware of the kind of life that now opens before them. It is imparted in a preliminary period of training and instruction given for a month in each of the two years prior to enlistment. Every day the officer, chosen for his tact and understanding of the life and problems of the particular group to which he is assigned, answers innumerable questions from youths and their elders. As a result, knowing not only their duties but their many privileges and opportunities, most of the recruits eagerly await their induction into the Red Army. While celebrated more decorously than of yore, it is usually a more festive and gala occasion. There are farewell speeches and presents to the young recruits from the farms, offices, or mills to which they belong. Through the embannered streets, with bands and accordions they are accompanied by their comrades to the recruiting stations. There often they are greeted and entertained by the leading singers, dancers, skaters, fencers, and Stakhanovites of the community.

The Red Army inculcates into its men the feeling of self-respect and importance. In keeping with Lenin's injunction—"Take care of the Red Army as the apple of your eye"—everything is done to enhance the morale of its soldiers. Only there are no "soldiers" in the Red Army. To avoid the old stigma attached to that word it calls them "Red Armyists" and, by the treatment it gives them, it invests the new name with a new meaning. It houses them in clean barracks with clean beds and clean sheets. It puts them into uniforms of about the same cut and cloth as their commanders, into long shining leather boots, the desire of every Russian. The shorter term of service is further shortened by days off and long vacation leaves. It cuts down drill hours from eight to five, filling out the extra time with sports, study, and amusements.

This concern for the welfare of the Red Armyist extends to his family. It receives certain tax exemptions, aid for its invalid members, advice on how to curb insolent officials. This adds greatly to the Red Armyist's prestige amongst his friends and relatives. In camp and barracks they come to visit and consult him, and on furlough home he is generally the hero and idol of the community. The children follow him about. The women give him their best cabbage-soup and pasties. Even the old men defer to him. No one stands higher than the man with the red star on his helmet—not even those exalted beings, the shock-brigaders and Stakhanovites. "What is a worker to a worker?" asks a catechism for Pioneers. The answer is "A brother." "And to whom is the worker brother?" "The Red Armyist."

With all these privileges go corresponding obligations. They are summed up in the "Red Oath" which, both in content and in the solemn manner of administering it, again enhances the sense of responsibility and self-esteem in the young recruits. It is a particularly impressive spectacle in Moscow when the Red Square—filled with the Soviet leaders and delegations of Communists, Socialists, and Trade Unionists from abroad, the foreign diplomatic corps and military attachés—re-echoes with the voices of tens of thousands of Red Armyists repeating in unison:

> I, son of the working people, a citizen of the Union of Soviet Socialist Republics, take upon myself the proud calling of warrior in the Red Army. I promise before the working-class of the Soviets and of the whole world to carry this title with honor, to master conscientiously the science of war, and to protect as the apple of my eye the property of the people from theft and destruction. I promise to observe revolutionary discipline, to obey strictly all orders of the commanders. I promise to refrain and to restrain my comrades from every act unworthy of a Soviet citizen, to direct all my actions and thoughts to the great goal of the liberation of all toilers. I promise at the first call to spring to the defense of the nation, and, in the fight for the Soviet Union, the cause of Socialism, and the brotherhood of all people, to spare neither my strength nor my life. If through evil intent I violate this solemn oath let universal contempt be my lot, and may the stern hand of revolutionary law punish me.

The Red Army is at once highly disciplined and democratic. Officially it is The Workers' and Peasants' Army, its name justified according to its handbook, on three grounds: "It is the only army in the world that defends the rights and interests of workers and peasants. It consists from top to bottom of toilers living by their own labor and not that of others. It is commanded not by the sons of landlords, nobles, and capitalists, but by the toilers themselves." Stressing the last point it states that under the Tsar scarcely ever did a proletarian become an officer as the war colleges were the exclusive preserve of the rich and privileged. Now the system is reversed. With the exception of a few old specialists of proved loyalty to the new regime, the general staff is largely of worker-peasant origin. So are the first three to receive the title of Marshal. Commissar and commander-in-chief,

Voroshilov, is the son of a Cossack shepherd, a slate-picker at the age of six and a metal-worker at fifteen. The head of the forces that guard the Far East frontiers, Blücher, is the son of a Ural workman. The cavalry hero, Budenny, who raced his men night and day over a thousand miles of steppe to appear suddenly before the gates of Warsaw, is the son of a poor peasant. Dramatically they sprang to leadership in the storm and fire of actual wars. Their colleagues must now pass through the longer, more patient, prosaic training of the academies. But they all come out of the ranks. They all are blood and bone of the working class.

With this revolution in the social origin of the commanders goes a complete change in their relations towards the rank-and-file. Gone is the old caste spirit, the sharp dividing barriers, and exaggerated formalities. Instead of the familiar "thou" used for children, animals, and inferiors, the Red Armyist is addressed as "you," as an equal. Instead of saluting on every occasion, the men salute to report or to receive an order—while off duty they do so only if they desire. Instead of "Your Excellency!" "Your Nobility!" they call him simply "Comrade Commander." And that is what he is supposed to be, a comrade. Only in drill and on the march is he a superior. The rest of the time he is to his men a senior soldier, a counselor, and friend. Around the campfires, in their clubs, canteens, and sport fields one may see them dining, reading, playing football or chess together on terms of close fellowship and intimacy.

This camaraderie does not imply that discipline is lax. On the contrary, it is very strict. Any willful violation of the code means immediate deprivation of freedom and privileges. Sometimes the men take it upon themselves to mete out punishment to the offender. One of their methods is social ostracism. On the night before maneuvers a sailor came on board his torpedo-boat in a drunken state. In the morning he was met with a conspiracy of cold silence. No one would recognize him, speak to him, have anything to do with him. He didn't belong. To be thrown into a dungeon would have been easier to bear than thus to be shunned and scorned by his shipmates. For in the words of John Ball: "Fellowship is heaven, lack of fellowship is hell." Repentant and reinstated, this sailor became one of the foremost shock-workers on the fleet.

Having abolished the "old discipline of the cane, the fist, and the knout," the Red Army strives to create a "conscious" discipline—one that rises out of a mastery of every rule and regulation, and of the reasons for them. These, with great pains and in simple language, the handbook explains to the recruit: "Can a factory operate with the workers coming and going at will? Can a big farm produce if each man goes out to plow, or sow, or reap, when and how it pleases him? No! There must be one head to give directions and the rest must carry them out. So it is in the Army, for war of today demands the utmost accuracy, speed, and team-work. Suppose a courier delays a few minutes in delivering his message. It may result in the rout of the whole army. Suppose a sentry guarding a powder magazine falls asleep and the enemy blows it up. It may mean the destruction of thousands of men and supplies. Therefore it is the duty of the Red Armyist to learn to carry out unconditionally, implicitly, every order of his commander." The aim, however, is not a blind but an intelligent obedience, arising out of knowledge, initiative, and self-control. These are the qualities that the Red Army wants in its men. To develop them it supports a vast elaborate system of education—technical, cultural, and political.

The Red Army is a school and workshop. With the aim of making "every Red Armyist a conscious fighter for Socialism with the rifle and the book," every effort is put forth to develop his mind and intelligence. To show him that the old army was not concerned in such training the handbook cites a general of the Tsar as saying to his officers: "When you are in the presence of a common soldier, forget that he is a human being. He is a mujik, an animal gifted with the power of human speech—nothing more. He has as much use for intelligence as a horse for silk stockings. His sole obligation is to be blindly obedient to every command. To make him so he should be kept ignorant, unthinking, and illiterate." This, of course, is the old regime at its worst. Still, as a matter of fact, 80 per cent of its soldiers were unable to read or write.

In complete reversal of this policy the Soviets at the very outset raised the slogan, "Every Red Armyist a literate man!" Often in hunger and rags he was compelled to grapple not only with the enemy, but with the alphabet, the letters sometimes ingeniously made out of twigs, "learning to read while he rode, to figure while he fought."

Thanks to universal compulsory schooling these primary classes are no longer necessary. Practically all recruits go at once into the higher courses, covering the whole educational field up to the university. While no longer lacking in the three R's, unfortunately many are quite ignorant of the rudiments of science and technics—the basic things essential to modern mechanized warfare and industry. For service in both these fields the Red Army prepares its men. It trains them to handle a tractor as well as a machine-gun, to convert phosphates into fertilizers as well as into gunpowder, to build bridges as well as to blow them up. Every opportunity is afforded the Red Armyists to acquire a trade or profession. And most of them do. Every year the technical schools of the army are turning out thousands of first class automobilists, blacksmiths, chemists, drillers, electricians, likewise hundreds of artists, musicians, librarians, inventors.

The Red Army is a "hearth of culture." Under the Soviets "culture" is a wide embracing term. It includes everything from politeness to polo-playing, from soap to symphonies and fox-trotting. While the Labor Union, Cooperatives and collective farms undertake to instruct their members in all these matters, in the Red Army they are to be seen as in a microcosm and at their best. Activities are centered in the 350 Houses of the Red Army and Fleet, open on equal terms to commanders, the rank-and-file, and their families. Some of them are really palatial, equipped with buffets, gymnasiums, concert and cinema halls, rooms for radio, reading, and recreation. Here in leisure moments the men come to lounge and listen to the regimental poet, buffoon, and story-teller. In serious hours they gather in study groups in the "Lenin Corners," which become the "Lenin Tents" when they go into summer camp.

It is a reading army. There are 2,000 libraries where the men have direct access to the shelves with fifteen million volumes, part of which go with them on maneuvers.

It is a writing army. More than 150,000 *armkors,* army correspondents, take part in the work of the press. They write for their daily *Red Star,* for the two score military journals, for the 10,000 wall-newspapers, filling them with anecdotes, poems, criticisms, sketches, drawings. They write home millions of letters, telling their friends and relatives about their daily life, the new laws, taxes, and decrees. In turn come back millions of letters telling the Red Armyists what the folks at home are thinking and doing, and incidentally serving the government as an invaluable barometer of the people's sentiments.

It is an acting army. To their dramatic instincts the men give expression in skits on themes of the day, in marionette shows, in reviews involving thousands of actors, in elaborately staged spectacles at the big Red Army Theatre in Moscow. Very popular is "The First Cavalry Army," written by a participant of that almost legendary night-and-day dash across the steppe. "Naib Khan's Compromise" depicts the assault of anti-Bolshevik Moslems upon a state farm on the Afghan border. "A Blow at the Steppe," the struggles of demobilized men to reclaim the arid wastes with irrigation. "Steel-Clad Enthusiasm," with the sub-title, "They are getting ready," follows a White general from capital to capital as he seeks to rally the imperialists to crush the Soviets. The army produces for the screen as well as the stage, in all of which the men participate as set-builders, scene-shifters, playwrights, actors, dancers and singers.

It is a singing army. The recruits from the villages may be taught new songs—but not how to sing. Most of them are gifted with rich and resonant voices and they like to use them. They sing alone, in little groups of two to twenty accompanied by the harmonica, in whole platoons, companies, and divisions in parts and unison. They sing in barracks, on the way to the bathhouse with towels tucked under their arms, on the long trek along the dusty roads out to maneuvers, keeping time not to the beat of drum and fife but the rhythm of their own voices. A lusty clear-voiced soloist strikes up the opening bars, and the whole company comes sweeping into the chorus. In the whole Soviet scene, nothing is more striking than the Red Army silently swinging by in ankle-long greatcoats, then suddenly bursting into song—a mighty volume of sound that rings and echoes through the city streets or rolls majestically across the meadows. "The church-mass," said Voltaire, "is the opera of the people." In Russia it is the Red Army.

It is a studying army. Besides the required courses almost every man voluntarily enrolls in one of the 70,000 study groups, known as "circles." There are "Literary Circles" reading aloud the classics, modern novels, and poetry; and sometimes the authors come to read to them. "Science Circles," experimenting in their own laboratories with test-tubes and chemicals, or going out on visits to observatories and institutes. "Musical Circles," with choral groups, ensembles, and instruction in theory, harmony, and technique. "Marxist Circles," with the ABC of his economics for novitiates and seminars on philosophy for the experts in dialectics. "Foreign Language Circles," teaching all tongues from Basic English to Japanese, imperative for all serving as scouts, spies, and agitators, especially those to be dropped in parachutes behind the enemy lines. There are all kinds of circles: "Art," "Anti-religious," "Drama," "Sports." From these the men may choose according to taste and talents. The commanding staff, however, on the principle that the best fighter is the one who knows exactly what he is fighting for, favors those dealing with state affairs and politics.

The Red Army is an institute of politics. In entering the army one retains all his civil rights. He holds his membership in Labor Union and cooperative, continues to vote and run for office. This practice in politics is illuminated by courses in economics, civics, and history—taught by his commander. He is as thoroughly drilled in Marxism as in musketry. Altogether some 450 solid hours of the Red Armyist's time is devoted to these required studies. He learns the story of the Red Army from those first stormy days when it fought under the battle cry, "War to the palaces! Peace to the cottages!" to the present time when it is ensconced in these palaces—and in scores of new ones. He learns of the 189 peoples comprising the Soviet Union—Armenians, Bashkirs, Chuvash, Tatars—many of whom he meets in his own regiment. In place of the instinctive intolerance and ridicule toward those of a different breed and culture, there is generated a spirit of mutual respect and good will, a powerful factor in promoting unity and solidarity in the nation. He learns of foreign lands and his interest and vision lifted across national boundaries comes to include all the toiling, struggling peoples throughout the world. The five-pointed star he wears is the symbol of the five continents where they live and in the Red Oath he promises "for the sake of their brotherhood to spare neither my strength nor my life."

Supplementing these formal lectures are "evenings" of conversation and debates made more alluring by many ingenious devices. Among these a favorite is "political roulette." To each of the thirty-six numbers on the wheel is attached a question: "What is the League of

Nations?" "What countries are friendly to the Soviets?" "What are the duties of a Communist?" A Red Armyist steps up to spin the pointer while the whole company crowds close, eagerly watching the number it points to, wondering how he will answer the question that goes with it. If he fails, it passes to the next. To add zest there are small prizes like pencils, matches, and cigarettes—bigger ones for the harder questions. With banter, jesting, and laughter the contest goes on for hours. Even though one wanted to escape this training in politics, he couldn't. From all sides it assails him—in play-time and in drill, radio, cinema, poster, and press. The result of all this is to bring great numbers into the Party. Out of every 100 entering the army, 15 are Communists. On leaving it the number runs to 60 per cent and still higher among the commanders. In the general staff, the youngest and most revolutionary minded in the world, over 90 per cent carry the red card of membership. Thus it is not only a Red Army in name but in reality. For the most part it is made up of Reds and of course in a red country the good citizen is a Red.

The Red Army turns its men into good citizens as well as good warriors. On completing their service term a small fraction—those with military talents and inclination—go on to the academies. The others return to the offices, farms, and factories from which they emerged, as missionaries of Soviet ideas and discipline and culture. "Instead of alcohol, cards, and disease which the soldiers of the Tsar took back to the village," says the handbook, "the Red Armyist carries with him books, the electric-lamp, and the latest knowledge of crop-raising." In every field they are aggressive shock troops of Communism. They lead the campaigns against kulaks and speculators who call them "red vipers inoculated with devil's blood in the army." They champion the cause of teachers, doctors, and agronomists to whom they are "the red warriors against darkness, disease, and superstition." They are elected to all key-positions in their communities. Most of the presidents of village Soviets are former Red Armyists, red sailors, and red airmen. Likewise a majority of the chairmen of Collective and most of the heads of Machine-Tractor stations.

In their yeomen services the Soviets find some compensation for the big outlay on its war apparatus. To it, the 1937 budget allotted 20,000,-000,000 rubles—a levy of over 20 dollars on every man, woman, and child. While that is less per capita than in France, England, or Japan, it is a tremendous burden for a nation upbuilding itself from its foundations. The Soviets would like to scrap the whole military machine and direct all its funds into productive channels. But that they do not dare to do. At any rate it is getting immediate tangible returns from its investment in the Red Army, Navy, and Air Fleet. They are producing effective citizens to be transformed again into effective fighters at the outbreak of war.

86. Why do the Soviets Count on Winning the Next War?

First, they have the largest standing army in the world. It consists of 1,500,000 troops ready to swing into action at a moment's notice. As to the quality of staff-work, discipline, and morale, the testimony of foreign military experts is unanimous. With half the rank-and-file and 90 per cent of the officers avowed Communists, they have a clear idea of what they are fighting for. And, with no defects or delays tolerated in the industries supplying the armies, they are excellently equipped for fighting. "Our aim is to spare the blood and strength of our Red Armyists by the highest degree of mechanization and motorization," says Voroshilov. How far this has progressed is attested by the members of the British, French, and Czech military missions at the autumn field maneuvers. Said the Czech General Luza, "It is richly equipped with the most up-to-date technique which has been mastered to perfection."

The casual observer gets a glimpse of this at the great reviews of May and November. After the parade of steel-helmeted infantry—well fed, uniformed, booted, and marching with long bayonets at "thrust" position—come batteries of light artillery, anti-aircraft guns, and howitzers. Then tanks of all kinds, high speed whippets, amphibians, turreted "land battleships" with cannon, followed by charging Cossack and Caucasian cavalry. Then gas, chemical, and bridge-building brigades, fleets of motor-lorries laden with sappers and miners; radio, signal, and search-light cars; battalions of motor-cyclists with demountable guns on their handle-bars and of bicyclists leading police dogs—every device for securing coordination and mobility in the Soviet forces at the front.

But to move these masses of men and weapons quickly and smoothly to the fronts! That is a problem that staggered the general staff of the old regime. And today, in spite of great advances, the railways are still a weak cog in the war machine. But at the outbreak of hostilities they will not be compelled to transport great masses of troops for great distances. The armies are already there in the two danger zones close to the frontiers. A million men comprise the armies of the West, ready to meet the menace of the Germans. Some five thousand miles to the East is the independent Red Banner Army of the Far East ready to grapple with the Japanese. Both these forces are supported by a chain of concrete forts along the two frontiers.

The Soviet Union has also thousands of miles of coastal frontiers to protect. Until recently the main strength of the Red Navy was in its torpedo-boats, destroyers, and submarines capable of staying long under water, and of distant non-stop voyages without refueling. Now it is embarking on a program of building big battleships, cruisers, and naval bases—which cannot be done in a hurry. But if the Soviets as yet lag far behind the great powers on the sea, they are unsurpassed in the air. The air armada consists of over 7,000 units, with its pursuit and scouting planes reaching a speed of 350 miles and over, with a cruising range of 1,250 miles. Squadrons of transport planes are capable of moving a whole regiment swiftly to any crucial point. Or they can drop thousands of parachutists with arms, machine-guns, and even parts of tanks to be quickly assembled, and deliver a surprise attack on the enemy from the rear. Planes laden with ten tons of gas and flame bombs climb to a four-mile altitude well out of range of most gunfire from the ground; air dreadnoughts flying 250 miles an hour carry thirty tons of explosives; hundreds of regular bombers are within easy striking distance of Tokyo and other centers of Japan.

If the war depends upon a quick decision in the air, for that the Soviets are well prepared. If it is to be waged with chemical weapons and gases, it is quite probable that they are equally well prepared. At Geneva repeatedly they pressed for the abolition of liquid fire, asphyxiating and blistering gases, infecting the enemy with virulent disease germs or destroying his crops with insect pests but their efforts were unavailing. However, with the extensive chemification of the country there is no reason to assume the Soviets are lacking in these sinister contributions of science to civilization. If the enemy uses them the Soviets will use them and perhaps some new and deadly devices of their own. Their efficacy however is still a matter of conjecture. There are ghastly pictures of the horrors that will be wrought by bombs and bacteria raining down from the sky, but the military experts themselves do not know their real value. They do know the value of well-disciplined, hardened soldiers. Of these the Soviet Union has a million and a half in its first-line defense. Upon them it depends to bear the brunt of the first assaults while the country gets on a war footing and brings up its reserves.

Second, the Soviets have enormous reserves of man power and raw materials. The first-line reserve consists of the nine million who after finishing their two years in the Red Army have been mustered out. Not only have they been trained but after returning to civil life there are short periods of further training aiming to keep them fairly fit and familiar with military affairs. The second reserves are the fifteen million members of the Air and Chemical Defense Society, sharpshooting circles, aviation clubs, hunters' brigades. This is not a huge unwieldy mass, a citizenry such as Bryan depicted "springing to arms overnight to repel the invader." They are already accustomed to firearms, gas-masks, grenade throwing. Many have taken part in actual maneuvers in scouting, liaison work, trench-digging. Others are skilled tractorists, parachutists, or pilots. In a short period most of them could be transformed into effective fighters.

Altogether well over twenty millions are available for service. The number actually to be mobilized depends upon the war and its duration. Also it depends upon two other questions. First, how many workers can be safely taken out of civil occupations without crippling the economic life of the nation? In this regard, thanks to women's entrance into industry, the Soviets are in a good position. Women are trained to take the places of men at the lathes, pumps, drills, forges, and tractors, releasing millions for the fronts. Second, how many can be kept at the fronts, adequately equipped with arms and munitions? Here again, thanks to state control of all industries, the Soviets are in a good position. Without any delay or negotiating with private owners, civil industries can be straightway transformed into military ones. The huge caterpillar-tractor plants can turn to the making of tanks; the fertilizer factories to nitrates and gunpowder; the chemical laboratories to poison gases; the aircraft plants to the building of bombers and pursuit planes. Adding their quota to the regular munition plants going full blast, they can keep a steady stream of supplies pouring into the devouring maws of the war-machine. In turn they can draw upon the well-nigh inexhaustible resources of the Soviet mines, forests, and grain fields. If it is to be a long drawn-out war of attrition, then the Soviets can go ahead with the assurance that in their sixth of the world they have ample resources of men, food, and minerals.

A third factor advantageous to the Soviet Union is its great expanse, its climate, and its general terrain. In military operations, especially on the defensive, these may easily prove to be assets of the first order. The huge area permits the erection of armament plants at a safe distance from the frontiers. It gives the Red Armies ample space territories in which to maneuver and to retreat if necessary. It allows them to cede temporarily region after region without losing the war or greatly impairing their fighting power. In a last interview before I took the Trans-Siberian train to Vladivostok in the spring of 1918, Lenin said to me: "The Allies are bent on smashing the Soviets. On your way you will probably see Japanese and Americans landing at Vladivostok. The British probably will push down from the North. The French and perhaps the Germans up from the South. We may have to abandon Moscow and retire towards the Urals. But there we can hold on a long, long time." To that plan the Bolsheviks were not compelled to take recourse. Moscow was not taken because the driving force of the invaders was spent before they could reach it. The distance, the difficulties in transport, and in pacifying the rear were too much for them.

These factors would likewise play havoc with any invading armies today. Supposing the Japanese should by a sudden thrust at Lake Baikal take over all East Siberia. Or the Nazis should attain their objective and possess themselves of the coveted parts of the Ukraine. In neither case would that be an irretrievable disaster to the Soviets. The Red Armies would still have wide bases in which to rest, rearm, and re-equip themselves. Meantime in the occupied territories every effort would be made by every means to keep the enemy in a state of tension and terror. From underground, the Communists would direct the activities of hosts of spies, agitators, snipers, and bands of partisans. The last are lineal descendants of the guerilla fighters who wore down the Grand Army of Napoleon by assaults on the baggage trains, night raids, and forays. All these arts for harrying, harassing, and hamstringing the enemy were highly perfected in the recent years of civil war. In them the people of Russia are adepts, and for their practice the forests and swamps of Russia are admirably adapted.

Then there is that old and redoubtable strategist who has won so many campaigns for Russia, General Winter. The sub-zero

cold to which Russians are inured is a grueling ordeal for soldiers from Western Europe and the Orient. And after winter
comes spring, transforming the country into a morass, and most
of the roads into quagmires. Transport is paralyzed and conditions
which are a terrible handicap to advancing troops may be actually
an asset to defenders. "Russia may be invaded but not conquered."
That is particularly true today because in addition to the formidable barriers of space and climate, the invader must reckon with
a new temper and spirit in the people.

*From the start of any war the Soviets will have practically
solid support of the people.* No time will be lost in mobilizing
public opinion. It will be done by the first bomb that falls on
Soviet soil, by the first assault on those countries—France, Czechoslovakia, Mongolia—with whom the Soviets have entered into a
compact to protect against an aggressor. That is the result of the
government's long tireless struggle for peace. It was first to ratify
the Kellogg Pact for the outlawry of war. It has offered to all
nations pacts of non-aggression, pleaded with them to sign them.
It has overlooked all sorts of affronts, "endured provocations to
which strong nations do not usually submit." (Nathaniel Peffer)
It has zealously backed every proposal at Geneva for real disarmament. These facts are the common knowledge of all citizens.
Even those otherwise critical of Soviet policies in general, fervently acclaim these efforts to keep the peace. If war comes, it
will be a last resort. Convinced that it is only after their leaders
have exhausted every means of averting it they will rally *en masse*
to the Soviets.

But are there no disaffected elements ready to find in war an
opportunity to settle their scores with the Soviets? No people with
grievances, grudges, complaints? Traveling over the Soviet land one
meets plenty of them. So numerous were they that, in my first journeys
into the villages, I was hard put to explain it. I knew that centuries
of visitations from plundering Tatars, tax-gatherers, and predatory
agents of the state and landlords had made the peasants wary of the
stranger coming into their midst. From Gorky I had learned that
they were a crafty and cunning lot, given to dwelling upon their

troubles, and disinclined to gratitude. So I didn't expect to hear the peasants singing paeans of thanksgiving to the Revolution. But I did expect some recognition of the benefits it had bestowed upon them. Instead of that I heard mostly of the evils with which it had afflicted them—high cost of city products, low prices of grain, misdeeds of Communists, red-tape, bureaucrats, the drive for collectivization. Everywhere my ears were smitten with lamentations and a litany of woes. Most vociferous was the lanky red-haired Dibenko in the village of Dikanka, who held forth frequently, eloquently, and in language of great strength on his sorrows. One day I found him in the Soviet hall vehemently denouncing his tax-bill of 46 rubles. Declaring that the Soviets were choking him, that the Bolsheviks were brigands, he called upon me to behold in him an upright citizen brought to ruin by his government.

Now it happened that I had just discovered that before the Revolution Dibenko was a landless, poverty-stricken laborer. From the Soviet he had received gratis some 30 acres of rich, black loam of the Prince Kochoobey Estate. He had acquired a new house, a yoke of óxen, two sons were students on scholarships in Kharkov. Taking him aside I asked, "Now, honestly, Dibenko, why is it you have always told me only about your troubles? What about your land, your oxen, your boys in school—about those things you never have said a word?" Taken aback, he laughed and then, half abashed, half in genuine astonishment, he exclaimed, "And I always thought Americans were sensible people, that they had heads and not cabbages on their shoulders! Why should I talk about the things I've got? I'm going to talk about the things I haven't got. And the louder and longer I talk the better chance I have of getting them." Putting this forward as a self-evident truth, he followed with some folk sayings as to the futility of political quiescence and passivity. "A stump is quiet, but what's the use of it!" "It's the good-natured cow that is milked the most."

Then with all barriers down he went on in softer mood, "After all, the Soviet is flesh of my flesh, bone of my bone. For three years I fought and bled for it in the civil war. It is my own. And haven't I the right to criticize my own? But don't you see that when my tongue scolds often my heart burns within me?" From such encounters I learned not to attach too much significance to the plaints of the peasants. In part, they rose out of a deliberate policy of putting on a poor front. In part, they were giving vent to their new-found right to abuse and berate their government. In part, they were based on grievances that were genuine enough.

But however stormy the assaults they were no indication of their fundamental attitude to the Soviets. Like Dibenko, they castigated it as their own child. But they would not allow others to do so. If an outsider essayed to join in the tirade, the man loudest in denunciation would often be most zealous in its defense. Such was the testimony of the terrorist anti-Soviet leader Savinkov at his trial, "To our amazement the mujiks who damned you most in our presence were the very ones we found fighting in the front ranks of your Red Armies. . . ." So I came to the conclusion that anyone who counted on the apparent disaffection of the Russian peasants didn't know them. While ready at any time to rise up with complaints and abuse on their lips against the Soviets, at the same time they were ready to rise up against anyone who would overthrow the Soviets with guns in their hands. They might have their own quarrels with their government, but it was a family affair and upon the outsider who presumed to interfere in it they would turn with furious resentment.

That is exactly what happened when the Allies intervened in 1918. Not only the masses, but even Brussilov, Nikolaev, Kamenev, and thousands of other officers in the Tsar's army, forgetting their differences with the Soviets, fought wholeheartedly in defense of their country. That happened when the Soviets were miserably poor and weak, when they had little to give the people, besides slogans, hopes, promises. Now most of these have become actualities. They now have Labor Unions, Cooperatives in which millions are actively participating, a vast network of giant plants, farms, schools, crèches, which they regard as their own. The standards of life are rapidly rising with prospects of an ever richer, more abundant life in the future. The invader who threatened these conquests would face the united efforts of an outraged people. They would hold out to the last ditch, the last copeck, the last drop of blood. It would be a holy war, with patriotic motives reinforced by international ones. They would be fighting, not only to defend their own factories, farms, and firesides, but to liberate the very armies they would be fighting against. For the Soviet peoples regard their country as the fatherland of the workers of all lands. In protecting it they would be battling not only in their own interests, but in behalf of their brothers throughout the world.

Finally, in favor of the Soviets is a considerable body of public opinion in foreign countries. This was one factor in defeating the attempt of the first coalition of 1918 to crush the Soviet state. Thanks in part to the protests of sympathizers, the activities of "Hands Off Russia!" committees, the strikes of dockers from Hamburg to Seattle against loading munitions for the White Armies, the refusal of railwaymen to transport their troops, the interventionists were driven off. "Without the support of the workers of the world," says Stalin, "long ago we would have been torn to pieces." With every year this support and sympathy is steadily increasing. Now there are 65 Communist Parties in the world pledged to fight the instigators of any assault on the Soviet Union, to turn the imperialist war into a civil war. The Second Socialist International likewise lays upon its millions of members the solemn obligation to defend the Soviet Union. Hosts of the leading intellectuals declare that the defeat of the Soviets would be a catastrophe to humanity. Even the man on the street, who dislikes the home brand of Communists, has a vague idea that in Russia they are conducting a "great experiment," and is all for letting them alone.

Sentiment, ranging from mild tolerance to zealous enthusiasm for the Soviets is to be found in all strata of the population. A cross section of it will be represented in any conscript army mobilized against them. Of this the Soviets know how to take the utmost advantage. How effectively they did so in 1918-1921 is a matter of history. One of the devices was to keep pounding away at their adversaries with a steady drumfire of questions: "Why did you come to Russia, Allied Soldiers?" "Why should workmen of France and England murder their fellow-workers of Russia?" "Do you want to destroy our Workmen's Republic?" "Do you want to restore the Tsar?" "You are fighting for the bond-holders of France, the land grabbers of England, the imperialists of America and Japan. Why shed blood for them?" "Why don't you go home?"

Red leaflets with these questions were thrown up into the air and blown by winds to the other side. Red soldiers rose up to shout them across the trenches. Red sentries with hands uplifted rushed forward crying them out. The Allied troops pondering over these queries were shaken. Their morale broken down. They fought half-heartedly. Italians, Czechoslovaks, and British became deserters. The sailors of the French Fleet at Odessa mutinied. The Michigan lumberjacks, revolted at slaying Russian woodsmen in the forests at Archangel, demanded to go home. The Whites in tens of thousands, whole battalions and ambulance corps, went over to the Revolution. One after another the armies of intervention crumpled up or melted away like snow in a Russian spring. Even the most iron-disciplined troops could not withstand the disintegrating impact of the Revolution. Says General von Hoffman, "Our victorious army on the Eastern front became rotten with Bolshevism. Our military machine became the printing press for the Bolsheviks. We got to the point where we did not dare to transfer certain of our divisions to the Western front. It was Lenin and the Bolsheviks that broke our morale and gave us defeat and the revolution you now see ruining us."

What the Bolsheviks did with propaganda in the last war, they will do again in the next one. Only they will do it with vastly more confidence, vigor, and technique. Along with the tanks and howitzers moving to the fronts will go batteries of linotypes and printing-presses. They will spray the opposing ranks with the deadly shrapnel of facts, arguments, appeals. They will treat every soldier not as an enemy but as a potential ally, a misguided brother to be instructed and set aright. Loud-voiced radios will ceaselessly inveigh against the folly and crime of workers killing their Soviet brothers. Swift planes will carry the message far into the rear. Sensationalists picture them speeding away with thermite flame-bombs on windy nights to fire the flimsy wood and paper cities of Japan. Maybe they will, but not if Soviet strategists deem that will arouse the rage and resentment of the Japanese masses and rally them closer to their government. More likely, reserving their bombs for the munition plants and the staff-headquarters of the generals, they will appeal to the masses to sabotage the imperialist slaughter that only increases their misery in order to swell the money-bags of the rich. They will call upon them to persuade their kinsmen at the front to ground arms, to turn against their officers, to desert *en masse* to the Soviets.

It was in response to just such appeals in 1917 that the Kaiser's soldiers with outstretched arms swarmed over the trenches to fraternize with the soldiers of the Tsar and the war on the Eastern front was over. Again those scenes may be re-enacted on a scale so colossal as to astound the world. Such a mass strike against war would have tremendous repercussions, creating back-fires of rebellion in many lands. Not without reason does Stalin say: "It can hardly be doubted that a war against the U.S.S.R. will lead to the complete defeat of the aggressor, to revolution in a number of countries in Europe and Asia, and the overthrow of their bourgeois landlord governments." And Voroshilov warns, "If the Fascists sow a wind, they will harvest the storm which will sweep them from Europe."

87. Will Japan Fight the Soviets?

Historians depict the inevitability of the collision "between the westward-moving Japanese and the eastward-moving Russians." Strategists draw maps of the campaign with arrows pointing to the places where the armies will collide. The press flares into headlines about the impending conflagration in the tinder-box of Asia. It flames out, too, in the speeches of the Fascist-militarist clique. "Peace in the Far East can be obtained only by a crusade against the Red Devils," declares Nodsol. "The continental epoch

of Japan has arrived," exclaims Kameichi. "The founding of the
new state in Siberia will be the most heroic deed of our reborn
people." To these provocations Marshal Blücher of the Red Army
replies, "If anyone stretches out his paws toward our resources,
he may be sure that, for every ton of coal, every cord of wood,
and every pound of flesh, we will fight long and stubbornly."

Warlike words are followed by warlike deeds. Japan pours 150,-
000 soldiers, including some of her crack regiments, into Manchukuo; across the borders the Soviets have twice the number in
their Red Army and reservists on the new collective farms and
industries. Japan builds a network of 200 airdromes and landing-
fields up to the borders of Outer Mongolia; the Soviets mobilize
a big fleet of bombing planes six hours away from the Nipponese
ports and capital. Japan launches a flotilla of speed-cruisers upon
the Sungari River; the Soviets assemble a squadron of submarines
in the Golden Horn of Vladivostok. Japan pushes a series of
strategic railways and motor-roads up to the Siberian frontiers;
on their side the Soviets build a string of forts and blockhouses, a
new railway north from Lake Baikal to the Pacific paralleling the
imperiled Trans-Siberian "life-line." Almost daily there are
clashes between border patrols, the shooting down of airplanes,
execution of spies. The Tokyo papers publish the communiqués
from Japanese generals about incursions of Soviet troops into
their territory. The official Moscow *Izvestia* retorts, "However
many communiqués the Japanese generals may issue, they cannot
gloss over the fact that very often they have to address requests
to the Soviets for the delivery of corpses of Japanese officers who
had crossed the Soviet frontier, while there are no analogous
cases of the Soviets addressing such requests to the Japanese."
Japan, on November 25, 1936, signed an anti-Communist Pact
with Germany, which, under the pretext of halting Red activities,
creates a military bloc against the Soviets. The Soviets immediately halted the important agreement which was about to give
the Japanese invaluable fishing rights for a period of eight years
and granted them for only a year.

This tension has lasted now for years. Will it end with a big explosion setting fire to the Far East and perhaps the whole world? Who wants war and what for?

That the Soviets do not want war is attested by all authorities. "In the Far East," says Yakhontoff, "Russia has ceased to be an aggressor, actual or potential, real or imaginary." And this, for the excellent reason, that there is nothing for it to be aggressive about. Land? So spacious is Siberia that it has less than three inhabitants to the square mile. Resources? Siberia is rich in coal, iron, water-power, gold, graphite, wheatlands, forests of cedar, larch, maple, and velvet cork. Investments in Asia to protect? Neither the Soviet state nor its citizens own wealth-producing properties abroad. Markets? The Soviets have an ever expanding and insatiable market at home and in the Far East import vastly more than they export.

In a war with Japan the Soviets have little or nothing to gain, and much to lose. It would divert their energies from the colossal tasks of reconstruction and weaken their power of resisting a Nazi invasion from the West. To avoid a conflict in the Far East the Soviets have pursued a policy of conciliation and concession for twenty years. They allowed Japan to set up its puppet state of Manchukuo in what was formerly a Russian sphere of influence. They removed a constant source of friction by cession of the Soviet-owned railway that runs through it. They have urged repeatedly the signing of a non-aggression pact, intimating that demilitarization of the frontiers might follow. They have pressed for the formation of a joint commission to define clearly the vague boundaries and put an end to forays and bloodshed.

The Soviets are set on peace, but there are limits beyond which they will not go or allow the Japanese armies to go. These limits are its frontiers and those of Outer Mongolia with which they are bound by a treaty of mutual assistance. If Stalin's statement, "We do not want an inch of foreign soil," is a declaration against any war of aggression, the other half of it, "We will not yield a single inch of our soil," is a declaration of determination to fight a war of defense.

If the Soviets are for peace, so is a considerable body of public opinion in Japan. The declaration of Prince Saito, "We have no aggressive designs against our northern neighbor," reflects the attitude of the liberals led by Count Makino of the Imperial Household, Saionji, last of the Genro, the fast-growing Socialists, and many big business interests. But there are powerful forces whose hearts like the German Nazis are set upon conquest, glory, and world dominion. These are the militarist-Fascists, the so-called "Younger Officers"—often men over fifty years of age—most of the three million army reservists, the Black Dragon, Ken Koku Kai, and three hundred other nationalist and secret societies. They acclaim the religion of arms and playing upon the loyalty and mystical patriotism of the people, urge them through war to realize the divine mission of Japan. In his "Tasks of Japan," General Araki declares that "the great ideals we have developed in three thousand years of history we must spread to the entire Far East and the whole world." General Matsui calls for a crusade to liberate "our blood-brothers," the Mongols, Buriats, Tunguz, Yakuts, Estonians, and create under the Flag of the Rising Sun a Pan-Turanian Empire reaching to the Atlantic. Another imperial dreamer Count Okuma declared that "in the middle of the twentieth century Japan will meet Europe on the plains of Asia and wrest from her the mastery of the world."

"Manchuria and Mongolia are the Belgium of the Far East," states the Tanaka Memorial to the Mikado. "In our wars with Russia and the United States we must make them bear all the horrors of war." Although it is dismissed as a forgery, the movements of the Japanese armies strikingly coincide with the policy enunciated in the document. While consolidating their position in Manchukuo, they are pushing into Mongolia with the alleged intent of striking north into Siberia. What are the motives impelling them to such an adventure? What has Japan to gain from conquest?

Economically it would deliver into her hands a great store-house of natural riches. It would give her complete control of the coastal fisheries now obtained by lease from the Soviets; the oil to fuel her fleet now obtained by concession from the Soviet half of Sakhalin, the coveted gold, graphite, coking coal, and first-grade iron ore for which she now goes to India. It would also, assert the empire-builders, provide an outlet for the surplus population now increasing at the rate of over 800,000 a year. This is a specious argument for in Siberia the winter is longer and climate colder than in Manchukuo which is so little to the liking of the Japanese that a bare half-million have settled there since it was opened to colonists over thirty years ago.

Strategically the possession of Siberia would be of great military value. It would remove the menace of Vladivostok, "a pistol pointed at the heart of Japan," enclose the Sea of Japan within its own territory, and secure its dominion over all North Eastern Asia. Conquest of the Lake Baikal region would give Japan complete control of the economic axis of Asia, eliminate the menace of air assaults on her cities, and prevent any co-operation between the Red Armies of China and the Soviets. With this great hinterland in its hands the Japanese could more confidently embark on a war with America.

Politically, the Fascists maintain that it would establish a huge buffer state between herself and the "dangerous thoughts" emanating from Moscow—a new *cordon sanitaire* against the bacillus of Bolshevism which threatens to sovietize China and take great areas out of the orbit of exploitation by Nipponese capitalists. "Japan is the watchdog against Red influence," declares General Tada. "China is obstructing and hindering the watchdog."

Psychologically another victory over the Colossus of the North would immeasurably increase the prestige and morale of the Japanese. A proud and sensitive people they have been stung by their exclusion from the United States, and their rebuffs in many of their dealings with the West. These humiliations would be wiped out by a triumph over the white race that would establish their lordship in Asia and strengthen their hegemony in the Pacific which occupies a third of this planet and around whose rim live half the people of the earth.

With these glittering prizes the Fascist-militarists urge the nation to embark upon the great adventure. Over against them stand the sober-minded realists pointing to the hazards it would involve. At home it would put a terrific strain upon Japanese finances even now in a precarious condition. It would further lower the living standards of the masses increasing the already widespread distress and discontent. In Manchukuo it would augment the difficulty of policing the vast territories already annexed but not pacified, and galvanize the guerilla bands into fresh raids and forays. In China it might arouse the smoldering resentment of 400,000,000 people to break forth into furious rebellion. Finally, there is the possibility of a crushing defeat by the Red Army, infinitely more powerful than that of the Tsar. As the Japanese are well aware, that would be an irretrievable disaster. If there are great things to be won by victory, there are as great or greater things to be lost by defeat. It would mean the probable relinquishment of territory already acquired on the mainland, the weakening of power to confront the American and British fleets, the forfeiture of all claims to supremacy in the Pacific. It might well start a Socialist Revolution in Japan itself, destroying the old feudal order of the Mikado and wiping out the militarists themselves.

These are the hazards. But so alluring are the prizes that they insistently cling to their plans and go ahead agitating and preparing for the great day. They may postpone the assault for some time in order to perfect their military machine and protect their cities with anti-aircraft devices. They may be compelled by some secret provision in the anti-Communist Pact with the Nazis to wait till the German armies strike from the West. Or they may seize the first favorable opportunity on the theory of now or never. For time is working on the side of the Soviets. Every year, month, day, their economic and military might is growing.

Indeed even now the Japanese militarists may regard it as too late and seek a *modus vivendi* deflecting the conflict into other regions or to some more propitious time.

88. What Books to Read About the Soviets?

As large as the country is the list of books about it. In the *Rossica* collection in Leningrad there are some 20,000 histories, monographs, diaries and brochures about Russia written by foreigners, twenty for every year during the ten centuries of its existence. To this output the Revolution has given a tremendous impetus. Now they are coming out at the rate of over a hundred a year, so fast that publishers are hard put to find new titles for them.

Most numerous are the impressions of travelers who have sojourned for a few months, weeks or days in the country. Hesitant about writing a book about their own country after a life-long residence in it, once they arrive in this country—utterly alien in spirit, language and institutions—they are seized by an irresistible desire to set forth their ideas and reactions. And some of them are not only interesting, but valuable. It is possible to understand a country without knowing everything about it—and vice versa. The newcomer is often sensitive to sights and sounds which the long time resident takes as a matter of course and fails to record. His intuitions may be more true and valid than the judgments of the most erudite. Scholars like Milukov and Harold Williams, who lived twenty years in Russia and knew twenty of its languages, were utterly wrong in their repeated predictions of Soviet downfall and disaster. One reason they went astray was that they could not or would not sense the dynamic spirit of the Revolution. Others did see or feel this, and although they did not know one-tenth as much as the famous Russian experts, they proved more trustworthy guides and prophets. Even casual impressions, therefore, have a place in the Soviet bibliography.

There are books laudatory and books damnatory. Books depicting the masses as slaves with reversed arms marching down to perdition, or as freemen under crimson banners pressing on to the millennium. Portraits of leaders as demagogues and despots or as selfless statesmen and seers. Exposés of corruption and bureaucracy. Tributes to triumphs in industry and science. Small wonder that the reader is lost in this welter of conflicting reports. Whom shall he believe? They are all honorable men. They all profess to be setting down the facts as they are. And for the most part they do. But there are all kinds of facts. By an arbitrary choice one can prove anything he wants. And he can do so out of the mouths of the Bolsheviks themselves.

Soviet newspapers are filled with accounts of blunders, break-down, executions—ample material for drawing up the most blasting indictment of the regime. They are filled, too, with stories of Arctic conquests, giant mills, new cities rising in steppes and forests—ample material for the most glowing panegyric. The picture that emerges depends upon the selection of the facts. And that in turn depends upon the author, the views he holds, the thesis he wants to prove. In 1927 two observers visited the little village of Saburova where I lived. One returned home to assert that the old Russian Church was quite dead, and in evidence thereof cited the fact that not a single marriage in the village was solemnized by the priest. The other returned to proclaim that the Church was as powerful as ever, and in evidence thereof he cited the fact that every child born in this village was christened by the priest. Each presented to the public a diametrically opposite state of affairs. And he did so not by misstating facts but by concentrating on different ones. But even on the basis of the same facts observers reach quite opposite conclusions. To one, a half-literate peasant in a responsible post demonstrates that "the workers really rule." To another it demonstrates the stupidity of the Soviets in appointing their officials.

In short, all books about the Soviets are colored by the personal prejudices, predilections and bias of the author. So obviously do the books about any country. But this is particularly true in the case of Russia. With the best will in the world it is difficult to be objective about a country which confirms or challenges so many of one's deep and long cherished ideas and beliefs.

Even if one could be dispassionate there are other obstacles in the way of a just and comprehensive appraisal of the Russian Revolution. First, it is too stupendous an event for the ablest mind to grasp in its entirety. Into twenty years it has crowded the four great revolutions—political, religious, industrial and agricultural —which in England and other countries were spread over several centuries and are still uncompleted. Secondly, it affects the lives of 175,000,000 people—seven times more than in the French Revolution, sixty times more than in the American Revolution—and it affects them more profoundly and fundamentally. Thirdly, it is too recent an event for the most far-seeing mind to appraise fairly its present results, much less its consequences for the future. To the request for an estimate of the French Revolution, a Chinese savant recently replied, "We are altogether too close to it to make any right judgment upon it as yet."

Pertinent here is the oft quoted excerpt from Macaulay's *Essay on Milton:* "We deplore the outrages which accompany revolution. . . . Its immediate effects are often atrocious crimes, conflicting errors, skepticism on points the most clear, dogmatism on points the most mysterious. It is just at this crisis that its enemies love to exhibit it. They pull down the scaffolding from the half-finished edifice: they point to the flying dust, the falling bricks, the comfortless rooms, the frightful irregularity of the whole appearance; and then ask in scorn where the promised splendor and comfort are to be found. If such miserable sophisms were to prevail, there would never be a good house or a good government in the world." A number of writers attempt to take this long-range view of the Revolution. Naturally the books they produce incline to the favorable. Not oblivious or blind to the negative aspects, they regard them as temporary and, like this book "The Soviets," stress the positive and constructive—those trends and tendencies that hold promise for the future.

To sum up with a truism. The "truth about Russia" is many-sided. No author has corraled it all and with every author it is colored by his particular concepts, convictions, desires and feelings. As a human being, he is a well-wisher, antagonist, athe-ist, Jesuit, Liberal, Anarchist, Communist. . . . He inevitably writes from his own point of view and there is no reason why he should not. But there is every reason for the reader to keep in mind what that point of view is and make his corresponding res-ervations and deductions. Especially should he be cautious and wary of those that proclaim they are "impartial" and "unbiased." . . . Most nearly objective are the specialized books on Soviet law, education, theatre, medicine, workers' life, foreign policy—the fruits of painstaking first-hand investigation by experts in these fields. In the following bibliography of 450 books in English appear most of the significant ones along with others not so significant. It includes the enthusiastically pro-Soviet, the vio-lently anti-Soviet as well as those valiantly trying to be neutral.

BIBLIOGRAPHY

I. General Surveys

Brailsford, Henry Noel: *The Russian Workers' Republic,* 1921.
Chamberlin, William Henry: *Russia's Iron Age,* 1936.
    Soviet Russia, 1930.
Davis, Jerome, editor: *The New Russia—Between the Third and Second Five Year Plans,* 1933.
Dillon, E. J.: *Russia, Today and Yesterday,* 1930.
Duranty, Walter: *I Write as I Please,* 1935.
Eddy, Sherwood: *Russia Today,* 1934.
    The Challenge of Russia, 1931.
Feiler, Arthur: *The Russian Experiment,* 1930.

Friedman, Elisha M.: *Russia in Transition,* 1932.

Harper, Samuel N.: *Civic Training in Soviet Russia,* 1929.

Hindus, Maurice: *Humanity Uprooted,* 1929

    The Great Offensive, 1933.

Hopper, Bruce: *Pan-Sovietism,* 1931.

Malevsky-Malevitch, P., editor: *Russia, U.S.S.R.,* 1927.

Pocket-Guide to the Soviet Union: Intourist, Moscow, 1932.

Raiguel, George Earle, and Huff, William Kistler: *This is Russia,* 1931.

Scheffer, Paul: *Seven Years in Soviet Russia,* 1931.

Tuckerman, Gustavus, editor: *Duranty Reports Russia,* 1934.

Webb, Sidney and Beatrice: *Soviet Communism: A New Civilization?* 1935.

Williams, Harold: *Russia of the Russians,* 1916.

For recent general information, see the *Moscow News,* daily and weekly editions; *Sovietland* and *U.S.S.R. in Construction,* periodicals published in Moscow; *Soviet Russia Today,* published in New York; *The Slavonic Review,* a large general survey published three times a year in London; the excellent *Research Bulletin* issued monthly by the American-Russian Institute in New York.

II. Russian History, the Revolution, Civil War, and Famine

Albertson, Ralph: *Fighting Without a War,* 1920.

Asch, Sholom: *Three Cities* (3-volume novel), 1933.

Beatty, Bessie: *The Red Heart of Russia,* 1918.

Boleslavski, Richard, and Woodward, Helen: *Way of the Lancer,* 1932.

Bryant, Louise: *Six Red Months in Russia,* 1918.

Bunyan, James, and Fisher, H. H.: *The Bolshevik Revolution, 1917-1918,* 1934.

Bunyan, James, editor: *Intervention, Civil War, and Communism in Russia,* 1936.

Bykov, P. M.: *The Last Days of Tsar Nicholas,* 1936.

Chamberlin, William Henry: *The Russian Revolution,* 1935.

Chernov, Victor: *The Great Russian Revolution,* 1936.

Coates, W. P., and Zelda K.: *Armed Intervention in Russia 1918-1922,* 1935.

Eckhardt, Hans von: *Russia,* 1932.

Fisher, H. H., and Varneck, Elena: *The Testimony of Kolchak and Other Siberian Materials,* 1935.

Fisher, H. H.: *The Famine in Soviet Russia 1919-1923,* 1935.

Florinsky, Michael T.: *The End of the Russian Empire,* 1931.

Fülop-Miller, René: *Rasputin: The Holy Devil,* 1928.

Furmanov, Dmitri; *Chapayev* (biography), 1936.

Golder, Frank Alfred, and Hutchinson, Lincoln: *On the Trail of the Russian Famine,* 1927.

Golovin, N. N.: *The Russian Army in the World War,* 1931.

Gorky, Maxim: *Forty Years,* 3 vols.: *The Bystander,* 1930; *The Magnet,* 1931; *Other Fires,* 1933.

Graves, Major-General William S.: *America's Siberian Adventure,* 1931.

Grinko, V. I.: *Features and Figures of the Past: Government and Opinion in the Reign of Nicholas II,* 1937.

Gubsky, N.: *Angry Dust* (autobiography), 1937.

Headstrom, Birger Richard: *The Story of Russia,* 1933.

Heifetz, Elias: *The Slaughter of the Jews in the Ukraine,* 1921.

Hill, Elizabeth, and Mudie, Doris, editors and translators: *The Letters of Lenin,* 1937.

Illustrated History of the Russian Revolution, 1917-1927. Ten Years' Progress Reported by Authoritative Russian Leaders, 2 vols., 1928.

Ivanov, Vsevolod: *The Armoured Train 14-69,* 1933.

Kearsey, Alexander Horace Cyril: *Study of Strategy and Tactics of the Russo-Japanese War, 1935.*

Kerensky, Alexander: *The Crucifixion of Liberty,* 1935.

Kluchevsky, V. O.: *History of Russia,* 5 vols., 1911-1931.

Kokovtsov, Count: *Out of My Past,* edited by H. H. Fisher, translated by Laura Matveev, 1936.

Krasnoff, P. N.: *From Double Eagle to Red Flag,* 1926.

Kropotkin, Peter: *Memoirs of a Revolutionist,* 1899.

Lenin, V. I.: Collected Works, 20 vols., 1922-1937. Among the most important are *Imperialism and the Imperialist War; From the Bourgeois to the Proletarian Revolution; The Revolution of 1917; Materialism and Empirio-Criticism; State and Revolution.*

Leroy-Beaulieu, Anatole: *The Empire of the Tsars and the Russians,* 1896.

Lobanov-Rostovsky, A.: *The Grinding Mill,* 1935.

Masaryk, Thomas Garrigue: *The Spirit of Russia*, 2 vols., 1919.

Mirsky, D. S.: *Russia; A Social History*, 1931.

Olgin, Moissaye: *The Soul of the Russian Revolution*, 1917.

Pares, Sir Bernard: *A History of Russia*, 1926.

Pilnyak, Boris: *The Naked Year* (novel), 1923.

Pokrovsky, Mikhail N.: *History of Russia from Earliest Times to the Rise of Commercial Capitalism*, 1931-1933.

Price, M. Philips: *My Reminiscences of the Russian Revolution*, 1921.

Ransome, Arthur: *Russia in 1919*, 1919. *The Crisis in Russia*, 1921.

Reed, John: *Ten Days that Shook the World*, 1919.

Ross, Edward Alsworth: *The Russian Bolshevik Revolution*, 1921.

Sayler, Oliver M.: *Russia, White or Red*, 1919.

Serafimovich, A.: *The Iron Flood* (novel), 1935.

Sholokhov, Mikhail: *And Quiet Flows the Don* (novel), 1934.

Sisson, Edgar: *One Hundred Red Days*, 1931.

Skariatina, Irina: *A World Can End*, 1931.

Stalin, Joseph: *The October Revolution*, 1934.

Stewart, George: *The White Armies in Russia*, 1933.

Tager, Alexander B.: *The Decay of Czarism; The Beiliss Trial*, 1935.

Tolstoy, Alexey: *The Road to Calvary* (novel), 1923.
    Darkness and Dawn, 1936.

Trotsky, Leon: *History of the Russian Revolution*, 3 vols., translated by Max Eastman, 1932.

Tyrkova-Williams, Ariadna: *From Liberty to Brest-Litovsk*, 1919.

United States Senate Document No. 62, 1919.

Vernadsky, George: *History of Russia*, 1929.

Wallace, Mackenzie: *Russia*, 1905.

Walsh, Edmund: *The Fall of the Russian Empire*, 1928.

Williams, Albert Rhys: *Through the Russian Revolution*, 1921.

Wreden, Nicholas: *The Unmaking of a Russian*, 1935.

III. Government, Party, and Peoples

Barbusse, Henri: *Stalin*, 1935.

Batsell, W. R.: *Soviet Rule in Russia*, 1929.

Brailsford, Henry Noel: *How the Soviets Work,* 1928.

Brameld, Theodore B.: *A Philosophic Approach to Communism,* 1933.

Burns, Emile: *A Handbook of Marxism,* 1935.

Davis, Jerome, editor: *Contemporary Social Movements,* 1930.

Fox, Ralph: *Communism,* 1936. *Lenin,* 1935.

Gurian, Waldemar: *Bolshevism: Theory and Practice,* 1932.

Harper, Samuel N.: *The Government of the Soviet Union,* 1937.

Hecker, Julius: *Moscow Dialogues,* 1934.

   The Communist Answer to the World's Needs, 1934.

Hicks, Granville: *John Reed; the Making of a Revolutionary,* 1936.

Keynes, J. Maynard: *Laissez-Faire and Communism,* 1926.

Kisch, Egon Erwin: *Changing Asia,* 1934.

Kohn, Hans: *Nationalism in the Soviet Union,* 1933.

Krupskaya, Nadezhda K.: *Memories of Lenin,* 1930.

Kunitz, Joshua: *Dawn over Samarkand—The Rebirth of Central Asia,* 1935.

Laski, Harold: *Communism,* 1927.

Levine, Isaac Don: *Stalin,* 1931.

McCormick, Anne O'Hare: *The Hammer and the Scythe: Communist Russia Enters the Second Decade,* 1928.

Maillart, Ella K.: *Turkestan Solo,* 1935.

Margolin, Arnold D.: *The Jews of Eastern Europe,* 1926.

Maxwell, Bertram W.: *The Soviet State,* 1934.

Mikhaylov, N.: *Soviet Geography,* 1935.

Mirsky, D. S.: *Lenin,* 1931.

People's Commissariat of Justice of the U.S.S.R.: *Report of Court Proceedings in the Case of the Anti-Soviet Trotskyite Center,* 1937.

Popov, N. N.: *Outline History of the Communist Party of the Soviet Union,* 2 vols., 1934.

Radek, Karl: *Portraits and Pamphlets,* 1935.

Rosenberg, Arthur: *A History of Bolshevism from Marx to the First Five Years' Plan,* 1934.

Ruppin, Arthur: *The Jews in the Modern World,* 1934.

Russell, Bertrand: *Bolshevism: Practice and Theory,* 1920.

Stalin, Joseph: *Foundations of Leninism,* 1932.

   Problems of Leninism, 1932.

   Marxism and the National Colonial Question, 1933.

Strachey, John: *The Theory and Practice of Socialism,* 1936.

Strong, Anna Louise: *The Red Star in Samarkand*, 1929.

Van Kleeck, Mary: *On Economic Planning*, 1935.

Webb, Sidney and Beatrice: *Soviet Communism: A New Civilization?* 1936.

White, W. C.: *Lenin*, 1936.

Yarmolinsky, Avrahm: *Jews and Other Minor Nationalities under the Soviets*, 1928.

IV. Economic Life: Agriculture, Finance, Five-Year Plan

American-Russian Chamber of Commerce: *Handbook of the Soviet Union*, 1936.

American Trade Union Delegation Report: *Russia After Ten Years*, 1927.

Borders, Karl: *Village Life Under the Soviets*, 1927.

Bourke-White, Margaret: *Eyes on Russia*, 1931.

British Trade Union Delegation Report: *Russia To-day*, 1925.

Bron, Saul G.: *Soviet Economic Development and American Business*, 1930.

Brutzkus, Boris: *Economic Planning in Soviet Russia*, 1935.

Burns, Emile: *Russia's Productive System*, 1930.

Burrell, George A.: *An American Engineer Looks at Russia*, 1932.

Campbell, Thomas D.: *Russia, Market or Menace*, 1932.

Chase, Stuart; Dunn, Robert; Tugwell, Rexford, editors: *Soviet Russia in the Second Decade*, 1928

Citrine, Walter: *I Search for Truth in Russia*, 1936.

Coates, W. P., and Zelda K.: *The Second Five-Year Plan*, 1934.

Cole, G. D. H.: *Economic Planning*, 1935.

Crowther, James G.: *Soviet Science*, 1936.

Dobb, Maurice: *Russian Economic Development since the Revolution*, 1928.
Soviet Russia and the World, 1932.

Dobbert, Duranty, and others: *Red Economics*, 1932

Dunn, Robert: *Soviet Trade Unions*, 1928.

Ehrenbourg, Ilya: *Out of Chaos* (novel), 1934.

Farbman, Michael: *Bolshevism in Retreat*, 1923.
Piatiletka: Russia's Five-Year Plan, 1931.

Fischer, Louis: *Machines and Men in Russia,* 1932.

Freeman, Joseph: *The Soviet Worker,* 1932.

Gladkov, Feodor: *Cement* (novel), 1929.

Gorky and others, editors: *Belomor; An Account of the Construction of the New Canal between the White Sea and the Baltic Sea,* 1935.

Grinko, G. T.: *Five Year Plan of Soviet Union,* 1930.

Hindus, Maurice: *Broken Earth,* 1926

> *Red Bread,* 1931.

> *The Russian Peasant and the Revolution,* 1920.

Hirsch, Alcan: *Industrialized Russia,* 1934.

Hoover, Calvin B.: *Economic Life of Soviet Russia,* 1931.

Hubbard, L. E., *Soviet Money and Finance,* 1936.

Ilin, M.: *Men and Mountains,* 1935.

> *New Russia's Primer—The Story of the Five-Year Plan,* 1931.

Jasienski, Bruno: *Man Changes His Skin* (novel), 1936.

Kataev, Valentine: *Time, Forward!* (novel), 1933.

Katzenelenbaum, S. S.: *Russian Currency and Banking, 1914-1924,* 1935.

Kautsky, Karl: *Bolshevism at a Deadlock,* 1931.

Kingsbury, Susan H., and Fairchild, Mildred: *Factory, Family and Woman in the Soviet Union,* 1935.

Lamb, Edward: *The Planned Economy in Soviet Russia,* 1934.

Leonov, Leonid: *Soviet River* (novel), 1932.

> *Skutarevsky* (novel), 1936.

Mavor, James: *An Economic History of Russia,* 2 vols., 1914.

Miller, Margaret S.: *The Economic Development of Russia,* 1926.

Molotov, V. M.: *The Success of the Five Year Plan,* 1931.

Monkhouse, Allan: *Moscow, 1911-1933,* 1933.

Nodel, W.: *Supply and Trade in the U.S.S.R.,* 1935.

Obolensky-Ossinsky, V. V., and others: *Social Economic Planning in the U.S.S.R.,* 1931.

Page, Myra: *Moscow Yankee* (novel), 1935.

Panferov, F.: *Brusski; A Story of Peasant Life in Soviet Russia,* 1930.

Pasvolsky, Leo, and Moulton, H. G.: *Russian Debts and Russian Reconstruction,* 1924.

Price, George M.: *Labor Protection in Soviet Russia,* 1928.

Reddaway, W. B.: *The Russian Financial System,* 1935.

Robinson, Geroid Tanquary: *Rural Russia Under the Old Regime,* 1932.

Rukeyser, Walter Arnold: *Working for the Soviets,* 1932.

Sholokhov, Mikhail: *Seeds of Tomorrow* (novel), 1935.

Smith, Andrew: *I Was a Soviet Worker,* 1936.

Sokolnikov, Gregory Y.: *Soviet Policy in Public Finance, 1917-1928,* 1931.

Soule, George: *A Planned Society,* 1932.

Stalin and others: *Socialism Victorious,* 1935.

State Planning Commission of the U.S.S.R.: *The Soviet Union Looks Ahead,* 1929. *The U.S.S.R. in Figures,* 1934.
  Summary of the Fulfillment of the First Five-Year Plan, 1933.

Stekoll, Harry: *Humanity Made to Order,* 1937.

Stepniak: *The Russian Peasantry,* 1888.

Strong, Anna Louise: *This Soviet World,* 1936.
  The Soviet Conquers Wheat, 1931.

Timoshenko, Vladimir P.: *Agricultural Russia and the Wheat Problem,* 1932.

Turin, S. P.: *From Peter the Great to Lenin,* 1935.

Tverskoi, K. N.: *The Unified Transport System of the U.S.S.R.,* 1935.

Walsh, Edmund A.: *The Last Stand,* 1931.

Ward, Harry F., *In Place of Profit,* 1933.

Williams, Albert Rhys: *The Russian Land,* 1927.

Wooton, Barbara Francis: *Plan or No Plan,* 1935.

Yakovlev, Y. A.: *Red Villages: The Five-Year Plan in Agriculture,* 1931.

Yurovsky, L. N.: *Currency Problem and Policy of the Russian Union,* 1925.

Zagorski, S. O.: *State Control of Industry in Russia During the War,* 1929.

For current information, see the magazine *Economic Survey,* published by the Chamber of Commerce in Moscow, and *Russian Economic Notes,* translations from Soviet newspapers published by the United States Department of Commerce, Washington.

V. Social Life: Women, Religion, Education, Courts

Avdeyenko, A.: *I Love* (novel), 1936.

Baldwin, Roger: *Liberty Under the Soviets,* 1928.

Berdyaev, Nicholas: *The End of Our Time,* 1933.

Boldyreff, Tatiana W.: *Russian Born,* 1935.

Bukharin, Deborin, Uranovsky and others: *Marxism and Modern Thought,* 1935.

Burroughs, H. E.: *Tales of a Vanished Land,* 1930.

Calcott, Mary Stevenson: *Russian Justice,* 1935.

Cole, Margaret I., and others: *Twelve Studies in Soviet Russia,* 1933.

Colton, Ethan: *The XYZ of Communism,* 1931.

   Four Patterns of Revolution, 1935.

Conus, Esther: *Protection of Motherhood and Childhood in the Soviet Union,* 1933.

Counts, George S.: *The Soviet Challenge to America,* 1931.

Dennen, Leon: *Where the Ghetto Ends—Jews in Soviet Russia,* 1934.

Dewey, John: *Impressions of Russia and the Revolutionary World,* 1929.

Fediaevsky, Vera, and Hill, Patty Smith: *Nursery School and Parent Education in Soviet Russia,* 1936.

Field, Alice Withrow: *Protection of Women and Children in Soviet Russia,* 1932

Goldberg, David: *Sussman Sees It Through,* 1935.

Griffith, Hubert: *Playtime in Russia,* 1935.

Haines, Anna: *Health Work in Soviet Russia,* 1928.

Halle, Fannina W.: *Woman in Soviet Russia,* 1933.

Harper, Samuel N.: *Making Bolsheviks,* 1931.

Hecker, Julius F.: *Religion Under the Soviets,* 1928.

   Religion and Communism, 1935.

   Russian Sociology, 1935.

Hindus, Maurice: *Moscow Skies* (novel), 1936.

Huxley, Julian: *A Scientist Amongst the Soviets,* 1932.

Ilf, Ilya, and Petrov, Eugene: *The Little Golden Calf* (satire), 1932.

Kallen, Horace M.: *Frontiers of Hope,* 1929.

King, Beatrice: *Changing Man: The Education System of the U.S.S.R.,* 1937.

Kingsbury, John, and Newsholme, Sir Arthur: *Red Medicine: Socialized Health in Soviet Russia,* 1933.

Kitchin, G.: *Prisoner of the G.P.U.,* 1935.

Koerber, Lenka von: *Soviet Russia Fights Crime,* 1935.

Marie, Grand Duchess of Russia: *Education of a Princess,* 1931.

Mehnert, Klaus: *Youth in Soviet Russia,* 1933.

Members of the Expedition: *The Voyage of the Chelyuskin,* 1935.

Monkhouse, Allan: *Moscow 1911-1933,* 1933.

Nearing, Scott: *Education in Soviet Russia,* 1926.

Ognyov, N., *The Diary of a Communist Schoolboy,* 1928.
  The Diary of a Communist Undergraduate, 1929.

Pinkevitch, Albert: *The New Education in the Soviet Republic,* 1929.
  Science and Education in the U.S.S.R., 1935.

Romanov, Panteleimon: *Three Pairs of Silk Stockings* (novel), 1931.
  Without Cherry Blossoms (short stories), 1932.

Rosenberg, James N.: *On the Steppes,* 1927.

Semashko, N. A.: *Health Protection in the U.S.S.R.,* 1934.

Sigerist, Henry E.: *Socialist Medicine; The Protection of Health in the
  Soviet Union,* 1937.

Smith, Jessica: *Woman in Soviet Russia,* 1928.

Spinka, Matthew: *The Church and the Russian Revolution,* 1927.
  Christianity Confronts Communism, 1936.

Stepun, Fedor: *The Russian Soul and Revolution,* 1935

Tchernavin, Tatiana: *Escape from the Soviets,* 1933.

Tchernavin, Vladimir V.: *I Speak for the Silent,* 1935.

Tobenkin, Elias: *Stalin's Ladder,* 1933.

Tolstoy, Alexandra: *I Worked for the Soviet,* 1934.

Trotsky, Leon: *The Revolution Betrayed,* 1937.

Williams, Frankwood E.: *Russia, Youth and the Present-Day World,* 1934.

Wilson, Lucy W.: *The New Schools of New Russia,* 1928.

Winter, Ella: *Red Virtue,* 1933.

Woody, Thomas: *New Minds: New Men?* 1932.

Zelitch, Judah: *Soviet Administration of Criminal Law,* 1931.

VI. Theatre, Art and Literature

Bourman, Anatole, and Lyman, D.: *The Tragedy of Nijinsky,* 1936.

Beaumont, Cyril W.: *Vaslav Nijinsky,* 1932.

Boleslavski, Richard, and Woodward, Helen: *Lances Down,* 1932.

Buxton, David R.: *Russian Medieval Architecture,* 1934.

Byron, Robert: *First Russia, Then Tibet,* 1933.

Carter, Huntly: *The New Spirit in the Russian Theatre,* 1929.
  The New Theatre and Cinema of Soviet Russia, 1925.

Chaliapine, Feodor: *Pages from My Life* (autobiography), 1927.

Conway, Sir Martin: *Art Treasures in Soviet Russia,* 1925.

Cournos, John, editor: *Short Stories Out of Soviet Russia,* 1929.

Deutsch, Babette, and Yarmolinsky, Avrahm, editors and translators: *Russian Poetry,* 1930.

Eastman, Max: *Artists in Uniform,* 1932.

Flanagan, Hallie: *Shifting Scenes of the Modern European Theatre,* 1928.

Freeman, Joseph; Kunitz, Joshua; and Lozowick, Louis: *Voices of October —Art and Literature in Soviet Russia,* 1930.

Fülöp-Miller, René, and Gregor, Joseph: *The Russian Theatre,* 1930.

Gorky, Bukharin, Radek, and others: *Problems of Soviet Literature, Reports at the First Soviet Writers' Congress,* 1935.

Hammer, Armand: *The Quest of the Romanoff Treasure,* 1932.
    Faberge, the Cellini of the North, 1937.

Holme, Geoffrey: *Art in the U.S.S.R.,* 1935.

Houghton, Norris: *Moscow Rehearsals,* 1936.

Kaun, Alexander: *Maxim Gorky and His Russia,* 1927.

Lyons, Eugene, editor: *Six Soviet Plays,* 1922.

Markov, P. A.: *The Soviet Theatre,* 1934.

Mirsky, D. S.: *A History of Russian Literature, from the Earliest Times to the Death of Dostoyevsky (1881),* 1927.
    Modern Russian Literature, 1925.
    Pushkin, 1926.

Nemirovitch-Dantchenko, Vladimir: *My Life in the Russian Theatre,* 1936.

Nijinsky, Romola: *Nijinsky,* 1933.

Noyes, G. R.: *Masterpieces of the Russian Drama,* 1933.

Patrick, G. Z. J., *Popular Poetry in Soviet Russia,* 1929.

Reavey, George, and Slonim, Marc: *Soviet Literature,* 1933.

Sabaneyev, Leonid: *Modern Russian Composers,* 1927.

Sayler, Oliver: *The Russian Theatre,* 1922.
    In the Moscow Art Theatre, 1925.

Seifulina and others: *Flying Osip, Stories of New Russia,* 1925.

Simmons, Ernest J.: *Pushkin,* 1937.
    English Literature and Culture in Russia (1553-1840), 1935.

Stanislavsky, Constantin: *My Life in Art,* 1933.

Struve, Gleb: *Soviet Russian Literature,* 1935.

White, W. C.: *Made in Russia* (handicrafts), 1932.

Yarmolinsky, Avrahm: *Russian Literature,* 1931.

    Editor, *The Works of Alexander Pushkin,* 1936.

Zostchenko, Mikhail: *Russia Laughs* (humorous stories), 1935.

For current events and information in this field see the magazine *International Literature,* edited by S. Dinamov and published in Moscow.

VII. Foreign Relations and Trade

American Foundation, Committee on Russian-American Relations: *The United States and the Soviet Union,* 1933.

Arnot, R. Page: *Soviet Russia and Her Neighbors,* 1927.

Buchanan, Sir George: *My Mission to Russia and Other Diplomatic Memories,* 1923.

Budish, J. M., and Shipman, Samuel S.: *Soviet Foreign Trade, Menace or Promise,* 1931.

Bullitt, William C.: *The Bullitt Mission to Russia,* 1919.

Conolly, Violet: *Soviet Economic Policy in the East,* 1933.

    Soviet Trade from the Pacific to the Levant, 1935.

Cresson, William P.: *Francis Dana,* 1930.

Cumming, C. K., and Pettit, Walter W.: *Russian-American Relations,* 1920.

Davis, Kathryn Wasserman: *The Soviets at Geneva,* 1934.

Dean, Vera Micheles: *Soviet Russia, 1917-1935,* 1935.

Dennis, Alfred: *Foreign Policies of Soviet Russia,* 1924.

Department of State: *Foreign Relations of the United States—"1918 Russia,"* 1931.

Dutt, R. Palme: *World Politics,* 1936.

Fischer, Louis: *The Soviets in World Affairs,* 2 vols., 1930.

    Why Recognize Russia? 1931. *Oil Imperialism,* 1926.

Florinsky, Michael T.: *World Revolution and the U.S.S.R.,* 1932.

Francis, David: *Russia from the American Embassy, April 1916-November 1918,* 1921.

Gankin, Olga Hess, and Fisher, H. H.: *The Origins of the Third International: A Documentary History,* 1937.

Hagedorn, Hermann: *The Magnate; William Boyce Thompson and His Time*, 1935.

Hard, William: *Raymond Robins' Own Story*, 1920.

Harper, Samuel N., editor: *The Soviet Union and World Problems*, 1935.

Henri, Ernst: *Hitler over Russia?* 1937.

Huntington, W. Chapin: *The Homesick Million: Russia-out-of-Russia*, 1933.

Knickerbocker, H. R.: *The Red Trade Menace*, 1931.
   Fighting the Red Trade Menace, 1931.

Lattimore, Owen: *Mongols of Manchuria*, 1935.

Lobanov-Rostovsky, Prince Andrei: *Russia and Asia*, 1933.

Lockhart, Robert Hamilton Bruce: *British Agent*, 1932.

Maxwell, Buchler and Pflaum, comp., *Recognition of Soviet Russia*, 1931.

Novikoff-Priboy, A.: *Tsushima* (novel), 1936.

Paleologue, Maurice: *An Ambassador's Memoirs*, 1923.

Plotkin, M. A.: *Legal Status of Foreigners in U.S.S.R.*, 1934.

Robertson, Jasper Rood: *A Kentuckian at the Court of the Tsars*, 1936.

Schuman, Frederic Lewis: *American Policy toward Russia since 1917*, 1928.

Sokolsky, George: *Tinderbox of Asia*, 1932.

Taracouzio, T. A.: *The Soviet Union and International Law*, 1935.

Vernadsky, George Vladimirovich: *Political and Diplomatic History of Russia*, 1936.

Yakhontoff, Victor A.: *Russia and the Soviet Union in the Far East*, 1931.
   Eyes on Japan, 1936.

Yanson, J. D.: *Foreign Trade in the U.S.S.R.*, 1934.

VIII. Impressions, Travelogues, and Diaries

Abbe, James: *I Photograph Russia*, 1934.

Alexander, Grand Duke of Russia: *Once a Grand Duke*, 1932.
   Always a Grand Duke, 1933.

Barbusse, Henri: *One Looks at Russia*, 1931.

Berkman, Alexander: *The Bolshevik Myth*, 1925.

Brown, E. T.: *This Russian Business*, 1933.

Brown, W. Adams, Jr.: *The Groping Giant*, 1920.

Chesterton, Mrs. Cecil: *Sickle or Swastika*, 1935.

My Russian Venture, 1931.

Counts, George S.: *A Ford Crosses Soviet Russia*, 1930.

Darling, Jay N.: *Ding Goes to Russia*, 1932.

Delafield, E. M.: *I Visit the Soviets*, 1937.

Douillet, Joseph: *Moscow Unmasked*, 1930.

Dreiser, Theodore: *Dreiser Looks at Russia*, 1928.

Durant, Will: *The Tragedy of Russia*, 1933.

Farson, Negley: *Black Bread and Red Coffins*, 1930.

The Way of a Transgressor, 1936.

Franck, Harry A.: *A Vagabond in Sovietland*, 1935.

Frank, Waldo: *Dawn in Russia*, 1932.

Freeman, Joseph: *An American Testament*, 1936.

Gauvreau, Emile Henri: *What So Proudly We Hailed*, 1935.

Gibson, William J.: *Wild Career*, London, 1935.

Gide, André: *Return from the U.S.S.R.*, 1937.

Goldman, Emma: *Further Disillusionment in Russia*, 1924.

Living My Life, 1931.

Harrison, Marguerite: *There's Always Tomorrow*, 1935.

Herriot, Edouard: *Eastward from Paris*, 1934.

Holmes, Burton: *The Traveler's Russia*, 1934.

Lamont, Corliss and Margaret: *Russia Day by Day*, 1933.

Lansbury, George: *What I Saw in Russia*, 1920.

Lee, Ivy: *Present Day Russia*, 1928.

Long, Ray: *An Editor Looks at Russia*, 1931.

Lyons, Eugene: *Moscow Carrousel*, 1935.

Mackenzie, F. A.: *Russia Before Dawn*, 1923.

McWilliams, R. F. and M. S.: *Russia in 1926*, 1927.

Muggeridge, Malcolm: *Winter in Moscow*, 1934.

Muldavin, Albert: *The Red Fog Lifts*, 1931.

Nansen, Fridtjof: *Through the Caucasus to the Volga*, 1931.

Newman, E. M.: *Seeing Russia*, 1928.

O'Flaherty, Liam: *I Went to Russia*, 1931.

Pares, Sir Bernard: *Moscow Admits a Critic*, 1936.

Ponafidine, Emma Cochran: *Russia—My Home*, 1931.

Porter, Anna: *A Moscow Diary*, 1926.

Robinson, William: *Soviet Russia as I Saw It*, 1932.

Ruhl, Arthur: *White Nights and other Russian Impressions*, 1917.

Sheean, Vincent: *Personal History*, 1935.

Sheridan, Clare: *Mayfair to Moscow*, 1921.

Skariatina, Irina, and Blakeslee, Victor: *New Worlds for Old*, 1935.
    The First to Go Back, 1933.

Smith, Marjorie: *From Broadway to Moscow*, 1934.

Stevens, Thomas: *Through Russia on a Mustang*, 1891.

Strong, Anna Louise: *The Road to the Grey Pamir*, 1931.
    I Change Worlds, 1935.

Thompson, Dorothy: *The New Russia*, 1928.

Travers, P. L.: *Moscow Excursion*, 1935.

Villard, Oswald Garrison: *Russia from a Car Window*, 1929.

Violles, André: *A Girl in Soviet Russia*, 1929.

Vorse, Mary Heaton: *Footnote to Folly*, 1935.

Waters, Brigadier-General W. H.: *Russia, Then and Now*, 1935.

Wells, Carveth: *Kapoot*, 1933.

Wells, H. G.: *Russia in the Shadows*, 1920.

White, William C.: *These Russians*, 1931.

Wicksteed, Alexander: *My Russian Neighbors*, 1934.

Wilson, Edmund: *Travels in Two Democracies*, 1936.

Wilson, Helen C., and Mitchell, E. R.: *Vagabonding at Fifty*, 1929.

Wright, Russell: *One Sixth of the World's Surface*, 1932.

Index

18